D0097751

Critical Theories of
PSYCHOLOGICAL DEVELOPMENT

PATH IN PSYCHOLOGY
Published in Cooperation with Publications for the Advancement of Theory and History in Psychology (PATH)

Series Editors:
David Bakan, *York University*
John Broughton, *Teachers College, Columbia University*
Robert Rieber, *John Jay College, CUNY, and Columbia University*
Howard Gruber, *University of Geneva*

A CRITICAL PSYCHOLOGY: Interpretation of the Personal World
Edmund V. Sullivan

CRITICAL THEORIES OF PSYCHOLOGICAL DEVELOPMENT
Edited by John M. Broughton

DEVELOPMENTAL APPROACHES TO THE SELF
Edited by Benjamin Lee and Gil G. Noam

FRANTZ FANON AND THE PSYCHOLOGY OF OPPRESSION
Hussein Abdilahi Bulhan

HUMANISTIC PSYCHOLOGY: Concepts and Criticisms
Edited by Joseph R. Royce and Leendert P. Mos

PSYCHOSOCIAL THEORIES OF THE SELF
Edited by Benjamin Lee

THEORETICAL PSYCHOLOGY: The Meeting of East and West
A. C. Paranjpe

WILHELM WUNDT AND THE MAKING OF A SCIENTIFIC PSYCHOLOGY
Edited by R. W. Rieber

Critical Theories of PSYCHOLOGICAL DEVELOPMENT

Edited by
John M. Broughton
Teachers College
Columbia University
New York, New York

PLENUM PRESS • NEW YORK AND LONDON

Library of Congress Cataloging in Publication Data

Critical theories of psychological development.

(PATH in psychology)
Includes bibliographies and index.
1. Child psychology—Philosophy. I. Broughton, John M. II. Series. [DNLM: 1. Child Development. 2. Child Psychology. 3. Personality Development. 4. Psychological Theory. WS 105 C934]
BF722.C73 1987 155.4 86-30383
ISBN 0-306-42431-2

A Division of Plenum Publishing Corporation
233 Spring Street, New York, N.Y. 10013

Printed in the United States of America

To
Klaus Riegel
for fostering the critical development
of so many young psychologists

CONTRIBUTORS

Jessica Benjamin, *Institute for the Humanities, New York University, New York, New York*

John M. Broughton, *Department of Developmental and Educational Psychology, Teachers College, Columbia University, New York, New York*

Susan Buck-Morss, *Department of Government, Cornell University, Ithaca, New York*

Rainer Döbert, *Institute of Sociology, Frei Universität Berlin, Berlin, West Germany*

Ed Elbers, *Department of Psychonomics, Faculty of Social Sciences, Rijksuniversiteit Utrecht, Utrecht, Netherlands*

Jürgen Habermas, *Department of Philosophy, University of Frankfurt, Frankfurt am Main, West Germany*

Adrienne E. Harris, *Department of Psychology, Rutgers University, Newark, New Jersey*

David Ingleby, *Department of Development in Society, Rijksuniversiteit Utrecht, Utrecht, Netherlands*

Richard Lichtman, *Wright Institute, Berkeley, California*

Gertrud Nunner-Winkler, *Max Planck Institute for Psychological Research, Munich, West Germany*

J. Jacques Vonèche, *Department of Psychology and Educational Sciences, University of Geneva, Geneva, Switzerland*

Valerie Walkerdine, *Institute of Education, University of London, London, England*

ACKNOWLEDGMENTS

I would like to thank the contributors to this volume, who not only entrusted their chapters to me, but also offered advice on the book and, over the years, have greatly deepened my interest in and affection for a political psychology. There are a lot of other contributors, whether they realize it or not, and at the risk of omitting many I should like to name some.

The influence of Marta Zahaykevich runs throughout my work, to the point where—I am proud to say—a lot of it is as much ours as mine. Her warmth and strength, as well as her good judgment, critical acumen, and political commitment, are the major reasons that things come to fruition in my life. In the bad patches of this work, she came home anyway. Her laughter in the silence kept me going and kept me lively.

Clifford Hill, whose friendship has been a port in many a storm during this period, gave his loving attention to the details of the manuscript and commented with frankness and good taste in both office and sauna.

During the preparation of the manuscript, I was fortunate to receive sage counsel on the state of psychology and its possibilities from the following: Janet Allen, Erika Apfelbaum, Carla Bluhm, Bo DeLong, Mark Freeman, Hans Furth, Howard Gruber, Will Kennedy, Richard Kitchener, Deanna Kuhn, Ian Lubek, Vince Luschas, Jack Meacham, Pierre Moessinger, Elyse Morgan, Paul Philibert, Mari Radzik, Irving Sigel, Jonas Soltis, Thomas Southwick, Helen Weinreich Haste, Philip Wexler, Robert Wozniak, and James Youniss.

There are those who over the years have contributed much to my general appreciation for the nature of the relation between life and the human sciences: Howard Gadlin, Maxine Greene, Kathleen Hill, Dwayne Huebner, Bernard Kaplan, Joel Kovel, Maria Millagros Lopez, Klaus Riegel, Douglas Sloan, Edmund Sullivan, Michael Watts, Ricardo Zuniga, and J. J. Cale.

In addition to these individuals, I owe a debt of gratitude to the friendship and stimulating cooperation of Lawrence Kohlberg, and the constellation of students and others he has generated over the years at the Harvard Graduate School of Education. I have also learned a great deal from working in the Society for a Critical Psychology, the Group for a Radical Human Science, and a study group convened by Paul and Bell Chevigny, and from my acquaintance with the Ideology and Consciousness Collective in England.

Four study groups at Teachers College have boosted my enthusiasm for scholarship, redeemed my faith in institutions, and rekindled my desire for intellectual collegiality over the past few years: one on high technology, conceived by Michael Timpane; a second, on feminism, involving many creative and innovative graduate students; a third, on women and education, convened by Judith Brandenburg; a fourth, on interpretation, sustained by the valiant efforts of Raymond McDermott, Patrick Lee, Robert McClintock, and Hervé Varenne (as well as others already mentioned). I have also benefited considerably from the chance to work with the *Aegis* program in adult education at Teachers College.

Rocky Schwarz, Bruce Azumbrado, and their cohorts gave me assistance of a quality and generosity above and beyond the call of duty in the preparation of the final manuscript.

Finally, my family in England have been continuously, well, familiar. Their support and affection, in spite of the distance, have been of more importance to me than they perhaps have realized or I have cared to admit.

When I look at the dimensions of this community, spread out over a number of countries, and ponder how many other individuals and groups I ought to have mentioned, I am reassured that there is some congruence between the content of this particular volume and the way in which it came into being: It was no simple expression of the intellectual development of a few individuals. If a model of development could account for the evolution of even one book on development, it would be progress indeed.

JOHN M. BROUGHTON

PREFACE

Something instructive occurred in the process of entitling the present collection. Both editor and publisher sought a simple and succinct rubric for the various pieces of work. But they rapidly and reluctantly reached the consensus that, by either intellectual or marketing criteria, the insertion of the adjective "psychological" to qualify the noun "development" was a communicative necessity. Much to the chagrin of the developmental psychologist, the term *development* still connotes—to the world at large as well as the general community of publishers, librarians, and computer archivists—the modernization of nation states. Inside and outside the university, I find that, when asked, "What are you interested in?" I am not at liberty to reply, "The concept of development," without being absorbed immediately into a discussion of Third World studies. The approach of the present volume should be taken as an exhortation to psychologists to take the genealogy of "development" seriously. The history of the discipline is not so different from the history of the word and, as we shall discover, the concern with developmental progress cannot easily be separated from the urge for dominion.

This volume presents a selection from the recent critical scholarship on psychological development. The emphasis is on rethinking the field of developmental psychology at the level of theory. Although theorizing itself is not well understood in the field of psychology, we mean to intensify professional self-scrutiny at the point where fundamental assumptions exert their leverage and pursue their productive power. It is at this point that decisions are made, usually quite unreflectively, about which research programs will be allowed to hypertrophy and to be applied in which ways, and which research approaches will be construed as irrational or rendered virtually inconceivable.

The examination of the meaning of such assumptions and of the practice of fostering their entrenchment is usually portrayed as a conceptual endeavor. As such, it is typically left up to psychologists emeriti who are, after all, entitled to a life of superannuated reverie in their lazy-boys. On occasion, conceptual reflection is even permitted to some intellectual historian who happens to stumble upon developmental psychology and mistake it for a serious scholarly undertaking. This is not the pattern of the present volume. Theorizing is not a speculative luxury to be afforded only at the margins; it is the heart of the matter. The chapters represent a serious ambition, not just to muse about historical trends or to comment cleverly on the shortcomings of the field and then return to more academic disciplines, but to generate a new direction of investigation, a new kind of framework for practicing psychological science, and a new level of responsibility in thinking through the significance of development for human life in general. The crime attempted here is an "inside job" rather than one of breaking and entering: the *modus operandi* emerges from direct familiarity with the discipline, and the perpetrators are motivated by a careful reexamination of their own experiences of supervising and holding forth on child, adolescent, and adult development under the aegis of a professionalized Western civilization.

The selection of work presented here has been made according to a number of criteria. First, writing was sought that showed some philosophical understanding. Thus, consideration was not given to treatments of conceptual issues as though they were merely methodological in nature and meta-theoretical reviews that stay at the level of describing trends. Moreover, a certain acquaintance with the history of philosophy was presupposed, including recent advances in critical philosophy.

A second criterion was that the work should express clearly a political vision of development. Typically, psychology has separated itself from politics, despite its involvement in policy formation and the obvious political implications of its funding sources and their priorities. A major goal of the present collection was to undo that normative self-deception.

However, there was a third concern that the book not be limited to political critiques. Instead, it was designed to explore a range of orientations to development as a discipline and as an object of policy. It was allowed that the focus could be on the more intellectual or the more practical aspects of theory, or some combination of the two. Most commonly, the chapters chosen concentrated on either the social and historical production of developmental theory or the meaning of development as a social and historical phenomenon. In several instances, both were dealt with, and in that case it was felt to be important that clarity be maintained with regard to the relationship between the ideal and the material.

Fourth, it was stipulated that the work should focus on the constitutive role of society and history, not just their influence on developmental processes. The volume therefore stands against relativisms, since it preempts the usual dualism of individual and society, in which each is postulated as ontologically external to the other. A major question posed by all chapters is: How is it that human development and historical and cultural transformations coincide? This stance pre-empts the treatment of society, culture, and history as "variables" and excludes the usual positivist vision of development as a dependent variable.

Fifth, and closely linked to the last requirement, it was expected that the critiques should do more than pay the usual lip service to "socio-historical context." Purely programmatic statements were avoided, as were lamentations about the ignoring of context in mainstream developmental psychology. The ideal type in mind was an adventurous exploration of a particular approach illustrating the constitutive process, whether at the level of psychological development or at the level of theories about it.

One might be tempted to call the domain of concern "the new developmental psychology," were it not for the fact that the disciplinary mainstream always presents itself in such terms. Nevertheless, it was made a requirement, our sixth, that the research included here be clearly innovative. What Kuhn has called "normal science" could conceivably be conducted within a critical paradigm as well as a conservative or liberal one. Hence, it was a prominent concern that any alternative psycho-social models presented exhibit something more than the extension of traditional left thinking. For example, in seeking work on the "Marx–Freud synthesis," the concern was to look at advances beyond the attempted integrations that have been available for 30 or 40 years. The hope was that, as a whole, the critical studies would provide a manifold of alternative avenues to the synthesis of psychological and social approaches, thereby transforming the traditional relationship between conceptual and political.

This sixth requirement implied a seventh. The interest in critical approaches was taken to require a responsibility on the part of the authors to be critical not only about mainstream psychology but also about the so-called "critical" approaches themselves. For example, while being sympathetic to the affinities between psychology and the social sciences, it was generally considered important to keep in mind that human life does not lack biological dimensions.

Last but not least, there needed to be a specific obsession with development in the work. Much critical psychology has suffered from its broad purview. Where development has been mentioned, it has often been touched on only in passing, or dismissed as an artifact of individualism or the ideology of progress. As critics, we wished to play a paradoxical role, enhancing the dignity of the topic of development in the very act of providing a critical framework for approaching the subject.

The parts of this volume are related to each other in too intricate a manner to have made it wise to divide the chapters officially into sections. However, by way of a prefatory overview, allow me to describe the contents of the book as though they were arranged according to the following scheme of four segments.

My introductory chapter represents an attempt to diagnose the ills of developmental psychology and to prescribe, if not a cure, some possible types of treatment. There is an expanded discussion of the chief dimensions of a critical approach sketched above in terms of criteria for choosing the contributions to the volume. Rather than pronouncing them by fiat, some effort is made to justify and explain them, with particular concern to avoid the usual misinterpretations of society, history, and politics that are current among psychologists. If anything characterizes my own approach it is that we must read development "at the slant," underline it, italicize it, put it in quotation marks. Not that it is not to be taken seriously, but it is certainly not to be taken literally. Hopefully, the overview remains consistent with the precepts of the whole book, resisting the temptation to give an abstract, synchronic analysis of the situation, and taking into account the social and historical formation of critical developmental psychology itself.

There is a certain irony to the next four chapters. All the contributors share a profound scepticism with regard to the use of chronological age as a salient feature in accounting for development. Nevertheless, their awareness of the social construction of development includes an acknowledgment that, like it or not, the periodization of the life course in terms of age is entrenched not only in educational institutions, but also in that institution called Developmental Psychology. The authors of Chapters 2 through 5, therefore, take it upon themselves to challenge the apparent naturalness, necessity, and immutability of infancy, childhood, adolescence, and adulthood. In so doing, they deconstruct and demystify the individualizing function of age, its concealing of socialization practices in a biological disguise, and its role in the maintenance of patrimony. They achieve this by focusing on maturation, organization, sequences, and competences, not as literal accounts of developmental realities but as symbols of ideology, power, and the historical formation of psychological discourse.

Adrienne Harris reinterprets the popularity of infancy research in terms of a concerted social effort to modernize development at its roots. There is something about the contemporary technological and bureaucratic enterprise, she argues, that requires a new kind of baby, a new kind of mother, and a tighter fit between the two. The scientific organism, now a dependent variable, now an independent one, has become the prototype for all infants. Harris points to the formative role of the inquirer. The hypertrophy of professional attention serves not so much the neutral interests of scientific discovery as the regulation of the relationship that is taken to be prototypical of all relationships. Mother and child construct the dialogue. What could be more natural than this earliest of democratic cooperations? But mothers and babies are increasingly construed as communication devices, to be turned on and tuned in. Intimacy is a militarized wireless operation, dominated by the decoding of signals and the encoding of strategically optimal responses. Behind the utopian promise of electronic bliss lies a dream of purely technical caretaking and an escalation of the authority of the expert. Jerry Bruner says . . . Berry Brazelton says . . . Danny Stern says . . . Jerry Bruner says. . . . The modern lullabye.

Jacques Vonèche wakens us from our infantile slumbers. Once a child himself, he laments the frozen landscape of modern childhood, the stilled voices of the preoperational. He was a colonial child of the Congo, speaking only Swahili. Now what troubles him is the implosion of imperialism—the colonization of the child. Vonèche points to the norm that has made many of our careers possible: Childhood as an object of examination and an opportunity for gentrification. Surveillance and regulation by educators produce a normal, child-like subject, a self-regulating component of the urban and suburban system. Psychology and the sciences of education—bodies of knowledge, or the knowledge of bodies? Do they not elevate their methods and themselves by marking the standard deviants in the bourgeois normal distribution and shunting them off for special treatment? Discovery, or production? The professionals have rescued the feral child from bestiality, but they themselves are not yet out of the woods.

Valerie Walkerdine changes the subject from childhood to adolescence. There is no natural, sequentially ordered progress through youth, no inevitable trials and tribulations of the transition to adulthood. There is only the initiation into certain gendered discourses. Romance wasn't built in a day. The transition to feminine sexuality is a gradual seduction by the literature of fantasy, particularly the preadolescent comic book, in which plucky lasses confront adversity while hoping for a sexual release. The instructions are clear: Pucker up and await the kiss of the frog prince, the phallus in Wonderland. Through the pleasure of the looking-glass text, "I" becomes "She." But, as suggested by Lacan, the desiring woman subject arises only through a subjection. The comic contains the tragic and fact turns out to be far stranger than fiction.

Richard Lichtman, as befits the Californian, moves on from youth to decay. Like Adorno in Los Angeles, he is struck by the illusion of adulthood as a capital investment coming to maturity. He indicates how to read in development the experience of life as capitalism advances to the rear. Societies decline to acknowledge their degeneracy, instead renaming it "progress." Only the lonely can be autonomous. Adulthood "stages" are premised on abstract time. Psychological life is a consolation for the loss of social life and historical significance. The army celebrates in retreat; subtraction appears as addition; scars are sported as emblems. The production of desire coincides with the desire for production. The question we are left with: How is transformation of the social situation possible? Or, as a Marxist friend used to quip, "Consumption be done about it?"

The dismantling of the timetable of life in these four chapters is followed, in Chapters 6 and 7 by two rather different discussions of recent developments in the Marx–Freud domain, drawing on European thought. The attempts to synthesize the theories of these two great theorists are particularly significant for developmental psychology. Even though neither Marx nor Freud was a developmentalist, strictly speaking, it could be said that Marx had a stage-sequential theory of historical progression and that it was the Freudian socialists who first brought to Marxism a psychological and developmental dimension. Chapters 6 and 7 continue the concern so far with the continuity between psychological elaboration and institutional life, and the close relation between authority and its internalization in psychological forms. But they introduce issues that are hardly mentioned in the first five chapters, such as the unconscious and its relation to false consciousness, alienation of labor and its relation to psychopathology, and primary process and its relation to political resistance. These issues are set in the context of social history and the history of critical paradigms in the human sciences.

Ed Elbers discusses the strengths and weaknesses of the Holzkamp school of *Kritische Psychologie* in Berlin, focusing on the particular successes and failures of the work of Osterkamp. Her historical account, borrowing from Leont'ev, rescues the maligned category of "motivation" by coupling development with both phylogenesis and social reproduction. We labor together to develop, and we are healed through practice rather than insight. Elbers comes not to bury mainstream psychology but to appraise an alternative psychology, and he does not fail to remind us that critical psychology itself cannot claim immunity from criticism. In so doing, however, he emulates his forbears in the Zuider Zee, managing to recover some of the *terra firma* of Marxist psychology that has too long been submerged.

David Ingleby updates the Marx–Freud debate by furthering the project of a critical psychiatry in the light of critical theory and post-structuralism. Since false consciousness presupposes a psychological self-deception, a concept of the unconscious seems essential to any critical psychologist. Yet the common assumption that Freud can be recuperated to provide this for us is betrayed by the biologism, conservatism, and individual–society dualism in his theory, and the authoritarianism in his practice. The possibility of insight is undermined by the fact that psychoanalysis is so well fitted to the generation of ideology. It is through recent research in cultural history that a political edge might be restored to depth psychology. What Walkerdine illustrates in practice, Ingleby justifies at the metatheoretical level—the productivity of post-structuralism.

The last three chapters, while offering quite diverse approaches to development, share their concern to speculate about innovative approaches to the elaboration of a synthetic alternative to mainstream psychology. They focus on the revision of traditional cognitive and clinical views of development in the light of Hegel, feminism, critical theory, family sociology, and aesthetic philosophy. They are deliberately eclectic, and therefore depart from much theory building on the left which, unfortunately, has tended to be narrow, dogmatic, and hostile to interdisciplinary coordinations.

Jessica Benjamin, like Ingleby, concludes that while we may have learned a great deal from psychoanalytic theory and the history of its practice, we must move on. The Freudian model will not do, she concludes, although not for the reasons that Ingleby suggests. What traditional psychoanalysis and its offshoots take to be the natural developmental emergence of individuality and autonomy is a program for the preservation of infantile narcissism through the reproduction of traditional authority. As for Walkerdine, it is gender that is at the heart of the issue. In the early, preoedipal relation to the mother, nurturance is artificially split from autonomy. Separateness is reified and deified as masculinity, thereby grounding the patriarchal model that reproduces gender hierarchy, misogynism, and rational violence. Like Ingleby, but in contrast to Harris, Vonèche, and Lichtman, Benjamin seasons her account with the recent findings of mainstream empirical psychology. Like Osterkamp, her critique of psychology does not prevent her from appropriating some of its findings for the purposes of her own argument. In so doing, she foreshadows a possible rapprochement between critical and traditional theory.

Susan Buck-Morss creates a complex and challenging framework for understanding development by operationalizing the theoretical concepts of the critical theorist Adorno. Few people have been able to link critical theory to development without compromising the former, but she manages to avoid the usual pitfalls with the help of Klaus Riegel's concept of dialectical operations. This allows her to advance development to a stage beyond Piaget, exposing the pretensions of logic and scientific method by tracing their historical origins within capitalist exploitation. Adorno described dialectics as "the ontology of the wrong state of things." Like Walter Benjamin, Buck-Morss deconstructs conventional social science to tell the story of how modernism casts its long shadow of abstract rationality over literary and aesthetic sensibility. Like Jessica Benjamin, she has a sobering message: what we take to be the development of reason may actually represent a dangerously regressive depersonalization that can only result in compliant anesthesia. She is the trickster—turning Enlightenment rationality upside down. Development is now its own mirror image, based on the root metaphor of nonidentity, with its corollaries of ambiguity, nonreciprocity, and disequilibration.

Rainer Döbert, Jürgen Habermas, and *Gertrud Nunner-Winkler* explore the implications of Habermas's work on dialogical ethics in the context of Döbert and Nunner-Winkler's empirical studies of "Adoleszenskrise." It is fitting that this volume close with a constructive program for research embodied in such an ambitious theoretical synthesis. In a remarkable instance of fruitful nonidentity, they rebuff the critique of Piaget by Vonèche and Buck-Morss. They map a thorough recuperation of cognitive developmental psychology, restoring its self and its biographical context by integrating it with ego psychology and family sociology. The outcome is an alternative developmental theory centered on the original concept of interactive competence.

As the above summary promises, the tension between traditional theory and critical theory, first spelled out by Horkheimer (1937/1972), is supplemented in this volume by numerous tensions among the positions of the contributors. These chapters may well comprise a historical and political unity in the broader context of the history and politics of psychology. But by no means does that imply that a point of closure has been reached. It is precisely the dramatic dynamism within critical developmental psychology that provides convincing evidence that it is alive. Hopefully, critical theories of psychological development will be brought into relation with other paradigms and will be operationalized in terms of further empirical projects and emancipatory practices. If this transpires, established developmental psychology could conceivably find the healthy vitality of the critical approach quite infectious.

JOHN M. BROUGHTON

References

Horkheimer, M. (1972). Traditional theory and critical theory. In *Critical theory: Selected essays*. New York: Herder & Herder. (Originally published 1937)

CONTENTS

Chapter 1

John M. Broughton

AN INTRODUCTION TO CRITICAL DEVELOPMENTAL PSYCHOLOGY

> *From this the poem springs: that we live in a place*
> *That is not our own and, much more, not ourselves*
> *And hard it is in spite of blazoned days.*
>
> Wallace Stevens, *Notes Toward a Supreme Fiction*

What Is Developmental Psychology?

Developmental psychology is a manifold of diverse human activities. It is not just a scientific discipline combining theory with practice and research. It is also wholly a part of society, a social institution with a professional structure and a public presence. Not only does it influence social behavior, but it also represents a special form of continuous participation in the political process. It not only reflects ongoing social activities but joins concertedly in their formation, regulation, and reformation.

Developmental psychology segments, classifies, orders, and coordinates the phases of our growth and even defines what is and is not to be taken as growth. It creates a developmental discourse that, like language itself, both engenders and preempts the range of conditions of possibility within which the human life course can make sense. Its interpretive function allows it to produce as well as consume meaning.

John M. Broughton • Department of Developmental and Educational Psychology, Teachers College, Columbia University, New York, New York 10027.

Developmental psychology sets goals and formulates ideals for human development and provides the means of realizing them. Rather than simply observing development, it develops us. By observing and speaking about the most intimate parts of our life history and personality, it enters into the realm of the private, participating in our formation as subjects as well as objects. It fashions us as specific forms of subjectivity within the intentional matrix of the world-historical situation.

However, developmental psychology does not exert these influences spontaneously, nor as an autonomous agency. As institution, discourse, practice, theory, method, or fact, it emerges in response to and as a representation of the imaginations, desires, and fantasies of the very same human individuals and collectivities in whose formation it plays such a decisive role. Each of us, and each of our social aggregations, in some respect contributes to these various activities of developmental psychology—the layperson as much as, if not more than, the professional psychologist. These contributions are made at a level of activity of which we are seldom conscious. They are often made unwillingly as well as unwittingly.

This description of developmental psychology is not the received view. To the contrary, there is considerable consensus among developmental psychologists that their field is an academic subdiscipline contained within the behavioral sciences, one that objectively observes and measures age-related changes exhibited by human individuals, more or less independent of concrete context or history. This consensual position would hold that developmental psychology functions autonomously in quest of advances in specialized knowledge, technical sophistication, and precision of measurement. The field sustains repeated incremental advances as a function of specific discoveries, methodological innovations, and clarifications of terminology. This progressive process of construction is independent of political motive or aim. As a science, it can serve no particular political purpose but rather possesses a privileged immunity from the machinations to which societal institutions are subject. Its business is confined to the registering of the realities of human development, which are of the order of naturally occurring facts, not produced entities. Developmental psychology therefore plays no role in the formation of the development it studies, nor do its acts of investigation shape the object of inquiry. It takes no liberties with language but analyzes its data and discloses its findings by means of standard linguistic usage. Its commitment to rigorous and replicable methods of experimentation, measurement, and observation guarantee its ethical neutrality and respect for the privacy of its subjects, that is, its objects of study.

Such is the credo of established developmental psychology. In a recent examination of the published abstracts of the 1985 conference of the Society for Research in Child Development, I found that all but 30 of the approximately 1,200 papers presented fit this paradigm exactly. A reading of the recent four-volume *Carmichael's Handbook of Child Psychology* (Mussen, 1984) reveals the same pattern of conformity. A comparison of the Carmichael handbook with its earlier editions or of Collins's (1982) reprise with the previous generations of metatheory (Harris, 1957; Stevenson, 1966) discloses that nothing much of significance has changed. The entrenched American tradition of empiricist and positivist psychology has sustained virtually perfect reproduction at the hands of developmentalists.

One rarely sees the dominant credo spelled out explicitly. Its complex of claims is felt to be so well established that it can be presupposed. It is comprised of self-evident "givens" that seem to be the only possible grounds upon which developmental psychology could exist. To call them into question would be heretical; it would imply that the questioner was not a developmental psychologist and could never be one.

This chapter confronts the problematic fact that our social arrangements encourage an unconscious truncation of human development and that, due to the unquestioned givens of the discipline, a primary responsibility for this state of affairs devolves upon developmental psychology. This unfortunate connection between modern life and modern science is subjected to critical scrutiny here in the optimistic belief that, were conditions more favorably disposed toward it, the possibility of a more distinguished ontogenesis might be realized. However, as currently constituted, developmental psychology asserts itself as a professionalized discipline in such a way as to curtail the very processes of growth that it claims to analyze and foster. The political–economic structure of the discipline has become such that its members tend to fixate more upon the growth of their profession, their careers, and their market relationships than they do upon the fate of the developing persons who are the occasion of their vocation. As a consequence, developmentalists provoke the very problems that they appear to discover and then ameliorate.

Like psychologists in general, developmentalists tend to be guided by the modernist vision so thoroughly described by sociologists from

Max Weber to Talcott Parsons. In the eyes of the devotee of modernization, a more highly differentiated, specialized, and relativized institutional structure, empowered to operate in a more complex, stable, and authoritative manner, is necessarily a more advanced one. Modern individuals develop only insofar as they accommodate to these macroscopic criteria, reproducing them in miniature (Sullivan, 1977). Unwittingly, the typical developmental psychologist, subscribing to this vision, looks back over the history of the emergence of his or her discipline from the body of psychology and takes the given pattern of this trajectory as an absolute precedent, a necessary model for all development. The imperative of institutional upgrading is thereby converted into the coercive system of individualized achievement (Looft, 1971). It is woven into the very political fabric of the discipline, then, that the course of actual human development will be dictated and regulated by the evolving needs and interests of the profession, rather than the latter taking its identity from a responsive attention to the needs and concerns of the developing people who are the object of its various operations (Henriques, Hollway, Urwin, Venn, & Walkerdine, 1984; Lubek, 1980).

The following notes are intended less to provide a manifesto for an alternative orientation to development than to situate that emerging approach and the critical psychology from which it has grown, to provide a historical and political backdrop for the various contributions to this volume. This introduction is concerned with identifying the occasional outcroppings of dissent as substantial reminders of a respectable scholarly tradition. At times close to an annotated bibliography in form, the following sketch of a nascent orientation embodies the promise that it is possible to reconceive diverse critical works both within psychology and in the surrounding penumbra of the human sciences in terms of a more or less unified ambition: an interrogation of the ideology of individual psychological progress and the severely limited form of human development that it tends to produce.

The Lack of Self-critique in Developmental Psychology

There is a distinguished tradition of self-critique in psychology (Broughton, in press; Sullivan, 1984). However, when we turn to developmental psychology, we find an interruption of this tradition. Developmentalists are a sanguine breed, blithely going about their business as though they were immune to the existing criticisms of psychology or knew nothing of them. The various prestigious publications that survey the field[1] and individual reviewers of its progress[2] confine themselves systematically to reporting certain trends—changes of orientation that are usually methodological in nature. The emergence of relativistic strategies of research design and analysis, such as interactionism, contextualism, and situationism are commonly celebrated. A safe neutrality is sustained throughout: No fundamental shortcomings in the discipline are acknowledged. There are no serious criticisms of developmental psychology voiced in these reviews. Moreover, any criticisms of the field that have been made by psychologists or other scholars[3] are tactfully ignored. "Business as usual," "Whistle while you work," and "Don't rock the boat" seem to be the watchwords of these scholarly sentinels.[4]

Closer examination reveals that the posture of neutrality is not authentic. There is a hidden advocacy of a specific and extreme kind: a trumpeting of the virtues of that which dominates. Here, at least, Machiavelli is apparently borne out: Might makes right. Any new trend, once it has gained a critical mass of adherents, finds a suitable mouthpiece through which to congratulate itself. This peculiar form of narcissistic gratification is secured by the invocation of supposedly neutral

[1]See, for example, Baltes & Brim, 1984; Hetherington, 1983; Horowitz, 1975; Lamb, 1984; Lipsitt & Spiker, 1984; Mussen, 1984; Perlmutter, 1984; and Reese, 1983.

[2]See, for example, Baltes, Reese, & Lipsitt, 1980; Bruner, 1983; Cairns & Valsiner, 1984; Field, 1982; Flavell, 1982; Honzik, 1984; Howe & Cheyne, 1985; Leahy, 1982; Masters, 1981; Parke & Asher, 1983; and, regarding general methodology, Lewin, 1979, and Nadelman, 1982.

[3]I do not wish to minimize the occasional efforts that have been made to develop alternative visions of the psychology of development. For example, in North America, there are the important explorations by Skolnick (1976), Buss (1979a, 1979b), Kessen (1979), and Kessel and Siegel (1983) and the inventive contributions of Glick, Gruber, Harris, Sullivan, and Wozniak in the Proceedings of the Teachers College Jean Piaget Memorial Conference (Broughton, Leadbeater, & Amsel, 1981). From outside the profession came the landmark ideology-critique of Buck-Morss (1975) and several influential histories of childhood, such as that by Sommerville (1982). The European contribution is perhaps more salient, starting out with the socialist developmental psychology of Henri Wallon (1941, 1945) and two critiques from phenomenologists, Merleau-Ponty (1964) and Bachelard (1969), and followed by the often critical collections edited by Armistead (1973), Richards (1974), Lock (1978), Sants (1980), Modgil and Modgil (1980, 1985), Hoyles (1981), Modgil, Modgil, and Brown (1983), and Henriques *et al.* (1984).

[4]It should be admitted that there are occasional reviews that escape the conventional tone of self-satisfaction, for example, those of Meacham, 1977; Labouvie-Vief and Chandler, 1978; Sigel, 1981; Kuhn, 1983; Wapner and Kaplan, 1983; Kaplan, 1984; and White, 1984. These authors engage in a more reflective and perceptive assessment than mainstream reviewers. However, they tend to do so by applying a developmental perspective to the field itself, thereby continuing to express a certain confidence in progress.

values, absolute and unquestionable, requiring no further justification. Of these, currently the most popular and most self-evidently objective is *sophistication*. Speaking of the recent changes in methodology, for example, Maccoby (1980) concludes simply, "The approach is more sophisticated" (p. 29), and Field (1982) declares, "One is impressed with the increasingly sophisticated human being, whether infant or aged, that is being revealed by increasingly sophisticated research" (p. xv). These are presumably sophisticated judgments revealing increasingly sophisticated developmental psychologists. But are they really sophisticated self-evaluations or simply sophistry?

The Hidden Crisis in Developmental Psychology

As Karl Marx observed, "Just as one does not judge an individual by what he thinks about himself, so one cannot judge . . . a period of transformation by its consciousness" (1976, p. 21). He pointed to the way in which ideological formations work to preserve a superficial impression of continuity precisely at points of deep historical discontinuity (Marx, 1978; Marx & Engels, 1947). The lesson of intellectual history is that it is precisely at times of crisis that empiricist, relativist, and situational approaches tend to gain a purchase (Mannheim, 1936). Could it be that the "neutral" yet sanguine outlook characterizing the self-evaluation of developmentalists is actually a defense mechanism, a concealment of discontinuity with the semblance of continuity? Is smugness a bluff?

Developmentalists may lag behind the other subdisciplines of psychology in the emergence of critical self-awareness precisely on account of a certain utopian optimism latent in the very notion of *development*. As suggested by certain critical commentators (Gordon & Green, 1974; Holzman, 1984; Jacoby, 1975, 1985), the metaphor of psychological growth may be one of the measures to which modern culture resorts in order to anaesthetize itself to the painful rending of personal and social fabrics. The delicate tapestry of scholarly work has not been the least of those tissues torn, and on this account a certain self-protectiveness may be understandable.

Crumbling Foundations and Spurious Innovations

Although therapists must respect their clients' defenses, they are also responsible for restoring a certain perception of reality. A close inspection of the grounding of the current psychology of development reveals that it is not so secure as it might seem. The central commitments of the established discipline—positivism and cognitive functionalism—no longer seem to possess a self-evident validity. Positivism is still paid lip-service in developmental psychology; yet it has been widely undermined by the trenchant critiques of psychologists and philosophers alike[5].

The hegemony of cognitive functionalism in developmental psychology persists (Howe & Cheyne, 1985; Sampson, 1981), despite the fact that the coherence of the cognitive position is in serious question (Dreyfus, 1979; Moroz, 1972). Moreover, key figures within the ranks of cognitive psychology have reluctantly arrived at the conclusion that cognitive and informational approaches are, in principle, inadequate to the task of even the simplest psychological explanation (Ingleby, 1973; Neisser, 1976; Rappoport, 1985; Weizenbaum, 1976; Winograd, 1980).[6]

But, surely, the new 'increasingly sophisticated' approaches in the field legitimate a certain confidence, don't they? Unfortunately, the recent innovations of developmental psychology turn out to be more public relations than substance:

1. Interactionism, presented as a discovery by the new metatheorists (e.g., Magnusson & Allen, 1983; Sigmon, 1984), turns out on examination to be just the other face of conventional individualism (Waterman, 1981). The "person or situation" controversy, having lost its command over social psychology, has turned to the task of colonizing the less sophisticated domain of developmental psychology (Gadlin & Rubin, 1979).
2. The successes of infant research, lionized by the Sunday color supplements, pivot on the dubious merits of technical refine-

[5]For critiques of positivism by psychologists, see, for example, Giorgi, 1970; Armistead 1973; Mussen, 1977; and Rappoport, 1985. For critiques of positivism by philosophers of science, see, for example, Radnitzky 1968; Lakatos, 1970; Rozeboom, 1972; Bhaskar, 1978, 1982; and Rorty, 1979. For critiques of positivism by philosophers of psychology, see, for example, Merleau-Ponty, 1963; Harré & Secord, 1972; Taylor, 1973; Gergen, 1979; Larsen, 1980, 1985; Gergen & Gergen, 1982; Manicas, 1982; and Secord, 1982. The burgeoning scepticism about positivism has even started to make inroads among developmental metatheorists (Looft, 1971; Smedslund, 1977; Harris, 1982).

[6]Despite the triumphalist rhetoric that celebrates the "cognitive revolution" (Maccoby, 1980), the cognitive approach is not as discontinuous with the past of psychology as some would like to have us believe. It is actually a direct descendent of behaviorist psychology (Broadbent, 1961) and shares the latter's dualistic mechanism (Jones, 1975). It is therefore subject to many of the rather telling critiques visited upon behaviorism (see, for example, Chomsky, 1959, 1972; Merleau-Ponty, 1963; Taylor, 1964).

ments that allow the discovery of cognitive competences at younger and younger ages (Masters, 1981; Dates, 1979). "Earlier is better" is the maxim of the hour, as if to retreat to mystical wonderment at the foresight of "human nature" and thereby avoid the burdensome task of having to explain development (see Chapter 2).

3. The burgeoning of "the Vygotskian approach" (van IJzendoorn & van der Veer, 1984; Wertsch, 1981, 1985), turns out on closer examination to be only an elaboration of the standard functionalist paradigm, and one that enhances its more mechanistic features (Zahaykevich, 1984).
4. The fad for "action theory" (Eckensberger & Meacham, 1984) is hardly more than old American functionalism and pragmatism in new bottles (Sigel, 1984).
5. The "life-span" movement, having failed to fulfill its initial promise (Freeman, 1984), merely reruns traditional individualist and positivist psychology (Dannefer, 1984) without anything more original than a hypertrophy of the methodological fetish (Kaplan, 1984), while its "dialectical" subgroup (e.g., Datan & Reese, 1976) makes much ado about trotting out the tired nag of behaviorism.
6. The new psychology of "self" (Loevinger, 1976; Smith, 1978) is simply systems theory in the reified form of an intrapsychic entity (Broughton, 1985a; Broughton & Zahaykevich, 1980, in preparation; Wexler, 1982).

In sum, it can be said that the "tradition of the new" maintains the circulation of academic capital in the interest of entrenched constituencies without any evidence of significant advance in the understanding of human development (Mussen, 1977; D. Olson, 1985).

Malpractice and Misapplication

Not only are the metatheoretical foundations and the research record of developmental psychology weak, but also its current *practice* is in a sorry state. The practical attempts to foster development are almost exclusively confined to the educational sphere. There is very little attempt to derive therapeutic procedures, at individual, group, or community levels, from developmental concepts or findings. Even within the educational domain, developmental psychology has had conservative effects, not least of which is its regressive tendency to confuse education with schooling. That much touted discovery, "adult development," has been used primarily as a legitimation for the construction of marketable reschooling devices for the disenchanted and the disenfranchized (Zahaykevich, 1983a).

With the increasing attenuation of educational psychology as an effective subdiscipline (Harré, 1985), developmentalists have been eager to move into the schools and fill the gap (Walkerdine, 1984). But it has turned out to be a much needed gap. Even in the domain of curriculum and pedagogy, there is a dearth of instances that one could point to saying, "Here, developmental psychologists have taught teachers something significant" (Claxton, 1985; Vonèche, 1980). The recent developmental justifications for the fad of instructional technology and the promotion of microelectronic learning are not only intellectually barren (Broughton, 1985b; Sloan, 1985) and lacking in research grounding (Pea & Kurland, 1984) but are also positively harmful, serving the needs of social control and the corporate economy rather than the needs of developing children (Greene, 1985; Jacobsen, 1985; C. Olson, 1985; Sullivan, 1985; Vonèche, in press). Not only has developmental psychology fostered the narrow vision of education as schooling; it has confounded development with the political socialization to which schools lend themselves so willingly (Bernstein, 1975; Noble, 1985; Zahaykevich, 1983b). In general, applied psychology has been a dismal failure (D. Olson, 1985), and applied developmental psychology, in particular, remains in disarray (Ginsburg, in press). Even the concept of the *application* of psychology is a confused and dubious one (Walkerdine, 1985).

The Decline of Development

As theory, research, method, social role, and institution, the psychology of development suffers from a certain degeneracy. But the very nature of development itself, often ignored in the hustle and bustle of professional life, is also cause for concern. Officially appointed to survey the contemporary conditions of child growth, Brim (1975), Keniston (1978), and De Lone (1979) independently arrived at the same conclusion: The welfare of our young is increasingly at risk, jeopardized by our current social arrangements and the direction of their rearrangement. Their findings converge with the tasteful jeremiad of Senn (1977). What is more, the conditions facing young mothers are declining rapidly as well (Kaufman, 1985). The dissipation of kinship and community networks and the rise of inauthentic forms of social life (Benne, 1975) have left parents less capable of child rearing (Lasch, 1977).[7]

Diverse testimony before the House of Representatives Select Committee on Children, Youth, and Family (1984a, 1984b, 1984c) confirms the impression that psychology, at that point where it is needed most, has been found most impotent (Sarason, in press). Its complacent self-satisfaction, advertised regularly through official channels such as the dreary *APA Monitor* and the trendy *Psychology Today,* seems to increase precisely in proportion to its inability to deal with the burgeoning social problems facing our young and their families. How ironic, then, to see the resurgence of empiricism, with its trust in the situation, context, or environment as explanatory concepts.

In summary, the actual state of affairs in developmental psychology does not appear to be what its spokespersons pretend. The most salient achievement of the discipline would appear to be that of a qualitatively new stage of self-deception. The idea that human beings can be characterized chiefly in terms of their natural tendency to develop and the developmental practices that urge young and old alike to submit to the process of development have become increasingly mystifying as we have come to feel more keenly the need for the reassurance they afford. As the young science amasses knowledge and grows into the adult society of fellow institutions, perhaps it is also developing in itself a systematic desensitization.

What Is Critical Developmental Psychology?

In a series of lectures originally entitled *The Crisis of the European Sciences and Psychology,* Husserl (1970) argued that it is the crux of any critical approach that it call into question precisely those givens in a discipline that are not regularly made the object of systematic examination and interrogation. Critical developmental psychology follows in this tradition. It aims at a thorough restoration of sensitivity to that body

[7]There are sporadic attempts at speaking out critically about the possible ways in which developmental psychology may be damaging rather than fostering the welfare of children and parents. However, such analyses tend to meet with abrupt dismissal. For example, Suransky (1982), with a strong endorsement from Freire (1982), has recently protested the containment and alienation of children by the institution of schooling (Smith, 1983). Bruner (1983) quickly rejected the critique as merely "the debris of Suransky's indignation," while poor old Paulo was damned as "breathless" (p.88).

of psychological knowledge numbed by an unreflective acceptance of the received view of what *development* is. Moreover, it seeks to question the assumption that development is forever condemned to take the same form that it does here and now.

However, the critical approach within developmental psychology exemplified here founds itself on more than Husserl's critique of scientistic objectivism. True, psychology as a natural science is disputed throughout this volume. It is also true that a central category rehabilitated within our critical approach is *subjectivity* as we shall see below. But critical developmental psychology has taken as its primary task the reconstruction of knowledge about human development in the light of a *historical, social,* and *political* understanding of the conditions under which that development takes form.

We need, now, to examine each of these adjectives in turn, taking care not to confuse the critical conception of historical, social, and political with their more traditional varieties. It is not so much that developmental psychology is apolitical, asocial, or ahistorical, but rather that it is a discipline that has traditionally been political, social, and historical in a presumptuous, self-deceptive, and oppressive way.

Development as Historical

Much of the influence of critical perspectives upon development derives from the dialectical psychology movement of the 1970s and early 1980s, a fascinating crosscurrent that originated chiefly in the work of Klaus Riegel (see, for example, Riegel, 1979). It was Riegel who first provided paradigmatic examples of how historical scholarship could inform our understanding of the ideological dimensions of developmental theories. In effect, he borrowed from intellectual history the methods of the sociology of knowledge and introduced them into developmental psychology (see, in particular, Riegel, 1972).

Riegel came to developmental psychology from gerontology through criticism of methodological problems in aging research. Sad to say, this seems to have fostered a confounding of his scholarly ideas with the methodological innovations of the equally Germanic life-span psychology movement (for a summary of this see Baltes, Reese, & Lipsitt, 1980). This school, however, has trivialized history, equating it with mere social change, and reducing it positivistically to a variable confounded with psychological change (Kaplan, 1984). As Freeman (1984) has documented, the life-span movement has had a largely regressive effect, returning developmental psychology to natural science and logical empiricism by exhuming Hempel's (1942) "covering law" model of explanation.

The neoconservative retreat to psychology's positivistic past has served to blunt the critical edge of Riegel's sociohistorical approach: his ideology critique has been reduced to a technique for the analytic control of cohort effects. Dialectical psychology, in the derivative form that it now takes, actually serves to isolate development from history and to prevent us from perceiving the historical nature of both development and the study of it. The very reappearance of ancient empiricist epistemology in the fashionable garb of life-span developmental psychology testifies to how ahistorical that psychology is. History is not an external variable impinging upon either subjects or disciplines. Rather, it has a subjective dimension (Minkowski, 1970) and is constitutive of subjectivity itself (Kovel, 1982), both biographically and culturally. For this reason, one cannot identify analytically and then "control for" historical effects. History is not a cause to which some "effect," developmental or otherwise, can be attributed. History is not a chain-link fence or input–output device to be reconstructed in terms of a set of antecedent conditions upon which other conditions are consequent. Such a view is "pre/post-erously" out of touch with scholarly historiography.

Historical time is not a simple continuous dimension (Gabel, 1975). It is only through a process of ideological reification (Lukacs, 1971) that our concept of temporality has been allowed to degenerate to such a one-dimensional level. Historical phenomena cannot be conceived of as bringing about localized alterations in human life at a given chronological point. That would constitute a "spatialization" of time, to borrow a term from Lukacs. History defies the Euclidean principle that one cannot be in two places at the same time. We do not conduct historical research in a purely archival or retrospective manner, as though looking back to another, distant place. Rather, the whole of the past lives vitally in the present, providing the very conditions of possibility of the forms of future life, individual and social (Collingwood, 1946; Dilthey, 1976). Moreover, self-consciousness of history and its continuing "action at a distance" in contemporary life further articulates and modulates the various types of historical influence.

It is this vital, subjectified vision of history that allows a critical psychology of human development to comprehend the dialectic between history and life history. In the domain of the subject, too, temporality is such that biographical understanding is nothing like a mere recounting of a sequence of places and events, ordered chronologically. There are some who would benefit from the illusion that the course of our lives really is captured in the records of the Census Bureau and the Internal Revenue Service. However, the bureaucratic organization of work, domicile, and economy comes nowhere near exhausting the meaning of life, fortunately for us. Much as the human experience of time is transformed with each shift in the form of civilization and each alteration of its self-awareness (Thompson, 1963), so, too, the subjectivity of persons and relationships takes on different existential and affective qualities, central to which are enhanced and diminished connections to past experience. This is why psychotherapy is much more central to helping people develop than the current disciplinary boundary between clinical and developmental psychology would indicate.

Development as Social

Central to the critical dialectical psychology that has emerged over the past decade is the aim of reconnecting developmental trajectories to societal structures. However, this mandate should not be taken as indicating that we should limit our revolutionary efforts to the consideration of development in its social context. The latter is a truism that amounts to little more than an overused textbook title. The exhuming of contextualism from its *fin-de-siècle* pragmatist grave is just another piece of evidence for the redundancy of liberalism. Within liberal ideology, the social, cultural, historical, political, technological, and so on are all homogenized into an external environment. The creed of interactionism ensues: "The individual affects the environment *and* the environment affects the individual." Person and situation, cast as text and context respectively, then bear to each other the reversible functional relationship of independent variable to dependent variable (Broughton, 1985c).

In this formula, almost magically, cybernetics displaces Newtonian causality with circular causality. Despite appearances, however, the traditional psychological dualism of individual and society is hardened. There is here a cunning sleight of hand that actually preserves the traditional positivist vision of development rather than challenging it. The old worldview appears to be replaced, but it is actually reduplicated, emphasizing again the catchword of orthodox Western democracies: *reciprocity* (cf. Gouldner, 1973). In the process, the relation between inside and outside is rendered even more mechanical, as human life and growth are reduced to bidirectional exchanges of subsystems with the superordinate systems that govern them. The abstract geometry of this reversibility, lauded in Piaget's theory of operational intelligence, serves the ideological function of concealing subordination, control, and privilege (Harris, 1975).

Critical developmental psychology demystifies this domination disguised as transactional equality. It seeks not simply the socializing of psychology, which, after all, already has its own social psychology firmly imbedded in the positivist tradition. Rather, it construes development itself as social, in every respect. Much as the critical understanding of history restored to it a collective activity, so, too, the critical understanding of society acknowledges the extent of its productivity. Rather than conceiving of social effects on individual development, the very possibility of development and of individuals is premised upon a particular social formation. There is a refusal of the traditional view of society and culture as a mere environment, which exerts its influence upon the developmental course by steering it in certain directions rather than others. Instead, the sociocultural matrix is reconceived as something much more ontologically powerful: it is capable of constructing that very field of alternative directions and of producing the very form that developing takes regardless of the direction in which it moves.

Society and development are therefore in a structural relationship to each other, not a functional one (Buck-Morss, 1975). The very conditions of possibility of development, as we know and experience it, are constituted by society. For psychology, the critical instance of such a constitutive productivity is the *individual* form that development takes in Western democracies. Not only individual commonalities and differences have a social origin, but also the presupposed given of individuality itself, as a phenomenon possessing historical and social specificity. As Geertz (1973) has pointed out, among the world's cultures this notion of a bounded, unique, more or less integrated unity is quite rare and is confined exclusively to societies of the particular type that we inhabit in the particular epoch in which we find ourselves (cf. Gadlin, in press). What appears to us to be the natural dimension of development is, in fact, "second nature"—an acquired morphology that only imitates exclusiveness and necessity.

Development as Political

As Durkheim and Mauss (1963) pointed out long ago, bodies of knowledge are sketches of desired achievements—representations that implicitly embody the advocacy of particular values and ideal objects. These intentional objects science strives to produce and reproduce in the very act through which it appears to "discover" their prior and permanent facticity.

The founding political act of a critical developmental psychology is to identify the ways in which psychology serves to extend and elaborate the societal and institutional effort to produce a certain kind of object. The aim of such a discipline is to sustain an object of study amenable to those methods that it has grown accustomed to employing effectively and through which it retains an authority so far entrenched that its legitimacy no longer comes under scrutiny[8]. These orthodox methods, including the orthodoxy of domination by method itself, appear to be admirably adapted to a scientifically 'neutral' kind of observation of individuals. In fact, such methods are techniques for *individualizing* our collective form of life, thereby rendering it susceptible to more intrusive regulatory organization.

A glance at any standard academic journal in the field will reveal the lengths to which developmental psychology is willing to go—by means of the deployment of operational criteria of excellence and other selection mechanisms—to preserve the individualistic illusion. Developmental psychologists are heavily invested in promoting that form of social life that best fits their own apparatus for the production of development (Ingleby, 1974). Once the illusion is well enough manufactured that the marks of its artificial origin escape notice, the illusion becomes self-fulfilling. It certainly has to be admitted that *development* has become *developments*: our respective life courses now look, to all intents and purposes, as though they were individual in nature. The human race is certainly cunning enough to generate life-like prostheses.

An approach that involves reaching down in this way to find the underlying roots of the discipline—the ulterior motive, the implicit striving, the unwitting foreclosure of possibilities—is a political orientation quite at odds with the currently modish political psychology (see,

[8]A quotation from Canguilhem (1980), brought to my attention by Valerie Walkerdine, is pertinent here: "'What is psychology?', becomes 'What do psychologists hope to achieve, doing what they do?' In the name of *what* have they set themselves up as psychologists . . . ? In the immanence of scientific psychology the question still stands: 'Who has, not the competence, but the mission to be a psychologist?' Psychology is still based upon a duality, not that of factual consciousness and the norms entailed by the idea of man, but that of a mass of 'subjects' and a corporate elite of specialists equipped with a self-appointed mission'" (p. 49).

for example, the journal of the same name). The latter is most commonly comprised of plain vanilla psychologists extending the scope of their academic achievements, applying orthodox, usually cognitive, approaches to political content. The study of political development, for example, is thereby reduced to the investigation of the sequence and rate of acquisition of certain political beliefs or decision-making skills (see, for example, the work of Lane, 1972).

Of course, a critical developmental psychology cannot confine its inquiry to reflexive critiques of the profession itself. It moves through such a reinterpretation of the political function of psychologists to a revisioning of how political socialization actually transforms the growth of experience, in concrete groups and types of children, adolescents, and adults. This concern brings with it a natural preoccupation with practice, the forms of engagement with nature and society, be they work, communication, identity formation, intimacy, social action, or emancipatory struggle—these being the kinds of domains of activity in which the essence of the political lies in the postmodern era (Habermas, 1973, 1974). It is interesting to observe that, with virtually no exceptions, such topics never find their way into the standard research publications.

The Psychological Dimension

As may be apparent from the above comments, a critical approach to development entails a thorough reworking of what the subject matter under investigation is and ought to be. The last three subsections suggest ways in which the concerns of history, sociology, and political science—or at least the critical wings of these disciplines—coincide with the concerns of developmental psychology. But what, then, is to prevent the latter from merely dissolving before our eyes, being absorbed into those other disciplines, as a mere subspeciality?

Although it is not often asked by left-leaning psychologists, an important question remains: What is *psychological* about a critical psychology? I would suggest that the progressive objectification of development in terms of its historical, social, and political characteristics must be offset by an equally rigorous subjectification in terms of the meaning that these qualities of life have for people (cf. Taylor, 1971). This is the core of what it means for a critical approach to reconstruct, and even reconstitute, the interpretive relationship that each and all of us have with the historical, social, and political meaning of our experience.

Within the historical, sociological, and political reanalyses of development, the phenomenological significance of living such a development must be repeatedly identified. Despite the powerful productivity of culture, we are not all formed alike. Indeed, we are not always like ourselves, from day to day or year to year. There is a spontaneity and unpredictability that inheres in the way that each dramatic passage in the psychic process unfolds and reaches its climax. The accent falls upon different notes at different moments and the resulting sound takes on ever new overtones in relation to other melodies that resonate in the interiority of the subject. The intrapsychic and intersubjective orchestra of perception, desire, will, and expression is equipped to generate an enormous repertoire of music, and no simple reductionism, from whatever discipline it emerges, is capable of constraining our celestial conductor to a single tune.

Developmental psychology, then, is irretrievably *hermeneutic* in nature (Freeman, 1985; Honey, in press; Sullivan, 1984). Even the phenomena of development must be understood in the full course of their construal by those who develop, and those who develop with them. The same developmental advance may have a quite different meaning for immigrants than for citizens, for example. Note that here I resist the temptation to say "for an immigrant" or "for a citizen." The forms of subjectivity engaged in that interpretation by which we arrive at the meaning of experience may well not be individualized in form.

A critical developmental psychology is obliged to resist that tendency to objectivism that pervades the social sciences, the foundational given that Husserl so discerningly urged us to question. We may well *appear* objectively to develop and yet hide within ourselves a stunted and disowned subjectivity (Winnicott, 1971). "We live in a place that is not our own and, much more, not ourselves," harking back to Wallace Stevens. This is where interpretive approaches of a psychodynamic nature must play a part, given the demonstrably dynamic origins of that undeveloped self that escapes consciousness. Of course, limitations of this kind in the formation of selfhood have cultural origins no less than personal ones (Jacoby, 1975; Kovel, 1982). The unconscious must be understood interpretively wherever and however it is manifest—in terms of social and political history as well as life history. Hermeneutic approaches provide the hope for fostering insight into all that is human in us but is yet to develop, and they suggest collective and interpersonal practices for both liberating and coming to own that yet-to-be.

The Origins of Critical Developmental Psychology

The critical developmental psychology outlined above would be risking self-contradiction unless it were to announce clearly that it is not just an abstract position. It is certainly not the outcome of an incremental process of factual discoveries or technical sophistications.

The critical approach has taken a specific shape as a function of various formal and informal communities, comprising collegial, teacher–student, and friendship relationships formed among particular people. Central to this history was the large and eclectic Dialectical Psychology Group organized in the early 1970s by Riegel (with its *Dialectical Psychology Newsletter*, edited by Howard Gadlin); a subgroup called the Society for Critical Psychology formed in the late 1970s to explore neo-Marxist perspectives; and the New York-based Group for a Radical Human Science, which was the outgrowth of that subgroup and gave rise to the journal *PsychCritique*[9]. Other journals played a part in the evolution of these collective activities: for example, the American *Psychology and Social Theory*, the Euro-American *Human Development*, and the British *Ideology and Consciousness*. An important feature of the activities of these groups and journals has been the energetic participation of developmental psychologists.

Although critical developmental psychology is an endeavor shared by a considerable number of people of different nationalities working in various directions, it may be worth our while to focus for a moment on some of the characteristics of the contributors to this particular volume, who are more familiar to me than others. This may help to situate not only our book but also critical developmental psychology as a general endeavor.

[9]An interesting document of relevance here is the statement of purpose formulated by over 75 participants in the Group for a Radical Human Science (1981a), which reads as follows: "We are an organization of radicals working in fields concerned with the relationship between psyche and society. The alienating forces of capitalism, sexism and racism which have isolated us politically are the forces which necessitate our coming together. In the context of a grossly inadequate system of health care, social services, and human sciences, the Group for a Radical Human Science seeks to provide: (1) a forum for discussion and analysis of the social mediations of those forces of domination and their impact on the individual; (2) a means for organizing our work so as to reduce the deadening power of professional, class, gender, and racial hierarchy; (3) a stimulus and guide for improving our theory and practice in the classroom, in treatment, and on the job; (4) a base for training ourselves and all those interested in a liberatory understanding and care of the psyche" (p. 4).

Those contributing here by no means constitute an organized group, and they are not homogeneous with respect to intellectual perspective, relative emphasis on theory or practice, professional level, historical generation, or country of origin. Only with difficulty could they claim to make up anything as formal as a school of thought or an "invisible college." However, most of them know most of the rest. Most have had some affiliation with the groups that grew out of Riegel's organizational efforts. Most grew up in an era of affluence and accelerated technical progress. They all have affiliations with institutions of higher education and/or research, where all function as social scientists and almost all as psychologists. Although Belgium, Canada, England, Germany, the Netherlands, and Switzerland are represented here, the non-American authors are relatively Americanized in professional orientation.

Although some of these contributors were radicalized through earlier events and experiences, they share a history of concern and involvement with the transcontinental upheavals of the 1960s and 1970s. The humanistic and socialistic attempts of that period to envisage a combined personal and political liberation were formative for each individual and for their relationships to each other and to their work. In particular, the experience of conflicts centered on capitalism and militarism, sexuality, racial and gender hierarchy, and the injustices of educational and mental health institutions has exerted a profound impact on their individual and collective activities and ideas (see, for example, Benjamin, 1979; Döbert & Nunner-Winkler, 1975; Habermas, 1970; Ingleby, 1967; Vonèche, 1974a, 1974b, 1974c).[10]

For most of the contributors, a crucial aspect of this historical period was the rapid burgeoning of the social sciences and, in particular, the rise in popularity of psychology—in the late 1970s, one of the dominant choices of undergraduate concentrations in American colleges. For several, this played a role in the acquisition and pursuit of a professional vocation in psychology and led to a more or less optimistic view of the discipline. It may even account partially for their shared interest in development, a topic the appeal of which has always seemed most seductive in periods of economic growth (Sullivan, 1981).

However, sooner or later, often through concrete political experiences, serious doubts about the social function of psychology arose.

[10]The intellectual and personal dimensions of this historical trajectory are recorded in an oral history assembled by the Group for a Radical Human Science (1981b).

Major turning points in my own political education were involvement in a university mental health committee as an undergraduate and, as a graduate student during the Viet Nam era, grappling with the work of Jensen and Herrnstein on race and intelligence and participating in the Harvard anti-war strike and the subsequent founding of a temporary but revolutionary 'open university' there.

For many, the political experiences of that period in turn raised questions about the propriety of being a psychologist, especially one who insulated political interests from professional ones. Many colleagues abandoned academic psychology because they became disenchanted with the fact that any radical reformulation of psychology was difficult to sustain in the face of the liberal, humanistic "personology" that then dominated the reaction against behaviorism and empiricism[11]. Others reached the conclusion—often mislabeled "burnout"—that the only possible action consistent with their radical critiques of psychology was to dissociate themselves from it entirely. "Left psychology" seemed a contradiction in terms, and so they left psychology. Their critique of social science, and particularly of research methodology, seemed to preclude the possibility of working constructively for change from within their discipline or profession. Moreover, the intellectual life itself seemed oppressively opposed to activism.

The contributors to this volume differ from that pattern: they have all striven to pursue politically relevant work within psychology. They all think, write, and publish actively. Although there is a literary sensibility to much of the writing here, the authors have not become disenchanted with science. They all retain respect for research and about half continue to conduct an empirical research program. Rather than reaching the conclusion that their discipline could only psychologize politics, they have set about the task of politicizing psychology.

There is a subtle tension between marginality and centrality in this

[11]Such feelings of anomie were by no means ungrounded. Psychology in general and developmental psychology in particular were hardly progressive forces in the face of the political emergencies of the 1960s and 1970s. Other than Keniston's *Young Radicals* (1968) and Hampden-Turner's *Radical Man* (1971), one is hard put to think of any major work of the period that took seriously the concrete political implications of developmental research and theorizing. Instead, there was a predominant attitude of business as usual, with occasional time out to protect established authority by diagnosing the developmental retardation and psychopathology inherent in student radicalism (see, for example, Feuer, 1969, Lorenz, 1972, and Wolfenstein, 1967, and also the political psychology of Harold Lasswell, 1930, arguably the founding work for the psychopathology of rebellion).

position. Critics of the 1960s and 1970s tended to the centrifugal, seeking a more or less peripheral location. They appear to have experienced political space as grossly Euclidean. In contrast, the contributors to this volume would seem to have taken relativity theory seriously, pursuing their transformative impulse centripetally. Most have assumed administrative responsibilities and arbitrative roles within their institutions, seeing a connection between pressing their critical commentary and pursuing its material consequences into the operational structure of the bureaucracy and its dilemmas of governance.

One hesitates to romanticize such management activities. However, there is a noticeable difference between this participatory engagement with institutions and the countercultural rejection of "the system" in the 1960s and 1970s. At worst, one could say that the system has assimilated its opposition (Foss & Larkin, 1982). At best, one could say that despite their overall reactionary tone, the 1980s have allowed criticism to be distinguished from merely unconventional conduct. The experiences of the last generation seem to have made possible a subtler and more sophisticated imagery of how power works (Simone, 1985). There is also a somewhat more tolerant, if not sympathetic, attitude toward institutional life, under the assumption that institutions too may have their subjective moment, one that contains the possibility of resistance and insight as well as self-deception and surrender. However, the fact that under certain conditions power corrupts cannot be blithely dismissed, least of all in post-Watergate America. The problem that Gramsci (1971) posited as the possibility of the "organic intellectual" remains: How are psychologists committed to a critical posture to deal with their frequently embarrassing access to authority and legitimacy (cf. Harris, 1981; Wexler & Whitson, 1982)? This task would appear all the more significant now that economic and ideological factors are threatening the professional future of the next generation of potential critical psychologists, one that may find the possibilities and privileges of such access severely curtailed.

It must be admitted that the previous generation, including the present contributors, was in many respects a privileged one. The general fact of affluence, the lingering ideal of social welfare, the harrowing reality of Viet Nam, and the shock of Watergate conspired to make the role of radical social scientist an almost acceptable one in the university's division of labor. This was distinctly less so in psychology than in, say, sociology or political science, but a spirit of tolerance was still discernible even in the behavioral sciences.

As Gunther Grass has often reminded us, America (unlike Germany, for example) has the shortest of political memories, and the historical delegitimization of authority in the United States occurring in the 1960s and 1970s is now considered so much water under the bridge. Militarization, the rearming of the world policeman, is again fashionable in office and in public favor. The peace movement is foundering. Savage, politically motivated funding cuts in the social sciences accentuate the apparent value of mainstream and defense-oriented research. Cognitive science flourishes, in part as a function of the fact that it is viewed by the government as "weaponizable," to use the currently modish Washington term. In light of these issues, for the young developmentalist to carry the torch of critical psychology is to risk getting badly burned. Certainly, as a teacher and advisor, one hesitates to hand it on.

Nevertheless, as Terry Eagleton (1985) has recently reminded us, the role of critic is a traditional one, and, as Richard Rorty (1983) has pointed out, the critical appropriation and passing on of tradition is the primary purpose of intellectual life. This does not entail being a mere conduit for the blind passing on of the already given. Rather, it presupposes a reflecting, judging, and rejuvenating collectivity whose members, in various combinations, interweave the full range of those discourses that have been experienced and—to restore a theological term eschewed by psychology—loved. Without the repetition of this friendly gesture, the recursive possibility of giving what has already been received from the hands of the admired—their scenarios for the future as well as their antidotes to amnesia—historical community would wither, and all traditions would collapse into the single tradition of the new.

The world of psychology is not only thoroughly modernized and rationalized, but also deeply profane. Its ritual, its mythopoesis, and its person-ality have been commodified and exchanged; there is little more than a mess of pottage to show for it. This, however, makes taking up the role of the critic even more vital. To be the bearer of history, its loyalties and convictions, the moral force of which inheres in living and sharing a full life, can only contribute to the formation of a significant identity for psychologists, dignified by their consistent alignment with the emancipatory moments of both the intrapsychic and the social whole. Is this not what we glimpsed when we were young academics, drawn to the psychological, but not yet to psychology? Is this intuitive desire for a collective union of internal and external freedoms not what we felt to be development and what, at one point, we so much wanted to raise to a reflective level, understand, and act upon?

It is to be hoped that some of the young and young at heart—the "undeveloped"—will read the following chapters and feel sufficient warmth and inspiration to engage with them, use them, criticize them, and improve upon them, as part of their own development, and as a way of reinvigorating their relationship with the psychological. My own experience, however, suggests the need for a certain caution. It would appear unlikely that the critical quest can be engaged in at a merely intellectual level. Moreover, it cannot be a primarily professional concern. At the risk of hypocrisy, I would argue that to make a career out of criticism would amount to a contradiction in terms. I would go so far as to say that critical developmental psychology cannot be contemplated or sustained without a personal, perhaps visceral, commitment. On this account, we are perhaps entitled to speculate that a critical approach to the field both requires and guarantees a real act of human development on the part of the psychologist.

Sad to say, under present conditions, this posture—what I would like to think of as an authentically developmental orientation—is almost bound to require a certain dissociation from the momentum of the ongoing, established profession. There is a kind of educating that only travel can provide, and the journey entails leaving home. Once abroad, one cannot expect reality to be always sympathetic to the solitary traveller. Hence the need for travelling companions; dissociation may require the discovery of new forms of association.

At the beginning of the quest for the Holy Grail, not knowing in which direction to go, the trusty knights "set out into the darkest part of the forest." The search for a critical psychology also requires that we confront our fear of the dark. Many will find the content dealt with here somber, disturbing, even threatening. We have attempted to be dextrous with the sinister. We have tried to remain aware of the thin line between critical vigor and perverse aggression and to stay on the sunny side of it. Nevertheless, when one enters the shadow on the subjective side of oppression, there are unavoidably disintegrative and sadistic qualities that have to be negotiated and even reexperienced.

Perhaps the critic also needs faith, trusting that

> One must have chaos in one,
> To give birth to a dancing star.

Nietzsche, *Thus Spake Zarathustra*

References

Armistead, N. (1973). *Rat myth and magic: A political critique of psychology*. London: Author.

Bachelard, G. (1969). Reveries toward childhood. In *The poetics of reverie*. New York: Grossman.

Baltes, P. B., & Brim, O. E. (Eds.). (1984). *Lifespan development and behavior*, (vol. 6). New York: Academic Press.

Baltes, P. B., Reese, H. W., & Lipsitt, L. (1980). Lifespan developmental psychology. *Annual Review of Psychology, 31*, 65–110.

Benjamin, J. (1979, September). *Starting from the left and going beyond*. Paper presented at the Second Sex Conference, New York Institute for the Humanities, New York University, New York.

Benne, K. D. (1975). Technology and community: Conflicting bases of educational authority. In W. Feinberg and H. Rosemont (Eds.), *Work, technology and education*. Urbana: University of Illinois Press.

Bernstein, B. (1975). *Class, codes, and control* (Vol. 3). London: Routledge & Kegan Paul.

Bhaskar, R. (1978). *A realist theory of science*. Atlantic Highlands, NJ: Humanities Press.

Bhaskar, R. (1982). Emergence, explanation, and emancipation. In P. F. Secord (Ed.), *Explaining human behavior*. London: Sage Publications.

Brim, O. G. (1975). Macro-structural influences on child development and the need for childhood social indicators. *American Journal of Orthopsychiatry, 45*(4), 516–524.

Broadbent, D. E. (1961). *Behaviour*. London: Eyre and Spottiswoode.

Broughton, J. M. (1985a). The psychology, history and ideology of the self. In K. Larsen (Ed.), *Dialectics and ideology in psychology*. Norwood, NJ: Ablex.

Broughton, J. M. (1985b). The surrender of control: Computer literacy and the political socialization of children. In D. Sloan (Ed.), *The computer in education: A critical perspective*. New York: Teachers College Press.

Broughton, J. M. (1985c). The genesis of moral domination. In S. Modgil & C. Modgil (Eds.), *Lawrence Kohlberg: Consensus and controversy*. Lewes, England: Falmer.

Broughton, J. M. (submitted for publication). *A critical history of developmental psychology*.

Broughton, J. M., & Zahaykevich, M. K. (1980). Personality and ideology in ego development. In V. Trinh van Thao & J. Gabel, *Dialectics and the social sciences*. Paris: Anthropos.

Broughton, J. M., & Zahaykevich, M. K. (in preparation) From authoritarian personality to ego development. In B. Seidman (Ed.), *Studies of socialization across the lifespan*.

Broughton, J. M., Leadbeater, B., & Amsel, E. (Eds.). (1981). Reflections on Piaget: Proceedings of the Jean Piaget Memorial Conference. *Teachers College Record, 83*(2), 151–217.

Bruner, J. (1983). State of the child. *New York Review of Books*, Oct. 27, 84–89.

Buck-Morss, S. (1975). The socio-economic bias in Piaget's theory and its implications for cross-cultural study. *Human Development, 18*, 35–49.

Buss, A. (1979a). *Psychology in social context*. New York: Irvington.

Buss, A. (1979b). *A dialectical psychology*. New York: Irvington.

Cairns, R. B., & Valsiner, J. (1984). Child psychology. *Annual Review of Psychology, 35*, 553–577.

Canguilhem, G. (1980). What is psychology? *Ideology and Consciousness, 7*, 51–62.

Chomsky, N. (1959). Review of *Verbal behavior* by B. F. Skinner. *Language, 35*, 26–58.

Chomsky, N. (1972). Psychology and ideology. *Cognition, 1*, (1), 11–46.

Claxton, G. (1985). Educational psychology: What is it trying to prove? In G. Claxton, W. Swann, P. Salmon, V. Walkerdine, B. Jacobsen, & J. White, *Psychology and schooling: What's the matter?* London: Institute of Education, University of London.

Collingwood, R. G. (1946). *The idea of history*. London: Clarendon Press.

Collins, W. A. (Ed.). (1982). *The concept of development: The Minnesota symposia on child psychology* (Vol. 15). Hillsdale, NJ: Erlbaum.

Dannefer, D. (1984). Adult development and social theory: A paradigmatic reappraisal. *American Sociological Review, 49*, 100–116.

Datan, N., & Reese, H. W. (1976). *Lifespan developmental psychology: Dialectical perspectives on experimental research*. New York: Academic Press.

De Lone, R. (1979). *Small futures*. New York: Harcourt, Brace and Jovanovich.

Dilthey, W. (1976). The construction of the historical world in the human studies. In J. Rickman (Ed.), *Dilthey: Selected writings*. Cambridge: Cambridge University Press.

Döbert, R., & Nunner-Winkler, G. (1975). *Adoleszenskrise und Identitätsbildung*. Frankfurt: Suhrkamp.

Dreyfus, H. (1979). *What computers can't do: A critique of artificial reason*. San Francisco: Freeman.

Durkheim, E., & Mauss, M. (1963). *Primitive classification*. Chicago: University of Chicago Press.

Eagleton, T. (1985). *The Function of criticism*. New York: Schocken.

Eckensberger, L., & Meacham, J. A. (1984). The essentials of action theory: A framework for discussion. *Human Development, 27*(3–4), 166–172.

Feuer, L. (1969). *The conflict of generations*. New York: Basic Books.

Field, T. (Ed.). (1982). *Review of human development*. New York: Wiley.

Flavell, J. H. (1982). Structures, stages, and sequences in cognitive development. In W. A. Collins (Ed.), *The concept of development: The Minnesota symposia on child psychology* (vol. 15). Hillsdale, NJ: Erlbaum.

Foss, D., & Larkin, R. (1982). Seven ways of selling out: Post-movement phenomena in social and historical perspective. *Psychology and Social Theory, 3*, 3–12.

Freeman, M. (1984). History, narrative, and life-span developmental knowledge. *Human Development, 27*, 1–19.

Freeman, M. (1985). Paul Ricoeur on interpretation: The model of the text and the idea of development. *Human Development, 28*, 295–312.

Freire, P. (1982). Foreword. In V. Suransky, *The erosion of childhood*. Chicago: University of Chicago Press.

Gabel, J. (1975). *False consciousness*. Oxford: Blackwell.

Gadlin, H. (In press). The deconstruction of self. *New Ideas in Psychology, 4*(3).

Gadlin, H., & Rubin, S. (1979). Interactionism. In A. Buss (Ed.), *Psychology in social context*. New York: Irvington.

Geertz, C. (1973). *Interpretation of cultures*. New York: Basic Books.

Gergen, K. (1979). The positivist image in social psychology. In A. Buss (Ed.) *The social context of psychological knowledge*. New York: Irvington.

Gergen, K., & Gergen, M. (1982). Explaining human conduct. In P. F. Secord (Ed.), *Explaining human behavior*. London: Sage Publications.

Ginsburg, H. P. (In press). What is applied developmental psychology anyway? Review of F. J. Morrison, C. Lord, & D. P. Keating (Eds.), *Applied developmental psychology. Contemporary Psychology*.

Giorgi, A. (1970). *Psychology as a human science*. New York: Harper & Row.

Gordon, E. W., & Green, D. (1974). An affluent society's excuses for inequality: Developmental, economic, or educational. *American Journal of Orthopsychiatry, 44*(1), 4–18.

Gouldner, A. W. (1973). *For sociology*. New York: Basic Books.

Gramsci, A. (1971). *Selections from the prison notebooks*. London: Lawrence & Wishart.

Greene, M. (1985). Philosophy looks at microcomputers. *Computers in the Schools, 1*(3), 3–11.

Group for a Radical Human Science. (1981a). Statement of purpose of G.R.H.S. *PsychCritique Newsletter, 1*, 4.

Group for a Radical Human Science. (1981b). An oral history of the group. *PsychCritique Newsletter, 1,* 2–3.

Habermas, J. (1970). *Toward a rational society.* Boston: Beacon.

Habermas, J. (1973). *Theory and practice.* Boston: Beacon.

Habermas, J. (1974). On social identity. *Telos, 19,* 91–103.

Hampden-Turner, C. (1971). *Radical man.* Cambridge, MA: Schenkman.

Harré, R. (1985). Foreword. In G. Claxton, W. Swann, P. Salmon, V. Walkerdine, B. Jacobsen, & J. White, *Psychology and schooling: What's the matter?* London: Institute of Education, University of London.

Harré, R., & Secord, P. (1972). *The explanation of social behaviour.* Oxford: Blackwell.

Harris, A. E. (1975). Social dialectics and language: Mother and child construct the discourse. *Human Development, 18,* 80–96.

Harris, A. E. (1981). Radical pedagogy. *PsychCritique Newsletter, 1,* 5–6.

Harris, D. B. (Ed.) (1957). *The concept of development: An issue in the study of human behavior.* Minneapolis: University of Minnesota Press.

Harris, D. B. (1982). Foreword. In W. A. Collins (Ed.), *The concept of development: The Minnesota symposia on child psychology* (vol. 15). Hillsdale, NJ: Erlbaum.

Hempel, C. G. (1942). The function of general laws in history. *Journal of Philosophy, 39,* 35–48.

Henriques, J., Hollway, W., Urwin, C., Venn, C., & Walkerdine, V. (1984). *Changing the subject.* New York: Methuen.

Hetherington, E. M. (Ed.). (1983). *Handbook of child psychology: Socialization, personality, and social development* (vol. 4). New York: Wiley.

Holzman, L. (1984). The politics of childhood. *Practice,* 2(3), 148–151.

Honey, M. (In press). The hermeneutics of the clinical interview. *Human Development.*

Honzik, M. P. (1984). Lifespan development. *Annual Review of Psychology, 35,* 309–333.

Horowitz, F. D. (Ed.). (1975). *Review of child development research* (vol. 4). Chicago: University of Chicago Press.

House of Representatives Select Committee on Children, Youth and Families. (1984a). *Youth and the justice system.* Washington, D. C.: U.S. Government Printing Office.

House of Representatives Select Committee on Children, Youth and Families. (1984b). *Child care.* Washington, D. C.: U.S. Government Printing Office.

House of Representatives Select Committee on Children, Youth and Families. (1984c). *Children's fears of war.* Washington, D. C.: U.S. Government Printing Office.

Howe, N., & Cheyne, A. (1985, April). *Recent trends in developmental research.* Paper presented at the Society for Research in Child Development, Toronto.

Hoyles, M. (1981). *Changing childhood.* London: Writers and Readers.

Husserl, E. (1970). *The crisis of the European sciences and transcendental phenomenology.* Evanston, IL: Northwestern University Press.

Ingleby, D. (1967). Psychological theory and human experience. *Cambridge Review,* Jan. 28, 172–176.

Ingleby, D. (1973). New paradigms for old. *Radical Philosophy, 6,* 42–46.

Ingleby, D. (1974). The psychology of child psychology. In M. P. M. Richards (Ed.), *The integration of a child into a social world.* Cambridge: Cambridge University Press.

Jacobsen, B. (1985). Does educational psychology contribute to the solution of educational problems? In G. Claxton, W. Swann, P. Salmon, V. Walkerdine, B. Jacobsen, & J. White, *Psychology and schooling: What's the matter?* London: Institute of Education, University of London.

Jacoby, R. (1975). *Social amnesia: The roots of conformist psychology from Adler to Laing.* Boston: Beacon.

Jacoby, R. (1985). Politics and therapy: Keeping the tension. *New Ideas in Psychology,* 3(2), 80–95.

Jones, B. (1975, June). *Cartesian preconceptions in the shift from behaviorism to cognitive psychology.* Paper presented at Cheiron: The Society for the History of the Behavioral Sciences, Carleton College, Ottawa.

Kaplan, B. (1984). A trio of trials. In R. M. Lerner (Ed.), *Psychology: Historical and philosophical perspectives.* Hillsdale, NJ: Erlbaum.

Kaufman, B. A. (1985, August). *The impact of federal child care subsidies on women's economic equity.* Paper presented to the Society for Research in Child Development, Toronto.

Keniston, K. (1968). *Young radicals.* New York: Harcourt, Brace and Jovanovich.

Keniston, K. (1978). *All our children.* New York: Harcourt, Brace and Jovanovich.

Kessel, F., & Siegel, L. (Eds.). (1983). *The child and other cultural inventions.* New York: Praeger.

Kessen, W. (1979). The American child and other cultural inventions. *American Psychologist, 34*(10), 815–820.

Kovel, J. (1982). *The age of desire.* New York: Pantheon.

Kuhn, D. (1983). On the development of developmental psychology. In D. Kuhn & J. A. Meacham (Eds.), *The development of developmental psychology.* Basel: Karger.

Labouvie-Vief, G., & Chandler, M. J. (1978). Cognitive development and lifespan developmental theory: Idealistic and contextual perspectives. In P. B. Baltes (Ed.), *Lifespan development and behavior.* New York: Academic Press.

Lakatos, I. (1970). Methodology of scientific research programmes. In I. Lakatos & A. Musgrave (Eds.), *Criticism and the growth of knowledge.* Cambridge: Cambridge University Press.

Lamb, M. E. (1984). *Advances in developmental psychology,* (Vol. 3). Hillsdale, NJ: Erlbaum.

Lane, R. (1972). *Political man.* New York: Free Press.

Larsen, K. (Ed.). (1981). *Social psychology: Crisis or failure.* Monmouth, OR: Institute for Theoretical History.

Larsen, K. (1985). *Dialectics and Ideology in Psychology.* Norwood, NJ: Ablex.

Lasch, C. (1977). *Haven in a heartless world.* New York: Harper & Row.

Lasswell, H. (1930). *Psychopathology and politics.* Chicago: University of Chicago Press.

Leahey, R. (1982). *Developmental psychology.* Mimeograph. Los Angeles Association for Advanced Training in the Behavioral Sciences.

Lewin, M. (1979). *Understanding psychological research.* New York: Wiley.

Lipsitt, L., & Spiker, C. (1984). *Advances in child development* (vol. 18). New York: Academic Press.

Lock, A. (1978). *Action, symbol, and gesture.* London: Academic Press.

Loevinger, J. (1976). *Ego development.* San Francisco: Jossey-Bass.

Looft, W. R. (1971). The psychology of more. *American Psychologist, 26,* 561–565.

Lorenz, K. (1972). The enmity between the generations. In M. W. Piers (Ed.), *Play and development.* New York: Norton.

Lubek, I. (1980). The psychological establishment: Pressure to preserve paradigms, publish rather than perish, win funds, and influence students. In K. Larsen (Ed.), *Social psychology: Crisis or failure.* Monmouth, OR: Institute for Theoretical History.

Lukacs, G. (1971). *History and class consciousness.* Cambridge: MIT Press.

Maccoby, E. (1980). *Social development.* New York: Harcourt.

Magnusson, D., & Allen, V. L. (1983). *Human development: An interactionist perspective.* New York: Academic Press.

Manicas, P. (1982). The human sciences: A radical separation of psychology and the social sciences. In P. F. Secord (Ed.), *Explaining human behavior.* London: Sage Publications.

Mannheim, K. (1936). *Ideology and utopia.* New York: International Library in Philosophy, Psychology and Scientific Method.

Marx, K. (1976). *A contribution to the critique of political economy.* Peking: Foreign Languages Press.

Marx, K. (1978). *The 18th Brumaire of Louis Bonaparte*. New York: China Books.
Marx, K., & Engels, F. (1947). *The German ideology*. New York: International Publishers.
Masters, J. C. (1981). Developmental psychology. *Annual Review of Psychology, 32*, 117–151.
Meacham, J. A. (1977). The decentration of developmental psychology: A review of recent books. *Merrill-Palmer Quarterly*, 1977, *23*(4), 287–295.
Merleau-Ponty, M. (1963). *The structure of behavior*. Boston: Beacon Press.
Merleau-Ponty, M. (1964). Maurice Merleau-Ponty at the Sorbonne. *Bulletin de Psychologie, 18*, 109–301.
Minkowski, E. (1970). *Lived time*. Evanston: Northwestern University Press.
Modgil, S., & Modgil, C. (Eds.). (1980). *Toward a theory of psychological development*. Slough, Bucks.: NFER Publishing.
Modgil, S., & Modgil, C. (Eds.). (1985). *Lawrence Kohlberg: Consensus and Controversy*. Lewes, England: Falmer.
Modgil, S., Modgil, C., & Brown, G. (1983). *Jean Piaget: An interdisciplinary critique*. London: Routledge & Kegan Paul.
Moroz, M. (1972). The concept of cognition in contemporary psychology. In J. Royce & W. W. Rozeboom (Eds.), *The psychology of knowing*. New York: Gordon & Breach.
Mussen, P. H. (1977). Presidential address: Choices, regrets, and lousy models. *APA Division on Developmental Psychology Newsletter* (Dec.), 9–15.
Mussen, P. H. (Ed.). (1984). *Carmichael's handbook of child psychology*. New York: Wiley.
Nadelman, L. (1982). *Research manual in child development*. New York: Harper & Row.
Neisser, U. (1976). *Cognition and reality*. San Francisco: Freeman.
Noble, D. (1985). Computer literacy and ideology. In D. Sloan (Ed.), *The computer in education: A critical perspective*. New York: Teachers College Press.
Oates, J. (1979). *Early cognitive development*. London: Croom Helm.
Olson, C. P. (1985). The dream of educational computing: Response to Papert. *New Ideas in Psychology, 3*(3), 297–307.
Olson, D. R. (1985). The enemy without: Review of E. Sullivan, *A critical psychology*. *Interchange, 16*(2), 39–44.
Parke, R. D., & Asher, S. R. (1983). Social and personality development. *Annual Review of Psychology, 34*, 465–509.
Pea, R., & Kurland, M. (1984). On the cognitive effects of learning computer programming. *New Ideas in Psychology, 2*(2), 137–168.
Perlmutter, M. (1984). *Parent–child interaction and parent–child relations in child development: Minnesota symposia on child psychology* (Vol. 17). Hillsdale, NJ: Erlbaum.
Radnitzky, G. (1968). *Contemporary schools of metascience*. Goteborg: Akademievorlaget. (Reprinted by Regnery, Chicago, 1973).
Rappoport, L. (1985). Renaming the world: On psychology and the decline of positive science. In K. Larsen (Ed.),*Dialectics and ideology in psychology*. Norwood, NJ: Ablex.
Reese, H. W. (Ed.). (1983). *Advances in child development and behavior* (Vol. 13). New York: Academic Press.
Richards, M. P. M. (Ed.). (1974). *The integration of a child into a social world*. Cambridge: Cambridge University Press.
Riegel, K. F. (1972). The influence of economic and political ideologies on the development of developmental psychology. *Psychological Bulletin, 78*, 129–141.
Riegel, K. F. (1979). *Foundations of dialectical psychology*. New York: Academic Press.
Rorty, R. (1979). *Philosophy and the mirror of nature*. Princeton: Princeton University Press.
Rorty, R. (1983). Post-modern bourgeois liberalism. *Journal of Philosophy, 80*(10), 583–589.
Rozeboom, W. W. (1972). Problems in the psycho-philosophy of knowledge. In J. Royce and W. W. Rozeboom (Eds.), *The psychology of knowing*. New York: Gordon & Breach.
Sampson, E. E. (1981). Cognitive psychology. *American Psychologist, 36*, 730–743.
Sants, J. (1980). *Developmental psychology and society*. New York: St. Martin's Press.

Sarason, S. (in press). Psychology and society: An interview. *New Ideas in Psychology, 4*(3).
Secord, P. F. (Ed.). (1982). *Explaining human behavior.* London: Sage Publications.
Senn, M. J. E. (1977). *Speaking out for America's children.* New Haven: Yale University Press.
Sigel, I. (1981). Child development research in learning and cognition in the 1980s: Continuities and discontinuities from the 1970s. *Merrill–Palmer Quarterly, 27*(4), 347–371.
Sigel, I. (1984). Reflections on action theory and distancing theory. *Human Development, 27*(3–4), 188–193.
Sigmon, S. B. (1984). Interactionist psychology: A fourth force? *Psychological Reports, 54,* 156.
Simone, T. (1985). The fate of 'the self' in the post-modern period. *PsychCritique, 1*(2), 74–80.
Skolnick, A. (Ed.). (1976). *Rethinking childhood: Perspectives on development and society.* Boston: Little, Brown.
Sloan, D. (Ed.). (1985). *The computer in education: A critical perspective.* New York: Teachers College Press.
Smedslund, J. (1977). Piaget's psychology in practice. *British Journal of Educational Psychology, 47,* 1–6.
Smith, D. G. (1983). The erosion of childhood: Good news or bad news? *Journal of Curriculum Theorizing, 5*(2), 128–133.
Smith, M. B. (1978). Perspectives on selfhood. *American Psychologist, 33*(12), 1053–1063.
Sommerville, J. (1982). *The rise and fall of childhood.* Beverly Hills: Sage Publications.
Stevenson, H. (Ed.). (1966). The concept of development. *Monographs of the Society for Research in Child Development, 31*(5) (Whole 107), 1–108.
Sullivan, E. V. (1977). Kohlberg's structuralism. *Monographs of the Ontario Institute for Studies in Education, 15.*
Sullivan, E. V. (1981). Comments. In J. M. Broughton, B. Leadbeater, & E. Amsel (Eds.), Reflections on Piaget. *Teachers College Record, 83*(2), 199–201.
Sullivan, E. V. (1984). *A critical psychology.* New York: Plenum Press.
Sullivan, E. V. (1985). Computers and educational futures. *Interchange, 16*(3), 1–18.
Suransky, V. P. (1982). *The erosion of childhood.* Chicago: University of Chicago Press.
Taylor, C. (1964). *The explanation of behaviour.* London: Routledge & Kegan Paul.
Taylor, C. (1971). Interpretation and the sciences of man. *Review of Metaphysics, 25,* 1–51.
Taylor, C. (1973). Peaceful coexistence in psychology. *Social Research, 40*(1), 551–578.
Thompson, E. P. (1963). *The making of the English working class.* New York: Vintage.
Van IJzendoorn, M. H., and Van der Veer, R. (1984). *Main currents of critical psychology.* New York: Irvington.
Vonèche, J. J. (1974a). Fausses alternatives: Normal–malade, différent–aliéné. *Choisir, 172,* 2–4.
Vonèche, J. J. (1974b). Le normal en psychopathologie. *Choisir, 175,* 10–14.
Vonèche, J. J. (1974c). La déviance. *Choisir,* 176–177, 2–29.
Vonèche, J. J. (1980). Toward a developmental theory. In S. Modgil & C. Modgil (Eds.), *Toward a theory of psychological development.* Slough, Bucks.: NFER Publishing.
Vonèche, J. J. (1985). La distinction toujours! Response to Papert. *New Ideas in Psychology, 3*(3), 315–317.
Walkerdine, V. (1984). Developmental psychology and the child-centered pedagogy: The insertion of Piaget into early education. In J. Henriques *et al.* (Eds.), *Changing the subject.* New York: Methuen.
Walkerdine, V. (1985). Psychological knowledge and educational practice: Producing the truth about schools. In G. Claxton, W. Swann, P. Salmon, V. Walkerdine, B. Jacobsen, & J. White, *Psychology and schooling: What's the matter?* London: Institute of Education, University of London.
Wallon, H. (1941). *L'évolution psychologique de l'enfant.* Paris: Armand Colin.

Wallon, H. (1945). *Les origines de la pensée chez l'enfant* (vols. 1 & 2). Paris: Presses Universitaires de France.

Wapner, S., & Kaplan, B. (1983). *Toward a holistic developmental psychology*. Hillsdale, NJ: Erlbaum.

Waterman, A. (1981). Individualism and interdependence. *American Psychologist, 36*(7), 762–773.

Weizenbaum, J. (1976). *Computer power and human reason*. San Francisco: W. H. Freeman.

Wertsch, J. V. (Ed.). (1981). *The concept of activity in Soviet psychology*. White Plains, NY: Sharpe.

Wertsch, J. V. (Ed.). (1985). *Culture, communication, and cognition: Vygotskian perspectives*. New York: Cambridge University Press.

Wexler, P. (1982). *Critical social psychology*. Boston: Routledge & Kegan Paul.

Wexler, P., & Whitson, T. (1982). Hegemony and education. *Psychology and Social Theory, 3*, 31–42.

White, S. H. (1984). The idea of development in developmental psychology. In R. M. Lerner (Ed.), *Developmental psychology: Historical and philosophical perspectives*. Hillsdale, NJ: Erlbaum.

Winnicott, D. W. (1971). *Playing and reality*. Harmondsworth, England: Penguin.

Winograd, T. (1980). What does it mean to understand language? *Cognitive Science, 4*, 209–241.

Wolfenstein, E. V. (1967). *The revolutionary personality*. Princeton: Princeton University Press.

Zahaykevich, M. (1983a). Review of Menson's *Building on Experiences in Adult Development*. *Lifelong Learning, 6*(10), 22–23.

Zahaykevich, M. K. (1983b). Personal construct theory and social change: Response to Bannister. *New Ideas in Psychology, 1*(2), 72–74.

Zahaykevich, M. K. (1984, April). *Parents as teachers: A speech act interpretation*. Paper presented at Graduate School of Education, University of Rochester.

Chapter 2

Adrienne E. Harris

THE RATIONALIZATION OF INFANCY

In this chapter I examine the impact of *technological* or *instrumental rationality,* considered as a worldview, as a cognitive style, and as a mode of inquiry, upon psychological studies of infancy and early childhood. This work joins a relatively new trend in psychology, more thoroughly developed in Europe than in North America (Buss, 1975; Richards, 1974; Sève, 1978; Shotter, 1974). This new tendency, for which the rubric *dialectical psychology* serves most aptly (Riegel, 1975, 1976; Wozniak, 1973), entails a critical reflection on all aspects of psychological knowledge, seeing as interrelated the growth, function, and dissemination of underlying interests in theory and in empirical research. This critical or hermeneutic approach treats theory and research in psychology as a *text,* susceptible to structural analyses both of the deep and surface meaning. More importantly, the psychological text is placed and interpreted within a *countertext,* that is, the historical and current social and structural conditions in which it is embedded. A binding assumption here is that the elements within and between text and countertext coexist in some complex and nontrivial relationship. The identification and analysis of these relationships is the task of a dialectical treatment.

Here I will concentrate on two areas within the domain of scientific psychology: infancy research and studies of first language acquisition. Several considerations motivate these choices. First, in the past two

Adrienne E. Harris • Department of Psychology, Rutgers University, Newark Campus, Newark, New Jersey 07102.

decades, both fields have undergone staggering change and growth. Child language and infancy research programs have been the targets of massive funding for basic research, for training, and more recently for applied work and interventions.

In infancy research a primary engine for development has been the advances in measurement technique and methodology, while in developmental psycholinguistics the impetus has come from the domain of theory, powered initially by the influential and trenchant transformational grammar of the early work of Chomsky. If we consider contemporary psychology both as a structured domain of knowledge and as a social structure, we see that the fields of infancy and child language research constitute major installations, highly developed points of production for psychological knowledge with links to mass distribution as well as to specialized distribution.

In child psychology, in contemplating both historical origins and the current situation, we have the intriguing task of describing and understanding the routes from scientific psychology to mass culture and to the specialist–expert for the family. This expert is embodied variously as the family doctor, the pediatrician, the school psychologist, the psychotherapist, or the social worker (Davin, 1978; Ehrenreich & English, 1978; Lasch, 1977; Sears, 1975). In identifying psychology as a social structure, we can trace lines of connection between university-based points of production of empirical research and of theory and points of mass distribution: clinics, mental health services, infant stimulation programs, preschool programs, how-to-parent paperbacks stocked in airport newstands and the supermarket checkout counter. The front line purveyors of this knowledge-cum-social practice are the social worker, school psychologist, mental health worker, even the "life-style specialist." These figures, acting as guides and as gatekeepers, translate and transform psychological knowledge, each with a class-specific style and objective (Donzelot, 1979).

In thinking about why such dramatic development should have occurred in the study of infancy and child language and how the social, practical, and theoretical strands are interwoven, we must be careful not to allow the analysis to deteriorate into either a mechanical application of deterministic principles or a paranoid view of the shaping of scientific knowledge. It is true that the prevailing tendency in psychology is to encapsulate theory and research and to insist that it is insulated from social and political influence. It is tempting to want to develop a dramatic antidote to that perspective (Jacoby, 1975; Lasch, 1977). However, the story of these interrelations of social and scientific life, of theory and policy, of popular concern and imagination, and of the rise of expertism to shore up family life and child development, is an exceedingly complex one. In this chapter, I hope to delineate some features of that analysis, identifying at this initial stage some outlines to the story.

Infancy studies and the literature on child language share an uncritical reflection of the historically conditioned relations of production (and reproduction) in which they have developed. There is a remarkable absence of concern or attention for the relation of social and political-economic factors to the dominant epistemology. In this regard, studying infants and studying language development are representative of much work in psychology. Those of us who practice within this discipline must puzzle over two phenomena: the underdevelopment of a critical apparatus in psychology and simultaneously the export and application of "the psychological" explanation to many features of social and political life. As a result, in North America, at least, psychology has been and continues to be a massive interpretive apparatus, flourishing without internal critical restraint or comment as a tool for social and self-understanding.

Infancy and early child development studies are, I believe, coupled in another sense. Considered as an ensemble, they represent a vision of early growth brought into the technological purview. In the theory, the empirical demonstrations, and the techniques of application and intervention, instrumental rationality penetrates earlier and earlier into human life. Techniques of study both illuminate infant process and create or *construct* a view of the human infant's capacities which have consequences for the infant and his social and human surroundings.

Before beginning a more detailed examination of these two areas, we can explore a little more carefully what is meant here by *critique* and what is entailed in a claim that current research on infancy and language constitute an imposition of technological or instrumental rationality on our understanding of infant experience and infant competence.

Ideology Critique

Inherent in the dialectical approach is a strong commitment to ideology critique (Mannheim, 1936), a tradition with a strong indebtedness to critical theory and to the work on the sociology of knowledge developed by the Frankfurt school (Jay, 1973; Horkheimer & Adorno, 1972) and maintained currently by a chief European inheritor of that tradition, Habermas (1975). This approach, in its operating procedures and method, also owes much to hermeneutics (Gadamer, 1965). The surface character of the research or theory in question is treated as a literary text, subjected to an active, engaged, constructive interpretation. The surface forms are penetrated to reveal underlying relations and structures which are in turn related to aspects and constructs outside the surface text. We may consider aspects and features not specifically located in the text that is contemporary psychology, as elements in a countertext, interdependent and connected to the body of psychological thought under examination but also contextual rather than central. Economic conditions, state policy, all the features of the social and historical praxis in which social science is embedded are considered as countertext.

Empirical research and clinical studies in psychology can be seen as a series of displays, dramatic rituals, scenarios, case histories, and emblematic routines. We subject these displays to a structural analysis, pulling out the underlying relations both internal to the work and externally linked to aspects of the historical and intellectual countertext. Such analytic strategies are comparable, in formal terms, to the structural-functionalist approach familiar to developmental psychologists who have been exposed to Piaget, Werner, or Vygotsky (Piaget, 1962; Wozniak, 1973; Vygotsky, 1962, 1978). This form of argument works through the technique of analogy, as Broughton (1979, 1981) has pointed out. The argument also depends on a systems-theoretical approach of the sort that Habermas (1975) employs in *Legitimation Crisis*. A *structural* analysis of psychology and its context provides a scaffolding upon which another level of speculative argument is built. From the structural analysis, one then moves to a discussion of the ideological *function* of psychological knowledge.

The grounding assumption here is that the development of social systems proceeds through the productive appropriation of outer nature on the one hand (through technology, mastery over nature) and the social appropriation of inner nature (human subjectivity, consciousness, social praxis) on the other.

Social appropriation is mediated through many structures. Some, like family or parent, have been more readily acknowledged in psychological or sociological discourse than others. It is not our task in this chapter to account for all the features and processes in social appropriation. For our purposes, it is sufficient to note that increasingly, in the last century, the legitimation for various techniques of social appropriation has been the psychological (Newson & Newson, 1974). Legitimation has moved from the religious to the medical and now to the psychological domain (Bakan, 1967; Foucault, 1965).

Psychology functions as ideology here in its promotion as a legitimating tool. Particular activities, techniques for socializing and managing children, have been given normative status. Endowing such activities with this status is, in essence, an act of conferring legitimacy. When the behavior of children and women are concerned, the rationale or legitimacy for these norms has shifted in the last century. Child-rearing practices were initially evaluated on religious grounds, later on medical grounds, and finally on psychological grounds. Discipline and, in particular, the management of sexuality in children were undertaken initially for the child's soul, later to prevent physical illness or enervation, and finally to maintain psychological health. The fear of damnation is replaced by the fear of illness and decline. A fear of medical disaster is then replaced by the fear of madness or psychopathology. These fears and the strictures that give rise to them act as complex and often internalized forms of social control.

If there is a cutting edge to social appropriation, it is the socialization of the infant. It is the central claim of this chapter that psychology, in its many manifestations, is one of the primary and critical venues whereby social appropriation penetrates earlier and earlier into human life. Within psychology, some greet this appropriation optimistically and positively. Bornstein and Kessen (1979), in a state of the art review of infancy research, note the erosion of the conceptual boundary between talkers and nontalkers. This erosion is achieved by the interpretation of infant life as increasingly rational, planned, goal-directed, and intentional. It is the nature and consequences of that erosion that we examine here.

Habermas's analysis does more than identify processes of social and productive appropriation. Events and activities in both spheres are treated as developing in parallel and interdependently. Psychology can, therefore, from this vantage point, be seen as an ideological apparatus of the state. As such, psychology as a discipline contributes to the techniques and the legitimation of particular forms of child rearing and child management that in design (if not perfectly in execution) connect to particular requirements in the world of work. The hypothesis that work, scientific psychology, and socialization experience are connected raises some interesting questions. What is the intended impact of psychology upon social appropriation? How are the entrepreneurial and intellectual energies of professionals in psychology meshed with these policy intentions? What features of child development are currently considered critical, and why? Finally, most intriguingly, is the connection of social formation, economic development, and an ideological apparatus like psychology a success? Is the relationship a neat dovetailing of interests and intentions, a fudged attempt at social management, or a contradictory mixture of repressive and emancipatory potential?

Kovel (1978) has analyzed the congruence of increased personal subjectivity and the organization of desire as these factors are connected to changing needs of advanced capitalist economies and the modern state. In talking about modern personality structure he notes two points of influence. First, there may be special consequences for personality flowing from the modern preoccupation with childhood as a special, privileged period. Second, there is the "universal imperative of rationalization" under capitalism which has important implications for the organization of work and workers. *Rationalization* is used here in both a familiar and unfamiliar sense. In considering rationalization as state policy, as a characterization of modern work and modern institutions, we focus on the centralized, hierarchically controlled, planned and directed aspect of these phenomena. Other features of modern work and institutional life are also important. Pure technique, technological skills, and systems abstracted from real process are valued. Activities are motivated on rational, structural grounds and not on pragmatic or concrete conditions.

It is perhaps less familiar to extend this concept to the domain of subjective experience, social relations, and consciousness. Bureaucratized, technological, and abstracted labor is best undertaken by particular kinds of workers. Schools, technical training, and educational experience at all levels include in their objectives the production of a worker–thinker–social participant for whom abstract, alienated, and technological work seems "natural." What is argued here is that the impetus to rationalization both in the management of consciousness and in the management of persons in work, play, and domestic life is extending into the earliest stages of human life and into the farthest reaches of consciousness. Centralized day care and its particular programs, geared to the production of children skilled at analysis, self-control, conceptualization, and abstract reasoning are but two levels of this rationalizing process. That this process is general and pervasive in social life can be illustrated with an anecdote from the movie *Atlantic City*. The old gangster, still a numbers runner, sits at dinner with a young woman being trained as a dealer for the new casinos. She attends a school for dealers, can rattle off abstract rules for baccarat and blackjack. He is cranky and resentful, thinks the casinos are too stuffy and safe. In a fascinating moment in the film, she asks him his social security number. He says he never had one. In that moment, betting and crime as cottage industry, as illegal and outside social control, meet up with the newly rationalized gambling technology. Centrally planned and hierarchically controlled large casinos are the new "rationalized" factories for gambling.

We see, then, that early childhood experience and child personality is an evolving and enlarging subjectivity that scientific psychology as a discipline penetrates, studies, and constructs. From both contemporary cultural criticism (Lasch, 1977) and social history (Shorter, 1975; Stone, 1977) an analysis is emerging that links changes in power relations within the family, changes in the structuring of individual subjectivity, and an increasingly intrusive state entering personal and family life through the avenues of professional expertise and bureaucratization of reproductive services (day care, early childhood education, welfare). Much of the argument thus far has been concerned with the development and shaping of new needs, new consumptive habits. Much current critical preoccupation with narcissism as a modern characterological defect has focused on the enlargement of subjectivity, of desire, and of expectations (Lasch, 1977). However, as Kovel (1978) notes, "*desire* is to develop intertwined with the equally contradictory moment of *rationality*." Cognitive and communicative *competence* are as much the goals of psychological and state intervention as desire.

It is instrumental reason as a goal of development or as a paradigm for infant mental life that is of concern here. In developmental psycholinguistics, from studies of the individual child through studies of interactive dialogue, and in infancy research, the insights and theoretical breakthroughs have effectively pushed rationalization, intentionality, and purposive functioning (often of a deep and highly specified sort) deeper and deeper into infant subjectivity. In judging the impact of psychological study on actual people we must consider at least two distinct possibilities. The first is that this approach, far from simply illuminating hitherto unknown facts, does begin to structure experience so that rational and cognitively competent activity does arise earlier, that is, that psychological study has real constitutive consequences for the objects of that study. A second possibility is that contemporary psychology with its insistence on rationality in fact mystifies and suppresses another aspect of infant life, namely, its resistant, fluid, ambiguous character.

Instrumental Reason

If we look at the terrain of modern social life, rationalization or technological reason manifests itself in some surprising outcroppings. Berger, Berger, and Kellner (1973) capitalize on analogies between modern consciousness and modern production. The fit with paradigms and constructs in psychology is striking. Our subjective experience is fragmented, our mechanical minds abstracted and split, our activity atomized. Our tendency is to carve the social and physical world into bits, component parts; our tropism is toward reifying the vivid and dynamic ensemble of social relations. We could here be describing the modern factory, the modern bureaucracy, the modern head. Consciousness and cognitive style reflect a preoccupation with goals, end states, teleology. The penetration of technological rationality into consciousness is both a matter of the process of thinking and the products of thought itself. In fact, as Schaffer (1977) has pointed out in a critique of the language and epistemology of psychoanalysis, division may itself be the reflection of a positivist, technological perspective. Planful, goal-directed being and thinking predominate. Goals are split off from means and values. Emotionality and affect are the targets of management and organization. In this state of consciousness, individuals are endlessly replicable pieces of social or productive machinery. Thought itself is treated as a hierarchically organized set of systems and subsystems governed by or rather administered by some subjectless, desireless plan (Anohkin, 1969; Miller, Galanter & Pribram, 1960). In this chapter we extend this analysis of the socially and historically constructed consciousness both to the experience of very young individuals and their families, at a conscious or preconscious level (Cole & Scribner, 1974), and to the organization of scientific understanding (Buck-Morss, 1975; Unger, 1975).

In applying this analysis to developmental psychology, there are several points of danger. First, we are not advancing the claims of mechanical Marxism, arguing for a simple or deterministic reflection of economic and social praxis to ideology and to the social and human sciences. These spheres of social, intellectual, and productive life have an intricate and dialectical relationship to each other. This issue becomes particularly subtle when the human science involved is psychology. For in considering that psychology has an ideological content and function we stress a multiple activity in which psychology constitutes or constructs certain aspects of social and individual life, normalizes and legitimates personality functioning, simultaneously reflecting and entering the historical process and the socially located individuals being "studied." The psychological is thus both a real and illusory category. This requires an elaboration of Durkheim's famous comment: "Whenever a social phenomenon is directly explained by a psychological phenomenon we may be sure that the explanation is false." Psychological knowledge, because it is offered as material for self-knowledge, has real impact and can be internalized as false consciousness, thereby becoming really operative and self-fulfilling. This process has added complexity when the psychological knowledge is about preverbal individuals (i.e., infants and young children) for whom the material of psychology is not directly accessible. Such knowledge may alter how infants are seen by virtue of its impact on parents and others who socialize children and consequently alter how infants are treated.

Instrumental rationality, conceived of here as an epistemology, has had impact on developmental psychology of both a liberal and a reactionary force. It remains to be seen how and whether such work can provide the base for a recuperative or emancipatory psychology. In infant research and in developmental psycholinguistics, the advances of the last 20 years have introduced theories and research strategies both more supple and more intricate than the behavioral or learning-mediation models they supplanted. Through the prism of modern psychological research we see the young human as active and engaging. The insights, metaphors, and procedures gleaned from systems theory, technologically based communications theory, information-processing paradigms, and structuralism (permeated as they are with mechanism), nonetheless offer a vision of the human infant as possessing an active, structuring intelligence, engaged in transforming encounters with the environment. They provide a perspective on mind that is deep and sophisticated, and they lead, at least, to a highly adequate account of the formation and character of bourgeois thought. What is problematic is the claim to account for transhistorical descriptions of mind and thinking (Cole & Scribner, 1974), as well as their aptness as accounts of early development. At issue is whether the last two decades of research and theory in infancy and language acquisition have been voyages of discovery or acts of social architecture serving the development of bureaucratized man, now seen as rational, goal-oriented, and technocratic from birth. More plausibly, has contemporary developmental psychology served both projects, simultaneously engaging in the elaboration and socially based construction of persons?

Infancy Studies

Within the past 20 years, infancy research has undergone an astonishing transformation. The "competent" (Stone, Smith, & Murphy, 1973) infant has replaced psychology's earlier conception of infant life as chaotic, unfocused, almost decorticate. There are several landmark studies in this development. Wolff's account of infant states establishes a perspective on early infant life (Wolff, 1959, 1966). This work ties together a physiological substrate with various psychosocial adaptations engaged by mother and infant and with later adequacy in development. What is established here is a premium on focused alert activity as an adequate ground in which perceptual and sensory functioning is elaborated. The ensuing work on infant perception presents us with infant capacity in visual pursuit, visual tracking, and pattern recognition, in initiating and sustaining attention, in depth perception, and in other organismically functioning sensitivities to the social and perceptual environment. The main points of influence here would seem to be Piagetian theory, with its focus on a functionally equilibrating system of actions and schema-based reactions to the environment and information processing—a great sea change in cognitive theory, which now dominates empirical research on infancy.

The infant, viewed from this vantage point, is a mechanical and teleological wonder. Techniques for response measurement (cardiac rate, operant responses, infrared recording of eye movement) give us the "new look" in infancy. No longer buzzing blooming confusion, the infant is hard at work, focusing, attending, all atomized activities, eyes tracing movement, programmed to avoid looming objects, differentiating figure from background, auditory system specialized for language reception and phonemic distinctions.

If the vanguard of infancy research has consisted of those researching sensory and perceptual systems, they have been closely followed by psychologists studying skilled performance, motor skill, and the productive side of behavior (Bruner & Connolly, 1976; Lunzer, 1968). Strongly cybernetic in its flavor, redolent with discussions of software and hardware in the performance apparatus, this research area is a curious mixture of Piagetian notions of sensorimotor intelligence and models of hierarchical plans and the structure of behavior.

The infant, identified and described in Piaget's descriptive accounts, is an active processor, a problem solver: hands moving to rattle, feet kicking mobile hanging over crib, grasping, lifting, pushing, coordinating acts, tinkering with action patterns, always experimenting, always learning how to work. Infant as baby assembly worker, atomized parts of mind and body in the service of an adapting intelligence, itself at the service of an evolving hierarchical structure. Infancy, in this treatment, is the business of building structure, building habits of thought and consumption, as well as goal-directed behavior in the service and in the guise of technology.

If this account of the infant's crib as our newest version of the dark satanic mills seems lurid, listen to the parents of young children questioning anyone with credentials as a psychologist. Overwhelmingly and from all classes, their concern is with activities and products which will improve performance. Look at the programs for preschools, particularly those serving culturally disadvantaged or high-risk populations. Parental concern connects to the aims of curriculum: remediation, preparation for the skilled production of knowledge and information. Child's play is work, as a Yale-produced film series on early development somewhat enigmatically tells us.

The possibilities of distortion in recent infancy research has been noted recently by Turkewitz (1979). Reviewing the last decade's work on infant perception, he notes the tremendous concentration on visual and auditory processing. The infant's functioning is clearly preparatory for adultlike analyzing, categorizing, selecting, and coordinating, stressed at the expense of smell, balance, taste, and touch, facilities which are highly salient for infant experience. In auditory perception the work on categorical discrimination carries the message that infants have the capacity to make quasi-adult discriminations, at least in regard to phonemic boundaries (Eimas, Siqueland, Juscyk, & Vigority, 1971). While this work has been controversial and much argued over (Trehub, 1979), studies of categorical perception have had a strong impact on current understanding of infant capacities for language.

There is a second orientation in infancy research, emanating from ethology and from systems theory showing a strong preference for biologically-flavored explanations of human behavior. This tradition, which has branches in Great Britain and in America, is an odd mixture of mechanistic and organismic features. British research promotes the natural infant possessed of innate sociability and innate subjectivity (Trevarthen, 1977, 1978; Schaffer, 1977: Newson & Newson, 1974). The young child is viewed as "innately primed to participate in complicated social rituals." The behaviors in question here include turn taking, burst-pause sequences of motor and sensorimotor action and gazing, rhythmic coordinations that are interpersonal (Condon, 1974). The infant as cyberneticist "naturally self-sustaining and self-rewarding" engages in a delicate tuning operation within a "mutually comprehensible" framework. In an admirable attempt to assert the primacy of social situations for development of individual functioning, the infant is designated social from the outset.

Note that there are at least two ways of thinking about this assertion. One, articulated by Newson and Newson (1974), is that "how early this can be seen will depend to a very great extent upon our social skill in drawing a baby's attention to objects as salient entities within the compass of his attention and upon our *experimental ingenuity* in detecting differential responses in subsequent encounters" (my emphasis). The conflation of observation and construction in this comment is striking. Alternatively, Shotter (1978), using an argument familiar to the psychoanalytic tradition, in particular to Lacanians, talks about the social activity in parenting in which infant activity is woven into dialogue. The central point to make here is that one wants to differentiate claims concerning the social origins of dialogue, language skills, personality, or cognitive development from the assertion that infants participate as fully social and socially knowledgeable beings. In failing to make that distinction, the constructive aspect of social interaction is thereby lost.

North American work on early interaction (Lewis & Freedle, 1977; Lewis & Rosenblum, 1974) seems more to focus on natural mothering. This is a curious recapitulation of the natural mothering assumptions present in much developmental theory and object relations theory arising in Europe and Britain at the end of the Second World War (Bowlby, 1969; A. Freud, 1965; Winnicott, 1974). Mitchell (1974) connected the appearance of that theoretical development with social and state policy in Britain aimed at the reestablishment of family life and the removal of women from the work force after the Second World War. Inevitably, one wonders whether the current reemergence of this perspective is also connected to changing shapes in the economy and pressures on women to retrench within family and purely reproductive labor.

From the pioneering work of Stern, using microanalytic techniques of observation, a characteristic treatment of mother–infant interaction emerged. The interaction of mother and infant is presented in idealized terms in which mothering appears as a staged drama of symbiosis, nurturance, and receptivity (Stern, 1974, 1977; Brazelton, Koslowski & Main, 1974). Apparently unmediated by learning or social situation, parent–infant interaction is presented as an intricately meshed series of moves and countermoves, responses to preprogrammed signals. It is reciprocal and, above all, natural. In the laboratory or "naturalistically" in the home, these experimental demonstrations, films, and transcripts are like medieval religious paintings, tryptichs of madonna-like maternal preoccupation with mother and infant locked in mutual gaze. Even that image is degraded here. The overlay of systems theory, of communication theory, and of ethologically influenced interpretations of behavior as signals for innate releasing mechanisms cleanses the situation of anything affective, erotic, inchoate.

In the studies of dialogue as well as this work on early interaction, the infant appears as an equal participant in the liberal democracy of the family. The dialogue with the caretaking parent begins at birth: infant's eyes, gazing, smiles, cries, physical aspect of vulnerability all act to "control" the caretaker. The vocabulary of this new research tradition—with its terminology of *caretaker, control, interaction, mutuality*—masks the social reality of power, disguises and blocks from our awareness the surrounding world (whether sustaining or isolating). Current treatments of dialogue do not analyze power. Everyone and anyone can initiate. Each participant's signals control the other. Gender seems to have left the relationship. All is natural and inevitable. "Mother and infant are excellent operant conditioners of each other" (Lipsitt, 1976). In this manner, contemporary psychology continues its tradition of reproducing the social as the biological. Lipsitt, for one, welcomes the return to "fundamental biological interest," to the study of "phylogenetically adaptive differences in the sexes." "Congenital response propensities" are treated as instances of self-regulation and social regulation.

What is lost? What disguised? For one thing, the bewildering sense in much modern family life that in relationships among family members everyone feels powerless. The ambiguity of power, the tyranny of helplessness, are never touched on. The linguistically and socially powerful mother initiates her child into a social and linguistic system in which that child will discover, among other things, the powerlessness of women. In her parenting, the woman must participate in her own loss of legitimacy. Chodorow (1978) and Dinnerstein (1976) have written extensively on this phenomenon and on the implications of early object relations and preoedipal experience. They trace out the implications for adult personality of early child-rearing situations in which the primary caretaking figure is a woman. In the work of these feminist theorists, mother–infant interaction is seen in quite a different light from the cooled-out cybernetic systems approach. The initial relation of mother and infant is complex and contradictory. The powerful mother figure promotes vulnerability and dependency, and within that system infant fear, rage, and resentment can be unleashed. One resolution of this conflict for the infant comes in a later alliance with the other figure in the family triangle, the father. One implication, then, is that socialization proceeds to the inevitable moment of splitting and dissociation from the early dependencies on the mother, and alienation from that relation. Lacan (1968), from a slightly different perspective, is reflecting on the same process. The entry of the child into the world of words is never merely acquisition of technical control and symbolic power, but entry into the world of the father. Through a complex and ambiguous voyage, learning to speak entails alienation from the mothering figure and from one's own subjectivity. The infant's desires, intentions, and needs are all recoded in the social symbol system and in that subtle alteration a dialectical nonidentity of subjectivity and symbolic expression develops.

In the child language literature, the idealization of reciprocity and mutuality leads to a very different understanding of the mother's role in this process. Mother is seen as the skilled and efficacious reader of infant capacity and state. Bruner (1975), for example, designates the mother as the Language Acquisition Device, all effortless code switching as she calibrates infant receptivity against her own patterns of intonation and utterance. The constructive and socializing aspects of her readings of the child are treated in the psycholinguistic literature as pure interpretation. It is, moreover, a notion of interpretive activity that is distinctly nonhermeneutic.

The dialogue of mother and infant is seen as an overdetermined system of connecting signals taken as transhistorical penomena, unaltered by culture and learning. It is at this point that one observes the intersection of social science and ideology. Mothering that is unlearnable and unmediated stands as a natural and normative vision of appropriate behavior with an infant. In the same study in which this theoretical perspective is elaborated, Brazelton (1974) notes that a rather large number of mothers in his observation fail to meet the conditions of sensitive reciprocity. This approach, I believe, constitutes a piece of ideological apparatus, identifying good and bad mothering, outside of any social or political understanding of that relation.

In this context, Brazelton, by virtue of his research activities, his professional stature, and his high visibility as a popularizer of psychological-pediatric wisdom, stands in the line of descent from Winnicott. In exploring analogies between the work of these two men we discover relationships, specific to the *human* sciences, between the development of knowledge and its organizing and prophetic impact on the objects of study through the distribution of that knowledge as normative advice. The alliance between scientific psychology and family medicine is a long-standing one (Donzelot, 1979). The legitimation of particular forms of child rearing was popularized and massively served up to people through parent education movements, popular literature, and an army of social workers and educators who united the functions of education and surveillance in their entry into working-class households (Davin, 1978; Ehrenreich & English, 1978).

Although the personnel conducting research and those distributing and popularizing are often distinct, it is interesting that in the instance of Brazelton and Winnicott they are conjoined. Winnicott, the pediatrician-psychiatrist with a long work history in the clinic, worked on a number of theoretical advances in the 1940s, within the domain of early object-relations and ego psychology, in the company of Anna Freud and others working or associated with the Tavistock clinic in London. After the Second World War, he was involved in a quite massive program to popularize and educate. His most salient contribution in that regard was probably the series of radio talks on the BBC (Winnicott, 1965).

His message to mothers in the postwar period was the call to total devotion to the needs and responses of the infant. Father was a shadowy helper. The central event of parenting was intricate, obsessive, attentive work with the child, a preoccupation that would be termed pathological in any other situation. Consuming maternal attention, Winnicott insisted, only looked like psychopathology; it was actually the acme of mental health. How to achieve it? How to ensure it? Here, Winnicott, the maturationist, talks against learning, intellectualizing. Healthy mothering required the women to reconnect to biology, to natural instinct, to intuition.

Brazelton, the pediatrician-psychologist, similarly bridges the worlds of knowledge production and knowledge distribution. He is the creator of a major testing device for neonatal responsiveness and for emblematic research studies on reciprocity in mother–child interaction

(Brazelton, 1969; Brazelton, Koslowski, & Main, 1974). He is also the author of various popular books offering advice to mothers (Brazelton, 1974). These books carefully partition the first years, creating a highly specific step-by-step progression of tasks and achievements (rated for slow and fast infants). Like Winnicott, Brazelton appears to share the maturationist outlook.

Aside from the potentially intense and anxiety-producing impact of this material on parents and consequent demands upon infant performance, this presentation of the key features of infant life legitimates early development as innately and inherently rational and rationalizable. The steps of the first year have the effect of atomizing infant life, subdividing it into hierarchically interlocked systems of actions and responses. In short, reflecting the consensus in basic research (Stone, Smith, & Murphy, 1973; Bornstein & Kessen, 1979), Brazelton's popular books encourage parents to see the technological capacities of their infants at increasingly early ages.

In this review, the concentration has been on the research and theory within empirical and behavioral psychology. What is missing, of course, is any consideration of the work on infancy developing within psychoanalytic thought. There, clearly, there is a line of development and interest, from Klein and from ego psychology, from the object relations school of Fairbairn (1954) and Winnicott and the more recent considerations of early infant life in the work of Schachtel (1959) and Mahler, Pine, and Bergman (1975).

In considering the relationship of that tradition to the work reviewed here I would make two points. First, in looking for the influence of psychoanalytic thought upon infancy research (primarily in the work of Bowlby, Ainsworth, and Stern), one sees that it is the more pristine and mechanical aspects of systems theory that have overriden the consideration of infant life as conflict filled, fluid, and inchoate. In short, the irrational aspects of infant life have been effectively lost in the movement from psychoanalytic theory into behavioral research.

Second, these traditions of thought about early development exist in a centrally contradictory relationship. Psychoanalytic work posits a fundamental asynchrony between affective experience, defensive cognitive structure, and efficacy. Infant experience of vulnerability and infant phantasy are out of phase with defense or competence capacities. In the behavioral, empirical, and cognitively based models of infant life, the infant is adequate to the stimulation (internally and externally arising) in the environment. Equilibration and management are the hallmarks of the engagement of child and social or physical world. For the most part, these two disparate traditions are neither reconciled nor strongly engaged in discourse. The separation of these domains and the consequences for understanding development is an issue worth pursuing.

Language Acquisition

In developmental psycholinguistics, the revolutionary changes arose in the domain of theory. Chomsky's work on transformational grammar, initiated in the late 1950s at MIT, was in an intellectual context in which one important practical preoccupation was "code cracking." Linguists and communication theorists (some funded through the United States Army Signal Corps) were concerned in that period to develop procedures for the interpretation of codes. Transformational grammar, with its initial strong claims to meaning-independent rules, has an interesting fit with that overarching project. The search for a universal grammar, which without recourse to meaning or context could decode novel utterances, provides one initial intellectual influence (among many) in which Chomsky's anti-Bloomfieldian and antibehavioral linguistic theory developed.

If we turn to the impact of this theory upon psychology, we note several matters. First, the perspective on speaking and understanding speech encountered by psychologists in taking on Chomsky's work was counterintuitive and counterpsychological. The primacy of syntactic rules (structural and generative) in relation to which semantic and phonological interpretations could take place made the act of speaking implausibly idealist, in fact unimaginable. Secondly, the idea of *generativity* in grammar has been interpreted more dynamically in psycholinguistic theory than the original formal conception intended. The attempt to translate a system of formal rules into real time processing strategies is an instance of structural isomorphism, that is, the transposition of structural description into a model of language knowledge and language processing. Add to this a perspective on language rules as innate in mind and universal, and the refurbishing of Cartesian dualism as the ground for contemporary psycholinguistics is complete. Despite disclaimers against considering transformational grammar as a theory of performance, there is a history of rationalist claims flowing in and out of linguistics and to psychology for which Chomsky himself (1968) as well as students and colleagues in psychology (Brown, 1973; McNeill, 1970, and others) bear some responsibility.

By 1965, transformational grammar had begun to shift from the strong claims with regard to universal meaning-independent syntax and to develop formal rules that appear to be a mixture of grammatical and semantic considerations, for example, selection restriction rules (Chomsky, 1965). As linguistic theories made more use of meaning for interpretation, the next wave of psycholinguists engaged in what Brown has termed "the rich interpretation," whereby context, informant (usually mother), and activity are used to make judgments about sentence meaning and thence about the structure of language knowledge. Bloom's early work (1970) is illustrative here. Structures of noun-plus-noun combinations analyzed in terms of transformational grammar were given syntactic (subject–object) and more semantic (possessive, agent–action, genitive) categorizations based quite heavily on corroborative evidence from context and maternal interpretation.

This shift to semantic-based models of language knowledge continued with the entrance of generative semantic theories, case grammars, and some cognitive theory into developmental psycholinguistics. Bowerman (1973) and Greenfield and Smith (1976) make powerful use of case grammar, for example, again making the isomorphic leap from structural description to structural knowledge. In these studies, word, action, and situation are tied in closer operational connection and the interdependence of language and context is illuminated. Interestingly, however, context, social frame, action, and the like are for the most part tools for disambiguation. Information outside the speech stream becomes part of the procedures for making structural assignment (at a formal level by the linguist, at an intuitive level by the parent).

A next step, taken simultaneously by Bloom (1973), Schaffer (1977), and others (Shotter, 1974) and influenced by the newly influential semiotic tradition, was to see social context and action as actually integral to meaning and structured construction. Halliday's work, for example, might be seen as an uneasy peace between rationalist models of knowledge and the grounding of child language in intentions to mean, to act, and to do. For some, the central influence has been cognitive developmental theory (Bates, 1976) or the information-processing approach to cognition (Bever, 1970). For others, the powerful influence has been Werner and Kaplan's work on symbolic function (Werner & Kaplan, 1963; see also Sigel & Cocking, 1979) and the neo-Firthian linguistic tradition introduced to psychologists by Halliday (Nelson, 1979).

Child language studies have shifted from the exclusive focus on underlying structure and individual competence characteristic of the first decade of developmental psycholinguistics. The interest now is in the social matrix, in social use of rules of language activity, in pragmatics and the intrusive determining role of context. Moreover, the term *context* is increasingly widely construed as terrain, task, social relationships, and discourse history or contingencies. Influenced by Searle (1969) and related traditions in the philosophy of language (Austin, 1962; Grice, 1957) and ethnomethodology (Garfinkel, 1967; Goffman, 1974), the current concern with pragmatics still relies at base upon certain assumptions about communicative competence and the informed intellectual and intentional apparatus of dialoguing individuals.

These assumptions are as follows. Dialogue involves (ideally) a shared, mutually negotiated exchange of interpretations. In ideal or undistorted communication, speaker and hearer are appropriately each other's object and their own subject, sharing matched expertise about rule systems (social, pragmatic, and linguistic) and sharing input and output conditions (see Searle, 1969, pp. 57–59). Observations of the conversations of young children suggest that such dialogues are remarkable for the incidence of smooth sequencing of turns, allocation of conversational space, and negotiation of what is or has been occurring (Dore, 1975). At least as manifested behaviorally, children talking to each other and to teachers have an impressively rich conversational competence.

The main theoretical substrate for this new research perspective is Searle's analysis of meaning and intentionality as revealed in speech acts. In the manifest content of illocutionary acts performed in a context and in a set of social relations, one can discover evidence of more latent belief systems and assumptions about how the world and in particular the language world is to be understood. Meaning is identified as the intention of speaking subjects to produce a specific effect in the hearer through the performance of some utterance because speaker and hearer share competence concerning the rules governing the utterance's interpretation and use. Conversations are often clarification and fine tuning of shared assumptions. In several studies of the speech acts of young children, flexibility and variety in structure as well as the social and discourse context appears to play an important role in the observer's argument that intentions to trigger a particular understanding in the hearer fuel the production of utterances (Dore, 1977).

I think there is one kind of dialogue or dialoguing relationship in which these assumptions are inappropriate or rather should be imposed on the dialogue situation carefully. Against the view of dialogue as democracy or consensus, of infant control over parents (Lewis & Rosenblum, 1974), of conversation as negotiation (Goffman, 1974; Bateson, 1973), I want to propose the dialogue of speaking parent and developing child as asymmetrical and in some sense exploitative (Harris, 1975). In the early stages of mother–child dialogue, there is one highly evolved competent communicator, namely, mother. Linguist–observer and parent bring to these dialogues assumptions about language structure and language use and as interpreters and participants in dialogue act (consciously and unconsciously) on the assumptions Searle suggests. The child, however, is only a gradual initiate into this system. If shared codes are the prerequisite for undistorted communication, they are not preexistent in mind.

The study of an illocutionary effect of speech acts has a prototypic form in the work of Peirce (1955), for whom the produced sign was to be distinguished from its interpretent (roughly, how it is decoded or understood) in the hearer. In parent–child dialogue, as verbal communication develops, there are initially minimal overlapping assumptions, and it is only gradually that children come to mean exactly or even inexactly what their parents have interpreted them as saying. Snow and Ferguson (1977), among others, have suggested that children learn what they mean from hearing their parent's interpretation. This view of evolving understanding brings the notion of meaning closer to that entailed in analyses of fuzzy set (Hersh & Camarazza, 1976). It is not, of course, that children are without intentions in their early communicative productions. Rather, their behavior (vocalizing, eye contact, demonstrative actions, and so on) is given signal significance in a social environment. All parents have experienced the resistance and rebellion of children; nonetheless, in the stages of parent–child dialogue when language control is unfolding, one part of the dyad is in control of the social definitions of actions and utterances and weaves the output of children into the fabric of discourse. Parents interpret and proceed in conversation in the only way people can, that is, assuming a shared competence long before such assumptions are definitively justified. In embedding child output in adult constructions, in supportive actions, and in setting up physical and linguistic contingencies that sustain the adult's understanding of what the child is intending, the interpretive assumptions are in many or most cases legitimated interpretations.

From Volosinov's (1973) work on speech acts, I take the view that all signs must arise in interindividual territory, that signs in a social system already have ideological content, that there is a "dialectical nonidentity" between subjectivity and social field and that the overlay of sign on infant intent must be partial and will rarely if ever be perfectly coterminous with it. What this means, among other possibilities, is that the origins of alienation are inextricably bound up in the process of both the experiential task of self–other differentiation and the social task of interaction. The duality of production and social interaction, labor and love, social and practical cognition is manifest publicly in the language learning conducted in dialogue.

Against the view of democracy or liberal negotiated compromise in dialogue, I want to pose the unequal power dynamic of socialized parent socializing the child precisely through the process of interpretation. If much of dialogue is reflection on what has just been said and meant, then in the conversation of mother and child one can observe the productions of children *given* particular interpretations (by embedding, expansions, commentary, and so on). Greenfield, Bloom, and others note the efficacy and efficiency of the child's simplest productions. Mothers accept output, however minimal syntactically and phonetically, and treat the utterance as not merely intentional, which it surely is, but often as participating in the same intentional effects as any user of those words. Simply put, in observed conversation between mother and infant, linguist and parent are Searlians with sufficient power—social power in the relationships and communicative power as competent speakers—to ensure that the child becomes one.

At this point it might be worthwhile to look at some commonalities between the individually based child language studies of the 1960s dominated by transformational grammar and the pragmatic, illocutionary act concerns of current work in the 1970s. Certainly the linguistic terrain surveyed is different and unquestionably the current models are more truly interactive and social in their focus. These two general theoretical enterprises are, however, linked in their assumptions about the nature of the speaking individual–child and in their assignment of a deep instrumentality to infant mind. Competence in transformational grammar's terms is rule knowledge. Pragmatic theories widen the conception of rules (and speak only rarely to the question of their genesis) looking at infant turn-taking, attention-eliciting devices, and communicative contact as behavior guided by competence in social and sociolinguistic rules.

Language competence as an attribute of mind is a rational competence. It is competence over an abstract exchange system. It is possible to see the evolution of functional but subjective language acts (as Halliday, 1975, describes the protolanguage of his son) into the public semiotic system as a shift comparable to that in an economic sphere moving from use value to exchange value. The relevance of such systems as metaphors for thinking and conceptualizing has been suggested by Buck-Morss (1975) and by the cross-cultural work of Cole and Scribner (1974). Current psycholinguistic and developmental theory now proposes that control over such abstract systems arises increasingly early in infant life.

Conclusion

To draw together both these traditions in contemporary child psychology and psycholinguistics, we may summarize the following tendencies. There is the strong, often exclusive, focus on individual development and an innate mind as the origin of primary categories of understanding and experiencing. There is, conjoined with this preoccupation, a strain of mentalism, which has two faces in psychology, one reactionary and one progressive. There is the mentalism and nativism of the intelligence movement with its "natural" justification for social stratification and hierarchy. There is also a more progressive, indeed, liberal view, which Chomsky's work has been important in asserting. There mentalism is conjoined with a notion of universalism, a theoretical perspective that proved particularly illuminating for workers in nonstandard dialects (Labov, 1972), who were able to demonstrate the structural sophistication, and thence to make claims for the cognitive sophistication, of a variety of ghettoized languages (e.g., Black English, Ameslan).

When language has been studied in interaction, the perspective is of parent–child relations as liberal democracy, all checks and counterbalances. Reciprocity is stressed at the expense of any understanding of power or distortion. Thus far, the reintroduction of context has not led to a sufficiently deep analysis of the social setting within which language experience develops and is experienced. One aspect of this rather limiting understanding of context is undoubtedly connected to the format for empirical investigation of child-language development, and of mother–infant interaction. In part by virtue of the labor-intensive nature of this sort of empirical work, rather idealized diorama-like presentations of language behavior have been the primary objects of study. Taking the

20-odd children reported in Brown's seminal account of developmental linguistics and the presentations of parent–child interaction from the laboratories of Stern, Brazelton, Lewis, and others, we see mother and child extracted from their networks of support and social labor, the mother, in particular, free from the minutiae and distractions of household work.

The isolation of mother and infant in the research paradigm can be seen as an ironic reflection and mystification of the social isolation of many women who parent. Single-parent households headed by women are a rapidly increasing statistic. The presence of a functioning support system for such families is highly problematic. Stack's (1974) work on black urban poor describes a supportive system of real and fictive kin. Following Rapp's analysis (1978) of household and class, we might expect that the working poor and lower- and middle-class families (and perhaps urban nonethnic poor) exist in considerable isolation from extended families and from supportive networks and services. Slater (1970) speaks of the isolation of the middle-class woman, even in intact families, where she is responsible for substantial amounts of reproductive labor done often as a quite solitary set of activities. Support systems may themselves be becoming bureaucratized. Although in-depth analyses of day-care centers as they function for education and parent support are still relatively rare, a recent account of one university- and community-funded day-care program in California does corroborate this view (Joffee, 1977).

When contemporary developmental psychology presents development arising in a two-person (mother–infant) dyad, it performs an ideological function. It reflects processes that are real and illusory. The vision of ideal parenting requires a sympathetic, empathic mother operating in figurative isolation. Working well, the mother offers an idealized version of reproductive labor. Working badly or insensitively, she becomes the target scapegoat for personal difficulties, in the family or in the developing child (Arieti, 1974; Lasch, 1977; Brazelton, 1974).

The treatment of children in most recent work on social and communicative development has some remarkable similarities to the treatment of women in the obstetrical literature (Oakley, 1980). In both instances there is an unusual fusion of biology and mechanism with an undercurrent of danger. It is women's destiny to bear children to interact with them; it is children's destiny to enter relations in an operational and democratic connection, to be communicatively competent at birth. Women, in obstetric literature, are often literally reduced to their reproductive organs, baby-making machinery hooked to the machinery of medical intervention. Infant in psychological literature is mechanistic, information processor, goal-directed problem solver and communicator. Lewis and Rosenblum speak of the project of investigating infant "ideology," by which they seem to mean the cognitive plans or intentionalities propelling infant life.

Underlying both the biological and the mechanical understanding is the sense that women and children are or can be dangerous. The infant controls his caretaker, a manipulative machiavelli. To care for infants, mothers must rediscover their natural communicative skills, their empathic sensitized responses, which allow them to play out interactions under maximal but not overwrought conditions of infant arousal (Stern, 1974, 1977). In this literature, the postpartum mother, like her counterpart in the obstetric texts, must be reconnected to her biology under supervision. In the case of childbirth, this may entail coaching by men as the replacement for male obstetric management.

Infant experience, seen simultaneously as technological and natural, has been a central component of infancy studies over the past decade. It coincides with the appearance of sociobiological perspectives in other scientific domains. In the name of enriched methodology and more systems-oriented theories, a deeply biological view of early social interaction and early cognitive-linguistic development is emerging. What is the relation of this development in psychology to current conditions of social and political life? Is this a legitimating apparatus designed to press women back to purely reproductive work, a modern update of the impact of Bowlby's seminal work on attachment with its assertion of mother–infant connections as theoretically and pragmatically primary? Mitchell (1974) has noted the compatibility of social policy needs in postwar Britain, in regard to its strong requirements to reconstitute family life and move women out of the work place. If this is in part the intention, will it be successful?

The vast wealth of new information on the capacities of infants in all sensory modalities and in communication may well change the expectancies that parents and teachers place on young children. In establishing the possibility of an escalation of developmental tasks, newer and earlier contingencies on the child's performance may be set up. The position of mainstream psychology and of the researchers responsible for this work is usually that these findings are merely the outcome of improved techniques of measurement and observation. Certainly a critical reading of this work must acknowledge any technological breakthroughs. But at the same time it must draw attention to the impact of this understanding on the objects of study and their social surroundings. In particular, it must focus on the intricate interplay of identifying phenomena, constituting new but historically conditioned modes of interpreting those phenomena and legitimating a change in social behavior that the field is itself responsible for initiating. An answer to all these questions requires a dialectical analysis of the "miracle of the mediation of traditions" and will reflect both the totality of the impact of industrial and capital development on all social and scientific institutions, even on the character of everyday life, and, at the same time, the unevenness of that penetration.

We can note a variety of features of the contemporary scene. Women are increasingly in the work force, brought there by changes in consciousness, the need to sustain family income in an inflationary period, and for reasons of commodity-purchasing power. Simultaneously the economy lurches to a "hard landing." There are well-documented changes in the structure of families or households, a bureaucratizing of personal life, and substantial isolation for many people (mostly female) involved in child rearing. The procedures and policies of state apparatus struggling to rationalize social life must be multiple and complex. It is also likely that the strategies will differ for various social groups and classes (Donzelot, 1979; cf. Vonèche's Chapter 3 in this volume).

The biological emphasis, which in some infant researchers' conceptions can be taught to less optimal mothers, legitimates a natural mother-infant symbiosis. At the same time, the research and popular literature leaves open the possibility of more collective state-dominated systems of infant care in the use of terms like 'caretaker.'

Mothering, or rather caretaking, to use the currently popular and abstracted term for parenting vulnerable and dependent humans, becomes, thus, an activity or product extracted from real social beings. As a consequence, the construct "mothering" exists in the psychological literature as potentially flexible ideological tool. It may be 'naturalized' into women's work and female character or 'rationalized' into bureaucratic and state-dominated socialization. In the past decade, a major impetus for more collective or social forms of child rearing came from the women's movement. Whatever the impact of such new social structures on women's lives, we may question any shift in social life which leaves individuals at younger and younger ages in a more unmediated relationship to the state. What we may have here is an example of a critical and liberating movement which initiated social change only to find that, without any control over social or state apparatus and dominant forms of ideology, such social change was open and available for co-optation by the state. Rationalized infant life may not provide the liberating possibilities that feminists anticipated.

Finally, one must note the appearance of biologically flavored theories in the social and human sciences coincident with moments of rising conservatism (Harris, 1980). In many areas of psychology, most noticeably in the analysis of intelligence and in testing (Kamin, 1974; Bowles and Gintis, 1976; Jensen, 1980), psychology has invoked heritability and innate or genetic mechanisms. Such conclusions have the effect of legitimating nonintervention. This analysis *naturalizes* social stratification and the unequal allocation of resources. As such, this work is the perfect companion to the economic and social policies of the 1980s.

References

Anokhin, P. K. (1969). Cybernetics and the integrative activity of the brain. In M. Cole & I. Maltzman (Eds.), *A handbook of contemporary Soviet psychology*. New York: Basic Books.

Arieti, S. (1974). *Interpretations of schizophrenia* (2nd ed.). New York: Basic Books.

Austin, J. L. (1962). *How to do things with words*. Oxford: Oxford University Press.

Bakan, D. (1967). *On method: Toward a reconstruction of psychological investigation*. San Francisco: Jossey-Bass.

Bates, E. (1976). *Language and context*. New York: Academic Press.

Bateson, G. (1973). *Steps to an ecology of mind*. St. Albans, England: Paladin.

Berger, P. L., Berger, B., & Kellner, H. (1973). *The homeless mind*. New York: Random House.

Bever, T. G. (1970). The cognitive basis for linguistic structure. In J. R. Hayes (Ed.), *Cognition and language learning*. New York: Wiley.

Bloom, L. (1970). *Language development: Form and function in emerging grammars*. Cambridge, MA: MIT Press.

Bloom, L. (1973). *One word at a time: The use of single-word utterances before syntax*. The Hague: Mouton.

Bornstein, M., & Kessen, W. (Eds.) (1979). *Psychological development from infancy: Image to intention*. Hillsdale, NJ: Erlbaum.

Bowerman, M. (1973). *Early syntactic development*. London: Cambridge University Press.

Bowlby, J. (1969). *Attachment and loss: Vol. 1. Attachment*. London: Hogarth Press.

Bowles, S., & Gintis, H. (1976). *Schooling in capitalist America*. New York: Basic Books.

Brazelton, T. B. (1969). *Infants and mothers: Differences in development*. New York: Delacorte Press.

Brazelton, T. B. (1974). *Toddlers and parents*. New York: Delacorte Press.

Brazelton, T. B., Koslowski, B., & Main, M. (1974). The origins of reciprocity: Early mother–infant interaction. In M. Lewis & L. Rosenblum (Eds.), *The effect of the infant on its caregiver*. New York: Wiley.

Broughton, J. M. (1979). Developmental structuralism: Without self, without history. In H. Betz (Ed.), *Recent approaches to the social sciences*. Winnipeg: Hignell.

Broughton, J. M. (1981). Piaget's structural developmental psychology, part V: Ideology-critique and the possibility of a critical developmental psychology. *Human Development, 24*(6), 382–411.

Brown, R. (1973). *A first language.* Harmondsworth, England: Penguin.

Bruner, J. (1975). The ontogenesis of speech acts. *Journal of Child Language, 2,* 1–20.

Bruner, J., & Connolly, K. (Eds.). (1974). *The growth of competence.* London: Academic Press.

Buck-Morss, S. (1975). Socio-economic bias in Piaget's theory and the implications for cross-cultural study. In K. Riegel (Ed.), *The development of dialectical operations.* Basel: Karger.

Buss, A. (1975). The emerging field of the sociology of psychological knowledge. *American Psychologist, 30,* 988–1002.

Chodorow, N. (1978). *The reproduction of mothering.* Berkeley: University of California Press.

Chomsky, N. (1965). *Aspects of a theory of syntax.* Cambridge, MA: MIT Press.

Chomsky, N. (1968). *Language and mind.* New York: Harcourt, Brace and World.

Cole, M., & Scribner, S. (1974). *Culture and thought: A psychological introduction.* New York: Wiley.

Condon, W. S. (June, 1974). Speech makes babies move. *New Scientist, 11,* 116–121.

Davin, A. (1978). Imperialism and motherhood. *History Workshop, 5,* 9–66.

Dinnerstein, D. (1976). *The mermaid and the minotaur.* New York: Harper & Row.

Donzelot, P. (1979). *The policing of families.* New York: Pantheon Books.

Dore, J. (1975). *The development of speech acts.* The Hague: Mouton.

Dore, J. (1977). Children's illocutionary acts. In R. O. Freedle (Ed.), *Discource processes (Vol. 1): Discourse production and comprehension.* Norwood, NJ: Ablex.

Ehrenreich, B., & English, D. (1978). *For her own good: 150 years of expert advice to women.* New York: Anchor/Doubleday.

Eimas, P., Siqueland, E., Juscyk, P., & Vigority, J. (1971). Speech perception in infants. *Science, 171,* 303–306.

Fairbairn, W. (1954). *An object-relations theory of the personality.* New York: Basic Books.

Freud, A. (1965). *Normality and pathology in childhood: Assessments of development.* New York: International Universities Press.

Foucault, M. (1965). *Madness and civilization.* New York: Vintage Books.

Gadamer, H. G. (1975). *Truth and method.* New York: Seabury Press.

Garfinkel, H. (1967). *Studies in ethnomethodology.* Englewood Cliffs, NJ: Prentice-Hall.

Goffman, E. (1974). *Frame analysis.* New York: Harper & Row.

Greenfield, P. M., & Smith, J. (1976). *The structure of communication in early language development.* New York: Academic Press.

Grice, P. (1957). Meaning. *Philosophical Review, 26,* 377–388.

Habermas, J. (1975). *Legitimation crisis.* Boston: Beacon.

Halliday, M. A. K. (1973). *Learning how to mean.* London: Arnold.

Harris, A. (1975). Social dialectics and language: Mother and child construct the discourse. *Human Development, 18,* 80–96.

Harris, A. (1980). Review of *Bias in Mental Testing* by A. Jensen. *New Republic,* 13–14.

Hersh, D., & Camazarra, A. (1976). A fuzzy set approach to modifier and vagueness in natural language. *Journal of Experimental Psychology, 105*(3), 254–276.

Horkheimer, M., & Adorno, T. (1972). *Dialectic of enlightenment.* New York: Herder and Herder.

Jacoby, R. (1975). *Social amnesia.* Boston: Beacon Press.

Jay, M. (1973). *The dialectical imagination.* Boston: Little, Brown.

Jensen, A. (1980). *Bias in mental testing.* San Francisco: Freeman Press.

Joffee, C. (1977). *Friendly intruders.* Berkeley: University of California Press.

Kamin, L. (1974). *The science and the politics of I.Q.* Hillsdale, NJ: Erlbaum.

Kovel, J. (1978). Rationalization and the family. *Telos, 37,* 5–21.

Labov, W. (1972). *Socialization patterns.* Philadelphia: University of Pennsylvania Press.

Lacan, J. (1968). *The language of the self.* Baltimore: Johns Hopkins Press.

Lasch, C. (1977). *Haven in a heartless world: The family besieged.* New York: Basic Books.

Lewis, M., & Freedle, R. (1977). Mother-infant dyad: The cradle of meaning. In P. Pliner, L. Krames, & T. Alloway (Eds.), *Communication and affect: Language and thought.* New York: Academic Press.

Lewis, M., & Rosenblum, L. (1974). *The effects of the infant on its caregiver.* New York: Wiley.

Lipsitt, L. (1976). *Developmental psychobiology: The significance of infancy.* Hillsdale, NJ: Erlbaum.

Lunzer, E. A. (1968). *The regulation of behavior.* London: Staples Press.

Mahler, M., Pine, F., & Bergman, A. (1975). *The psychological birth of the human infant: Symbiosis and individuation.* New York: Basic Books.

Mannheim, K. (1936). *Ideology and utopia.* London: Routledge & Kegan Paul.

McNeill, D. (1970). *The acquisition of language.* New York: Harper & Row.

Miller, G., Galanter, E., & Pribram, K. (1960). *Plans and the structure of behavior.* New York: Holt, Rinehart and Winston.

Mitchell, J. (1974). *Psychoanalysis and feminism.* New York: Pantheon Books.

Nelson, K. (1979). Structure and strategy in learning to talk. *Monograph of the Society for Research in Child Development, 149,* (38).

Newson, J., & Newson, E. (1974). Cultural aspects of childrearing in the English-speaking world. In M. P. M. Richards (Ed.), *The integration of a child into a social world.* Cambridge: Cambridge University Press.

Oakley, A. (1980). *Women confined: Towards a sociology of childbirth.* Oxford: Martin Robinson.

Peirce, C. S. (1955). Structuralism. In J. Buchler (Ed.), *Philosophical writings.* New York: Dover.

Piaget, J. (1962). *The origins of intelligence in children.* New York: Norton.

Rapp, R. (1978). Family and class in contemporary America: Notes towards an understanding of ideology. *Science and Society, 42,* 278–300.

Richards, M. P. M. (Ed.). (1974). *The integration of a child into a social world.* Cambridge: Cambridge University Press.

Riegel, K. F. (Ed.). (1975). *The development of dialectical operations.* Basel: Karger.

Riegel, K. F. (1976). The dialectics of human development. *American Psychologist, 31,* 689–700.

Schachtel, E. (1959). *Metamorphosis: On the development of affect, perception, attention and memory.* New York: Basic Books.

Schaffer, H. R. (1977). *Interactions in Infancy.* New York: Academic Press.

Searle, J. (1969). *Speech acts: An essay in the philosophy of language.* Cambridge: Cambridge University Press.

Sears, R. R. (1975). Your ancients revisited: A history of child development. In E. M. Hetherington (Ed.), *Review of child development research* (Vol. 5). Chicago: University of Chicago Press.

Sève, L. (1971). *Man in Marxist theory and the psychology of personality.* Sussex, England: Harvester Press.

Shorter, E. L. (1975). *The making of the modern family.* New York: Basic Books.

Shotter, J. (1974). The development of personal powers. In M. P. M. Richards (Ed.), *The integration of a child into a social world.* Cambridge: Cambridge University Press.

Shotter, J. (1978). The cultural context of communication studies. In A. Lock (Ed.), *Action, gesture and symbol.* London: Academic Press.

Sigel, I., & Cocking, R., (1979). Cognition and communication: A dialectical paradigm for development. In M. Lewis & L. Rosenblum (Eds.), *Communication and language: The origins of behavior* (vol. 5). New York: Wiley.

Slater, P. (1970). *The pursuit of loneliness: American culture at the breaking point*. Boston: Beacon Press.

Snow, C., & Ferguson, C. (1977). *Talking to children: Language input and acquisition*. Cambridge: Cambridge University Press.

Stack, C. (1974). *All our kin: Strategies for survival in a black community*. New York: Harper & Row.

Stern, D. (1974). Mother and infant at play: Dyadic interaction involving facial, vocal and gaze behaviors. In M. Lewis and L. Rosenblum (Eds.), *The effect of the infant on its caregiver*. New York: Wiley.

Stern, D. (1977). *The first relationship*. Cambridge, MA: Harvard University Press.

Stone, L. (1977). *The family, sex and marriage in England, 1500–1800*. New York: Harper & Row.

Stone, J., Smith, H. T., & Murphy, L. B. (Eds.). (1973). *The competent infant*. New York: Basic Books.

Trehub, S. (1979). Reflections on the development of speech perception. *Canadian Journal of Psychology, 33,* 3680–381.

Trevarthen, C. (1977). Communication and cooperation in early infancy: A description of primary subjectivity. In M. Bullowa (Ed.), *Before speech: The beginnings of human cooperation*. Cambridge: Cambridge University Press.

Trevarthen, C. (1978). Secondary subjectivity: Confidence, confiding and acts of meaning in the first year. In A. Lock (Ed.), *Action, gesture and symbol: The emergence of language*. New York: Academic Press.

Turkewitz, G. (1979). The study of infancy. *Canadian Journal of Psychology, 33,* 408–412.

Unger, R. M. (1975). *Knowledge and politics*. New York: Free Press.

Volosinov, V. N. (1973). *Marxism and the philosophy of language*. New York and London: Seminar Press.

Vygotsky, L. V. (1962). *Thought and language*. Cambridge, MA: MIT Press.

Vygotsky, L. V. (1978). *Mind in society: The development of a higher psychological process*. Cambridge, MA: Harvard University Press.

Werner, H., & Kaplan, S. (1963). *Symbol formation: An organismic approach to language and the expression of thought*. New York: Wiley.

Winnicott, D. W. (1965). *The maturational process and the facilitating environment*. New York: International Universities Press.

Winnicott, D. W. (1974). *Playing and reality*. London: Penguin.

Wolff, P. H. (1959). Observations on newborn infants. *Psychosomatic Medicine, 21,* 110–118.

Wolff, P. H. (1966). The causes, control, and organization of behavior in the neonate. *Psychological Issues, 5,* 17.

Wozniak, R. H. (1973). Structuralism, dialectical materialism and cognitive developmental theory. In K. F. Riegel (Ed.), *Issues in developmental and historical structuralism*. Basel: Karger.

Chapter 3

J. Jacques Vonèche

THE DIFFICULTY OF BEING A CHILD IN FRENCH-SPEAKING COUNTRIES

Victor

When, before dawn on 9 January 1800, "Victor" (which was not his real name) came out of the woods near the village of Saint-Sernin in southern France, the knell of the ancient forms of childhood was ringing. Previously, parents had put up with bizarre children, poet children, sad children. The new parents were going to be different. Taking risks was running out of fashion. Child rearing would no longer be a venture: artist or wino, scientist or gay, Francis of Assissi or Marquis de Sade, Joan of Arc or Queen Margot, at random. The new ideal was the norm, and like all ideals it was arduous, fringed with uncertainty, and lined with anxiety. But, thanks to the goddess Reason, the French Revolution had come and French was being imposed on all as the standard tongue of the country. Napoléon Bonaparte had come into power and, as premier consul of France, was busy codifying everything at hand. *Liberté, egalité, fraternité* was being replaced with "property, equality, and liberty," the official proclamation by which Napoleon signed his *coup d'état* on the 18th Brumaire, an. VIII (i.e., month of mists of the eighth year of the Revolution). The statement prophetically ended with this phrase:

J. Jacques Vonèche • Department of Psychology and Educational Science, University of Geneva, Geneva, Switzerland.

"Citizens, the Revolution is established on the principles upon which it was founded: It is over."

The old forms of childhood were over too. Innocence had been granted to children by the men of the Renaissance along with its necessary corollary, *patria potestas* (father's authority). The conjunction of these two factors in the Reformation had authorized people like Calvin or Luther and their followers to moralize children by enshrining them within their families. Since then, there had been no more living in the same house with prostitutes, as in Erasmus's days; no more sleeping naked alongside a male servant in the same bed; no more sleeping with your babies, because of the risk of stifling them in midsleep (the medieval version of abortion on demand). Generations were to be raised on Sunday school and absolute ablatives, strangers to their own bodies and those of others, loving their parents dearly but at a distance, always modestly dressed, but dreaming of Oedipus erect while fagging in boarding schools. Everyone had a family to care for and to care for her or him. Those who did not had an orphanage. The entourage of saintly nuns and priests, deacons and deaconesses, ministers and sherpherdesses was the next best thing to being blessed with the sweetness of a real family. This had been the right way to grow up from the original innocence of selfless little things into the moral strength of adults.

And then came the Revolution. Finished with priests and religions, reformed or not; finished with nuns and orphanages; finished with deacons and boarding schools, nurseries of reactionaries. What happened next? A mess, the tremendous mess of the white Terror, the red Terror, all sorts of horrors. A little Corsican, Napoléon dawning under Bonaparte, was attentive to all these changes and when he took over the reins of the state, he replaced the orphanages with specialized schools and the saintly guardians of children with notables and experts. Reason replaced religion.

Therefore, when Victor came out of the woods, everyone knew what to do with him: catch him and normalize him by sending him to the experts on abnormal populations. Victor was no longer a moral dilemma for the people of southern France, for he had become a medical case. Since he could not speak, he had to be sent to the newly instituted School for Deaf-Mutes in Paris where he was supposed to undergo some diagnosis and treatment that would standardize him in relation to the normal boys of his age.

Thus, even the parentless boy who had once escaped civilization was not respected in his project of living like an animal. In the name of liberty and equality, the state had to make the mark of its property upon this human being by investigating him as if he were a machine. In so doing, the state literally applied the principles of La Mettrie, whose theory of machine-man was then in fashion, as well as Condillac's sensualism according to which all that differentiates a real man from a statue of him lies in the existence, inside the former, of sense-data experience. The avenue opened by this mechanical metaphor of the human condition had led us to put children into families and children and families alike into the hands of social technicians, physicians, judges, and notables of all sorts who were to assist them in living their lives according to the standards of bourgeois rationality.

The idea behind all this is, clearly, that human beings are incapable of enterprises of their own, that human action has no meaning, that the human mind is simply the locus of a certain number of processes that traverse the body of the agent, forming or not forming (this point is debatable according to the experts) structures that "speak across the subject," in Lacan's phrase, and are transparent only to those happy few who have been trained for that purpose. Man has been "naturalized" as an object, reduced to a simple taxi for genes by biology, a cookie jar for elementary particles by biophysics, a stage for the developmental ballet of structures by structural-genetic psychology, a space for tribes of responses by behavioral psychology, a locus of diseases for medicine, a focus of laws for legal sciences, or the driftwood of social movements recognized by sociology.

Victor's life in the midst of civilization is the perfect example of this process of reduction. Nobody cared to know more about his life in the woods of Aveyron. No one went along with him. He was leashed and gagged and taken to a school and then to Paris to be examined by doctors who segmented him into a speech-impairment case, a neurological case, a mental case, and so on, discussing at length what they should do with him before putting him in a foster family, the Guérins, and entrusting him to the care of the young and ambitious Jean René Itard, who was later to develop a number of new techniques of intervention, control, and domination of children.

The point to be made here is that these new techniques were invented under the guise of philanthropy, a word coined at the time to characterize those who believed that they knew better than others what was good for them. Victor, for instance, was studied by the Society of Observers of Man. This was a newly founded group of scientists and philosophers, a notable member of which was Pinel. This man, who had unchained the madmen of Bicêtre asylum, was the one who wrote the report on Victor for the society. Thus, the philosophy of the Enlightenment was responsible for freeing the madmen and putting an end to the belief that deaf-mutes were dumb, but the price to pay for this liberation was to be the standardization of childhood. Napoléon himself was busy taking care of the legal aspects of the question with the creation of his code of penal and civil laws. Medicine was beginning to regulate behavior by the introduction of hygiene, biometry, and preventive medicine. Thanks to education, the new philanthropists were building a complete system of external government of families and children around medical and legal knowledge and power.

It was taken for granted by the bourgeois power of revolutionary France that both extreme ends of society, aristocracy and proletariat, were ignorant of how to live properly. Hence the tremendous purge of the Terror, the moment at which Pinel, a physician, was named as the head of the Bicêtre instead of a police officer, as was the case under the kings of France. The conjunction of the two events is not coincidental. The thinkers of the Revolution decided that aristocracy was not educable because it was rotten and therefore it had to go or perish. In fact, the elimination of aristocracy was due to the fact that it had been in power and knew the rules of the power game. On the contrary, people belonging to the lower classes were considered to be plain ignorant. It was considered necessary for them to be schooled, in both senses of the word. Out of the previous melting pot, madmen, criminals, and deaf-mutes had to be streamed into different channels and sent to schools in accordance with their talents. For the first time in history, children were unanimously seen as being exploited in such a way as to form the "main nursery of enemies of social order." Notice that working classes were already considered dangerous. Victor was harbored by the Institute for Deaf-Mutes in Paris because he could have been "hunted" by the populace of the villages surrounding his woods. What was hidden behind this humanitarian preoccupation was the fact that Victor was a "bad example" for the population of the place: children could have been tempted to act like Victor and parents tempted to abandon their progeny. After all, *Le Petit Poucet* ("Tom Thumb") was a popular tale written by Charles Perrault without even a hint at the parents' bad conduct, but Perrault was incorrigibly *ancien régime* and could not have condemned parents.

It was possible for families to do nothing for their children and some parents even set the bad example themselves by resisting standardization: they refused the minimum hygiene and they failed to display the minimum stability or permanence required to educate children properly. Philanthropists struggled against such a chaotic situation by different means. Urban planning was the first one. Napoléon continued the work of Richelieu, who had razed all the walls of provincial towns to the ground to ensure the centralization of power in the king's hands, against the slightest will toward independence among provincial noblemen. This time around, the focus of urbanization was the ghetto or people's enclaves, where neither the police nor the doctors dared to go. Broad avenues were traced right into the ghetto, dispersing neighbors and families, and allowing, if needed, orderly police charges against potential demonstrators. This convassing of the city streets, inherited from Bentham's philosophy of panopticism, was followed and improved upon by Napoléon III, who later created the *grands boulevards* to separate the "right" people from the "wrong" people. Thus urban design was used as a means of creating big empty spaces where, under the guise of sanitation, hygiene, and welfare, unwanted demonstrators would be killed more easily and masses of people could be assembled to acclaim the monarch.

Besides urban design, there was the remedy of schooling the children of this increasingly aseptic society. Schools would limit the improvidence in reproductive characteristics of working classes and increase the providence in the organization of daily life. Civilization was entering the home. In fact, during the nineteenth century and up to the middle 1950s, France witnessed the development of a fantastic campaign in favor of schooling that culminated in the compulsory education law in 1880 and, in 1955, in the extension of this obligation up to the age of 16. In the interval, schools promoted all the values of the successive governments of France and thus became a powerful instrument of division among Frenchmen.

Schools were perfect parking places for children, keeping them busy and off the streets, but they could not always take care of the children all the time. A special effort had to be made to stabilize families into enough permanence to permit their taking care of their own childern. Unlike medieval families, modern families would have to take care of their children and to put them under strict surveillance if they themselves wanted to avoid the strict surveillance of magistrates and notables who disciplined them by canvassing city blocks with spies, by questioning neighbors, by police verifications of identity, and so on. Those parents who did express some sort of rebellion against this state of affairs automatically lost their *patria potestas,* their right to keep the children, who were then put into correction houses.

The stabilization of the family revolved around the now predominant role of the mother. If you wanted to keep the men at home so that they went to bed early and were ready in the morning to go to work at the factory, their labor forces fully restored, you first had to keep the women in the home. Not any sort of women: mothers, not prostitutes. Madame Guérin, who took care of Victor at the Institute for Deaf-Mutes, was a very good example of this new sort of woman who had learned very recently to cook decent meals in the right quantities for the family, to keep the home by tidying up rooms, putting curtains in windows, organizing indoor spaces according to their main functions—in short, by living up to the standard of "Home, sweet home." French women were assisted in this task by the philanthropists who had created schools for parenting (*École des Parents*), where women were to learn all the virtues of hygiene, prevention of venereal disease and alcoholism, and breastfeeding their babies themselves.[1] They were also to learn how to balance a working-class budget.

In sum, three sorts of methods were employed to surround families in order to fortify them and, at the same time, to govern them from without: (1) inquisitorial investigation, (2) classificatory expertise, and (3) interpretive knowledge. Philanthropy founded the method of social inquiries. Social work set about instituting a sort of peripheral approach to the family, by inquiring about the family's virtues, by fathering the schoolteacher's impressions and those of the neighbors and parents' bosses. In the neighborhood, the *bistro* (a word brought back from Russia by Napoléon's troops) or the publican played a central role, since pubs have always been the sitting rooms of the working classes.[2] Furthermore, the *bistro* was often the superintendent of the tenements in the neighborhood. The third feature of these investigations, besides the interviewing of notables and inquiries in the neighborhood, was the verification by the police of all the information gathered about the family before they handed their report to the superior authority of those who are called here "the experts."

The role of the experts was essentially that of a medicalization of the case handed out to them. A profusion of methods was developed by the

[1]Previously, city mothers sent their babies to the countryside to be breast-fed by strong peasant women, the pollution of Parisian air having been recognized from the Middle Ages.

[2]See the American "saloon" imported from the French *salon,* meaning sitting room.

medical profession to render its activities more scientific in appearance: anthropometric measurements of all sorts (leading to a typology of deviance according to physical appearance), mental tests of a totally impressionistic nature, careful description of sexual organs (primary and secondary), and examination of the sense organs (taken as the sources of intelligence). All this search for pathology was centered around three main notions: mental retardation, perversity, and hysteria, all three considered as pathologies typical of the working classes. A new class of medical doctors was assigned to this diagnostic task. For this task force, such an assignment was a blessing. It allowed the "alienist," the psychiatrist of the time, to come out of the closet of asylums to penetrate (if the metaphor is not too bold) society at large and regenerate it by spotting the vicious ones right from the beginning, that is to say, at school. Since the predominant view of the world was Lockean, the only philosophy consonant with the desire to impose an external control upon the family, mental retardation, perversity, and hysteria were attributed to the family. Think, for instance, of the Kallikak family.[3] And overshadowing this attribution there was the threat of imprisonment for those who did not conform to the ideal of bourgeois morality.

Above the experts who examined real cases was an upper echelon of experts who held the keys of interpretive knowledge. The scholars in this group rarely used direct investigation as a means of inquiry. They relied on information given by others and remained secluded in their cabinets of study. It is interesting here to observe the hierarchy of classes in terms of bodily contacts. The working classes were supposed to ignore their bodies except for working purposes. For instance, they exhibited no self-palpation, no anatomical knowledge; the body was merely a tool. The experts in charge of classification of the population used their own bodies as an instrument of investigation of the passive and ignorant

[3]The Kallikak family was the double lineage of a soldier who, during the American Civil War, had an illegitimate child by courtesy of a supposedly feebleminded barmaid (giving rise to the so-called "Kak" line of descent) and then later married within his social class and had more children with his wife (the so-called "Kall" line of descent). This story has been told with such restraint by geneticists that it is not at all clear that it is true, or that the barmaid was really a moron. What is clear, instead, is that no effort was made to analyze the objective conditions under which the "Kak" (from the Greek *kakos* meaning "bad") side of the family was living, that is, a milieu wherein there was no issue other than crime and dereliction, whereas the "Kall" side (from the Greek *kalos*, meaning "good") was described as composed exclusively of nice people. Hence the virtues of the "Kalls" and the vices of the "Kaks" were attributed to intrinsic properties of their respective genes. Once again, unsuccessful people are dangerous people, the social role of the bourgeoisie being to tame the working class and bring them to law and order.

bodies of the poor and suffering people. The top interpreters exhibited a total regression of body contact into the gaze; they would occasionally ask an interesting case to walk around the room, sit down, or lie down, all of these commands involving only distal contacts. Thus, the hierarchy of knowledge replicated the hierarchy of production. Control was becoming more and more remote. By opposition to the image of the body as a locus of pleasure and displeasure, inherited from the Middle Ages, the modern image of the body was purely functional. The distance between bodies increased, favoring individualism and secrecy by modesty and separation, with the consequence that external controls became easier to establish among people who were ashamed of feeling something in their own bodies, a feeling that could be taken as a sure sign of some deviance.

Thus, the role of the interpreters became that of establishing the causal relations existing between pathological (read "working class") families and children's troubles. This led to the appearance of a new profession: psychology. Its practitioners were going to be put directly in charge of manipulating the parameters amenable to an educational action upon the nonstandard individuals.

Marguerite and Armande

"Marguerite and Armande" (in reality, Madeline and Alice) were the two daughters of Alfred Binet, who himself was one of the chief interpreters of the end of the nineteenth century and the initiator (involuntarily) of all the unifactorial and multifactorial analyses of the relationship between the family, considered now as a hereditary capital of aptitudes, and the environmental heritage of solicitations. With Galton's work on the inheritance of talents in the same family (the Bachs in music, for instance), it was taken for granted that genius was genetically transmitted from one generation to the next. In France, however, the Lamarckian tradition was still strong and scientists still emphasized the role of the environment in the formation of children's minds in a given family. These were pre-Mendelian times during which natural selection was understood on the model of what animal breeders did when they wanted to improve horse races, for instance.

Beside this medical model of man, to which we will return later, another model appealed to the minds of psychologists of the time: the model of industry. The leap forward of industrialization in Western countries was so impressive that its methods and concepts were often imported into domains apparently foreign to their application. At the time of Binet, schools were such a domain. A political battle was being fought between the progressive minds, who wanted free and compulsory schooling for all children, and the conservatives, who opposed it with their characteristic imagination. To imagine what the situation was like at the time, one should revert to what happened in the United States when free admission was proposed for the City University of New York in our own day. The conservative reaction was the same and could be summarized in general as: "What? All these poor people in school? Don't you know they are stupid?" It seems hard to believe now that the reaction was the same regarding entrance into the first grade of elementary school at the turn of the century. But the fact is that everyone "in his right mind" felt that free admission to elementary school was a threat to the quality of schooling, a lowering of standards, a menace to the general education of the public, and even a clear case of jeopardizing public law and order engineered by the political left in order to get into power. At any rate, it was understood that "those poor kids" coming from poverty-stricken areas would never learn to read and write properly, the latter being clearly a privilege of the middle class and inaccessible to others.

In order to defend such a view of education, the conservative groups pressuring the French government decided to conceptualize education as an enterprise to pay off its investments. Students were considered as a product to promote and teachers as production-line workers specialized in different segments of production: Greek, Latin, mathematics, modern languages, and so on. Their main function was to ensure that the product, the graduating student, conformed to the standards of production. In order to evaluate this conformity, a procedure of sampling was established under the name of "examinations." These examinations were the bourgeois equivalent of the tournaments of feudal chivalry. Where aristocrats used to expose their own bodies to the blows of combat, the new bourgeoisie exposed its children. Note the difference. Moreover, examinations combined the techniques of a hierarchizing surveillance with those of normalizing sanctions. The strategies of surveillance consisted in isolating children from their peers and parents, and thus from any communication with unqualified personnel, for the good of their intellectual work.

The consequence of this policy was that children were prevented from ganging up against the authority of their masters in the same way that factory workers were prevented from forming trade unions. These strategies were inspired by the penal methods practiced at the time in order to subdue psychologically recalcitrant inmates. A vertical order was established in which anyone knew her or his superiors and inferiors but ignored her or his equals. In addition, teachers and students were not supposed to exchange any information on what was going to happen during the examination so that students could not possibly know ahead of time on what grounds they would be rated. Hence the new bourgeoisie was entirely pervaded by a drive toward outdoing others by passing a succession of examinations, considered as the locus for the exchange of knowledge. This gave rise to the system of *grandes écoles* so typical of France and based on the successful results at a *concours* ("competition") open only to those who spent enough time in a crammer or special preparation class. This system completely regulated the work market by introducing into the economy just enough working force to keep it going, since every year the quotas were fixed by government regulation. The sanction of the school mark was thus the hallmark of intelligence defined as a substance inoculated during school years into students who would later diffuse it into the social tissue. Again, the medical metaphor.

Before passing to a consideration of the medical metaphor, it must be understood that grades were supposed to hierarchize the student body into main categories like eggs: jumbo eggheads, large, medium, and small, with special sales for broken, damaged, or aged ones, each one according to its caliber. For the leisure classes, those disciplines such as Latin and Greek that are completely useless; for the working classes those subjects inherited from the German Pietists and from the Christian Brothers, that are useful and pragmatic, like manual work, agriculture, winery, business. The task of teachers was, like that of production-line workers, the channeling of raw material to the proper calibrating device, defective material being sent to special sections for special treatment. The medical metaphor, once again.

This process classified and provided information on students in such a way that even the least of them had a better documented vita than Charlemagne (once again, the inversion of the heroism of chivalry into the prosaic and the police index). The examinations were also a means of diagnosing students. The network of observations that teachers had to organize around students by noting their conduct, application, zeal, cleanliness, attitude in the classroom, obedience, and so on, as well as their performance in the different subjects of the curriculum, allowed the full evaluation of their singularity as well as the comparison among singular students in order to rate them on a scale.

This process, to which we are now so accustomed, was new at the time of Binet and relied on the new experimental medicine of Claude Bernard and Louis Pasteur. Medicine was then understood as the science of the singular by opposition to physiology, which was the science of the general. Statistical methods, discovered at the same time, functioned as the generalization of the singular or the articulation of the singular upon the general. By the use of statistics, a singular case is always and automatically part of a population. This localization of the individual case on a curve was the means by which existing social practices of acceptance or rejection were scientifically justified. The rejected case was no longer morally repulsive; it simply fell outside the allowed standard deviation.

The attitude toward masturbation and venereal diseases was characteristic in this respect. After the Reformation, they were the signs of immoral behavior, but they could be forgiven by God if sincere repentance and perfect contrition were shown. At the time of Victor, the position was unclear, and that is the reason why very little is known about Victor's sexual life, except the fact that he remained unmoved by the charms of the delicious Madame Récamier. On the contrary, at the turn of the century, despite the fact that substantial numbers of the male bourgeoisie practiced masturbation and died of venereal diseases, self-abuse and venereal disease were considered to affect only certain segments of the population: prostitutes, their working-class mates, and mental retardates. The essential point to keep in mind is that the medicalization of venereal diseases and masturbation made the condemnation of those guilty of these two diseases absolute; there is no recourse in the face of medical diagnosis, no appeal, no saving grace. One cannot be forgiven for one's own diseases or for falling outside the first and second deviations. Standard deviations are more inflexible than God.

This rigidity was also reflected in the conception of the body as the object for all sorts of contraptions. It was the time of corsets, crinolines, bearing ribbons, brassieres, panty hose, stiff shirts and collars, girdles. A complete industry for the imprisonment of the body in all sorts of prostheses flourished at the time, claiming marvellous moral effects due to the compression of stomachs, the discipline imposed on the spinal cord by bearing ribbons, and so on. This orthopedic practice culminated in the work of the father of Freud's patient, the notorious "President Schreber," whose pedagogy was based entirely on apparel that prevented children from doing all sorts of things, especially reaching out for their genitals.

Hence, there emerged within the rising science of psychology a disjunction between a phantasmic body imagined by Freud, Janet, and Flournoy, and the completely negated body as in cognitive psychology and the posterity of Binet. Binet himself described only the intellectual development of his own two daughters. His descriptions were couched in the medical language of singularity but justified by the use of statistics and experimental methods. Nevertheless, both Binet and Freud, working in their separate fields, were propagating the social representation of the happy family.

The invasion of new collective representations, such as the interiority of the family, the central state, and the technological and scientific advances imposed by both the state and the philanthropists, created in the minds of people an increasing tension that could not be resolved by the intervention of social workers at the level of families. The gap between social rules and social practices, especially in the lower middle class, was too wide to be filled by practical action only. Hence, the genius of psychoanalysis, which discovered this gap and filled it by creating a theory that joined medieval lust for life (think of *The Canterbury Tales*, for instance) with the new demands made upon women and men of the Victorian age by the law and order so typical of nation-states, under the guises of, respectively, the id and the superego. Thus, it was no accident that this new science was born in the new milieu of recently maranized (secularized) Jews. They occupied the right economic, social, and ideological position to accomplish this prowess of regulating society by giving the impression of freeing women and men, especially those of the high society who thought that the world was watching their deeds. Economically, they were the result of a new wealth. However, socially, as *nouveaux riches*, they could not be accepted into society in spite of their talents and diplomas. Moreover, being Jewish, they occupied in European mythology the position of the "bad guys" to whom one could confide that the pressures of modern life were too strong to be obeyed. They had, in addition, an experience not to be neglected: a very long tradition of what is called in Hebrew *pillpull*, or discussion of the different manners in which a very rigid law, the Decalogue, could be applied to complicated situations.

Neither was it an accident that "Anna O.," Freud's first patient, became the first social worker in the Germanic countries. If the bourgeoisie could afford to resolve the tensions between its own desires and rules by consulting a psychoanalyst, other social classes of a lower status needed the intervention from above by social workers to check the liberties taken such as abandoning children on the steps of churches, to control possible wild associations such as concubinage, and to impose a return to the family on hobos and other vagabonds because the family is a happy place. Families are happy places because of the sweetness of the home. In the bourgeois family, members weave links of affection among each other against the servants who have become more and more strangers to the family that they serve. Compare, for instance, the confidence of Marivaux's servants or Molière's with those in the comedies at the turn of this century. In the working-class family, the home is no longer the sort of haunt it was before, but the hideaway of people who control each other.

In each type of family, there was a "queen" of the home. In the bourgeoisie, there was a reevaluation of educational tasks centered around the increasing influence of the mother on children within the family and without which the children were supposed to become pathological individuals, intellectually and morally. A good bourgeois wife was also an asset in the transmission of the economic, social, and cultural heritage of the family. Outside the family, she was the instrument of her husband's cultural radiance (Freud's notion of "social penis"). In the working class, women aspired to stay home and raise the children. This contradiction between work and home led women to think of themselves as refractions of their husbands and children.

Children of the bourgeoisie were raised in a very sheltered environment in which the mechanisms of control were discrete. Bourgeois parents established a real sanitary belt around their children in spite of the cohabitation in the same building of various social classes. In the working class, children were under their mother's surveillance when playing on the street or in backyards. They were more and more channeled into spaces of higher order such as schools and houses where many social classes lived and controlled each other. Such children constantly had held over their heads the meance of being thrown out of the apartment because the influential bourgeois might get nervous about working-class children who did not "behave." The bourgeois parents, on the other hand, internalized this menace for their own children by advocating good behavior because they were to become future leaders who must set a good example.

All these attitudes were reflected in the Binet-Simon test. The pictures showed the social hierarchy: the bourgeois reading the newspaper under a lamp, poor people doing a moonlight flit, and so on. Family scenes were presented as romantic and charming. But the questions asked in the section called "comprehension" (understanding) were even more revealing of the philanthropists' outlook. For instance, children were asked to explain why it is better to give money to a charitable organization than to a pauper in the street. The question is: Is it indeed better? If the answer is yes, then it means that poor people have no self and should be checked constantly by those who know better. When one thinks that such questions were supposed to measure intelligence, one is more and more convinced that such tests were measuring how adequately children's knowledge of the social order matched up to the self-satisfied image that the ruling class had formed of themselves.

To conclude, both Freud and Binet attempted to bridge the gap between the demands of the industrial society and human instinct. Freud tried this by conceptualizing a trinitary mental structure in the psyche and the notion of the unconscious, an affective one indeed. Binet tried to bridge the gap by postulating a cognitive unconscious[4] and by measuring the deviation of the individual and his or her social intellectual abilities from the bourgeois norm for intelligent behavior. He thus measured a degree of acculturation rather than intelligence itself.

It is interesting to note at this point that both Freud and Binet did not enjoy a university chair. Both their own social origins and their preoccupations with the sick and the disadvantaged prevented them from gaining a high social position in academic circles but at the same time made them sensitive to a major social change. Fascinated as they were with the industry of machines, they conceptualized this change in mechanical terms. Mental processes were assimilated to hydraulic machinery by Freud and to physical operationism by Binet. Human action and praxis were fused with mental processes located and taking place in that sort of no man's land that they independently called unconscious, as if they needed to find a limbo to excuse the resistance of men and women to the regimentation and bureaucratization of their lives.

When one thinks that all this was taking place at the time when a young man in the Rhineland was reinventing the notion of alienation, one can hardly suppress a smile of compassion for Armande and Marguerite, but also for David Copperfield and Oliver Twist, without forgetting a little newborn: Jean Piaget.

[4]The quarrel about imageless thoughts is typical of the defense of this notion by Binet.

Jacqueline, Lucienne, and Laurent

These three children were born around 1930 in the home of Jean Piaget. Children had become sufficiently precious and accepted in society that their father could use their real names in his books. But there was a reciprocal movement of distantiation from the children such that a father did not feel awkward in exposing his own children to the public eye. There was thus a recentration of the family around the mother in the middle class, the father becoming an absentee who could therefore be an "impartial" observer. To all questions about the education of his children, Piaget used to repeat: "My wife is a perfect educator," as if education were none of his business.

This situation was typical of Western society after World War I and the great crisis of the late 1920s. In most homes, the father had become the chief and often only wage earner. His role was perfectly described by Talcott Parsons, so I shall not repeat the latter's discussion of the expressive and instrumental roles or the distinction between inferior and superior powers in the family. I will simply remind the reader of the relationship established by Parsons himself between his own theory of the family as a social system and Freud's psychoanalysis. Grossly speaking, the instrumental role covers the superego and the expressive one the id, making women wilder than men or presenting them as the invasion of tellurian and biological forces into an otherwise well organized and civilized world. Through menstruation, women's sex was an integral part of the great natural rhythms of the planets, men being a sort of spiritual excrescence independent of this universe. But, in addition, such a system presented men as totally enslaved to the capitalistic mode of production. Thus, the chasm between men at work and women at home was duplicated by an explanatory distinction between the instinctual forces of love and hatred that must be kept in the home and the instrumental forces of labor that must be objective, realistic, and cooperative.

This distinction was reflected in the new urban design. Houses tended to be more distant from the place of work. There was a need for the middle class to reconquer the nature lost in the inner cities. Thus, one could witness among these families an enormous migration toward the outskirts of existing cities. It was the time of the "villa." The consequence of such a move was the higher concentration of working-class neighborhoods in the inner city or on the industrial periphery of large cities. This meant a stronger separation of social classes, since the moral segregation was now doubled by a physical one. In addition, it meant the recognition by the ruling class that the great economic depression had domesticated the working class to the extent that even high concentration did not make it dangerous.

The execution of Rosa Luxemburg and Karl Liebknecht near the little bridge in Berlin, the imprisonment of Antonio Gramsci in Rome, the rise of fascism all over Europe, and the establishment of the Russian Revolution had silenced and would continue to silence the European working class for a long time. Workers had something to dream about in Russia so that they could suffer "the slings and arrows of outrageous fortune." Europe was in fact divided into two blocks but did not know it. The situation was clear and some relaxation was in the air.

Even the bodies were released from their contraptions. Fully bearded men of the Victorian age dared to show their naked faces and long-haired women dared to cut it short. Off with corsets and crinolines, stiff shirts and tailcoats. Working class costumes penetrated into the male bourgeoisie with short coats and a general simplicity of *garderobe.* Sunbathing became fashionable and even nudity in the avant-garde. There was a renewal of interest in sports of all sorts.

The distance among bodies tended to decrease, within certain limits, of course. Women were even allowed to shake hands with men without wearing gloves. At elegant suppers and dinner parties, women stopped wearing gloves at the table, thus eating their food with bare hands and maximizing the possibility of contact with other bare hands. Men and women bathed together in the sea. Compact modern cars allowed a certain proximity among bodies of different sexes that was undreamed of in drawing rooms. The working-class habit of kissing a woman on the cheek instead of the hand was gradually introduced at that time.

The general simplicity of dressing affected also the quantity of garments worn at one time in the middle class. The bra-less, girdle-less *garçonne* of the twenties allowed the shape of her body to be guessed through the light material of her dress, a timid return to the see-through dresses of Victor's times.

This general reaction against regimentation in the intelligentsia led to the movement for active pedagogy in which *spontaneity* was given a central role. But, at the same time, the most conservative segment of the population was pushing toward the conservation of the acquisitions of the previous period by enrolling in the fascist movement, which was favorable to a stronger regimentation of society. As a result, these times witnessed a deep contrast between the movement toward regimentation and the movement toward bureaucratization, with the final victory of the latter.

Fascism wanted to push to the extreme the distinction between the instrumental and expressive roles by making men emotionless warriors and women *le repos du guerrier* (warrior's spouse and repose). Therefore, it opposed psychoanalysis and psychology in general, for the same reasons revolutionary Russia did, because nonbehavioristic psychological theories and especially psychoanalysis pointed to that gap between social ideals and social practices in the standardization of people. Since the Victorian age had already pushed the repression of instinctual powers to an extreme, fascism could not win, regardless of its military defeat.

Fascism, needing compact masses to operate its demonstrations of power, could not win in Switzerland in spite of the century-long Swiss tradition of moralization, because this Protestant ethic was balanced with another century-long Swiss tradition, that of a science of the singular. Because of the contradictions created in such a hybrid country by different mother tongues, different religious confessions, and a secular opposition between city and country, in order to survive, the Swiss had to elaborate a complex science of the singular. They had to establish a social order in which fractionation was multiple enough to prevent the formation of critical masses of people in favor of one group over the others, be it linguistic, religious, or urban. Any cleavage that could possibly constitute a majority or a minority strong enough to make a difference had been clearly avoided for centuries by the breaking up of the national territory into several small cantons. This organization incorporated a variety of the above-mentioned cleavages so that any social movement could, in the last analysis, be reduced to the individual psychological case—hence the success of psychological sciences in Switzerland and the blooming of a Swiss section of the psychoanalytic International. Psychoanalysis was the theory of the Swiss practice of psychologizing dissent.

Hence, the social milieu surrounding Jacqueline, Lucienne, and Laurent could be reduced easily to the nuclear family plus the maid, and the rapports inside this family to objects such as Daddy's beret and pipe, toys and cribs, and occasionally a bit of nature (streams and moons, snails and flowers). The Piaget siblings lived in a world constituted of objects or "things and thoughts," to borrow the title of Baldwin's trilogy, rather than one made out of people having a certain idea (not to say an exact idea) of what children should look like. Their world, as reconstructed in their father's books, was rather Rousseauian. Of course, it all happened in Geneva. But this is no explanation. How could one prevent one's own children from demanding from other adults or older children what were, at least for a growing child, answers to very pressing questions? How could these children be happy with the sempiternal adult answer of: "What do *you* think?" A certain sanitary belt, if not an "iron curtain," must have been cast around these children. Is this not a certain form of dictatorship? Does it not remind one of existing practices in fascist countries? Is it not in contradiction with the claimed spontaneity of the child? What could be the long-term aftereffects of such rearing practices upon children? Have we not reached the peak of the social construction of innocence in the child as described so convincingly by Philippe Ariès? I feel that these questions are not incongruous with the general question we are asking in this chapter.

Thus, everything took place as though the institutions around these children—family, school, and other institutions for the protection of childhood—did not exist. This becomes more obvious when the "stages" of child development are shown to correspond exactly with the respective terminations of the influence of these institutions, a surprising coincidence that has escaped examination. For instance, the stage of concrete operations corresponds with the age of schooling children at the elementary level, and formal operations are attained at the end of compulsory education in most Western countries. Moreover, when Piaget describes himself as a young man in his various autobiographies, he uses a deciphering grid inspired by the literary idea of youth at the time of his own youth. I am currently working on how developmental psychology has continuously "scientifized" stages of ontogenic development that were initially literary or social ones. Greeks, with their system of "ages of life" based on the number 7, in which age 7 marked the attainment of reason, age 14 that of adolescence, and age 21 that of majority, and so on, were not too far from modern psychology. Apparently, one of two possible reasons makes this concordance possible: either the Greeks already had an elaborate developmental psychology, which is factually false, or these ages correspond to an inescapable biological sequence. In fact, since unschooled populations of the non-Western world do not exhibit such a sequencing of development, it is not a fact of nature but one of culture. This is even clearer in the very case of Piaget's autobiographies in which he becomes a character out of Romain Rolland's novel *Jean-Christophe,* or any other *Bildungsroman* of the period, as I shall show elsewhere.

For Piaget, the institutional fact became a fact of nature. This process of naturalization of social forces had a long history in developmental psychology. It served two main functions in the economy of the newly created science: a function of legitimation and one of conflation. An appeal to the theory of evolution legitimized developmental psychology as something radically different from mere baby watching, an innocent pastime for old spinsters. By refusing to leave childhood as an epistemological vacuum and instead conceptualizing it, more or less, as a period for recapitulating the long process of hominization separating modern adult mankind from apes, developmental psychologists managed to occupy a central position in the theory of knowledge of the time. Developmental psychology could no longer be dismissed so easily as baby watching had been previously. It had become a respectable pursuit of knowledge that legitimated all sorts of treatments inflicted upon children by benevolent "scientists." Beside this function of legitimation, the process of naturalization also served a function of conflating facts and norms, as in the concept of *maturity* so widely used in developmental psychology. Maturity in the social realm is indeed quite different from maturity in the biological domain. Watching a fruit mature is a mere observation that could be operationalized almost perfectly, as in Bridgman's operationism. Considering an individual as mature or immature is a judgment of value. By fusing the biological domain with the social realm thanks to the process of naturalization, psychologists transformed a norm into a fact. This magnificent accomplishment was to bring forth disastrous aftereffects, since it was to render natural and objective quite a large number of value judgments made by psychologists from their own egocentric viewpoint. As everyone knows, one does not argue with a fact. There is a saying for that in English: "A fact is more respectable than a lord mayor." Respectability was, at the time, the main concern of developmental psychologists. Hence the constant recourse to naturalization and the theory of evolution, in order to present the norm of a developmental law conceived by a given observer in a given context of meanings in the guise of an observable fact immanent to the object under scrutiny. The reference to the theory of evolution was also employed so that the history of science could be invoked as the norm for the social development of a given notion. By the usual paralogical leap, this norm was transformed into a fact observable in children who, strangely enough, were recapitulating these societal (historical, scientific) stages of development in a logical order.

This "taking the things of logic as the logic of things," as Marx once called it, yields the logico-mathematical model of development in which there is such a chasm between the theory (constructed datum) and its execution (preconstructed datum) that any real child can be taken as the mere reflection of an abstract and symbolic "epistemic subject," to use Piaget's phrase. This chasm excludes the practical functions of social insertion, political struggle, or economic position in favor of symbolic functions only. The latter, in turn, are freed, by this process, from any situational context. They are homogenized into epistemic constructs (objects constructed by the theory and as such unfalsifiable from within the theory) and separated from negligible historical (called *accidental* or *casual* in the vocabulary of the theory) individual or social behaviors. The latter constitute the preconstructed object, directly observable, against which the operation of theoretical construction has been executed in the first place.

This is what Piaget calls "reflective abstraction." It converts a practical succession into a representational one, from a praxis oriented toward a space, conceived as an ensemble of demand and taboos, into a reversible operation, constituted in a continuous and homogeneous space. This symbolization process reduces child development to nothing but the reflection of the logical order of scientific construction.

This incapacity to think a historical subject of knowledge is best typified in structuralism. As the internalization of the nation-state by a social class that has been overcome by the movement of society, structuralism is incapable of conceptualizing praxis otherwise than as mere execution. That is to say, it can only conceive it, and exclusively so, in the negative form of a by-product resulting from the construction of the various systems of objective relations. The consequence for structuralism of this separation between theory and praxis is devastating. It is always bound to one of these fundamental fallacies. It leaves open the question of production of invariants and regularities, as did Ferdinand de Saussure; or it reifies the abstract products of scientific knowledge as autonomous realities, as did the Gestaltists and Chomsky; or it grants considerable social efficacy to these products since they are supposed to act as strongly on the baby discovering object permanence as on Poincaré formulating the mathematical group of displacements. The latter is Piaget's solution.

If this last solution is correct, then the paralogical inference is completed: the passage, surreptitious as it is, from the model of reality to the reality of the model is accomplished. Natural thought must obey the rules of "natural" logic because it is constituted by regularities and invariants of all sorts. But notice that this is a passage from regularities that are necessarily statistical to regulations that are by definition normative and conscious. Such regularities, if they are to remain regularities and not regulations, cannot be postulated in the conscious life of the subject. It was, in fact, Kant's mistake to postulate such conscious statutory dispositions. Therefore, Piaget must reify such statutory dispositions into a system of unconscious cognitive self-regulations performing successive and inclusive forms of equilibrium. Such a solution releases Piaget from analyzing the practical conditions in which such statutory dispositions appear. It also allows him to move freely into the utopian view of moral development as a march toward perfect reciprocity in which each individual would become capable of silencing his or her private interests in order to redistribute wealth impartially in cases of lack of reciprocity. Thus, morality is reduced to a mere question of the natural balance of forces or equilibrium of exchanges.

To summarize this period, one could say that the world of Jacqueline, Lucienne, and Laurent was very abstract and remote. The role of the unconscious was predominant and utopia was reigning. An enormous legitimacy-producing machinery was being put forth. Faced with the impossibility of tracing back the very roots of hominization and the ultimate sources of knowledge, developmental psychologists were trying to legitimate the impossible. Since the establishment had failed to take the necessary course of action to prevent the Black Friday of economic crisis and the rise of fascism, it had ordered its intelligentsia to render action representational and abstract so that "dying for Madrid," as went the motto of the Spanish Civil War, became ludicrously theatrical and unreal, a mere figment of the imagination. It was nothing to be concerned with, since it was now a proven fact that history was an unnecessary convenience that could be disposed of by an adequate recourse to the structuralistic form of explanation.

The Others

Madrid was just the beginning. Auschwitz, Bergen-Belsen, Buchenwald, Dachau, Maunthausen, Treblinka. . . The names fell like drops of blood around the thorn crown of Germany, to be quickly followed by the unnamed colonial wars. The hope of socialism has been drowned in the Gulag. Children of today know that the world is a bloody place to be. They have lost a good deal of innocence that three centuries of childhood had tried to put into them. Thanks to the media, they are back in the world of adults. But this itself is different.

Urban planning has segmented the life of people into functions performed in different places: housing developments as dormitories, inner-city offices as working places, and some downtown sections as playpens. The economic differences among social classes have decreased significantly, but their social distance has increased reciprocally. Individual cars prevent human contacts in public places. In such a completely restructured social environment, where the rich spend their vacations in poor countries all over the world without even seeing them, bodies can rediscover each other in the nudity of sex or on beaches as a human right. But they are always under the control of an expert who teaches them how to have sex properly, how to touch others with the correct sensitivity. This is the age of good manners, protocol, and training under the guise of spontaneity, nonchalance, and relaxation. Extreme geographical places are the ultimate in luxury: the North pole or an empty beach on the Equator. This is the age of mass loneliness with a nostalgia for chosen solitude.

In a world progressively mediated by machines of all sorts, nature is in the ideological forefront under various forms: ecology, psychology, sociology, and economics. In ecology, the use of very sophisticated tools of investigation has helped us realize that we have been changing the environment. Such tools were undreamed of at the time when the Mediterranean populations, leaving the land for the sea in very large numbers, so completely changed the thickly forested Mediterranean environment that it became what we know today. We have forgotten that, for centuries, we kept nature as it is by unnatural means. The forests of Europe would not exist if men did not cultivate them very carefully.

In psychology, we witness a double movement of returning to nativism to explain social phenomena such as aggressivity and returning to mechanical, informational explanations in cognitive psychology (*artificial* intelligence). Aggressivity is considered an instinct and not as the possible outcome of years of struggle for heritage, power, or the possibility simply to survive. Sibling rivalry is natural and never the result of a nuclear family in a competitive society. The present emotional free exchange is presented as the liberation of impulse and not the narcissistic double retreat of the bourgeoisie which is sadly made aware of the fact that, in its present form, it is overcome by history. Hence, a renewed investment in the child as the incarnation of the future.

The title of Margaret Boden's book *Artificial Intelligence and Natural Man* typifies the double return that I have in mind here. The very opposition between the reduction of strictly intellectual processes to a sort of machinery (doubtless very complex) and the very naturalness of human beings passes by the opposition between rationality and cognition, on the one hand, and emotions and instincts, on the other. Cognition can be accounted for by purely bureaucratic models, whereas emotion literally cannot be accounted for, because it is a force, a wild natural impulse. Hence, an interest in children whose wildness has not yet been tamed into the rational-emotional dichotomy and in whom the genesis of bureaucratic processes can be observed, as well as the decay of instinctual processes considered here as pertaining to the executional side of things and, as such, theoretically unanalyzable. Thus, the very mechanical informational explanations become natural in their own way by a strangely familiar reversal of perspective.

In sociology, there is a direct attack on the mechanisms of oppression at work in our society. The great tradition of French sociology, from Michel Crozier's *Société Bureaucratique* to Pierre Bourdieu's *La Distinction* or Alain Touraine's books on the sociology of social movements, describes a blocked society in which the social determinants have covered the depths of human nature so profusely that the social forces are at a standstill. There is no way out. One is always dominated by someone, the only apparently free agent being the sociologist, and even that is not so certain. So one must look at the most dominated and the freest in society, youth, for an answer or a key.

In economics, because the discipline has based itself upon scarcity, there has been a denial of the complexity of the relationships between subjects and objects. This has occurred by means of a reduction of alienation to the plain notion of strangeness, in contrast to the Hegelian notion of alienation as separation (*Entäusserung*, a parting), a way of getting rid of a problem by schizophrenia, in the literal Greek meaning. Such an epistemological choice has generated economic models that prevent the passage from one system of production to the next by a sort of prisoner's dilemma: no one wants to lose his own advantages but everyone agrees that a new economic order is necessary, which is a paradoxical position to be in. Hence the present reconceptualization of primitive economies as economies of plenty instead of scarcity and the return to more natural ways of production and exchange.

As one can see, there is a paradoxical situation in the social sciences today, which is reflected most clearly in the attitude toward children. The best example of this attitude is given by the present mass production of educational toys. If we look at the educational toys of today, those creative playthings that are sold to middle-class parents, what do we see: plain wood, geometric forms, sandboxes, water containers. In sum, nothing very appealing, at least for a bourgeois, since those were the objects of the Pietistic pedagogy of the eighteenth century. These sorts of materials were in every classroom in poor neighborhoods. With such materials, the young Piaget built his early experiments on conservation, after the style of Decroly and the Calvinists of the Jura mountains when they created their schools for the needy. Why, then, this enthusiasm?

It seems to me that the enthusiasm about educational toys synthesizes all the aspects of the modern predicament, in three ways: on the cognitive level, a scholarly naïveté; on the affective level, free constraints; and on the social level, controlled audacity.

In order to be understood as educational, educational toys first require a certain education from the buyers—an aesthetic education warranting that such simple, plain objects are beautifully designed and therefore give their money's worth. Second, they require a certain familiarity with the psychological vernacular, since they are promoted in language that appeals to some minimal knowledge of the psychological vulgate. They become accessible only to those mothers of the middle class who have invested a minimal amount of their study or leisure time in the educational sciences. Third, the naïveté attributed to the child is indeed very elaborate: in the mathematical realm, Piaget and Bourbaki agree in saying that the child thinks in terms borrowed from set theory, and in geometry, the child recapitulates the entire Erlangen program of Felix Klein. Linguistically, the child rediscovers generative grammar. As one can see, this naïve little creature is a scholar in the full sense of the word. Graphically, the child is a spontaneous Miro, a natural Klee. No wonder, then, that the intellectual avant-garde of cybernetics and artificial intelligence as well as the artistic avant-garde of painting, sculpture, theatre, and cinema invade elementary classrooms; they are there with peers if not masters. So much so, that a bit of doubt sometimes crosses my mind that this learned company, having been incapable of becoming "like children," has simply decided to make children in its own image. How else could I explain that my daughters, Anne-Christine, Marina, or Isabelle, who strike me with their naïveté, have been, in turn, aristotelian, galilean, newtonian, and einsteinian in physics, and topologist, perspectivist, affine, and euclidean in geometry?

Emotionally, the children who enjoy educational toys must display a certain relaxation in their understanding of the difference between leisure time and working time, since these toys teach them, while playing, such things as classification, serialization, and number. The intercourse with such toys is never totally playful nor totally playless. They are intended for the middle classes whose time budget is not so clearly divided between the laborious hours spent at work serving a conveyor belt and the joyous time spent in pubs or with the chaps in town. In addition, such toys require a certain amount of space for the child's exclusive use, and the obedience to certain rules of play in contrast with the crowded spaces of the working classes and the unmethodical and rough games of the street. They are the perfect expression of an educated spontaneity.

Socially, these toys encourage a controlled audacity, since they promote constraint by the maintenance of the game's rules and freedom by playfulness of the presentation of the rules. The competitive side of these toys makes children more daring, but only up to the limit imposed by the rules. In this, they are actively conservative, too.

In summary: The very notion of nature that seems to be so pervasive today is based on a view of what is natural that is so elaborate as to be completely socially reconstructed. This could be a way of exorcising a nature lost long ago. But it could also be a way of exorcising children by making them so precious that they should be rare. The latter is verified in demographic curves of natality, as well as in the marginalization of youth, that represent more than 50% of the unemployed in French-speaking countries.

One should not read the general investment in the education of children as a reconversion of scientists and artists into education. It seems to me that it indicates a fading away of the distinction between the pedagogical and the creative that is beneficial to neither of the two fields. Children are placed close to production centers and must perform correctly in the steeplechase of their curriculum. They must walk at a certain age, speak at another, and so on—in brief, they must perform according to specified standards in all fields of activity. If they do not act as young Stakhanovites, the pediatrician or the psychologist picks them up from the floor and puts them back on the assembly line after some special treatment.

To this colonization of childhood corresponds a symmetrical infantilization of adulthood. Since the return of the natural and spontaneous is always mediated by a mentor, adults are forced to learn spontaneity in the scholastic mode at such privileged places as encounter and bioenergetics groups, creative writing classes, and health clubs.

Instead of a *rapprochement* between school and life, we witness here a confusion of the two. In the commendable desire to close the gap between school and real life, our time has succeeded in making living a form of schooling.

Chapter 4

Valerie Walkerdine

NO LAUGHING MATTER

GIRLS' COMICS AND THE PREPARATION FOR ADOLESCENT SEXUALITY

This chapter is a consideration of how girls are prepared for initiation into romantic love and other heterosexual practices. I have chosen to examine this preparation for adolescent sexuality as it is mediated by children's fiction, especially girls' comics. Such an inquiry allows us to discuss the relation between cultural forms and the psychological production of feminine desire.

At the primary school level, young girls are confronted with, and inserted into, ideological and discursive practices that position them in regard to specific patterns of meaning and regimes of truth serving to produce and reproduce femininity. In such positionings, the organization of psychological life permitted by family dynamics is of primary strategic importance for the preparation of feminine sexuality. These family dynamics, as psychoanalytic studies have indicated, encourage the young girl to detach her desire from the mother and reattach it to the father or, rather, to the phallic representation of the paternal. Cultural forms embody such dynamic shifts symbolically. They assist in the preparation of means for inserting the girl into romantic heterosexuality by capturing the psychological conflicts that are dealt with in phantasy situations and by presenting possible resolutions for these conflicts.[1]

This chapter draws on material previously presented in Walkerdine, 1984a.

[1]In psychoanalysis the term *phantasy* is used rather than *fantasy*. This is because the term is intended to be wider in usage than simple imaginary production, relating broadly to the "world of the imagination" (Laplanche & Pontalis, 1973, p. 314).

Valerie Walkerdine • Institute of Education, University of London, 58 Gordon Square, London, WC1 HONT, England.

It will be the purpose in what follows to identify and examine some of the cultural practices that locate the girl in the struggle over heterosexual femininity. As Freud (1908/1956) has suggested, "The constitution will not adapt itself to its function without a struggle" (p. 117). The girl does not passively assume a female role model; she does not easily accommodate the demands of standard feminine practices. Because heterosexuality is achieved as a solution to a set of conflicts and contradictions in familial and other social relations, the adoption of femininity is at best precarious and incomplete. Rather than telling us something basic about the nature of the female body or mind, the observation that the girl appears to accept voluntarily the position to which she is traditionally fitted demonstrates the power of those practices through which a particular resolution to the struggle is produced. In particular, because they are specifically designed to engage with the production of girls' conscious and unconscious desires, girls' comics prepare for a "happily ever after" outcome, in which the finding of the "prince" or "knight in shining armor" emerges as the obvious solution to a set of problematic and often overwhelming desires.

Sexism in Children's Literature

The issue of stereotyping in children's literature has been of persistent importance in feminist analyses of educational materials, curricula, and practices (e.g., Dixon, 1977; Lobban, 1975). For example, the sexist bias in children's literature has been shown to be reflected in the presentation of stereotyped images that offer a distorted picture of social reality, for example, by showing women always at work in the kitchen and concealing the fact that many women engage in paid labor outside the home. To counteract such bias, Pinkerton (1982) has suggested that we should "extend children's thinking beyond stereotyping . . . by providing a wide range of material . . . which presents broader images" (p. 30).

Such analyses and recommendations have been most significant in raising the issue of the content of children's literature. However, these approaches are characterized by two related kinds of assumptions, both of which turn out to be illegitimate. First, they assume that with the provision of a "wide range of experience" there will take place a relatively unproblematic transformation in children's views of themselves and of possible courses of action. Second, they assume that this change will occur through the mere adoption of nonstereotyped activities: for example, by girls' engaging in the physical form of work typically practiced by boys.

These assumptions carry with them the image of a passive learner, or rather a rationalist one who will change as a result of simple exposure to the correct information about how things "actually" are. They presuppose that as soon as the tissue of distortion is lifted from the little girl's eyes, she, too, will want to participate in those activities from which she has been forbidden by virtue of her gender. However, it seems doubtful that even young girls are so malleable, or that the nature of their motivation is such a simple matter.

Rather, cultural practices produce social positions for women, and what the latter want is determined by the inscription of desire in those positions. Recent work in the field of cultural practices has emphasized the way in which texts such as books, films, advertisements, and the like operate in terms of systems of signification, in which the text has to be actively read in order to engage with the manner in which images and other signs, verbal and nonverbal, are constructed. The critiques of sexism and stereotyping in children's literature, despite their importance, have tended to underestimate the important role of the text itself in producing both particular meanings and specific forms of engagement on the part of the reader.

It is not a simple matter of information that does or does not "tell the truth." It is not a situation in which distasteful roles and images can be jettisoned and replaced with more palatable ones. Rather than biasing the communication of an external reality, texts—through the practices for their production—*present their own reality.* In their construction of meanings, they create positions for the subject in the text itself by providing the occasions for identification. The texts contribute to the definition of who and where women are, and to their desire to be who and where they are. The content of children's literature is not simply grafted onto a waiting, labile subject. Instead, the positions and relations created in the text emerge from existing social and psychological struggles and provide a fantasy vehicle which inserts the reader into the text. It is this complicated process of engagement which deserves our attention.

Modern Psychoanalytic Theory of Female Sexuality

If fiction presents fantasies by the use of textual devices which engage with the desires of the reader, then this would suggest a very different understanding of the development of gender than the one most commonly asserted. Those approaches stressing roles and stereotypes suggest a girl who is already rational, who takes in information or takes on roles. By contrast, psychoanalysis offers a dynamic model in which there is no simple or static reality perceived by children. Central to the psychoanalytic reality is the production of complex and tortuous relations, conscious and unconscious, centered upon the girl's relations with her family. The account that psychoanalysis offers presents a subject who is more resistant to change than a rationalist account might suggest and who is engaged in a struggle in relation to the achievement of femininity.

Recent advances in the study of texts have made use of psychoanalysis in understanding the production of textual identities. They provide a potential avenue for exploring the cultural practices that produce phantasies and the relation of those to the development of sexuality. Such accounts make use of the work of Jacques Lacan (e.g., 1977), who has taken advantage of developments in linguistics and semiotics to rework Freud's account of psychic development. This means that Lacan has been able to understand the production of textual fictions and psychic phantasies in the same terms.

Lacan reworked certain basic concepts from Freud, but they both share the stress on the oedipal relation and the castration complex as central to an understanding of female sexuality (Mitchell & Rose, 1982). Although there have been some feminist appropriations of psychoanalysis, they have tended to stress preoedipal relations with the mother and consequently do not understand the father (or phallus, in Lacanian theory) as central to sexuality. Moreover, such accounts have not so far analyzed cultural practices or ideological relations with either the same tools or the same depth as Lacanian-influenced theories of representation. For these reasons there follows a very brief exploration of certain key concepts in accounts of female sexuality.

Freud located the production of sexuality in the relations of the family. His various clinical researches converged on the conclusion that actual interactions or family relations are lived by the participants through the framework of complex systems of psychic phantasy relations—hence the importance of the working through in fantasy of certain wishes, particularly in relation to the mother. Freud insisted that the pain of separation from and the loss of continuity with the maternal body pushes the infant into a struggle to possess the mother, to be dependent and yet to control her availability. The experience of psychic distress caused through the inevitable failure of the mother to meet the child's insatiable demand sets up a particular dynamic between them. Freud distinguished between need and wish (or desire). He recognized that the phantasy created in the gap between possession and loss was not made good by any "meeting of needs" because the satisfaction would only be temporary and the object of desire would both constantly shift and be out of reach. The presence of siblings produced a rivalry and therefore jealousy in relation to the mother, setting up its own particular familial dynamic. However, the presence of the father, whose possession of the mother creates further rivalry, is of crucial importance to Freud's account of the production of sexual difference. Although the little boy struggles for possession of his mother—in competition, therefore, with the father—the little girl can never possess the mother. Freud therefore postulates the struggle for the transfer of desire from the mother to the father to account for female heterosexuality.

Subsequent schools of psychoanalysis (particularly object relations accounts) have tended to differ from Freud along a variety of dimensions. The first difference concerns the countering of the stress on oedipal, and in that sense paternal, relations with the mother. Although Freud agreed that he had underexplored the importance of the preoedipal attachment to the mother, he fought against the way in which theoretical focus on the relations with the mother occurred at the expense of the downplaying of sexual differentiation. Along with the stress on the mother, particularly in object relations accounts, there is also the diminution of emphasis on wish or desire and the development of normative accounts based on the fulfillment of need (see Mitchell & Rose, 1982, especially Mitchell's introduction). Such accounts move toward the possibility of practice of the adequate meeting of the child's needs by the mother.

The stress on the meeting of needs has been countered by the approach offered by Lacan. This has emphasized the gap between needs for bodily comfort, food, and so on and the way in which demand always exceeds satisfaction. Freud demonstrated the way in which infants hallucinated the milk which had been withdrawn by the breast, or played games in which the presence and absence of the mother was controlled in fantasy. In this sense, Freud concentrated on the creation of phantasy in the gap between need and wish fulfillment. Lacan developed this by his stress on desire. He argued that the satisfaction of need is an illusion and one sustained by practices that produce phantasy or imaginary resolutions. Although infants are clearly gratified by the mother, this gratification "contains the loss within it" (Mitchell & Rose, 1982, p. 6). The price paid for consciousness is the first recognition of the mother as other, and therefore of the me/not me split.

Lacan uses the example of an infant's gaze at its own reflection in a mirror to stress the idea that singularity and identity are illusory. The infant is dependent and relatively powerless, but an illusion of unity and control is created by apprehending the mirror image. Lacan's account then stresses the importance of the acquisition of language by the child as the means for control over both the initial loss of the mother and the capacity for self-reference, the illusion of control. He uses two terms: the *imaginary* and the *symbolic*.

The imaginary relates to the imaged state of self-recognition in the mirror. The imaginary is the location of phantasy resolutions, the illusion of the meeting of needs, of ideal complementarity, or merging with the other. As we shall see, this is why the phantasies of completion and resolution to psychic conflicts offered in children's fiction are so important. They proffer possible resolutions, held out as the meeting of needs for and phantasies of identity or wholeness.

The symbolic is the site of control in language that fixes meaning. The fixing of meaning offers certainty and knowledge: the idea that we can have control over our loss by knowing the truth. This truth is identified not with a real father as such but by what Lacan calls the "paternal metaphor." Lacan uses the term *phallus* to describe that in which the symbolic is invested, the breaking of the mother–child dyad. If the child first imagines control through language, then it is the father—not as real father, but as imagined guardian of "the word"—who holds the key to the symbolic order and thus to control.

Lacan describes complex relations that operate in language and fantasy and then operate on conscious and unconscious relations of identification. The problems of sexual difference relates to the contradictory paternal and maternal identifications involved in being/having the mother, making good the loss, and having/being in control by having or being the phallus. It is in this sense that sexual identity is taken never to be a secure achievement because there is no easy fitting into available roles. However, because language and phantasy play such a crucial part, identities created in the everyday locations that the child enters—in schooling, in texts, and so forth—offer occasions for imaginary closure. They engage with psychic conflicts, identifications, and resolutions. They are therefore crucial to change and yet problematic at the same time.

The Nature of Children's Fiction

A moment's consideration will reveal how pervasive phantasy is in the cultural productions that adorn our everyday lives. Fabulous and tantalizing rewards are dangled before us constantly through the media, particularly in the form of prizes for various competitions, which often take the form of all-expense-paid trips to exotic and remote parts of the world. I, an ordinary person, can suddenly be special: phantasy and reality meet. Of course, it could be said that we are at liberty to ignore these incitements. Surely, we can just switch off the radio or television. But what if such messages are not the kinds of things that we can choose to ignore? What if their very power resides in the way that they provide a vehicle for, and even create, the form and content of our struggle to "be someone"? Modern cultural practices contribute to our very biographies in this way by stimulating the production not only of realizations of the bourgeois dream but also the dream itself.

The Appeal of Phantasy

Girls' comics are a particularly powerful form of the dream and its realization because they engage, at the level of phantasy, with the hopes and fears mirrored in the reference to the media. More than that, they implicitly offer guidance as to how young girls may prepare themselves to be good enough to "win" the glittering prizes: the man, the home, the adventure, and so forth. They do this, but they do it at a level that the alternative images or role models for girls simply cannot reach. They work on *desire.*

In her analysis of the adolescent magazine *Jackie,* Angela McRobbie (1982) discusses the codes through which adolescent femiminity is constructed and therefore may be read. The positions that magazine offers relate to heterosexual practices about "getting and keeping a man," and although preteen comics do not do this in any overt sense, what happens is that they engage with the construction of femininity in such a way as to prepare young girls for the fate that awaits them.

How, then, are young girls prepared? In most cases, textual devices turn around stories based on classic fairy tales. They end with "happy ever after" solutions, mostly around the insertion of the girl into an ideal family. Meanwhile, in getting there, the girls in these stories are apparently hapless victims of circumstance, scorned, despised, and hard-done-by. The resolution in the family is, I will argue, the oedipal resolution played out. The happy family is produced through the traumas associated with the loss and abandonment of the mother in favor of the oedipal love of the father. And, as we know, the father simply precedes the prince, or knight in shining armor. The heterosexual practices of *Jackie,* then, offer a solution, a way out of the misery of the femininity struggled over in the pages of these comics.

The comics that I have chosen to examine below are two of the most popular among junior school girls in Britain: *Bunty* and *Tracy.* For the most part, these stories develop themes of family relationships. To do so, they use particular kinds of narrative device. I shall not attempt a comprehensive examination of these devices, particularly the use of strip cartoons or the style of drawing, but will concentrate particularly on the devices that allow certain very distressing issues to be the focus of the stories. And the stories are very distressing indeed: dreadful events befall their heroines.

How can comics full of frightful stories sell so well and be so gripping? Why are the heroines of the stories more often than not helpless victims? I shall attempt to answer these questions by outlining the themes of the stories, mentioning some remarks made by Freud which relate to similar content that emerged in his clinical work.

There are 18 strip stories in these two comics. They are nearly all about girls who are victims: of cruelty and circumstance. Eleven are about girls who do not have, or do not live with, their parents. Indeed, the circumstances are so fantastic that they would, on the surface, appear to bear very little relation to the lives of their young readers. I say "on the surface," because it is precisely the organization of *phantasy* (rather than of reality, as presumed by the realist approach of antisexist literature) that is so important in understanding the relation of such literature to the organization of desire. After all, it is phantasy that is the tool of psychoanalysis par excellence.

In his early work, Freud (1908, pp. 237–241) considered the significance of phantasy in the generation of the material that formed the subject matter of the analysis itself. He posited various structures and mechanisms through which, in his terms, reality was "mediated" by phantasy, implying that the material of everyday life is not experienced directly through simple mechanisms of perception. He argued that it was quite common for children to phantasize about alternative parentage: "Chance occurrences . . . arouse the child's envy, which finds expression in a phantasy in which both his parents are of better birth" (p. 239). Such phantasies have certain impacts on the lived relations of the family. In addition, they serve to permit certain difficult circumstances to be managed.

Phantasy and Reality

What is the effect of phantasy and how does it operate? These issues will be explored in two ways. First, the content of the two girls' comics in question will be examined. Then, this content will be related to other cultural practices in which phantasies are produced, particularly phantasies connected with romantic heterosexual love.

The very "unreality" of the stories presented in these magazines is one of their chief strengths, not one of their weaknesses. They engage with exactly the types of issues raised by Freud, fostering the experience of problematic emotions and suboptimal circumstances through the use of devices that permit identification of the young readers with the heroine in the text. They not only allow the process of working out certain conflicts but also encourage certain resolutions or products in the form of specific life styles and practices.

The market targetted for these comics appears to be prepubescent working-class girls. The stories themselves involve phantasies about family, sexuality, and class, constructing heroines who are the victims of foul deeds yet persist in the face of personal injustice. This struggle takes the form of a feat of endurance that always eventuates in triumph but is essentially *private*. In contrast, boys' comics deal chiefly with overt bravery and visible fights against injustice—activities that are openly celebrated and rewarded, in *public*.

Traditionally, in relation to matters of sex and class in children's literature, such material has been regarded as biased, as unreal, and therefore bad, and consequently requiring the antidote of an appropriate "realism." But such realism is based on a rationalist politics of cognitive transformation—change accomplished through dictating the correct, undistorted account of reality. But reality is not something that can be hidden or distorted in any simple sense. Rather, what is called for is an examination of the materiality of the phantasies created in literature such as these comics, in terms of both what is spoken and how, what is understood, how dilemmas are posed, and what kinds of resolutions are proffered.

With respect to texts, readers construct readings and, simultaneously, readers are constructed. This gives rise to a complex interplay that does not recognize a simple split between a preformed psychic subject who reads and a text in which meaning is produced (Henriques, Hollway, Urwin, Venn, Walkerdine, 1984; Adlam, in press). The realist approaches to reading that prevail in the critical work on children's fiction treat readers as preexisting subjects of given class, gender, and race, who are formed through certain material relations of production. They have a "lived" reality, a material ground, which stories promote or obstruct. According to this approach, more real texts would be those that reflect the reality of life (predominantly working-class life).

What are such children to do with such realist texts when confronted with what is represented in them as their reality? What if the readers do not recognize their lives and themselves in the texts? What if they are resistant to recognizing what is portrayed? What about their desires to have something and be someone different?

Traditional fairy stories are hardly realistic; they are quite fantastic, bearing little or no resemblance to the lives of ordinary children. Yet they act powerfully in terms of important themes about potential realities. The realist, "tell it like it is" stories do not touch on such possibilities at all.

Comic book stories, on the other hand, touch directly on such possibilities. They describe difficult lives and miserable circumstances, but in such a way as to offer solutions, both phantasied and practical, affording escapes in the form of alternative constructions of what and who one might be. The stories romanticize poverty and portray masochistic ways of celebrating it rather than bemoaning it. Poverty is shown to be desirable precisely because it can be suffered virtuously, transcended nobly, and left behind rapidly. Poverty is always accidental.

Contingent, too, are the wicked families who oppress those in their charge. The sorry state of children is the natural result of tragic circumstances. Making these troublesome conditions fantastic is the chief narrative device employed to render them tolerable: the child protagonists are translocated into a different geographic location or historical period and into surrogate families. In the majority of stories, the children are fated not to live with their biological kin but with substitute families in which they are subjected to cruel and unusual treatment.

Such narrative devices help make possible the engagement of the reader with difficult material. Where an identification with a reality presented as mirroring the life of the readers may well be rejected as "unlike me" or "too close for comfort," identification at the level of phantasy remains a possibility. The distance or difference renders these stories more, not less, effective. And such an effectivity is far beyond the reach of a simple realism.

Attempts to alter children's outlook through the use of realist texts and counterstereotype description concentrate on *images*. These may be true or false, good or bad. They are not rationally or passively appropriated but actively engaged with and constructed as imaginary fulfillments of wishes. Fiction is not a mere set of images, but an ensemble of textual devices for implicating the reader in the phantasy. Since the phantasies created in the text draw on wishes already present in the lives of young children, the resolutions offered relate to their own, already experienced desires. In consequence, a complex psychic organization of an image occurs rather than a simple and direct response to that image. The reader who engages in such a fiction lives a real life that is, at the same time, organized in relation to phantasy. To interpret children's fiction in this way yields quite a different view of its presentation, its impact on, and its significance for the lives of young girls.

Fiction and Phantasy in Girls' Comics

Types of Narrative

We shall now proceed to an examination of the detailed content of serial stories in two of the most popular of prepubescent girls' comic books, *Bunty* and *Tracy*, with the purpose of identifying and interpreting the major themes underlying that content. I shall focus on 18 stories from *Bunty*, 1982, *1282* and *Tracy*, 1982, *150*, selected to represent the predominant types of plots and themes. Setting aside for the moment the 11 stories about girls who do not have or do not live with parents, the narratives of the remaining seven stories can be summarized as in Table 1.

Even when the girls are presented in an ordinary family setting, the stories tend to center on the resolution of certain problems, often concerned with internal family relations. The girls are often the object of gross injustices: they are continually misunderstood and misjudged. A repetitive theme is that, despite everything, the girls engage in selfless and brave acts of helpfulness to others. This theme is typically captured in the weekly resumés—"The story so far. . . ."—given at the head of each picture strip. Moving on to the more typical ("orphan") tales, let us

Table 1. Summary of Narrative Line in Bunty and Tracy *Stories*

Story 1. A girl is helpful and does kind deeds except when she puts on a glove puppet, then her character undergoes a total transformation and she becomes angry, vicious, and generally evil. As soon as she removes the puppet, she has no recollection of her bad deeds.

Story 2. A girl is perfect at school—clever, beautiful, helpful, and sensible—but her cleverness and good deeds make her the object of envy. She becomes unpopular and as a result unhappy.

Story 3. A girl lives with her mother, who has lost her job. The girl fears she will have to sell her treasured camera but averts this eventuality by using it ingeniously to make money by taking and selling photographs that turn out to be related to good deeds for others.

Story 4. A girl has a mother who is a teacher and who has chosen to teach in a rough "comprehensive" school where she persists in her attempts to reform the children. Through ingenious good deeds the girl helps her mother to manage the school, but without her mother finding out who was responsible.

Story 5. A Victorian serving girl who has been frozen for a century in a block of ice (!) is found by a family wih a daughter of similar age who passes the serving girl off as her cousin.

Story 6. A girl gymnast from an Eastern bloc country is helped to escape by a British girl gymnast.

Story 7. A girl's horse is the object of another horse's jealousy. The heroine's horse nevertheless helps this other horse unselfishly.

take as an example the story, "Joni the Jinx." One of the weekly captions reads: "When orphan Joni Jackson was adopted by Kate and Robert Stewart, she looked forward to the kind of happy family she had always dreamed of. But things didn't quite work out as planned. . . ." In this story, the adoptive parents are eager to do their best for Joni, but when they get to discussing how to present themselves properly to the social worker, the latent tensions between husband and wife are brought to the fore, resulting in an argument. Joni, thoughtful and helpful as she is, takes this to be her fault in the sense that it is her presence that has occasioned the disagreement (Figure 1).

"Cherry and the Chimps" is a story about an orphaned girl whose parents were lost in a plane crash. A wicked couple finds her living with chimpanzees in Africa. They use her as a servant to run their chimp circus act for them, and they constantly abuse her (Figure 2).

Figure 1. Thoughtful and helpful: Joni the jinx. Copyright 1982 by D. C. Thomson & Co. Ltd., Dundee, Scotland. Reprinted by permission.

Figure 2. Girls as victim: Cherry is abused. Copyright 1982 by D. C. Thomson & Co. Ltd., Dundee, Scotland. Reprinted by permission.

Cherry's misery is alleviated only by the reappearance of her real parents who, it turns out, were not actually killed in the plane accident (Figure 3).

"She'll Stay a Slave" is a story about Jenny, also an orphan, who is enslaved by her cruel cousin (Figure 4). Jenny is, predictably, very clever and helpful, despite the fact that her wicked cousin is always exploiting her and trying to spoil her efforts. The résumé caption reads, "Jenny Moss lived with her Aunt Mary and Uncle John. Her cousin Paula treated her like a slave and Jenny put up with it as she mistakenly believed that Paula had saved her life after an accident. Jenny was one of three girls being considered for a scholarship to Redpark College—but Paula tried to spoil Jenny's chances of winning as she did not want to lose her 'slave'."

The stories' endless victimizations come in further and more macabre varieties. One concerns a girl whose grandfather, a ventriloquist, coerces her into acting as his dummy because he is ill. Another involves a girl who is pressed into service by wicked relatives in a circus act in which she has to behave like a robot (Figure 5). She takes both pain and humiliation without a word because she believes these relatives are paying the hospital bills for her sick brother. Another plot centers around Victorian orphan sisters, one of whom, after a a series of worsening disasters, suddenly turns blind (Figure 6).

Recurrent Themes

Certain themes recur persistently in the story lines of these comic serials. First, let us consider the predominant tendency toward producing girls as victims. Certain recurrent elements function in the plots to circulate specific meanings and present key signifiers on the phantasy

Figure 3. Family romance: The rescue and reunion. Copyright 1982 by D. C. Thomson & Co. Ltd., Dundee, Scotland. Reprinted by permission.

Figure 4. The scheming relative: Jenny's cousin exploits her and undermines her every effort to succeed. Copyright 1982 by D. C. Thomson & Co. Ltd., Dundee, Scotland. Reprinted by permission.

Figure 5. Altruism and deceit: Meg's performance. Copyright 1982 by D. C. Thomson & Co. Ltd., Dundee, Scotland. Reprinted by permission.

level. Chief among these are miserable circumstances and intentional acts of cruelty, which are presented as occasions for adventure. Cruelty as excitant is used at the phantasy level to romanticize practical obstructions and intractable situations and to advocate a passive rather than active posture in the face of aggression. Analytically, this might be supposed to correspond to a disowning and projection of angry feelings and hostile impulses.

The daunting life worlds encountered by the heroines are offset by their own unselfish helpfulness. This virtue endows them with the capacity to achieve great feats, as long as these actions are taken out of a concern for the other. However, there is always the threat of failure: how could one ever be selfless enough? The protagonist's key personality characteristic of altruism is highlighted by the unremittingly self-interested, ruthless, and treacherous nature of the other children or older relatives in the stories. As noted by McRobbie (1982), the good, timid girl is typically blond, whereas the bad ones, scheming "bitches," are brunettes.

Modest and uncomplaining selflessness is self-justifying, leading to a confidence in one's own virtue and righteousness and thereby provid-

Figure 6. Disaster strikes again: Sarah's brave deed and its dark reward. Copyright 1982 by D. C. Thomson & Co. Ltd., Dundee, Scotland. Reprinted by permission.

ing a potential resolution to the dilemma: good deeds are ends in themselves. Bad times are celebrated as the condition that makes possible personal triumph through self-abnegation and wishful thinking. The value system of these texts produces thought-for-self, desire, or self-assertion as unacceptable and necessarily evil qualities that will inevitably lead to a bad end. The various contrivances of the plot conspire to produce at its center the archetypal bourgeois individual, feminine and actively passive, to whom material circumstances are subordinated.[2]

Psychic suppression of need is reinforced by the vision of the longed-for happy family. The heroines sustain their belief in their power to bring about the transformation of the artificial surrogate family structure into the desired and genuine one. The latter takes the form of the typical bourgeois setting of the nuclear group, typically portrayed as residing in a comfortable house furnished with the requisite possessions and secured by the needed monetary resources. In this way, class and gender relations are structured through the same medium.

It is notable that relations between the female protagonists and their sisters are frequently salient, whereas relations with brothers are rarely explored. Relationships with parents are typically displaced onto other relatives, adoptive parents, grandparents, or adventitious couples who by various means take possession of the girl. Rivalrous sentiments always originate in one or another of these spurious or unnatural figures, rather than obtaining between genuinely related siblings and alongside good feelings. The heroine always transcends jealousy through her vanquishing of or distancing from the impostor(s), and this provides a neat resolution for the conflicts that arise in the course of the story.

It is consistently the "other" who experiences the negative emotions of anger, jealousy, and so on. In the rare exceptions (as with the girl who becomes evil only upon donning the glove puppet—see Figure 7), the bad qualities enter only from outside, and so the protagonist is again the victim rather than the responsible agent. Heroines are incapable of justifiable anger, greed, or jealousy. They overcome through their

[2]This is not to say that those in "possession" of a bourgeois life style, for example middle-class women, are possessed of the objects of their desire. The achievement of the dream in reality often brings with it anxiety states in recognition of yet unfullfilled desires: alcoholism, addiction to tranquillizers among women, suicidal tendencies in the wealthy, and so forth. This is precisely the point: that we are to equate the resolution of the bourgeois dream with the fulfillment of an impossible phantasy. However, it is equally true that there are many who will live the dream as "normal." On the other hand, it is, of course, common for many working-class parents to tell their children off for always wanting something.

Figure 7. The dissociated experience of negative emotion: The puppetry of Polly. Copyright 1982 by D. C. Thomson & Co. Ltd., Dundee, Scotland. Reprinted by permission.

very compliance. Anger and rebellion are preserved as totally negative signifiers, to be expressed at peril.[3]

Splitting is the recurrent technique underlying these various maneuvers, especially the splitting between good and evil. In psychoanalytic terms, it is allied with psychic mechanisms of *projection,* in which certain qualities are disowned and located exclusively in the other. Interestingly, it is through projection of the split-off parts that the heroines become victimized. In a sense, passivity is actively produced as the outcome of a struggle internal to the self.

A rather anomalous feature of the stories is the academic achievement of the heroines. They are usually clever—often at mathematics, the very domain in which they are typically supposed to be weak (Walden & Walkerdine, 1982; Walkerdine, 1985). (See Figure 8). This kind of cleverness, interestingly enough, although it may embarrass the heroines, is not construed as nonfeminine, as many of the stereotyping arguments would seem to indicate.

There is a kind of leeway in the term "good girl" that makes being helpful and like mother at home compatible with being good, helpful, and even clever in the classroom (Walkerdine, 1981). In consequence, girls' performance fares very well indeed in comparison with that of boys at the primary school level, the problems in performance appearing later. This slippage in signification between helpfulness and academic achievement is well illustrated by "She'll Stay a Slave," the story in which the girl who is proposed for a scholarship is still able to succeed despite busying herself with as many good deeds as possible.

Similarly, the girl who is top of her class also looks the best in the school because she takes pride in her school uniform (Figure 9). This chain of signifiers, stretching from neatness and helpfulness to academic attainment, is notable in that there are no pejorative connotations attached to academic performance at this stage. However, there is a marked split between the arts and the sciences. Although heroines are often represented as good at math and science, the latter are tedious subjects. Romance and excitement are confined to the arts. An interesting illustration of this splitting is provided by a futuristic science fiction tale entitled "I Want to Dance," in which the heroine wins a scholarship to a prestigious boarding school where the girls are called by numbers

[3]It is significant that when interviewing nine- and ten-year-old girls as part of my current research, the girls told me that anger and selfishness are bad qualities in themselves, some to the extent that they could not see that they possessed any qualities they felt to be good.

Figure 8. Academic femininity: Rebecca's success. Copyright 1982 by D. C. Thomson & Co. Ltd., Dundee, Scotland. Reprinted by permission.

and not names and are made to study even when asleep. Music is outlawed—so much so that the heroine destroys a precious tape recorder in order to avoid being expelled (Figure 10). Here, through textual splitting, excitement and romance are aligned with the arts, and the scientific-mathematical becomes the natural regimen for girls' education. It is the absence of desire from the sciences and its exclusive presence in the arts (I *want* to dance) that is crucial in the formation of such semiotic chains in the education of girls. The desirability of the comic book "art" itself, as opposed to formal texts, is an embodiment of this same dichotomous argument.

Figure 9. Appearance as achievement: Rebecca's neatness. Copyright 1982 by D. C. Thomson & Co. Ltd., Dundee, Scotland. Reprinted by permission.

Figure 10. The splitting of desire from science and its alignment with the arts: Denny's sacrifice. Copyright 1982 by D. C. Thomson & Co. Ltd., Dundee, Scotland. Reprinted by permission.

The Fairy Tale

The comics that we have been discussing illustrate some of the ways in which a self-consistent, unitary subject, with class and gender membership and access to the dream life, is produced textually by means of the psychological articulation, displacement, and enactment of desire. Now let us consider some of the other practices and products of popular culture that embody such phantasies.

In the narrative practices of popular culture, the outcome offered to the reader is the attainment of a bourgeois family, with the provision of specific locations and corresponding reinforcements for girls that contrast with those for boys. In addition, such stories also allow girls to confront emotional dilemmas. Although the outcomes of these confrontations are negative as well as positive, the practices that permit such engagement may well be important in producing certain kinds of qualities usually attributed to women. Because the equivalent literature for boys does not engage with these emotional dilemmas at all, there are fewer practices that engage with the resolution of such difficulties. Instead, boys avoid the necessity of resolving them by virtue of their trajectory toward the public domain. In consequence, it is not possible to sustain a simple argument for or against such literature, or even for or against a conceivable alternative literature that might remove certain possibilities from girls by making them more like boys.

The archetype of the comic narratives is the fairy tale. The research that has been reported on the relation of fairy tales to psychic dramas has typically construed fairy tales as built upon basic myths of family relationships. The paradigmatic study of the relation of psychoanalysis to the fairy tale is *The Uses of Enchantment*. In this book, Bettelheim (1977) argues that fairy tales can assist children in the resolution of conflictual psychic material.

> Fairy tales have unequalled value, because they offer new dimensions to the child's imagination which would be impossible for him to discover as truly is own. Even more important, the form and structure of fairy tales suggest images to the child by which he can structure his daydreams and with them give better direction to his life. (p. 7)

Precisely for these reasons, phantasy in stories and play is central to modern school practices with young children.

Jennifer Waelti-Walters (1982), in her feminist critique of Bettelheim, argues that—in line with Bettelheim's consistent use of the male pronoun—such fairy tales might well have a positive effect for boys in allowing them to achieve autonomy but that, in contrast,

> they hold girls back. They offer only one security: that of being loved by father or his substitute. This is a deliberate prolongation of the oedipal stage with its implied substructure of dependency and physical dissatisfaction/sexual immaturity. Hence it is the negation of ontological security necessary for a child to achieve autonomy." (p. 7)

Although it is true that fairy tales, like comic stories and other cultural products, offer dependence as a resolution to the oedipal drama, one must remain critical of the assumption that women, like men, should aspire to the presumed opposite of dependence—the ideal of autonomy. Autonomy is only the ideal of the bourgeois individual as independent free agent, an aim particularly characteristic of liberal American feminist approaches to the psychology of women (Walkerdine, 1984b).[4]

The inculcation of bourgeois morality became the chief thrust of the fairy tale only in the nineteenth century, when the emergence of a

[4]Autonomy is created through the phantasy of possession, which is lived as reality as a result of certain practices that support the presumption that the individual has achieved control over the object of desire. This can be manifest particularly in those for whom class and gender apparently guarantee that possession and who invest what they possess in practices that promote such want through a constant supply of the means of acquisition: money, status, success. Examples of the promotion of autonomy at considerable cost are those classroom practices that support the idea of child power and control by the total subservience of women to the meeting of children's needs.

literate working class made such socialization both possible and necessary. One can see this shift in the historical transformation of the Cinderella story, from a tale for gentlefolk to a rags and riches story (Hoskin, 1984; Rose, 1984).[5] The inculcation of bourgeois morality, aspirations, and modes of conduct led to a narrative showing that those with money could possess, while those without could at least behave properly. Such an observation reminds us that it is necessary to understand the family romance and oedipal drama in the context of the historical production of those practices that are aimed at the constitution of the bourgeois individual (Foucault 1977, 1979; Henriques *et al.*, 1984).

Romance: Preparing for "Mr. Right"

The themes that appear in traditional cultural forms such as fairy tales and in contemporary cultural forms such as comics act as powerful signifiers evoking struggles that are central to the production of femininity and female sexuality. Although the significations we have been discussing are not often overtly sexual, in certain important ways they may help to prepare girls for current adolescent heterosexual practices that appear to offer an escape from conditions of victimization. Although heterosexuality is not an overt issue, other features of femininity are generated in the comics in such a way as to make "getting your man" the sole outcome.

Producing femininity in this form, aimed at finding "Mr Right," takes place through the creation of certain "regimes of meaning." Girls are victims of cruelty but they rise above their circumstances by servicing and being sensitive to others. The girl who services is like the beautiful girl whose reward for her good deeds is to be freed from her misery by a knight in shining armor. The semiotic chain slides into romance as the solution, with the knight as savior. Servicing helps to reproduce the autonomy of men and children. It is here that girls are produced as victim ready to be saved. Cruelty and victimization are the key features, but it is precisely those features that are salient in the production of women as passively sexual.

In his analysis of gender in children's fiction, Dixon (1977) examines *The Sheikh,* the book that was made into the Rudolph Valentino film, *The Sheikh of Araby.* In that volume, the key significations of slavery, victimization, and submission are linked explicitly to a woman's sexual

[5]I am indebted here to the unpublished work of Jo Spence on this topic.

initiation and the dawn of romance. The heroine, a headstrong woman, insists on going into the desert alone, where she is captured and raped by the Sheikh, whose catch-line is "What I want, I take." At one point, after she runs away, "He catches her and now we knows she loves him although he's an Arab, and to him a woman is a slave" (Dixon, 1977, p. 29). The use of the signifier *slave*, central in girls' comics, is here explicitly used in relation to sexual submission, with all the other links in the chain such as rape being exciting. "Women really like it all" is the familiar implication.

Dixon ends his analysis of the book by saying, "The reader is left to presume that they both lived happily ever after. Perhaps, as sadist and masochist they did" (Dixon, 1977, p. 29). The problem is that this implies that the material is all rather silly. However, what is clear is that the production of girls and women as victims and the signification of vicitimization as exciting is actually linked to sadomasochistic practices.

As suggested by Lacan's (1982) treatment of the ecstasy of St. Theresa, vicitimization and martyrdom carry similar significations, in this case women giving themselves for and to Christ.[6] In her article "Sexual Violence and Sexuality" (1982), Ros Coward also analyzes representations of female sexuality that promote women in poses of passivity connoting sexual pleasure. In one of these, the "victim" appears dead. Coward entitles these pictures, "The representation of female sexual pleasure: submission and the ultimate passivity, death" (p. 19). As she says,

> This leads on to the question of the code of submission, which is similarly problematic. This is the dominant code by which the female sexual pleasure is represented as simultaneously languid and turbulent, the combination of orgasm and passionate death. The explicit association with death which is frequently seen is extremely disturbing: women are shown in passionate submission, their posture evoking at best romantic deaths, at worst sexual murders. This overlayed on the potentiality of photography unconsciously to suggest death, creates a regime of disturbing and erotic photographs. Not only do they reinforce ideologies of sexuality as female submission to male force, but they also powerfully re-circulate the connection between sexuality and death which is so cruelly played out in our society. (p. 18)

By virtue of the circulation of this regime of meanings, cruelty is bound to sexual excitement. This linkage is not confined to pornography. We can see similar meanings being circulated through the sexual representation of women in the comics. What is of greatest significance

[6]The debate within the Women's Movement around the publication of an article on sadomasochism in an issue of the magazine *Heresies* highlights this issue.

is the relation between the representations at the level of phantasy and the production of meanings through which desire is understood and in which desire is invested.

The romantic resolution of desire for adolescent girls is well illustrated in McRobbie's analysis of romance in *Jackie* (1982). McRobbie observes that romance is the key to sexuality, not sex *per se*. The moment of bliss, as signified by the first kiss, is the dominant motif. Girls' lives are portrayed as dominated by the emotions of jealousy, possessiveness, and devotion, which generate the conflicts between girls. Other girls are made into enemies, typically because the heroine must get a boy and keep him. What one girl can achieve in getting a man is constantly threatened by others with the same designs; insecurity is constantly reproduced. The contradiction, which is underplayed in the magazine but is brought out by McRobbie, is that although getting and keeping men is a constant struggle for girls, the potential for romance is ubiquitous—from bus stop to disco.

The arrival of the knight in shining armor is the typical solution. What this solution conceals is that keeping a man is itself a serious threat to happiness ever after. It is because having a man is identified as the natural resolution to problems of female desire that it continues to act so powerfully, even in the face of contradictions. The getting and keeping of the man demonstrates that the girl is "good enough" and "can have what she wants."

Whereas in *Bunty* and *Tracy* the heroine is fated to suffer in silence, the fatalism of *Jackie* resides in the inevitable destiny of loss, the loss of a boy. Girls who lose their boyfriend to another are expected to suffer in silence and not to make a fuss or get angry. They are supposed to work toward the next relationship in a hopeful spirit—"Better luck next time." Rather than examining the past relationship, or relationships in general, the heroine is encouraged to put work into attracting the next boy, in the conviction that the subsequent knight must be Mr. Right.

Jackie differs from *Bunty* and *Tracy* in that it contains no school stories. The very excitement produced by school adventures in the comics slides over into romance, as signifying excitement, reward for selflessness, beauty, and the resolution of desire. This slippage is illustrated by Brewster (1980). In her chapter in the collection *Learning to Lose*, she quotes one of the women who edited the book as admitting that, despite a very successful primary school career, "during adolescence I simply changed my concept of success and I worked no less diligently at being feminine than I had done at being first in my class."

Nevertheless, as we have seen, there are aspects of the school curriculum that are presented as exciting in the comics. These are the arts subjects (as in "I Want to Dance"). In my own school memories, the principal investment in the study of French was romantic. It seemed to be the passport to romance. We were captivated by the beauty of the language, the smell of Gauloises, French trains, the excitement and romance of dark and exotic French men (on those trains, or in the Gauloises advertisements.) In my biography, the continuation of academic work was motivated by just these possibilities of excitement. The exotic dream of escaping holidays in Blackpool and winging off to the continent sustained hours and hours of painful mental labor.

Loss is also of central significance in Eichenbaum and Orbach's (1982) feminist appropriation of psychoanalysis which stresses the relation to the mother.

> From girlhood to womanhood women live with the experience of having lost these aspects of maternal nurturance. This nurturance is never replaced. Women look to men to mother them but remain bereft. The needs for nurturance do not increase any the less for the loss. The loss, which causes tremendous pain, confusion, disappointment, rage and guilt for the daughter, is buried and denied in the culture at large as well as in the unconscious of the little girl. (p. 362)

As we have seen in the comics, loss is not so much buried and denied as dealt with by active maneuvers such as splitting (there are good girls and bad girls, naughty and nice, kind and horrible). In fantasy, one split identity is elevated above the other. We are not all good girls who are selfless and have repressed anger. Some of us are and were angry, jealous, horrid. But bad girls are punished, and thereby positioned in various ways. Identities are created to deal with those characteristics, and those identities are gender-specific. Being a naughty girl is a very different matter from being a naughty boy (Walkerdine, 1984b). Certain ways of resolving loss are culturally sanctioned for a given gender, whereas others are prohibited and punished. Such sanctions and resolutions are presented in the phantasies created in the comics. They are also created in the practices making up the daily lives of the young girls.

Eichenbaum and Orbach understand the issue of the anxiety created by the loss of the other in terms of the dependency relationship set up between mother and daughter, which prohibits the development of strong ego boundaries in the little girl. However, as Lacan (1977) has stressed, the idea of a strong ego is illusory. The existence of a bounded, coherent, and autonomous subject only exists in the imagination. One problem is Eichenbaum and Orbach's formulation, then, is that in stressing ego boundaries they seem to offer a resolution that makes women more like men. This suggests that rather than femininity relating to specifically prescribed and proscribed positions, women simply have fallen short in some way or other.[7] Although Eichenbaum and Orbach (along with other similar feminist psychoanalytic writers, such as Chodorow, 1978) stress the problem of masculinity, their answer lies with the mother: by having men "mother," the issue of dependency needs may be resolved. Such a resolution ignores the paternal metaphor, the central and strategic issue of the control of truth. The complex relation that swings the subject from the maternal to the paternal, from the imaginary to the symbolic, is what both fixes identity and also assures a subject who is not fixed for all time but constantly demanding and resisting a singular identity.

The qualities so clearly expressed in the comics—vicitimization, selflessness, and helpfulness—relate to loss and to the forming and relocation of desire in the person of the ideal male savior. That women have a continued sense of lack of worth, of rejection and guilt, relates specifically to the constellation of meanings associated with the qualities necessary to become the object of desire of the man, and therefore potentially to quench the overwhelming desire in relation to the loss of the mother.

Lacan's most important contribution is his assertion of the centrality of signification that allows us to understand the production of meaning and of the links in the chain of desire. Comics as constellations of meaning are not removed from, but actually take part in, that formative process. They help to produce the very semiotic chains through which desire is recognized and the very discourses and practices that fix desire and channel its resolution into particular cultural forms. Comics do not "tell it like it is"; there is no psychic determinism that they represent. Their very constellations of meaning provide vehicles for the content of gender differentiation and for the resolution. If they did not do so, they would not be so successful as cultural products. Psychoanalysis does not help us to understand the internalization of norms of femininity through processes of identification. This would be to operate as though girls, in identifying with the texts of comics or with the position of their mother, "became feminine." Rather, what we must understand is the relation of cultural products and practices to the production and resolution of de-

[7]I have argued elsewhere that such accounts diminish the position of women and their own desires, seeing their primary function as one of care giving, (Walkerdine, 1983a).

sire. Such relations are not fitted easily onto girls but are struggled over. We must grasp the way in which that conflict is lived and the relationship between specific content and the solutions proffered to psychic and material struggles. A statement by Rose (1983) is helpful at this point:

> All this happens at a cost, and that cost is the concept of the unconscious. What distinguishes psychoanalysis from sociological accounts of gender (hence for me the fundamental impasse of Nancy Chodorow's work) is that whereas for the latter, the internalization of norms is assumed roughly to work, the basic premise and indeed the starting point. of psychoanalysis is that it does not. The unconscious constantly reveals the 'failure' of identity. Because there is not continuity of psychic life, so there is no stability of sexual identity, no position for women (or for men) which is ever simply achieved. Nor does psychoanalysis see such 'failure' as a special case of inability or an individual deviancy from the norm. 'Failure' is not a moment to be regretted in a process of adaptation, or development into normality, which ideally takes its course (some of the earliest critics of Freud, such as Ernest Jones did, however, give an account of development in just these terms). Instead 'failure' is something endlessly repeated and relived moment by moment throughout our individual histories. It appears not only in the symptoms, but also in dreams, in slips of the tongue and in forms of sexual pleasure which are pushed to the sidelines of the norm. Feminism's affinity with psychoanalysis rests above all, I would argue, with this recognition that there is a resistance to identity which lies at the very heart of psychic life. Viewed this way, psychoanalysis is no longer best understood as an account of how women are fitted into place (even this, note, is the charitable reading of Freud). Instead, psychoanalysis becomes one of the few places in our culture where it is recognized as more than a fact of individual pathology that most women do not painlessly slip into their roles as women, if, indeed, they do at all. (p. 9)

In order to reach a deeper comprehension of the situation of women, we must realize that it is not a case of a series of roles, identities, or images that are fitted onto girls. Nor is it a matter of certain stereotypically feminine behaviors that are sanctioned in preference to others. Rather, we must understand the relationship between those practices that not only define correct femininity and masculinity but that *produce* it by creating positions of occupancy and by channeling psychic conflicts and contradictions in particular ways. Good girls are not always good, but where and how is their badness lived? What is the struggle resulting from the effort to be or live a unitary identity? In the comics, good girls and bad girls are utterly different, mutually exclusive personalities. It is exactly such "personality theories", promoted in school (Walden & Walkerdine, in press), that help to create a "truth" informing those current practices that position girls in identity. In such practices, relational dynamics and shifting identities are denied in favor of a fixed and measurable unity. In consequence, the possble varieties of formation are ignored: naughty girls might be maladjusted *or* juvenile delinquents, for example.

The Canalization and Fixing of Desire

As soon as we identify any kind of fit between the meanings produced within the comics and those expressed in dialogue or interview, we can no longer argue easily that girls are simply shaped or molded from the outside by stereotyped images. Nor are the readers of comics simply constituted by the relations of signification within the text, as some structuralist accounts have implied. Approaches that stress conformity to stereotypes or passive imposition of structures miss the centrality of desire to understanding the complexity of the relationship between cultural products and subjectivity. Cultural practices do not simply engage in a process of imposing normalization. They participate in the formation of desire, fueling its flames, and thereby canalize it, directing it toward investment in certain objects and resolutions. Reading is nevertheless an active engagement, a struggle for both meaning and identity, and the role of desire and action means that readers do not identify with the heroines always in the same way.

It is the production of girls as characters within stories, as objects within particular discourses, that generates and sanctions certain sorts of intellectuality and certain forms of femininity. Educational practices are a locus at which the production of intellectuality and the production of femininity intersect. At this point of convergence, we must examine the process by which desire becomes channeled and fixed in relation to particular ideological content, a process of psychosocial mapping.

Elsewhere (Walkerdine, 1981) I have used the concept of *positioning* in discourse in order to elucidate the multiple and contradictory ways in which individual subjectivities are produced and fixed in terms of the positions that a particular discourse makes it possible to be taken up. Although this notion permits one to understand the multiple rather than singular nature of subjectivity, my previous treatment did not address the way in which a specific individual is produced in relation to any particular nexus of positionings. I was therefore subject to the accusation of having espoused a kind of "discourse determinism." A further development of the argument is therefore required: an account of the relation of the production of desire to its fixing and grafting onto particular signifiers in the discourse. In order to further this development, I shall draw heavily on Venn's (1982) formulations.

In returning to the concept of positioning, it is necessary first to stress the historical specificity of discourse: What counts as the norm is historically variable. When we say a particular girl is good, "good" is a position fixed in relation to the truth values of particular discourses at a given point in time. For example, what counts as "good at math" depends on those discourses related to modern schooling that govern what counts as mathematical and how mathematics is construed and generated, discourses which are themselves subject to historical change (Corran & Walkerdine, 1981; Walkerdine, 1983b). The position "good" will be signified and recognized in terms of the set of methods for assessing attainment, particularly marks or grades. Also, "good" represents a positioning differentiated in terms of gender. Good at math for girls is not necessarily the same as good at math for boys.

The slippage between the signification of "good" in terms of attainment and "good" connoting "well behaved" is important to understanding how girls can maintain a position within early education that allows them to be both feminine and clever. It is the relations between the significations present within different discourses and the positions afforded by those discourses that are at the root of the production of identity. Identification—the fixing of a subject in a position—cannot take place outside the normative structure of discourse. But the fact that one position rather than another is taken up depends on the mechanism of desire. What practices count as teaching and learning mathematics provides the conditions of possibility of a position. For instance, for a teacher in a progressive infant school, "good teaching" does not include putting children in desks in rows. Insofar as the discourse validates the position of the teacher when she employs a more informal arrangement, it also contributes to the production of her identity as "good teacher."

In Lacan's terms, it is precisely the relationship between particular significations that produces the chaining of the unconscious and the incorporation of those signifiers in constellations—"regimes of truth," in Foucault's terminology. I would disagree, then, with Elizabeth Cowie (1978), who argues that content is not important. It does not follow from the return to content, however, that we have to fall back on stereotyping or structural determination as the explanation.

It is the relationship between the production of discursive practices, regimes of truth, and apparatuses of social administration that provide the machinery for the generation of positionings. The actions of a girl are given various readings in order to locate her in relation to the normative evaluations embodied in the discursive practices. The particular positions generate specific significations that key into desire and so channel it. The chief signifiers fix the girl's identity as a subject position in relation to a regime of truth and meaning and thereby allow her to be publicly recognized.[8] She is subjectified through her subjection to the normative structure that these signifiers imply. The "interdiscourse," the slippage of signifiers between one discourse and another, allows for a chaining that links together a complex of positionings and sediments the continuity between them.

Femininity can be understood as just such a constellation of meanings, a convergence of positionings. For example, in the case of girls, "good" is located as signifying similar relations within a variety of practices (home, school, romance, selfless helpfulness, fashion-consciousness, and so on), and it is this complex of significations that crystallizes out that overdetermined matrix of similarities which we recognize as feminine. In Gramsci's term, such a complex is "hegemonic."

At the same time, there are differences in content of the same signification as we shift positions in the interdiscourse that allow for the emergence of discontinuities and contradictions that split the subject. For example, a professional woman is both powerful and powerless, depending on whether she is positioned as a professional or as a woman. Where the two significations meet, they are bound to produce problems at the level of the reading of the woman's actions and of others' reactions to her. Such problems will have to be recognized and resolved in some way by the woman. Anxiety around desire will be expected in such a situation.

In development, although there may be a temporary appearance of noncontradictory identity, similar conflicts may arise as soon as the girl enters a new set of practices, such as adolescent heterosexuality. The resolutions of these conflicts of desire, for instance, in terms of the image of Mr. Right, will have widespread implications for her future positionings as an adult woman—how she cultivates her own feminine "charms," for example. These in turn will have particular psychic conse-

[8]I explore the concrete identification of such processes in interview materials in my "Working Papers" (Girls and Mathematics Units, Institute of Education, University of London), currently in preparation.

quences, which will be played out in relation to others through the mechanisms of projection and introjection that we saw illustrated above in the girls' comics.

It is important to realize that in the complex of discourses and their various intersections, particular others will not necessarily have the same significance to different girls. A good example here is a conversation that I recently had with my sister. We were recalling our childhood experience of our father. Had there been a fly on the wall, it would surely have thought we were talking about two different men. I recalled a father who was all good, for whom I worked hard; I felt that I was "his girl." My sister remembered a father who was weak and ill and in relation to whom she felt too powerful. It is precisely such ambiguities that make it impossible to simply read off the positionings of girls through a simple model of their insertion into family and school. The relationship between positioning, signification, and desire is too complex for such a model.

New Strategies of Intervention: What Are the Possibilities of Subjective Transformation?

Once one realizes the significance of desire and phantasy in the incorporation of girls into discursive practices through cultural products such as comics, it becomes less surprising that the rationalist interventions stressing new, counterstereotypical content fail to work. The reactionary response to such failures has been, "If counterstereotyping fails to produce new social conditioning, then the traditional definitions of femininity must be valid." But given the argument in this chapter, quite a different account can now be given of the failure of those interventions.

The rationalist approach, which points to the need for alternative literature for girls, often aggravates the very problem it is designed to ameliorate. For example, feminist literature for girls often depicts women engaged in activities traditionally undertaken by men. In such images it is the mother who, as it were, wields the phallus: In a 1983 alternative book produced for and by beginning readers under the auspices of Division 5 of the London Education Authority, there is an illustration of a mother holding a spanner (wrench). In another feminist text, where a traditional fairy tale is reworked, the heroine, instead of marrying the prince, goes off to be a feminist decorator, garbed in dungarees.

This phallic element is quite relevant to psychoanalytic interpretations of textual material. According to modern psychoanalytic theory, a major problem for girls in the formation of female gender is the move away from desire for the mother that accompanies the recognition that she, originally perceived as the omnipotent Phallic Mother, does not, in fact, possess the phallus. Although social changes have brought about a situation in which women can indeed fill positions that invest them with the phallus, this is not to imply that such positions provide coherent or noncontradictory identities.

Lacan has argued that the phallus is a "fraud," since men do not possess it either but rather perpetually struggle to attain it. For women to aspire to be the Phallic Mother is equally fraudulent. This should not be taken as an argument that modern shifts in work-related practices are unimportant, or that girls should not grow up in relationship to a powerful mother, or that phantasied approaches toward the phallus are not significant in encouraging awareness of opportunities. However, the phallus cannot insure safety, much as marriage does not guarantee living happily ever after.

Alternative fiction must be planned with an awareness of the identities and positions that traditional fiction produces for girls and with attention to the complex relational dynamic that underlies the struggle involved in constituting femininity (or masculinity). It also must be planned with an awareness of the ambiguity of textual revision: the alternative texts may have quite variable meanings and quite different consequences. It is true that fantasies of machine-minded mothers and feminist decorators may well provide the vehicle for an alternative vision. However, they could equally feed a *resistance* to the feminist alternative. How might other fantasies be generated that offer different paths for dealing with desires and conflicts? Could resolutions that are not black and white, projective and introjective, be considered? Could there be resolutions that do not conform to the type of "future reward for present pain"? Could there not be characters who are not produced by simply splitting human nature into good and bad?

By examining how present cultural practices deal with conflicts and offer resolutions to them, it may be possible to reach an understanding of how those practices work, what they speak and what they do not, what fantasies they do and do not tolerate, what forms of sexuality they encourage and what they foreclose. Since conflicts of desire persist throughout life, it might be possible to envisage, by way of new interventions, texts promoting fictive engagements with both present and future struggles, with both small and large resolutions, from presence or absence of the mother to the arrival of Mr Right, or the prince. If current fictions produce such powerful effects, we too, if we are to find other possibilites, must work on the production of dreams.

Two concepts, elaborated in the work of Venn (1982) may be useful in a consideration of possible subjective transformation, the articulation of possible dreams. These are the notions of *forgetting* and the *recanalization of desire.* In Lacan's account of the production of the subject, the subject is not pregiven but is produced out of the separation from the mother–other. Until the infant can mark and recognize that separation, it is not constituted as a subject. Pecheux's (1982) concept of forgetting refers to the way in which the subject places in its own way the greatest possible obstruction to change when it ignores the constituted character of the self and imagines itself to be the rational and free subject of the *cogito.* If we posit ourselves as subjects of free choice, we become incapable of recognizing the constitutive character of the regimes of truth that produce us. It is the mechanism of desire that is responsible for this forgetting. It operates to repress our separation and pain of loss. Moreover, as Foucault (e.g., 1977, 1979) has pointed out in his analyses of the administration of the social, those discourses and practices that sediment us in positions of bourgeois free agents produce in us a false understanding of ourselves as presocial individuals possessing fixed and determined attributes, such as cleverness.

Our loss of the constitutive character of our subjectification through the fixing of our desires calls for a *deconstruction,* a practice that allows us to take apart the taken-for-granted in the construction of subjectivity and to examine its socially and historically specific character. In their feminist approach to art practices, for example, Parker and Pollock (1981) point to the political significance of such a deconstruction:

> Within the present organization of sexual difference which underpins patriarchal culture, there is no possibility of simply conjuring up and asserting a positive and alternative set of meanings for women. The work to be done is that of deconstruction. The 'otherness' of woman as negative of man and the repression of woman within our culture is not without radical possibilities for challenging the oppressiveness of patriarchal systems for both men and women. In art practice, women can engage in work to expose these ideological constructions by questioning the traditional institutions of artist and art, by analyzing the meanings which representations of women signify and by alerting the spectator to the ideological *work* of art, the effects of artistic practices and representations. (pp. 132–33)

Brewster (1980), inquiring into why the performance of many girls in math and science starts out as good but then becomes poor, concludes:

> There is no clear and categorical explanation. One can only ask, what happens to girls in secondary school that they should come to *forget* what they had already acquired at an earlier age? What are the pressures on them to forget; what are the advantages of forgetting? (p. 10)

I would argue that it is precisely the changes relating to the insertion of the girl into heterosexual practices and her relocation to a new constellation of meanings that makes forgetting a significant part of subjective transformation. Venn (1982) refers to this kind of process as "recanalization of desire":

> Subjective transformation. This process has similarities with transference. It is not a rational or purely rational exercise, since rational arguments alone are not sufficient to change hearts and minds: they simply present another possible and competing 'field of identity' or ideomorph, but without engaging with the subject's investments. So it seems to me that the process of changing subjects and of politicization must involve, in addition, another (or others) who can function as Other: a leader/hero, a mentor, friend, lover, or a cohesive group enabling a cathartic recanalization of desire, and thus, the relocation of the subject. (p. 318)

Is it possible that it is such a recanalization of desire that cathartically diverts the girl and gives rise to forgetting? If so, what must we then do to produce a recanalization that lacks such problematic consequences? Venn mentions heroes and lovers. Phantasy is crucial because heroines can resolve conflicts in a variety of ways and lovers can take up a variety of positions.

We should hold fast to the significance of the phantasied here, rather than that of everyday functional reality. The needed other is not a role model because the construct of role model, with its accompanying practical interventions to achieve attitude change, does not require the same investment of desire or call for the same deconstruction of signification that transformation in the universe of fiction and phantasy does.

By deconstruction's revealing the gaps and silences, previously unspoken problems may be voiced. Those problems, although suppressed in the discourse, are experienced by women every day. But to be confronted, they must first be spoken and made to signify. The act of voicing and deconstruction are preludes to the recanalization of desire, that imperative in our struggle for self and social transformation.

After all, it was only the princess's desire that transformed the frog into a prince.

References

Adlam, D. (in press). The condition of the psychological subject. *New Ideas In Psychology, 4*(2).

Bettelheim, B. (1979). *The uses of enchantment.* New York: Knopf.

Brewster, P. (1980). *Learning to lose.* London: Women's Press.

Chodorow, N. (1978). *The reproduction of mothering.* Berkeley: University of California Press.

Corran, C., & Walkerdine, V. (1981). *The practice of reason. Vol. 1: Reading the signs of mathematics.* London: University of London Institute of Education.

Coward, R. (1982). Sexual violence and sexuality. *Feminist Review, 11,* 25–32.

Cowie, E. (1978). Woman as sign. *m/f, 1,* 49–63.

Dixon, B. (1977). *Catching them young. Vol. 1: Race, sex and class in children's fiction.* London: Pluto.

Eichenbaum, L., & Orbach, S. (1982). *Outside in, inside out.* Harmondsworth, England: Penguin.

Foucault, M. (1977). *Discipline and punish.* London: Allen Lane.

Foucault, M. (1979). *History of sexuality* (Vol. 1). London: Allen Lane.

Freud, S. (1956). Family romances. *Standard edition of the complete psychological works of Sigmund Freud* (Vol. 9). London: Hogarth Press and the Institute of Psychoanalysis. (Originally published in 1908)

Henriques, J., Hollway, W., Urwin, C., Venn, C., & Walkerdine, V. (1984). *Changing the subject.* London: Methuen.

Hoskin, K. (1984). Cobwebs to catch flies: Writing (and) the child. In R. Steedman, C. Urwin, & V. Walkerdine (eds.), *Language, gender, and childhood.* London: Routledge & Kegan Paul.

Lacan, J. (1977). *Ecrits: A selection.* London: Tavistock.

Laplanche, J., & Pontalis, J.-B. (1973). *The language of psychoanalysis.* London: Hogarth Press and the Institute of Psychoanalysis.

Lobban, G. (1975). Sex roles in reading schemes. *Educational Review, 27*(3), 179–192.

McRobbie, A. (1982). Jackie: An ideology of adolescent femininity. In B. Waites, T. Bennet, & G. Martin (Eds.), *Popular culture, past and present.* London: Croom Helm and the Open University Press.

Mitchell, J., & Rose, J. (1982). *Feminine sexuality: Jacques Lacan and the Ecole Freudienne.* New York: Norton.

Parker, R., & Pollock, G. (1981). *Old mistresses.* London: Routledge & Kegan Paul.

Pecheux, M. (1982). *Language, semantics and ideology.* London: MacMillan.

Pinkerton, G. (1982). Challenging sex stereotypes: Ideas for the classroom. *ILEA Contact,* November 12, 26–32.

Rose, J. (1983). Femininity and its discontents. *Feminist Review, 14,* 4–20.

Rose, J. (1984). Peter Pan, language, and the state. In R. Steedman, C. Urwin, & V. Walkerdine (Eds.), *Language, gender, and childhood.* London: Routledge & Kegan Paul.

Venn, C. (1982). *Beyond the science–ideology relation.* Unpublished doctoral dissertation. University of Essex, England.

Waelti-Walters, J. (1982). *Fairy tales and the female imagination.* Montreal: Eden Press.

Walden, R., & Walkerdine, V. (1982). *Girls and mathematics: The early years.* London: Heinemann.
Walden, R., & Walkerdine, V. (In press). *Girls and mathematics: From primary to secondary schooling.* London: Heinemann.
Walkerdine, V. (1981). Sex, power, and pedagogy. *Screen Education, 38,* 14–25.
Walkerdine, V. (1983a). *Feminism, psychoanalysis, and mothering.* Paper presented at the Socialist Society Conference on the Family, London, England.
Walkerdine, V. (1983b). *The historical construction of the scientific truth about girls.* Paper presented at the Second International GASAT Conference, Oslo, Norway.
Walkerdine, V. (1984a). Some day my prince will come. In A. McRobbie & M. Nava (Eds.), *Gender and generation.* London: Macmillan.
Walkerdine, V. (1984b). Power, gender, and resistance. In R. Steedman, C. Urwin, & V. Walkerdine (Eds.), *Language, gender, and childhood.* London: Routledge & Kegan Paul.
Walkerdine, V. (1985). Science and the female mind: The burden of proof. *PsychCritique, 1*(1), 1–20.

Chapter 5

Richard Lichtman

THE ILLUSION OF MATURATION IN AN AGE OF DECLINE

Psychology is the dominant ideological paradigm of our age. It is the prism through which the reality of society is transformed into the mythology of individualism. Two striking instances of this tendency appeared at the beginning of the century. James Ward's classic *Psychological Principles* (1920) set down the following methodological pronouncement: "Taking individual experience as defining the scope of psychology, we began our study with our own experience, since other experience can be intelligible only in these terms" (p. 361). And William James introduced his influential *The Varieties of Religious Experience* (1902) with the following prescription: "If the inquiry be psychological, not religious institutions, but rather religious feelings and religious impulses must be its subject, and I must confine myself to those more developed subjective phenomena recorded in literature produced by articulate and fully self-conscious men, in works of piety and autobiography" (p. 4). It is not the focus on mind that distinguishes twentieth-century bourgeois thought from earlier historical reflections; it is, rather, the separation of mind from the social institutions in which it is embodied.

What gives psychology its particular power? Why does it appear so persuasive and even self-evident as a mode of explanation? The answer lies finally in the manner in which psychology reflects the isolation, antagonism, fragmentation, and subjectivism of contemporary life. Psychology is not historically possible as an independent discipline until

This chapter draws upon material previously published in Lichtman, 1981.

Richard Lichtman • Wright Institute, 2728 Durant Ave., Berkeley, CA 94704.

capitalism sunders individuals from their traditional social ties and reconstructs them as privatized monads confronting an opaque reality. Then it becomes necessary.

But to say that psychology *reflects* individual experience is not to say that it *copies* what precedes it. However much experience depends upon a lived conceptual framework, psychology, as a formal science, constitutes its own order. For it could not realize its function unless it provided an abstract, coherent, and formally ideological *articulation* of ordinary experience. Its purpose is not to mirror but to legitimize experience, a task it can only complete by redefining the individual as the primary agent of social life, and the causal initiator and locus of a complex system of technically manipulable determinants. This reconstruction of everyday life brings individual experience into the ideological order of bourgeois justification. Isolation, estrangement, and loneliness are codified as autonomy, independence, and self-reliance. The more thoroughly this psychology permeates common sense, the more thoroughly individual suffering can be reconceptualized as resignation, acceptance, or even, under more extreme conditions, wholly effaced in the illusion of "growth" and "development."

One of the most important strands of contemporary psychological ideology is *stage theory*, the view that the individual passes through a sequence of necessary and universal junctures in the course of development. Why are these theories so popular at the present time? Bourgeois theorists often provide an internal cognitive explanation, that Freud's theories offered a restrictive and inadequately articulated view of the range of human growth from earliest infancy to the end of life. This view seems unpersuasive.[1] Countless Freudian misconceptions go wholly unnoticed in theoretical circles (Lichtman, 1982). Nor can any theoretical difficulty in itself explain the enormous proliferation of popular versions of the developmental perspective. The general public has very little interest in theoretical adequacy as such; unless some common concern is evoked, the most gaping deficiency will go unnoticed.

Let me approach the answer obliquely, through speculative analogy. Laissez-faire theory began to flourish in the United States in the post–Civil War period at precisely the time in American history when the possibility of free competition in the market place was becoming an

[1]In my view, Freud has no explanation of development. Only the defensive apparatus can be said to develop; the instinctual flow of energy merely moves from one erogenous zone to another.

anachronism. Again, the Full Employment Act was passed by Congress in 1946, when it was abundantly clear that full employment has ceased to exist as a real possibility under capitalism. The relationship between reality and ideology always carries the imprint of inversion, for the reality that violates bourgeois doctrine must be presented as the opposite of its actual condition. The same holds true of stage theory, which presents an idealized version of development, one of the main functions of which is to obfuscate the growing sense of a lack of meaningful maturation among an increasing portion of the American public. Levinson (1978), to whose theory we will turn shortly, inadvertently happens upon the truth: "There is a growing desire in our society to see adulthood as something more than a long featureless stretch of years with childhood at one end and senility at the other" (p. x). We shall see how his own work speaks to this desire and how the bourgeois vision of continuous progress is mapped onto the otherwise featureless expanse of the capitalist terrain.

The Use of Exchange Time

Despite an occasional nodding reference to social factions, the fundamental work being produced at present on the subject of aging is asocial and ahistorical. Stages of development are implicitly or explicity held to be universal. This reification alone should be enough to disqualify the theory. Instead, little if anything is said of the whole enterprise of social anthropology, history, or comparative social studies, and on the basis of a dozen instances, or perhaps several times that number, global judgments are rendered without caution. A miniscule sample of the middle class (usually caucasian) of one or a handful of contemporary capitalist countries is taken as sufficient ground to render pronouncements on the human condition.

But even within our own culture in the last several hundred years, capitalism has profoundly altered the nature and meaning of *time, passage, growing up, growing old, aging* and *dying* itself (see, for example, Ariès, 1960 and 1976). Thomas Hardy brilliantly captures the essence of an earlier period in one poignant passage: "Tess started on her way up the dark and crooked lane or street not made for hasty progress; a street laid out before inches of land had value, and when one-handed clocks sufficiently subdivided the day." Here one finds in a single coherent structure the rejection of speed and direct linear movement, the relationship between spatialization, fragmentation, and value, and a measure of time derived from the activity it organically adverbializes.

The reference to *value* in Hardy's passage is important, for it leads us to consider two very different meanings of the term. If we contrast economies of use, in which goods are produced to be directly consumed or bartered for immediate consumption, with the economies of exchange, in which commodities are produced to be sold for money for the purchase of new commodities in a process without end, we can see that each of these modes of production requires of necessity a different form of time. Time and value are inseparable. In systems of use value, time is lived, organic, heterogeneous, integral, biological, and intrinsic. In the mode of exchange value, time is conceptual, homogeneous, mechanical, extrinsic, and independent. There is a fundamental shift from quality to quantity brought on primarily by the introduction of abstract value and abstract labor, each unit of which is necessarily worth precisely the same as the next. Through the clock, which contributed both to the creation and measured recording of this atomization, each unit of time becomes equivalent to the next, and all become, for economic purposes, indistinguishable.

In capitalist ledgers every unit of time is worth the same, the first moment of the morning and the last of the evening. The fact that fatigue, wear, decay, and dissolution accumulate during the working day and that consequently the lived experience of the last moment of the day, the last day of one's work, and the last year of one's life are wholly different from the first—all of this is irrelevant to the capitalist. The capitalist has no interest in qualitative transformation as he has no way of measuring its meaning, unless, of course, exhaustion leads to accident, absence, or some other measurable cost of production. What happens with the advance of capitalism is that time becomes absolutized; it is severed from the activity of which it is the time. It becomes instead an independent, objective, alienated medium that forces the new content of social life to conform to its mechanical and repetitious anonymity. In organic communities of use, time tends to accommodate to the rhythms of nature and lived experience. Lived time always has direction, whereas abstract time is, by its very definition, reversible. Human purpose is directed toward ends, and the phases of that developing purpose are as qualitatively different as the growing fund of meaning embedded in its developing realization. But in advanced capitalism, the imperative of profit requires that accumulation command and labor succumb to the sheerly mathematical considerations of maximized profit.

Use time, as contrasted with exchange time, is oriented to human tasks, first, because in such cultures people attend to external requirements—seasons, tides, natural growth, and decay. Thus, in pastoral and agricultural societies time tends to be cyclical. This suggests that time is formed in the process of what it measures and that although Kant might argue that time is a universal and necessary intuition, there is clearly a dimension of temporality that is, as Durkheim insisted, socially constructed and variable. Second, in societies of use there is less separation between work and the remainder of life, so that the qualitative time of play, ritual, and social amenity fuse with labor to lend it their quality. Third, in organic communities the work day lengthens or contracts according to the nature of the task to be completed. As Mumford (1934) maintained:

> The clock, moreover, is a piece of power-machinery whose 'product' is seconds and minutes: by its essential nature it dissociated time from human events and helped create the belief in an independent world of mathematically measurable sequences: the special world of science. There is relatively little foundation for this belief in common human experience: through the year the days are of uneven duration, and not merely does the relation between day and night steadily change, but a slight journey from East to West alters astronomical time by a number of minutes. In terms of the human organism itself, mechanical time is even more foreign: while human life has regularities of its own, the beat of the pulse, the breathing of the lungs, these change from hour to hour with mood and action, and in the longer span of days, time is measured not by the calendar but by the events that occupy it. The shepherd measures from the time the ewes lambed; the farmer measures back to the day of sowing or forward to the harvest; if growth has its own duration and regularities, behind are not simply matter and motion, but the facts of development; in short, history. (p. 15)

When abstract time becomes the new currency of social life, one does not rise with the rhythms of the day nor lie down with them. One does not necessarily eat when one is hungry but when the meal is sanctioned by an objective schedule ultimately justified by "efficiency" in the coordination of labor. And as work reshapes time, the length of the labor does not conform to the "natural" conditions of light and darkness. Rather, the invention of the wick, the lamp, and the electric light undo previously natural rhythms to prolong the profitability of the working day. And as time homogenizes, space, which not only in Einstein's theory but also in lived experience is inseparable from the meaning of temporality and passage, quantifies. "Space as a hierarchy of values was replaced by space as a system of magnitudes" (Mumford, 1934, p. 20). The discovery of the laws of perspective was an aspect of that larger process which insisted that the understanding of any thing or event in the world was inseparable from locating it in space and time. It was the invisible lines of longitude and latitude that permitted Columbus his act of faith. In the process, space reformulated time, which came to be divided, filled up, and with the machinery of labor-saving technology, even expanded. "Down they forgot as up they grew" (e. e. cummings).

Capital accumulates; human beings disintegrate. The growth of the machine means the decline of craft; control by the machine, loss of human direction. A distinction began to develop between employer's time and worker's time. The first was tied to the growth of profit, the second to the death of craft. For "the employer must *use* the time of his labour, and see it is not wasted: not the task but the value of time when reduced to money is dominant. Time is now currency: it is not passed but spent" (Thompson, 1967, p. 61).

The developing use of the clock and the quantification of time affected the priority of the temporal senses. Previously it was sound that marked common passage—the tolling of a bell, the bleating of a horn, the song of a people. The change from aural to visual punctuation was also a change from the collective world in which one sound reached those, and only those, who could perceive it, to the privatized world of evolving capitalism in which each could carry his or her own index of collective coordination. The clock tower marked the transition.

With the division of labor came the need for the synchronization of labor. Work was artificially divided and financially connected. The rationalization of time became a primary instrument in disciplining the labor force (Marx, 1867/1967). The commodification of time was inseparable from exploitation. For the capitalist, the homogeneous unit of time was to be filled with productivity and emptied of waste; that is, it was to be made thrifty. There developed a unique historical conception of the temporal efficiency of human production that included the husbanding of one's energies, the rationalization of desire, and the instrumentalization of human want. The "reasonableness" not only of human action but of subjectivity itself was measured more and more by the ratio of outcome per unit of expended energy. Upon the Christian injunction against idleness was superimposed the capitalist requirement of efficiency in the use of one's personal energy. To effect the largest consumption of the other on the basis of the least possible expenditure of one's self became the new bourgeois paradigm of mature development.

To horde labor thus was possible only in a system of abstract labor time, where each unit of lived expenditure could be translated into multiples of a single, homogeneous measure and stored as such. The commodification of labor time as money affected such diverse human phenomena as the quantification of happiness in the utilitarian calculus of pleasures and the privatized accountancy of passion in the balance sheet of containment and release. But this new personal metaphysic was also the basis of a profound social accusation—that the poor suffer through their profligacy or their laziness, that is, through too great or too little an expenditure of their selves, and that in their misuse of time they are punished by the inexorable laws of social physics.

The forms of time were also the forms of public and private life. Popular sports and holidays were curtailed, and the quantified time of the workplace permeated the public realm while recreational time was relegated more and more to the privacy of the family. Of course, with the introduction of "labor-saving" technology into the home, the modes of time became confused and the haven of the family, including its ostensible pardon from the merciless imposition of exchange time, found itself more and more thoroughly routinized and rationalized. And as the reach of commodified need and state administration extend more profoundly into the entirety of life under capitalism, the released time of the home is more thoroughly organized as an adjunct to profitable production. Beyond the home or within it, sexuality, mind-altering drugs, and assaultive art promise to break the hold of quantified temporality for something that more nearly resembles the Bergsonian *durée*. But their existence is always more precarious as they are quickly marketed for their transcendent appeal. Thompson's (1967) reflection of the transformation of the British working-class movement holds here too by analogy, except that in the world of marketed consumption there is little if anything to act as resistance:

> The first generation of factory workers were taught by their masters the importance of time; the second generation formed the short-time committees in the ten-hour movement; the third generation struck for over-time or time-and-a-half. They had accepted the categories of their employers and learned to fight back with them. (p. 86)

The overwhelming majority of stage theorists pays little or no attention to the historical and social transformation of time. There is, of course, the obligatory obeisance, but its function is cosmetic. Although nothing could be more intimate to the mind than passage and memory, and although it is equally clear that these are culturally mediated experiences, the variable character of these dimensions is merely omitted. This leads to two significant consequences: the nature of aging is separated from the social context of its occurrence, and the social structure of advanced capitalism is taken for granted in the articulation of the ostensibly universal movement of life. The result of this double reification is the profound contraction of the most fundamental magnitude determining the nature of human possibility—temporal change.

Contemporary capitalism involves a contradiction between two modalities of experienced temporal gratification. The first mode is that of production, which requires orderly, coordinated, structured, disciplined labor and its concomitant 'delayed' gratification. Since one of the primary activities of the self is the binding of time through the construction of extended action, this function of "productive" time requires the instrumental connection of specialized, rationalized, calculable moments of homogeneous accumulation. With the delay of gratification, the temporal boundary of the self is expanded and its temporal substance attenuated. But contemporary capitalism also requires the indulgence of consumption for the sake of continued production, and this requirement underscores the importance of immediate gratification and the continued eliciting of commodified impulsivity. The ritualized "here and now" of the growth movement is the psychological reflection of this mandate to pleasure which functions as an individual lure to ensure the more rapid circulation of capital in the circuit of novelty. Neither mode of time nor their juxtaposition can secure satisfaction, however, for either the moments of time are endured in sullen frustration for the sake of a mythical justification, or the moments of frenetic immediacy follow upon each other in discontinuous staccato. What is lost is the experience of enriched duration, in which the funding of experience nurtures the roots of previous phases.

The forms of immediate gratification, particularly the demand and obligation to consume, are, on the scale of present mass society, historically unique. Of course, this new mode of time is inseparable from a unique formation of desire and of the self whose contours are shaped through this novel structuring. It is not merely that at each moment the character of need and that of longing are made different from what they are in other societies. It is, rather, that the whole arc of life is reconstituted and the meaning of its phases reconstructed, for, certainly, the present function of immediate gratification is inseparable from planned obsolescence, which is in turn intimately tied to the very notion of aging itself. The natural breeding ground for novelty, change, immediacy, and "fun morality" is youth, and when this factor is joined with the productive definition of time in terms of accumulation, it is easy to see that past the apogee of efficient work, one is moving inexorably toward extinction. Ariès (1960, 1976), in his writings on childhood and dying, has shown how much these notions have changed over the centuries even in the West. Stages, like adolescence, which we take for granted, had no previous existence, even in our own tradition. It is abundantly clear that in the wholly distinct ontology of traditional societies age represents the accumulation of experience and wisdom and that in this light the entire meaning of approaching death is transformed.

The Ideology of Progress

Age is socially constructed and defined. There are, of course, changes that occur in body and mind over time. These "facts" are adduced by stage theorists in their argument for the universality of human development. Two basic considerations invalidate this naive positivism, however. First, it is impossible to separate the nature of change from the society in which it takes place. Just as the natural environment is stamped with social presence, so in turn are the body and mind of human beings. Beyond certain very broad changes, it is impossible to ascertain the supposedly natural occurrence of disease, senility, sexual potency, and similar events. But even if such determinations were possible, they would prove irrelevant, for the meaning of nature is itself a social determination and the significance of such change as occurs is the product of the society in which the signification occurs. The demarcation line for "old age" in our society is established in the vicinity of 65 not for any intrinsic, natural change which occurs in the organism at that time. It was largely because the structure of capitalism required a resolution of mass unemployment during the Depression that 65 was chosen as the age most likely to remove the optimum number of workers from a swollen work force. The result in a society that equates productivity and wealth with social value and human dignity itself is the characterization of old age as redundant uselessness.

When age is defined as dissolution we have a potent instance of a self-destroying prophecy. But it is not sufficiently noted in the traditional developmental literature that the anticipation of age casts a debilitating shadow over the middle stages of life. If all one can look forward to is decline, the meaning of one's life as it proceeds will be marked by a deepening sense of despair. Retirement is most often a social exile, as the prevision of old age is mobilized for social control, for the threat of extinction that reaches back into middle years affects the alternatives and life priorities that precede it. Retiring people from work and making their later years dependent, devalued, and debased encourages harder work at earlier periods and forces choices that would not have been made if the later years of life could have been anticipated with serenity. It is hard work that is supposed to stave off destitution in old age. When the worst happens and individuals fail—in illness, dependency, or decay—it is they who are blamed for the deficiency of their preparation, rather than the system of enforced destructiveness. Capitalism constructs the debasement of old age and individualizes its penalty. In the face of an approaching meaningless death, the pains of unlived life are made less horrendous by comparison.

The relationship between old age and false consciousness is crucial to capitalist legitimation. The myth of progress—national and personal—is deeply ingrained. Were the myth credible, the approach of death might seem to bring with it the realization of fulfillment. But this is not possible, as Weber (1958) noted in a profoundly beautiful comment on the writings of Tolstoy:

> All his broodings increasingly revolved around the problem of whether or not death is a meaningful phenomenon. And his answer was: for civilized man death has no meaning. It has none because the individual life of civilized man, placed into an infinite "progress", according to its own imminent meaning should never come to an end; for there is always a further step ahead of one who stands in the march of progress. And no man who comes to die stands upon the peak which lies in infinity. Abraham, or some peasant of the past, died "old and satiated with life" because he stood in the organic cycle of life; because his life, in terms of its meaning and on the eve of his days, had given to him what life had to offer; because for him there remained no puzzles he might wish to solve; and therefore he could have had "enough" of life. Whereas civilized man, placed in the midst of the continuous enrichment of culture by ideas, knowledge, and problems, may become "tired of life" but not "satiated with life." He catches only the most minute part of what the life of the spirit brings forth ever anew, and what he seizes is always something provisional and not definitive, and therefore death for him is a meaningless occurrence. And because death is meaningless, civilized life as such is meaningless; by its very "progressiveness" it gives death the imprint of meaninglessness. (p. 140)

Weber derived meaninglessness from infinite progress. What should we say of the situation of imminent decline? If "continuous enrichment" cannot provide satisfaction, how much grief must be engendered by the disaccumulation of culture? More and more, public mentality is permeated by pessimism and the expectation of defeat. But for some with the wealth to distract or narcotize themselves, a pervasive illusion of recurrent excitation glosses the surface of bewilderment. Those suffering deprivation are closer to the truth; they are most lucidly aware of the receding movement of the dream. The approach of death brings the purest vision, for the aged are best situated to judge the meaning of their lives and the extent to which their hopes have been fulfilled. So they are segregated and silenced. The clear public vision of their weary exhaustion would not merely stand as an indictment; it would rob the living of their deceit. Terror is not conducive to legitimation.

There are several ways in which society can deal with this threat to the legitimizing myth of social progress. First, as we have already noted, it can deal with it by isolation. But the aged can also be encouraged to costume themselves in the toys and garments of youth—an ironic reversal of children's "dress up" games. The aged can be seduced into acting out the gaudiest and most vulgar pretenses of adolescence, a pitiful spectacle which abounds in prefabricated retirement communities. Or the aged can be brought to believe that their complaints are the result of a natural deterioration, the consequence of senility rather than discovery. Or the claim of sacrifice can be brought into play. Through this stratagem, which is so profoundly important to the ideology of capitalism, one does not deny the failure of one's now spent life but regards it as the necessary preliminary for the success of one's children. They are to reap the benefit of disaster.

But this last device is also in jeopardy, for either expansion or stagnation occurs. In the first case, accumulation and progress continue, with the result that individualism is enhanced and the ties of the family weakened, as De Toqueville (1904) brilliantly noted:

> Among democratic nations new families are constantly springing up, others are constantly falling away, and all that remain change their condition; the woof of time is every instant broken, and the track of generations effaced. Those who went before are soon forgotten; of those who will come after no one has any idea; the interest of man is confined to those in close propinquity to himself. (p. 586)

In the second case, the economy moves into a long period without expansion and begins even to contract; then one cannot readily sacrifice for one's children, for the progress that justifies our lives by theirs cannot lend conviction to the hope of their advance.

Levinson and the New Theodicy

Daniel J. Levinson's *The Seasons of a Man's Life* is typical of the ideology of developmental psychology. It is also one of the more popular books of its kind. On the basis of a sample of 40 men chosen from four occupations (workers, executives, biologists, and novelists) in one limited geographical area, Levinson constructs a theory of universal and necessary stages:

> The life course has a particular character and follows a basic sequence. . . . The journey from birth to old age follows an underlying, universal pattern on which there are endless cultural and individual variations. . . . Each has its necessary place and contributes its special character to the whole (pp. 6–7). Even the most disparate lives are governed by the same underlying order. (p. 64)

It is not merely the absence of any carefully selected cross-cultural evidence that vitiates Levinson's universal claim; it is the failure to define or even take note of crucial terms. How, for example, do we distinguish the underlying, universal pattern from its variations, or identify the criterion that permits allocation to one of these categories or the other? Furthermore, although Levinson appears to credit social factors in his reference to variations, they play no meaningful role in his work. The claim of universality is an empty assertion the function of which is to provide ideological security rather than theoretical conviction.

But note that the stages are not merely necessary; they are also appropriate or right, "in contributing their special character to the whole." The term *contributing* is of course derived from the ideological character of Levinson's perspective; no independent evidence is offered on its behalf. The general approach is to reconstruct the process of aging along the lines of a theodicy of progress and then offer this itinerary as a guide for the distraught and perplexed. The more this self-conception insinuates itself into the public consciousness, the more the passage of life will be misconceived in its terms.

It is no accident that Levinson wholly confuses nature and society. "By twenty, most of the mental and bodily characteristics that have been evolving in their pre-adult years are at their peak levels" (p. 21). These characteristics include height, strength, "sexual capability," memory, "abstract thought," and the ability to learn specific skills. It does not seem to occur to Levinson that in other societies these traits may mature differently and acquire different meanings, or that along with the material increase of a capacity its value may decline. What is the importance of strength in a computerized society? What, after all, is the peak level of sexual capability? The latter question cannot be asked, let alone answered, except by following the positivist assumption that sexuality can be reduced to physiological response.

"The instinctual energies, too, pass their maximal level and are somewhat reduced in middle adulthood" (p. 25). What are these declining instincts? They include "the capacity for anger and moral indignation, self-assertiveness and ambition, the wish to be cared for and supported" (p. 25). This account makes one long for the old instinct theory of MacDougall, who in comparison with Levinson appears the very soul of parsimony. What is at work here is transparently clear: Levinson reifies the destructiveness of capitalism, its slow, insidious depletion of the human spirit, and presents the result of this socially induced decay as a natural decline. In some instances, such as the loss of moral indignation, he describes what is probably an actual occurrence and wholly misconstrues its cause. In others—as in the wish to be cared for—he falls prey to current male stereotypes and falsifies the evidence. Both aspects of this mystification serve to accommodate individuals to the paucity of their lives.

We are unlikely to be surprised, then, when Levinson replaces his vulgarization of Freudian instinct theory with his ideological version of Jung:

> As Jung conceived the term, and as it is commonly used by psychologists, individuation is a developmental process through which a person becomes more uniquely individual. Acquiring a clearer and fuller identity of his own, he becomes better able to utilize his inner resources and pursue his own aims. (p. 33)

The more deeply we become enmeshed in the worlds of work and family, the obligations of supporting children and parents, the accumulation of some modicum of property and status, the more we can utilize our untainted "inner resources" and "reduce the tyranny of both the demands society places on us and the demands of our own repressed (instinctual) unconscious" (p. 33). No matter how sonorously Levinson intones the pious platitude of the social self,[2] his working thesis remains the centrality of the "archetypal unconscious," an inner source of self-definition and satisfaction. "Archetypes are, so to speak, a treasury of seeds within the self" (p. 33).

[2]The reader might consult Levinson (1978, pp. 46–49) for an example of decorative, totally superfluous social posturing. As liberalism is required to genuflect to social responsibility, so liberal theory is forced into a similarly uncomfortable position.

If maturity is the capacity to tolerate contradictions, Levinson's work is the very model of ripeness. Although individuation is supposedly a process of acquiring a more unique identity, it occurs by throwing off society and turning instead to the "archetypal unconscious," which one might have thought the paradigm of undifferentiated commonality for all individuals. But just as one is settling into this difficulty, Levinson informs us that the self and the social world "interpenetrate," that each is "inside the other," (p. 47) and that we "cannot grasp the full nature of the self without seeing how diverse aspects of the world are reflected and contained within it" (p. 48). This remark appears promising until we realize that it is suspended above the body of the work and bears no functional relationship to the whole mass of Levinson's universalistic reification. It is the level of abstraction that tells the story, as Marx long ago informed us. So long as Levinson remains enmeshed in homilies, he appears to have both his necessary, underlying sequences and his disarming recognition of social reality. Therefore he has no difficulty in informing us that in analyzing the "life structure . . . the most useful starting point . . . is to consider the *choices* a person makes and how he deals with their consequences," (p. 43) and he can immediately add that

> society makes available to each of its members a limited range of individuals, groups, material resources, occupations and possibilities for social involvement and self-fulfillment. . . . Through its own structure, society brings about a patterning in the choices a man makes. (p. 48)

What saves the enterprise is the careful avoidance of any social, economic, or moral analysis of the structure of society and its relation to the apparent choices of its members.

The social reification of the analysis is supported by a wonderfully congruent metaphysic, a teleology that centers upon the notion of *task*. For example:

> A special task of middle adulthood is to become more aware of both the child and the elder in oneself and in others. (p. 28)

> The primary task of every stable period is to build a life structure. (p. 49)

> [In the early adult transition] the first task is to start moving out of the preadult world: to question the nature of that world and one's place in it. . . . The second task is to make a preliminary step into the adult world, to explore its possibilities. (p. 56)

> The young man has two primary yet antithetical tasks: (a) He needs to explore the possibilities of adult living: to keep his options open, avoid strong commitments and maximize the alternatives. . . . (b) The contrasting

> task is to *create a stable life structure:* become more responsible and "make some sense of my life." (pp. 57–58)

> A developmental crisis occurs when a man has great difficulty with the developmental tasks of a period; he finds his present life structure intolerable, yet seems unable to form a better one. (p. 58)

There are several important points to note in regard to the use of the term *task*. First, the term is neither defined nor defended, even though it is absolutely central to the work: "The specific character of a period derives from the nature of its tasks. A period begins when its major tasks become predominant in a man's life. A period ends when its tasks lose their primacy and new tasks emerge to initiate a new period" (p. 53). Now the term *task* involves the notion of purpose. A person can undertake a task in the obvious sense of attempting to achieve a particular result. But Levinson is certainly not using the term in this way, for it is clear that there are many persons who do not consciously undertake the tasks that Levinson has defined as crucial. It is Levinson who supplies the material content of these tasks, although he wishes to be regarded as the discoverer, rather than the inventor, of "The order [that] exists at an underlying level" (p. 41). In short, the idea of a universal sequence of sequential purposes is simply asserted without any relevant evidence offered on its behalf.

Second, if we now ask for a description of "normal" development we discover it bears an uncanny resemblance to prevailing social ideology. We learn, for example, that "in all societies, a man is expected to marry and to take certain responsibilities within a familial system" (p. 45). Never mind that the meaning of such family obligations varies without end. The real point of Levinson's natural teleology is to legitimize the present family in advanced capitalism: "The family provides protection, socialization and support of growth during our pre-adult years. With adequate development, we can be relatively self-sufficient members of society as we enter adulthood" (p. 20). Independence, self-sufficiency, a range of choice and social exploration are the happy consequences of contemporary life, except, and this is the third important point, that these terms are so redefined as to serve the purpose of accommodation.

"Broadly speaking, a life structure is satisfactory to the extent that it is *viable in society* and *suitable for the self*" (p. 53). As we have no independent measure of what is suitable for the self, we are left with social viability as a guide. Since Levinson informs us that a transition period comes to an end "when the tasks of questioning and exploring have lost their urgency" (p. 52), are we to conclude that the individual has outgrown the need to question this society or that it is not socially viable to continue the exploration? Our "inner dreams and values" may not be "workable in the world." The burden lies with the individual to change in the face of this disparity.

> In the end, we must effect a reconciliation with the sources of the flaws and corruptions in our lives. The sources are multiple: they are in ourselves, in our enemies and loved ones, in the imperfect world where each of us tried to build a life of integrity. (p. 38)

Of course we may continue to fight for our convictions, but recall that the instinctual energy of our moral passion has peaked and begun its decline. Our task is to make peace with the world. After retirement, having paid our "dues to society," we are free to pursue the "interests that flow most directly from the depths of the self" (p. 36).

Finally, it is clear that the teleology Levinson asserts is a normative sequence in the sense that each task "may be carried out well or poorly" (p. 53). The criterion of judgment is the individual–social accommodation we have noted. But what are we to say of situations in which development does not occur?

> For large numbers of men, life in the middle years is a process of gradual or rapid stagnation, of alienation from the world and from the self. Severe decline and constriction are common enough so that they are often seen as part of normal middle age. In many populations, a good deal of decline is *statistically* normal in the sense that it occurs frequently. It is not, however, developmentally normal. Drastic decline occurs only when development has been impaired by adverse psychological, social and biological circumstances. (pp. 26–27)

Since nothing in Levinson's account ventures to indict society for any substantial failure in human development, the underlying recommendation can only be for a more productive assimilation on the part of the individual. This should be possible since society is benign and our underlying telos is toward growth; supposedly, we grow unless impeded. But why are we not free to reverse this teleology and contend that we stagnate or decay unless socially nurtured or that our normal tendency is toward neither fulfillment nor dehumanization except in so far as society elicits one or the other response from us?

The underlying task of Levinson's work is to protect society from criticism by implicitly accepting its basic structure while simultaneously indicting the individual and continuing to offer individual hope. This liberal project is accomplished by separating the telos of development from actual individual choices and then imposing upon the individual the obligation of recognizing "the fundamental task which human development requires." The entire enterprise comes to knowing, accepting, and accommodating to the ultimate rhythms of human existence:

> If conditions for development are reasonably favorable, and if impairments from the past are not too severe, middle adulthood can be an era of personal fulfillment and social contribution. *This requires, however, that a man come to terms with the developmental tasks* of Midlife Transition. (p. 27) [italics added]

Therefore, despite Levinson's previous contention that the move out of the preadult world consists in questioning "the nature of that world and one's place in it," the fact remains that ultimately choice consists in accepting or refusing the inexorable telos of social accommodation. Levinson does not note the bourgeois nature of the "effort to be more fully one's own person—to be more independent and self-sufficient, and less subject to the control of others" (p. 144). He therefore remains unaware of the manner in which capitalist individuality acts to sustain the social system in which individuals are defeated and pulverized. He has absolutely no sense of false consciousness as an affliction of liberal culture. When he comes to list the central concerns of a man's life—occupation, marriage and family, friendship and peer relationships, ethnicity and religion—he makes no reference to participation in the public realm of political action, social culture, or civic polity. The interests that Levinson ascribes to individuals are precisely those that constitute the privatization of contemporary life. His assertion that the most useful starting point for analysis is "to consider the choices a person makes" is perfectly predictable; it is the deepest strand of bourgeois ideology. The recognition of imposed social structures remains merely a gesture of intellectual courtesy. In his account of the "novice phase" of development Levinson describes the young man's alternatives: "In a technologically advanced, fragmented and changing society such as the United States, he has the advantage and burdens of greater choice. More options are available in his environment" (p. 76). Is this abstract telos that moves from preadulthood to adulthood the common universal archetype, or is one's concrete existence as upper-class patrician, ghetto black, working-class unemployed, or affluent professional intellectual of any account? In a fragmented society, has one the choice of wholeness; faced with constantly changing technological society, can one choose organic stability? Consider a contrasting reflection on the exigencies of development under capitalism:

> *Growth, like any ongoing function, requires adequate objects in the environment* to meet the needs and capacities of the growing child, boy, youth, and young

> man, until he can better choose and make his own environment. It is not a 'psychological' question of poor influences and bad attitudes, but an objective question of real opportunities for worthwhile experience. . . . Our abundant society is at present simply deficient in many of the most elementary objective opportunities and worthwhile goals that could make growing up possible. . . . It is lacking in honest public speech, and people are not taken seriously. It is lacking in the opportunity to be useful. It thwarts aptitude and creates stupidity . . . it has no Honor. It has no community. (Goodman, 1956, p. 12)

So Paul Goodman constructed an argument of considerable power showing that the difficulty lay not in the extent of choices, but precisely in the total absence of meaningful choice. But Levinson follows writers like Erikson who popularized the notion of "identity crisis" as a situation of existential commitment among viable possibilities. The fundamental question to be explored by contemporary social theorists of capitalist society is how the putative free choices of individual citizens emerge from and reconstitute the exploitation of the social order.

Levinson's obfuscation of social exploitation reaches its apogee in the following passage:

> However, the boyish self (which emerges in the late thirties) is also a source of opposition and discontent. He wants to attain great heights through magical omnipotence rather than the sweat of his brow. He wants things to go effortlessly his way, without wanting to consider the conflicting needs or requirements of others. When sufficient recognition is not forthcoming, the little boy feels totally deprived and humiliated. When a boss or other authority is restrictive or imposing, it is the little boy who feels utterly helpless and intimidated. The boyish self becomes the ingratiating sycophant, the ever-agreeable 'nice-guy' or the impulsive, self-defeating rebel—but not the persevering worker or the leader who uses his authority for constructive, humane ends. It is the little boy inside the man who transforms the ordinary mortals with whom he is involved—bosses, wives, mentors, colleagues—into tyrants, corrupters, villainous rivals, seducers and witches. (p. 146)

It would be difficult to construct a more invidious apology for capitalist dehumanization. A reductive Freudian ideology is harnessed to an arrogant, patronizing attack upon the victims of social exploitation. Despite the fact that capitalism thrives on the creation of fantasies of omnipotence, that millions of mystified laborers accede to every rule and are nevertheless crushed for their sacrifice, that a competitive structure forces the life plans of one individual to undermine the hopes of another, and that through the sweat of one's brow seeps the life blood of one's humanity, nurtured by the ideology of liberalism in a vain desire for humane fulfillment, Levinson can simply avert his gaze and join the forces of oppression. When bosses appear restrictive and imposing, since we know that bosses are in fact magnanimous and kind, we must look to a neurotic transference rooted in childhood. When powerlessness and the lack of human recognition lead to humiliation, we are not to consider this an appropriate response, but merely another manifestation of personal pathology. When irrational authority slowly reveals the ideals of bourgeois culture for their inverted truth, look to oedipal projections, infantile omnipotence, a childish rage against mature resignation. Look anywhere but in the face of power.

Death and the Accommodation of Despair

It is often the case that literature provides a truer picture of the human condition than does social science. Consider Albee's (1959) reflection on the American Dream:

> What I wanted to get at is the value difference between pornographic playing cards when you're a kid, and pornographic playing cards when you're older. It's that when you're a kid you use the cards as a substitute for a real experience, and when you're older you use real experience as a substitute for the fantasy. (p. 27)

The American dream is decomposing. Its credibility derives from the period of American expansion and international hegemony. From the earliest moments of this country's existence, its "manifest destiny" has been inseparably linked to a morally righteous crusade for world domination. Of course, the exercise of global power was justified through its ostensible liberation of backward peoples from their unfortunate barbarism. As we accumulated wealth and opportunity, the ideology of continual progress appeared self-evident; the progress of individual lives through an isomorphic development seemed equally obvious. But now, the basis of the dream is coming to an end: the dream unravels, producing anxiety, confusion, hatred, and retreat. Experience and fantasy pursue each other in endless rounds, each consuming the other in an insatiable regress. It is in this context that stage theory arises. As Berger and Luckman (1966) note:

> The symbolic universe also makes possible the ordering of the different phases of biography. In primitive societies the rites of passage represent this nomic function in pristine form. The periodization of biography is symbolized at each stage with reference to the totality of human meanings. To be a child, to be an adolescent, to be an adult, and so forth—each of these biographical phases is legitimated as a mode of being in the symbolic universe (most often, as a particular mode of relating to the world of the gods).

> We need not belabor the obvious point that such symbolization is conducive to feelings of security and belonging. It would be a mistake, however, to think here only of primitive societies. A modern psychological theory of personality development can fulfill the same function. In both cases, the individual passing from one biographical phase to another can view himself as repeating a sequence that is given in the 'nature of things,' or in his own 'nature.' That is, he can reassure himself that he is living 'correctly.' The 'correctness' of his life program is thus legitimated on the highest level of generality. As the individual looks back upon his past life, his biography is intelligible to him in these terms. As he projects himself into the future, he may conceive of his biography as unfolding within a universe whose ultimate co-ordinates are unknown. (pp. 99–100)

It is precisely the function of stage theory to teach us how to live correctly by rooting our conception of passage in the necessary sequences of our "nature." But our symbolic universe is not without its own gods—of expansion, progress, and accumulation.

What undermines security in our own time is that we can only look back on an intelligible past if we can believe in a continually more intelligible future. This is the weakness of the legitimizing myth of progress; no moment can grant satisfaction except in so far as it is placed between the preparation of the past and the consummation of the future—hence the relevance of the idea of sacrifice, as I have suggested. For if one toiled faithfully in the field of capitalist self-denial for some promised satisfaction which seemed always to elude one's grasp, if life were increasingly worn smooth by work, exhausted in monotony, pulverized by isolation, there was still the final solace: One could die believing that one's suffering was justified by the eventual success of one's children. Success is the god that redeems the unlived life. In the paradigmatic American nightmare, *Death of a Salesman,* Willy Loman exchanges his failure for the illusion of success. The means of this miraculous transubstantiation is the abstract exchange value of his insurance policy, which converts dead labor into the hope of life and in the process of being "redeemed," redeems its subject.

I have maintained that the contraction of capitalism permeates the life cycle of the self. Stage theory provides a personal itinerary, a dramaturgy of progress in the face of a growing sense of the meaninglessness of contemporary life. I believe that the same considerations apply as well to theories of infancy and childhood development. Prevailing interpretations map the requirements of capitalist character structure onto the phases of early life; isolation masquerades as separation–individuation, bureaucratization as ego adaptation, resignation as maturity, and the internalization of domination as self-determination. Object relations theorists ascribe to infants attributes that could not possibly characterize the rudimentary powers of such unformed lives but derive their plausibility from the apparent naturalness of their adult counterparts. One finds constant reference to the infant's omnipotence long before it can be credited with any meaningful conception of causality, hatred of the other before any conception of the other has emerged, primary narcissism when it is acknowledged that the infant still lacks a conception of its self, relations to other objects before any self–object relation can be conceptualized. The assumed necessary characteristics of adults are retrojected, in rudimentary form, into the conception of the infant's natural endowment. Thus, the specific form of capitalist competition—the need to differentiate, defend, and promote one's self against violent rivals for scarce supplies of material goods, meaningful relations, nurturance, and social esteem—is construed as a universal stage of individuation. But bourgeois individuation is an absolutely unique form of achieving social identity and has no counterpart among a large proportion of the world's cultures.

The final disgrace of stage theory is the flood of works on death. The notion that there is some universal sequence of stages in dying (see, for example, Kubler-Ross, 1969) is too preposterous to require more than passing scorn. Not only do diverse metaphysical and religious beliefs constitute different meanings of life and death in diverse cultures, but there are some social orders in which our notion of death is simply unintelligible. The point of these theories has really nothing to do with their cognitive validity. They must be understood from the perspective of their ideological function. They have a latent meaning that can be translated as follows: death is necessary; everything necessary must be accepted; the acceptance of necessity is natural, beautiful, and transcendent; if death can be accepted with grace, nothing that appears evil in life is beyond acceptance if not affirmation; if death can be regarded as the final fulfillment of life, the very notion of limitation is vaporized and other apparent indignities to the human spirit pale into insignificance.

The truth is that death extinguishes what is of potentially infinite value. There is no more truth than in Dylan Thomas's "Do Not Go Gentle into That Good Night." A society that exploits and disfigures so many of its members and then counsels acquiescence in the final destruction of their emaciated existence is worthy only of contempt. The current preoccupation with death arises less through a new honesty in dealing with a previously feared condition than it does through the prevailing despair that accompanies the growing conviction that the promise of life cannot be realized. There is consequently a great need for consolation. The new psychology takes up the anguish of dying to assure the victims that they have not lived in vain. Death can truly be accepted to the extent that life has been fulfilled. But the current ideology of graceful dying is the dirge of an embittered death that chooses even in the end to deny its painful truth.

References

Albee, E. (1959). *The zoo story.* New York: American Library.

Ariès, P. (1960). *Centuries of childhood.* New York: Vintage.

Ariès, P. (1976). *Western attitudes to death from the Middle Ages to the present.* London: Marion Boyars.

Berger, P. L., & Luckmann, T. (1966). *The social construction of reality.* New York: Doubleday.

De Toqueville, A. (1904). *Democracy in America.* New York: Appleton.

Goodman, P. (1956). *Growing up absurd.* New York: Random House.

James, W. (1902). *The varieties of religious experience.* New York: Modern Library.

Kubler-Ross, E. (1969). *On death and dying.* New York: Macmillan.

Levinson, D. T. (1978). *The seasons of a man's life.* New York: Ballantine Books.

Lichtman, R. (1981). Notes on accumulation, time and aging. *Psychology and Social Theory, 1,* 69–76.

Lichtman, R. (1982). *The production of desire.* New York: Free Press.

Marx, K. (1967). *Capital* (Vol. 1). New York: International Publishers. (Originally published 1867).

Mumford, L. (1934). *Technics and civilization.* New York: Harcourt, Brace and World.

Thompson, E. P. (1967). Time, work-discipline, and industrial capitalism. *Past and Present, 38,* 56–97.

Ward, J. (1920). *Psychological principles.* Cambridge: Cambridge University Press.

Weber, M. (1958). Science as a vocation. In H. H. Gerth & C. W. Mills (Eds.), *From Max Weber.* New York: Oxford University Press.

Chapter 6

Ed Elbers

CRITICAL PSYCHOLOGY AND THE DEVELOPMENT OF MOTIVATION AS HISTORICAL PROCESS

Marxist critics of psychology are more or less united in their judgment of the discipline. They reproach it for considering the individual as an ahistorical being and for not studying the relationship between the individual and the structure of society. Because of these defects they conclude that psychology, or a large part of it, is a component of the prevailing ideology, which they further criticize (using the Marxist concept of ideology) as a pillar of capitalist society.

Marxists, however, differ in their approach to the question of what a psychology without these defects would look like. Some of them advocate a psychology based directly on the writings of Marx himself. Others consider this an impossibility but demand nonetheless that a psychology must be in agreement with the basic anthropological and methodological premises of Marxism. These appeals to Marxism have produced many different—indeed, often incompatible—standpoints with regard to psychology. Goldmann (1959), for instance, felt that Piaget's work was very close to Marx's dialectical materialism, whereas Naville (1946) had the same idea about Watson's radical behaviorism. Between Reich and Althusser, there were three generations of Marxists who oriented themselves toward Freud. Others felt more drawn toward Pavlov. And more recently Vygotsky has been considered to be the foremost

Ed Elbers • Department of Psychonomics, Faculty of Social Sciences, Rijksuniversiteit Utrecht, P.O. Box 80.140, 3508 TC Utrecht, Netherlands.

Marxist psychologist. The question remains, however: Can there be such a thing as a Marxist psychology?

This question has been answered in the affirmative by a group of German Marxist psychologists, mostly active in West Berlin, whose aim it is to develop what they call a critical psychology within Marxism. The sparse attention they have received in the English-speaking world (Brandt, 1979; Stroebe, 1980; van IJzendoorn & Van der Veer, 1983, 1984) does not do justice to the originality of their ideas and even less to their productivity.[1] In forming his program for a Marxist psychology, Klaus Holzkamp—whose studies of the foundations of psychology have made him the foremost representative of the Berlin school of critical psychology—dissociates himself from a stereotyped image of Marxism. Holzkamp (1977a) writes that many Marxist psychologists contend that the individual's activities and consciousness are determined by the objective conditions of life. They repeat, true enough, one of the basic tenets of Marxist thinking but embrace therein only one aspect of human reality. Holzkamp claims that this viewpoint was in fact already criticized by Marx (1845, 1975) himself in the first thesis on Feuerbach, in which he states as an objection to the then prevailing forms of materialism "that the thing, reality, sensuousness, is conceived only in the form of the *object or of contemplation,* but not as *sensuous human activity, practice,* not subjectively" (p. 421). These Marxist psychologists criticized by Holzkamp lose sight of the fact that to a certain extent people themselves consciously create the objective conditions of their lives.

Holzkamp warns that this "subjective" aspect must not be interpreted as "individual." The reproduction of social life is a collective process. The subjects of the historical process are not separate individuals, but rather social forces that, in a class society, conflict. Holzkamp contends that a society can be characterized by the relationship that exists between objective and subjective determination of the social conditions of life, that is, the degree to which people are subject to their circumstances and the extent to which, cooperating as members of particular social groups or classes, they are masters of those circumstances. He maintains that individuals, by contributing as members of a particular social class toward controlling social life, can by the same token increase their hold on the conditions of their own lives.

Thus, Holzkamp characterizes as the object of Marxist theory the

[1]The only English publication of a member of the school of critical psychology is Keiler (1981).

relationship between objective and subjective determination of the historical process. The political aim of Marxist theory is the development of the subjective factor in history. The commitment of critical psychology, in particular, lies in developing the subjective component in individual life, the broadening of self-determination. As we shall see, the critical-psychological idea of self-determination stands apart from traditional conceptions of autonomy and independence because it stresses an individual's dependence on cooperation with others to form and organize the common conditions of life. It is therefore a nonindividualistic concept, consonant with the Marxist conception of the subjective determination of social life.

In this chapter, I do not so much wish to examine Holzkamp's claims as a Marxist, but rather the success of the theory in psychological terms. On the last page of a little book in which he collected his criticisms of modern psychology, Holzkamp (1972) announced that he would now turn from merely criticizing psychology to developing a critical psychology, which would comprise all the traditional fields of psychology. A year later, he first presented the functional-historical method as the method of critical-psychological investigation and applied it to the field of perception and cognition (Holzkamp, 1973). This study functioned as a paradigm that guided his pupils, who since then have published on such topics as language, thinking, motivation, socialization, and biological problems of psychology. These studies lack the encompassing character of Holzkamp's book on perception, with the exception of an extensive treatment of motivation by Ute Osterkamp (Holzkamp-Osterkamp, 1975, 1976), which, together with Holzkamp's publications, ranks among the major achievements of critical psychology. Osterkamp not only deals with motivation but also develops a theory of personality development, of the origins of psychic disturbances, and of psychotherapy. Throughout this chapter I will use Osterkamp's study on motivation as an example of critical psychology. I will begin by presenting the functional-historical method and the most important parts of the critical-psychological theory of motivation, and after that I will endeavor to evaluate them.

The Functional-Historical Method

The functional-historical method is based on the historical approach to psychological phenomena, originally proposed by the Russian psychologist A. N. Leont'ev (1959, 1973). This approach is based on the idea that the individual is the product of three histories: phylogenesis, the history of society, and ontogenesis. In line with the Marxist principle that to explain something means to understand its coming into being (Holzkamp & Schurig, 1973), psychology must invoke these three histories in the study of human personality.

Holzkamp changed Leont'ev's conception somewhat, first of all by assuming that a functionalist principle is at work in each of the three histories, which ensures that those psychic characteristics of living creatures remain that are advantageous for survival. In phylogenesis that means the survival of the species, and in both history and ontogenesis, the maintenance of social life. Second, Holzkamp prescribed exactly the steps that should be taken in a functional-historical analysis, which deviate in some respects from Leont'ev's formulation. The first step, the natural-historical analysis, comprises the study of the biological features of the human species. The second step establishes the psychological characteristics arising from the condition that people reproduce their existence in a society. (These characteristics are examined here in general terms without reference to specific social and historical circumstances.) In the third step, the various forms these characteristics assume in a concrete social situation are studied.

Each of these steps is equally essential, and the steps succeed each other in a logical sequence, the results of one step being used in the next. The first step, on its own, is insufficient. Osterkamp criticizes the champions of human ethology and sociobiology because they fail to make a distinction between natural-historical and social-historical development and thereby fail to recognize the need for the second and third steps. Osterkamp admits that, at first sight, the second step is problematic. People do not live in general social conditions, but always in specific ones. She regards this step, however, as a necessary abstraction. If we want to examine how psychological characteristics are influenced and deformed in capitalistic conditions, we must first of all have a conception of these characteristics. It is not primarily the biological traits that are repressed in a capitalist society, but rather those characteristics that ensue from life in a society. The second step, therefore, in which these social characteristics are distinguished from the purely biological, is an indispensable link in the chain.

Osterkamp's Theory of Motivation and Personality Development

In her study of human motivation, Osterkamp applies the three steps of the functional-historical method. In this section I will follow her line of thought and summarize the results of her analysis.

In a comprehensive reconstruction of the phylogenesis of the human species (the first step of analysis), she investigates the biological characteristics important for human motivation. In this respect, she is less concerned with physiological and morphological characteristics than with behavioral dispositions. Osterkamp bases her work principally on ethological studies (by Lorenz, among others) and endeavors to establish which tendencies become manifest in the course of human evolution. The fact that the capacities of animals to adapt to their environment increase in the course of natural history is considered by Osterkamp to be of central importance. The lower animal species are characterized by instinctively set reaction patterns, whereas the higher animals possess species-specific learning abilities and consequently a greater freedom in confronting the environment. The animal's ability to preserve its acquired experiences by learning makes it less vulnerable to the vicissitudes of the environment. Hand in hand with the increased learning capacities, curiosity and exploratory behavior develop, designed to lessen the unknown elements of the environment.

The activities that are functional in the avoidance of danger and in providing for primary needs develop at some time in natural history into what Osterkamp considers an independent need to control the environment. In this way, the need system is doubled. In addition to the elementary physiological needs (hunger, thirst, and sexual drives), a need to control the environment appears in the course of evolution, anchored genetically in the higher species. This need for control brings about social relationships that are independent of the reproductive function and that manifest themselves in the increased degree of organization of the animal group, in various forms of socialization, and even (in the case of higher animals) in the formation of traditions.

The qualitative change between natural and social history takes place in an area of transition between animal and man that is not precisely definable chronologically. The subhuman hominids were the first to intervene in their environment and to adapt it to their needs, rather than being adapted by it. The evolutionary advantages of this change were so great that the biological possibilities of intervening in the environment increased still further. The production and use of tools made possible the planned, collective, and cumulative changing of nature—that is, labor. For Osterkamp—following in Marx's footsteps—labor is the basis of life in any society, the specific means by which people exercise control of their environment and reproduce the conditions of their existence.

In Osterkamp's psychology, therefore, labor plays a central role. Separate individuals can guarantee their own conditions of life only by participating in the social labor process. Osterkamp stresses the close connection between individual and social existence, maintaining that to increase the collective control of social conditions automatically creates more possibilities for individuals to master their own circumstances. Labor is also the basis of historical and social development. In contrast to the experience of animals, which is lost when each individual dies, the experience of human individuals is reflected in the products of the social labor process: objects, symbols, technical procedures, class structures, cultural and social traditions. With the help of these, the experiences of one generation are passed on to the next.

In the second step of analysis, Osterkamp attempts to establish the consequences of the genesis of labor. In the first step, she inferred the biological characteristics that man shares with the higher species of animals (such as curiosity, need to control the environment, and social organization). These now have to be further determined in relation to labor. Although they form the natural basis for the functioning of the individual, their character changes in the context of life in a society. According to Osterkamp, the behavior patterns developed during the evolutionary process exist only as transformed in a society, mediated by the social labor process. Curiosity behavior, for instance, is reflected in conscious exploration of the environment in the context of safeguarding the collective existence and, in a later phase of history, in the scientific study of nature. The biological dispositions toward social behavior are transformed within society into cooperative relationships, relationships that have a bearing on the collective control of social life.

The social shaping of biological characteristics takes place in ontogenesis. Osterkamp (following here Leont'ev's psychology) characterizes the developmental process with the concept of *appropriation:* the individual appropriates a part of social experience. Children acquire skills and knowledge by which they strengthen their grip on their own conditions of life and by which, later on, they can contribute to the reproduction of society. The role of the adult in the development of a child lies in the transmission of cultural experience. By formulating expectations, making demands, imposing rules, and giving instruction, the educator assists children in acquiring various skills with which they can direct their lives in accordance with the possibilities available at a given time.[2] In the socialization process, the educators utilize the biological drives inborn in all children. Parents who want to teach their child to eat with a spoon—and using a spoon can be regarded as a form of control on life—will put a spoon in the child's hand and thereby play on the innate exploratory instinct and eagerness to learn. The parents, in this case, will also direct the child's hand and give appropriate instruction. Eventually, children no longer want to be fed, once they discover that by relying on themselves they become less dependent.

Osterkamp stresses the support that children need in their development toward greater mastery of their environment. Their abilities to control their own environment are still limited and, in their exercise of this limited degree of control, they remain dependent on the protection and help of their educators. Knowledge is a very important component of the skills that children develop, and learning to recognize and assess the possibilities of action forms part of the process of appropriation that educators guide. For these children, understanding the possibilities for expanding the grip on life, in combination with their basic productive motivation as human beings, leads directly to their willingness to use those possibilities.[3]

In ontogenesis, man's biological tendencies to control the environment are thus transformed and absorbed into skills and needs that are characteristic of the possibilities offered by society for giving purpose and shape to life. The process of appropriation generates *productive* needs and abilities, as Osterkamp calls them. The term "productive" is an awkward choice because of its strong association with the process of

[2]To conceptualize the crossing point of individual and society, Osterkamp uses the concept of *forme d'individualité*, which she borrows from Sève (1972). A form of individuality is a matrix of activities (subject to historical change) that must necessarily be carried out for the preservation of society and which in the course of time have been summarized in one profession, social function, or position. The development of personality can be understood as the integration of an individual in one or more forms of individuality. Both Sève and Osterkamp use this concept only to carry out analyses of a global kind (e.g., the form of individuality of the wage-laborer) but make no historical analyses of concrete individuals or social groups. As it is formulated now, the concept of form of individuality appears to add nothing to the theory of appropriation and cultural transmission. Therefore, I will not dwell on it in the text.

[3]Osterkamp's theory can be classified as a cognitive theory of motivation (see Madsen, 1974).

industrial production. Productive needs and abilities, however, have to do with the control of the conditions of life in a wider context, which includes social areas such as labor, science, technology, and politics. Next to the productive needs, Osterkamp places the "sensory-vital" needs, conceptualized as the needs for rectifying physical deficiencies and stress conditions of the body. The sensory-vital needs have a homeostatic character; they occur, in other words, when an equilibrium is disturbed. Osterkamp subdivides the sensory-vital needs into sexual needs and organic needs (for food, regulation of body temperature, and so on). In these two motivational systems (productive and sensory-vital needs) which, according to Osterkamp, human beings possess, we see the twofold need system characteristic of higher animals repeated at the human level.

There is a close connection between sensory-vital and productive needs. The material conditions for satisfying the sensory-vital needs are created within the social production process. The satisfaction of sensory-vital needs therefore demands the development of a willingness and capacity to participate in the production process, that is, the development of productive needs and capabilities. Because the production of means of satisfying the sensory-vital needs is open to historical change, it follows that these needs themselves are, to a certain extent, open to change. We do not satisfy our hunger by eating raw meat but prepare our food in a way that fits the dictates of our culture. Nevertheless, the objects at our disposal for satisfying the sensory-vital needs are to a greater or lesser extent fixed, and therefore Osterkamp regards the possibilities of extending the sensory-vital needs as being very limited. That which is specific to human motivation does not lie in the refinement of sensory-vital gratifications, but in coming to terms with a fortuitous and uncontrolled existence through the development of productive capacities and needs.

Now we come to the third step in the functional-historical analysis. What are the motivational characteristics of human beings living in a capitalist society? Osterkamp states that the individual appropriation of social experience in this society has a double and conflicting character, in line with the contradictions within capitalist society. Capitalism exercises a greater degree of control over physical and social reality than has ever been exercised before in any kind of society. Control of natural processes by science and technology, in particular, has expanded enormously. Compared to this, the process of social development is in a state of anarchy because of the fact that to a large extent it has been left to private enterprise and to competition between economic forces. The development of abilities and corresponding needs in children bears the mark of these contradictions.

In the socialization process, the child is set on the road to perform a function in capitalist society, with the result that some abilities are given extra stimulus while others are curtailed. Osterkamp maintains that the abilities most people develop lag behind the level of control that could be reached given the possibilities inherent in a capitalist society. Abilities are developed only to the extent that they contribute to the preservation of the prevailing class structure. The majority of the population may and must make a contribution toward the reproduction of society but is excluded from fundamental decisions about society and therefore about their own conditions of life. In the process of socialization, for instance, the members of the laboring classes appropriate all kinds of useful technical abilities, but without developing at the same time those abilities that would enable them to participate in major decisions about the aims of society.

In order to analyze this restricted socialization process, Osterkamp examines the child's interaction with educators and teachers in the process of development. The effects of education cannot, in her view, be understood sufficiently by a social learning interpretation which uses principles like imitation, instruction, reward, and punishment, because it does not explain why people are prepared to accept a lower degree of control than is in principle possible given the social means available. Therefore, Osterkamp develops a psychodynamic theory of the development of personality, in an extensive commentary on the work of Freud. She agrees with Freud that conflicts and coming to terms with them play a central role in the development of the personality, but she has a different conception of the structure of these conflicts and of their consequences for the individual.

In the developmental process, conflicts arise as a result of the demands that educators make on children, in the form of rules and expectations. In the early years of childhood, the sensory-vital and productive needs are, as yet, comparatively unconnected. The parents respond immediately to eating, drinking, clothing, washing needs, and so on, but before long they expect the child to assist in planning and regulating the gratification of these. Because the child does not have much experience in regulating the sensory-vital needs and has learned only few means by which to gratify them, the parents' demand to regulate them can be overwhelming. Typical conflict situations can then arise, for instance, around toilet training and table manners.

The conflict situations that Osterkamp describes here resemble in many ways the struggle between the pleasure principle and the reality principle in psychoanalysis. She assumes, however, that such conflicts can be dealt with in a positive way when the parent is able to make it clear to children that the rules of behavior are in their own interests because observance of the rules enables them to increase their grip on the conditions of their lives. When the educator is able to convince the children that the instructions are useful, he or she appeals to their productive needs, so that the children can then overcome the conflict and, productively motivated, accept the educator's wishes. The most important condition for coping with these kinds of developmental conflicts, on the child's part, is therefore to understand that carrying out the instruction in question will improve control over the conditions of life and by the same token make the child more independent.

In a society in which the majority of the population takes no part in the most important decision-making process regarding social life, not every demand that an adult makes on children results in their becoming more independent. Some of the demands made in fact are intended precisely to deter them from exercising a greater control over their circumstances. In these cases educators are not able to make the purpose of an instruction clear to children and can therefore only impose it by force. This enforcement consists of punishment or threats to withhold practical and emotional assistance. The children's only way out of these conflicts is to suppress their own impulses and, in conformity with the commands of the adults, to regard them as unjust or morally wrong. Osterkamp believes that repressing conflicts in this way can result ultimately in a permanent tendency to stop questioning the underlying reasons for adult demands and to accede to them immediately. The children internalize the adults' external compulsion and exercise this as internal coercion against themselves. They learn to condemn and suppress their behavioral impulses of their own accord and voluntarily accept the rules laid down by adults. Osterkamp speaks of an internal control mechanism that, because of its close affinity to Freud's theory (to which I will return later), she calls the *superego*.

Another kind of conflict that Osterkamp describes is characteristic not only of children but also of adults. Conflicts arise when individuals want to increase their influence over their own lives but are impeded by the environment. This kind of situation arises when, for instance, a child's increased capacities outgrow the scope allowed him or her by the parents. The environment thus blocks further development of the productive capabilities and needs. In order not to jeopardize the support of the adults, the child has no other choice but to accede to the conditions laid down by the parents or educators. This leads to a reinforcement of the superego. Adults, too, meet this kind of situation, which, according to Osterkamp, is common in a capitalist society. The absence of opportunity to give conscious shape to social life limits the possibilities of the individual to act. Individuals, productively motivated to arrange their lives as they see fit, find themselves confronted with a dilemma: they must either accommodate themselves to and accept the controls available or go against the tide and try to increase those controls. In the latter case, they run a risk of losing more than they gain. Workers can come face to face with this kind of dilemma, for instance, when agitating for more democracy in their factory. If this leads to dismissal, they have not only failed to achieve their goal but, once unemployed, are left with even fewer possibilities of control.

In such situations, the handling of conflicts requires developing means to act in a cooperative manner. The risks attached to critical aspirations can be overcome only within a collective group. The individual is powerless against capitalist society. Workers who advocate workers' control can reduce the risks involved and increase their chances of success by operating within a trade union. Osterkamp therefore considers the organized workers' movement an important social force toward increasing control over social conditions and thus also toward contributing to positive solutions of psychic conflicts.

In this way, Osterkamp reinterprets the psychoanalytic concept of the *superego*. She makes use of the term "superego", for want of a better one. Nevertheless, we must not lose sight of the wide difference between the two interpretations of the concept. Osterkamp regards superego development as resulting from failure to deal with conflicts in situations wherein it is in principle possible to cope with them in a positive way. In Freud's work, subjects in the Oedipus situation have no alternative but to suppress their own impulses; the desire for love is exchanged for an identification with the demands and prohibitions of the parents. In Freud's view, individuals can participate in social life only on condition that they renounce their libidinous longings. But in Osterkamp's version, instead of being a necessary consequence of socialization, the superego is a symptom of *unsuccessful* socialization: the subjects accommodate themselves blindly to uncomprehended demands from authorities and so reconcile themselves to a situation of dependence in which they act in a way expected of them from others and not because such behavior is in their own interest. What is for Freud a general human conflict, a fate, is for Osterkamp something that only appears in a social context in which the integration of the individual in cooperative relationships is hampered, as is the case in a capitalist society.

Osterkamp's interpretation of the development of personality is built on these ideas. As the child gets older, under the influence of conflict experiences, a personality structure develops that, as time goes by, will play an increasingly important part in the way the child reacts to conflict situations. The conditions that determine a positive or negative outcome of a conflict situation lie initially beyond the child himself or herself. They are situational conditions, such as the degree to which the educators are able to make the purpose of their rules clear to the child, the prevailing pedagogical ideologies, the objective possibilities for developing productive abilities, and the degree to which the educators themselves are able to influence their own conditions of life. Developmental conflicts and their positive or negative outcomes precipitate personality traits and continue, as such, to play a role. In favorable circumstances, a personality can develop that is able to cope adequately with conflicts. Such a person exercises a certain control over the conditions of life and by joining others in cooperative relationships can increase his or her control. Unfavorable circumstances can, however, cause a strong superego to develop, in which the inclination to avoid conflicts gains the upper hand and in which defensive tendencies stand in the way of the individual's ability to react adequately to conflict situations. The causes of failure to cope with conflicts thus shift in ontogenesis from external causes to personality characteristics. Social repression is internalized and becomes a personality trait. Unlike Freud, who believed that the experiences in the first years of an individual's life are of decisive significance for the rest of life, Osterkamp does not limit the period in which the personality develops to the first phase of life. She speaks rather of a lifelong process.

Osterkamp differs with Freud over the nature of defense mechanisms. Whereas, in Freud's theory, they are purely individual strategies of the ego used to conjure away conflicts, according to her they are social mechanisms, transmitted by culture, through which critical ideas and impulses are repressed. They are ideologies and attitudes of mind that prohibit critical questions, for example, the idea that society is unchangeable, which is a central element of bourgeois ideology. Osterkamp localizes these ideological defense mechanisms in the superego because they can be regarded as social norms and prohibitions with which the person identifies himself or herself. Individuals use these mechanisms of their own accord to repress conflicts between the need to increase their control over their own existence and the environment that allows them only limited control. Real possibilities for increasing the capacity to act are barred from their consciousness, with the result that they become insecure, increasingly unable to weigh the risks of their behavior, and increasingly guilty about their critical impulses. They reconcile themselves to an existence in dependency.

Comparison with Other Psychological Theories

When we compare Osterkamp's theory of productive needs with other theories of motivation, its strength becomes apparent. Superficially, the idea of productive needs bears a resemblance to current conceptions of motivation in psychology. The ego psychologists, beginning with Hartmann, criticized Freud's pessimistic vision of man as being dominated by the dark forces of the unconscious. Hartmann assumed the existence of an autonomous and conflict-free ego, developing independently of the id (Fine, 1979, p. 339). The humanistic psychologists, Rogers and Maslow, also opposing Freud's ideas, shared the view that human behavior is motivated by an "actualization tendency" (Weiner, 1980, p. 411). In developmental psychology, one also finds concepts referring to control over the environment. Kagan (1979a), for instance, puts forward a motive for resolving uncertainty and a motive for mastery by way of explaining the behavior of children.

Osterkamp's view differs from all these concepts in two ways. In the first place, she deduces the existence of productive needs from a functional-historical analysis, by retracing the origins of the double motivational system in the evolution of the human species, rather than simply postulating them. By appealing to evolutionary evidence, she avoids merely presenting lists of motives, a feature that renders many theories of motivation somewhat arbitrary. The second, and more fundamental, difference is that the productive needs are not anthropological constants, but historically specific. Their form and the way they are expressed are dependent on how the society organizes and reproduces the capacities of individuals, and they are consequently subject to historical change. This implies, by the same token, that the possibilities for realization of the productive needs are dependent on the social conditions and the means offered by that society to exercise control over existence. In theories of the autonomous ego, personal growth, and the mastery motive, individuals depend only on their own powers, whereas in Osterkamp's theory it is quite rightly suggested that the individual's potential to develop cannot be separated from the collective means of influencing the course of society and the possibilities for associating with others to control social, and therefore individual, conditions of existence. Thus, in critical psychology, "being autonomous" has the meaning of associating with others to control and change the collective conditions of life. This nonindividualistic conception of mastery and control distinguishes her theory from current psychological conceptions of autonomy and self-reliance.

Moreover, Osterkamp's theory is very much in accordance with modern psychological research on early development—a source of support, in fact, that she does not utilize sufficiently. Most present-day developmental psychologists assume that babies and young children turn spontaneously toward the world and positively enjoy their growing capacity to involve the environment in their activities. It was only from about the 1960s that this standpoint became influential, although it was first introduced by Piaget (1936). Piaget is recognized at present as the main inspiration for current infant psychology (Kagan, 1979b; Yarrow, 1979). He observed the interactions of babies with their physical environment and explained sensori-motor development and the origins of intelligence as an intrinsically motivated assimilating activity. Schaffer (1971) demonstrated that social responses are also based on spontaneous motivation, rooted in the baby's perceptual preference for social stimuli. Freud's supposition that sociability is a secondary drive, based on a baby's physical dependence, is no longer tenable. On the basis of this, both Piaget and Schaffer reject the psychoanalytic theory of the development of babies.

In one respect, however, Osterkamp is closer to Freud than to the modern developmental psychologists. Like Freud, she assumes that children's behavior must be regulated by their educators and that the transmission of social rules gives rise to conflicts. This viewpoint shields her from the overoptimistic attitudes advocated by some developmental psychologists (e.g., Trevarthen, 1980) on the subject of the social capacities of babies[4] and prevents her from exchanging the concept of socialization for the presupposition of a preestablished harmony between the baby and its social world (as, for example, in Ainsworth, Bell, & Stayton, 1974). Osterkamp gives an affirmative answer to the question of whether children are social beings at birth, although she does not regard the social reactions of babies as truly human. The innate social responses have to be restructured as the child moves into cooperative relationships, the most important aspect of which is the gaining of control over the situation. In these cooperative relationships, biologically determined impulses are transformed into truly human productive needs by the acquisition of skills. In the course of this restructuring process, which, on the one hand, is called "appropriation" when referring to the child, and, on the other hand, "the transmission of cultural experience" when referring to the educators, a biological being becomes a member of society. Because modern developmental psychology does not investigate the cultural shaping of innate reactions, it remains largely at the biological level.[5]

Osterkamp's reinterpretation of the superego as the result of failed socialization offers a way out of the problem that many left-wing psychoanalysts have been battling with for many years. Freud assumed a fundamental opposition between individual and society, man's natural instinct being hostile to society. In the socialization process, the needs of children are increasingly frustrated by their educators. Children are compelled to curb their instincts because they cannot be reconciled with life in a social context. This leads to the development of the superego in which the rules of the society are internalized. In his *Civilisation and Its Discontents,* Freud (1930/1961) was very pessimistic about the struggle for social and political change because he assumed that every society is based on suppressing natural instincts, the inevitable consequence of which is suffering. Left-wing Freudians found themselves confronted by the dilemma of how they could accept this theory and at the same time join in the struggle for social change. Reich attempted to solve the prob-

[4]See the discussion by Ingleby (Chapter 7 in this volume).

[5]Since 1979, Holzkamp and his colleagues have been carrying out a longitudinal investigation of early childhood development. Their aim is to study the development of cooperative relationships between parents and children and to examine the conditions under which their opposite—merely social relations in which a common perspective is lacking—arise. Until now, Holzkamp (1979) has only announced the existence of the project, without publishing results.

lem by simply denying that there is any basic conflict between individual and society (Robinson, 1969). According to his theory, the sexual drives of the id are healthy and normal and provide the basis for social life. The political and economic characteristics of Western culture inhibit sexual gratification and for that reason lead to neuroses. Marcuse (1966; cf. Robinson, 1969, pp. 147–244) drew a distinction between "basic" and "surplus" repression, recognizing thereby that life in a society requires at least a minimum of repression. All repression in excess of that minimum is the fault of various forms of political domination. When economic exploitation ceases, he argued, life will take on a genuinely erotic quality.

Reich and Marcuse share in common with Freud the belief that the sexual drives are the most important ones in human beings. Osterkamp, however, tries to show that the structure of human motivation comprises two systems: the sensory-vital (which embraces the sexual needs) and the productive. Humans, by their very nature, are oriented toward life in a society, but society can only be explained by reconstructing the genesis of needs for cooperative control of the environment in the course of human evolution. There is no fundamental conflict between individual and society. Development is not the curtailment, but rather the unfolding of productive and sensory-vital needs by the appropriation of social reality. The fact that certain social circumstances impede this development is no reason to assume that it is an inevitable result of the clash between human nature and society.

Is a Principle of Functionality Essential in Historical Analysis?

Despite the interesting suggestions Osterkamp's writings permit with reference to these divergent problem areas, not all elements of the critical-psychological enterprise can, in my view, survive the test of criticism. The basic idea of investigating psychological phenomena as the outcome of three histories—phylogenesis, the history of society, and ontogenesis—is a most important suggestion. But the way in which Holzkamp and Osterkamp carry out this project, by looking at the historical development of psychological characteristics in the light of their functionality, spoils some of the effect.

Let us have a closer look at this principle of functionality, which represents the materialist premise of Marxism in critical psychology (Jäger, 1977). The aim of the functional-historical analysis is to explain the origin of psychological phenomena by their functionality for the preservation of life. Functionality has, of course, not the same connotation in the three histories. In phylogenesis, being functional means contributing to the preservation of the species; in the history of society the functionalist principle applies to the survival of social life; in ontogenesis it pertains to the maintenance of individual existence through participation in the cooperative control of society.

It is plausible that functional analyses can be carried out in investigations of the biological characteristics of the human species, and Osterkamp's description of the development of two need systems in the course of evolution is a convincing cornerstone of her theory of motivation. In fact, in this sense, a functionalist principle forms the basis of the Darwinian theory of evolution, which Osterkamp therefore employs. But as a means to study the development of psychological characteristics in history or in ontogenesis it appears to me hard to defend.

To regard psychological phenomena as products of a continuous social effort to expand control over the circumstances of the existence of a society, and to consider them functional for that control, is a risky hypothesis that may blind us to the manifold and complex motives and intentions of human action in history. Strangely enough, although Holzkamp and Osterkamp prescribe an historical analysis, they can be reproached with a lack of real interest in human history. The changes that Holzkamp made in Leont'ev's historical approach in fact result in a phylogenesis–ontogenesis scheme, from which history has fallen away. After studying the biological aspects of man and after determining man's general characteristics as a member of society, an examination is made of the transformation of those general human characteristics in ontogenesis under capitalist conditions. Hardly any attention is given to the history of society and to psychological changes that may have occurred in the course of history. The only change in man's history subjected to deeper analysis is the animal–man transformation period in which the human species evolved. In contrast to this, capitalism is considered almost from a structuralist viewpoint as a social formation with fixed and unique characteristics and not as a historically changing phenomenon in itself. In her books on motivation, Osterkamp gives little sign of being interested in the changes that have taken place within bourgeois society. She connects psychological phenomena directly with capitalism as a social structure. Distinctions such as "early" versus "late" capitalism do not appear in her work.[6] This overschematic view of history in critical psychology is also evident from the absence in the writings of Holzkamp and Osterkamp of any trace of interest in historical-psychological and cross-cultural research.

For the study of ontogenesis, too, the functional principle appears problematic. The critical psychologists do not contend that the development of each separate individual is functional but argue, as Holzkamp (1973) argues, that we can explain the survival of social life only if we presuppose that human beings on the average possess psychological characteristics that are functional for that survival. This process is functional for an individual only indirectly in so far as the survival of the individual is dependent on the continued existence of society. Of course, some human characteristics must be functional, but both contemporary history and clinical psychology show the important role played in the socialization process by all kinds of traditions, patterns of upbringing, social norms, and ideals, which by all means can be dysfunctional. In fact, how can the genesis of a superego in the middle classes, as described by Osterkamp, be reconciled with functionality? The superego is perhaps functional for the survival of capitalist society, but certainly not for the maintenance of human life in general (Verbij, 1981; Meeus & Raaijmakers, 1984). Holzkamp's argument proves neither that functional elements are predominant nor that functionality must be a basic assumption of the critical-psychological method. Rather, the functionality of the psyche is itself an historical entity and the amount of functionality of human behavior in various social and economic circumstances and in different social groups could be an object of interest for radical psychological research. In my view, critical psychology should abandon the functionalist principle as a postulate for its method. Rather than pressing phylogenesis, the history of society, and ontogenesis into the strait-jacket of one unitary method, each step in the historical analysis should have its own method.

[6]There is a group of critical psychologists of labor involved in the study of technological changes of the last few decades and their consequences for society (Haug *et al.*, 1975), but their findings have not had any impact so far on Osterkamp's theory of motivation.

Can Affective Relationships Be Reduced to Cooperation? Some Comments on Osterkamp's Theory of Psychic Disturbances and Therapy

Although Osterkamp's emphasis on the cooperative aspect of many social relationships contrasts favorably with the cultivation of unmediated interpersonal relationships in modern psychology, she exaggerates by making cooperation the basis of every real social relation. She places merely social relationships, which do not contribute to broadening the collective control of society, in opposition to cooperative relationships. Every affective relationship that is not rooted in cooperation is regarded as regression to a prehuman level. In my opinion, it is a mistake to play off these two forms of social relationship against each other in this way. Human relationships do not allow themselves to be reduced totally to the collective reproduction of life in the labor process. A whole area of social exchange—in distinct paradigms called "object relations," attachment," or "affective relations"—is rendered invisible. This one-sidedness of the theory is closely connected with the equally limited view of society prevalent in critical psychology. Osterkamp neglects superstructural phenomena and places labor at the core. However, human social life is not *only* control and labor, unless one regards expressions like music, sport, and literature as coming under this heading. Osterkamp views mankind too much from the point of view of work, cooperation, and politics and too little from the point of view of play, social interaction, and culture. The limitation of this viewpoint is nowhere clearer than in the critical-psychological interpretation of psychic disturbances and psychotherapy.

Osterkamp's (1978) view of psychic disturbances follows naturally from her interpretation of the superego. The total or partial paralysis of the ability for adequate action in cases of psychic disturbance is nothing more than a further impediment of the control possibilities that already have been curtailed by the superego. As a result of a history of failure to cope with conflicts, an accumulation of defense tendencies can arise in individuals through which they increasingly lose control over their environment and develop a predisposition to meet tensions with disturbed behavior.

Holzkamp and Osterkamp (1977) use this idea to interpret the problems of an adolescent boy, Lothar, who was treated by the therapist

Kappeler, who has similar ideas. In interpreting the development of the boy and the background of his neurotic problems, they dismiss interpretations that place in the center events of a personal nature: in Lothar's case, the death of his mother at his birth, his upbringing by his grandmother, the death of this grandmother when he was 6 years old, and the second marriage of his father. Chance events like these, they say, do not reach the human level of specificity; the psychic health of young chimpanzees can also be injured by the death of a mother. Therefore, they claim, such events are unsuitable to explain tendencies to avoid confrontations with the environment or to renounce the control of existence. On the contrary, they propose to explain psychic disturbances in terms of a life history in which cooperative relationships and productive skills could not be developed. Tragic events such as Lothar experienced should be regarded only as aggravating factors that play a role of secondary importance. Then they attempt to make Lothar's problematic behavior plausible by pointing to objective conditions of his situation: the class position of his father, who climbed up from worker to civil servant, his resulting petit-bourgeois ideology, the limited financial resources of the family, and the authoritarian school system.

It seems difficult to justify this attempt to explain a psychic distrubance solely in terms of the social characteristics of a life history and to consider only as aggravating factors events such as the death of the grandmother who brought the boy up. Surely, the opposite would be more plausible: the seriousness of the loss of an attachment figure is dependent on the socially determined characteristics of a family. There is some, although not unequivocal, evidence, that the death of a loved person for a child in a culture in which the extended family is the rule rather than the exception and in which many adults take it upon themselves to care for the child is easier to cope with and less likely to leave traumatic scars than in the Western world where the nuclear family predominates with the mother as the central figure.[7] The critical psychologists' fixation on cooperative relationships inhibits them from attaching to psychic phenomena a relative autonomy with regard to social labor and thereby seriously weakens their theory.

The same is also true of their concept of therapy. Because Osterkamp regards mental disturbance as a serious lessening of the ability to act, the purpose of critical-psychological therapy is to help the client

[7]The influence of cultural practices and family conditions on the process of mourning is discussed succinctly by Bowlby (1981). Alas, he gives only a little cross-cultural evidence.

to recover a conscious and active control over his or her life. As always in Osterkamp's work, this conscious influence over the conditions of one's own life means participation in the collective control of society. By defining the purpose of the therapy in this way, Osterkamp distances herself from the psychoanalytic concept of therapy in which understanding and the working out of problems from the past lie at the heart of the matter. According to her, the closed and private character of the psychoanalytic therapy situation, in which a client's mentioning of social and political problems is usually interpreted as defense, is totally unsuitable to help the client to determine again the course of his or her own life. Therapy in the critical-psychological conception is not regarded as a form of treatment, and therapeutic discussions are of minor significance. On the contrary, the client is directed toward the normal life situation outside the therapy, and therapy itself is given the function of preparing the ground for the client's everyday life and of evaluating it. In the course of therapy, therapist and client examine together the control possibilities that are present in the client's situation. The client's task is then to make use of these possibilities in actual terms, for which insight is a first requirement. Moreover, it may be necessary to introduce and practice various skills within the course of the therapy.

Osterkamp assigns only a minor role to the emotional aspects of the client's problems and to his or her emotional development during the course of the therapy. The client's emotional life plays a role principally during the diagnostic stage. Emotional expressions are regarded as expressions of the client's inability to control his or her life consciously and serve therefore as a useful source of information about the nature of his or her relationship with the environment. Osterkamp appears to attach little importance to the working through of conflicts from the past that have left their emotional marks on the individual. She seems to assume that insights into new possibilities for action automatically precipitate a restructuring of the client's emotional life. The relationship between therapist and client is also not analyzed as above all an emotional relationship. Osterkamp offers no theory of transference, and she considers identification of the client with the therapist as a hindrance to recovery. Contrary to the neutral character of psychoanalytic therapy, she demands a partiality from the therapist in the "therapeutic alliance" which entails that the therapist help the client with advice and with moral and practical support in his or her efforts to come to grips with existence. In the course of therapy, the cooperative relationship between therapist and client must give way to cooperative relationships outside therapy.

In order to overcome their isolation, clients must be integrated again into social relationships. According to Osterkamp, cooperation is a prerequisite for a successful therapy. For instance, Holzkamp and Osterkamp regard Lothar's participation in the college students' opposition, which made a great noise in Berlin at that time, as a really important step forward in the boy's developmental process. By contrast, Lothar's love relationship with a girl friend who helped him to conquer his solitude is considered to be only of secondary importance.

To sum up, in this conception of therapy one finds an emphasis on cooperative rather than affective relationships. Nevertheless, Osterkamp's insistence on cooperative relationships has its merits, too. In contrast with most forms of therapy—the here-and-now demands of Gestalt therapy, the pragmatism of behavioral therapy, the apolitical character of most psychoanalytic therapy—the relativization of what can be accomplished by a therapeutic treatment is refreshing. Reintegration of the client into cooperative relationships can certainly be a necessary condition of successful therapy. There are some problems in the face of which a therapist can do little: for instance, the difficulties of mothers of small children isolated in the city, or depression among the unemployed. Feminist groups striving for the availability of day-care centers and labor unions may have more to offer here than a therapist, unless he or she is prepared to induce people to acquiesce in their fates.

The Relationship to Mainstream Psychology

How does critical psychology regard its relationship to mainstream psychology? As a means of overcoming the arbitrary and disintegrated theory formation characteristic of current psychology, Holzkamp (1977b) makes a strong plea for the functional-historical method. However, he does not discard the many theories and approaches in modern psychology as of no value but feels that in many cases their findings could be incorporated into the more comprehensive psychological theory that the critical psychologists are developing with their own method. For this reason, Holzkamp and Osterkamp devote space in their writings to appraisals (albeit short) of Piaget, Gibson, Gestalt psychology, behaviorism, and so on. Then they come to the conclusion that most of the theories are not so much untenable as valid in much more restricted circumstances than their supporters would suppose. The criticism leveled by critical psychology at other theories is thus directed towards demonstrating their limited validity and to rejecting their exaggerated claims of universality.

Therefore, it pays to dwell more closely on Osterkamp's criticism of Freud, the only thorough assimilation by critical psychology of mainstream ideas.[8] Osterkamp expects that critical psychology can, on the one hand, benefit from the insights into human subjectivity and into the problems of human relationships gathered in psychoanalysis and, on the other hand, distinguish between what is fruitful in Freudian theory and what is not. An analysis of Osterkamp's critique of Freud reveals three aspects:

1. A number of elements of the psychoanalytic theory are rejected as being scientifically untenable, for instance, Freud's drive theory and his socialization theory. The drive theory is replaced by the theory of the two need systems, and Freud's socialization theory is rejected in favor of the theories of appropriation and transmission of cultural experience.

2. Some concepts are subjected to reinterpretation within the confines of critical psychology. Let us take the superego as an example. Osterkamp criticizes the superego theory because of its ahistorical character. The superego, *à la* Freud, is an ahistorical concept because it is rooted in the drive theory, which presumes the active presence of general human drive impulses in every individual. By disconnecting the superego from the drive theory and relating it to her own motivation theory, she is able to interpret it as the residue of failed conflict resolution in certain concrete historical and social circumstances.

3. Finally, Osterkamp wonders that psychoanalysis, for all its faults and inadequacies, is nonetheless still able to reflect so adequately the subjective problems of individuals in a bourgeois society. Her answer is that in certain historical circumstances some of Freud's analyses are valid; Freud's superego theory, for instance, is appropriate to members of the middle class in a capitalist society. It is true that Freud incorrectly regards the development of a superego as a condition of, rather than a hindrance to, participation in social life, but his ideas on the working of the superego and its function in the development of psychic disturbances are correct.

This constructive view of mainstream theories distinguishes critical psychology from Marxist critics who see psychology only as an ideology

[8]Strangely enough, though, in her reflection on psychoanalysis, Osterkamp confines herself solely to the work of Freud. Without any argument she claims that all divisions and revisions within the psychoanalytic camp have been steps backward and that all attempts to integrate Freud's ideas into psychological theories of personality have failed.

in varying disguises and refuse to consider the degree of plausibility of the various psychological theories to be worthy of further study.

However, in formulating their own theories, the critical psychologists are curiously indifferent to empirical evidence collected by other researchers. Up to the present time, the development of the theory has taken place only at a theoretical level. I propose absolutely no objection to theoretical work, but there must be some systematic link with empirical material, if only to bridle a propensity to speculation. It is not without reason that the theory of the two need systems is so successful. This theory arose from extensive analyses of ethological research. The theories of psychic conflicts, psychic disturbances, and therapy, however, suffer from a lack of clinical evidence. The fact that Osterkamp has no experience as a therapist is not the most important objection. She could always have made use of the research findings and case histories of others, not only as sources of inspiration but also as tests for her own theory. There is also a total lack of data on the social epidemiology of psychic disturbances, which Osterkamp could have used to elucidate her theory.

Conclusion

To conclude, let me summarize my answer to the question: How valuable is critical psychology?

1. The idea of an historical approach in psychology is an important contribution. Holzkamp's connection of the historical method to a functionalist principle, however, is neither convincing nor essential for a historical study of the human psyche. Moreover, the changes that Holzkamp made in Leont'ev's original formulation of an historical approach in psychology lead to neglecting historical-psychological and cross-cultural psychological phenomena. Holzkamp's historical method, paradoxically, is not historical enough.

2. Nevertheless, Holzkamp and Osterkamp have succeeded in developing some psychological concepts in which an historical dimension is incorporated and which emerge favorably from a comparison with traditional ideas in psychology. In the first place, there is the theory of the two need systems and of the historical character of the needs and capabilities that individuals develop, which is an alternative to both sociobiological and psychological theories of motivation, including psychoanalysis. The concept of the superego as the result of failed socialization in specific historical circumstances is a powerful suggestion counter

to Freud's commitment to the idea of a natural conflict between individual and society, of which the superego is supposedly the inevitable outcome. The theories of appropriation and cultural transmission can certainly stand comparison with traditional theories of socialization and with modern criticisms of the idea of socialization. In addition, the non-individualistic interpretation of autonomy comprises an original critique of modern ideas of self-reliance and personal freedom.

3. A serious flaw is the idea of social relationships as structured around labor and the common control of reality. This tenet, typical of critical psychology, leads to a neglect of affective relationships. The critical-psychological treatment of psychic disturbances and therapy are, as a consequence, far from convincing. A looser connection between base and superstructure (labor and psychological phenomena) would be a much more fruitful premise.

In the light of these points, can we conclude that a Marxist psychology is possible? When, in the summer of 1975, Klaus Riegel read a lecture at the Psychological Institute of the Free University Berlin, Holzkamp rather condescendingly remarked in the discussion that, however important Riegel's work in the positivist climate of American psychology, critical psychology had reached a much more advanced theoretical position as a Marxist psychology. This judgment reflects, perhaps, an excessively linear idea of progress in Marxist psychology. But critical psychology certainly presents a most interesting program for a Marxist psychology. In elaborating this program Holzkamp, Osterkamp, and others[9] have obtained impressive results. And it is certainly true that critical psychology has progressed beyond either a criticism of contemporary psychology or the sort of programmatic declarations beyond which many attempts at a radical psychology have never gone. It follows from this that interest in critical psychology should really not be confined to small groups of psychologists outside mainstream psychology in the German-speaking countries, Denmark, and the Netherlands.

[9]The Psychological Institute of the Free University Berlin edits two series of books: the *Texte zur kritischen Psychologie* (published by Campus Verlag in Frankfurt) and the *Studien zur kritischen Psychologie* (Pahl-Rugenstein in Köln). The *Texte* comprise studies of central importance for the development of critical psychology (until now 13 books, in addition to those of Holzkamp and Osterkamp, by O. Dreier, F. Haug, S. Jaeger, E. Leiser, R. Seidel, U. Schneider, V. Schurig, I. Stäuble, and G. Ulmann). The series *Studien* consists of work of related interest (32 books). The school of critical psychology has its own journal *Forum Kritische Psychologie* (Argument Verlag in Berlin). Holzkamp published another work in 1983 (see references).

ACKNOWLEDGMENTS

I am grateful to David Ingleby, who encouraged me to write this article, made some valuable suggestions, and helped me with the final English version.

References

Ainsworth, M. D. S., Bell, S. M., & Stayton, D. J. (1974). Infant-mother attachment and social development: 'Socialisation' as a product of reciprocal responsiveness to signals. In M. P. M. Richards (Ed.), *The integration of a child into a social world*. London: Cambridge University Press.

Bowlby, J. (1981). *Attachment and loss: Vol. 3. Loss: sadness and depression*. Harmondsworth, England: Penguin.

Brandt, L. W. (1979). Behaviorism: The psychological buttress of late capitalism. In A. R. Buss (Ed.), *Psychology in social context*. New York: Irvington.

Fine, R. (1979). *A history of psychoanalysis*. New York: Columbia University Press.

Freud, S. (1961). *Civilisation and its discontents*. In *Standard edition* (Vol. 21). London: Hogarth. (Originally published 1930)

Goldmann, L. (1959). La psychologie de Jean Piaget. In *Recherches dialectiques*. Paris: Gallimard.

Haug, F., Baumgarten, M., Gluntz, U., Ohm, C., Schütte, I., Van Treeck, W., Wenk, S., & Zimmer, G. (1975). *Automation in der BRD*. Berlin: Argument.

Holzkamp, K. (1972). *Kritische Psychologie: Vorbereitende Arbeiten*. Frankfurt: Fischer.

Holzkamp, K. (1973). *Sinnliche Erkenntnis: Historischer Ursprung und gesellschaftliche Funktion der Wahrnehmung*. Frankfurt: Athenaeum Fischer.

Holzkamp, K. (1977a). Kann es im Rahmen der Marxistischen Theorie eine kritische Psychologie geben? *Das Argument, 19*, 316–336.

Holzkamp, K. (1977b). Die Überwindung der wissenschaftliche Beliebigkeit psychologischer Theorien durch die kritische Psychologie. *Zeitschrift für Sozialpsychologie, 8*, 1–22, 78–97.

Holzkamp, K. (1979). Zur kritisch-psychologischen Theorie der Subjektivität. II: Das Verhältnis individueller Subjekte zu gesellschaftlichen Subjekten und die frühkindliche Genese der Subjektivität. *Forum Kritische Psychologie, 5*, 7–46.

Holzkamp, K. (1983). *Grundlegung der Psychologie*. Frankfurt: Campus.

Holzkamp, K., & Osterkamp, U. (1977). Psychologische Therapie als Weg von der blinden Reaktion zur bewussten Antwort auf klassenspezifische Lebensbedingungen in der bürgerlichen Gesellschaft—am Beispiel des 'Examenfalles' von Manfred Kappeler. In M. Kappeler, K. Holzkamp, & U. Osterkamp (Eds.), *Psychologische Therapie und politisches Handeln*. Frankfurt: Campus.

Holzkamp, K., & Schurig, V. (1973). Einführung. In A. N. Leont'ev, *Probleme der Entwicklung des Psychischen*. Frankfurt: Athenaeum Fischer.

Holzkamp-Osterkamp, U. (1975). *Grundlagen der psychologischen Motivationsforschung* (Vol. 1). Frankfurt: Campus.

Holzkamp-Osterkamp, U. (1976). *Grundlagen der psychologischen Motivationsforschung* (Vol. 2). Frankfurt: Campus.

Jäger, M. (1977). Wissenschaftstheoretische Kennzeichnung der funktional-historischen Vorgehensweise als Überwindung der Beschränktheit der traditionellen psychologischen Wissenschaftspraxis. In K. Holzkamp & K. H. Braun (Eds.), *Bericht über den ersten Kongress kritische Psychologie* (Vol. 1). Köln: Pahl Rugenstein.

Kagan, J. (1979a). Motives in development. In *The growth of the child: Reflections on human development*. Hassocks, England: Harvester.

Kagan, J. (1979b). Overview: Perspectives on human infancy. In J. D. Osofsky (Ed.), *Handbook of infant development*. New York: Wiley.

Keiler, P. (1981). Natural history and psychology: Perspectives and problems. In U. J. Jensen & R. Harré (Eds.), *The philosophy of evolution*. Brighton, England: Harvester.

Leont'ev, A. N. (1973). Über das historische Herangehen an die Untersuchung der menschlichen Psyche. In *Probleme der Entwicklung des Psychischen*. Frankfurt: Athenaeum Fischer. (Originally published 1959)

Madsen, K. (1974). *Modern theories of motivation*. Copenhagen: Munksgaard.

Marcuse, H. (1966). *Eros and civilization: A philosophical inquiry into Freud*. Boston: Beacon Press.

Marx, K. (1975). Theses on Feuerbach. In *Early writings*. Harmondsworth, England: Penguin.

Meeus, W., & Raaijmakers, Q. (1984). Kritische Psychologie in den Niederlanden: Eine Diskussion. *Forum Kritische Psychologie, 13*, 81–101.

Naville, P. (1946). Psychologie moderne et matérialisme dialectique. In *Psychologie, marxisme, matérialisme: Essais critiques*. Paris: M. Rivière.

Osterkamp, U. (1978). Erkenntnis, Emotionalität, Handlungsfähigkeit. *Forum Kritische Psychologie, 3*, 13–90.

Piaget, J. (1936). *La naissance de l'intelligence chez l'enfant*. Paris: Delachaux et Niestlé.

Robinson, P. A. (1969). *The Freudian left: Wilhelm Reich, Geza Roheim, Herbert Marcuse*. New York: Harper & Row.

Schaffer, H. R. (1971). *The growth of sociability*. Harmondsworth, England: Penguin.

Sève, L. (1972). *Marxisme et théorie de la personnalité*. Paris: Editions Sociales.

Stroebe, W. (1980). The critical school in German social psychology. *Personality and Social Psychology Bulletin, 6*, 105–112.

Trevarthen, C. (1980). The foundations of intersubjectivity: Development of interpersonal and cooperative understanding in infants. In D. R. Olson (Ed.), *The social foundations of language and thought*. New York: Norton.

Van IJzendoorn, M. H., & Van der Veer, R. (1983). Holzkamp's critical psychology and the functional-historical method: A critical appraisal. *Storia e Critica della Psicologia, 4*, 5–26.

Van IJzendoorn, M. H., & Van der Veer, R. (1984). *Main currents in critical psychology*. New York: Irvington.

Verbij, A. (1981). De historische methode. In P. Van den Dool & A. Verbij (Eds.), *Van nature maatschappelijk*. Amsterdam: SUA.

Weiner, B. (1980). *Human motivation*. New York: Holt, Rinehart & Winston.

Yarrow, L. J. (1979). Historical perspectives and future directions in infant development. In J. D. Osofsky (Ed.), *Handbook of infant development*. New York: Wiley.

Chapter 7

David Ingleby

PSYCHOANALYSIS AND IDEOLOGY

When anyone mentioned change, the gentry asked confidently: "Can the sun rise in the West?":

William Hinton, *Fanshen*

In this chapter I shall try to analyze one element of the political character of psychoanalysis, namely, Freud's belief in the inevitability of conflict between individual and society and the consequent futility of social change.

Freud published his definitive views on this subject in *Civilization and Its Discontents* (1930/1961), and their validity became more or less a compulsory question for leftist intellectuals of the 1930s to answer. Why, the reader may ask, should we return to the subject now, after half a century? Chiefly, I would answer, because the wheel appears to have come full circle: after having been regarded for decades as obscurantist and reactionary, psychoanalysis is now once again being perceived as a radical viewpoint. This reinterpretation stems from three main sources. One is the women's movement which, following Juliet Mitchell's *Psychoanalysis and Feminism* (1973), has relented in its traditional hostility to psychoanalysis. Another is Lacanian theory. The third is the critical theory of the Frankfurt school, represented today by such writers as Habermas and Jacoby. These recent approaches to psychoanalysis offer a fundamental reappraisal of its political character, partly by changing the criteria of assessment and partly by putting forward a different read-

David Ingleby • Department of Development in Society, Heidelberglaan 2, Rijksuniversiteit Utrecht, 3584 CS Utrecht, Netherlands.

ing of the theory itself. However, I shall argue that none of these "new Freudians" have properly come to terms with that part of psychoanalysis that carries the most profound political implications, namely, its insistence on the fundamental dualism of human nature, the opposition between desire and reason, nature and culture, individual and society. My purpose, therefore, is to analyze Freud's views on this opposition, to assess their merit, and to describe in this light how compatible his theory really is with radical political thought. First, however, it will be instructive to examine changing attitudes to psychoanalysis over the last 50 years.

The Fortunes of Freudianism

In this section I can offer only the crudest sketch of an intellectual history of psychoanalysis. The world of ideas is not the homogeneous, flat terrain that the following remarks suggest, and a different selection of writers and places would yield a different picture. Nevertheless, I think certain central tendencies can be detected in the reception accorded to psychoanalysis over the years.

Overall, psychoanalysis enjoyed a rise in popularity and respectability from the 1930s until about 1950. This is largely accounted for by the substantial exodus of analysts from Nazi Europe and their highly successful penetration of the United States medical profession. Between 1950 and the late 1970s, the pendulum appears to have swung the other way, with other groups showing an increasingly hostile or dismissive attitude to psychoanalysts. Only recently has psychoanalysis again become the focus of much intellectual excitement.

The character ascribed to psychoanalysis depends very much on the current state of its fortunes. In times and places where psychoanalysis is orthodoxy, commentators tend to perceive it as conservative and authoritarian; out of favor, its subversive and liberating elements become more salient.

The above generalizations are not meant to be taken too seriously, but they may help to put certain matters into perspective. For example, nowadays—when psychoanalysis has almost disappeared off the map—the hostility of philosophers and psychologists of the 1950s seems out of all proportion to its object, a shade unsporting, even, like hitting a man when he is down. What is easily lost sight of is the fact that psychoanalysis at that time was an extremely powerful opponent. In the United

States, analysts held influential positions in mental hospitals, medical schools, and university departments of psychology; Freud was endlessly discussed, both in serious books and in a flood of popular handbooks on "mental hygiene" and parenthood. Out of all this was born a wholly new cultural type: "psychological man" (Boyers, 1975). To criticize Freud at such a time was perhaps to open the door to a breath of fresh air; to do so when few people take him seriously, however, is to keep it firmly shut.

Another important consideration is that the character of psychoanalysis itself has been strongly influenced by the power it enjoys. In its American heyday, psychoanalysis became an instrument of the social engineers of "mental health"; its emphasis was on adaptation and away from social critique. Analysts had always tended to hold themselves aloof from outside criticism, believing that such criticism stemmed from irrational motives and could only threaten their survival. With survival assured, they maintained this stance even more rigidly, appearing to feel themselves to be an élite that no longer had need of public legitimation. Central to the development of these character traits was the institutionalization of psychoanalysis as a branch of medicine, something on which Freud himself had already cast doubt in "The Question of Lay Analysis" (1926/1960). Indeed, the new Freudians see the doctrine that grafted itself so successfully onto American psychiatry as a travesty of Freud's real approach, as we shall see below.

What has happened to this once-powerful empire? In some enclaves, hardly anything; the view from uptown Manhattan is probably as encouraging for analysts as it ever was. But there is no doubt that in the rest of the world, and particularly in the universities, psychoanalysis has suffered a serious decline. Behaviorism and organic psychiatry have undermined its hold in the clinical and theoretical fields; faster, easier, and more reproducible psychotherapies have overtaken it in the private market. Although psychologists still pay lip service to Freud, his influence has been reduced by a process of attrition: textbooks of psychology compete with each other for the most stripped-down version of his theories, and in this minimal form their plausibility diminishes still further. (For good illustrations of this trivializing process, see Schaffer, 1971; Oakley, 1972; Tajfel, 1973; Rutter, 1975; and Brown & Harris, 1978.) In social theory, although grand sociological systems with no place for psychology have declined, those who have endeavored (in Homans' phrase) to "bring men back in" have wheeled onto the stage an entirely pre-Freudian creature. In contemporary ethnomethodology and linguistic philosophy, for example, agents are characterized axiomatically as conscious, rational, and self-governing (cf. Harré & Secord, 1972); the unconscious is simply defined out of existence.

Jacoby (1975) describes the demise of psychoanalysis as part of the "planned obsolescence of ideas." But we will be seriously misled by this witty phrase if we imagine that the rejection of Freud was anything but a *reasoned* one. Though their reasoning may be faulted, the critics of this period were at pains to avoid the charge of irrational resistance. Three main targets of their attack can be distinguished.

1. Authoritarianism. Both the theory and practice of psychoanalysis seemed to offend liberal assumptions about human nature. Therapy demanded a humiliating submission of the patient and an apparent denial of his or her capacity for self-help and self-realization. To these tendencies the "third-force," "client-centered" approaches of Maslow (1962) and Rogers (1961) offered a highly successful critique and alternative.

2. Psychological reductionism. Sociologists in particular reacted against the apparent lack of social relativity in Freud. They responded either by tacking on a social dimension or by denouncing psychoanalysis as a means by which "the system" reduced human conflicts to individual dimensions and kept problem cases in line (cf. Berger, 1965). This reaction was shared by many Marxists, for example, by the French communist party, which in 1948 denounced psychoanalysis as a "reactionary ideology."

3. Unscientificity. Psychoanalysts, especially at the height of their power and prestige, seemed to the outside world to have a cavalier attitude to truth. Typically, attacks on the credibility of psychoanalytic theory were directed at the *manner* of theorizing, rather than the particular conclusions reached. Popper's concept of unfalsifiability, specifically fashioned to deal with psychoanalysis and Marxism as he saw them, was the main weapon used. Open season was declared on psychoanalysis, as philosophers and psychologists repeated the charges (cf. Eysenck, 1953; Farrell, 1963; MacIntyre, 1967; Borger & Cioffi, 1970). More generally, the rise of psychological methods borrowed from other laboratory sciences created disdain for Freud's "soft" approach, despite some efforts to reconcile the two.

Recent defenders of psychoanalytic theory, however, argue against these criticisms in the following terms.

1. Freud's view of human nature is seen as a realistic one, in contrast to the utopianism of his critics. People in modern society are indeed

split and deluded. The "unconditional positive regard" enjoined on therapists by Carl Rogers is totally inadequate to foil the devices of the unconscious. According to Jacoby (1975) or Holland (1978), notions of "self-realization" presuppose a healthy, intact subject which modern industrial society has rendered increasingly mythical. Thus, the reluctance to accept Freud's conflict-ridden image of man is seen as complicity with the forces that create the conflict. (Those who champion Freud's *description* of the human condition along these lines, however, usually manage to ignore his *diagnosis*. As we shall see, he regarded conflict as inherent in the human condition and not confined to a particular political order.)

2. Concerning the social dimension, psychological reductionism is seen as a vice of American Freudianism, but not of Freud himself. The biologistic, adaptationist bias of the medical profession is blamed for filtering out the social and historical dimensions of Freud's thought. According to Althusser (1971), the French communist party's rejection of psychoanalysis was based on a failure to distinguish it from its revisionist replicas: "the 'dominant ideas', in this case, were playing their 'dominating' role to perfection, ruling unrecognized over the very minds that were trying to fight them" (p. 178). Jacoby (1975) repeated what the Frankfurt school had argued all along, that psychoanalysis was not about nature so much as about second nature, quoting Marcuse (1962) as follows: "Freud's theory is in its very substance 'sociological', and no new cultural or sociological orientation is needed to reveal this substance." Furthermore, without understanding the psychological processes that mediated the production and reproduction of structures of domination, "mechanical Marxism" would remain as ineffectual in the 1970s as it had been in the 1920s as a predictor and catalyst of social change.

3. Critics of the unscientificity of psychoanalysis, it is argued, misunderstood the nature of both science and psychoanalysis. First, according to postempiricist philosophers, falsifiability was not a criterion that any science could actually satisfy. The necessary interdependence of theory and observation made it inevitable that certain theoretical principles could never be tested, only presupposed. To characterize Freud's method of argument as "Heads I win, tails you lose" was seen as a ludicrous misreading of the text (cf. Cosin, Freeman & Freeman, 1970). Second, doubt began to be felt during the crisis years of the 1960s and 1970s about the objectivity of the experiments and psychological tests proposed as scientific alternatives. Third—and perhaps most radically—

the view gathered strength that psychoanalysis, like the human sciences generally, could not *in principle* obey the logic of the natural sciences; it was an interpretative or hermeneutic discipline, concerned with the elucidation of meaning rather than of causal laws (cf. Rycroft, 1966; Habermas, 1968; Lacan, 1973; Shafer, 1976). Psychoanalysis, in short, had been tried in the wrong court. Wollheim (1974) assembled a collection of essays showing that philosophers could, after all, take Freud seriously; Jahoda (1977) argued that psychoanalysis should once more be recognized as a significant contribution to "the dilemmas of psychology."

To deal fully with each of these three issues is beyond the scope of this essay. To a large extent, the proposed revaluations of psychoanalysis appear to me plausible. Nevertheless, I doubt whether American Freudianism, or the critics of the 1950s, were as misguided in their interpretations as the new Freudians imply. What is being offered as a new reading of Freud often seems to be little short of a new theory. But it is not this debate that I want to enter here. I shall have little to say directly on the politics of psychoanalytic treatment, or on the epistemological problems surrounding the theory. Instead I wish to focus attention on a question that, although it has an important bearing on the issues of authoritarianism and reductionism, has been overlooked in the recent controversies: the question of the inevitability of alienation.

I shall argue that Freud's theory presupposes at a basic level an opposition between individual and society. This pessimism is often ignored, since it conflicts with the radical purposes for which psychoanalysis is being called into service, but it dooms any marriage between Freud and Marx to eventual divorce. I shall also suggest that this presupposition is largely *ideological* in character, being determined more by the political world view that Freud subscribed to—what I call the "zero-sum paradigm"—than by his empirical discoveries. But although the diagnosis of conflict Freud offers is largely a mythical one, his description of it cannot be dismissed so easily and remains an essential part of the armory of any social critic. The relationship between psychoanalysis and ideology that emerges is in fact a double one, for as well as generating ideology, psychoanalysis also creates ways of dismantling it. In particular, that part of Freudian theory with (apparently) the most pessimistic implications of all—the belief in man's infinite capacity for self-deception—can be turned into a tool for analyzing the compulsions and delusions that keep exploitative and irrational social systems in existence.

What is it to characterize Freud's views as "ideological"? In Marx and Engels's *German Ideology* (1845/1974), philosophers who attempted to rationalize the existence of repression by appeal to theological or metaphysical arguments were scathingly dismissed as "the thinkers of the ruling class . . . who make the perfection of its illusions about itself their chief source of livelihood." The claim put forward here is that many of Freud's psychological beliefs also derive at root from political commitments. Freud certainly believed that psychoanalysis had strongly conservative political implications, and this interpretation has been shared by those of the Right who wish to denounce Marxism and those of the Left who wish to denounce Freud. In America particularly, certain Freudian ideas have become such an unquestioned part of received wisdom that they constitute a major bulwark against arguments for social change. For example, in its Freudian reincarnation, the classical dualism of nature and culture serves as a key notion in Western ideology. There is thus a connection between political conservatism and Freudian beliefs, and my aim in this essay is to show it is a valid connection (i.e., not based on a misinterpretation of the theory). However, it is a connection in which the direction of causality runs from politics to psychology, rather than vice versa. In other words, Freud and his orthodox adherents think the way they do about human psychology because their politics are what they are, not the other way round. Despite all this, Freud—like the sorcerer's apprentice—initiated an enterprise that led in unforeseen directions. It is not paradoxical, therefore, that many radical thinkers have found it possible to use his ideas as part of a social critique and an attack on conformist ideology. However, I shall argue that psychoanalysis as Freud left it cannot be recruited wholesale to these purposes but must be cleansed painstakingly of its own ideological assumptions.

It cannot be stressed too strongly that the point of examining the political implications of psychoanalysis is not simply to decide whether or not it is acceptable to people who have already made up their minds about the root of human evil. If it produces plausible findings that contradict our political preconceptions, then certainly we must reject the latter, not the former. But even from the point of view of a disinterested search for knowledge, it is important to know what prejudices a theory is likely to incorporate so that we can be alert to their effects. In the human sciences, it is impossible to theorize in a way that does not reflect one's political commitments. Therefore, ideology critique is essential to scientific progress, quite apart from considerations of political praxis.

It is also important to emphasize that to call some of Freud's beliefs ideological is not to say that he *consciously* selected them to fit in with his politics, or even that it was his own political views that they furthered. In most instances, he was simply recycling the prejudices of a common sense that was itself already ideological, for the notion that a society without contradictions is a logical impossibility was, as I shall try to show, a dominant theme in nineteenth-century thought and one with obvious political underpinnings.

For this reason, what Freud personally thought about politics is not all that germane to the argument. It has been demonstrated over and over again that judicious selection from Freud's comments on society can create the impression either of a bigoted reactionary or of a passionate revolutionary. It is not uncommon, however, for people with radical attitudes to produce ideas with thoroughly reactionary implications, or vice versa. The point is what the *theories,* not the authors, have to say about society. Nor can we trust even an author's own political interpretation of his theory. Books that are excellent in every other way, such as Roazen's *Freud: Political and Social Thought* (1969) or Bocock's *Freud and Modern Society* (1976), fail to grasp the political point of psychoanalysis because they do not confront the task of examining the detailed implications of Freud's psychological theory but instead concentrate on his ventures into sociology or anthropology. More to the point is Horowitz's *Repression* (1977), which starts from the same questions as the present essay but reaches somewhat different conclusions.

Basic Repression

For Freud, civilized man was inescapably at loggerheads with himself and with other men, and increasingly so as civilization progressed. Both intelligent behavior and social organization entailed conflicts with human nature that made frustration inevitable. In Freud's metapsychology, the relationship between ego and id was essentially one of colonization. This set severe limits on what could be achieved by therapy, and the optimistic project of using psychoanalysis to produce a happy reconciliation between individual and society—as American Freudianism, by and large, sought to do—was a hollow travesty of Freud's own philosophy. "Transforming hysterical misery into common unhappiness" was the most that Freud claimed to do for his own patients (1895/1955). Neither, of course, could Marxism free us from our chains, for the chains were part of our humanity itself.

To mitigate the severity of Freud's diagnosis, Marcuse (1962) introduced a distinction between *basic* and *surplus* repression, the former being that which was required to maintain civilized behavior generally, the latter being added to this by forms of social domination. But so far as Freud was concerned, the removal of surplus repression would make hardly a dent in the sum of human misery. It is perhaps for this reason that Wollheim (1971) ends his book on Freud with the following solemn admonition:

> No greater disservice can be done to Freud than by those, who in the interest of this or that piety, recruit him to the kind of bland or mindless optimisim that he so utterly and so heroically despised. (p. 235)

Certainly, Freud himself felt that his theories left little room for improvement of the human condition through social change; in *Civilisation and Its Discontents* he states that the psychological premises on which communism is based are "an untenable illusion" (p. 50). Such views may come as a surprise in the light of some of Freud's other attitudes, for instance, his belief that sexual repression was excessive, that homosexuality should be tolerated, and so on. Reich, for example, argued that, in this essay, Freud had cut off his nose to spite his face, since in his view its basic motivation was to administer Reich a rebuke for having associated psychoanalysis with "disreputable" left-wing movements (see Robinson, 1970, p. 31). Below, however, I shall attempt to show that Freud's interpretation of the political implications of his own theory is quite correct in its conclusions, though not always in the route by which it reaches them.

In the following sections, therefore, I shall examine the different ways in which psychoanalysis can be thought to imply the inevitability of conflict. In each case I shall ask: How strict is the implication, and on what hidden premises does it depend? How securely grounded is that particular portion of psychoanalytic theory, and to what extent does the system as a whole depend on its retention?

The Roots of Conflict

Freud's belief in the inevitability of conflict was, to use one of his own terms, "overdetermined": several different lines of reasoning led him to the same conclusion. At the outset we can isolate three major lines, and I shall devote a section to each.

Freud often falls back on the notion that "reason" and "instinct" are in essence opposed. This I shall call the *axiomatic* approach. For the most part, however, he ascribed conflict to contingent aspects of human nature (i.e., features that might be different in some other, imaginable world). Here we can isolate particular *instinctual needs* from the innate *cognitive structures* of the human mind.

The Axiomatic Approach

Occasionally Freud makes it clear that, for him, the opposition between reason and instinct is a self-evident one, inherent in the concepts themselves. In accepting this presupposition, he was merely subscribing to the dominant conceptual framework of his time. That natural desires were inherently unreasonable was, for the average citizen of the nineteenth century, an unquestionable piece of wisdom, and we will be committing a pardonable solecism if we regard Freud as a typical Victorian in this respect. This dualism can of course be traced back to Descartes and still further, although it was not without its critics, such as Rousseau, in the romantic epoch.

We see Freud elaborating this idea in his discussion of aggression in the case of Little Hans (1909/1956). Here, he refers to "a universal and indispensable attribute of all instincts and impulses—their 'impulsive' and dynamic character, what might be termed as their capacity for initiating motion" (p. 28). This attribute, Freud goes on to suggest, lends to all conduct an aggressive (and, by implication, antisocial) character.

Horowitz (1977) demonstrates the same sort of preconception in his assertion that human drives are inherently "distant from reality" (p. 9). Having accepted this idea, of course, Horowitz commits himself to a form of basic repression that effectively preempts much of his subsequent discussion. A little conceptual analysis, however, soon shows that this notion is not a logically necessary one. For if what we mean by *instinct* is simply an end that the organism innately seeks, then instincts have to be "controlled" merely because they lack form, not because they have the wrong form. In this sense it is a "category mistake" to see an opposition between reason and instinct because they are logically not the kinds of entities that can be in conflict. Rationality is concerned with means, instinct with ends, and insofar as rationality provides the means of gratification of instinctual needs, it removes a conflict rather than creating one.

Clearly, there are no grounds here for regarding the relationship between ego and id as one of repression. The relationship between cognitive and motivational mechanisms is essentially one of cooperation, not competition. Opposition can only arise because instincts themselves conflict with one another, or because the human mind inherits irrational modes of thought in addition to instincts themselves. However, making this elementary point does not go very far toward refuting Freud's pessimism; precisely such postulates form the basis of his whole theoretical system.

Specific Instincts

In speaking of instincts, I am adopting the (nowadays) unfashionable view that Freud ascribed a biological origin to human desires. It is true that most of the time when *instinct* appears in English editions of Freud, the original German is *Trieb,* which means only "drive" or "impulse." Hence, the impression is given in Strachey's translation that Freud was much more of a biological reductionist than was really the case. Freud certainly stressed that *Triebe* themselves were removed at several stages from biological needs, having undergone complex transformations as the outcome of the history of the organism's interaction with the environment. Nevertheless, to eliminate the biological component altogether (as Lacan, 1973, seems to be trying to do) is to propose an entirely new theory far removed from Freud's. The two drives most responsible for conflict were, for Freud, aggression and libido.

Aggression. In *Civilization and Its Discontents* Freud (1930/1961) invokes man's "inclination to aggression" as a major source of his inability to live comfortably in civilized society. "In consequence of this primary mutual hostility of human beings, civilized society is perpetually threatened with disintegration" (p. 49). This diagnosis, however, is somewhat surprising in view of Freud's earlier work, in which aggression is not seen as a basic instinct. Although most analysts have overlooked the contradiction, I shall follow Reich in regarding Freud's renunciation of his own theories as a retrograde step.

Up to 1920, in fact, Freud strenuously opposed those such as Adler who claimed that aggression was an innate drive. He preferred to see it as a secondary phenomenon, a tactic adopted by the instinct of self-preservation (cf. the frustration–aggression hypothesis of Dollard *et al.*, 1939), or as a component instinct of libido. "I cannot bring myself to assume the existence of a special aggressive instinct alongside of the familiar instincts of self-preservation and of sex, and on an equal footing with them" (Freud, 1909/1956, p. 140).

When, in 1920, Freud combined self-preservation and libido into a single instinct, eros, he removed the main source of dualism in his theory, and the death instinct (thanatos) was created in order to give intrapsychic conflict a biological base once more. Reich, of course, would have preferred Freud to see internalized forms of domination as the source of this conflict. But to do so would have radically altered the ideological nature of the theory, and I suggest that it was this consideration that dominated Freud's thinking at this point. Wollheim (1971) ascribes the creation of the death instinct to a fondness for dualism for its own sake. But Reich's suggestion that the compulsion was political, not merely intellectual, is a convincing one.

In any case, the death instinct is far from being a straightforward aggressive drive. It is, of course, a reworking of Freud's old belief that the nervous system strives to reduce excitation. This tensionless state, or nirvana, was essentially a form of suicide, and it was only a defensive *projection* of the drive toward it that caused aggression—a pretty roundabout way of explaining why people kill each other! On scientific grounds, Freud's earlier theory is surely more attractive, and he himself appears to have conceded this in not insisting that his followers accept the death instinct.

When his followers did accept the theory, as in the case of Melanie Klein, we can see even more clearly how little it is warranted. Ironically enough, it is Klein's own theory that dispels most effectively the notion that senseless violence is ever found in the child. Her close attention to the context and function of aggression showed that it is always an *intelligible* response to frustrating situations. Whether the urge to destroy is directed outward, or inward to the child's phantasied "internal objects," it always makes sense as a defense, protecting the child against a real or imaginary threat and manipulating the environment. Moreover, although the child's anger makes sense, it does so within its own imperfectly constructed world. Thus it is not valid to infer from the child's murderousness toward objects in its inner world to a disposition in the mature adult to kill. The very young child cannot entertain the wish to destroy a real person because it does not yet have the concept of real people or, indeed, of reality itself. Thus, it is erroneous to suppose that the total, blind rage of the infant underlies the mature emotional response or is a purer, more honest version of it; the two exist in separate worlds.

What we see from this discussion, in fact, is that it is the *unrealistic* character of the child's or adult's thinking that is primarily to blame for their destructiveness; specifically, it is the inability to realize that the object destroyed is the same as the one that is loved. This "splitting" is a manifestation of "primary process" (see below), and it is the latter that should therefore be regarded as the fundamental source of human conflict.

But even given all this, might a belief in innate aggression for its own sake be warranted by evidence from outside psychoanalysis? In the view of ethologists such as Konrad Lorenz (1966)—a view often falsely equated with Freud's—it clearly is. But Bennett (1974) and Montague (1968) show how shallow such arguments are. There is clearly no future in simply denying the enormity of "man's inhumanity to man"; in this century alone, mankind has killed over one hundred million members of its own species, to say nothing of the unnecessary slaughter of other species. Yet it is another thing to argue that this indicates an innate need to kill for the sake of killing. Most killing is performed in culturally sanctioned, technologically sophisticated cold blood. Such aggression is not an end in itself, requiring a fixed daily quota in Lorenzian fashion, but is usually dictated by political, religious, or economic logic. For the most part, the postulate of an aggressive drive appears to be merely an alibi to avoid taking responsibility for such actions, whether at an individual or a social level. Indeed, there is a macabre irony in the spectacle of ethologists peering earnestly at primate colonies to detect the secret springs of human aggression while back home their governments manufacture and distribute conflict as efficiently and as globally as Coca-Cola.

Libido. 1. The inertia principle: The first feature of instincts that Freud regards as militating against a happy life is contained in his assumption that the tendency of the nervous system is to keep excitation to a minimum—the inertia principle, which appeared as early as the "Project for a Scientific Psychology" (1895/1954) and was never abandoned. (Strictly speaking, of course, this principle is not confined to libido but dominates the operation of any instinct.) What the inertia principle chiefly implies is that any form of exertion will be unwelcome, unless it corrects an immediate state of need. The ideological implications of this notion are seen most clearly if we contrast it with Marx's view that the objectification of oneself in the products of creative labor is inherently fulfilling. Freud implies that any form of work, whether physical or mental, will be an irksome chore unless it reduces a current tension. Neither animals nor humans are as lazy or uncreative by nature as this doctrine implies. We now know that the nervous system does not strive for quiescence but keeps arousal at a certain optimum level; total sensory deprivation is, in fact, a form of torture (Zubeck, 1964). Freud's later constancy principle acknowledges this fact, but in this, the opposition to inertia comes from secondary processes and is still seen as less natural. Animals, like humans, prefer complex and stimulating environments to simple and monotonous ones; exploratory behavior and curiosity appear to be intrinsically motivated, being stronger, not weaker, when other drives are satisfied (Watson, 1961). In human infants, psychologists have been led to posit an "effectance motive" to cover the way in which infants appear to take pleasure in action for its own sake.

Freud's doctrine was not founded on any neurological evidence whatever, and it seems to be most satisfactorily explained as a variant of the general belief that humans are by nature idle and have to be goaded into activity. "The great majority of people only work under the stress of necessity, and this natural human aversion to work raises most difficult social problems" (Freud, 1930/1961, p. 17). The ideological significance of this belief lies in the fact that it offers a nonpolitical explanation of the alienation that most people in fact experience, both in education and in work. The schoolchild and the worker are seen as unavoidably alienated because they have to struggle constantly with their own inertia. Thus it becomes paranoid to suppose that, in Marx's words, "some other man" has imposed unnatural tasks upon them. Hence, even before Freud defines the specific aim of instincts, he characterizes their operation in such a way as to make Marx's goals unattainable. The inertia principle betrays the ahistoricism of Freud's approach: if he observed a tendency in people toward apathy, inertia, and the avoidance of stimulation, we can conclude fairly certainly from what we know about neurophysiology that this must have been due to the uncongenial nature of the demands being made on them. It is not hard to understand this, since the people Freud observed were engaged in the most massive accumulation of surplus value in human history.

2. Oral and anal sexuality: In the pregenital phases of libidinal development (oral and anal), Freud sees the instinctual aims of the infant as incompatible with the requirements of civilization. Specifically, weaning and toilet training inflicted traumas that left a permanent neurotic residue.

Although Freud provided ample evidence that these traumas occur, it is strange that he should have thought them inevitable. Dr. Spock (thankfully) is quite right when he tells us that both a preference for solid foods and sphincter control come naturally to the child in their own good time. What is interesting is why this time is not early enough for civilized societies. In the type of upbringing Freud described, conflict seems to be artifically created, and it is tempting to accept Fromm's (1973) interpretation, that this mode of socialization is functional in that it generates neuroses which certain social institutions can subsequently exploit. It never seems to have occurred to Freud that many of the difficulties that we put in the way of the infant are needless ones. Even in Spock-run households where weaning and toilet-training are taken as they come, the child is likely to be fed on a 4-hourly schedule (rather than the 2 or 3-hourly one that appears to be physiologically natural) and deprived of physical contact to an extent that demonstrably creates anxiety and malaise (Ainsworth, 1967). All this leads plausibly to the view that the conflicts of socialization in ostensibly advanced societies are far from inevitable but instead serve a purpose to which Freud himself unwittingly may have given us the key, in showing the normal neuroses to which they give rise.

3. Genital sexuality. The antisocial character of sexual love is a recurring theme in Freud's writings. In some ways, his complaints on the subject have a faintly ridiculous air. For example, sexual love is said to be intolerably exclusive, but are not sexually contented people easier to get on with than frustrated ones, and can we not manage without their company for a few hours a day? Males and females are born in equal numbers, so we do not even have to exploit our bisexuality to solve the problem of scarcity.

But all this points to the real problem that Freud uncovered. It is the particular way in which sexual drives are channeled and regulated that gives rise, in Freud's case histories to "hysterical misery." The root of this lies not in the restrictions imposed on adults but in the structure within which the child's love life is confined—the oedipal triangle.

Again, however, there is something a little bit suspicious about the supposed inevitability of oedipal conflict. If it is such a burden, why do we go to such pains to make sure that everyone has it inflicted on them? Why are the boy's passions so insistently channeled toward the one unattainable object, his mother, and why is the girl encouraged to feel that the one thing worth having is the thing she has not got, a penis? Again, if we follow Reich (1930/1972) or Deleuze and Guattari (1977), the real meaning of all this becomes clear when we see what important advantages the Oedipus complex has for an authoritarian, patriarchal society.

Thus, much of the frustration of libido that Freud describes, though it is real enough, seems something less than inevitable; most of it can probably be reclassified under Marcuse's category of surplus repression. It would seem quite feasible to provide an environment in which a child equipped with the basic Freudian instinctual apparatus could grow up without acquiring the neurotic compulsions that seem to play such a large part in maintaining the irrationalities of the present social order. However, it is still doubtful whether a population equipped only with this apparatus would in fact get very far along the road toward a society in which "the fulfilment of all was the condition of the fulfilment of each." For Freud condemned man to social discord as much by what he left out of his instinct theory as by what he put into it. The missing ingredient, as we shall now see, is sociability.

4. The lack of sociability: The infant portrayed in Freudian theory, standing stonily aloof from human company, is one of the curiosities of psychology, paralleled only by Piaget's account of the lonely scholar in the pram. Recent psychology has emphasized what every parent knows, that infants take a great delight in relating to others. This delight is censored out of Freud's theory almost as efficiently as sexuality was from the child psychology of his predecessors, and it is in ideology that one must surely seek an explanation for this omission. Nevertheless, Freud qualifies in important ways the bland optimisim of the "infants-are-born-social" school.

Freud's view of the nature of attachment was summed up by Schaffer (1971) as a "cupboard love" theory. In other words, the mother was seen as important to the infant primarily as a provider of food and basic care. For three or four years, the child's main source of gratification was supposed to be autoerotic or narcissistic, that is, primarily centered on its own body. Only at the phallic phase did another person become the true object of desire. This oedipal desire, as everyone knows, was doomed to frustration; according to Freud, a man's first love, for which all other loves are merely substitutes, must forever remain unrequited.

Having reduced sociability to this bare minimum, Freud then had the task of explaining what holds society together. As Bocock (1976) says, "Freud inherited the Hobbesian problem of order," but chiefly because he chose to adopt the Hobbesian definition of human nature. The solution he offered was in terms of transformations of oedipal desire, and the internalized moral promptings of the superego. Inevitably, the nature of the glue holding us together constrains the structure that can be built; the type of society that can be built using Freudian adhesive is, as he correctly deduced, a patriarchal, authoritarian, and essentially irrational one. As it is very hard to believe that Freud's picture of the infant was forced on him by observation, it is simpler to assume that he started from the assumption that the existing social order was the only possible or natural one and constructed a theory of the infant's biological endowments that would have this as its inevitable outcome.

Although Freud's views on sociability are typical of his age (cf. J. B. Watson or Piaget), they are quite at variance with the picture that has emerged from recent work. This is not to say that what is more up to date is necessarily more objective; there is an important ideological ingredient also in theories of innate sociability, as I have argued elsewhere (Ingleby, 1974). (Freud's view tends to rationalize conflict, the opposite view, to deny it. Both effectively obscure its origins in social structure.) Moreover, much of the work on attachment gained credence in the post-World War II drive to reconstruct the nuclear family (see Mitchell, 1973, pp. 227–231). However, the observations that contradict Freud's view are hard to dismiss altogether on such grounds.

In the first place, there is good evidence that the infant is not solely interested in people as a source of food. Schaffer and Emerson (1964) showed that 30% of infants' primary attachments were to their fathers, who did not feed them, while according to Wolff (1965), social responsiveness was higher when infants were fed than when they were hungry. There may still be a place for the concept of orality, in the sense that many emotionally intense interactions with adults center around feeding, but the secondary drive or cupboard-love hypothesis is not supported by these findings.

Another line of research has stressed the degree to which the infant is preadapted to social interaction. Richards (1974) emphasized how finely tuned the infant's visual and auditory mechanisms are to receiving human communications. Although, as Riley (1978) pointed out, this does not tell us much about the infant's social dispositions—"the human infant usefully drawn to the parental voice rather than to the creaking door"—such information does nevertheless suggest that communication has a high priority biologically.

More striking evidence comes from recent work by Trevarthen on "precocious communication" (Trevarthen & Hubley, 1978; Trevarthen, 1979). According to this, newborn infants demonstrate many of the elements of "intersubjectivity"—a capacity for imitation, empathy, and turn taking. Before the infant has mastered language, it is capable of sophisticated games and dialogues. Klein (1975) argued similarly that object relations occur in infants long before Freud's phallic phase.

Trevarthen claims, indeed, to have discovered "instincts for human understanding and for cultural cooperation." It would appear, then, that the Hobbesian problem of order that Freud set himself was more of a pseudo-problem. In a sense, sociable conduct may be far more natural than unsociable conduct.[1] Clearly, the infant has a talent for ordered social relations to a far greater extent than Freud's views allowed.

Nevertheless, Freud's views cannot be dismissed as sheer mythology, and they qualify in important respects the Rousseauian view that emerges from work such as Trevarthen's. Klein perhaps provides the key to a reconciliation. Although she believed the infant has strong *feelings* about other people, she posited an *awareness* of them that is initially quite fragmentary and distorted. In the "paranoid-schizoid position" (see Segal, 1979), the infant imagines itself capable of magically introjecting other figures, and of projecting its own experience into them. Moreover, it splits them into "good" and "bad" halves in such a way as to avoid experiencing contradictory emotions toward them. It is a long time before the child can relate to people as more than "part objects," and during the phase in which the child is coming to terms with his or her reality, "transitional objects" such as dolls (Winnicott, 1965) may have to play an important role in smoothing the path. Only when the "depressive position" is fully mastered can the infant treat others as whole, independent, and enduring—and heaven knows, this achievement even then is precarious enough! Hence, although the child may have very strong social drives, his or her *objects* are not other people as they really are but as he or she experiences them. The gap between the two may be so great as to leave the mother feeling (as she frequently does) that the infant is treating her not as a person but as a thing.

In this way, we may be able to reconcile Freud's view of infants as incapable of object relations with Trevarthen's apparently opposite view that they demonstrate intersubjectivity. Everything hinges on how we define *object*. If we mean the person as they really are, then infants are not capable of object relations, whereas if we refer to the person as

[1]An observation by Tulkin and Konner (1973) suggests, in fact, that competitiveness is something that has to be learned. They found that skill in cooperative games was lower in American schoolchildren than in their Mexican counterparts, the contrast increasing according to the number of years the children had spent in school.

experienced by the infant, then they certainly are. Once again, what handicaps the infant in social life seems to be not so much a question of motivation as of cognition. The crucial obstacle to social harmony thus becomes "primary process," which we shall now consider in detail.

Primary Process

Because most psychologists, following Freud, have regarded his theory as chiefly a dynamic one (i.e., concerned with motivational mechanisms), it may sound odd to claim that his main postulate is in fact cognitive—the notion that thought is systematically distorted in the service of desire.

That the id comprises more than drives is implicit in Freud's way of talking. Its irrationality is said to lie in its unwillingness to accept deferred gratification and in its capacity for simultaneously entertaining contradictory ideas—it "knows no conflict." But logically speaking, how can a drive know anything? Indeed, is there any reason why a drive should be abated simply because it cannot be immediately gratified or because of the existence of another drive the fulfillment of which is incompatible with it? Should we lose our hunger just because dinner is two hours away, or should we cease to want our cake just because we have eaten it?

Clearly, the id comprises not just wishes but also thoughts and beliefs. The division of labor between it and the ego is imperfect because it presents not just problems but also intended solutions to them (as is implicit in Freud's analogy of a horse and rider: after all, a horse has a mind of its own!). It is therefore not merely the motivational core of personality but almost a separate personality in its own right, as was perfectly clear in Groddeck's original concept of *das Es.*

What is the principle governing the id's beliefs and thoughts? As is well known, Freud defined it as the pleasure principle. But this term is hardly ever correctly understood, since most people interpret it simply as the striving to satisfy biological needs, not as the attempt to satisfy them by wishful thinking, which is what Freud usually intended. For Freud, hallucinatory wish fulfillment was the natural aim of an instinct. In order for adaptive behavior to occur, the ego had to suppress this tendency and interpose the reality principle (Freud, 1911/1958). The difference between this and the pleasure principle lies not simply in their tactics, but in the nature of the goals they pursue. The pleasure principle seeks not merely primitive pleasures but *imaginary* ones. The reality principle has little to do with the supposed wisdom of renouncing biological needs (though even so distinguished a Freudian as Herbert Marcuse writes as if it did—cf. Walton & Gamble, 1972); it simply counsels their active pursuit instead of daydreaming.

Thus, the human mind is ill-adapted not simply to society but to *reality itself.* The program of the pleasure principle is "at loggerheads with the whole world, with the macrocosm as much as with the microcosm" (Freud, 1930/1961, p. 13). The reality principle that opposes this program is thus concerned with upholding not only the laws of man, but those of nature, too, though significantly Freud (like Hobbes) did not trouble much about the distinction between the latter two. The fundamental obstacle to adaptation in Freudian theory is not, in fact, a drive, but a mode of cognition: primary process.

As Wollheim (1971), alone among Freud's commentators, emphasizes, the notion that motivation affects cognition figured in Freud's theory even before the discovery of psychoanalysis itself. In the nervous system hypothesized in the "Scientific Project," frustration could lead to hallucinatory wish fulfillment. This mode of thought was seen to full advantage, Freud argued, in dreams ("the Royal Road to the unconscious"), and in Chapter 7 of *The Interpretation of Dreams* (1900/1953) he expounded in detail its mode of operation.

As I have argued elsewhere (Ingleby, 1983), primary process extends to something more complex than simple hallucinations; cognitive *structure* as well is influenced by desire. Thus, people will cling to ways of construing the world that serve no current adaptive function simply because they cannot bring themselves to admit that the past is dead. In Piagetian terminology, they refuse to "accommodate" their schemas but instead compulsively "assimilate" reality to them.

Three basic Freudian concepts illustrate the role of primary process in maintaining out-of-date schemas: complexes, fixations, and transference. The *complex* is a scenario that haunts the individual, in terms of which he or she unconsciously construes any situation that lends itself to the goal of reliving the past. According to Laplanche and Pontalis (1973, p. 73), it is "a basic structure of interpersonal relationships and the way in which the individual finds and appropriates his place in it." The classic instance is, of course, the Oedipus complex. *Fixation* is "an attachment to archaic modes of satisfaction, types of object and of relationship" (p. 162). Here, the usual manifestations are oral or anal fixations, where the feeding or excreting situation is used to structure later situations to which it may be quite inappropriate. In *transference,* earlier objects are identified with a present figure (usually the analyst, although of course transference does not occur only during psychoanalysis). Freud usually spoke of transference as involving actual persons from the past. Klein, however, felt that primitive objects could form its basis, and hence children still attached to their parents could exhibit transference to a therapist.

Thus we see that in Freudian theory primary process came to govern a whole range of everyday experiences—in addition, of course, to dreams, imagination, symbolic play, neurotic symptoms, and parapraxes. All wish-fulfilling modes of cognition became subsumed under the general concept of phantasy, and phantasy was seen as an inevitable substrate of most experience, thus drastically undermining the traditional distinction between "sane" and "mad" people.

So far, I have argued that this tinge of madness in the normal personality is the fundamental obstacle Freud posited to harmonious social relationships and undercuts any arguments about specific drives. In the light of these drastic implications, how are we to evaluate the postulate of primary process? I shall discuss four ways in which we may seek to evade this pessimistic notion, only the last of which has much success.

Piaget's Argument. Although in his early work Piaget uses the notion of hallucinatory wish fulfillment extensively, the concept is in fact incompatible with his famous principle of equilibration, and he came to be quite insistent that there is no such structural link between affect and cognition. Affectivity is "like gasoline, which activates the motor of an automobile but does not modify its structure" (Piaget, 1954/1981, p. 5).

Piaget accepts that much of the child's thinking is "magical" but denies that it serves primarily a defensive function. For him, it is a temporary stage, a necessary starting point, which is for the most part soon phased out. The magical world of the child is simply the easiest way of construing sensory evidence, since the concept of external reality has to be built out of invariances the inference of which is a task of ever-increasing logical complexity. For Piaget, intelligent adaptation is the essence of life itself; the mollusc, the child, and the scientist are all engaged in a continuous and progressive search for equilibrium with the outside world. The conflict between pleasure and reality principles is thus seen not as one between nature and culture, or between two parts of the mind, but between successive stages. There are no emotional blocks or resistances to the transition between stages; the problems to be surmounted are entirely logical ones.

However, as I have argued (Ingleby, 1983), this view simply does not enable us to make sense of the data. In many cases, phantasies are more complex than the reality to which they are supposedly an approximation. There are good grounds from therapeutic evidence for believing that emotional blocks are the obstacle to many cognitive achievements. There is now, in fact, a growing tendency in developmental psychology to regard Piaget's postulate of structural independence between affect and cognition as empty axiomatizing.

The Biological Argument. At first sight, the concept of primary process seems implausible on evolutionary grounds. It is hard to see how any species could make the evolutionary jump required to develop the reality principle out of nothing. While the principle remained undiscovered, creatures would pass their days like opium addicts, basking listlessly in a state of illusory gratification. Such behavior is strikingly absent in animals. In this sense, their cognition is far more realistic than our own.

Freud, in fact, considered this objection in a footnote to his paper, "Formulations Concerning the Two Principles of Mental Functioning" (1911/1958). The answer he gave there is interesting because it shows how sophisticated his concept of evolution was compared to that of latter-day sociobiologists or ethologists. This maladaptive state was tolerable, according to Freud, precisely because the infant spends so much of its life shielded from reality by its caretakers. Characteristics evolve in the context of a specific environment, and part of this context may be a social institution such as parenting.

We may still ask what the biological point of such a propensity might be. The answer that Freud suggests is that an organism that can slide effortlessly between reality and imagination can solve problems by "vicarious trial and error" and can develop systems of symbolic representation and communication that create whole new realms of adaptation. Hence, it may be that the capacity for phantasy is the chief reason for the biological superiority of the human race, as well as its most persistent threat.

Social Origins. Alternatively, we may challenge Freud's belief that magical thought is innate by pointing to the fact that many phantasy systems are part of the individual's cultural inheritance—myths, magic, religion, and ideologies, not to speak of the shared delusions that arise in intimate relationships. Freud certainly neglects this fact, but it still does not explain the individual's readiness to participate in such belief systems and the reluctance to abandon them when their irrationality is demonstrated.

The Reflexivity Problem. The chief obstacle to the belief that human thought is *primarily* dominated by wish-fulfilling phantasy is that it is, in fact, a self-refuting one. Like Marx's theory of false consciousness, psychoanalysis has to provide a reflexive account of how it can be trusted. Otherwise, it merely implies that it, too, is a phantasy. To say that all men are deluded is simply another variant of the famous Cretan saying, "All Cretans are liars."

Hence, it is in fact logically necessary that strict limitations to the operation of primary process should exist, and Freud is somewhat unsuccessful in explaining what imposes these limits. As I have argued (Ingleby, 1983), the reality principle and sublimation are inadequately explained in his theory; Freud never satisfactorily accounts for reasonable human conduct. As stated by Laplanche and Pontalis (1973) "the lack of a coherent theory of sublimation remains one of the lacunae of psychoanalytic theory" (p. 433).

The Zero–Sum Paradigm

I hope to have shown in the above that Freud approached the field of psychology with strong preconceptions about the inevitability of conflict between man and other men, nature, and himself. (The conflict between man and woman is another part of the story, too, but one to which I have not been able to do much justice here.[2] In the case of libido, it is primarily because Freud assumes that the patriarchal nuclear family is inevitable that he sees frustration as necessary. Primary process, however, constitutes an apparently innate mode of unreasonableness that militates against adaptation to any form of society. I have argued that it is the latter, cognitive postulate of Freud's that most seriously undermines a belief in social progress.

Although I am thus proposing that part of Freud's pessimism should be regarded as warranted, I have argued that most of it is not, and it is therefore interesting to consider where his beliefs about human nature might have come from. Chiefly, it would appear that it is Freud's tendency to ignore the social context of his observations that leads him

[2]See, however, Chodorow (1978, Chapter 9).

to make the inferences he does. Freud's method was essentially ahistorical in that he attempted to infer the nature of what had been repressed from its unconscious form after repression without taking into account the possibility that whatever led to its being repressed in the first place might also have affected its form. Had he done so, the act of repression would have lost its self-justifying appearance, and Freud would have had to seek elsewhere the reasons for man's self-alienation.

Freud characterizes the id in the same way that white Americans characterized the Red Indian and colonial peoples generally have characterized the victims of their exploitation. The Indian had to be brutally repressed, so the myth ran, because his behavior was lawless and wanton. It was the same with the "criminal violence" of the Algerians under the French—so coolly demythologized by Fanon (1967)—and so too with the lawlessness of children, mental patients, the working class . . . and the id.

But these myths can be sustained only by leaving out of view the political facts of the case. The restoration of historical perspective brings back the justice and intelligibility of what has been repressed. We see that the domination and exploitation of the colonized person *produces* the characteristics that are supposed, by entirely circular logic, to justify it. Thus, the behavior of the Indians does not reflect the intrinsic character of their culture but that of the oppression they experienced (Waters, 1969). Similarly, the seething chaos of the unconscious does not reflect man's biological predispositions so much as the savage force by which they are suppressed.

In order to understand what Freud found in the unconscious, then, we must bear in mind the violence with which nineteenth-century Europe exploited its citizens, something to which Freud was remarkably insensitive, as his discussion of the case of Schreber demonstrates (Shatzmann, 1973). (For all this, we must hastily disavow the attitude that Freud's observations were somehow unrepresentative of civilization before and after.)

Thus, we can see that the myth of inherent opposition between nature and culture was congruent with Freud's own conventionally conservative politics precisely because this myth renders invisible the objective contradictions in society. Viewed in this light, Freud's theories seem not so much a challenge to the received ideology of his time as a new and sophisticated reformulation of it.

What is this ideology? I have called it the zero–sum paradigm because it sees human relationships as essentially competitive rather than cooperative. Any relationship to society involves the individual in a renunciation of his own interests. As Luce and Raiffa (1957) define it:

> A strictly *competitive* (or, equivalently, *zero–sum*) two person game is one in which the two players have precisely opposite preferences. It is, therefore, a game in which cooperation and collusion can be of no value. Any improvement for one player necessitates a corresponding loss for the other. (p. 85)

Of course, this is also the ideology of "possessive individualism" (see Macpherson, 1962). Although this view of society has its roots in the eighteenth century, it has enjoyed a sudden and spectacular revival in recent years, as part of the philosophy of monetarism. The concept of free enterprise embodies an implicit assumption that enterprise that is free is competitive because human nature is such that people would never of their own accord enter into cooperative arrangements. (The fact that even under capitalism they persist in doing so is always conveniently overlooked.) Laissez-faire economies, instead of being seen as the forced contrivances that they are, are implied by their very name to be the outcome of letting things happen naturally.

The assumption that free enterprise is competitive entails in turn the notion that cooperation in the common interest must be coerced. Thus, socialism is identified *a priori* with iron rule and the end of liberty. Christianity is regarded in much the same light. For Freud, "Love thy neighbour as thyself" was a ridiculous and repressive injunction. "The commandment is impossible to fulfil: such an enormous inflation of love can only lower its value, not get rid of the difficulty" (Freud, 1930/1961, p. 80). The same argument is repeated closely by Szasz (1961). In short, therefore, we need not seek the origins of Freud's beliefs in his discoveries, his private political views, or his personal state of mind; they were very much a part of his time and of ours as well.

The Necessity of Revisionism

It should be clear by now that Freud's theories, in the form in which he left them, are not compatible with Marxism, or even with a liberal belief in progress. This raises problems for the new Freudians, who maintain that it is only subsequent misreadings of Freud that have given rise to the impression of reactionary ideology. Jacoby (1975) sees Marcuse as unfolding Freud's concepts into a revolutionary vision of history. But this unfolding turns out to be of precisely the same kind as that of the conjurer who unfolds a handkerchief to reveal a flight of pigeons or a white rabbit. Jacoby is scathing in his attack on revisionist versions of psychoanalysis, but without a substantial amount of revision Freudian theory cannot be used legitimately for any but its traditional conservative purposes.

Of course, it may be the belief in progress that ought to be revised in the light of Freud. But in view of the foregoing discussion, I do not think Freud's arguments for the permanence of the existing order can be sustained, with the possible exception of primary process, to which I shall return below.

What would Freudian theory look like, then, if its more obviously ideological components were removed? I would argue that provided primary process remained intact, little of substance would be lost. The inertia principle is neurologically false anyway, the death instinct is a speculative afterthought, and the inevitability of the patriarchal nuclear family was never a truly psychological postulate in the first place. A psychoanalytic account of child development that takes into account the infant's sociability already exists in the British school of object relations theory. Obviously the question deserves a more careful answer than these few lines provide. But I do not think that the removal of ideological preconceptions from psychoanalysis would leave the theory either unrecognizable or unworkable. Unfortunately, until the necessity of this task is appreciated, progress on it is bound to be slow.

What of the remaining postulate, primary process? It could be argued that a species with such a talent for self-deception as Freud ascribes to the human race had but a miserable prospect of discovering a rational mode of social organization and could only make things worse if it tried to seek one. However, primary process is not so incompatible with Marxism as this argument implies. First, as we noted above, the theory that all thought is a delusion is self-refuting. Although Freud's theory of rationality is unsatisfactory, psychoanalysis needs such a theory in order not simply to be acceptably optimistic, but to be coherent as a theory at all. Second, Marx himself (who, incidentally, shares this problem) places considerable emphasis on self-deception or false consciousness in his account of the production and reproduction of social systems. Although self-deception for Freud operated primarily to maintain mental (rather than social) order, there is no reason why false consciousness and emotional defenses should not take the same form (the paradigm, case being, perhaps, that of religion).

Hence, Freud is useful to a critical view of society not simply because he describes the inner conflicts of its members so faithfully in contrast to the bland reassurances of humanistic psychology. He also offers a detailed explanation of the compulsions and delusions that make people more at home in an oppressive society than they would be in a free one and hence suggests what changes are necessary in order to make social progress psychologically possible. It is this psychological problem that Marxists after World War I, and feminists after the 1960s, turned to psychoanalysis to solve: Why was it that when the conditions for social change seemed ripe people seemed emotionally incapable of accepting a new order? The Freudo-Marxists answered this question in terms of the normal neuroses and compulsions, which from one point of view serve as emotional defenses and from another as social ideologies.

What Reich, Fromm, Marcuse, and others essentially were arguing was that a society that runs on fairy tales requires that, in certain fundamental respects, its members should not grow up, particularly the less privileged ones. The task for radical psychoanalysis, then, is to show how crippling compulsions arise in the course of normal socialization and persist because they serve so well the maintenance of oppressive institutions. Freud himself inevitably started this line of criticism by blurring the distinction between sanity and madness, arguing that religion, mass movements, and character traits manifested, in psychological terms, the same structure as neuroses.

Freudo-Marxism versus the Poststructuralists

To sum up, I think we should use Freudian theory as the critical theorists have used it, but not without first undertaking some unashamed revision of its foundations. As the original Frankfurt school argued, Freud provides the key to the shared unconscious forces that hold repressive power structures in place, and, as Habermas later argued, its method of critical self-reflection can provide the paradigm for a truly emancipatory theory. However, in this section I will have to deal with some of the more recent critiques of both these notions, which originate in what I have called elsewhere (Ingleby, 1984) the poststructuralist school of Foucault, Donzelot, Deleuze and Guattari, and Castel. These writers, rejecting the alliance of Freud and Marx urged on the French communist party by Althusser, have argued that psychoanalysis is so deeply rooted in the structures that maintain social order that the project of using it for emancipatory ends is doomed from the start.

In one of his last works, Foucault (1978) develops the notion that the form in which power is embodied in the modern state is productive rather than repressive. Social control agencies such as psychiatry (of which psychoanalysis is seen as an intrinsic part) do not so much impose constraints as create new forms of subjectivity by the introduction of new discourses. Freud's discourse about sexuality and family life is seen as a further development of the dialogue of the confessional and the clinical consultation. We have all been taken in by the myth, Foucault claims, that Freud shattered some kind of Victorian conspiracy of silence about sexuality. In reality, the church and the medical profession had talked incessantly about sexuality (especially in children) and in doing so had exerted the productive power of structuring sexuality within the categories of their discourse.

Donzelot (1979) utilized the same concept of power in his analysis of the agencies that regulate family life. For him, Freud plays a central role, since it was he who struck the necessary balance between "the necessity of imposing social norms of health and education, and that of maintaining the autonomy of individuals and the ambition of families as a principle of free enterprise" (p. 232). Freud's achievement in the social sphere is compared by Donzelot to that of Keynes in the economic: just as Keynesian economics maintained the mainspring of capital—the profit motive—but regulated it with a system of checks and balances, so Freud devised a therapy that enhanced autonomy in some respects yet retained the family as "the horizon of all individual paths" (p. 232).

Two other works buttress the poststructuralist condemnation of psychoanalysis: Deleuze and Guattari's *Anti-Oedipus* (1977) and Castel's *Le psychanalysme* (1972). Both argue that the idea of a true Freudianism, waiting to be discovered in all its pristine radicalism beneath the mildew and tarnish of ideological distortions, is a chimera that has led the Left seriously astray. The focus of Deleuze and Guattari's critique is the insistent "familialism" of psychoanalysis. Far from liberating us from the tyranny of the "the papa–mama matrix," they say, it seeks to impose its rule even more thoroughly. If the patient does not have an Oedipus complex of his own, then—before going any further—the analyst will install one for him.

Castel focuses on the inequality of power in the relationship between patient and analyst. The autocracy of the latter is maintained inviolate by the banishment of certain topics from the discourse altogether. Any questions to do with the analyst's exercise of his powers are treated as material for interpretation only; they cannot be permitted to have a realistic referent. Thus, free association is the perfect complement of the bourgeois ideal of free speech: anything may be said, on the understanding that none of it has to be acted upon.

How are we to evaluate these criticisms? Even if they apply to most of what goes under the name of psychoanalysis, do they necessarily apply to all? Such a question is of increasing practical concern, especially to those who wish to use psychoanalytic therapy in the name of specific radical causes (such as feminism).

Castel's criticisms show that Habermas's characterization of psychoanalysis as emancipatory is founded on a somewhat idealized and partial understanding of the method. One of the preconditions of genuine dialogue is a commitment by both parties to try and see each others' viewpoints as valid. A situation in which one person's utterances are routinely reduced to the status of material for interpretation clearly fails to meet this condition. Lomas (1981) also points out that such a situation might also be rather bad for people, especially if their ontological foundations are at all shaky to start with. Thus, when Conrad and Schneider (1980) describe psychoanalysis as "reopening the dialogue" with madness which had been broken off since the classical age, the dialogue is a pretty one-sided one; the id is accepted into polite society on much the same terms as Tuke accepted the madman, that is, as "the perfect stranger."

The basic inequality of power between patient and analyst stems ultimately, I believe, from the origins of psychoanalysis within the medical model. Critics such as Lacan are right to argue that it is the medical profession's dominion over psychoanalysis that has obscured its revolutionary content, but it is not clear whether this fundamental authoritarianism can be removed simply by putting the method into lay hands. By all accounts, the Lacanian analyst seems to exercise an even more autocratic kind of power than the orthodox Freudian, since he does not even offer the analysand an intelligible reason for placing faith in him.

Nevertheless, the nature of the analyst's authority must not be oversimplified. Merely to say that he abolishes the power of the real father and appropriates it to himself only describes the early stages of an analysis in which regression and dependence are encouraged. The cure does not reside in this, but in the overcoming of the transference by the joint work of patient and analyst. In this process, the analyst actively undermines precisely those magical powers with which the patient has invested him. If the analyst reinforces the rule of Oedipus, then, it is not (as the priest did) by simply providing a more imposing father figure. Rather, it is as Donzelot put it, by making the family "the horizon of every individual path."

Again, however, most analysts would reply that this is to mistake the problem for the solution. If the patient's preoccupations are repeatedly interpreted in terms of the papa–mama matrix, it is because this is whence they come. Only when the unconscious familial phantasies have been brought into the light by interpretation can the patient be released from their grip and become free to choose some other horizon than the family for his path. Far from trapping people within familial structures, then, progressive analysts would reply that their job consists precisely in liberating them from these structures.

This is a powerful objection and one which is not easy to meet. Deleuze and Guattari have a reply which is all too simple: it is that however far from the original papa–mama matrix the analyst takes the patient, the discourse still remains firmly within the realm of the personal, and the concept of person is inextricably bound up (they say) with the rule of the family. For Deleuze and Guattari, on the other hand, there are no persons, only "desiring machines"; "the unconscious knows no persons." This is not the place to attempt a proper critique of this ontology, but it suffices to indicate that its acceptance involves taking a step—the abolition of the concept of person—which by no means all critics of familialism are necessarily committed to. Indeed, I would argue that the notion that the only basis for personal relationships is the family is itself a pretty obvious piece of familial ideology.

So perhaps the end of analysis is, after all, a relationship with the patient thoroughly cleansed of all parental overtones, which enables the patient systematically to dismantle the familial scenarios that have previously structured and dominated his or her life. Ought we not to accept this as the emancipation we have been looking for?

Not quite, for though this therapy may not exactly be familial, it is nevertheless infantilizing through and through, confirming the patient in a mute submission to magical powers lying outside himself or herself. To look for these powers in the analyst is, of course, a mistake, since by the end of the therapy he or she, like the Wizard of Oz, has entirely abdicated them. No, the powers are invisible ones, to which the analyst is just as subject as the patient. They are the magical powers of psychoanalysis itself, powers drawn from the twin gods of medicine and science and saluted in the ritual obeisance to hierarchies of certification and catechisms of technique. It was these powers that Lacan attempted to demolish but, failing to perceive their true nature, succeeded only in reinstituting. For Lacan regarded orthodox psychoanalysis as the fetish of an obsessional religion, whereas its true character is patriarchal. This patriarchal power was carefully preserved by Lacan, both in the Lévi-Straussian formalism of his theory and in the charismatic basis of his practices.

We arrive, thus, at the conclusion that the poststructuralists' interpretation of the political character of psychoanalysis is after all correct, though not for the precise reasons that they give. This critique serves as an important warning to those on the Left, however well intentioned, who would seek to recuperate the benefits of Freud for more radical concerns without appreciating the profundity of the revision this entails both in theory and practice. Furthermore, this critique is consistent with—indeed, vital to—Foucault's notion that our present civilization is based on the interruption of a dialogue with madness and all it stands for. But it leaves us with very little idea of what such a dialogue would be like and how it could be recommenced.

Lacan, it is true, has shown the way, in his insistence that the unconscious is not to be simply subordinated to secondary process but allowed to speak with its own voice. For him, this means primarily a change of linguistic style, a shift from rigidly rationalistic prose to a more poetic, allusive language that permits contradictions and different levels of meaning to coexist. Lacan's own notoriously obscure writings represent his desire to practice what he preaches in this respect (though French intellectuals have seldom been keen to subordinate what they wish to say to the duty of making reasonable sense). But what structure of relationships does such a dialogue presuppose? The Lacanian analyst's relationship to his analysand, preserving as it does the paternalism of the medical model in its unequal distribution of power, surely cannot suffice. A more appropriate structure will be found only by those who are willing to experiment with new and humbler modes of confronting madness. Only in this way, perhaps, will we manage to restore a genuine dialogue with our unreasonable selves.

References

Ainsworth, M. D. S. (1967). *Infancy in Uganda*. Baltimore: Johns Hopkins University Press.

Althusser, L. (1971). Freud and Lacan. In *Lenin and philosophy and other essays*. London: New Left Books.

Bennett, S. (1974). Is there an innate human aggressive drive? *The Human Context 6*, 399–404.

Berger, P. (1965). Towards a sociological understanding of psychoanalysis. *Social Research 32*, 26–41.

Bocock, R. (1976). *Freud and modern society*. London: Nelson.

Borger, R., & Cioffi, F. (1970). *Explanation in the behavioural sciences*. Cambridge: Cambridge University Press.

Boyers, R., (Ed.). (1975). *Psychological man*. New York: Harper & Row.

Brown, G. W., & Harris, T. (1978). *Social origins of depression*. London: Tavistock.

Castel, R. (1972). *Le psychanalysme*. Paris: Maspero.

Chodorow, N. (1978). *The reproduction of mothering: Psychoanalysis and the sociology of gender*. Berkeley: University of California Press.

Conrad, P., & Schneider, J. W. (1980). *Deviance and medicalization*. St. Louis: Mosby.

Cosin, B. R., Freeman, C. F., & Freeman, N. H. (1970). Critical empiricism reconsidered: The case of Freud. *Theory of Social Behaviour 1*, (2), 121–151.

Deleuze, G., & Guattari, F. (1977). *Anti-Oedipus*. New York: Viking.

Dollard, J. & Doob, L. W., Miller, N. E., Mowrer, O. H., & Sears, R. R. (1939). *Frustration and aggression*. New Haven: Yale University Press.

Donzelot, J. (1979). *The policing of families*. New York: Pantheon.

Eysenck, H. J. (1953). What is wrong with psycho-analysis? In *Uses and abuses of psychology*. Harmondsworth, Middlesex: Penguin.

Fanon, F. (1967). *The wretched of the earth*. Harmondsworth, Middlesex: Penguin.

Farrell, B. A. (1963). Psychoanalytic theory. *New Society 38*, 11–13.

Foucault, M. (1978). *The history of sexuality: vol. I, An introduction*. New York: Pantheon.

Freud, S. (1954). Project for a scientific psychology. In M. Bonaparte, A. Freud, & E. Kris (Eds.), *The origins of psycho-analysis*. London: Hogarth. (Originally published 1895)

Freud, S. (1953). *The interpretation of dreams. Standard Edition* (Vols. 4 and 5). London: Hogarth. (Originally published 1900)

Freud, S. (1956). A phobia in a five-year-old boy. *Standard Edition* (Vol. 10). London: Hogarth. (Originally published 1909)

Freud, S. (1958). Formulations concerning the two principles of mental functioning. *Standard Edition* (Vol. 12). London: Hogarth. (Originally published 1911)

Freud, S. (1960). The question of lay analysis. *Standard Edition* (Vol. 20). London: Hogarth. (Originally published 1926)

Freud, S. (1961). *Civilisation and its discontents. Standard Edition* (Vol. 21). London: Hogarth. (Originally published 1930)

Freud, S., and Breuer, J. (1955). *Studies in hysteria. Standard Edition* (Vol. 2). London: Hogarth. (Originally published 1895)

Fromm, E. (1973). *The crisis of psychoanalysis*. Harmondsworth, Middlesex: Penguin.

Habermas, J. (1968). *Knowledge and human interests*. London: Heinemann.

Harré, R., & Secord, P. F. (1972). *The explanation of social behaviour*. Oxford: Blackwell.

Holland, R. (1978). *Self and social context*. London: Macmillan.

Horowitz, G. (1977). *Repression*. Toronto: University Press.

Ingleby, D. (1974). The psychology of child psychology. In M. P. M. Richards (Ed.), *The integration of a child into a social world*. Cambridge: Cambridge University Press.

Ingleby, D. (1983). Freud and Piaget: The phoney war. *New Ideas in Psychology, 1*(2), 123–144.

Ingleby, D. (1984). Mental health and social order. In A. Scull & S. Cohen (Eds.), *Social control and the modern state*. London: Martin Robertson.

Jacoby, R. (1975). *Social amnesia*. Boston: Beacon.

Jahoda, M. (1977). *Freud and the dilemmas of psychology*. London: Hogarth.

Klein, M. (1975). *Love, guilt, and reparation.* London: Hogarth and Institute for Psychoanalysis.
Lacan, J. (1973). *Écrits.* London: Tavistock.
Laplanche, J., & Pontalis, J-.B. (1973). *The language of psycho-analysis.* London: Hogarth.
Lomas, P. (1981). *The case for personal psychotherapy.* Oxford: Oxford University Press.
Lorenz, K. (1966). *On aggression.* London: Methuen.
Luce, D., & Raiffa, H. (1957). *Games and decisions.* New York: Wiley.
MacIntyre, A. (1967). *The unconscious.* London: Methuen.
Macpherson, C. B. (1962). *The political theory of possessive individualism.* Oxford: Clarendon Press.
Marcuse, H. (1962). *Eros and civilization.* Boston: Beacon.
Marx, K., & Engels, F. (1974). *The german ideology.* London: Lawrence & Wishart. (Originally published 1845)
Maslow, A. (1962). *Toward a psychology of being.* Princeton, NJ: Van Nostrand.
Mitchell, J. (1973). *Psychoanalysis and feminism.* London: Allen Lane.
Montague, A. (Ed.). (1968). *Man and aggression.* Oxford: Oxford University Press.
Oakley, A. (1972). *Sex, gender and society.* London: Temple Smith.
Piaget, J. (1981). *Intelligence and affectivity: Their relationship during child development* Palo Alto, CA: Annual Reviews. (Originally published 1954)
Reich, W. (1972). *The sexual revolution.* London: Socialist Reproductions. (Originally published 1930)
Richards, M. P. M. (1974). First steps in becoming social. In M. P. M. Richards (Ed.), *The integration of a child into a social world.* Cambridge: Cambridge University Press.
Riley, D. (1978). Developmental psychology, biology and Marxism. *Ideology and Consciousness 4,* 73–92.
Roazen, P. (1969). *Freud: Political and social thought.* London: Hogarth.
Robinson, P. (1970). *The sexual radicals.* London: Temple Smith.
Rogers, C. R. (1961). *On becoming a person.* London: Constable.
Rutter, M. (1975). *Helping troubled children.* Harmondsworth, Middlesex: Penguin.
Rycroft, C. (1966). *Psychoanalysis observed.* London: Constable.
Schaffer, H. R. (1971). *The growth of sociability.* Harmondsworth, Middlesex: Penguin.
Schaffer, H. R., & Emerson, P. E. (1964). The development of social attachments in infancy. *Monographs of the Society for Research in Child Development 29.*
Segal, H. (1979). *Klein.* London: Fontana.
Shafer, R. (1976). *A new language for psychoanalysis.* New Haven: Yale University Press.
Shatzmann, M. (1973). *Soul murder.* London: Allen Lane.
Szasz, T. (1961). *The myth of mental illness.* New York: Harper & Row.
Tajfel, H. (1973). The roots of prejudice: Cognitive aspects. In P. Watson (Ed.), *Psychology and race.* Harmondsworth, Middlesex: Penguin.
Trevarthen, C. (1979). Communication and cooperation in early infancy: A description of primary intersubjectivity. In M. Bullowa (Ed.), *Before speech: The beginnings of human cooperation.* Cambridge: Cambridge University Press.
Trevarthen, C., & Hubley, P. (1978). Secondary intersubjectivity: Confidence, confiding, and acts of meaning in the first year. In A. Lock (Ed.), *Action, gesture and symbol.* London: Academic Press.
Tulkin, S. R., & Konner, M. J. (1973). Alternative conceptions of intellectual functioning. *Human Development 16,* 33–52.
Walton, P., & Gamble, A. (1972). *From alienation to surplus value.* London: Sheed & Ward.
Waters, F. (1969). *The book of the Hopi.* New York: Ballantine.
Watson, A. J. (1961). The place of reinforcement in the explanation of behaviour. In W. H. Thorpe & O. L. Zangwill (Eds.), *Current problems in animal behaviour.* Cambridge: Cambridge University Press.

Winnicott, D. W. (1965). *The maturational process and the facilitating environment: Studies in the theory of emotional development*. London: Hogarth.
Wolff, P. H. (1965). The development of attention in young infants. *Annals of the New York Academy of Sciences, 188*, 815–30.
Wollheim, R. (1971). *Freud*. London: Fontana.
Wollheim, R., (Ed.). (1974). *Freud: A collection of critical essays*. New York: Anchor.
Zubeck, J. P. (1964). Effects of prolonged sensory and perceptual deprivation. *British Medical Bulletin 20*, 38–42.

Chapter 8

Jessica Benjamin

THE DECLINE OF THE OEDIPUS COMPLEX

Contemporary psychoanalysis has, metaphorically speaking, shifted its focus from Oedipus to Narcissus. It no longer attributes central, unequivocal importance to those instinctual conflicts and their resolution that develop through the triangular relationship of child and parents, the Oedipus complex. Instead, pathologies of the self, or narcissistic disorders, have increasingly become the focus of psychoanalytic practice and discussion. More generally, issues that begin in the mother–infant dyad, the preoedipal issues of early individuation and self-formation, take precedence over neurotic conflicts pertaining to defense against instincts or drives. As articulated by Kohut (1971), chief exponent of the focus on narcissistic disorders, our age is witnessing a transition from the problems of Guilty Man to those of Tragic Man, from the thwarted search for drive satisfaction to the desperate search for fulfillment of the self. Such formulations of change by psychoanalysts have, in turn, been popularized in contemporary social criticism—with greater and lesser accuracy—in terms of "the new narcissism." In this rhetorical usage, the pejorative meaning of the word *narcissism* and the invidious comparison between Oedipal Man and the New Narcissist are readily discernible. Here the decline of the Oedipus complex is seen as linked to the decline of authority and morality that engendered Guilty Man's

Jessica Benjamin • Institute for the Humanities, New York University, New York, New York 10003.

conflicts with his drives but spared him Tragic Man's disorganization of the self.

The decline of the Oedipus complex, referring both to a decline of interest in it and an actual diminution of oedipal conflicts in psychic life today, has been variously interpreted. Some analysts are inclined to see a profound change in the nature of individual psychology, others to see a change in the visibility and salience of certain conflicts brought about not only by social conditions but also by the development of the psychoanalytic approach. That is, the attention to earlier, preoedipal conflicts could be explained by a change in analytic treatment and method that illuminates such problems as well as by a change in the complaints of individuals who come to the attention of the mental health professions. My purpose here is not to question the notion of a change in individual psychology, though I think it may not be as far-reaching as some have claimed, but to suggest what such a change might mean. Specifically, I will address the meaning of this change from the point of view of contemporary challenges to paternal authority and to traditional gender roles. That is, assuming that the Oedipus complex did represent accurately some truths about the development of the individual in our culture, what kind of individuality was it and what would a change in this individuality mean?

I shall first discuss the theory of the Oedipus complex as a model of how human beings achieve autonomy. I will go on to show how it implies the necessity of an authority relationship between parent and child and the internalization of that authority as superego. It also implies a relationship between the sexes in which male dominates female. I will then suggest that psychoanalytic views of human development that grew out of an interest in preoedipal or narcissistic issues may be associated with a different view of authority and the parent–child relationship. This includes a discussion of how domination develops as a way of resolving the early conflict between nurturance and autonomy. Then follows an analysis of how the oedipal resolution consolidates early tendencies to solve that conflict by emphasizing separateness over connectedness, by repudiating the mother. This solution can be seen to stem from the sexual division of labor in our society. Finally, I shall propose that the oedipal solution to the conflict between nurturance and freedom actually preserves the early narcissistic wishes for control and oneness in a dangerous way. Thus, I question the normative use of the oedipal model and some aspects of the distinction between oedipal and preoedipal or narcissistic issues.

From Oedipus to Narcissus

The Oedipus complex was the centerpiece of Freud's theory of individual development (see, for example, Freud, 1923/1961). Its significance derived from the fact that it not only identified the etiology of neurosis in a specific set of instinctual conflicts but also proposed how a successful resolution of these conflicts contributes to the development of psychic structure. In the Oedipus complex, the triangular relationship between parents and child as experienced by the little boy—and boys alone were the prototype for this theory—is crystallized. The male child loves his mother and wishes to possess her, hates his father, and wishes to replace or murder him. Induced by the fear of the father, the threat of castration, the child renounces his incestuous wish toward the mother and internalizes the paternal authority that demands this renunciation. The father's insistence on renunciation is also an insistence that the child become autonomous, sever the maternal bond, and give up his wish for an exclusive relationship with the mother. Those desires that the child once proclaimed quite openly—"I'm going to marry you when I grow up, Mommy"—now undergo repression or, better yet, are sublimated into more civilized filial feelings. Henceforth, the boy's superego will perform the paternal function within his own psyche, proclaiming autonomy at the price of sexual renunciation and former dependency. Structurally, this process means a differentiation within the psyche, the development of the superego through identification. The successful resolution of the Oedipus complex means also the transition from fear of external authority to self-regulation; authority is replaced by independent conscience, prohibition by self-control, need for approval by autonomy.

It is the structure-building function of the Oedipus complex that is of importance to the social critics who bemoan its decline. Recently, and most powerfully, Lasch has articulated this critique of contemporary narcissism in his books *The Culture of Narcissism* (1979) and *Haven in a Heartless World* (1977). Lasch's account draws on 40 years of psychoanalytically oriented social criticism, beginning with the works of the Frankfurt school.[1] He has captured the public imagination with his de-

[1]Most of the fundamental themes of Lasch's critique of narcissism were anticipated by the writings of the Frankfurt critical theorists. On the decline of paternal authority, see Horkheimer and Adorno (1972) and Horkheimer (1949). On the use of psychoanalysis for social theory, see Adorno (1967, 1968). On the decline of the Oedipus complex, see Marcuse (1955, 1970). Their position was further developed by Mitscherlich (1969). Most

scription of a new cultural prototype, the narcissistic personality of our times. Ruthlessly self-seeking and self-involved, lacking in a sense of responsibility toward others or society, the New Narcissist is a caricature of self-interested individualism. Lasch explains that the new narcissism is the product of parents who could not or did not exercise authority. The failure of parental authority is, in turn, attributed to the weakening of parents' autonomy and individual decisiveness by the interference of experts, social agencies, and prescriptive literature. The disenfranchised parent, no longer trusting her or his ability to rule at home, is the counterpart of the man in the gray flannel suit, who does not control or take responsibility for his work because he is only a cog in the bureaucratic wheel. By contrast, the model figure who unifies authority and autonomy is described as something like the nineteenth-century father who runs his own business and his family with a just but firm hand.

Lasch's critique of contemporary parenting and its consequences for individual psychology draws on one side of a controversy in contemporary psychoanalytic discussions of narcissism. It will be worth clarifying some aspects of this controversy before proceeding to the significance of the Oedipus complex and the meaning of its decline. From the standpoint of classical psychoanalysis, the patient with oedipal conflicts is more advanced developmentally than the patient whose ego is weakened by difficulties pertaining to the preoedipal phase. There is general agreement that the earliest and most profound problems are found in those individuals who have been unable to achieve a stable sense of the mother's existence and to differentiate in relation to her. In classical psychoanalytic theory, the child is seen as beginning in a stage of primary narcissism in which it feels entirely fused with the mother. Self and other are, as yet, undifferentiated in the child's mind. The primary psychological task of this early phase is *differentiation:* formation of an independent ego, recognition of the distinct existence of others apart from the self, and realization of the self as an ongoing separate entity. Until differentiation occurs, the unconditional and unfailing support of the parent is experienced as part of the self. Consequently, the self feels *omnipotent.*[2] Feelings of omnipotence and grandiosity are components of

recently, the idea of the decline of the individual has been presented by Jacoby (1975). For a critical discussion of these important and early contributions to understanding the familial and psychic changes brought about in late capitalism, see Benjamin (1977, 1978).

[2]The most comprehensive formulation of a psychoanalytic theory of early differentiation can be found in Mahler, Pine, and Bergman (1975). Many researchers on infancy would

early narcissistic experience that must be modified by the process of differentiation.

The decisive problem to which the myriad uses of the term *narcissism* seem to refer is the person's ability or inability to see the other as an independent subject in her or his own right. That is, the individual must relinquish omnipotence. It is here that the controversy opens. What must the earliest objects, the child's parents, provide in order that differentiation occur and early grandiosity and omnipotence feelings be modified? What must the analyst do if this modification has never successfully taken place?

The point of view expressed by Lasch is that parental authority, internalized as superego, is the fundament upon which differentiation is based. He derives his position chiefly from the work of Kernberg, who represents a more classical view of narcissistic disorders than does Kohut. Kernberg argues that the problem should not be seen as a developmental arrest, that is, a failure of something to occur that modifies early narcissistic relatedness. Rather, he sees a pathological, defensive structure which like other defenses must be dissolved by interpretation. Concerning the achievement of mature object relatedness, Kernberg attributes great importance to the development of the oedipal superego. "The developmental state of the superego (particularly the ego ideal) and the nature of the predominant outcome of the oedipal conflicts influence the degree to which an object relation is "anaclitic" that is, dominated by "regressive, infantile features" (Kernberg, 1975, p. 324). It is the oedipal superego that insures that the individual does not regress to less clearly differentiated relationships, that pathological narcissism does not develop.

It is this position on narcissism that Lasch, with some liberties, makes use of to argue that in recent history there has been an alteration of the superego. Because of the breakdown in authority, the new superego "derives most of its psychic energy in the absence of authoritative social prohibitions from the destructive aggressive impulses within the id" (Lasch, 1979, p. 40). He maintains that there is an essential difference between the representation of authority derived from such id-

---

dispute the claim that infants initially perceive the mother as part of the self. The attribution of narcissism and omnipotence feelings to infants is seen by some, e.g., Stern (1985) and Peterfreund (1978), as an adultomorphism. Although I agree with this criticism, I am here interested in criticizing psychoanalytic theory on its own terms, developing an "immanent critique."

influenced, preoedipal fantasies and the representation "resting on later impressions and therefore reflecting a more realistic assessment of parental powers" (p. 41). This view of development holds that the archaic fantasies and aggression brought by the child to its relationships must be counteracted by experience with real authority, in the form of loved and respected models of social conduct. The kernel of this argument is that differentiation is predicated upon the parental exercise of authority, albeit a benevolent or reasonable authority. The erosion of "all forms of patriarchal authority" and consequent "weakening of the social superego" (p. 40) leave individuals at the mercy of their destructive impulses.

The views expressed by Kohut on the development of narcissism do not afford the same implicit defense of authority nor do they attribute such importance to the superego. Kohut's explanation of narcissistic disorders in terms of developmental arrest poses the problem largely in terms of a failure to receive positive responses to early narcissistic strivings (Kohut, 1971).[3] The better satisfied the early strivings for self-display and autonomy, the less likely the individual will cling to a grandiose image of the self. To achieve a stable, flexible self requires two types of early experience: the opportunity to merge with another person's cohesive self and the mirroring by an audience of one's own self-expression. Given such experience, the child can react to minor loss and frustration by soothing or affirming itself and thus adopting the object's functions. For Kohut, the emphasis in the analytic situation should be on the empathic appreciation of the need being expressed rather than on the analysis of defenses. In early development, it is appropriate gratification that allows narcissism to develop naturally from fantasies of omnipotence to real autonomy. Kohut even suggests—somewhat overzealously, I think—that it may be the failure of parental responsiveness to the child's assertiveness that calls forth the intensity of sexual and hostile attitudes that comprise the Oedipus complex.[4]

What is useful in Kohut's perspective is the focus on the process of differentiation not in terms of authority but in terms of respect for sub-

[3]This view emphasizes the need for inner structures of a different kind. In his recent work, Kohut (1977) attributes scarcely any role to the superego.

[4]In his recent work, Kohut (1977) suggests that the Oedipus complex as we know it may be the result of "empathy failures" on the parental side, the failure of the environment to respond to the child's "whole self." He asks whether "it is only the self of the child whose primary affectionate and competitive assertiveness is not responded to that is then dominated by unassimilated lust and hostility?" (p. 247). This position seems to imply that a perfect environment would obviate all unconscious conflict—a dubious proposition.

jectivity. A good example of this is the setting of limits. He suggests that parental inability to say no points to an inability to tolerate separateness, to see the child as "an independent center of initiative" (Kohut, 1977, p. 274). Here it becomes clearer that a child's relinquishment of omnipotence is predicated on the parent's attainment of psychic differentiation. Behind the exercise of authority or responsibility lies something else. When Kohut says that the child needs to experience the parent as an omnipotent ideal object, he means that the parental check on the child's impulses should be felt as stemming from the parent's own confident, cohesive selfhood.

The contemporary discussion of narcissism, then, suggests at least two rather different views of what the decline of the Oedipus complex means. The crux of Freud's theory, and of those contemporary reformulations most loyal to it, seems to be the claim that, unless some form of authority is internalized, the individual will remain dependent on others for what she or he ought to embody in the self. But, from the other point of view, this assumption can be questioned by asking: Why should authority be central to autonomy? or, more broadly, Why should differentiation be linked to domination? My purpose is to ask whether the oedipal model, with its affirmative view of authority, is an ideal or universal path of development to individuality. This is not to say that the theory of the Oedipus complex is simply wrong or irrelevant. In those aspects that pertain to the affirmation of childhood sexuality and the power of the unconscious imagery that expresses it, the theory legitimately remains central to much clinical endeavor. I do not question the importance of the child's early struggle with gender identity and sexual love for the parents; I do question the broad structural claims for the oedipal conflicts in the development of the ego and superego. I am challenging the use of the theory as a normative model of socialization which assumes that internalization of authority and, more broadly, a specific form of male gender identity are necessary to differentiation. It is this model that I propose to investigate, not as a universal, but as an *ideal type* of socialization in our culture. I propose to explain what the Oedipus complex and its decline can tell us about gender domination in our society. I assume that the oedipal model probably reflects quite accurately the way that individuality has been developed in our culture, but this development can no longer be accepted as the only possibility of human development. The apparent crisis of this pattern of socialization suggests that we should question rather than defend this form of individuality and its connection to authority.

The Problem of Omnipotence

The oedipal conflict has been reinterpreted in light of contemporary analytic concerns as the culmination of the preoedipal struggle to differentiate, to relinquish infantile omnipotence, and to overcome early narcissism. It can be viewed as the end point in the process of separating from the mother and father, an end point reached by renouncing the one and internalizing the other. The oedipal wish to make the mother an exclusive love object has been interpreted as a later expression of the narcissistic longing for fusion and return to omnipotence. Chasseguet-Smirgel (1976) has suggested that we might view "the wish to be big like father and to thus possess mother . . . (as resulting from) nostalgia for primary fusion, when the infant enjoyed fullness and perfection" (p. 357). However, actual fulfillment of the incest wish would mean return to oneness, dedifferentiation or loss of an independent self. It is this danger of complete narcissistic regression that the superego protects against by prohibiting incest (p. 349).

But the superego itself represents a transformation of early narcissism, growing out of the earliest ego ideal. The origins of the superego, Freud throught, lay in the early identification with the omnipotent parental object in the period when self and object were one:

> Man has here again shown himself incapable of giving up a satisfaction he once enjoyed. He is not willing to forego the narcissistic perfection of his childhood . . . he seeks to recover it in the new form of an ego ideal. What he projects before him as his ideal is the substitute for the lost narcissism of his childhood in which he was his own ideal. (Freud, 1914/1957, p. 94)

It is the superego, heir to the early longing for perfection and omnipotence, that should modify and insure renunciation of that longing.

There is an ambiguity in this formulation that is the marrow of the difficulty of the affirmative view of authority. The superego is both part of the problem and part of the solution, a contradiction that Freud was more aware of than many of his successors. In his lengthy disquisition on the need for authority in *Civilisation and Its Discontents,* Freud develops this contradiction in terms of the superego's role in curbing aggression. The expression of aggression, he suggests, provides

> an extraordinarily high degree of narcissistic enjoyment, owing to its presenting the ego with a fulfillment of the latter's old wishes for omnipotence. The instinct of destruction, moderated and tamed . . . provide(s) the ego with the satisfaction of its vital needs and with control over nature. (Freud, 1930/1961, p. 121)

But the superego grows out of internalization. It is fueled by the "same harsh aggressiveness" (p. 123) that it turns against the ego in its efforts to curb this satisfaction of the omnipotence wish.

Thus, in both of Freud's formulations on the origins of the superego, whether pertaining to the desire for perfection or the pleasure of aggression, the superego never escapes the taint of omnipotence. It is a sublimation, not a cure for omnipotence, using the grandiosity and aggression of early narcissism to fuel its demands for self-control. Herein lies the irony: The very authority that keeps omnipotence in check originates in what we experience, or wish to experience, as omnipotence, but this experience really corresponds to the state of our greatest dependency.

Analogously, the superego has the double function of protecting and limiting the absolute claims of the self. It is fueled by narcissism and also serves to curb it. The superego seems to forbid omnipotence or fusion in all aspects—being one with, being like, or possessing the source of perfection. Yet it does not do so completely. For it promises gratification in the future: If you are good and realistic and independent now, if you defer gratification and control yourself, you may one day possess and control someone like mother. It is this promise that makes for the specifically *rational* character of paternal authority. The child wants to destroy authority, but instead identifies with and internalizes it. The power or threat behind the promise, as with the carrot and the stick, is gradually lost to consciousness. Bowing to reality, submitting to parental authority, has this dual element of prohibition and promise of fulfillment.

The Repudiation of Femininity

The oedipal promise foreshadows the structure of the future relationship between adult men and women, the outline of gender domination. As Freud conceived it, the superego was the internalization of two seemingly opposite injunctions (and here the male derivation of this theory becomes acutely apparent). The father's command, "You may not be like me," means that the superego forbids incestuous union with the mother. The command "You ought to be like me" enforces the distinction between the mother, who is object of love, and father, who is object of identification (Freud, 1923/1961, p. 34). The mother, love object, now represents lost dependency; the father, object of identification, now functions as the ideal of future autonomy. The child is no longer permitted to identify with the mother because this would also be a form of fusion, a more primitive one, even, than possession of her. So both commands have the function of forbidding fusion and dependency. The identification with the mother, being feminine like her, is now experienced as dangerous regression and dedifferentiation.

The repudiation of femininity is the central thread that runs through the Oedipus complex. The "negative Oedipus complex" in which the boy seeks to be loved by his father and (like a girl) identifies with his mother is, in Freud's view (1923, p. 33) a part of the complete Oedipus complex. But the successful resolutions of both the negative and positive aspects of the complex point in the same direction—an intensified identification with the father, a disidentification with the mother. The boy's identification with the father and his choice to protect his penis, or masculinity, by submitting to his father are both made at the expense of the identification with the mother. Recent feminist psychoanalytic thought, especially the work of Chodorow (1978, 1979), has illuminated the consequences of this process of male identity formation. According to Chodorow, the fact that women are chiefly responsible for the early care of the young means that woman = mother is a unity in the child's mind and constitutes the first basis for identification. Because boys must break with this early identification in order to preserve their masculinity, the achievement of gender identity (as distinguished from object choice) is more precarious for them than it is for girls. As a result, Chodorow argues, male identity is characterized by a preoccupation with difference, separateness, distance, and boundaries in a way that female identity is not.

The full meaning of the Oedipus complex emerges when we consider the link between the achievement of individual identity and the repudiation of the mother. This link may help to illuminate how the narcissistic issue of relinquishing omnipotence is restated and resolved in the oedipal phase. According to the classical model, these issues are resolved by the intervention of the father, his prohibition of incest, and early maternal identification. The problem with this purported resolution becomes evident when we consider that women have never been regarded as equal, independent subjects by men. If the repudiation of identity with the mother leads, as it has thus far, to a denial of her subjectivity, how can the oedipal resolution be said to foster relatedness with the other as an independent subject? The ability to see the other as an independent subject, which represents the decisive step away from the omnipotence fantasy of infancy, has seldom been part of either the relationship between the sexes or the male attitude toward the mother.

Along these lines, Dinnerstein (1976) has proposed that paternal authority grows out of men's narcissistic rage at both the power of the mother and the frustration of the wish to remain in symbiotic oneness with her. In her analysis the theme recurs that authority, which ought to be the solution to the problem of omnipotence, actually reinstates the problem in disguised form. Only when the issues of gender domination are resolved can an individual self develop that is truly capable of accepting the existence of the other person without compromising its own.

The power of the oedipal paradigm derived from its ability to explain simultaneously the development of gender identity and the development of individual selfhood. That it did so by collapsing individuality and masculinity is highly significant. The oedipal father represented our peculiar form of individuality; his authority represented the only alternative to remaining undifferentiated, his freedom until now the only freedom. He taught us the lesson that she who nurtures us does not free us and that he who frees us does not nurture us but rather rules us.

Equally significant in this constellation is the split and polarity that is institutionalized between two essential needs, for nurturance and for freedom. Acceptance of the oedipal solution means accepting this polarity. Either we differentiate or remain dependent; either we bow to reality or we remain infantile; either we deny our needs or we are enslaved by them. The Oedipus complex institutionalizes and reifies this polarity, giving it social form and assigning gender to it. The superego redefines the utopian longing to recover the unity of these needs as the prohibited and dangerous regression to total dependency and loss of self. The necessity of the superego, of authority, and of gender polarity are all bound up with this split between nurturance and freedom.

This polarity, which is in fact the polarity of gender, is at the heart of our investigation of the Oedipus complex. On the basis of the foregoing discussion of the superego, its origins in the experience of narcissism, and the repudiation of femininity, we can now address several specific sets of questions. First, there is the question of the necessity of paternal authority and its internal form, the superego, in preventing regression or enforcing differentiation. We must ask why dependency should retain its exclusive allure even after we are no longer helpless. Why is the mirroring of autonomy not sufficient to anchor autonomy? In short, do human beings not want to differentiate? The second set of questions has to do with the splitting between autonomy and dependency, between nurturance and freedom, which is enjoined by the oedipal superego. We must ask why identification and object love must be directed to opposing parents in the Oedipus complex. Why does independence or individuality consist of rejecting identification with one parent? And why does this split get projected along gender lines? Finally, there is the paradox that the superego emerges from the same impulses that it is needed to control. We must inquire into the consequence of giving up omnipotence by projecting it onto paternal authority and then internalizing it in modified form. Is the dependency hidden in the illusion of omnipotence not the well-kept secret of the superego? Is this method of control any less dangerous than the regression it is supposed to prevent? Is this realistic, rational authority less dangerous, its claim to power smaller, than the naked domination it is supposed to replace?

Recognition and the Formation of Self

As the earlier discussion of narcissism theory suggested, the exploration of early conflicts around differentiation may offer a different perspective than that afforded by the oedipal model. The emphasis on early dyadic experiences and problems of the ego or the self has led to a deemphasizing of drives. From the examination of such experiences, both inside and outside of classical psychoanalysis, positions have emerged that challenge the primacy of oedipal experience in psychic life and development. These perspectives imply that the development of autonomy might be voluntary, dependent upon the responsiveness but not on the authority of the parent. According to Freud's view of the drives and the ego as initially monadic, unrelated to objects or external reality, sociability was imposed from without. Object relations theory (e.g., Guntrip, 1961), an offshoot of orthodox psychoanalysis, has for some time maintained a different view of the drives. It has argued that the primary drive, or libido, seeks not release of tension or pleasure, but the object as another person. Subsequent research in ethology and human infancy (e.g., Bowlby, 1969) bears out the perspective that humans are motivated by an impulse toward attachment to specific persons from the beginning of life. This attachment is not based simply upon physiological need or dependency, as Freud thought, but is an essentially social impulse. Attachment develops through the active participation of both child and parent. It is an impulse that pushes toward a deepening awareness of the other's independent existence, the culmination of which is mutual *recognition.*

Recognition of the other's independent existence, a vital aspect of differentiation, goes hand in hand with the assertion of one's own independence. The ability to recognize significant others and to initiate and regulate social interaction begins to develop by the fourth month of life (Stern, 1977, p. 1). In addition to its early capacity for sociability, the infant shows a disposition to assert itself, to explore and master the environment as well.[5] It is not possible here to propose a new interpretation of Freud's metapsychology that would do justice to the old and yet make sense of new empirical evidence and theoretical developments. Let us simply say that it is possible to understand human development through a variety of conceptual systems. In the effort to understand the development of the *self* and the intersubjective reality of self and other, a new set of categories seems to suggest itself. In formulating the growth of the self, the process of differentiation, we can identify two fundamental directions: the strivings toward the other, for connection, attachment, closeness; and the strivings toward assertion of self, for activity, mastery, and exploration.[6] These two capacities define a human nature that strives to become independent and differentiate self from other, as well as to remain connected to and protected by a sense of oneness with a loved and trusted companion. These strivings or capacities are intertwined from the beginning of life, and both constitute the process of successful differentiation, even as they both contribute to successful attachment.

Such innate dispositions assumed, the vehicle of differentiation ap-

[5]Ainsworth has developed Bowlby's work to explain development in terms of a "more inclusive concept of a balance between exploratory and attachment behavior" (Ainsworth, Bell, & Stayton, 1971, p. 18). One of the earliest formulations that stresses the activity impulse of infants is that of Schachtel (1959). Research psychologists in the last decade have documented the active differentiating side of infant life, especially infants' search for experiences of contingency which confirm the sense of efficacy (Goldberg, 1977).

[6]Although the terminology I use to describe these two tendencies may be somewhat arbitrary, the intention behind them should be clear. The rejoicing of the infant at the sight of the loved parent returning home and the joy of the infant who has just climbed a ladder and stands crowing at the top are distinct experiences that refer to attachment and self-assertion respectively. These two capacities cannot develop independently of one another, though our conventional usage implies that they can by making *independence* the opposite of *dependency*. It has therefore been suggested that we think not in terms of dependency but of attachment—the loving bond—which can be as strong on the part of an independent person as a dependent one, if not stronger (Ainsworth, 1969).

pears to be not prohibition and injunction by authority, but recognition by a loved other: appropriate mirroring of autonomous activity and secure confirmation of connection and closeness. Is this perhaps an overly optimistic, "oversocialized" view of human nature? I do not think so. In my view, the notion of such primary strivings—I shall call them object and activity strivings—opens the way for profound conflict. This notion helps to explain those conflicts that define psychological life in our culture, conflicts between autonomy and mutuality, nurturance and freedom. The two tendencies easily, if not inevitably, assume an antithetical relationship to one another. The splitting of object and activity strivings is the key to that split between two kinds of objects in the Oedipus complex—between the ideal object of attachment and the mirror of exploration, between the objects of love and identification. This polarity becomes the greatest obstacle to differentiation, although it appears in our culture as a necessary path to it. To conceptualize this polarity, we must imagine a possible unity that the oedipal model has pulled apart. Ideally, as the study of preoedipal experience suggests, both capacities must be recognized and responded to in the same relationship. We must now consider how these strivings become divided and opposed to one another. The opposition begins in what I call the paradox of recognition.

Human beings require recognition to develop a sense of their own agency. Autonomous selfhood develops, and is later confirmed, chiefly by the sense of being able to affect others by one's acts. Ultimately, such confirmation also allows us to develop an appreciation of the other's subjectivity, to recognize another person. Such recognition of the other is as much the culmination of true differentiation as is autonomy. Developing the awareness of self and the awareness of the other are really parts of the same process. Paradoxically, the need for recognition means that we are dependent upon another person to acknowledge our independence. In our very attempt to establish independence from the other person, we are dependent on that person to confirm or recognize our independence. It is this paradox that governs our first relationship, the relationship between infant and primary parent (object attachment). The child is in the position of metaphorically having to destroy the authority of the one it loves and depends on in order to be independent. Because it is so difficult to endure this paradox, the impulse to split these vital needs easily takes over. This paradox is the key to how the needs for autonomy and for recognition become split and opposed, as well as to the connection between domination and differentiation.

This theoretical construct corresponds remarkably to the finding of Mahler, Pine, and Bergman (1975, pp. 76–108) in their observation of infants and their mothers. The paradox of recognition corresponds to the dynamic which they term "the rapprochement crisis." In the rapprochement phase, the toddler insists that the mother "share" in all his or her new discoveries and performances, seeking validation for his or her self-assertion. Although more independent, he or she is not so content as earlier to discover the world without this constant affirmation. The toddlers' contradictory wish is to be, and to be recognized as "separate, grand and omnipotent on the one hand, and to have mother magically fulfill their wishes, without their having to recognize that help was actually coming from the outside, on the other" (p. 95).

The most important attempt to explain these interconnections, the first articulation of this paradox, was Hegel's (1807/1952, pp. 141–150) discussion of the struggle for recognition (cf. Benjamin, 1983). The struggle for recognition becomes a struggle to the death—as if only by risking death (of the self) can one's autonomy (the self) be established. Each self struggles to achieve its selfhood in the eyes of the other. So each is caught between the need to negate the other and the need to be recognized by the other as an equal. Hegel asserted that in order to exist for oneself, one had to exist for another, that persons must affect one another through their acts. In order to be recognized by someone, one must recognize him or her in return. Hegel's point is that absolute independence is not possible (for self-conscious beings) because mutuality is a condition of independence. Recognition of the other person's independence means accepting one's own dependency rather than denying it; the person whom we need to recognize us is outside our control. Should we obtain control over the other, the other would no longer be an independent subject capable of conferring recognition upon us. However, as human beings do not wish to give up their absolute independence, they often do attempt to obtain power over the other person as if by doing so they could solve this dilemma of the need for recognition. The struggle for recognition culminates in the relationship of domination, master and slave.

Hegel's interpretation of the problem suggests that the refusal to give up omnipotence occurs not because we cling to dependency but because it is too painful to acknowledge it. Although Hegel, like Freud, believes that human beings do not voluntarily give up omnipotence, he confronts the ego with the intrinsic necessity of giving up independence in order to obtain it. The intervention of authority—the acceptance of domination—is not necessary to achieve independence, however. Rather, caught between the inherently social nature of selfhood and the desire for absolute independence, the ego creates domination. Because of this conflict, one self subjugates another. Indeed, each self struggles to be the subjugator. Hegel's metaphor of the struggle for recognition is not a justification of authority but an explanation of its origins as domination (*Herrschaft*). Domination is a substitute for or escape from differentiation, from recognizing another's independent existence.

Domination is a substitute for differentiation not only for the subjugator but also for the dominated. This gives us an added perspective on the acceptance of domination, the internalization of authority. Here, so beautifully put by George Eliot, is an illustration of the oedipal resolution, "I will accept your [the father's] power if you will let me become like you." She wrote of the heroine Dorothea in *Middlemarch:*

> We are all of us born in moral stupidity, taking the world as an udder to feed our supreme selves: Dorothea had early begun to emerge from that stupidity, but yet it had been easier for her to imagine how she would . . . become wise and strong in his strength and wisdom, than to conceive with that distinctness which is no longer reflection but feeling that he had an equivalent centre of self, whence the lights and shadows must always fall with a certain difference.

To immerse ourselves in the power of the father rather than to become autonomous on our own, to accept his principle of difference rather than our difference from him, is easier. Yet it is the very opposite of that feeling by which we know the other to be a separate, equivalent center, to be truly different from ourselves.

True differentiation involves not only the awareness of the separation between self and other, but the appreciation of the other's independent existence as an equivalent center. The most vital aspect of differentiation is the ability to see the other person as an independent subject, someone who is both similar to and different from, connected to but separate from, the self. True differentiation means accepting dependency not as dangerous regression but as enjoyable connection. It lies not in the splitting of autonomy and recognition but in accepting the tension of their paradoxical relationships. It means tolerating the ambivalence of being connected to and separate from another without the defense of imagining oneself becoming like some all-powerful other. Only by giving up the aspiration to complete control can both self and other be experienced as vibrantly distinct.

As I have stated elsewhere (Benjamin, 1983), the struggle for recognition entails a dialectical tension. If one person completely controls another, the other ceases to exist as a person who can recognize him or her. If the other does not offer that sense of uncontrollability but appears to succumb entirely to the first person's power, then this other will no longer appear as a person. So, at some point in the earliest struggle for recognition, the mother must actually remove herself from the child's omnipotent sense of control. She must establish her existence as another subject, as a person, so that the child, too, can have a sense of selfhood. If the mother is not herself able to tolerate this degree of differentiation from her child, to inflict this pain upon her or him, or if she is able to do so only by asserting her own total control over the child, the child's narcissism will either be unrealistically inflated or wounded. The outcome of the early experience of differentiation from the mother–child dyad (for this dyad is the usual context in our society) depends upon the mother's responses in the first years of life. Although the father is a significant contributor, the idea that later paternal intervention is the key to differentiation has little to do with concrete reality.

So far, I have argued that human beings do wish to differentiate, to become autonomous, but that autonomy itself is an ambiguous phenomenon. It cannot be realized as absolute independence but only in conjunction with what in our culture is often defined as its opposite: mutual recognition. Mutuality is often experienced as intolerable because it involves acknowledging both dependency and the other's independence. To the extent that such dependency is perceived as a threat to autonomy, the individual must protect herself or himself by identifying with someone whom she or he imagines to be truly strong and independent. The process of escaping differentiation by this use of authority parallels the escape in which domination or control over the other substitutes for mutual recognition.

The superego can be seen not as a necessary agency to insure differentiation but as a mechanism of these false forms of differentiation. By forcing the repudiation of dependency, the superego reflects the authority it derives from, an authority who also keeps secret his dependency and appears ideally autonomous. In other words, a one-sided or false differentiation is promoted by the solution in which one subject tries to repudiate his or her own dependence and insure the submission of the other. This sort of independence, which is not based on the mutual and reciprocal appreciation of distinctness, is promoted by the internalization of the father as an ideal of absolute autonomy.

The Polarity of Gender

This form of differentiation can, I believe, be seen as institutionalized in the Oedipus complex through the polarity of gender. Man–father achieves absolute autonomy because woman–mother represents dependency. Individuality, then, is constituted by what is male, by the permanent assignment of man to the role of subject. Women are denied subjectivity and are assigned to the role of object. Originally, it is through this denial of subjectivity to women that men lose the mirror of their subjectivity. Recognition occurs not through the love relationship, but only in the competitive struggle with other men. Man's domination of woman has found expression in the oedipal relationships in which the split between male and female is reproduced in each generation. Let us examine more closely how this process of splitting between love and identification, nurturance and freedom, is embodied in the Oedipus complex and how the form of individuality that we are familiar with grows out of these splits.

The oedipal father is the enforcer not of true differentiation but of splitting and polarity. In our model of the preoedipal experience, the tension between recognition and autonomy occurs in relation to one figure, traditionally the mother. In the oedipal model, identification, that is, validation for autonomy, is projected onto the father; love, that is, acceptance by the other, is projected onto the mother. Each partner becomes the object of one striving. The price of autonomy is, of course, relinquishment of the love object and therefore repression of the object striving itself. Thus the father demands not only that the two tendencies be split but also that the object striving be subordinated to the activity striving, that autonomy develop at the expense of mutual recognition. He denies the contradictory unity of differentiation, which includes not only the assertion of self but also the recognition of the other.

Although the splitting of this unity does not begin at the oedipal level, it is consolidated and institutionalized in terms of gender at this point. The contradiction begins in the preoedipal experience of differentiation and gender identity, based on the paradox of recognition: the felt tension between dependency and autonomy, attachment and separation. The classical preoedipal model has not wholly grasped this tension. To a large extent, the preoedipal model has been construed teleologically in terms of the oedipal model, as if the oedipal conflicts represented a graduation from the earlier stage. Indeed, this has led to the mistaken clinical assumption that the presence of preoedipal conflicts implies greater pathology or weakness of the ego in the patient, an equation that does not always hold up.[7] Furthermore, differentiation has been conceived from the beginning largely in terms of independence and separation rather than in terms of the positive capacity to appreciate the mother's subjectivity. The ability to recognize her selfhood is confounded with sexual renunciation, giving up the hope of possessing her. But of course recognition means more than this. Similarly, in the classical preoedipal model, self-assertion and activity are seen as only separations from, not as connections to, other subjects. In actual fact, a baby's assertiveness develops as much through trying to affect the parent as though detaching itself from the parent.

In this sense we could say, as Chodorow (1979) has put it, that the classical preoedipal model sees differentiation through the lens of male experience, for it stresses separation from rather than recognition of the mother. The denial of identification with the mother is the great imperative of male differentiation in both phases. The little boy is to think he is or must be nothing like the one he loves and who loves and nurtures him. This repudiation of identity also functions as a denial of dependency. It is an attempt to differentiate by dominating or objectifying the other person. Unconsciously, denying the mother's subjectivity and the need to identify with her confirms the sense of omnipotence—in this case, of self over object. Furthermore, not merely the identification with the mother but also identification as a mode of relating is repudiated. The two elements of recognition—identification and distinguishing self from other—are split. One no longer feels both the same as and different from the other; one only feels different (cf. Miller, 1973). Similarly, one feels not connected and separate, but only separate. The capacity for identifying with, feeling like, is henceforth feminine, an aspect of the forbidden narcissistic fusion (see Engel, 1980). Female children, whom Freud saw as remaining narcissistic, could develop the capacity for identification but, in his view, at the expense of their autonomy, conscience, and ability for object love. The girl's narcissism is only partially fulfilled; her need for mirroring of activity and autonomy is denied.

Since, for men, the mother is deprived of subjectivity, the identification with her would mean a loss of subjectivity. Activity, nonidentifica-

[7]With the increased vision given by the theory of separation–individuation, it is possible to see how preoedipal issues shape the conflicts of patients who, because of their relatively strong ego functions, previously would have been treated as oedipal patients. This approach moves away from the idea of fixation and does more justice to the accretion of personality in the context of relationships in the first years of life.

tion, and difference are equated with the father and with individuality (subjectivity) itself. But object love without identification does turn the mother into an object—she is only different, The Other. Since boys are forced to achieve their individuality by repudiating dependency and the identification with the mother, they become fit for the stalemate of one-sided differentiation. Since girls are denied identification with the father, who stands for difference and separation, they are unable to achieve the accepted form of autonomy. Each gender is able to represent only one aspect of the self–other relationship; each gender plays a part in a polarized whole. One is independent, the other dependent; one is master, the other slave.

Neither gender can appreciate difference, for each is forbidden the identification with the other parent. Hence identification with someone who is, in part, different is virtually an unknown feeling. One can only imagine identifying with someone essentially like oneself, someone who is in the same category. Identification then assumes an all-or-nothing quality, it threatens dedifferentiation, the regression to loss of identity. It is not developed as one part of the object striving for recognition, the part that feels likeness within difference. Furthermore, only identification with the father's activity, with the father as activity principle, is considered to be a form of differentiation. The process of recognition, the commingling of activity and object strivings that makes up true differentiation, is totally devalued and repressed. To differentiate under the aegis of the oedipal father is to do so one-sidedly. The oedipal father has become an embodiment of this form of differentiation—of the principle of difference over likeness, activity over intimacy. He represents and enforces the principle of polarity—the conflict of opposites—as the context for individual development.

The peculiar rationality that grows out of male experience has been criticized by Gilligan (1977, 1982) in regard to a counterpart of the oedipal model, Kohlberg's theory of moral development. Kohlberg, following Piaget, posits stages of development from self-interest through conformity to universal values. Successful socialization culminates in increasing independence of environment, in ego autonomy. Kohlberg (1971) found that women tended to remain at stage 3 of development, judgment based on interpersonal considerations, in their moral determination. He found that more men moved on to universal values such as justice and the right to self-fulfillment in their discriminations, whereas women were moved by identification and tied to specific contexts and relationships.

Gilligan (1977, 1982) criticized this conclusion from a feminist perspective. In her alternate version of the experiment, Gilligan found that women do proceed to the universal stage of moral development and that attainment of independence is a crucial part of this transition. But this transition takes a different form because women, in order to become independent of their environment, must revise their understanding of responsibility for others to include responsibility for themselves (whereas men begin with a sense of responsibility for self, self-interest). Women must move to a comprehension of caring that means not self-sacrifice but respect for one's own needs as well. When they do so, they attain as universal values notions of psychological truth, caring, and nonviolence that remain substantive. Their thinking remains connected and relational, their analysis of events concrete and contextual. They strive to reconcile a sense of urgency with concern for the other. In contrast, men appear committed to formal, abstract values such as equal rights for everyone. With the female model as normative, it becomes clear that men's rationality—formal rather than substantive, and excluding the subjectivity of the other—is only a step away from objectifying, instrumental reason. Male individuality is based on differentiating cognitively. Men aspire to and attain a cognitive appreciation of the difference between their needs and others', but without the commitment to the other's context or to empathic appreciation.

Beyond the Sexual Division of Labor

Thus far I have described an ideal type of differentiation and its consequences for our system of gender and our type of individuality. It is important to bear in mind that the oedipal model is an ideal type and that contradictions and polarities arising from oedipal socialization are far less clear in "real life." This conceptual scheme does shed light upon the intimacy of the connection between autonomy and authority in our culture. As Freud developed it, the oedipal model purported to speak for nature rather than for history; it assumed the inevitability of domination and gender difference. This inevitability and immutability no longer seem so self-evident. According to the model, we must have someone outside the first dyad to recognize our difference from the mother—to free us. This seems quite reasonable and does not conflict with the idea that humans have as much desire for independence as for merging. It simply means that our drive for independence must be recognized, find resonance, in a person other than the one we are becoming independent from. But why should this person be essentially different from the first? Why not simply two (or many) mothers? What is not convincing about the oedipal father's intervention in the dyad is the element of polarity, opposition. To provide recognition of the child's independence, the father need not enforce the principle of difference, embody the repudiation of dependency, deny the mother's common subjectivity. He need not have been a less nurturant or nonparticipating parent in the child's earliest life. These aspects of his role are a function not of the inevitable source of differentiation but of institutionalized gender domination.

Similarly, the mother's inability to model autonomy is also a function of her debasement in the present gender system. The metaphor of the Oedipus complex refers to the child's struggle with and acceptance of the fact that he is not the center of his mother's life. In the oedipal model, the father sets this limit. In true differentiation, the child perceives its mother as an equivalent center not only because she belongs to father (or, in the modern version, loves father). Rather, the child must be able gradually to experience the nurturing relationship with her as a relationship between persons, a relationship that has limits. The mother sets a limit to the child's narcissism not only by loving another but also by feeling and acting as a person who cannot be controlled totally by anyone. The mother who is not infantilized, not shut out of the public world, not dependent for her existence on her husband, is more likely to experience herself as a person in her own right. Feminists (e.g., Chodorow, Dinnerstein, and Miller) have therefore argued that both parents should have an equal role in raising children and both have a foot in the world of adults. But this demand covers a far broader terrain than the rearing of children. It implies a challenge to the entire sexual division of labor. It also challenges the separation of domestic/personal and productive/public spheres in our society, a separation that has been absolutely intrinsic to the growth of capitalism. It is this separation that, on the societal level, embodies the split between activity and recognition; the former is depersonalized and the latter is privatized. To women as mothers is assigned the promethean task of raising individuals who can harmoniously balance what society pulls asunder. The family must bear the entirety of the individual's needs for recognition, needs that our small, child-centered families tend to cultivate intensely.[8]

[8]Kovel (1982, p. 119) suggests that as the family becomes more like a greenhouse, cultivating an individuality that has no place in the public sphere, women in particular become the locus of conflicting demands for individual independence and restful domesticity.

The sweep of changes implied by dual parenting, then, is enormous. Nor should we imagine that such changes in our culture and social structure would put an end to human ambivalence. Rather, they would mean that the relief and pleasure as well as the pain of being a separate person are experienced together. This ambivalence would not be resolved defensively by denying the need for nurturance and dependency, by attributing these needs only to babies and not to adult individuals, or by controlling the other person so as to conceal one's feeling of dependency. Differentiation would not occur through the principle of polarity but through sustaining the unity of opposites in tension.

The analysis of the Oedipus complex as a polarization of drives that ought to remain interdependent raises a number of highly important, if presently insoluble, issues. What is the historical relationship between the rule of the father and the polarity within our culture between nurturance and freedom? Is some form of authority inevitable because human beings are incapable of enduring a mutual recognition that maintains these drives in tension (as Hegel's analysis might indicate)? The argument in favor of paternal authority is that without the father's rational authority the mother would permit endless fusion, blurring all differences and keeping her child in a swamp of undifferentiated narcissistic bliss. Such a view of the other clearly can be seen as a *result* of the gender polarity. This is how women–mothers appear once domination is institutionalized. This view of maternal love is also an expression of the revulsion and distortion that repression confers upon a forbidden wish, in this case a wish for fusion. The view of regression to narcissistic fusion as dangerous and requiring the vigilant prevention of the superego is equally likely to be the result, rather than the origin, of repression. Whereas regression appears as an absolute, a journey away from civilization with no return, to a more flexible ego it may be only an excursion. One may wonder if the regressive wish of men to remain dependent is not the wish for what is denied them. Analogously, one might find in the secret heart of women just the opposite, the longing for the activity and independence that have been the lot of men. Does not each sex crave what the other is permitted to express, the other pole of selfhood? In short, to what extent have the sexual division of labor and gender domination created what appears to us as natural forms of individuality and, indeed, polarity itself?

The purported decline of the Oedipus complex would make some of these speculations more real. Were we truly able in one fell swoop to wipe out centuries of socialization and confront the conflicts of earliest differentiation without institutionalized gender polarity, we might answer these questions. As it is, we can only wonder whether human beings are capable, no doubt with great anxiety, of suffering true differentiation. Our present state seems to offer less than such a total decline of the Oedipus complex. The change decried by Lasch and others as the end of oedipal socialization is something more like a loosening of it. This loosening reflects the lack of the powerful, idealized paternal authority of yesteryear, the increasing participation of women in the public sphere, a far more intense generational conflict, the growth of a child-centered, emotionally intense family culture. Although these factors have significantly changed the psychological relationship to authority, it is hardly clear that they have led to a decline in individuality or a failure of differentiation. They have led to a heightening of the contradiction between assertive activity and emotional connection. As Kovel has so aptly put it, "In capitalism an enhanced individuality encounters a deadened public world." Public life "is nowhere enriched . . . to the level of demand created by the development of the personal sphere" (Kovel, 1982, p. 117). In fact, we are raising children with more individuality into a world where there are fewer opportunities for them to be author of their acts or to be recognized as such.

The depersonalization of authority and the less authoritarian role of parents have led to a new perspective on fathering, male identity, and the very nature of normal individuality. As one psychoanalyst put it, work with patients that Freud would have rejected (borderline, psychotic, preoedipal patients) of whom presumably far more come to clinical attention, has led to a questioning of the exclusion of "empathy and identification from normality" (Loewald, 1979, p. 773). It has led to a respect for the "quest for irrational nondifferentiation of subject and object" (pp. 772–773) as containing its own truth that challenges our received order of objectivity, rationality, and reality. For many psychoanalysts, then, the opposite conclusion from Lasch's is emerging, that is, a questioning of the old ideal of individuality rather than the impulse to restore it.

These psychological changes do not necessarily mean that men no longer control society. The association of the male gender with the qualities and the practice of rationality and autonomy has not changed despite the diminishing opportunities for public exercise of individual powers. However, the image and practice of male individuality have suffered certain shocks. The superego's best kept secret, the father's dependency on the woman he controls, is out of the bag. As the dependent woman is no longer so reliable, this image of the father is no longer so convincing. Indeed, we might ask about the extent to which such changes in fixed gender roles have revealed self-esteem as a major clinical issue. The one-sidedness of male individuality, its inability to provide a solution to the tension between the needs for autonomy and oneness, has also been exposed. Further, the paradox between autonomy and authority has been intensified. The combination of affirmative and destructive attitudes toward the authority on which autonomy was based is difficult to maintain when each previous generation of authority appears less rational to the new one. Thus, despite the persistence of our one-sided form of individuality, we are witnessing great dissatisfaction as previously hidden contradictions rise to the surface.

The Myth of Oedipus

The crisis of authority exposes more clearly the paradoxes that were always inherent in the link between authority and autonomy and between domination and differentiation. The final paradox to be considered is the use of an authority based on the ideal of omnipotence to control omnipotence. Thus far, I have investigated two aspects of the Oedipus complex. First, I have asked whether the oedipal solution—the path to differentiation through domination—is necessary because otherwise human beings would refuse to give up the fantasy of omnipotence. To this I have answered that the human strivings for recognition and autonomy do not make this solution necessary but that their potential for conflict may explain why this form of development occurs. Second, I have addressed the psychological consequences of this solution, the kind of differentiation that oedipal socialization allows. I argued that the Oedipus complex embodies the polarity of gender and through it leads to a polarization of human capacities. These capacities would, in true differentiation, be united with one another—mutuality and autonomy, nurturance and freedom, identification and separation—in a creative tension. Breaking this tension, oedipal socialization promotes a one-sided individuality that is identified solely with those capacities attributed to the male or father.

According to the oedipal model, the nature of the narcissistic bond with the mother necessitates the role played interpersonally by father and internally by superego, Either we seek to retain her as the omnipotent object that we once experienced her to be, in which case we do not really separate from her, or we seek to become as we imagined her, omnipotent ourselves, as the only viable notion of how to be independent. "Mother does not need me, she is perfect; I will become perfect, cease to need *her*." This is the fantasy image of a person who cannot be affected by us, the unmoved mover, who need not recognize or be recognized by us. In Freud's view, the very act of trying to establish independence derives from our aspiration to such omnipotence. Only the brutal head-on collision with the other shatters this fantasy. Seemingly, it is up to the father to be this other. He demands the renunciation of fusion with the mother, but he does not replace it with permission to fuse with him. Furthermore, he is supposed to represent a less omnipotent authority as a model of autonomy. That is, he is perceived as neither object nor omnipotent ideal but as a rational, if authoritative subject. What becomes of this fantasy of omnipotence and perfection after the oedipal collision with the father? Does this form of differentiation truly succeed in containing human aspirations to omnipotence and narcissistic longings for regression? Or does it not, by repressing them, allow their reappearance in a more dangerous form?

I will argue that the aspiration to power—the attempt to deny dependency by controlling the other—is the result of this repression of omnipotence and not the inevitable form in which narcissistic longings are expressed. It converts the struggle for recognition to a struggle for control over the other, over woman, over nature. The oedipal version of autonomy means that the mother's subjectivity must be denied and her nurturance rejected. It has often been stated that, as a body symbol, the phallus stands for the opposition to and differencing from the mother, the attempt to replace her imagined omnipotence with one's own. Equally important are the mental and cultural myths that embody the repudiation of the mother and aspiration to her omnipotence. Thus, oedipal socialization culminates in a deep sense that individuality is the accomplishment of autonomous activity at the price of mutual recognition. More generally, the principle of polarity, of either/or, becomes a normal way of experiencing the world. The image of human subjectivity is "purified" of the other (female) pole of human experience. A subject is no longer one who nurtures others, who identifies with others. *He* is above all defined by his opposition to a world of objects, nature, woman, all that is other. The elements of mind that correspond to the male stance in differentiation reflect the emphasis of difference over sameness, separation over identification, as well as the depersonalization of the other. As Keller (1978) has argued, the male stance in differentiation corresponds to a rationality that is objective, controlling, analytic, antiemotional.

The world orientation that emerges through the male posture in differentiation corresponds, then, to a peculiar form of rationality. Although I cannot develop this contention at length here, I have elsewhere proposed (Benjamin, 1978, 1983) that this rationality should be understood as *male rationality* because it is psychologically rooted in the male rejection of the mother, of her nurturance and her existence as a subject. The depersonalizing or objectifying attitude and the instrumental attitude toward others are reflected in this rationality. I have also suggested the parallel between male rationality and what Weber called "instrumental rationality," which he saw as the dominant type of rationality in modern society (Benjamin, 1978). Instrumental or goal rationality means the orientation of activity to product rather than to process or to human values and needs. It is oriented to control, calculability, and impersonal objectivity. In Weber's view, it is this principle of occidental rationality that allowed capitalism to develop and triumph in the West. I believe it is not unfounded to suggest that instrumental rationality is the generalization of the male pole of the psychosocial division of labor. Because the male position is the dominant position, this rationality was and is hegemonic in our culture. It can be viewed as an ideology that is born of women's subordination and that serves to perpetuate it.

The process of societal rationalization means the replacement of personal forms of social intercourse by impersonal, abstract, bureaucratic institutions. It means the replacement of personal authorship in the determination of goals and values by impersonal social forces that seemingly have no author whatever. But the triumph of instrumental rationality, however much it undermines the visible forms of paternal authority, is actually the exaggerated and extreme form of male domination, the generalization of male rationality. The waning of paternal authority, and hence of the Oedipus complex itself, does not so much change the basic structure of domination as reveal it more clearly.

Speaking very schematically, the progress of rationalization means that rationality can no longer be contained within the personal, paternal forms that gave it life. It is now institutionalized in ways that challenge the more personal aspect of male subjectivity, the sense of rational individual authorship. The most dangerous upshot of this development is not that the loss of the internalized father allows the recurrence of the most primitive, regressive form of narcissism, nor that the erosion of personal, community, and kinship ties allows the problem of exploiting others for one's self-esteem to emerge as an analytic problem and source of suffering (instead of being tolerated as the socially sanctioned way of treating one's wife or one's children). The most serious consequence of the dominance of instrumental rationality is most assuredly the destruction of nature. The "taming of the destructive instinct" has its own nemesis. It is in the technological rationality that has taken nature as its object to be exploited and controlled that the nemesis of male domination is most frighteningly apparent. The aspiration to omnipotence is nowhere more clearly evident than in the rape of nature. For although the oedipal father may prohibit the blissful union with mother and the mother nature, he does promise control, possession, and the subordination of her as object. The use of such authority, individuality, and rationality as the oedipal father embodies to hold omnipotence in check only creates an ideology and practice of control that is far more destructive.

The notion of narcissistic omnipotence is ambiguous, connoting both the desire to be one with the world (eros) and the desire to control and be all there is (aggression). Omnipotence, which is always a fantasy rather than an experience, refers either to the pole of absolute merging or of absolute separation–self-sufficiency. As absolutes, both represent death of the self. As polarities, they are expressed through gender division, the irreconcilability of the urge toward oneness and separateness. In the course of this essay, I have used the term *omnipotence* as a fantasy of the absolute self, to be one and all, and fusion with the mother or the world. I have suggested that the patent efforts of men to control women must be understood foremost in the context of the ultimate need–desire for oneness with the beloved source of love and secondarily as a fear of or revulsion against such fusion. The fantasy of omnipotence, in my view, refers first to this image of perfection in oneness. It is only later, as the paradox of recognition develops, that dependency is repudiated. From this perspective, I have asked what happens when the quest for omnipotence is suppressed by an idealized figure whose power derives from that same omnipotent idealization, the superego that grows from the earliest ego ideal, the father who replaces the mother. I would suggest that, in the course of development, longings for perfect selfhood change from a preoccupation with love to a preoccupation with power and control. This probably occurs under the impact of loss, frustration, and feelings of helplessness. Although it is true that the child develops a more realistic representation of its parents as it grows older, its narcissistic longings are also preserved and modified by oedipal socialization into a quest for paternal power. It is this identification with paternal power that, in retrospect, legitimates the transformation of the struggle for recognition into the struggle to subjugate the other. The attempt to replace the mother's omnipotence with one's own becomes a quest for control, not for bliss. This transformation in desire is consolidated, as I have so far charted it, through identification with the individuality and rationality of the oedipal father.

The theme of control over destiny is, of course, the subtext of the original Oedipus myth. The outcome of the myth is entirely opposite to the outcome that the Oedipus complex, in its ideal form, is supposed to produce. The oedipal father is overtaken by the very destiny from which he sought to escape and the very thing he sought to control. I am referring here to the father of Oedipus, Laius, who sought to prevent his prophesied death at the hands of his son by setting him out to die. In this act he insured that everything he feared would take place. Oedipus survived unaware of his true parentage and returned to his place of origin, where he unknowingly murdered his father and committed incest with his mother. But knowingly or not, the main point is that such control of destiny as the father imagines is not really possible. It is highly significant that, contrary to Freud's usage of the myth, the problem begins with the father who is seeking to avoid what in some sense is the fate of all fathers—to die and be superceded by their sons. The maternal principle represented in the myth by the malevolent sphinx triumphs in the end by bringing chaos, disorder, and death. The riddle of the sphinx, which only Oedipus solves, reminds us that we begin and end our lives in helplessness: "What walks first on four legs, then on two, then on three?" Attempts to control events otherwise end in the vengeful return of the repressed, the intolerable experience of helplessness.

The myth of western history shows that the attempt to control nature and woman as nature has been unparalleled in its destructiveness. The belief that internalization of rational authority protects us from our inner drive for omnipotence seems to parallel the misguided efforts of Laius to save his kingdom. In the attempt to control, to repress, the disaster one imagined is actually set in motion. Internalization is, after all, the reproduction of the guilty desire to replace authority by becoming it. Internalization is the translation of the desire to merge with an all-powerful other and/or submit to his authority into a desire to be such a person. The image of adult independence as such all-powerful control is one version of omnipotence. The persistence of this urge to be one with such an authority is equally dangerous whether expressed as conformity (submission to external power) or internalization (identification with that power). In reality, individuals often swing from one stance to the other, as the contradictory imperatives to be one of a kind and be like everyone else simultaneously suggest.

Internalization proceeds by our turning the force of omnipotence against ourselves; we may not be able to control the world, but we can at least control our own omnipotence. We may not be able to be truly independent of all other creatures, but at least we can control and objectify them so as to appear completely autonomous. It is fallacious to believe that only through internalization of authority do human reason and morality develop. Certainly development of these capacities requires practice and recognition. Thus, one must not confound the internalized principles of paternal morality and guilt with the inner wellsprings of sociability and autonomy; not confuse the injunctions of the superego with our native potential to respect others and ourselves that develops with the experience of mutual recognition. It is important to distinguish these abilities from the respect for individuality that appears in our culture as power, self-control, and the machismo of the lone wolf. The defense against omnipotence as fusion is fueled by the narcissistic wish embodied in our image of autonomy, to be one and all alone.

In *Dialectic of Enlightenment,* Horkheimer and Adorno proposed that the reasoning ego has always contained this narcissistic kernel that finally culminates in the rationality of control. They argued that the omnipotence of thought adheres not, as Freud said, to magical primitive thinking which respects the independence of nature but rather to Western science, which inherited Adam's fiefdom, dominion over every living thing. The voice of the realistic, rational superego is thought to curb the limitless strivings for narcissistic grandeur, to chasten the sense that I am the world and the world is mine, in short to nip omnipotence in the bud. However, this reasonable internal father seems to be invested with scarcely less omnipotence than we once attributed to mother or wished for ourselves. Where could one find a better spokesman for the oedipal voice of reason than in the man who wrote of his resolution with more than a hint of self-congratulation: "My third maxim was to try to conquer myself rather than fortune, and to change my desires rather than the order of the world, and generally to accustom myself to believing that there is nothing entirely in our power except our thoughts . . . and this alone seemed to me to be sufficient to prevent me from desiring anything in the future that I could not obtain" (Descartes, 1637/1968, p. 47).

No doubt Descartes thought himself modest, claiming only himself and his thoughts for the sphere of omnipotence. Freud knew better, yet he could not but also succumb to the same ideal of autonomy and the same Faustian imperialism toward nature that it implied: "Where id was, there ego shall be. It is a work of culture not unlike the work of reclaiming the Zuider Zee" (Freud, 1933/1964, p. 80). Contemporary psychoanalysis often permits a more critical awareness of the trouble caused by this arrogant ego, its exclusion of the irrational, the subjective, the empathetic. Reason may conquer nature, but now can reason alone, especially the rationality of control, help us find a way into the world of other subjects?

I have been trying to suggest that the authority of reason has collapsed because it carries the secret wish for omnipotence within it, a wish that we once attributed to less reasonable hopes. Reason has become materialized in the social world not as reason but as rationality, as the domination of impersonal, abstract bonds and of exchange value over the living web of social ties. I have argued that the psychology of our rational culture was transmitted by the internalization of paternal authority. This process has been accurately reflected and scientifically codified as the oedipal model. Thus the oedipal model seems to reflect the truth of our culture, the fatal polarity between autonomy and recognition, nurturance and freedom, subject and object. If it is true that the father or the paternal principle is no longer the vehicle of this rational autonomy, if his authority is not embodied in impersonal institutions, if autonomy and rationality are, as psychological traits, increasingly degendered and distributed among men and women, this reflects not the triumph of archaic impulses but of the rationality of control.

It is not hard to understand those who fear that now nurturance and maternal love have become infected with the ruthless rationality of the public sphere, that private life has been invaded increasingly by institutions of mass culture. The progress that we have made—the degree to which less machismo and more nurturance have become acceptable for men and more independence and less submission have become acceptable for women—may seem to them small by comparison with the overwhelming destructiveness of our social systems. The immediate gains of the disruption of the private sphere caused by the waning of paternal authority may not seem worth the cost. The painful effects of unstable families are perhaps more visible than the emancipatory effects. The long range goals of androgyny, of parenting based on mutuality, equality, and true differentiation, must seem wholly utopian in the context of our overwhelmingly instrumental culture and rationalized society.

Yet there are some grounds for optimism. The salience of oedipal conflicts may have decreased both because of the changes in parental authority and because of the emergent expression of needs for "preoedipal" experience, formerly "archaic" or female. True, the repudiation of the need for dependency and recognition, once embodied in the oedipal father, seems alive and well throughout our culture. He was heir to our narcissism, preserving it in the particular form of rational paternal individualism; and if he is no longer needed, it is because his legacy has achieved such enduring impersonal form. If this means that rational individualism no longer works psychologically, revealing its roots as a defense against helplessness and the ambivalence of differentiation, then we are faced with the alternative of reviving more primitive defenses (pathological narcissism) or of setting ourselves the task of living with this ambivalence and tension. But at least we are in a position to begin thinking about reunifying aspects of human life that have been split and preserved as antagonisms in the gender system. We are in a position to think about the dangerous, destructive consequences of investing our omnipotence in rationality, a rationality that seeks to control the world, to dominate nature and to be as powerful as the imaginary omnipotent mother. We are in a position to face our narcissism, to find more constructive ways to nourish it and to satisfy our utopian longings for self-knowledge and perfection. If we do not disclaim Narcissus in ourselves it is because, as Marcuse (1955) wrote, his image is that "of the Great Refusal: refusal to accept separation from the libidinous object (or subject). The refusal aims at liberation—at the reunion of what has become separated" (p. 154).

References

Ainsworth, M. D. S. (1969). Object relations, dependency, and attachment. *Child Development, 40,* 969–1025.

Ainsworth, M. D. S., Bell, S. M., & Stayton, D. (1971). Individual differences in the strange-situation behavior of one year olds. In H. R. Schaffer (Ed.), *The origins of human social relations.* London: Academic Press.

Adorno, T. W. (1967). Sociology and psychology, Part 1. *New Left Review, 46,* 85–103.

Adorno, T. W. (1968). Sociology and psychology, Part 2. *New Left Review, 47,* 110–132.

Benjamin, J. (1977). The end of internalization: Adorno's social psychology. *Telos, 32,* 42–64.

Benjamin, J. (1978). Authority and the family revisited: A world without fathers? *New German Critique, 13,* 35–58.

Benjamin, J. (1983). Master and slave: The fantasy of erotic domination. In A. Snitow, C. Stansell, & S. Thompson (Eds.), *Powers of desire.* New York: Monthly Review Press.

Bowlby, J. (1969). *Attachment and loss: vol. 1. Attachment.* London: Hogarth.

Chasseguet-Smirgel, J. (1976). Some thoughts on the ego-ideal. *Psychoanalytic Quarterly, 45,* 349–360.

Chodorow, N. (1978). *The reproduction of mothering.* Berkeley: University of California Press.

Chodorow, N. (1979). Difference, relation and gender in psychoanalytic perspective. *Socialist Review, 9*(4), 51–70.

Descartes, R. (1968). *Discourse on method* and *The meditations.* Harmondsworth, England: Penguin. (Originally published 1637)

Dinnerstein, D. (1976). *The mermaid and the minotaur.* New York: Harper & Row.

Engel, S. (1980). Femininity as tragedy: Reexamining the new narcissism. *Socialist Review, 10*(5), 77–104.

Freud, S. (1957). On narcissism: An introduction. *Standard Edition* (Vol. 14, pp. 67–102). London: Hogarth. (Originally published 1914)

Freud, S. (1961). *The ego and the id. Standard Edition* (Vol. 19, pp. 3–66). London: Hogarth. (Originally published 1923)

Freud, S. (1961). *Civilisation and its discontents. Standard Edition* (Vol. 21, pp. 59–145). London: Hogarth. (Originally published 1930)

Freud, S. (1964). *New introductory lectures. Standard edition* (Vol. 22, pp. 3–182). London: Hogarth. (Originally published 1933)

Gilligan, C. (1977). In a different voice: Women's conceptions of self and morality. *Harvard Educational Review, 47*(4), 481–517.

Gilligan, C. (1982). *In a different voice: Psychological theory and women's development.* Cambridge, MA: Harvard University Press.

Goldberg, (1977). Social competence in infancy: A model of parent–infant interaction. *Merrill-Palmer Quarterly, 23,* 163–171.

Guntrip, H. (1961). *Personality structure and human interaction.* New York: International Universities Press.

Hegel, G. W. F. (1952). The independence and dependence of self-consciousness: Master and slave. In *The phenomenology of spirit.* Hamburg: Felix Meiner. (Originally published 1807)

Horkheimer, T. (1949). Authority and the family today. In R. Anshen (Ed.), *The family: Its function and destiny.* New York: Harper.

Horkheimer, T., & Adorno, T. W. (1972). *The dialectic of enlightenment.* New York: Seabury.

Jacoby, R. (1975). *Social amnesia.* Boston: Beacon.

Keller, E. F. (1978). Gender and science. *Psychoanalysis and contemporary thought, 1,* 409–433.

Kernberg, O. (1975). *Borderline conditions and pathological narcissism.* New York: Jason Aronson.

Kohlberg, L. (1971). From 'is' to 'ought': How to commit the naturalistic fallacy and get away with it in the study of moral development. In T. Mischel (Ed.) *Cognitive development and genetic epistemology.* New York: Academic Press.

Kohut, H. (1971). *The analysis of the self.* New York: International Universities Press.

Kohut, H. (1977). *The restoration of the self.* New York: International Universities Press.

Kovel, J. (1982). *The age of desire.* New York: Pantheon.

Lasch, C. (1977). *Haven in a heartless world: The family revisited.* New York: Basic Books.

Lasch, C. (1979). *The culture of narcissism: American life in an age of diminishing expectations.* New York: Norton.
Loewald, H. W. (1979). The waning of the Oedipus complex. *Journal of the American Psychoanalytic Association, 27*(4), 769–778.
Mahler, M., Pine, F., & Bergman, A. (1975). *The psychological birth of the human infant.* New York: Basic Books.
Marcuse, H. (1955). *Eros and civilization.* Boston: Beacon.
Marcuse, H. (1970). The obsolescence of the Freudian concept of man. In *Five lectures.* Boston: Beacon.
Miller, J. B. (1973). New issues, new approaches. In J. B. Miller (Ed.), *Psychoanalysis and women.* Harmondsworth, Middlesex: Penguin.
Mitscherlich, A. (1969). *Society without the father.* New York: Harcourt, Brace and World.
Peterfreund, E. (1978). Some critical comments on psychoanalytic conceptualizations of infancy. *International Journal of Psychoanalysis, 59,* 427–441.
Schachtel, E. (1959). *Metamorphosis.* New York: Basic Books.
Stern, D. (1977). *The first relationship.* Cambridge, MA: Harvard University Press.
Stern, D. (1985). *The interpersonal world of the infant.* New York: Basic Books.

Chapter 9

Susan Buck-Morss

PIAGET, ADORNO, AND DIALECTICAL OPERATIONS

In an earlier article (Buck-Morss, 1975) I brought together two previously separate areas of discourse, Piaget's theory of cognitive development and Adorno's philosophy of negative dialectics. The essay was an attempt to account for the fact that in the cross-cultural application of Piaget tests, non-Western children score significantly lower than their Western peers, implying that the cognitive development of the former, particularly in Third World countries, is in some way retarded (see Dasen, 1972).

The gist of my argument was this: Piaget chose to examine the development of formal operations because he wanted to establish a psychology that was universal, hence "scientific," according to his definition, and he made the assumption that formal structures of thought were universal precisely because they were abstract, whereas particular content, which could be separated from form, was inessential, contingent on cultural and environmental factors. But according to Adorno (who was following the early work of Lukacs (1971/1923), this separation of form from content, far from being universal, was itself the product of history: the abstract form of cognition that the present era has accepted as second nature, although appearing to be divorced from the

This chapter, which is a revised version of "Piaget, Adorno, and the Possibilities of Dialectical Operations," appeared in H. J. Silverman (Ed.) (1980), *Piaget, Philosophy, and the Human Sciences* (Atlantic Highlands, NJ: Humanities Press).

Susan Buck-Morss • Department of Government, Cornell University, Ithaca, New York 14853.

social world, is in fact its mirror image. Specifically, the abstract formalism which Piaget focused upon in thought emerged historically in urban commercial cultures and became the dominant logical structure when, with the rise of Western industrial capitalism, it became the dominant social structure. With the advent of wage labor, production as well as exchange acquired abstract value, and the purely formal language of mathematics (the language of commercial transactions) became the expression of the social relations of production as well as those of the marketplace. It is thus not surprising that in Third World countries, especially in rural areas where social structures of kinship have not yet been preempted by those of market exchange, children do not develop their capacities for abstract, formal cognition, and in testing for this the development of other cognitive modes may have gone unnoticed.

Piaget recognizes indeed that the child's cognitive development does not occur in a vacuum but depends on his or her acting upon objects. But those objects are simply given, the furniture of the child's environment, which provide the occasion for cognitive development but do not determine it substantively.[1] Even at the level of concrete operations, where some of his most interesting work has been done, Piaget assumes that the most significant thing is not so much what the child can do in this concrete world but how quickly he can do without it. It is the form, not the arbitrary contents of the classification and conservation tests, that is important. They test for the ability to identify an abstract quality that remains constant despite change in the object's appearance and despite the fact that human beings have acted upon it. This directly parallels the ability to conceptualize commodities and labor in mathematical terms of abstract exchange.

Built into Piaget's theory is an epistemological mistake. A socioeconomic bias impairs his vision and prevents him from seeing that at the level of formal operations thought has far from left the mundane world behind but only incorporated it more deeply, at a social structural level, rather than merely a perceptual, empirical one—as, indeed, has Piaget himself. For he is no more divorced from interaction with the objective world than are the children in his experiments. The truth of his theory emerges precisely when, from the point of view of his own scien-

[1]In considering cognitive development as an analogy to biological evolution, Piaget (1971) acknowledges that objects might themselves influence the development of mathematical cognitive structures and recognizes that if objects really influenced subjective structures, "my interpretation would need some rather basic revision. It would just be one of those unfortunate things that happen" (p. 342).

tific intentions, it fails. That is, truth emerges not in establishing a universal psychology but in accurately, if unintentionally, reflecting the structure of his own society, for which his tests are indeed a very good indication of how well a child can function cognitively.

This argument provides a dialectical exercise, an applied illustration of Adorno's critical method (cf. Buck-Morss, 1977). Its aim is not merely to demonstrate that superstructure and substructure, consciousness and social reality, are dialectically interrelated but also to provide an intellectual experience that, in contrast to Piaget's tests for reversible operations already achieved, invites a new level of insight, one that is in fact irreversible. For if the argument has made its point, it puts the texts of Piagetian literature in a new context so that they can never be read in quite the same way again.

We can put this to the test with an example. The Harvard psychologist Kohlberg has developed a theory of moral development paralleling Piaget's theory of cognitive development. Kohlberg assumes that abstract mental processes are by definition universal, free of particular social content, and defines moral maturity as the ability to divorce morality from content and to think in accord with formal moral principles. In a seminal article providing an introduction to his theory Kohlberg (1969) reports on a series of experiments to illustrate the development, in stages, of abstract comprehension generally:

> 1. *Preconceptual* (age 3–4). Money is not recognized as a symbol of value different from other objects and it is not understood that money is exchanged in purchase and sale transactions. . . .
> 2. *Intermediate* (age 4–5). Children recognize that money transfer is required in stores, but do not recognize that the transfer is an exchange of equal economic value. The exchange of work for salary is not understood, nor is the scarcity of money understood. . . .
> 3. *Concrete operational* (age 6–8). Children recognize money transactions as involving a logical relation of reversible, reciprocal, and equal exchange values. They understand that the storekeeper must pay money to others for his goods; they understand the work–salary exchange, and the scarcity or "conservation" of money.

Here the tables are turned on the tester, for the empirical research Kohlberg cites in fact documents that the child is learning not abstract thinking but concrete economics: these are the developmental stages in being introduced to the riddle of commodities. Without knowing it, and precisely against his intent, Kohlberg's text allows an immanent criticism of his formalist position and in the process provides evidence for our own.

Decentering, Dialectics, and Equilibrium

The immanent critical procedure of allowing a text to bear witness against itself was characteristic of Adorno. I am tempted to call it a process of *decentering*, although he himself did not, and although the word, now the pet term of a wide variety of structuralists including Piaget, has lost precision of meaning. But perhaps the very ambiguity of the term helps to clarify the difference between Adorno and Piaget.

In Piaget's theory, decentering refers to the moment at each stage of cognitive development when, in order to reconcile disparities between conceptual schema and empirical experience, an egocentric cognitive position is relinquished in favor of a more "objective" one.[2] This process is complete by adolescence, when the child's space has become universal, the child's time historical time, and earlier illusions of omnipotence have been replaced by comprehension of the external laws of causation.

Significantly, Piaget concentrates on just those formal categories of time, space, and causality that the bourgeois philosopher Kant maintained were the *a priori* of rational experience.[3] But, for Adorno, Kant's Copernican revolution in philosophy implied another kind of egocentrism. It assumed as the structure of experience an identity between the rational subject and the empirical objects that it reasoned about. Adorno (1973a) described his own philosophy as giving Kant's "Copernican revolution an axial turn" (p. xx) toward *non*identity, by exploding all attempts of the rational subject to find itself in the world that, Adorno claimed, was decidedly not rational. As a materialist Adorno insisted on the priority of the external world, that—implying another kind of decentering—imposed its structure (the formal, reified structure of commodity production) on consciousness,[4] and which it was the task of reason to think against rather than adapt itself to.

[2]In mental development "successive constructions always involve a decentering of the initial egocentric point of view in order to place it in an ever-broader coordination of relations and concepts, so that each new terminal grouping further integrates the subject's activity by adapting it to an ever-widening reality." Ultimately this entails submission to social constraints. Piaget continues: "Parallel to this intellectual elaboration, we have seen affectivity gradually disengaging itself from the self in order to submit, thanks to the reciprocity and coordination of values, to the laws of cooperation" (Piaget, 1967, p. 69).

[3]Piaget's affinity to Kant is also clear in his constructivism, that is, his stress on the moment of the subject's spontaneous activity in cognition that is the hallmark of Kantian philosophy. For a discussion of the connection between Kantian thinking and sociopolitical reality after 1848, see Buck-Morss (1977, pp. 70–71).

[4]Kant said reality is what it is because of man's perception of it; Adorno said man's

In contrast, and in complicity with his own definition of decentering, Piaget's theory of *equilibration* holds that cognitive structures generate higher, more stable (albeit not static) forms when faced with contradictions that its existing forms cannot resolve, or, to use his biological metaphor, when it is subject to stimuli from without for which it cannot compensate (1967, p. 151). It has been suggested that this conception is a dialectical one (Youniss, 1974). If this is so, then it is so only at the most simplistic, undialectical level—we might refer to it as stage 1 of dialectical thinking—which is found in the crude schematization of Hegelianism into the catchwords, thesis, antithesis, synthesis, or in the automatic evolutionism of Engels' *Dialectics of Nature,* which was known in Adorno's time as "vulgar Marxism" (cf. Lukacs, 1923/1971, pp. 1–26). The limitation of this conception of dialectics is that it posits a dialectical interrelationship between subject and object (in this case, between the child and his environment) while at the same time thinking it can bracket out the observer, as if the theorist were not himself a part of the dialectical process he was describing. As Adorno and his colleagues have argued, this attempt to describe dialectics from the outside either leads into the static deadend of metaphysics (Horkheimer, 1932) or posits an automatic progress by means of a dialectical evolution that from the perspective of the twentieth century appears indefensibly optimistic (Buck-Morss, 1977, p. 48).

Adorno was fully aware of his own sociohistorical relativity. His theory intervenes actively in promoting historical change because it does not just describe a dialectical operation, but *is* itself one—at stage 3, at least—and he takes us there with him. What Piaget views positively as a natural tendency of the mind to seek stable states through assimilating and accommodating the outside world in its given form, Adorno (setting that whole world in question) views negatively as a lamentable social condition. For him, it is a tendency towards conformism nourished by the mindless culture of mass society, and represents a retardation rather than an advance. Reason, faced with real contradictions, mistakes them for logical contradictions and spends its energies trying to eliminate the latter rather than the former. If this tendency appears natural, Adorno would argue, then this is because social reality has become "second

perception is what it is because of reality's structure. As Adorno phrased it in a letter to Walter Benjamin, written in 1935, "The fetish character of commodities is no fact of consciousness, but dialectic in the emanating sense that it produces consciousness" (1970a, p. 112).

nature," accepted unquestioningly, which means that consciousness must struggle against it all the more strongly.

In fact, it would be accurate to define Adorno's goal as achieving cognitive instability, a disequilibrium between structures of consciousness and those of reality. This is really the heart of his philosophy of "negative dialectics." It sets off a disequilibrium in thinking by stressing nonidentity, and it does this in two ways. First, it takes advantage of the ambivalence between word and thing, arguing, for example, that second nature is not truly natural, since it is the historical product of a particular social structure. But the social structure is not truly social either, because of the alienation and isolation of its members. Such a critical procedure throws patterns into disequilibrium by pointing out the difference in identity, that is, the assumed identity between word and thing (cf. Buck-Morss, 1977, pp. 43–62). Second, the process can be reversed, pointing out the identity in difference, showing how two seemingly opposed phenomena in fact have identical structures, as in our initial argument that the structure of abstract formal cognition reflects the social structure of commodity exchange.

It must be made clear that Adorno's procedure in no way implies reductionism. When he analyzes a psychological theory, he indeed translates it into terms of social reality, but when he analyzes a social phenomenon, his focus shifts to the psychological structures that sustain it (Buck-Morss, 1977, pp. 185–6). There is no hierarchy to the translations from one mode to another but only a shifting of centers (Adorno, 1973, pp. 31–34). The result is a totally altered conception of causality. For Adorno there is no unequivocal historical "source" of the present, but only a creative, continually renewed discovery of the constellation which the past makes within a constantly changing present. The process is not unlike poetic "troping," whereby an idea undergoes a series of metamorphoses without any one form's being dominant over the rest.[5]

But Adorno's transformations are not simply variations of a myth. Nor are his negations merely inversions within a system. The function of myths is to provide logical models for overcoming social and cultural contradictions. They thus have the capacity to make coherent and acceptable whatever is self-contradictory in the ideological system. De-

[5]Bloom (1975) has suggested that every act of writing (creation) and reading (interpretation) is a metaphorical substitution or misreading of a preceding text. Each is a representation or re-seeing of tradition whereby the present generation frees itself from the domination of ancestors by joining them. Here the point of origin is the past source of present creativity, not a prior cause in which the present can be mechanically reduced.

scribing origins, they reconstruct the past in order to explain away a present anomaly. The function of Adorno's arguments is precisely the opposite. Every one of them, by decentering thought and heightening awareness of contradictions, deconstructs a system, dismantles a myth. Indeed, he made "antisystem" the motto of his philosophy and equated it with a process of demythification (Buck-Morss, 1977, pp. 49–50).

Science, Art, and Myth

If in Adorno's theory the translation of structures from one modality to another replaces the search for causal origins, this results from the fact that the model for his philosophy was aesthetic experience, not scientific experiment. "Perhaps from early on in the bourgeois era," he wrote, "the experiment became a surrogate for authentic experience" (Adorno, 1942, p. 61). It is significant that Adorno studied musical composition with Schönberg's disciple Alban Berg. Musical meaning emerges in the interruptions of anticipated patterns (Collaer, 1961, p. 68) rather than, as with experimental science, in the consistencies of results. Moreover, the internal coherence of aesthetic compositions is achieved by articulating the antagonisms between idea and reality rather than reconciling them. As Proust has written, the artwork is constructed out of the "superimposition of two systems" (in Brée, 1969, p. 55), the world of experience and the aesthetic order, and these worlds remain nonidentical in a relation of tension that determines the aesthetic form.

Adorno did not want to make philosophy aesthetic. As he wrote, "Most bitterly irreconcilable is that which is similar but which feeds on different centers" (Adorno, 1970a/1935, p. 14). Rather, he refused to see science and art as binary opposites and instead counterposed knowledge to myth. He defined myth as a closed system, reproducing the ever-identical. In this sense, it could be argued that the experimental standardization that has befallen Piaget's tests is far more mythical than art, whereas knowledge as experience of the unanticipated, the new, possesses that moment of discovery and freedom that was the original impulse of science.[6]

[6]In fairness to Piaget, his theoretical discoveries were based on an open, decidedly creative method of research that made use of a small sample with whom he was very much involved (e.g., his own children) and thus violated some fundamental ground rules of scientific methodology. But in the standardized application of Piagetian tests, consistency rather than discovery has become the criterion for truth. For a revealing criticism of this

The possible claim that Piaget's approach is more "scientific" than Adorno's cannot be substantiated philosophically or empirically. Not only does Piaget's equation of cognitive and biological development (e.g., Piaget, 1971) amount to the metaphorical translation of psychology into the terms of natural science, but also it must be conceded that science itself is a metaphor, (cf. Turbayne, 1970), a belief system in which, as in magic, internal coherence has become a substitute for truth. In *Primitive Classifications*, Durkheim and Mauss (1963, p. 71) note two social functions of belief systems: one, a speculative function, making intelligible the relation between things; the other, a moral function, to regulate the conduct of human beings. The scientific belief system that dominates in present-day society seems to have difficulty doing either. Yet the hold of science remains tenacious. As Polanyi (1958) has observed, the situation is not unlike that described by Evans-Pitchard among the Zande in Africa, who resisted giving up their magical belief systems even when elements in it were demonstrated to be wrong. In our society,

> Any contradiction between a particular scientific notion and the facts of experience will be explained by other scientific notions. . . . Secured by its circularity and defended further by its epicyclical reserves, science may deny, or at least cast aside as of no scientific interest, whole ranges of experience which to the unscientific mind appear both massive and vital. . . . I conclude that what earlier philosophers have alluded to by speaking of coherence as the criterion of truth is only a criterion of stability. It may equally stabilize an erroneous or a true view of the universe. (p. 291)

The point is, of course, that the "criterion of stability" has crucial political implications. Science is not a neutral language, and the whole notion of value-free knowledge is one of the most insidious myths. By trying to explain given reality rationally, scientific explanations tend toward the "equilibration" of social systems, whereas Adorno's decentering method applies reason against the grain of reality. The important political point is that power lies not only in control of the means of production within a society but in the *control of the production of meanings* as well.

The Development of Dialectical Operations

Piaget has written "the principal goal of education is to create men [sic] who are capable of doing new things, not simply repeating what

---

testing by a psychologist who experimented with 1,400 children in three countries, see J. Smedslund (1977).

other generations have done" and that its second goal "is to form minds which can be critical, can verify—and do not accept everything they are offered" (quoted in Duckworth, 1964, p. 75). Yet his choice of paradigms—the scientific experiment with its abstract, formal operations—works unwittingly against this goal because it has no means to place the "given" itself in question. An education system based on this model may produce intelligent functionaries—technocrats who, in science, social analysis, or any other field, apply their rational faculties within existing cognitive and social structures.[7] But it will not encourage the development of human beings capable of structural innovation.

Piaget (1973) insists that "to understand is to invent" (p. 18), stressing the active role of the subject. But invention turns out to be no more than a rediscovery of the already dominant mode of thought, the "rediscovery of truth" (p. 34), through interaction with an unchanged world. He acknowledges the importance of play in cognitive development. Yet play is not understood to be like the creative fantasy of the artist that in the name of denied pleasure protests against reality by constructing another world.[8] It is merely the "predominance of assimilation over accommodation" (Piaget, 1962, p. 150), which means that instead of the child's submitting to reality, reality is forced to submit to the child. Play for Piaget is pleasureful only in the sense of "freedom from conflicts" (p. 149), of achieving mastery over "models of activity" and "acquiring thereby a feeling of virtuosity or power" (p. 89). It is "prac-

[7]Compare Gouldner's (1975–76) distinction (building on T. S. Kuhn's theory of paradigms) between intellectuals and conventional scholars: "Intellectuals, then, are scholars who reject, make problematic or critically focalize the boundaries hitherto implicit in normal scholarship and the scholarly paradigms on which the scholarly community had, till then, centered, and their elaborated speech variants. Searching out and transcending the conventional boundaries of 'normal scholarship,' they are an irritant to conventional scholars, who condemn them as deviants. Rather than operating safely within the familiar boundaries of an established paradigm, intellectuals violate boundaries. They mingle once separate disciplines; they pass back and forth between ordinary and artificial languages; between the 'common sense' and technical tradition. Such boundary transgressions sometimes generate scandalous intellectual *incunabula;* but, sometimes, they are the basis of powerful intellectual breakthroughs and of rich innovations" (p. 23).

[8]Piaget (1962) rejects Freud's definition of play as the domination of the pleasure principle over the reality principle, noting that the repetition of even painful experiences is a "primary factor in play and more widespread than the pursuit of pleasure for its own sake" (p. 149). Contrast Adorno, who, although arguing that fantasy as an aesthetic experience is never an escape from reality, affirms Freud's radical dichotomy between the physical desire for gratification and its forced repression by the overly constraining structure of present reality. Adorno (1970a) claimed that art expresses the individual's fantasy of omnipotence, not as controller of existing reality, but as creator of utopian possibility, "the wish within the artwork for constructing a better world" (p. 22; see also the whole section, pp. 19–31).

tice" (p. 90) or "repetition" (p. 149), and its distinction from serious activities is thus only a matter of degree:

> Play is distinguishable by a modification, varying in degree, of the conditions of equilibrium between reality and the ego. We can therefore say that if adapted activity and thought constitute an equilibrium between assimilation and accommodation, play begins as soon as there is predominance of assimilation. (p. 150)

If we are concerned with the capacity not merely to think within existing cognitive systems and social systems but beyond them, then the constellation of fantasy, criticism, and disequilibration that characterizes Adorno's program indeed might be more relevant than Piaget's notions for a theory of cognitive development. What are the possibilities of studying the development of children's thinking in terms of negative, dialectical operations, based on principles of nonidentity,[9] which, because they shift the cognitive focus off center, constantly question and challenge not only "reality" but also the dominant cognitive schema purporting to describe it adequately?

In the first place, rather than stressing, as does Piaget, the child's ability to synthesize contradictions, we would be interested in just the opposite, the ability to tolerate ambivalence (cf. Riegel, 1973, p. 356) and, moreover, to enjoy its suspense as a moment of creative risk and potential for new discovery. For example, at the level of perception, in testing for the comprehension of space, we would not assume Piaget's bias toward Euclidean geometry or any formal, measurable system wherein the synthetic coordination of objects within an unequivocal, universal space is considered the cognitive goal. For Piaget (1962), fully developed spatial comprehension is described thus: "The construction results in a universe of permanent objects constituting a single practical space that is relatively decentered (in that it includes the child's own body as one element among many)" (p. 262). Instead, we would inquire into the child's ability to play with space so that its meaning is transformed, as in picture games like Spot the Object or to produce changing

[9]There is an important distinction between negative dialectics and the positive dialectics that the system of Hegelian idealism has in common with the "vulgar" Marxism of, for example, Engels' *Dialectics of Nature* (which has become the basis for official Soviet Marxism). This distinction is one between the stress that positive dialectics places on the reconciliation of contradictions, by an automatic process in which the cognitive efforts of the subject become predictable, and the emphasis in negative or critical dialectics, not on the resolution of contradictions, but on the contradiction of resolutions. Compare Riegel's (1976) definition: "Rather than searching for final answers, dialectical logic is concerned with the origin of the endless sequence of raising questions" (p. 372).

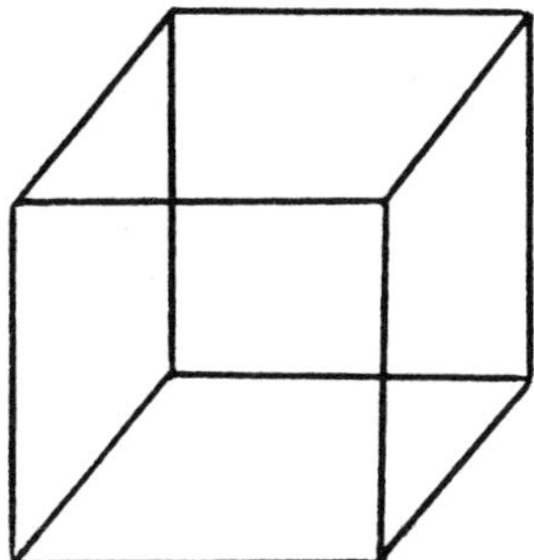

Figure 1. A Necker cube.

patterns out of static representations by shifting the relative depths of spatial planes, as in experiencing a Necker cube (see Figure 1).[10] Furthermore, we would not accept Piaget and Inhelder's (1955) equation of cognitive maturity with visual realism or mastery of perspective—a fif-fifteenth-century Florentine invention that reflected the bourgeois cosmology of a man-centered, secular universe. Instead, we would be interested in the child's ability to read deep and complex spatial arrangements, as in a cubist or surrealist work, or to grasp the paradoxical intellectual space in the paintings of Vassaly or the drawings of Escher. We would, therefore, be more interested in a continued development of what Piaget and Inhelder identify as preoperational "intellectual realism," rather than the perspectival "visual realism" of the operational phase.

In regard to time, our attention would not be directed at empty, formal time—clock time, which is a measurable constant regardless of what occurs within it and which functions as "the coordination of motions" (Piaget, 1969, p. 2). Instead, aesthetic experience would again provide a model, in the form of musical rhythm. Maturity would be defined as the ability to grasp increasingly irregular rhythms, moving from the 4/4, repetitive rhythm of a military march to the syncopated

[10]A Necker cube is a transparent figure the two optically square sides of which can be read alternately as the foremost and hindmost plane of the cube (Fig. 1). It may be noted that spatial ambivalence in designs existed in very early cultures. Levi-Strauss (1964) comments that the art of several Indian cultures in North and South America is "marked by an intellectual delight in double meanings (in Hopewell (Easter U.S.), as in Chavin (north of Peru), certain motifs bear one meaning when read normally, and quite another when read upside-down)" (p. 246).

rhythms of jazz,[11] to the more sophisticated, asymmetrical rhythms of non-Western music, and to the polyrhythmic superimposition of two opposed schemas. An example of the latter would be found in those passages of Beethoven's piano sonatas where the left hand plays triplets while the right hand plays couplets, or cases of rhythmic ambivalence, as in the third movement of the *Eroica* where, to cite Adorno, rhythm "rises up against the existing law until it produces from out of it a new one" (Adorno, 1936/1964, p. 112).

It should be noted that, on the perceptual level of time and space, our approach would represent more a shift in focus than a totally new project.[12] For, at least through the stage of concrete operations, Piaget's experiments are tied to content, and he is fully aware of the generative power of perceptual ambivalence in accounting for the dynamics of cognitive development. But Piaget views the child as constantly trying to regain perceptual equilibrium. Indeed, this is what motivates the child to construct new cognitive schemas. In contrast, we are suggesting that, as a form of play akin to artistic creation and as an operation vital to critical thinking, the child may be motivated to abandon perceptual equilibrium and to construct schemas that aid him in this process.

A fundamental difference in our approach would be its rejection of Piaget's formal model of mathematics with its stable, reversible operations. Instead, we would turn to *language* as the expression of cognitive development—not language as a system, but spoken language, with none of the ambivalence of its referents bracketed out.

Piaget's relative lack of concern for language might seem surprising, given the seminal role it plays in the structuralist movement with which he identifies. But it is precisely his acknowledged affinity with this group that has led him to make a sharp distinction between language

[11]Adorno (1936/1964) considered the stereotyped syncopation employed in popular jazz no real negation of standard rhythms because it was "purposeless; it leads nowhere, and is arbitrarily revoked through a dialectical, mathematical conversion of time-counts which leaves no remainder" (p. 112). (See also the exchange between Chevigny and Buck-Morss in *PsychCritique*, 1985, *1*(1), *Ed.*)

[12]In testing the child's concept of time, for example, Piaget (1969) investigates rhythmic perception. But true to his bias, he utilizes a metronome, which provides an abstract measurement of rhythms (motions relative to an absolute, formal time) rather than rhythms as they appear within a musical content that gives them meaning. Or, testing comprehension of two simultaneous motions of varying velocities (in our example, left-hand triplets counterposed to right-hand couplets), Piaget searches for the child's comprehension of identity, rather than nonidentity, that is, the fact that "total durations are equal" (p. 170), despite varying velocities.

and intelligence. French structuralists deal with language as a system of arbitrary signifiers, the meanings of which are fixed by social convention. As such, they are unconcerned with the generative process of speech, that expressive activity central to the linguistic development of the child. On the other hand, the American structuralist Noam Chomsky deals with the generative structure of language, but he does so with a notion of innateness that violates Piaget's most persistent tenet, the constructive nature of cognitive development, the fact that its generation is dependent on experience.[13] Piaget has avoided a conflict with fellow structuralists by arguing that since, for example, children combine or dissociate manually before they do it verbally, intelligence "antedates language and is independent of it" (Piaget, 1967, p. 98). Thought comes first and is a spontaneous, individual activity, but language "is a group institution. Its rules are imposed on individuals. One generation coercively transmits it to the next" (Piaget, 1970, p. 74). Language "profoundly transforms thought," but only in the sense that by submitting to its tyranny, thought "attains its forms of equilibrium by means of a more advanced schematization and a more mobile abstraction" (Piaget, 1967, pp. 92–93). What gets lost in his conception is the constructive moment of speech: to speak is to invent meaning, not only out of the dialectical tension between linguistic convention and the speaker's intention, but out of the gap between signifier and signified that, for Adorno, is the locus of the production of meanings and the point at which play, creativity, and the capacity for critical thinking converge.

In the beginning, the child's language is literal. Objects have priority in the child's world, and every name for them is a proper name. There is no gap between signifier and signified.[14] Adorno's close friend Walter Benjamin, recalling the Old Testament story of Adam as name-giver of God's creatures, called this the language of Paradise, before the Fall when, with the babble of human language, words lost their ade-

[13]For Piaget's discussion of the "fundamental problem" concerning the nature and origin of Chomsky's "fixed innate schema" and his proposed way out of this theoretical difficulty (that language structures are derived from concrete operations, and these produce structures that are neither wholly innate nor wholly acquired but discovered through experience), see Piaget (1970, pp. 81–96).

[14]"The fact is that adults think in terms of allegories and metaphors, whereas children think in terms of objects perceived in their world of objects. Their thinking is limited during the first years to images of things. . . . I know of a four-year-old child who gets furious whenever she hears an adult speak about ladyfinger biscuits" (Chukovsky, 1974, pp. 12–13).

quacy because they could not recapture exact and concrete knowledge of the particular (Buck-Morss, 1977, pp. 88–89). As mimetic reflection, as a simple image of the given, it could not represent anything but the given (Buck-Morss, 1977, pp. 89–90). He acknowledged its utopian promise for the future: the positivity inherent in a language of names would in fact be adequate for describing a just society. But for the present, language needed to be critical, using logic to express the illogic of society.

In light of this theoretical speculation, it is perhaps not without significance that when children do begin to use language as a self-contained system of signifiers, they take great pleasure in using the logic of language against the logic of reality. Adherence to grammatical rules can make sense out of nonsense:

> The cow sat on a birch tree
> and nibbled on a pea.

This rhyme is cited by Chukovsky (1974, p. 96), the Soviet child psychologist, in a book (reissued in Russia 16 times since its appearance in 1925) which argued strenuously against the position of those socialist-realist educators who wanted to eradicate such nonsense in order "to convert every child immediately into a scientist" (p. 110). Like Adorno, Chukovsky considered creativity a common component of art and science. Chukovsky notes: "The child thinks of words in pairs, he assumes that every word has a 'twin'—an opposite in meaning or quality" (p. 61). Just so, he continues, sense and nonsense are thought together. Hence, the child's appreciation of nonsense is an indication that he grasps reality in order "to be able to respond to these playful rhymes the child must have a knowledge of the real order of things" (p. 95). Yet at the same time, it is a form of protest, a creative use of language to suggest another reality. Language nonsense which violates the established order of reality, such as the three-year-old's invention: "The birds ring, the bells fly!" (p. 99) is called by Chukovsky the "Topsy-Turvies": "A most widely used method in these mental games is precisely a reversal of the normal relationship of things: ascribing to object A the function of object B, and the other way round" (p. 98). The method described is pure dialectics. Perhaps the child's game of Topsy-Turvies, where humor, knowledge of reality, and making believe all find expression, is the ontogenetic origin of negative dialectical operations.

The gap between signified and signifier, the object and its concept, thus prevents thought from being totally dominated by reality in its given form. However, so Adorno would argue, it also prevents the opposite, the domination of reality by thought. Because human language cannot reinstate the name, any attempt to absorb the object within the concept, which generalizes through abstraction, must do violence to the object's uniqueness. Adorno claimed that objects do not go into their concepts without leaving a remainder and therefore "no object is wholly known" (Adorno, 1973a, p. 14). Piaget would agree with this assumption (which is actually Kantian[15]), but he would lament the situation. Biological systems, he notes, which fulfill primary needs such as food and protection, must remain "open" because "the organism only succeeds in preserving its form through a continuous flow of exchanges with the environment" (Piaget, 1971, p. 350). But "an open system is a system that is perpetually threatened." In contrast, cognitive systems tend toward "closure": by registering environmental feedback, they form a circular structure that gives the organism power to regulate and control exchanges with the environment (p. 354).

Yet insofar as cognitive structures cannot be divorced from their content—and any language act that intends meaning is an example of this—such closure must remain incomplete. Piaget finds only one exception among cognitive structures, the closed system of mathematical logic, that "structure of structures" for which he has such a strong predilection: "Logico-mathematical structures do, in fact, present us with an example, to be found nowhere else in creation, of a development which evolves without a break" (Piaget, 1971, p. 355). Adorno considered this predilection for closed systems (the mark of idealist philosophy) in fact not so very far from the animalism which it strove to overcome. Abstract reason, he claimed, tends literally to gobble everything up so that nothing is left outside. Ultimately, all of material nature is consumed without a trace—as is in fact the case with mathematics. Adorno (1973a) wrote, using his own biological metaphors:

> The system in which the sovereign mind imagined itself transfigured has its primal history in the pre-mental, the animal life of the species. Predators get hungry, but pouncing on their prey is difficult and often dangerous; additional impulses and the unpleasantness of hunger fuse into rage at the victim. . . . The animal to be devoured must be evil. . . and finally all that reminds us of nature is inferior, so the unity of the self-preserving thought may devour it without misgivings. This justifies the principle of the thought as much as it increases the appetite. The system is the belly turned mind, and rage is the mark of each and every idealism. (pp. 22–23)

[15]It is Kant's distinction between reality (*noumenon*) and appearance (*phenomenon*). The noumenal realm of things in themselves forever escapes us, for we can only know objects as phenomena, as they appear to us in cognitive experience, through the grid of subjectivity.

In this sophisticated version of Topsy-Turvies, Adorno then points out that just as the logic of mathematics reflects the structure of abstract exchange and mathematics becomes a metaphor for commercial society, so thought as a "closed system," far from being independent or uncontaminated by matter, "really approximated" the system of the social world to which the individual is forced to conform, where "less and less was left outside" (p. 23). "If society could be seen through as a closed system, as system accordingly unreconciled to the subjects, it would become too embarrassing for the subjects as long as they remain subjects in any sense" (p. 24).

Children use language to construct nonsense worlds that protest against the limits of reality by transgressing them. But they also protect reality against the tyranny of language. In the form of riddles, language jokes, and puns—a persistent and apparently spontaneous form of children's play (Opie & Opie, 1959)—children are in complicity with objects, rescuing them from being consumed by the concept. These language games function because of the ambiguity of referents, the fact that the word does not identify the object totally.

> What's black and white and red (read) all over? *A newspaper.*
> What goes up the chimney down, but not down the chimney up? *An umbrella.*

In riddles, only when the object slips out of the meaning first anticipated by the question is sense restored. Puns, *doubles entendres,* and all ambivalences which emerge in the gap between signifier and signified are thus an occasion for the practice of dialectical operations.

Adorno referred to his own method as "riddle-solving," (Adorno, 1973b, vol. 1, pp. 334–335), and the name was apt. He analyzed spoken or written words as if they were puzzles or hieroglyphs. Their meanings are ambivalent, not identical to the speaker's own conscious intent. They are thus in need of a dialectical interpretation that could compensate for the limits of the concept by grasping truth at contradictory levels. "The determinable flaw in every concept makes it necessary to cite others; this is the font of the only constellations which inherited some of the hope of the name" (Adorno, 1973a, p. 53).

If we apply this kind of hermeneutic method to the statements of children, they take on significance as critical insights into reality. This text is given to us by Piaget's daughter:

> At 3;11(12): *"That little baby was bought. They found her in a shop and bought her."* . . . At 5;3(23), referring to the guinea-pigs she had just been given to help her to discover the true solution: *"Where do little guinea-pigs come from?—*

> What do you think?—*From a factory.*" . . . At 5;5(8): "Were the little guinea-pigs inside their mother? *I think they were.*" But two days later: "*They come from the factory.*" (Piaget, 1962, pp. 246–247)

For Piaget, this text exemplifies a "mythic" stage of "artificialism" (p. 250), a set of wrong answers on the path toward scientific understanding. Yet what the child is quite accurately reflecting is the ambivalence between natural and social sources of the materially given objects of experience. The persistence of the child in connecting creation to the social process, first in terms of store-bought commodities and then in terms of factory production, may be more on the right track than off.

The question of origins is a question of creation as well as causality, and here the contradiction is between the concept of creation as a conscious product of human activity—to quote Marx (1967, p. 332), an "act of self-creation"—and the reality of alienated labor, characterized by dependency on another to whom (again from Marx) "I owe . . . not only the maintenance of my life but also its *creation*, its *source*. My life necessarily has such an external ground if it is not my own creation" (pp. 312–313). To make is to be a subject; to be made is to be an object. This much Piaget's daughter knew:

> At 5;5(22): . . . What things make themselves?—*Pipes, trees, egg-shells, clouds, the door. They don't make themselves, they have to be made. I think trees make themselves, and suns too. In the sky they can easily make themselves.*" At 5;7(11): "How is the sky made? *I think they cut it out. It's been painted.*" At 5;7(12): "How do they make stones? How do they hold together? How are they made? . . .—*I think it's with cement.*" At 5;7(22), on seeing the sun set behind a mountain ridge: "So the sun moves too, does it? Like the moon? *Somebody makes it move [sic], somebody behind the mountain, a giant, I think.* (Piaget, 1962, p. 248)

The confusion in the child's mind between making and being made reflects a real one. It is not just the figment of a five-year-old imagination. The child's artificialism, the transformation of objects into subjects, is a humane inversion of the original distortion, the social transformation of subjects into objects. Such "wrong" answers are reflections of utopia, that form of Topsy-Turvies that would set the world aright. An interpretation that recognizes this not only describes the child's learning but learns from it.

Language and Society: The Image of the Trickster

Advanced levels of negative dialectical operations can be distinguished from the more elementary ones of puns and language jokes in that they involve whole texts, whole structures of meanings rather than individual words as they relate to the social structure rather than individual objects. It is with some misgivings that at this point I bring Habermas into the discussion. For, unlike Adorno, whose colleague he was in the 1960s at the Frankfurt Institut für Sozialforschung, Habermas (e.g., 1973), a powerful and complex theorist in his own right, has expressly addressed himself to the work of Piaget and Kohlberg, incorporating elements of both in his work with rather less criticism than I am voicing here. Moreover, Habermas has rejected Adorno's relentless negativity and worked out a positive dialectical theory of ego development in which *identity* is no pejorative term and ontogenetic and phylogenetic parallels produce strong Hegelian reverberations (see Habermas, 1975a). But if I may borrow eclectically from Habermas (given his own extraordinary eclecticism, this seems only fair play), when applied to the relation between structures of meaning and social structures, his theory of communicative action can be illuminating.

That theory focuses on a central contradiction in the speech situation. Implied in speaking is a reciprocity of understanding between speaker and listener, the prerequisite for a possible consensus of meaning. This mutuality has the structure of democratic equality; yet within present society it remains a utopian hope.[16] For if the structure of the social relationship between speaker and listener is one of domination, true reciprocity is impossible, and the act of communication itself will be distorted.

There is a Finnish *schwank* that expresses this contradiction clearly. To understand its humor is to grasp Habermas's problematic:

> Once a farmer and his servant were starting their meal, as the neighbors were eating too. So the farmer said, "Let's pretend eating, but not eat." The servant contented himself with it, and then when they went to the field to mow, the servant took the blade off the scythe and said, "Now let's pretend mowing, but not mow." (quoted in Köngas, 1962, p. 210)

The democratic structure of the language exchange, emphasized metaphorically by the parallel sentence structure, suggests an equality that does not exist. It is out of phase with the structure of domination between master and servant, and this nonidentity provides the occasion

[16]Adorno, who had an overriding concern for the individual never directly addressed the question of intersubjective communication. It could be said that, for him, the work of art was the expression of utopian hope, indeed, on the same grounds of "domination-free communication" which Habermas posited for communicative action. As Adorno (1973b, vol. 7, p. 250) wrote: "Artworks say we."

for the humor of the servant's trick. This trickster who tears the veil from the apparent reciprocity of the speech exchange is the prototype of the social critic.

The trickster is a seminal figure in folk literature, from the Homeric Hymn to Hermes and to the tales of Uncle Remus. Tricks differ from crimes in that they do not betray the shared bond of human communication and hence its utopian promise but instead play on the ambivalence of meanings,[17] acknowledging the rules of the game but turning the tables, using those rules against the game itself. The trickster lives above and beneath social constraints as well as within them. He demonstrates that the question of who controls the relations between signifier and signified in the production of meanings is a political question. Although he acts to save his own skin, in using language to outwit the powerful, he is clearly the ally of the powerless. As is true of Uncle Remus's Brer Rabbit stories, "It is not virtue that triumphs, but helplessness" (Harris, 1947, p. xiv). As the inventor of meanings, the trickster is the prototype not only of the social critic, but of the artist or paradigm-breaking scientist as well. Uncle Remus comments:

> One of the reasons that made old Brer Rabbit get along so well was he never copied any of the other creatures. When he made his disappearance before them it was always in some brand new place. (Harris, 1971, p. 42)[18]

Yet despite the revolutionary potential of the trickster, he is tolerated by the powerful so long as he remains at the peripheries of society where he can in fact function as an aid to social stability. Kerenyi (in Radin, 1969) writes:

> Disorder belongs to the totality of life, and the spirit of this disorder is the trickster. His function . . . is to add disorder to order and so make a whole, to render possible, within the fixed bounds of what is permitted, an experience of what is not permitted. (p. 185)

In the Roman Saturnalia, masters served slaves, but the topsy-turvy world of the Carnival owed its very meaning to the fact that it was an

[17]A favorite game of tricksters is the *double-entendre*. Odysseus uses the name "Udeis" which means "nobody," but also "hero," to trick Polyphemus the Cyclops (Horkheimer & Adorno, 1972, p. 64). The tortoise in a Nigerian folktale takes the new name "All of You" at a feast, and gets the lion's share of the food prepared "for all of you" (Achebe, 1972, pp. 87–88).

[18]Similarly, in the Homeric Hymn to Hermes the Thief (who became identified with the lower-class struggle for equality with the aristocracy in sixth-century Athens), "references to Hermes as an inventor are frequent, vivid, and elaborate. In all of them, the individual and original genius of the inventor is emphasized" (Brown, 1947, p. 75).

extraordinary event; hence, it served to define the boundaries of the real social world all the more precisely. The trickster is one of many cases of fringe figures—witches, magicians, fools, prophets—whose potentially revolutionary behavior is socialized within abnormal occasions of festival and ritual.[19] Their powers are confined to a peripheral realm; they act as buffers or mediators against the natural and supernatural worlds. Hence, prophets inhabit the wilderness[20] and to accuse someone of witchcraft is "the political idiom of out-casting and re-definition of social boundaries" (Douglas, 1973, p. 88).

The crucial question is one of legitimacy: these figures and the classes of social underdogs they represent must themselves acquiesce to the peripheral position that established authority allots to them. When medieval ideology condemned usury as a sin, as long as medieval capitalists accepted the Church's meaning of their activity, they could not challenge the nobles' political power:

> The medieval merchant accepted his own equation with the thief: he carried a thief's thumb as a talisman to help him in his business, shared his patron Saint Nicholas with the thief, and made Reynard the Fox [a famous trickster] his hero and his ideal. (Brown, 1947, p. 82).

But in periods of social disequilibrium, when the normal world has itself gone topsy-turvy, fringe figures may suddenly become central. Then witches call themselves visionaries, prophets turn into messiahs, and tricksters shed their masks of humor and are revealed as heroes.[21] When

[19]Mauss (1972) has noted as an essential characteristic of magic and witchcraft that "most of the conditions which must be observed are abnormal ones. However commonplace, the magical rite has to be thought of as unique . . . . All magical rites generally aim at endowing the ceremonies with an abnormal character. All movements are the opposite of normal ones, particularly those performed at religious ceremonies. Conditions, including those of time, are apparently unrealizable: materials are preferably unclean and the practices obscene. The whole thing is bizarre, involving artifice and unnatural features—very far removed from that simplicity to which recent theorists have wished to reduce magic" (p. 50).

[20]"Consider the distinctive appearance of prophets. They tend to arise in peripheral areas of society, and prophets tend to be shaggy, unkempt individuals. They express in their bodies the independence of social norms which their peripheral origins inspire in them. It is no accident that St. John the Baptist lived in the desert and wore skins, or that Nuer prophets wear beards and long hair in a fashion that ordinary Nuer find displeasing. Everywhere, social peripherality has the same physical forms of expression, bizarre and untrimmed" (Douglas, 1973, p. 118).

[21]When commercial classes in sixth-century Athens successfully challenged the ruling aristocracy and democratized political power, the cult of Hermes was ensconced alongside that of Apollo, "aristocrats of the gods," and at the same time Hermes' character was transformed, acquiring "the essential traits of the mythological type of culture hero,

the legitimacy of the powerful is undermined (a threat endemic to late capitalist societies, if we are to believe Habermas (1975b)), then objects escape the domination of old concepts and the world can be renamed. The cognitive method of Adorno (himself very like a trickster) is relevant in this context because it entails a shift in vision so that "apocryphal realms on the edges of civilization move suddenly into the center" (Adorno, 1942, p. 2). The dialectical reversal of meanings inherent in his method, what Nietzsche called a transvaluation of values, is no new invention. The seventeenth-century Jewish mystic Sabbatai Zevi claimed himself the Messiah by converting to Islam and averred that in the Messianic age "everyone who wants to serve God as he does now . . . [will] be called a desecrator" and what is now considered sinful will become a holy act" (Iggeret Hagen Abraham, 1668, quoted in Scholem, 1971, p. 72). The revolutionary message of Marxism is not different: "Under the dictatorship of the proletariat the relationship between legality and illegality undergoes a change in function, for now what was formerly legal becomes illegal and vice versa" (Lukacs, 1923/1971 p. 262).

The dialectics of critical humor, expressed in the *schwank* by the servant's trick against the master, keeps the utopian moment alive within speech even when within reality it may appear to have vanished. But Hegel's (1807/1967) story of the dialectic between master and slave (pp. 228–249), which begins humorlessly with a fight unto death—a struggle, it should be noted, for the same mutual recognition that underlies Habermas's notion of communicative action—goes further than illuminating the gap between language and reality. It renames reality by reversing the relation between signifiers and signified and in so doing illuminates the logic of social transformation. The slave realizes that as the active producer, he is in fact the master, whereas the master, totally dependent on another's labor, is the slave. The only way out of the

---

of which there is no finer example than the Greek Prometheus. Like Prometheus, Hermes is represented as 'pre-eminently intelligent.' . . . Like Prometheus again, Hermes is represented as a friend of mankind, a source of material blessings, 'the giver of good things,' 'the giver of joy'" (Brown, 1947, p. 21.) But the transformation of trickster into hero is not the only possibility. Peacock (1967) reports an example of mass culture co-option occurring in contemporary, urban Java, where transvestites, closely related to the figure of the trickster, provide nightly stage entertainment for proletarian audiences, singing songs that transform traditional cultural meanings in a way that makes cultural sense out of new industrial conditions, functioning to justify the inequities of those conditions, rather than critically illuminating them.

vicious circle whereby masters end up slaves is to eradicate the hierarchical structure altogether, so that social relations really become a reciprocity between equals, and reality thus lives up to the utopian promise of language.

Dialectics and the Child's World

The argument that a genetic epistemology should focus its attention on dialectical cognitive operations rather than on abstract formal ones is based not on grounds of political expediency, but on the grounds that it comes closer to truth. In this case the right theoretical tendency and the right political tendency converge (cf. Benjamin, 1973, p. 86). In order to comprehend reality, children must be able to think dialectically because the world of their experience is in fact dialectically structured. Moreover, the child's development is composed of precisely that tension between domination and submission, power and helplessness, independence and dependence, that forms the central contradiction of the larger social structure.

The fundamental paradox of children's existence is that they desire autonomy yet are dependent on adults. In order to gain power over their own environment, children give up a false sense of omnipotence and submit to the authority of the powerful—first their parents, then their teachers. By submitting to adults' tutelage, children acquire the knowledge and power to rebel against them. Piaget (1962) recognizes that learning is motivated by the child's respect for "an adult who has personal authority" and gives rise to "imitation of the superior by the subordinate" (p. 73). Hegel (1967, e.g., p. 136) clearly implies a parallel between the dialectic of master and slave and the relation between teacher and student: submitting to authority is necessary in the process of developing intellectual independence. The correlation between childhood and social powerlessness has long been recognized by myths in which the socially impotent are represented in the image of the child. Just as the Messiah comes with the birth of a baby, so when Hermes becomes identified with the lower-class struggle against the aristocracy, he first appears in myth as a new-born child (Brown, 1947, pp. 83–86).[22]

[22]It should be pointed out that the dependency resulting from certain natural characteristics, such as sex and race, has social origins and is not surmounted by growing to adulthood: "Whereas the difference between parents and children can be diminished, that between the sexes is accentuated" (Butor, 1973, p. 360).

Children themselves, of course, are at first unaware of the connection. Their struggle against authority, which begins in the second year against the mother and continues with the involvement of the father in the four-year-old's oedipal phase, is a private one and is not correlated with any objective comprehension of the class structure of society (Wacker, 1976, e.g., p. 47). The association between their own helplessness and that of the poor or socially outcast is instead made for them by adults and conveyed to them through fairy tales. If myths project social inequalities onto the image of the child, then fairy tales do just the opposite: they project the child's experience of inferiority onto a social image. Children are encouraged to identify in fairy tales with paupers who become princes, youths who slay ogres, or poor men who become rich and to see in these allegories the possibility for their own transformation (Butor, 1973, pp. 352–354).

Fairy tales are complex phenomena. To unravel their enigma, to separate their layers of meaning as a dialogue between generations, would indeed provide a model for a dialectical developmental psychology. Fairy tales are for children but not *of* children: "The child knows about fairyland only what the adult tells him" (Butor, 1973, p. 356). Told within a context of "vertical inequality between parents and children" (Ariès, 1962, p. 99), they require a categorical distinction between generations which in Western civilization, as Ariès tells us, was a relatively late invention, a discovery of the seventeenth-century bourgeoisie (cf. Berry, 1974). It was not until the late seventeenth century that fairy tales began to emerge as a distinct genre of children's literature. It is important for our purposes to note that storytelling as a game common to all ages and all classes "was destroyed at one and the same time between children and adults, between lower class and middle class. This coincidence enables us to glimpse already a connection between the idea of childhood and the idea of class" (Ariès, 1962, p. 99).

The fairy tale brings pleasure to adult and child alike, but surely not for the same reasons. The child's own narrative constructions have a different logic. The adult, with first-hand knowledge of the inequities and inadequacies of the social order, has the chance in telling the tale to make that order different, reconstructing the world in a more utopian form.

> A world inverted, an exemplary world, fairyland is a criticism of ossified reality. It does not remain side by side with the latter; it reacts upon it, it suggests that we transform it, that we reinstate what is out of place (Butor, 1973, p. 353).

The child who hears the story discovers in terms of a social allegory the logical possibility of resolving his own existential paradox—indeed, with the aiding and abetting of those very authorities whose domination he desires to overcome. Thus, the fairy tale is a constellation in which, for the moment, the utopian reconciliation of generational conflict and social conflict converge in one image.

Yet the image is an illusion, the projections a distortion. Were it otherwise, then every adult who told a fairy tale and every child who listened would support the socially oppressed. Despite parallels, the fusion of the dialectics of child and pauper entails a confusion of nature and history[23] that camouflages their real difference. One major difference is that childhood is a state that is outgrown naturally, as are those forms of helplessness, dependency, and inferiority peculiar to that state: "Vertical inequality is always surmounted in reality. Life will transform all children into adults" (Butor, 1973, p. 356). This inevitably happy ending is not guaranteed in the social history of oppression. Another major difference between the strife of generations and classes is that when children become adults they invariably reproduce the structure of inequality with respect to the next generation. This need not be true of relations between people in social reality.

In the dialectics of domination, the structures of class struggle and the oedipal situation have formal parallels, but they are out of phase with each other. They exist on different axes—class and generation—that intersect in a variety of specific constellations. The constellations are, I believe, various but not limitless, as their structure would become visible in the arrangement of a handful of key elements. To outline a social-historical, natural-historical typology of the ways in which social class and chronological age interact in relation to domination (no doubt the variables of sex and race would also be crucial) would be to continue the work of Adorno and his associates on character typology in *The Authoritarian Personality,* (Adorno, Frenkel-Brunswick, Levinson, & Sanford, 1950) which in turn built on the work of Erich Fromm and other colleagues at the Institut für Sozialforschung (see that institute's 1936 publication, *Autorität und Familie*). Here, by way of illustration, we might list several possibilities of types:

[23]Particularly interesting regarding the fusing of natural and social experiences of impotence is recent work in the psychosocial interpretation of dreams (Millan, in preparation).

it does when applied to the case of parents offering their children the choice: "All right, do you want to wash your ears and then brush your teeth, or brush your teeth and then wash your ears?"

But to claim that the structure of society prevents democracy from "living up to its concept" is really too weak to describe the seriousness—and the absurdity—of the child's world in the present historical era. Over the fundamental contradiction of class there hangs the shadow of another paradox—that the industrialized, militarized reality to which children must adapt in order to survive increasingly threatens survival. Moreover, those with power are as helpless as those without to escape the life-endangering consequences of that reality. In Vonnegut's (1963) novel, *Cat's Cradle,* Philip Castle tells the story of the time bubonic plague hit the tropical town of San Lorenzo where his father had founded a hospital. If the plague can be seen as a symbol of the destructive potential of the present world order, then the story can be read as a modern *schwank,* expressing the paradox of today's master class:

> When the plague was having everything its own way, the House of Hope and Mercy in the Jungle looked like Auschwitz or Buchenwald. We had stacks of dead so deep and wide that a bulldozer actually stalled trying to shove them toward a common grave. Father worked without sleep for days, worked not only without sleep but without saving many lives, either. . . . One sleepless night I stayed up with Father while he worked. It was all we could do to find a live patient to treat. In bed after bed we found dead people. "And Father started giggling," Castle continued. "He couldn't stop. He walked out into the night with his flashlight. He was still giggling. He was making the flashlight beam dance over all the dead people stacked outside. He put his hand on my head, and do you know what that marvelous man said to me?" asked Castle. "Nope." "'Son,' my father said to me, 'someday this will all be yours.'" (pp. 134–145)

Conclusion

> The object of a mental experience is an antagonistic system in itself—antagonistic in reality, not just in its conveyance to the knowing subject that rediscovers itself therein. . . . Regarding the concrete possibility of utopia, dialectics is the ontology of the wrong state of things. The right state of things would be free of it: neither a system nor a contradiction. (Adorno, 1973, pp. 10–11)

Fairy tales provide an image in which nonidenticals are fused, and in this imagining that reconstructs reality there exists a utopian promise. But the other pole of that promise is critical thinking that demythifies reality: here nonidenticals converge only when as concepts (children and oppressed, tricksters and heroes, masters and slaves) they are held apart. Fundamental to both fantasy and critical negation (as well as to humor) is the linguistic representation of the nonidentity between thought and reality. The abstract formalism of Piaget's cognitive structures reflects the abstract formalism of the social structure, and this is the source of their truth. But it is less adequate than dialectical thinking because it cannot reflect critically upon itself and because it cannot capture the ambivalence between the egalitarianism implied by abstract exchange and the social structures of domination in which that exchange takes place.

If there were a shift in focus from formal to dialectical operations, the new generation might indeed be encouraged to develop dialectical skills, for the hierarchical relation between adults and children tends to evoke in the latter what is looked for by the former. No one need fear, however, that this would mean raising a generation of revolutionaries. It is not social criticism that causes social disequilibrium, and the source of society's disorders lies elsewhere than in cognitive structures. But what might be hoped for is a new generation with the intellectual tools for comprehending change and the shift of meanings that it entails; with the cognitive independence, now reserved for a few, to be themselves producers of meaning. In the face of social disequilibrium, such a generation would not need to escape from the freedom that would be released. Rather than clutching at the crusts of an old order or being blindly led by demagogues into a new one, they could cultivate the creative potential of change and the utopian possibilities of renaming the world.

References

Achebe, C. (1972). *Things fall apart.* Ibadan, Nigeria: Heinemann Educational Books.

Adorno, T. W. (1942). Notizen zur neuen Anthropologie. Frankfurt: Adorno Estate.

Adorno, T. W. (1964). Über Jazz. In *Moments musicaux: Neugedruckte Aufsätze, 1928 bis 1962.* Frankfurt: Suhrkamp.

Adorno, T. W. (1970a). *Über Walter Benjamin.* Frankfurt: Suhrkamp. (Letter to Benjamin originally written 1935)

Adorno, T. W. (1970b). *Aesthetische Theorie.* Frankfurt: Suhrkamp.

Adorno, T. W. (1973a). *Negative dialectics.* New York: Seabury Press.

Adorno, T. W. (1973b). Die Aktualität der Philosophie. In *R. Tiedemann (Ed.), Gesammelte Schriften.* Frankfurt: Suhrkamp.

Adorno, T. W., Frenkel-Brunswik, E., Levinson, D., & Sanford, N. (1950). *The authoritarian personality.* New York: Harper.

Ariès, P. (1962). *Centuries of childhood: A social history of family life.* New York: Vintage Books.

Benjamin, W. (1973). The author as producer. In *Understanding Brecht.* London: New Left Books.

Berry, B. M. (1974). The first English pediatricians and Tudor attitudes towards childhood. *Journal of the History of Ideas, 35,* 561–577.

Bloom, H. (1975). *A map of misreading.* New York: Oxford University Press.

Brée, G. (1969). *Marcel Proust and deliverance from time.* New Brunswick, N.J.: Rutgers University Press, 1969.

Brown, N. O. (1947). *Hermes the thief: The evolution of a myth.* Madison: University of Wisconsin Press.

Buck-Morss, S. (1975). Socio-economic bias in Piaget's theory and its implications for cross-culture studies. *Human Development, 18,* 35–49. Reprinted in K. Riegel (1975), *The development of dialectical operations.* Basel: Karger.

Buck-Morss, S. (1977). *The origin of negative dialectics: Theodor W. Adorno, Walter Benjamin, and the Frankfurt Institute.* New York: Free Press.

Butor, M. (1973). On fairy tales. In R. Hall (Ed.), *European literary theory and practice: From existentialism to structuralism.* New York: Delta.

Chukovsky, C. (1974). *From two to five.* Berkeley: University of California Press.

Collaer, P. (1961). *A history of modern music.* New York: World Publishing.

Dasen, P. (1972). Cross-cultural Piagetian research: A summary. *Journal of Cross-Cultural Psychology, 3*(1), 23–39.

Douglas, M. (1973). *Natural symbols: Explorations in cosmology.* New York: Vintage Books.

Duckworth, E. (1964). Piaget rediscovered. *Journal of Research in the Science of Teaching, 2,* 170–182.

Durkheim, E., & Mauss, M. (1963). *Primitive classification.* Chicago: University of Chicago Press.

Gouldner, A. W. (1975–76). Prologue to a theory of revolutionary intellectuals. *Telos, 26,* 21–29.

Habermas, J. (1973). Das Rollenkonzept des Sozialisationsvorganges. In *Kultur und Kritik: Verstreute Aufsätze.* Frankfurt: Suhrkamp.

Habermas, J. (1975a). Moral development and ego identity. *Telos, 24,* 41–55.

Habermas, J. (1975b). *Legitimation crisis.* Boston: Beacon Press.

Harris, J. C. (1947). Introduction. *Uncle Remus: His songs and his sayings.* New York: Appleton Century.

Harris, J. C. (1971). *Brer Rabbit: Stories from Uncle Remus.* New York: Harper.

Hegel, G. W. F. (1967). *The phenomenology of mind.* New York: Harper & Row. (Originally published in 1807)

Horkheimer, M. (1932). Hegel und das Problem der Metaphysik. In *Festschrift für Carl Grunberg, zum 70 Geburtstag.* Leipzig: C. L. Hirschfeld.

Horkheimer, M., & Adorno, T. W. (1972). *Dialectic of enlightenment.* New York: Herder & Herder.

Kohlberg, L. (1969). Stage and sequence: The cognitive-developmental approach to socialization. In D. Goslin (Ed.), *Handbook of socialization theory and research.* Chicago: Rand McNally.

Köngas, E. K. (1962). A Finnish schwank pattern: The farmer–servant cycle of the Kuusisto family. *Midwest Folklore, 11,* 200–219.

Lévi-Strauss, C. (1963). The structural study of myth. In *Structural anthropology.* New York: Basic Books.

Lévi-Strauss, C. (1964). *Tristes tropiques.* New York: Atheneum.

Lévi-Strauss, C. (1973). History and dialectic. In *The savage mind.* Chicago: University of Chicago Press.

Lukacs, G. (1971). *History and class consciousness.* Cambridge: MIT Press. (Originally published 1923)

Marx, K. (1967). Economic and philosophic manuscripts. In L. Eaton and K. Guddat (Eds.), *Writings of the young Karl Marx on philosophy and society*. Garden City, NY: Anchor.

Mauss, M. (1972). *A general theory of magic*. London: Routledge & Kegan Paul.

Millan, I. T. (In preparation). *Mr. Mexico: Caracter e Ideologia del Ejecutivo Mexicano.*

Opie, I., & Opie, P. (1959). *The lore and language of schoolchildren*. Oxford: Clarendon Press.

Peacock, J. L. (1967). Javanese clown and transvestite songs: Some relations between 'primitive classification' and 'communicative events'. In J. Helm (Ed.), *Essays on the verbal and visual arts*. Seattle: University of Washington Press.

Piaget, J. (1962). *Play, dreams and imitation in childhood*. New York: W. W. Norton.

Piaget, J. (1967). *Six psychological studies*. New York: Random House.

Piaget, J. (1969). *The child's conception of time*. London: Routledge & Kegan Paul.

Piaget, J. (1970). *Structuralism*. New York: Harper.

Piaget, J. (1971). *Biology and Knowledge*. Chicago: University of Chicago Press.

Piaget, J. (1973). *To understand is to invent: The future of education*. New York: Grossman.

Piaget, J., & Inhelder, B. (1955). *The child's conception of space*. London: Routledge & Kegan Paul.

Polanyi, M. (1958). *Personal knowledge*. Chicago: University of Chicago Press.

Radin, P. (1969). *The trickster: A study in American Indian mythology*. New York: Greenwood Press.

Riegel, K. F. (1973). Dialectical operations: The final period of cognitive development. *Human Development, 16*, 350–365.

Riegel, K. F. (1976). From traits and equilibrium toward developmental dialectics. In W. J. Arnold (Ed.), *Nebraska symposium on motivation*. Lincoln: University of Nebraska Press.

Scholem, G. (1971). *The messianic idea in Judaism*. New York: Schocken Books.

Smedslund, J. (1977). Piaget's psychology in practice. *British Journal of Educational Psychology, 47*, 1–6.

Turbayne, C. M. (1970). *The myth of metaphor*. Columbia: University of South Carolina Press.

Wacker, A. (1976). *Die Entwicklung des Gesellschaftsverständnises bei Kindern*. Frankfurt: Campus.

Vonnegut, K. (1963). *Cat's cradle*. New York: Delacorte Press.

Youniss, J. (1974). Operations and everyday thinking: A commentary on "dialectical operations." *Human Development, 17*, 388–389.

Chapter 10

Rainer Döbert, Jürgen Habermas, and Gertrud Nunner-Winkler

THE DEVELOPMENT OF THE SELF

Our preoccupation with the topic of the development of the self was occasioned by an empirical study by two of the authors carried out at the Max Planck Institute (Döbert & Nunner-Winkler, 1975). We were interested in types of potential for conflict and apathy in the developing individual which might demonstrate that the acquisition of functionally necessary motivations and legitimations in contemporary society is subject to limitations. Such potentials cannot be explained with trivial psychological assumptions but rather have their origin in the realm of socialization.

From this viewpoint, adolescence represents a particular danger zone. In every society, the transition to adulthood is a precarious threshold. What must be examined is whether or not successive generations will adhere and conform to the given system. In societies of our type, this becomes more improbable because of a moratorium that offers to youths the possibility of acquiring the cultural heritage through formal

This essay originally appeared as the introductory chapter in an edited volume by the authors entitled *Entwicklung des Ichs,* published by Kiepenheuer and Witsch (Cologne) in 1977. For more information concerning this collection, see footnote 2. This version involves only very minor editorial alterations and was translated by John Broughton with the assistance of Hans Bremer and Suzana Libich.

Rainer Döbert • Institute of Sociology, Frei Universität Berlin, Berlin, West Germany. *Jürgen Habermas* • Department of Philosophy, University of Frankfurt Dantestrasse 4–6, Frankfurt am Main, West Germany. *Gertrud Nunner-Winkler* • Max Planck Institute for Psychological Research, West Germany.

education while also regarding that heritage critically. The study mentioned above concentrated on relations between the course of adolescent crisis, moral consciousness, value orientations, and, especially, fundamental political attitudes.

The Formation of Identity

The course that adolescence follows, the stages of moral consciousness, and the life orientations that are anchored in the personality system form the network of variables that we must use in the analysis of the development of the *I,* or as we shall call it here, the *self.*[1] This is the case for any description of the development of the self in terms of the sociologically relevant aspects of the process by which identity is formed in the adult members of our society. The concept of *identity* is the sociological equivalent of the concept of the self. Identity is the symbolic structure that permits a personality system to insure continuity and consistency under changing biographical conditions and different positions in the social space. A person must claim his or her identity for himself or herself and *vis à vis* others. Self-identification, the differentiation of self from others, must be recognized by these others as well. In other words, the reflexive relationship of the individual that is self-identified depends on the intersubjective relationships that he or she has with those others by whom he or she is identified. In the process of self-identification, the individual is supposed to maintain his or her identity in the biographical "vertical" (that is, as he or she passes through the different, often antithetical stages of life), just as much as in

[1]Throughout this chapter, the German *Ich* has been translated as "self" rather than as "I" or "ego." In English, "the I" and "the development of the I" would appear not to correspond well to the authors' intended meaning, whereas the term *ego* has come to have a narrowly psychoanalytic connotation. In recent years, the broader (although perhaps more ambiguous) term *self* has gained increasing currency in the fields of sociology, cognitive developmental psychology, and even psychoanalysis, the domains of greatest relevance to the present authors' theoretical framework. Nevertheless, the German *Ich-Identität* has been translated as "ego identity," since "self-identity" is a standard philosophical term meaning something seriously metaphysical rather than psychological and also because *ego identity* is a term in the current literature with a more or less specifiable and familiar meaning. It should be noted, however, that the German *Ich-Entwicklung,* translated here as "development of the self," could be understood as close in meaning to *ego development,* a term that has come to have a broader, more eclectic meaning than that attaching to *ego* alone. Nevertheless, I have preferred to retain the term *self* throughout for the sake of clarity and continuity.—*Trans.*

the "horizontal" (that is, in the simultaneous reaction to different, often competing structures of expectation). Both personal and social identity have a specific sociological meaning. As individuals are allowed to acquire their identity, they simultaneously secure the intersubjectivity of possible understanding between themselves and others. Thus, there is a structural connection between the forms of identity of individuals and the forms of social integration of the life context by means of which they associate and deal with each other. Extreme cases of loss of identity, as in psychotic withdrawal from the social world or the definitive leave-taking from it that we call suicide, are just as much the symptoms of a ruptured, distorted form of life context in the social group as they are signs of the course of individual illness.

The formation of identity is a complex process that we can conceptualize in the idealized case as a development from the natural *body-bound identity* of the small child, through the *role-bound identity* of the school child, up to the *ego identity* of the young adult (de Levita, 1971; Döbert & Nunner-Winkler, 1975, pp. 38–46; Dubiel, 1973; Habermas, 1973, pp. 195–231; Krappmann, 1969). From the perspective of a child growing into the symbolic universe of its environment, this process can be analyzed as a stepwise acquisition of competence. As the child learns to differentiate itself from its environment, it gains, so to speak, a "natural" identity attributable to the time-conquering character common to all organisms that maintain the boundaries of their differentiation. Even plants and animals are systems in an environment, so that each has not only an *identity for us* (the identifying observers), as a physical object does, but in a certain sense an *identity for itself*. However, the child only develops as a person to the extent that it learns to localize itself in a social environment. When it acquires the symbolic universals of the few fundamental roles in its familial environment, and later the action norms of larger groups, then the natural or organismic identity of the child is replaced by a symbolically supported role identity. The quality of the role identity as something that lends continuity rests on the stability of behavioral expectations that take hold of the person through his or her ego ideals.

This conventional identity can fracture during the adolescent phase. During this period, the adolescent learns the important difference between norms, on the one hand, and the fundamental ideas or principles that give rise to norms, on the other hand. Such principles can serve as criteria for the critical appraisal and justification of existing norms. Indeed, to the person judging in a principled way, all existing norms must appear to be only conventions. Among these existing norms, only general norms can be identified as moral because only these insure reciprocity of rights and obligations of everybody *vis à vis* everybody else. As soon as the kind of interactive reciprocity that is found in the role structure is elevated to the level of a principle, the self can no longer identify itself with particular roles and existing norms. It has to accept the fact that the traditional forms of life can prove to be just particular unreasonable forms. That is why the self must take back its identity behind the lines of all particular role norms and stabilize itself solely by means of the abstract capacity to present itself in any situation as that which can comply with a request for consistency even in the face of conflicting norms. These conflicts may be horizontal (incompatible role expectations) or vertical (the biographically determined succession of contradictory role systems). The ego identity of the adult is confirmed by the capacity to build up new identities while amalgamating them with superseded identities of the past, thus organizing itself and its interactions in a noninterchangeable life history.

Cognitive, Interactionist, and Psychoanalytic Approaches

The concept of developmental stages of identity is introduced here only provisionally and has not yet attained the status of a sufficiently validated construct. However, this notion guides us in classifying the literature treating the various aspects of the process of identity formation. The developmental problems linked with the concept of identity formation have been dealt with in three different theoretical traditions: (1) the cognitivist psychology of development founded by Jean Piaget, (2) the social psychology of symbolic interactionism that goes back to G. H. Mead, and (3) the analytic ego psychology derived from Sigmund Freud. In all the of these theoretical traditions, the developmental trend is characterized by increasing autonomy vis à vis at least one of three particular environments. In other words, development is characterized by the independence the self acquires insofar as it enhances its problem-solving capacities in dealing with: (1) the reality of external nature of both manipulable objects and strategically objectified social relations; (2) the symbolic reality of behavioral expectations, cultural values, and identities, such as they have been experienced from a performative perspective; and (3) the inner nature of intentional experiences and one's own body, in particular, those drives that are not amenable to communication. Piaget's theory of cognitive development tackles the first aspect, Mead's theory of interactive development the second, and Freud's theory of psychosexual development the third.

For all three theories, the transposition of external structures into internal structures is an important learning mechanism. Piaget speaks of "interiorization" when schemes of action—meaning rules for the manipulative mastery of objects—are internally transposed and transformed into schemes of comprehension and thinking. Psychoanalysis and symbolic interactionism propose a similar transposition of interaction patterns into intrapsychic patterns of relations, one which they call "internalization." This mechanism of internalization is connected with the further principle of achieving independence—whether from external objects, reference persons, or one's own impulses—by actively repeating what one has first passively experienced.

Certainly, we must not overestimate the convergences of the three approaches. But there is no denying the fact that the theoretical perspectives they stress complement each other.

The concept of *developmental logic* has been elaborated particularly by Piaget. According to him, the formative process of cognizant, active individuals passes through an irreversible sequence of discrete and increasingly complex stages of development. In this sequence, no stage can be skipped, and each higher stage implies the preceding one in the sense of a rationally reconstructible pattern of development.

Mead developed the concept of *ego identity*. The adolescent is constituted as an individual only by taking part in social interactions. Identity forms itself by socialization, that is, first by integration into a particular social system. This integration is achieved by acquiring symbolic universals. Then, through identification with increasingly more abstract groups and structures, the adolescent learns to organize his or her interactions autonomously in a noninterchangeable biographical context. Socialization means individualization.

Finally, for Freud, it is the concept of the *pubertal crisis* that is central. For him, development not only is discontinuous but also, as a rule, crisis-ridden (Erikson, 1959). The resolution of stage-specific developmental problems is preceded by a phase of destructuration and, in part, by regression. The experience of productive resolution of a crisis, that is, of overcoming the dangers of pathological paths of development, is a condition for mastering later crises.

The convergences between these three traditional theories strike us more forcibly today since assimilation has already taken place between them in one or the other direction. The integration of Freud's and Mead's approaches has proceeded farthest in sociology (Denzin, 1972; Parsons & Bales, 1955). Psychoanalytic ego psychologists have tried to link Piaget's theory of cognitive development with psychodynamic concepts (Anthony, 1957; Cobliner, 1967; Haynal 1975; Wolff, 1960). Cognitive psychologists concerned with moral development have found points of contact with the fundamental ideas of symbolic interactionism (Feffer, 1959, 1970; Feffer & Gourevitch, 1960; Flavell, Fray, Wright, & Jarvis, 1968). It might be noted that the perspective in which such syntheses are now produced more or less eclectically was already present in the early treatises of members of the Freudian Left (Dahmer, 1973), who attempted to make Marx and Freud compatible by means of the application of Hegel's ideas (Habermas, 1975).

Theoretical Framework

Although we do not yet possess a plausible theory of the development of the self that would sufficiently explain the complex processes by which identity is formed, we have nevertheless compiled a collection of diverse writings with a view to the task of developing such a theory (Döbert, Habermas, & Nunner-Winkler, 1977). Although we are sociological in orientation, this collection contained mostly treatises that could be called, in the proper sense of the word, psychological.[2] Despite

[2]The way in which we structured that selection of writings is perhaps interesting because it reveals the kinds of sources that we found instructive. What we term "theory of self development" is not a clearly defined area of research. Thus, the selection of the writings can but indirectly indicate the boundaries of the field as we see it.

The first part of the volume presented a concept of identity derived from the theory of action (Parsons, 1968) and also a theoretical model of the social system that is most important for the constitution of identity, namely, the family (from Hess & Handel, 1959). An essay by Stierlin *et al.* (1973) was used as an exemplary exposition of how specific family constellations influence the formation of identity during adolescence. The second part of the book introduced the dimensions that we consider relevant for an adequate psychological model of the development of the self. The sequence of dimensions—cognitive development (Muuss, 1967), role taking (Selman & Byrne, 1974), moral development (Turiel, 1969), and the development of the ego as a synthesis of cognitive and motivational factors (Loevinger, 1966)—reflects a hierarchy of increasingly complex structures. The third selection showed how, by recourse to those dimensions, the specific developmental problems of the adolescent can be described. Regarding the cognitive problems, we included Elkind's (1967) paper on adolescent egocentrism; motivational problems were illustrated by the work of Blos (1967), an excerpt from Jacobson (1973), and a paper by Podd (1978); moral aspects were covered by Kohlberg (1973) and Turiel (1974).

the risk of letting the sociological interests recede too far into the background, we felt then and still feel that it is necessary to explain the importance which a nascent and programmatic theory of the development of the self can have for sociology. This is particularly important given the fact that sociology and psychology lie surprisingly far apart in the spectrum of social sciences.

We shall begin, in this section, by sketching a theoretical framework. Then, in the following section, we shall proceed to characterize the development of interactive competence as the core of identity formation. Finally, in the last section, we shall attempt to discover whether such theorizing may signal a paradigm shift in sociology.

In the construction of our nascent theoretical framework, the following six issues have to be discussed.

Phases of Development

The different theoretical traditions of developmental psychology converge on the particular importance of two phases or forward thrusts in the development of the self. The first phase, which, according to our cultural definitions, leads to the child's being mature enough for schooling, is seen as an oedipal crisis from the psychodynamic viewpoint and as a transition from preoperational to concrete operational thinking from the viewpoint of cognitive development. The second phase, which, according to our cultural definitions, is characteristic of adolescents, is seen as the adolescent crisis or pubertal crisis from the psychodynamic point of view and as the transition from concrete operational to formal operational thinking from the viewpoint of cognitive development. Considered as sociological phenomena, the forward thrusts of these two developmental transitions depend on, respectively, growing into the parental family and becoming detached from it. Starting from such an interpretive conceptualization, we can say that there is a two-stage process of socialization that has motivational and cognitive aspects, although its essence lies in the acquisition of interactive capacities and the evolution of an identity.

For both stages, the functional developmental problems which have to be solved can be determined sociologically. By solving the oedipal

---

The three essays collected in the last part of the book (Adelson, 1971; Keniston, 1969; and Haan *et al.*, 1968) were used to illustrate how political attitudes and political activity can be seen as resulting from the specific formal dimensions presented in the preceding parts.

crisis and acquiring specific sex and generation roles, the child integrates itself into the social structure of the parent family. Thus, the child learns how to distinguish individual relations with particular persons from generalized behavioral or attitudinal expectations. He or she evolves internal controls of behavior and attitude, acquires a role-bound identity, distinguishes the family system from the family's social environment, and so on. During adolescence, the problem of detachment from the concrete ties of the love objects of early childhood is repeated on a higher level. Adolescents must not only relativize their familial role with respect to their peers but also transcend family bonds and actively take roles that relate to the total social system. In modern Western societies, we have to deal with specialized roles of professions and professional training, the abstract role of the citizen, the highly individualized role of a sexual partner, the parental role, and so on. In short, the adolescent must live up to the expectations of autonomy that are linked with adult status.

Identity Formation

A precise analysis of the developmental problems that the adolescent has to face leads us to the fact that the central task is the reconstruction of the role identity bound to the parent family. Detachment from the family must be followed by the attempt to find another basis of identity to replace family membership. Erikson has provided us with an exemplary investigation of this sequence of detachment and identity crisis. The form of the adolescent crisis may range from the inconspicuous to the dramatic. Where the crisis is intense, it brings about conflicts that some adolescents attempt to resolve more or less internally, whereas others act them out more visibly. The solution of the crisis experience is a function of the particular way in which the process takes place[3] Three ideal types of outcome can be distinguished.

In the first, unsuccessful, case, the adolescent fails to build up an identity. He or she does not achieve an unconstrained integration into

[3]In a serious identity crisis, for example, conventional role identity is fractured to such a degree that a restabilization on the conventional level would be improbable. Depending on the structure of communication within the family, the attainment of ego identity can be relatively free of crisis, but nevertheless such an outcome is rather infrequent. The modal solution consists of a change in the content of the role identity. The connection to the family of origin is transformed and new roles (e.g., work roles) are assumed with respect to the whole society, without a transformation occurring on the structural level (Döbert & Nunner-Winkler, 1975; Haan, 1974).

society, a balance between the different spheres of life, or a unified interpretation of his or her life history. This results in a diffuse, split-up, unstable, and insecure identity. We have not taken into consideration these phenomena, which belong to the border area between psychopathology and sociology. From the viewpoint of structure, the forms of damaged identity could be examined only if the pertinent forms of systematically distorted communication were investigated better than they have been so far and if they could be described theoretically. Of course, these phenomena also appear in less extreme forms in pathological deformations of everyday life. They are normalized and can hardly be distinguished from the other two types of identity formation that we postulate for the successful process of adolescence.

These second and third alternatives are as follows: The adolescent either reconstructs on the same structural level the fractured role identity that is linked with the family of origin or overcomes the role identity in favor of an ego identity. In the first case, his or her affiliation to more abstract groups replaces family membership as a basis for identity. As a rule, this is effected by membership in a definite professional or status group, usually related to membership roles of a regional, ethnic, national, political, or linguistic kind. These more abstract role identities, no longer bound to the family, must be acquired in the second case as well. However, in this instance, once formed, they are broken again. In this process, the adolescent learns how to generalize the faculty of overcoming old identities and of building up new ones and transferring them to any situation. The individual kernels of the role identities that have been given up are then nothing but the life-historical traces of a learning process that had led to identity formation's becoming reflexive. Identity formation is now a process that is triggered anew in any critical situation.

Orientation in Life

The adolescent stage is described frequently as the philosophical period of life. This at once brings to mind literary models of a youthful development that is typical of its epoch, of the surrounding civilization, and, above all, of the social stratum. However, the idealism of a high-flying, middle-class adolescent with intellectual interests and inclinations is only a particularly striking variety of a more general model. During the phase of adolescence, the young person finds a differential access of one kind or another to the cultural tradition prevailing at the time. He or she is bound to adopt that tradition in order to fill the temporal horizons of the adult status with the contents of a comprehensive orientation in life. Identity formations also comprise this content-specific aspect. Self-identification requires a self-interpretation that may be articulated in very different depths of focus. Certainly, this articulation of a life orientation depends on the opportunities available for access to the cultural belief system and on the opportunities actually taken. Whatever the possibilities of access, the outcome of the adolescent crisis also depends on what structures are offered by a cultural tradition. From the tradition, the adolescent adopts not only elements of content but also means of contructing an identity that is no longer bound to the family. In this respect, cultural traditions hold different potentials for stimulation according to their formal level. For example, they can encourage the transition to a postconventional identity or they can fix the remodeling of the role identity at a conventional level.

Research on the political consciousness of adolescents, such as that carried out by Adelson (1971), Keniston (1969), and Haan, Smith, and Block (1968), refers to parts of our cultural tradition the formal level of which provokes a rupture with authority-bound conventional thinking. It does so mainly by virtue of fundamental political ideas derived from a rational "natural rights" approach and from the theories of bourgeois society, through which the self-understanding of democracies with rival programs of the constitutional state and the welfare state, respectively, expresses itself. Many adolescents make no use of this potential for stimulation. However, the catalytic effect that, given appropriate circumstances, such a tradition may have on the solution of adolescent crises can be seen by considering the example of those experiments that are meant to foster children's moral consciousness by confronting individuals with exemplary arguments at a stage of moral judgment elevated just above their own (Turiel, 1969). Seen in this perspective, adolescents' selective utilization of the cultural potential for stimulating development becomes a phenomenon demanding explanation.

Cognitive Structures

Judging the outcome of the adolescent crisis in terms of the developmental stage of identity formation achieved, we employ (at least implicitly) a concept that Piaget initially introduced with respect to cognitive development. The stages of cognitive development can be described as problem-solving activities or operations that form a distinct structural whole. The internal relations existing between operations that are on the same level comprise structures the significance of which can be explained formally, that is, they can be given a rational reconstruction. However, that applies not only to the relations internal to a structure but also to the relations between structures on different levels. This concept of a developmental logic, which has not yet been analyzed sufficiently (Flavell, 1972), is also at the basis of our suppositions concerning the development of identity.

Obviously, there is a close relationship between identity formation and the stages of moral conciousness (Podd, 1972). Morality that follows principles must be established firmly in an identity formation that is role-independent. Probably, both are based on the same structure. In fact, the applicability of the concept of a developmental logic has been examined empirically only for the development of moral consciousness.

Cognitive development seems to adopt the function of a pacesetter for moral development. Thus, for example, the mastering of formal operations is a necessary though not sufficient condition for postconventional moral judgment that invokes definite principles. However, we cannot state yet whether or not cognitive development in the domain of dealing with manipulable objects is a self-regulatory process and thus advances autonomously or instead depends on the development of competences in the domain in which practical questions can be morally clarified, that is, the domain of communicative actions. Thus, the question arises of whether the capacity to execute operations reversibly in contrary directions is first acquired in social interactions and only later transferrred to cognitive operations. We shall be able to decide that empirically only when we know what function the acquisition of specifically interactive abilities serves in the development of the self. In this domain, we are only beginning to study processes of role taking experimentally.

Motivational Background

While the developmental logic can be investigated with the help of cognitive structures, one cannot deal with the mechanisms of development without analyzing psychodynamic processes. These have been examined primarily by psychoanalysis. In the classical treatment, development is described first from the perspective of the destiny of changing drives. In particular, there is a focus upon those recently acquired sexual drive urges of early adolescence that lead to the regressive reliving of oedipal fears and early childhood needs and so set in motion the individual's defenses. A successful defense occurs when early childhood object cathexes can be withdrawn, so that the youth frees himself or herself from his or her internalized mother and father images, which leads to a weakening of the superego and to depression. The previous object libido is transformed into narcissistic libido. It strengthens cognitively determined egocentrism (cf. Elkind, 1967) and moral instrumentalism (the protest instrumentalism exemplified especially by Kohlberg's stage 4½), which both appear during an intense adolescent crisis. The narcissistic libido has to be transformed again into a cathexis of or attachment to an object, through the choice of a partner and of life goals. As a result of this, there is a thorough reorganization of the ego and superego that is subjectively experienced as a developmental crisis, as ego psychology has demonstrated (Blos, 1967; Jacobson, 1964). Psychoanalytic investigations demonstrate that the maturational crises interlock in a cumulative interdependence. The prognosis is unfavorable for anyone who drags along the mortgage of unresolved developmental problems from prior crises (cf. Siegert, 1979).

We would like to touch upon another point in this connection. Because the transition to a postconventional stage of moral consciousness is intertwined with the construction of identity, two forms of reflection encounter one another in the developmental process, namely the *abstractive* reflection on which Piaget bases his explanation of cognitive structures and an *analytic* reflection about the life history of the self which touches upon the process of motivational development. The former type of reflection comprises a twofold movement. The child learns constructively, internalizing the formal properties of his or her spontaneous activities and action coordinations and drawing out the formal qualities from spontaneous activities, so forming a basis for new, more abstract activities. Piaget calls this process "interiorization." Progressive interiorization can also be understood as a reflexivity of manipulative exchanges that emerges with the increasing objectification of reality. In other words, at each developmental stage, the adolescent acquires a new category of activities that operates on the activities of the previous stage, taking them as its object. Schemes of sensorimotor activity deal with more primitive movements, that is to say, the coordination of simpler activities; concrete operations allow for the management of these already coordinated activities; formal operations, in turn, permit the manipulation of concrete operations. In the constructive steps of learning, children come to reflect on the formal qualities of their achievement.

In this way, cultural invariants with a general form are built; each competent subject, in the appropriate circumstances, acquires the same structures.

The remarkable thing about the development of a moral consciousness thus appears to consist in the fact that these structures do not evolve by means of a reflexive awareness of the general formal characteristics alone. The transition to post-conventional consciousness requires the occurrence of yet another kind of reflection, the critical self-reflection of the growing person who learns to see through his or her own particular development. How, then, are the two kinds of reflection related? The type of reflection that is a reconstructive recollection of universals that have been mastered already at an intuitive level requires mediation through the other kind of reflection that involves a critical distancing from the unconscious constellations of the self's life destiny.

Socialization Background

The developmental problems of adolescence can be taken to demonstrate that identity formation cannot be explained without a systematic integration of its psychoanalytic and cognitivist theoretical traditions. However, until now, no one has succeeded in clarifying this relationship between the psychodynamic aspects of identity formation and the growth of postconventional structures of moral consciousness.

As the key word *self-reflection* points out, it seems that changes in the system of defense mechanisms plays a mediating role (Haan, 1969; Lichtenberg & Slap, 1972; Mentzos, 1976). In turn, these barriers to intrapsychic communication are connected with distortions of family communications. Therefore, it seems reasonable to assume that a better understanding of the socializing interactions between parents and children can explain how the dynamic and logical sides of identity formation are connected. For example, Stierlin, Levi, and Savard (1973) have shown how the psychodynamic "separation crisis" is negotiated in the context of the distorted communication structure in the parental home. Hess and Handel (1959) have investigated some of the causes of such systemic communication pathologies that the nuclear family has to solve. During the last two decades, families with clinical potential, that is, exhibiting signs that according to an intuitive preunderstanding can be classified as symptoms, have been examined sufficiently that one can risk some tentative generalizations. The interactions and role structures in such families are too strongly or too weakly established in order to bring about that flexible relationship between nearness and distance, sameness and difference, dependence and independence, inside and outside, that goes to make up uninhibited intersubjective relationships that are especially important for the optimal ego development of children.

Nearness and Distance. The well-known research investigations undertaken by Lidz (1965) and Wynne, Rycoff, Day, and Hirsch (1958), and also by Stierlin (1974), Mohler (1972a, 1972b), and Kaufman (1972), confirm that the distance between various members in pathogenic families cannot be regulated according to the situation. The basic family roles (sex and generation) are either so sharply defined against each other that the boundaries between generations and sexes are too rigidly fixed or the roles are insufficiently differentiated. Such patterns often show through in all interactions. The consequence is that the social distances cannot be coordinated flexibly because either the group disintegrates into a split and estranged state or a desperately forced overintegration creates a coercive solidarity. In this case, we use the concept of "pseudomutuality," pointing to a kind of group interrelationship maintained only for the sake of appearances.

Similarity and Difference. Another important factor is the scope provided within the family for the self-representations of the individual members. In pathogenic families, the mutually confirmed congruence of self-portraits, that is, the presented and acknowledged identity of the members, is either so great that the family stereotypes are overpowering and hinder the development of individuality or so lacking that the collective unit is threatened by the absence of normative agreement. Thus, it is not the degree of stereotyping or the strength of the discrepancy that is decisive but the inability to synthesize the aspects of similarity and difference. Therefore, there arises in the family a need to mask the contrast between the self-portraits that are tolerated and the actual behavior of the various individuals.

Activity and Passivity. Uneven power distribution means that the scope of activity of an interaction partner is limited and controlled not only by the scope of another family member but also by his or her initiative. In symptomatic families, one can often observe rigidifications that originate in the dependence of one of the marriage partners on the other and in the formation of coalitions between at least one parent and one or more children (Lidz, 1965). In this regard, we might mention Oeverman's (1974) concept of an "affective solidarity" that exists between parents and which, in the families examined, is disturbed. The uneven distribution of activities amongst the members is not a problem in itself. The problem is the more or less inconspicuous dominance relationships in which the marginalized members' wishes to take initiative are prevented from fulfillment. Such relationships form the basis of strategies for exploitation within the family.

Demarcation of the Family System. A great number of observations supports the assumption that the symptomatic family does not develop a self-guiding capacity sufficient to regulate exchanges with the environment autonomously. On the one hand, very disturbed families are more isolated than inconspicuous families and have less well organized contacts with the environment. On the other hand, disturbed families are more exposed to external influences, typically those exerted by both parents' families of origin. Through his clinical experience, Ackermann (1968; Ackermann & Behrens, 1956) has developed the following typology of families: the family that is isolated from the outside world; the family that is integrated with regard to the outside but is not unified internally; the family that is not internally integrated; and finally the family that is disintegrated and regressive. This can be connected with the concept of "rubber fence" developed by the Wynne group. They use this term to refer to the diffuse delimitation of the pathogenic family which prevents a clear differentiation between inside and outside, and especially between particularistic relationships and the stronger universalistic ones. The net result is that the members of such families isolate themselves from the world around them.

In the symptomatic families, we often observe extreme values on the four dimensions we have just sketched. These families exhibit a systematic distortion of communication and a conflictual charge which is simultaneously cushioned and defended against by the interaction structures. Many findings suggest that children who have grown up in such a family environment establish intrapsychic defense systems that prevent an optimal solution of their age-specific developmental problems. Psychodynamic barriers also interfere with constructive learning processes, preventing any advance toward more complex structures of thinking, moral judgment, and action.[4]

[4]For more recent research and thinking on the relationship of moral development and family interaction, see Döbert and Nunner-Winkler (1985)—Ed.

The Development of Interactive Competence

If one organizes the development of the self into a theoretical framework, as we have started to do here, the sociological implications become obvious: The core of identity formation consists in the achievement of an interactive competence, that is, the ability to take part in increasingly complex action systems. Research on socialization, influenced by Mead, has interpreted this ontogenesis of universal action competence as a series of stages of role taking (play, game, universal discourse). Meanwhile, this concept has been made accessible to more rigorous experimental examinations from the cognitive point of view, according to which it is seen as an aspect of the gradual stagewise diminution of childish egocentricity (Keller, 1976, Selman, 1976; Selman & Byrne, 1974).

Selman differentiates three stages of role taking. First, the child learns that different interaction partners "see" the same situation from different perspectives and thereby learns to differentiate not only their perceptual points of view but also their interpretations, including thoughts, intentions, feelings, and motives. Of course, the child can only absorb these perspectives one after the other and cannot yet coordinate them. Not until the second stage does the child form reciprocal perspectives, learning to understand its own behavior and intentions from the perspective of the other. The child now knows that its actions can fulfill or disappoint the expectations of another person and that the other person's actions can do the same to him or her. This other person always has the position of an opposite; he or she is not a neutral third person, but a "you." Only at the third stage can the reciprocity of the perspectives that is connected to the communication roles of "I" and "you" be made the object of thought. Now, each interaction partner can not only take the role of the other but can also know from the viewpoint of a third person how his or her own perspective is bound up reciprocally with that of the other. The concept of the action norm that entitles all members of a social group to certain behavioral expectations will be formed only when the interactive egocentricity is sufficiently reduced that the child objectifies reciprocal expectation structures from the viewpoint of a disinterested group member. The communication role of the other is split up into the role of the *alter ego,* a participant opposite, and the role of the *neutral person,* who is only taking part in the interaction as spectator. There has been fairly extensive investigation of the developmental step from an interaction that is guided only by the concrete behavioral expectations of individual reference persons, to role-bound action that is also regulated by generalized behavioral expectations. However, the context of this step is less easily examined. A few tentative reflections are now offered concerning this complex issue of the acquisition of interactive competence.

Introduction of the Observer's Perspective into the Domain of Interaction

Let us return to the developmental problems confronting the child in the oedipal phase. The child's interaction with the parents is marked by the generation gap and the authority relation. However, interactions with peers, which the growing child is extending gradually, are characterized mostly by symmetrical power relations. Because of this structural dissimilarity, the relationships with peers cannot undergo a simple assimilation to the relationships in the family (cf. Piaget, 1965/1932). Rather, both areas of interaction must be coordinated on the level of roles. This implies a demarcation of the family system vis à vis at least one additional social system (and not only vis à vis a negatively defined extrafamilial environment). This functional imperative can be fulfilled by the child only if it changes its concretistic relationships to people into the normatively regulated relationships of an interaction system. In this way, perhaps one can imagine from a structural perspective the completion of the process by which the child grows into the symbolic universe of its own family.

This process also has a motivational aspect. Through the example of its own family, the child learns to master its first interaction system insofar as its hedonic motives for action are converted into role obligations. In order to explain this process, Parsons (1964) has reinterpreted the oedipal phase in terms of role theory. The role structure of the family, fixed by the culturally universal establishment of the incest taboo, demands from the growing child both the anticipatory learning of a sex role through identification and the simultaneous denial of any sexualization of the intrafamilial relationships. From this contingent biological task—identification with the role of the oedipal rival and denial of the immediate possession of the love object—the child learns by example the internalization of reciprocal behavioral expectations.

The studies of role taking clarify the structural aspect of the oedipal learning process that Freud investigated from the psychodynamic aspect. The steps that are decisive for the development of role concepts and for participation in normatively regulated interactions depend upon two fundamental attitudes that first of all must be differentiated and then interwoven systematically: the *performative* or participatory attitude exercised between interaction partners whose perspectives are related to each other reciprocally, using the communication roles of "I" and "you", and the *neutral* attitude, exercised with the observational perspective of a third person who participates in an interaction only as a spectator. With the transition to concrete operational thinking, cognitive preconditions are established that are necessary for an objectifying attitude toward manipulable objects, that is, for a decentered perception of a reality that is subjected to the conditions of physical measurement. As soon as this objectifying attitude is introduced into the domain of interaction as well, it becomes possible to represent the already established reciprocity of the action perspective *per se*. The system of personal pronouns expresses the decisive combination of the perspectival articulation of self and other with the possibilities of transformation between the participating and observing attitudes. These reciprocally articulated perspectives can now be apprehended from the third-person perspective. Social roles can constitute themselves only when the interaction partners can not only take the perspective of the other partner but also switch between the perspectives of participant and observer.

Thus, we are talking about a capacity of the self that, when making an utterance, is able to take the perspective of the other toward himself or herself, simultaneously to neutralize his own and the other's perspective from the third-person point of view, and then to return to his or her participant attitude. This permits the self to establish the interpersonal relations between himself or herself and the other not only spontaneously but also reflexively. Having attained such a competence, the self no longer acts only according to the expectations of the other; he or she knows that the other understands the self's utterance as the intentional fulfillment of the other's behavioral expectations. If the same condition is also fulfilled by the other, both sides can communicate in the knowledge that each has the complementary relationship of behavioral expectations and fulfillments in mind. As soon as this condition is fulfilled, two reciprocal behavioral expectations can be so coordinated that they form a system of reciprocal motivation. The other may expect that the self fulfills his or her behavioral expectation because the self may expect that the other fulfills the self's behavioral expectations. To the extent that self and other understand and internalize the constituted role as a system of reciprocally motivating behavioral expectations, stable motives for action can be formed independently from individual reference persons. Given this systematic internalization, the normative context of values that is institutionalized in roles and transformed into motives for action detaches itself from the sphere of communicative actions. Action and normative reality, still mixed together in symbolically mediated actions, are now separated out. Now, if speaker and hearer take up interpersonal relationships, they can differentiate between their utterances and the normative context of those utterances. Utterances are not only comprehensible or incomprehensible, true or false; now they can be appropriate or inappropriate in relation to recognized normative contexts.

Introduction of Hypothetical Thinking into the Domain of Interaction

Although these assumptions about the development of interaction during the oedipal phase are only partly examined here, we have enough indications to sketch a plausible picture. This is not the case, however, for the further development of interactive competence. The studies of communication pathology show that interactive abilities acquired in the adolescent phase are focused on a reflexive distancing from a naively conducted interaction. This withdrawal may occur by means of indirect communication (hints, irony, jokes, and the like) or by passing to a metacommunicative level of communication. All rational answers to situations of disturbed communication demand a reflexive thematization of speech, actions, or intentions. However, it is by no means clear in exactly which respects the interaction competence has expanded. If the participation in normatively regulated interactions can be construed as role behavior, what is the equivalent of role behavior at the next higher stage?

On the one hand, so we gather, there is a complex form of strategic action whereby the acting individual lets himself or herself be guided by hypotheses about the behavior-determining hypotheses of an opponent. On the other hand, there is argumentation in which validity claims that have become problematic are thematized and examined systematically.

For the cognitive domain, Piaget has shown how, at the end of the concrete operational phase of development, the child is confronted by problems that he or she cannot solve with the cognitive means currently available. During adolescence, interaction problems are probably accumulated in a similar way, problems that cannot be solved by interactive means of role behavior. Role conflicts are often managed by recourse to superordinate norms. However, the possibility of identifying disagreements, in certain circumstances, can lead to an awareness that there are norm conflicts which can no longer be solved consensually without questioning the validity of the superordinate norm. As long as the system of society has such a low level of complexity that these conflicts appear only by chance or, if structurally conditioned, only temporarily and phase-specifically, special transition norms (adolescence rites, marriage rites, and so on), are sufficient to cushion them. However, it is typical of modern societies that action areas develop that are no longer regulated exclusively by tradition. As soon as this occurs, there arise conflicts that cannot be handled from within the frame of normal role actions. Obviously this frame can be abandoned in favor of strategic action (in the sense of actions of rational choice). Or, it can be abandoned in favor of an attempt at solving problematic validity claims through argument, if there is the introduction of a fundamentally new attitude in the realm of interaction, a type of attitude we adopt toward hypotheses, namely, that tentative attitude which suspends validity claims.

With the transition to the formal operational phase, youths learn to think hypothetically. They learn to deal with postulated situations concerning which it is uncertain whether or not they exist. Hypothetical thinking demands argumentation because it is presumed that the truth claim of a hypothetical statement can be decided only by the giving of reasons. In each argumentation, there is, at least virtually, a division of labor between an opponent who attacks the controversial validity claim and the proponent who defends it. These two are bound together by the aim of a cooperative search for truth. The adolescent is trained to take a hypothetical attitude by participating in such arguments. We have seen that role participants have to be able to engage in the mutual transformation of the perspectives of the participant and the observer. How does the interaction change when a third, hypothetical, attitude is added?

The connection of role activity to a hypothetical attitude can be imagined in such a way that the acting persons no longer simply take the normative context as a given but rather suspend normative validity claims. Then they are faced with the choice of continuing role activity either through strategic behavior or discursive speech. In both cases, the normative reality of society is stripped of its affirmative validity claims. In strategic actions, in fact, these claims are just pushed aside, whereas during discourse they are made an object of systematic examination.

The person acting strategically substitutes for the orientation of role action, which is aimed at agreement, an orientation toward his or her own success; the participant in discourse indirectly maintains the consensual attitude of role actions on a reflexive level in the indirect form of a cooperative search for truth.

Since strategic actors face their social opponents with the same objectifying attitude as that with which they confront the physical environment, their actions can be connected directly to hypothetical thinking: the actors support their decisions with hypothetical forecasts concerning the opponent's options. The transition from role acting to discourse, in contrast, demands the transfer of hypothetical thinking from propositions to norms. The transition to the phase of formal operational thinking means that youths learn how to treat propositions hypothetically. The same hypothetical attitude toward action norms, however, is obtained only at the postconventional level of moral judgment. On this level, the development of interactive competence coincides with that of moral consciousness.

Both strategic action, that is, behaviors of rational choice, and argumentation are forms of indirect association; they are characterized by the hypothetical attitude of the interaction partners. In strategic actions, we influence an opponent's decision by manipulating his or her options. During argumentation, a suspended consensus is to be restored by means of discourse. These forms of indirect association mark borderline cases. The option to change to strategic action or discourse opens up a spectrum of possibilities of understanding in which already established normative interaction, that is, a role-bound consensual action, occupies a marginal position. Normally, first of all, definitions of the situation must be worked out and an implicit understanding about the respective communication assumptions must be established. The latter requires a context-dependent use of means of indirect understanding, a use which only in extreme cases becomes stylized into strategic actions or into argumentative talk.

The conventional and postconventional levels of interaction are approximately comparable from the point of view of building consensus. At the level of role action, the interaction partners can rely upon a consensus secured in advance by normative integration. To the extent that this agreement loses unquestionability on the next level, it must be replaced by interpretive work with the participants, which calls for forms of indirect communication.

The Origin of Interactive Competence

If these hypotheses are not totally misleading, a provisional scheme suggests itself for the development of interactive competence. For the preschool-age child, still situated cognitively at the preoperational level, the action-related sector of the symbolic universe consists primarily of individual concrete behavioral expectations and actions as well as the consequences of actions that can be understood as gratifications or sanctions. As soon as the child has learned to play social roles, that is, to participate in interactions as a competent member, its symbolic universe no longer consists of actions that express isolated intentions only, for instance, wishes or wish fulfillments. Rather, the child can now understand actions as fulfillments of generalized behavioral expectations or as offenses against them. When, finally, adolescents have learned to question the validity of social roles and action norms, their symbolic universe expands once again. There now appear principles according to which controversial norms can be judged. This treatment of hypothetical validity claims demands the temporary suspension of constraints on action or entry into discourse in which practical questions are clarified through argument.

In the sequence of these three levels, adolescents acquire the corresponding concepts of the *motives* of action and the *subjects* of action. With respect to the motivated components of actions, children cannot distinguish at first between natural causality and free will. Imperatives are understood in nature as well as in society as expressions of concrete desires. On the next level, children learn to differentiate between actions that they ought to make and actions that they want to make, between duty and inclination. They differentiate between the facticity of a desire or an expression of will and the validity of a norm. Finally, adolescents form the notions of *heteronomy* and *autonomy;* they recognize the difference between existing conventions and justifiable norms. The orientations guiding action become increasingly abstract, focusing first on concrete need, then duty, and finally autonomous will.

These levels of concepts of motive correspond to the increasingly general concepts of the acting subject. First of all, the concept of the subject is context-dependent. Only the existence of particulars is acknowledged: concrete actors and actions. On the next level, there is a differentiation of symbolic structures of the general and the particular, that is, norms vis à vis single actions and role carriers vis à vis individual actors. On the third level, it must be possible for the special norms to be thematized from the point of view of their generalizability, so that it becomes possible to differentiate between particular and general norms. At the same time, the actors are no longer understood as a combination of role attributes. Rather, they count as unique individuals who use principles to organize their own noninterchangeable biographies. In other words, on this level there must be a differentiation between individuality and "I in general."

If we start with the assumption that moral consciousness refers to the capacity to substitute interactive competence for a conscious solution of morally relevant action conflicts, then the developmental levels of moral consciousness must be derived as a special case from the developmental levels of interactive ability. Elsewhere, we have tried to make such a derivation plausible (Döbert & Nunner-Winkler, 1975, pp. 106–117; Habermas, 1975).[5]

A Paradigm Shift in Sociology

We have demonstrated above why and how a theory of the development of the self that could explain identity formation in relation to the ontogenesis of general action competences would be of sociological interest. By way of concluding, we would like to announce a still more far-reaching interest. A theory of the kind that we have delineated not only is informative from a sociological point of view but could even be a model of paradigm shift in sociological research.

So far, the sociological theory of action has been taken as a metatheory that clarifies basic conceptions such as actor, action, situation, action orientation, role, norm, value, and so on. These basic conceptions are used to establish the categorical framework for empirical theories. This methodological self-understanding has prevented sociology from giving its basic conceptualization a naturalistic turn. Obviously, concept formation in sociology is not unconnected to everyday conceptions in which the members of social groups construct the normative reality of their social environment. It is therefore but a short step to the design of the sociological theory of action as a theory that tries to reconstruct the universal components of the relevant pretheoretical knowledge of the sociological layperson.

By so doing, sociology would enter into a reflexive relationship with

[5]See also Habermas (1979, 1984).—Ed.

itself. It would not choose its basic assumptions conventionally, but rather develop them with the aim of characterizing the general formal qualities of the action competence possessed by socialized subjects and action systems. Indeed, phenomenological research has a similar intention, in that it aims to capture general structures of possible social life worlds. However, from the beginning, the execution of this program was weighed down by the weakness of a method copied from the introspective approach of the philosophy of consciousness. Only the points of departure taken by competence theory in linguistics and developmental psychology have created a paradigm that combines the formal analysis of known structures with the causal analysis of observable processes. The term *interactive competence* reflects the assumption that, just like language and cognition, the abilities of socially acting subjects can be investigated in terms of a universal competence that is independent of particular cultures.

To be sure, the model of role playing underlying the conventional theory of action could have given rise to an investigation of interactive competence. However, such an inquiry was obstructed not only by the aforementioned methodological self-misunderstanding but also by the neglect of the ontogenetic question. Ironically, role theory has dominated concept formation and problem finding in socialization research more than it has in any other sociological research area, without there having been any serious investigation of the acquisition of role competence. It took the external influence of the recently recognized psychology of cognitive development to actualize this overdue questioning. The suspicion mentioned by Gouldner and Oevermann, among others, that the conventional variations on role theory typically treat the limiting case of total institutions as though it were the norm can be reinterpreted today from the viewpoint of a developmental logic. As long as role theory deals with questions of ontogenesis only in terms of the acquisition of cultural content and not in terms of the development of interactive competence, it must remain uncritical toward itself. Whether it is with regard to life history or to social evolution, it cannot control the developmental level of the characteristics that it distinguishes through its framework of categories.[6]

Admittedly, sociology gets into difficulties with the new structural developmental paradigm. We are not referring here merely to those

[6]On the criticisms of conventional role theory, see Habermas, (1973), Joas (1973), and Geulen (1977).

difficulties that theories of this kind normally have to struggle with: defining operationally the exact limits of competence and performance, giving a sufficiently analytical explanation of the concept of developmental logic, and providing a plausible nexus between mechanisms that can explain the developmental dynamic and structures of consciousness ordered according to a developmental logic. For sociology, an additional difficulty exists. It must conceptualize the structures of consciousness at such a general level that the description of their formal properties remains neutral vis à vis the reference points of the system, namely, personality and society. Only then is it possible to treat the question of the interdependence of learning levels—ontogenetic or socioevolutionary—as an empirical question without already being prejudiced on the analytical level. Besides, the fruitfulness of the competence theory approach to macrosociological inquiry will also depend upon whether or not the concept of an institutional embodiment of culturally available structures of rationality turns out to be a justifiable one (Eder, 1976).

References

Ackerman, N. W. (1968). The family approach and levels of interpretation. *American Journal of Psychotherapy, 22,* 5–14.

Ackerman, N. W., & Behrens, M. L. (1956). A study of family diagnosis. *American Journal of Orthopsychiatry, 26,* 66–78.

Adelson, J. (1971). The political imagination of the young adolescent. *Daedalus, 100,* 1013–1051.

Anthony, E. J. (1957). The system makers: Freud and Piaget. *British Journal of Medical Psychology, 30,* 255–269.

Blos, P. (1967). The second individuation process in adolescence. *Psychoanalytic Study of the Child, 22,* 162–186.

Cobliner, W. G. (1967). Psychoanalysis and the Geneva school of genetic psychology. *International Journal of Psychiatry, 3,* 82–116.

Dahmer, H. (1973). *Libido und Gesellschaft.* Frankfurt: Suhrkamp.

deLevita, D. J. (1971). *Der Begriff der Identität.* Frankfurt: Suhrkamp.

Denzin, N. K. (1972). The genesis of self in early childhood. *Sociological Quarterly, 13,* 291–314.

Dubiel, H. (1973). *Identität und Institution.* Düsseldorf: Bertelsmann.

Döbert, R., & Nunner-Winkler, G. (1975). *Adoleszenskrise und Identitätsbildung.* Frankfurt: Suhrkamp.

Döbert, R., & Nunner-Winkler, G. (1985) Moral development and personal reliability. In M. Berkowitz & F. Osen (Eds.), *Moral education: Theory and application.* Hillsdale, NJ: Erlbaum.

Döbert, R., Habermas, J., & Nunner-Winkler, G. (Eds.) (1977). *Entwicklung des Ichs.* Cologne: Kiepenheuer & Witsch.

Eder, K. (1976). *Zur Entstehung staatlich organisierter Gesellschaften.* Frankfurt: Suhrkamp.

Elkind, D. (1967). Egocentrism in adolescence. *Child Development, 38,* 1025–1034.
Erikson, E. (1959). Identity and the life cycle. *Psychological Issues. 1,* (1), 1–171.
Feffer, M. (1959). The cognitive implications of role-taking behavior. *Journal of Personality, 27,* 152–167.
Feffer, M., & Gourevitch, V. (1960). Cognitive aspects of role-taking. *Journal of Personality, 28,* 383–396.
Flavell, J. H. (1972). An analysis of cognitive developmental sequences. *Genetic Psychology Monographs, 86,* 279–350.
Flavell, J. H., Fry, C., Wright, J., & Jarvis, P. (1968). *The development of role-taking and communication skills.* New York: Wiley.
Geulen, D. (1977). *Das vergesellschaftete Subjekt.* Frankfurt: Suhrkamp.
Haan, N. (1969). A tripartite model of ego functioning values and clinical and research applications. *Journal of Nervous and Mental Diseases, 148,* 14–29.
Haan, N. (1974). The adolescent antecedents of an ego model of coping and defense and comparisons with Q-sorted ideal personalities. *Genetic Psychology Monographs, 89,* 273–306.
Haan, N., Smith, M. B., & Block, J. (1968). Moral reasoning of young adults: Political-social behavior, family background and personality correlates. *Journal of Personality and Social Psychology, 10,* 183–201.
Habermas, J. (1973). *Kultur und Kritik.* Frankfurt: Suhrkamp.
Habermas, J. (1975). Moral development and ego-identity. *Telos, 24,* 41–55.
Habermas, J. (1979). *Communication and the evolution of society.* Boston: Beacon Press.
Habermas, J. (1984). *Theory of communication action* (Vol. 1). Boston: Beacon Press.
Haynal, A. (1975). Freud und Piaget. *Psyche, 3,* 242–373.
Hess, R. D., & Handel, G. (1959). *Family worlds.* Chicago: University of Chicago Press.
Jacobson, E. (1964). *The self and the object world.* New York: International Universities Press.
Joas, H. (1973). *Die gegenwärtige Lage der soziologischen Rollentheorie.* Wiesbaden: AULA.
Kaufman, L. (1972). *Familie, Kommunikation und Psychose.* Bern: Hans Huber.
Keller, M. (1976). *Kognitive Entwicklung und soziale Kompetenz.* Stuttgart: Klett.
Keniston, K. (1969). Moral development, youthful activism and modern society. *Youth and Society, 1,* 110–127.
Kohlberg, L. (1973). Continuities in childhood and adult moral development revisited. In P. B. Baltes & K. W. Schaie (Eds.), *Lifespan developmental psychology* (Vol. 2). New York: Academic Press.
Krappmann, L. (1969). *Soziologische Dimensionen der Identität.* Stuttgart: Klett.
Lichtenberg, J. D., & Slap, J. W. (1972). On the defense mechanism: A survey and synthesis. *Journal of the American Psychoanalytic Association, 10,* 776–791.
Lidz, T. (1965). *Schizophrenia and the family.* New York: International Universities Press.
Loevinger, J. (1966). The meaning and measurement of ego development. *American Psychologist, 21,* 195–206.
Mentzos, S. (1976). *Interpersonale und institutionelle Abwehr.* Frankfurt: Suhrkamp.
Mohler, L. R. (1972a). Cognitive style, schizophrenia and the family. *Family Processes, 11,* 125–146.
Mohler, L. R. (1972b). A family perspective on psychosomatic factors in illness. *Family Processes, 11,* 457–486.
Muuss, R. E. (1967). Jean Piaget's cognitive theory of adolescent development. In *Adolescence.* New York: Random House.
Oevermann, U. (1974). Rollenstruktur der Familie und ihre Implikation für die kognitive Entwicklung von Kinder. In G. Szell (Ed.), *Privilegierung und Nichtprivilegierung im Bildungssystem.* Munich: Nymphenburger Verlagshaus.
Parsons, T. (1964). *Social structure and personality.* Glencoe, IL: Free Press.

Parsons, T. (1968). The position of identity in the general theory of action. In C. Gordon & K. Gergen (Eds.), *The self in social interaction*. New York: Wiley.

Parsons, T., & Bales, R. F. (1955). *Family, socialization and interaction process*. Glencoe, IL: Free Press.

Piaget, J. (1965). *Moral judgment of the child*. New York: Free Press. (Originally published 1932).

Podd, M. H. (1972). Ego identity status and morality: The relationship between two developmental constructs. *Developmental Psychology, 16*, (3), 497–507.

Selman, R. L. (1976). Toward a structural-developmental analysis of interpersonal relationship concepts. In A. Pick (Ed.), *Tenth Annual Minnesota Symposium on Child Psychology*. Minneapolis: University of Minnesota Press.

Selman, R. L., & Byrne, D. F. (1974). A structural-developmental analysis of levels of role-taking in middle childhood. *Child Development, 45*, 803–806.

Siegert, M. T. (1979). *Adoleszenzkrise und Familienwelt: Prozesse der Identitätsstörung bei opiatsüchtigen Jugendlichen*. Frankfurt: Campus Verlag.

Stierlin, H. (1974). *Separating parents and adolescents*. New York: Quadrangle.

Stierlin, H., Levi, L. D., & Savard, R. J. (1973). Centrifugal versus centripetal separation in adolescence: Two patterns and some of their implications. In S. Feinstein & P. Giovacchini (Eds.), *Adolescent psychiatry* (Vol. 2). New York: Basic Books.

Turiel, E. (1969). Developmental processes in the child's moral thinking. In P. H. Mussen, J. Langer, & M. Covington (Eds.), *Trends and issues in developmental psychology*. New York: Holt, Rinehart and Winston.

Turiel, E. (1974). Conflict and transition in adolescent moral development. *Child Development, 45*, 14–29.

Wolff, P. H. (1960). *The developmental psychologies of Jean Piaget and psychoanalysis*. New York: International Universities Press.

Wynne, L. C., Rycoff, I., Day, J., & Hirsch, S. (1958). Pseudo-mutuality in the family relations of schizophrenics. *Psychiatry, 21*, 628–649.

POSTSCRIPT

The intellectual significance of 1968 struck me late. It made its way to me only indirectly via European psychology. So absorbed was I in trying to become a psychologist that it was not until 1975 that the reverberations of that momentous historical disruption penetrated my dull brain.

1975 was the year in which my friend from New Zealand, John Moir, and I celebrated the completion of our doctorates by embarking on an "adult" project. We set ourselves the task of assembling a collection of writings on James Mark Baldwin, a founding father of developmental psychology in the United States. Unlike Baldwin, we were both immigrants. We had found our home away from home in the school of cognitive-developmental psychology that had been initiated by Baldwin and elaborated by Piaget and Kohlberg. We were both impressed by the relevance of developmental psychology to education, especially as demonstrated by Kohlberg and the Harvard branch of the school. We both felt compelled to do something distinctly American.

In an effort to get better informed about the historical context of early psychology, we attended the annual meeting of Cheiron, the Society for the History of the Behavioral Sciences, at Carleton College in Ottawa. What we encountered was distinctly un-American. We ran into three attractive young characters in black leather jackets: Friedrich Otto Wolf, Siegfried Jaeger, and Irmgard Staeuble, representatives of the Holzkamp moiety of the psychology department at the Frei Universität in West Berlin. The five of us negotiated a number of steins, debated the point at which quantity turns into quality, and then played frisbee in the street at midnight. We discovered that if you hold a frisbee over a street lamp, it absorbs photons, and can then be made to describe looping incandescent trajectories across space—between the British and the Germans.

Our playmates invited us to a lunchtime workshop that they were presenting the next day. They said it was on "Critical Psychology." It was a sobering experience. We were horrified to learn that we were "liberals" and, as such, professionalized mongers of "ruling class ideas." The fortress of cognitive psychology and progressive education that had been our shelter as graduate students started to look like Jericho, as we heard for the first time the powerful trumpet blasts of ideology-critique. Both good public school types, inured to privileged education as fish to water, we took the demystification hard. Neither of us has quite recovered from it. Somewhere in the closet is a black leather jacket I brought back from London that year.

From Ottawa, we hurried back to Boston and immersed ourselves in the history of Marxist philosophy. We examined Kant, Hegel, and Feuerbach in a vain effort to rescue and resuscitate them. One night at the Hofbrau in Harvard Square, we finally came to the awful recognition that the critique of ideology was well-founded. Moreover, we came to admit that the intellectual content of the critical perspective—its sheer explanatory scope and incisiveness—far exceeded in significance that of the narrow cognitive psychology in which we had desperately sought shelter. Our naive faith in the Enlightenment, and the constructivist psychology it had spawned, faded away into a jaded apostasy. Our earlier choices took on the convincing appearance of historical mistakes, an object lesson in the choice of the wrong solidarities. The moment at which we entered the vestibule of our chosen profession was, by most happy misfortune, the same moment at which the entire edifice was condemned.

Since those days in Ottawa, each of us has tried to recapture a luminescence in the night. Speaking for myself, in that search I have been blessed with the good fortune of sturdy traveling companions and the advice of those who have gone before. I even discovered that two of my undergraduate psychology professors had been closet neo-Marxists and that my undergraduate advisor had married one.

My first job: teaching statistics to working class blacks and whites in Motown. I was intent on paying my dues and aware of being far in arrears. It was an evening course. Fifty-six times I struggled the quarter mile back to the parking lot in the dark with the A-V equipment under my coat. I was accompanied by the image of the good-looking woman in the front row, with the patch over her right eye. The previous week, she was looking good—no bandages. Afterward, she had left class and, in the parking lot, these dazzling headlights sliced through the night, and three guys. . . .

I pointed to the norm of the distribution and spoke of class consciousness. A number of students were already asleep. It was the pre-robotics era. Improving your mind is hard after nine hours of screwing in car seats: autoworkers and the American dream. I found out that there were a cardsharp and a fire-eater in my class. They kindly agreed to perform. Several students woke up. And then we discussed the ideological basis of the standard error of the mean.

I got another job. Like John Moir on his return to the antipodes, I found that graduate schools of education provide a haven for the stable marginal. However, my eventual tenure proceedings were perturbed by the accusation that I "showed contempt for empirical work." It wasn't entirely true, but I was relieved: someone in the faculty meeting had finally noticed the slight tic that appeared under my right eye each time an experimental psychologist sat near me. My chairperson was asked surreptitiously, "Do we really need a Marxist in Developmental?" I was not so much surprised as flattered. I never made it as a Marxist either, despite my proletarian period at Wayne State, despite study groups, political consciousness-raising, and the admonitions of a British socialist roommate. Like most members of my social class, I was always absorbed in ideas. My religious background could not be erased. On occasion, my face was known to shine. My Godspell album was discovered. My standing as a radical was severed at the roots. I protested that I was a 'critical' psychologist. My associates assumed I was referring to a medical condition.

My doctor looked through the index of this manuscript. He concluded that this collection is largely a phantasy of mine.

I am alone in my study. My wife is away at a conference. I pick up the phone and call the colleagues I feel most affinity to. They don't know I like to cook. They assume, "It's America, so it's potluck." All manner of edible complexes appear. The table groans. Man [*sic*] cannot live by bread alone, so I provide the beverage. The company speaks in many tongues. The associations are free. We talk shop, but it is fresh and exciting. Somehow, it all works. It is a dream soirée.

Eventually, the evening draws to a close. One for the road. Mandatory joshing of the host.

"In the morning, John will come in—"

"Broughton never gets up that early!" (*Laughter*)

"Well, then, in the afternoon, John will stick his nose in here and all the dirty dishes will be gone and he will find just a book on the table."

"Faintly glowing!"

"The book or his nose?" (*Laughter*)

"And he'll open it up, and —"

"Everything we've said will be in print!" (*More laughter*)

It is already early morning. The soirée is over. Coats. Scarves. Hats. Parting invitations. One more for the road gently declined. Exeunt. The guests wend their way back to the various corners of the globe. I switch out the last light. Feeling a little sad, I step outside for a moment. It is bible black. The stars down to earth. Right overhead an errant asteroid flares in our planet's atmosphere, describing an incandescent trajectory. I almost hear it thud to earth. For some reason I scream into the night.

My wife is shaking me gently. "It's only a dream. Go back to sleep."

"Oh, you're back."

"Back from where?"

"The conference."

"What conference?"

"Oh." I am beginning to wake up. "Anyway, get this one. You weren't there."

"Nice start."

"No offense. Anyway, I invited a bunch of social theory types to dinner and each of us presented ideas about a critical developmental psychology."

"Yeah, yeah. You and your nightmares. I suppose you all put on black leather jackets and played frisbee in the dark."

"No. No leather jackets."

(Pause) "John. Don't go back to sleep. There's a strange sort of glow coming from the dining room. Did you leave a light on?"

JOHN M. BROUGHTON

INDEX

firebirds rising

Enchantress from the Stars	Sylvia Engdahl
The Faery Reel: Tales from the Twilight Realm	Ellen Datlow and Terri Windling, eds.
The Far Side of Evil	Sylvia Engdahl
Firebirds: An Anthology of Original Fantasy and Science Fiction	Sharyn November, ed.
Fire Bringer	David Clement-Davies
Grass for His Pillow Episode One: Lord Fujiwara's Treasures	Lian Hearn
Grass for His Pillow Episode Two: The Way Through the Snow	Lian Hearn
The Green Man: Tales from the Mythic Forest	Ellen Datlow and Terri Windling, eds.
Growing Wings	Laurel Winter
Hannah's Garden	Midori Snyder
The Harp of the Grey Rose	Charles de Lint
The Hero and the Crown	Robin McKinley
The Hex Witch of Seldom	Nancy Springer
The Hidden Land	Pamela Dean
House of Stairs	William Sleator
I Am Mordred	Nancy Springer
I Am Morgan Le Fay	Nancy Springer
Interstellar Pig	William Sleator
The Kestrel	Lloyd Alexander
The Kin	Peter Dickinson
The Legend of Luke	Brian Jacques

Loamhedge	Brian Jacques
The Long Patrol	Brian Jacques
Lord Brocktree	Brian Jacques
Magic or Madness	Justine Larbalestier
Mariel of Redwall	Brian Jacques
Marlfox	Brian Jacques
Martin the Warrior	Brian Jacques
Mattimeo	Brian Jacques
Moon-Flash	Patricia A. McKillip
Mossflower	Carol Emshwiller
The Mount	Brian Jacques
The Neverending Story	Michael Ende
New Moon	Midori Snyder
Outcast of Redwall	Brian Jacques
The Outlaws of Sherwood	Robin McKinley
Parasite Pig	William Sleator
Pearls of Lutra	Brian Jacques
Primavera	Francesca Lia Block
Rakkety Tam	Brian Jacques
Redwall	Brian Jacques
The Riddle of the Wren	Charles de Lint
Sadar's Keep	Midori Snyder
The Safe-Keeper's Secret	Sharon Shinn
Salamandastron	Brian Jacques
The Secret Country	Pamela Dean
Shadowmancer	G.P. Taylor
The Sight	David Clement-Davies

Singing the Dogstar Blues	Alison Goodman
The Son of Summer Stars	Meredith Ann Pierce
Spindle's End	Robin McKinley
A Stir of Bones	Nina Kiriki Hoffman
The Sunbird	Elizabeth E. Wein
Taggerung	Brian Jacques
Tamsin	Peter S. Beagle
Treasure at the Heart of the Tanglewood	Meredith Ann Pierce
Triss	Brian Jacques
Waifs and Strays	Charles de Lint
Water: Tales of Elemental Spirits	Robin McKinley and Peter Dickinson
Waters Luminous and Deep: Shorter Fictions	Meredith Ann Pierce
Westmark	Lloyd Alexander
The Whim of the Dragon	Pamela Dean
The Winter Prince	Elizabeth E. Wein
Wolf Moon	Charles de Lint
Wolf Queen	Tanith Lee
Wolf Star	Tanith Lee
Wolf Tower	Tanith Lee
Wolf Wing	Tanith Lee
Wormwood	G.P. Taylor
Wren's Quest	Sherwood Smith
Wren's War	Sherwood Smith
Wren to the Rescue	Sherwood Smith

firebirds rising

an
anthology
of
original
science
fiction
and
fantasy

edited by Sharyn November

FIREBIRD
AN IMPRINT OF PENGUIN GROUP (USA) INC.

FIREBIRD
Published by the Penguin Group
Penguin Group (USA) Inc., 345 Hudson Street, New York, New York 10014, U.S.A.
Penguin Group (Canada), 90 Eglinton Avenue East, Suite 700, Toronto, Ontario,
Canada M4P 2Y3 (a division of Pearson Penguin Canada Inc.)
Penguin Books Ltd, 80 Strand, London WC2R 0RL, England
Penguin Ireland, 25 St Stephen's Green, Dublin 2, Ireland
(a division of Penguin Books Ltd)
Penguin Group (Australia), 250 Camberwell Road, Camberwell, Victoria 3124,
Australia (a division of Pearson Australia Group Pty Ltd)
Penguin Books India Pvt Ltd, 11 Community Centre, Panchsheel Park,
New Delhi - 110 017, India
Penguin Group (NZ), Cnr Airborne and Rosedale Roads, Albany, Auckland 1310,
New Zealand (a division of Pearson New Zealand Ltd)
Penguin Books (South Africa) (Pty) Ltd, 24 Sturdee Avenue, Rosebank,
Johannesburg 2196, South Africa

Registered Offices: Penguin Books Ltd, 80 Strand, London WC2R 0RL, England

Published by Firebird, an imprint of Penguin Group (USA) Inc., 2006

1 3 5 7 9 10 8 6 4 2

ISBN 0-14-240549-3

Printed in the United States of America

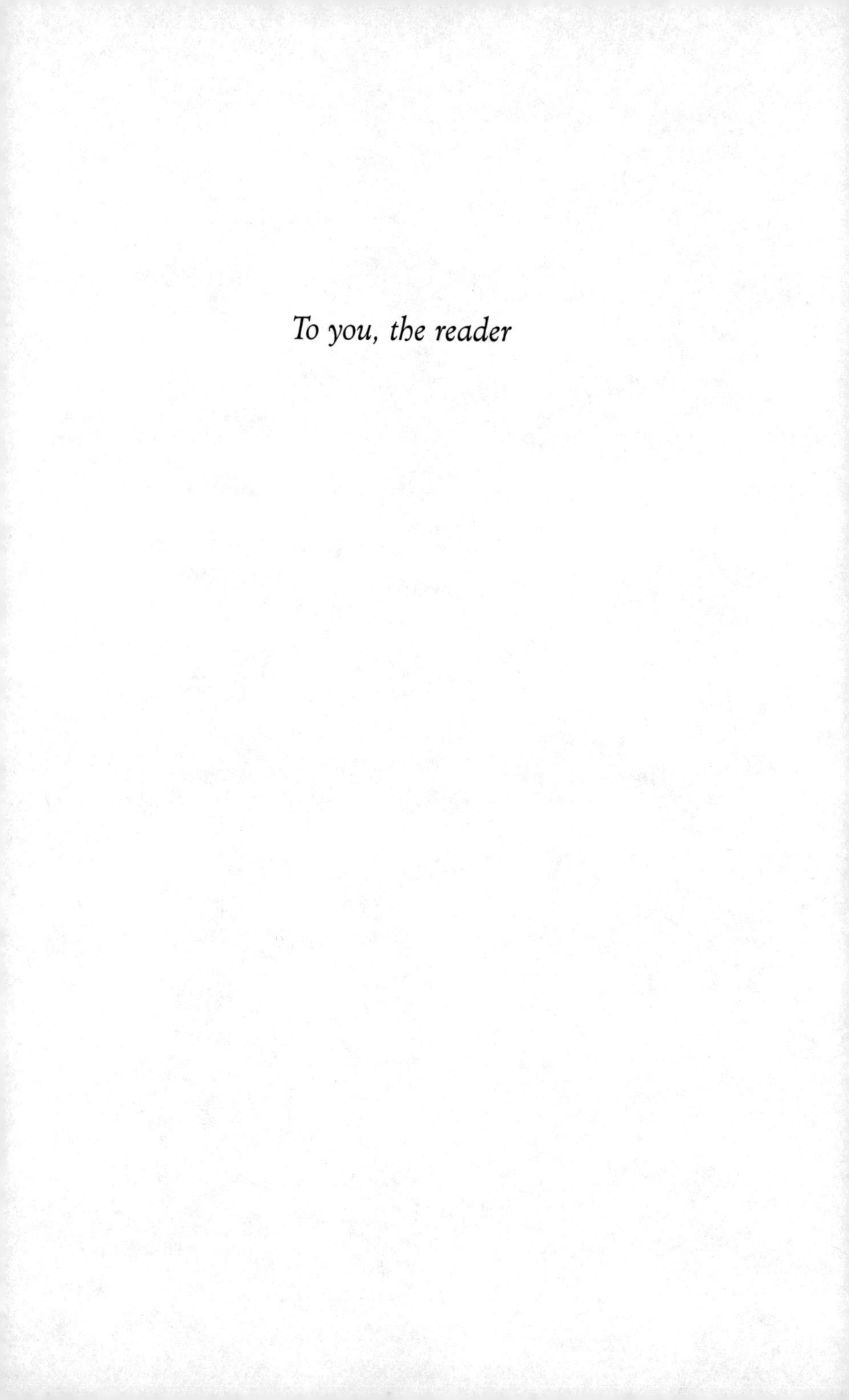

To you, the reader

contents

Firebirds Rising

Introduction

Welcome to *Firebirds Rising*, also known as "the second Firebird anthology." I tend to skip introductions, myself—they are usually too pedantic or give too much away—so this one will be brief, and I will not say anything about the stories themselves. No spoilers!

But every book has a backstory.

The *Firebirds* anthology was an experiment: *Can I do a representative anthology for this imprint? Is there an audience out there?* There was. The success of the first book meant that I was able to do a second one, and for that, I thank you. Firebird, more than most imprints, is driven by its readers. If you're interested in something, I'll do my best to find out more about it; if there's an author you think I should check out, I do. I got a lot of e-mail about *Firebirds*, and I'm still getting it.

One of the things people pointed out was the first book's lack of science fiction. It wasn't for want of trying; the sf

authors I queried didn't have stories for me. But I didn't have as many to ask then as I do now—the pool of available writers has grown with the Firebird list itself. Close to one-third of *Firebirds Rising* is sf. I'd love to shoot for 50 percent next time around.

Before I edited *Firebirds*, I wondered how one put together an anthology. Now I know. You start by just asking. I contacted all of the writers I'd published in Firebird and on the Viking list (where the original science fiction and fantasy I edit initially appears, in hardcover), as well as people I *wanted* to publish.

I was shocked; everyone said yes. And the stories started coming in.

Some were practically perfect just as they were; others needed some editing. Still others weren't right for the collection, which killed me; I hate turning things down when they're good, but they didn't fit. I got so many stories for *Firebirds Rising* that I've already begun work on a third collection—and more on that in a moment.

Once all of the stories were in and edited, and I had bios and notes from the authors, I needed to sequence the book. It reminded me of doing set lists, when I was in a band; what do you start with? what goes in the middle? what should be last? It is not easy, and every editor has a different method. I never expect anyone to read an anthology from beginning to end in one shot—I know I don't!—but I want it to be possible.

I can't wait to hear what you think of *Firebirds Rising*. My

e-mail is **firebird@us.penguingroup.com**, and I really do read everything everyone sends.

Speaking of which, remember that third collection I mentioned? It needs a title. Help me out. I'm serious . . . and I'll even credit you if you come up with the perfect one.

Sharyn November
October 2005

Tamora Pierce

Huntress

My dad left for good when I was ten. My mom kicked him out. "Fine!" he yelled. "I've had it with you, your family, and all that screwy New Age goddess crap! I should have left years ago! Now watch—you'll turn my own daughter against me!" He grabbed his bag and walked out. He didn't notice I was standing right there.

I should have said something. Instead I stared at my whatever-many-great-grandmother's portrait. It hung in front of where my dad had been standing. There was Whatever-grandma in Victorian clothes, laced in tight, with that crescent moon tiara on her head. He was so clueless he didn't even see Mom's family was into the goddess stuff back then, before anyone ever said "New Age" with capital letters. But that was my dad.

After the divorce, he found a girlfriend. They got married and had a kid. Kevin was sweet, but I stopped visiting. They were always joking, asking if Mom and my aunts had sacrificed any cats lately, or did I brew up some potion to get a boy-

friend. I told Dad it wasn't funny, and then that he was boring my socks off. Finally I just told him I couldn't come to visit because I had practice. He bought it. Clueless, like I said.

But when it came to Mom's family portraits, and her religion, he wasn't the only one who thought it was just too weird. By the time I was in sixth grade, the friends I brought home were noticing the crescent tiaras and full moon pendants. They'd notice, and they'd ask, and I'd try to explain. I'd make them nervous. Then the jokes and whispers began. In seventh grade, the witch stuff blended in with whispers that I was too weird, even stuck-up, maybe a slut. I didn't even know where that had come from, but sixth grade had taught me I couldn't fight any of it. I acted like I couldn't hear. I would read for lunch and recess, by myself in a corner of some room. I kept my head down. I didn't even try to make friends. I didn't see the point. Sooner or later I would have to take them home. There they'd see the portraits, and the jewelry. They'd ask their questions. Back to square one.

The only good thing about school was track. I'd found out I was good at it in grade school. With a summer of practice and middle-school coaches, no one on our team could catch me by the time the seventh-grade spring meets rolled around. I came in second in the district in all my events but one, and that one I won. Winning was like a taste in my mouth. Everyone I raced against was a possible source of whispers, but I couldn't hear them if they ran behind me. They'd have to catch me to make their words hurt.

In eighth grade I won all of my middle-school events at the All-District meet. A bunch of the high-school coaches wanted

me to come to their schools, but Mom had other plans. At the last meet of the year, she introduced me to the head coach from Christopher Academy. Christopher was offering a full scholarship, if I wanted it.

Wanted it? Christopher was one of the top private schools in the city, with one of the top track teams in the country. If I did well there, I could write my college track ticket. Better: nobody in my school could afford it. Nobody. And nobody else was getting a scholarship. My teammates didn't talk to me, but I heard everything. They would have told the world if they had gotten into the Christopher Academy. It was out of their reach. Christopher kids were like Beverly Hills kids on television, clean and expensive gods and goddesses. Nobody at my school would dare to talk to them. There wouldn't be any whispers in those expensive hallways.

When she saw I wanted this school and this chance, Mom went a little nuts. Over the summer, we moved from the old family apartment in the Village—and wasn't my Aunt Cynthia happy to take it when we left—to a squinched-up little place on the Upper East Side. Mom took a second job, tending bar at night, to cover the new expenses. Our apartment was near the school and near Central Park, where the Christopher runners trained. I could practice with the team and not have to worry about taking the subway home after dark, Mom said, putting her altar up in a corner of her tiny bedroom. I felt guilty. Mom and her sisters were true believers in the family religion. She wasn't happy with just a medallion, not even a proper hunt-goddess figure, instead of the shrine in our old place, but this was only for four years, I told myself. Maybe

the apartment wasn't so much, but I could have friends, and bring them over, and only have to explain horseshoes over the doorways.

Anyway, I wasn't a believer in the family goddess after middle school. If their goddess was so wonderful, why didn't she fix my life? She protected maidens, right? Wasn't I a maiden? My dad was right about that much—the worship was screwy.

After all that, ninth grade still wasn't exactly a popularity explosion. It was made clear to me that while I had a track scholarship, ninth graders did not show up the upperclassmen. They trained and they waited for their turn, their chance. They ran with the team. If I heard it once during those first weeks, I heard it a dozen times: I belonged to the Christopher *team,* the Christopher tradition, the Christopher way of doing things. I warmed a bench and kept my mouth shut.

And there was another problem. Things had changed. I had changed. It wasn't easy for me to make friends since I'd stopped trying years ago. I still waited for whispers to begin, though months passed without them. It was like I thought the gossip was a weed that would sprout when my back was turned.

I did make two ninth-grade friends from the track team. We had lunch together, walked home together, sat together on the way to meets. We ran when Coach told us to. We cheered the upperclassmen and held down a leg on the relay team. We raced other ninth graders from other private schools, and we envied the older runners. The seniors weren't that interesting. Their eyes were locked on the Ivy Leagues.

They didn't draw our attention the way a certain junior did.

Felix soaked up light in the halls and gave it off again, from his bronze-and-gold gelled hair to his tanned calves. He was so right, so perfect, that no one ever gave him a hard time for the long, single braid he wore just behind one ear. People gave him tokens to wear in it—beads, ribbons, chains—but he didn't take everything. Just because he wore someone's token one day didn't mean he wouldn't give it back to them the next. He wrote his own rules for the school, too. The staff let him do it most of the time, maybe because the auditorium had his last name over the doorway. It was listed five times on the brass plaque that announced the past headmasters of the school. Felix was what Christopher Academy was about, and his crowd was Christopher Academy, just like track was Christopher Academy.

He ran, but he didn't care about it. He'd slide out of boys' warm-up laps to come over and flirt with his sophomore and junior girls, or his "lionesses," he called them. The first time I heard him say it, in April of my ninth-grade year, he called it to our coach as we circled the baseball diamond in our section of the park, our feet thudding on wet dirt.

"What do you think of my lionesses, Coach?" he called, keeping pace with his girlfriends in the middle of the pack. "Let's take them to the Serengeti, get some blood on them, show them how to hunt." He fiddled with a strip of camouflage cloth that was wound into his braid, running a finger over a dark spot on it.

"Ewww, Felix," cried Han, a Chinese girl who'd been liplocked with him before practice. "Blood? No, thanks!"

"Can't break oaths sworn in blood, sweetness," he told her, falling back as we ran by. "Isn't that right, Corey?" he asked, slapping me on the arm.

He knew who I was. He called me by my last name, like I was any other member of the team, any other rich Christopher kid.

I forgot to be careful. I forgot that I was new, that I had to be one of the team and earn my place. Trying to outrun the blush that burned my cheeks, I sped up. I cut through his precious lionesses as they jeered at him, telling him he scared me. I stretched my legs until I caught up to the senior girls. They glanced back, saw me and glared. "Back of the pack, *freshman,*" one of them grumbled.

So I stopped being sensible. It was only practice. "Afraid you'll have to work for it?" I asked, and picked up my pace. They weren't really trying: it was a warm-up. My cheeks burning now because they thought they could get first place handed to them, I trailed the seniors, looking for a way through their bunched-up group. When they closed in tighter, I powered around them in the turn. By the time it dawned on them that they ought to show me who was boss, they couldn't catch me.

Stupid, I told myself, slowing after I thudded past the finish, my temper burned off. Stupid when you want friends, stupid when you don't want to stand out. Stupid when you're "with the team."

Across the field the boys were hooting at the runners. I turned around to see the lionesses, juniors and sophomores together, cut through and around the red-faced seniors. One

of them, redheaded Reed, looked back at the seniors and yelled, "You snooze, you lose."

Coach glared at me, then walked toward the seniors, clapping her hands. "You thought it was going to be easy, these final meets of the year?" she yelled to the seniors as the lionesses caught up with me. "You'd catch a break because it's your last year in the high-school leagues? Nobody cares! Younger girls are waiting to make their names, and they'll kick your asses. Two more laps before you quit for the day!"

"Showin' them, Corey." Reed tugged my braid.

"You rock," another one said quietly.

The lionesses collected me after practice. I looked at my two ninth-grade friends, but they shook their heads and grinned. They wanted me to go so I could tell them what it was like the next morning.

The way the lionesses acted it was no big deal, drinks and french fries at a diner on Madison Avenue, a sour-faced waitress watching as six of us jammed into a corner booth.

"Why don't you split up?" she wanted to know. "Make it easier on everybody?"

The older girls fell silent, staring at her. The air went funny. The waitress looked at them, then threw down the menus and left. The minute her back was turned, they began to laugh and nudge one another. "Shut *her* up," Reed said.

"Like that dealer," another muttered.

"Only he *ran,*" Beauvais, a platinum blonde, whispered. Reed elbowed Beauvais hard. She elbowed back but didn't say anything more as the waitress—a different waitress—came for our order.

I don't even remember if I talked very much, but I was there, with the kids everyone looked at. And the guys showed up, even Felix. I learned then that the guys were lions, to match the lionesses. Felix called them "my Pride," and said casually, "You should see them hunt."

Half of me wanted to stay, but half knew I was supposed to be home fifteen minutes ago. I had to run to be there when Aunt Lucy, who watched me while Mom worked, put dinner on the table. I expected a reaming, but my aunt was so happy I'd been with kids my age she didn't even yell. I pretended I didn't see her light a moon candle in thanks while I cleared the table. I guess I wasn't the only one who'd thought I was going to be a hermit all through high school.

After supper, we went for a walk. We talked with the neighbors for a while outside the building. I was playing with the baby of the couple downstairs, so I don't know how it started, but I heard the old guy who lived across the street say, ". . . just a dealer, so excuse me if I don't cry."

"Was it an overdose?" asked the baby's mom.

The old guy shook his head. "The cops say people were chasing him last night after dark, and he grabbed his chest and fell into the lake near the Ramble. Heart attack. A drug dealer, having a heart attack."

"Good riddance," said the baby's father. "But how could anybody see to chase him?"

"It was a full moon," Aunt Lucy and I said at the same time. She smiled at me and said, "Jinx," because we had echoed each other. She looked at the other grown-ups. "Plenty of light for a chase."

I shivered. The baby's mom saw and collected her from

me. "It's getting cold," she said. I didn't argue, though I don't think I had shivered because I was cold.

When I got to school in the morning, my life had definitely improved. Suddenly my two friends and I had more company at lunch. They liked that. I did, too.

I didn't exactly like it when, at the next meet, Coach pulled me out to run with the juniors and seniors. "You started this, you finish it, Corey," she muttered as she changed my place in the lineup. So I ran the way I did alone, and made the two best runners sweat to beat me. The Pride thought it was cool. They cheered for me at meets. At the All-District competitions, when I had the hundred-meter and the three-hundred-meter events, Felix gave me an ornament from his braid to wear, a little golden sun. I came in second in the hundred, first in the three hundred. He wouldn't take his sun back. He kissed me and told me to wear it instead.

I told myself he kissed all the girls. Then I went out and got a top-of-the-ear piercing done just for that earring. Once it was there, I looked at myself in the mirror and let myself dream about him.

The night after the last practice, I was on my way home when I saw one of the Neighborhood Watch people taking down the sketch of a rapist who had been working the Upper East Side. This one, with his spiky eyebrow piercing, had given me the shivers for weeks. "What happened?" I asked her. I was going home to an empty apartment—Aunt Lucy had finally convinced Mom a girl who was almost sixteen didn't need a babysitter—so I was being lazy about getting there. "They caught him?"

"They caught him," the woman said with a grim smile,

like she had been there. "The cops got an anonymous tip. He was at the bottom of Bethesda Terrace with a broken leg and a broken arm." I winced. That was a long, hard marble stair around the big fountain in Central Park. She told me, "Bastard said he was out for a run and he tripped. They found his rape kit under him, complete with souvenirs. He said a gang chased him. Good for them, that's what I say." She waved the flyers she'd already collected at me. "One down, plenty more to go."

I went on home, shaking my head. Whoever heard of a gang that chased somebody until they fell, then ran away? And who tipped off the cops? How did they know who he was?

I told the Pride about the rapist at lunch the next day.

"Cool gang," said Felix, laughing. He had a new addition to his braid that day, a spiky bar that could have been for an eyebrow piercing. "It captures criminals. A superhero gang. Maybe I can join. Do they wear cool jackets?"

We all cracked up. Maybe they called themselves a Pride, but I thought of bandannas and leather jackets and box cutters and low-rider cars when I thought "gang." These were trust fund babies. They were a world away from the ugly street and the gangs in the projects like the ones I knew. They were strong young animals dressed in light and fresh air, not dirt and blood.

"Hey, maybe it was us. We hang in the park when school's out," black-haired Jeffries said, tossing a rolled-up napkin from hand to hand. "Sure, it coulda been us. Except I'd probably just give a rapist my dad's card. He's always telling me even slime deserves a defense, right?"

Beauvais shoved him. “Like your dad would defend a *rapist*.”

“One with money,” Han said with a laugh. She sounded as Chinese as I did.

I smelled mint as Felix leaned back and whispered in my ear, “Sometimes we hang out after dark.”

I reached down for my backpack, hiding my chest so he wouldn’t see his effect on me. “Isn’t it dangerous?” When I sat up, I cradled my pack, just in case he looked at my too-perky tits.

“We go as a group,” Jeffries said. “Our gang, remember?”

“Have to be safe,” Reed told us, sprawled over her section of the table. “Parental units throw a fit if they find out you’re out in the scary old park.”

Felix ran a hand down my arm. Of course the bell rang and monitors came out to move us along to class. Felix grabbed my wrist and tugged me down till his lips brushed the little sun in the top of my ear. “The next full moon, come out with us,” he whispered. “We meet at the East Ninety-seventh Street entrance and go for a run to the Loch, just the Pride. You want to really be one of us, be one of my lionesses, right? You’d maybe even replace Reed one day as queen of the hunt. So come. Not a word to anybody, Corey. Pride business. Nine o’clock, the night of the full moon.”

I had laughed at the Pride as a gang. But as a way to erase the misery of the last few years? It was pure gold. The presidents of the new senior and junior classes for next year belonged to the Pride, as well as the captains of both track teams and both soccer teams. Okay, so Felix seemed to be the boyfriend of almost all the girls off and on. The guys didn’t

seem to mind. Rich kids were different. A little of Felix was better than none, maybe. Or maybe he'd settle for only me.

I wouldn't be alone anymore. I wouldn't be weird, or strange. I'd belong, not as a happy outsider, like Mom and her family, but as a happy insider, smooth and tan and laughing, like my dad and his new family. As choices went, this one was easy.

So I was there, the night of the full moon, dressed to run, but dressed for Felix, too, in a black tank top and running shorts that hugged what I had. I thought about leaving my crescent pendant at home, but left it on. How many people knew what it was anymore? A lot of girls wore them as jewelry without knowing they had a religious meaning, or caring if they knew. I added a snake earring and a couple of gem studs, fixed a gold chain in my braid, and I was ready to go. No bracelets, no ankle bracelets, not when I ran. I carried my phone, my water, a towel, and other things I hoped I might need in my backpack.

Felix and some of the other guys of the Pride looked me over and made happy noises. Felix backed a couple of them off with slaps on the chest that could have been serious. The lionesses wore shorts like me, or cropped cargo pants, short blouses, running shoes. The guys wore shorts and T-shirts, summer wear. When Reed finally showed, wearing cargos, we set out across the park, a group of about seven girls and eight guys. Other people were out; it was still early enough and the moon was starting to rise. We passed dog walkers and other runners, bicyclists, skateboarders, Rollerbladers, men sitting alone on benches with paper bags beside them, men seated

alone on benches waiting, arms stretched out on the backs of the benches, legs spread wide, a warning in flesh not to come too close. The girls of the group moved inside, the guys outside, though no one seemed nervous or even like they paid attention. I wondered what Mom was doing now.

There were peepers chirping all around us from the trees that circled the meadows. We moved out onto the grass and toward the rocks that led to the oldest part of Central Park, where trees from the old island had been left to grow beside Olmstead's carefully chosen plantings. I could hear an owl somewhere close by. There were bugs everywhere, big ones, some of them. A moth fluttered past. A rippling shadow darted after it and surrounded it. The bat moved on, but not the moth. Central Park, that seemed so people-friendly when we did our practices there during the day, was showing its real face now. I touched my snake earring, thinking about the hidden world, the one my family recognized.

We moved into a smaller meadow near the rocks and trees. "Our hunting ground," Felix said, looping an arm around my neck. "One of them, anyway. This one was our first ground. This is where we became a Pride. A person could get lost back in those trees."

"A person could get found," said one of the guys. The boys laughed.

The girls didn't. They put their stuff in a heap and began to stretch, getting ready to run. "Put your gear down," Felix said. "We'll keep an eye on it. Used to be around here we couldn't do that, but things have changed late—"

"You." A big guy, ragged and swaying, lurched over to us.

"You stinking kids. You play games with my friend and leave him in the street like *garbage*—"

Felix let me go and faced the homeless guy, fiddling with his long braid and its ornaments. "Which one was he?" Felix asked, sounding bored. "I guess you're talking about one of our hunts, loser."

"You made him run onto Fifth Avenue," the man accused. His eyes glittered in the moonlight as he watched the Pride fan out around him. Everywhere I saw shadowy figures moving, but none came to help or stop whatever was happening. This was a harder end of the park, closer to Spanish Harlem. I would never have come here alone.

"That one?" asked Jeffries with a yawn. "He wagged his dick at Han."

"My feelings were hurt," Han said with a pout. "It wasn't even a *good* dick."

"You chased him and got him killed," the big guy snarled. "I'm gonna fuck you up." He had knives, one in either hand. "Little rich bastards think you can run people to death."

My head spun as Felix put his arm around my neck again. "Okay, Corey, here's how it works," he explained, keeping his eyes on the big guy. "The lionesses have their claws. Right, girls?"

They held up their hands. They had slim knives I had never seen before, tucked between their fingers so a couple of blades jutted out of each fist, like claws. They were busily tying the blades to their palms with leather thongs so they wouldn't fall from their hands.

"We lions keep him from leaving the grass. The lionesses

drive him to you. You have to mark his face without him killing you. Then you girls drive him into the rocks"—Felix pointed—"and the lions chase him down and finish him. You get the trophy to mark your initiation." Felix smiled down at me. "Here. Your first claw." He handed me a long, slender knife. "The trick is to run him till he's too exhausted to see straight. One of these scumbags, it's not hard. They don't have any lungs left because they're eaten up by crack, and their muscles suck because they're too lazy to work. Don't worry about cops. We have watchers, and they don't investigate this kind of thing very hard. They have a saying for it." He looked at the homeless man. "No Humans Involved."

My mouth felt stuffed with cotton. I wondered if I'd been drugged, except I'd been drinking from my own water bottle all the way here. "That's not funny."

"Sure it is," Felix told me. "One strong, healthy runner against a degenerate bum. It's hilarious."

"You killed his friend?" I asked. I could hear my voice shake.

"No," Felix said patiently. "The stupid mope ran out in traffic and got killed. Another useless mouth who isn't getting state aid. Corey, you're either a lion or a mouse."

My brain clattered into gear. "The drug dealer that got chased. The rapist that got chased."

"Scum. Scum," Felix said patiently. His eyes sparkled oddly in the growing moonlight. "Girls, get this hump moving."

The lionesses surged forward, running out to circle around the homeless man. They looked small and slight against his shadowy bulk, but they surrounded him. He flailed with his

knives. One girl darted in, then another. The man bellowed.

"No!" I cried, and dropped my knife. "This isn't an initiation. It's murder." I looked at him, wanting him to be gold again, not this white marble boy with eyes like ice. "Felix, are you crazy? I swear I won't tell, but I can't do this."

He made a cutting motion. The lionesses fell back, except for Reed. She pulled something from a pocket in her cargo pants and showed it to the homeless man. He put up his hands, letting his own knives drop. She had a gun. So that was how they made sure things always went their way. She motioned with it. The homeless guy ran, stumbling. He fell once and lurched to his feet.

"Don't hope he'll bring the cops, Corey," Felix said. "His kind knows better. And since you ruined our hunt with him, you'll take his place. Which is fine with us."

I stared at him.

"See, the cops will listen to you," Felix explained. "And frankly, most of us would rather have you for prey."

"You don't belong," Han said. "Not at the Academy. You don't understand how to wait your turn, making us eat your shit at the meets this spring. Sure, we laughed. We knew you'd be coming out here with us." She smiled and drew her knives gently down my chest. They didn't cut—this time.

My choices were clear. Argue or move, fast. I broke left, out of Felix's hold, away from Han. Three lionesses blocked my escape on that side. I whirled and darted in the opposite direction, jinking around Reed, then Jeffries, feeling my knees groan as my shoes bit into turf. I dashed for the rocks, but the lionesses swept out and around me, long-limbed and beauti-

ful, moonlight gleaming on their muscled arms and legs. I'd lost surprise, and I knew all of them were good enough to give me a good run. I set out for the longer meadow to see if I could outlast them.

Bad luck: two of the lions joined them. I couldn't outrun or outlast lions. I kept running, looking for a way out. All I found was an audience. People had come to line the meadow's edge, homeless people, kids our age and older in gang colors—real gang colors. Hard-faced women and men, and men on their own, smoking, drinking, watching. There for a show. They knew. They knew this went on, and they came to see.

Still, I had to run. I searched for an opening not covered by a watcher or a member of the Pride. I don't remember how the first lioness crept up on me, but I felt that sharp sting on my back. I stumbled, swerved, clapped my hand behind me, and brought it up before my face. It glittered with blood. I spun and fell, tripping a lioness whose dad was president of some investment bank. She had been trying to be the second to cut me. I scrambled to my feet and bolted forward again, weaving between two more of the lionesses. Now the fear was filling my legs, turning my knees to jelly.

The next to rake my arm was Reed, who I liked. I got out of her reach and stayed away to ask, "Why are you doing this?"

Her eyes were wide and dark and hot. Her teeth shone in a moonlight grin. "Because I can," she said, and faked left, trying to drag my attention from Beauvais. I turned and dashed, tripped on a wrinkle in the ground, hit and rolled to my feet, flailing with my arms and legs for balance. I felt a blade catch in my shoe. It almost yanked me off my feet.

"Because you don't stay the best without *practice.*" Someone scored a long shallow cut across my head and ear and forehead, coming out of my blind spot.

I bolted and came up against one of the huge boulders that marked the edge of the broken ground leading up into the trees. I scrabbled and crawled onto it, panting, as the Pride moved in, forming a half circle around the base of the stone. Felix was there, toying with his braid. The lionesses stood with him, panting, some of them leaning on their knees. They were tired. I'd shown them some moves.

But my muscles were burning. I felt a bad shiver in my calves and hamstrings, a sign I was overworked. I ripped off my tank top, not caring if every creep in the park saw me in my sports bra. I tore the cloth into strips with hands that quaked. That shallow cut on the side of my head was the worst, dripping blood into the corner of my eye. I needed to get that covered up if I had to run again.

"Too bad you blew it, Corey," Felix said, his voice almost like sex. "Nobody's ever given the lionesses a run like this. The prey is usually blood sushi by now." He was getting off on this, maybe like he'd been getting off on the whole game of luring me in.

With my head and my arm bandaged, I grabbed my crescent pendant with one hand, squeezing it so hard the pointed ends bit into my palm, letting the pain clear my head. I wouldn't answer. I needed my breath for running. Screaming was useless. Screaming in Central Park at night was so useless. Here, away from the park's roads, the only way I'd get lucky would be if horse cops or undercover cops were somewhere

near, and I had a feeling that ring of creeps would warn Felix about them. They wouldn't want anyone to spoil the fun.

There was leaf and earth litter between my boulder and the one behind it. I carefully felt around at my side for what rocks or glass pieces might be there. I'd need them for weapons.

"Now, you can come down here and race the lionesses some more," Felix said. He threw a bottle of water up to me. "Or we can play the next level."

"Shit," I heard one panting lioness say.

"Pick door number two, Corey," another of them advised, her voice hoarse.

I stared at him, then at the bottle. For a minute a black haze fizzed over my vision. My life, my *blood,* was a *game*? I reached for the bottle, ready to throw it straight back at his head and say "Fuck you"—but there was the gun. Reed had a gun.

I should drink the water. I'd lost so much fluid. But that was a bad idea, too. I wouldn't put it past Felix to drug the water to slow me down. He couldn't gamble on the cops being somewhere else all night. He'd want to end this.

So I threw it at him after all. He dodged, but I struck Han in the shoulder. She swore at me. Felix only shook his head. "A waste. I didn't think you were a hothead, Corey."

I ignored him. I'd exhausted the mess of leaves beside me. All I had to show for it was a handful of small stones. It wasn't good enough. I blinked tears away so they wouldn't see me wipe them off.

"Here's the deal. You come down here, or you can go up there." He pointed past me, into the rocks and trees of the

wilder end of the park. "The lions will take over the hunt." They were already stepping back from the girls. Moonlight slid along the knives in their hands. "Hey, you might even find your way out up there. Or you might find a friend. Someone who's not with the Pride. Of course, they play kinda rough up here." He grinned as he unsheathed his knife. "And if the lions take you, we'll be wanting a little something extra for our trouble. Before we collect our trophy."

My stomach turned. They would rape me, he meant. "I'll get out, and you will be so dead," I croaked.

"When they find the drugs in your backpack? And Reed's family says we were at their place tonight? Our word against yours, Corey. Those very disturbing things you told my lionesses during all those after-practice get-togethers . . ." He shook his head. "Sad. You scholarship kids can be so troubled. So out of your element."

And I had wanted to be one of them? "At least if I don't get out of this I'll die clean," I mumbled to myself.

I looked at the meadow, and at the creeps. I looked at the lionesses. They were drinking water and adjusting their blades. I'd tried to break free out there. I wasn't sure I had the speed to do it now. The thought of letting any of that "audience" get their hands on me made my skin crawl. Turning my head, I looked back and up at the towering trees. Mom's family called these old parts of the park "godwoods." They said the old gods of the land still lived here.

Why was I thinking of their crap now? Look at me, trapped! Look at what their gods had done for me! Even the goddess that was supposed to look after me had done nothing. There

she rode in the sky, or so they'd always told me, just a flat white disk. I could count on nothing from her except scratches from the stupid pendant I wore! I began to cry in silent anger. Furious, I shook my blood-streaked fists at the moon.

That's when I saw the broken bottle at the edge of the litter on my boulder. I sat casually, dangling my legs over, hiding my side as I grabbed its long neck. It was warm in my hand. Finally, a weapon I could use to do some damage before the Pride cut me down. "Do I get a head start?" I demanded, wiping my eyes with my free arm. "You guys are fresh. I want it. I get into the trees before you so much as take the trail into the rocks."

Felix stared at me. "Damn, I wish you didn't have to die," he said finally. "You're a *real* lioness. A real—"

"What would you know of lionesses, you perfumed and gelded whelp?"

A moment ago, when I had looked at the open meadow, she had not been there. Now she strode across it like a queen, a tall, ice-blonde woman in a white tank top and jogging shorts. Her long limbs were so pale they almost seemed to glow. Her ponytail picked up the moon's gleam as it bounced behind her. Even the woman's eyes were silver, colorless and icy as she looked the Pride over.

I don't know how she got there or what she thought she was doing, but I couldn't have her stepping into my shitstorm. "Lady, get out of here!" I screamed, or tried to. My throat was too dry for more than a croak, and I coughed as I spoke. "Go on, get out of here, call the cops—do you have a cell phone on you? Run—get—"

She held up a long-fingered hand as she came to a halt ten feet from the nearest lioness. It was as if she had laid her hand on my mouth. "Hush, maiden. Your courtesy is well intended, but needless. Under the circumstances, it is gallant. I will not forget." She looked at the Pride, which swung out to encircle her. "You seek a hunt," she said. "I fear you will not give me a hunt that will satisfy, but times are corrupt. Tonight you shall be *my* prey."

Jeffries laughed. "Wait your turn, bitch."

She stooped and picked up a quiver, which she slung over her back, then an unstrung bow—a big one. I knew damned well they hadn't been on that grass before.

"Once, you would have known to whom you spoke, and understood your death was before you," the woman told Jeffries. She took a bowstring from the pocket of her shorts. Everyone watched her. They had to. It wasn't possible to look anywhere else as she gracefully fitted one end of the string to the end of the bow she had placed between her running shoes. With hardly any effort she bent the heavy bow and slipped the string over the free end. "For your foulness, I shall not soil an arrow on you. I have better things for those of mongrel breeding."

Jeffries gasped. He always bragged on his family going back to European nobility in the 1600s and did not like her comment about his breeding. Ignoring him, she put two fingers to her lips and blew a whistle that had everyone clutching their ears. As its echoes faded, I heard sounds in the brush behind me and around me. Dogs trotted down from the rocks and trees. It was then, I think, that a few creeps decided life was

better somewhere else. Some of those dogs were really big. They looked like they had rottweiler or wolfhound in them, but it was all part of a mix. Whatever the full mix was, it was dangerous. These were lean, hard-looking animals, cautious as they came out onto open ground.

The closer they got to Her—by now I understood the truth of Her being—the lighter they were on their feet, until they frisked around Her like puppies, tails wagging. They were glad to see Her. They were strays, their coats tangled, some ribs showing, but they weren't stray-cautious once they could smell Her.

"Fuck this." Reed broke the spell. She had her gun out and had pointed it at Her. "I don't know who—"

Up came the bow. I didn't even see the hand that took an arrow from the quiver. I glimpsed the arrow on the string, the ripple of muscle as She drew the string to her ear, and loosed. The arrow went through one of Reed's beautiful eyes. She fell, the gun still in her hand.

The goddess looked at Felix and the Pride. "I said, *you are my prey now.* You thought to hunt one who is under my protection. Now meet my price. I give you the chance you gave to her—the trees. Linger but a moment more, and I shall lose my patience." She looked at the dogs. "My children, see that one?" She pointed to Jeffries. "Tear him to pieces."

That set the Pride free of Her spell, if she had cast one. All of them, including Jeffries, bolted for the trees of the old forest. She let them go. Despite Her words, the dogs waited around Her feet, panting, scratching, rolling on the grass. She walked over, collected Reed's gun, and handed it up to me,

along with the bottle of water Reed had carried in a holder at her waist. I took both with shaking hands and would not meet Her eyes. The goddess did a few runner's stretches for her legs, then chirped to the dogs. Running easily, the bow in one hand and an arrow in the other, She headed up into the rocks. The dogs fanned out around Her and caught up, all business now.

It was a long time before I found the nerve to come down and check Reed. She was dead, her skin as cold as marble. The arrow that had killed her had vanished. There wasn't even a mark where it had struck her.

I looked around. All of the creeps were gone. That was probably a good idea. The goddess might decide they were worth hunting next. There was no telling what might offend Her.

For a long time the only sounds I heard were the dogs' baying, and an occasional shriek, up among those old dark trees. I drank Reed's water, then made myself collect my knapsack and everything I had brought. I kept the gun for now, in case anyone decided that I looked like easy prey. I wiped it clean with tissues as I waited. On my way home, I could toss it into a storm drain, into the sewers. At some point there would be cops. I didn't want them finding anything of mine and tracking me to my door like they did on television. I knew they wouldn't believe me, but I didn't want the psychiatrists, or the medication, or the attention. I just wanted to curl up on my bed and think of ways to apologize to my mother's family for past disrespect.

Thinking of them, I checked my cell phone. There were no

calls, though it was long past midnight. I wondered if Mom knew who I was running around with so late. The thought made me giggle. The giggle sounded a little strange, so I made myself quit. Instead I sat down and waited. It never occurred to me to just go home. I hadn't been dismissed.

Sometime before dawn the dogs returned one by one. They were tired. After a look around, and a pee at the base of the rocks, they decided I was harmless. They lay down close to me and got to work licking the dark stains from their fur. Last to appear was their mistress, carrying a small terrier I had missed in all the confusion. His muzzle, too, was dark. He was more interested in trying to kiss Her face than in cleaning himself up.

I scrambled to my feet, though my legs were jelly from all my running. She would not catch *me* showing Her disrespect. She stopped in front of me and nodded.

"As I thought. They were better prey than hunters," She said in that chill and distant voice. "Here is my sign, to safeguard you on your way home." She pressed a blood-smeared thumb to my forehead and drew a crescent there. It felt as cold as her voice. I swayed and tried not to faint, either from Her touch or from the thought that I now had Pride blood on me. "Tell your family they have served Me well. I am pleased." She dropped something on the ground between us.

I looked down at Felix's braid. "I didn't ask for this," I whispered. "Or for them to die."

She smiled. "I answer prayers as I will, maiden. Only remember the others who perished at their hands. They would

have taken more, in time." She yawned, and pulled the tie out of her ponytail. Ivory hair cascaded down over her shoulders. "Good night to you, maiden. Or rather, good day."

I watched as she strolled across the meadow, still carrying her terrier. A quick whistle called the rest of her pack. They followed her, panting, tails wagging. Somewhere in the middle of that long expanse of grass, with no trees or rocks to hide them, they all vanished.

Tamora Pierce is the *New York Times* best-selling author of twenty-three fantasy novels for teenagers, which are published worldwide in English and in translation in more than six languages. She is currently awaiting the publication of an anthology that she coedited, the publication of two other short stories in addition to "Huntress," and the production of her next audio book with Full Cast Audio. She would also like to get some sleep at some point. She lives in Manhattan with her husband, Tim Liebe, a Web designer and administrator, as well as their four cats and two parakeets.

Her Web site is **www.tamora-pierce.com**, and she maintains an active presence on **www.sheroescentral.com**, a message board she founded with author Meg Cabot.

Author's Note

The idea for "Huntress" came to me in 1990, when the case of the Central Park jogger and stories of teenagers "wilding," or playing criminal games in New York City's Central Park, were in the news. They came together in an unpleasant stew with images from the Robert Chambers 1988 assault on Jennifer Levin in that same park, and the story bubbled out of that. Originally my narrator was a bag lady, a schizophrenic former professor of mythology and folklore now known as Crayfish, who simply told what she observed. When Sharyn November asked me for a story for *Firebirds Rising*, I knew I would have

to rewrite "Huntress" from the point of view of a teenage outsider. Writing it from a lioness's point of view was too alienating—not everyone wants to swim through the thoughts of a sociopath. I would have written it, but if my husband refused to read it, I knew everyone else would hate it, too.

The thing is, I still wish I could do that. I still wish I could call the merciless Huntress down to deal with some of the girl-killers we have out there. I bet the number of murders of girls and young women would fall off sharply if word got out that their killers were showing up dead, and the killer was untraceable. I suppose that makes me a bad person. What do you suppose it makes the people who prey on those who can't fight back?

Nina Kiriki Hoffman

Unwrapping

Brenna, her arms around a black garbage bag stuffed with all the ingredients of her mummy costume, followed her best friend Nadia upstairs to Nadia's bedroom.

"Why won't you tell me what you're going to wear to the Halloween dance?" Brenna asked. "I get that you don't want Adam to know, and that's why you wouldn't talk about it at lunch." Adam and Jason had sat with them in the middle-school cafeteria, and not for the first time. It was the first time Jason had spoken directly to Brenna, though. "But we're alone now," she continued. "You can tell me."

Nadia smiled over her shoulder. "You'll see."

"Did you make your costume or buy it?" Brenna asked.

"You'll see."

Most of Nadia's house smelled like steamed broccoli, which Brenna hated. But Nadia's room smelled like incense and cinnamon. It looked like something out of the *Arabian Nights*. The bed was swathed in a rose satin coverlet. A pile

of plump pillows in shades of pink and red overlapped one another at the head of the bed. The red carpet was thick; when you walked on it, you felt like you were walking on bubble wrap without the pops, bouncy, never quite touching the ground. The curtains were dark red, and the walls were hung with quilted silk squares in red, gold, and purple scattered with small round mirrors.

Brenna dumped her garbage bag on the floor and sank into one of the puffy, red chairs by the wooden dresser. She'd been coming to Nadia's house for three years now, since they were both eleven, and she was still pleased and delighted every time she saw this room.

Nadia's mom, Emily, was an antiques dealer, so the house was full of interesting furniture, but no other room was the color of Nadia's. Nadia's room didn't belong to the house the same way Nadia didn't seem to belong to her family. Mr. and Mrs. Wood were pleasant and friendly and normal, brown-haired, brown-eyed, not too plump and not too thin. Her older brother, Lewis, also brown-haired and brown-eyed, was the sort of boy you noticed the second or third time you looked at a group of boys.

If Nadia was anywhere in a room, you knew it, not just because of her red hair and amber eyes, but because of her electric spirit. Brenna suspected that Nadia was adopted, but she'd never asked. Sometimes it was nice to let a mystery alone.

Brenna had brown-gold hair and hazel eyes. Whenever she and Nadia shared a bathroom mirror, Brenna felt like Nadia's shadow. It was a role she liked. She got invited everywhere

Nadia did because everyone knew Nadia didn't go anywhere without Brenna, but no one paid attention to Brenna, so she could enjoy herself watching other people. Even before she met Nadia, sitting in the shadows and watching was something Brenna had been good at: her older sister, Amy, was a genius and an artist. Being someone's shadow felt natural to Brenna.

Unlike Amy, Nadia actually listened to Brenna and liked her.

Nadia squatted and opened Brenna's bag, pulled out the rolls of white medical gauze Brenna's mother had brought home from the hospital. "All right, Bren. Take off your clothes."

"Nadia!"

"What, you think mummies wore clothes before they got wrapped? Not hardly. Just an amulet here and there inside the wrappings. I've got a nice green scarab to place over your heart."

"I'm not going to strip."

"I knew you'd say that." Nadia straightened. "So I got out my body stocking. You *will* wear it." She picked up a wad of stretchy beige cloth from the other puffy chair and handed it to Brenna.

Brenna shook it out. It was leotard material that covered the entire body except the hands and head; it had snaps at the back and at the crotch. "Eww," she said, examining the crotch and wondering how to get it to work.

"Right, that part isn't fun, so don't drink anything."

"I'm wearing my underwear and bra."

"Sure, sure."

"I'm going to the bathroom first."

"Good idea."

Brenna took the body stocking into Nadia's bathroom. The dance started in an hour, and it was supposed to last until midnight, maybe longer. Could she really go seven hours without peeing? Why hadn't she thought of that when she came up with her costume?

She stripped, peed, and pulled on the body stocking over her underwear. From the neck down, she looked like a creepy Skipper doll. She came out of the bathroom with her arms straight in front of her, jerk-walking like Frankenstein's monster. "Night of the Living Doll," she said in her spookiest voice.

"Oh yeah? Just you wait. Hold that pose." Nadia grabbed the gauze and started wrapping Brenna. She overlapped each layer neatly and evenly, and fastened the gauze with small gold safety pins every time she got to the end of a roll or a body part. Brenna watched as her arms and then the rest of her was enveloped in a white pattern that looked like wickerwork. Nadia held a palm-sized green scarab against the center of Brenna's chest and wrapped it there, continuing the pattern. Brenna felt its weight. Trust Nadia to make even this beautiful: everything she did came out like art.

How had Brenna found such a great friend? Nadia had sat next to her in the cafeteria on her first day at school. "What's in your lunch?" Nadia had asked, and Brenna had showed Nadia one of the reasons she usually sat alone: she had a whole avocado from the organic market. She sliced it at the

table to put on her cheese sandwich. Nadia had never seen an avocado before, or a satsuma mandarin orange. She loved them.

Brenna's first friend-capture method had been food.

Her second was listening, and answering weird questions without flinching. Nadia asked things nobody else did, like "What do you do when no one's looking that would embarrass you the most if anyone saw?" and "What do you think about just before you fall asleep?"

Brenna's third method was to be as honest as she could. Nadia trusted her judgment. No one else in her life ever had. Nadia listened to Brenna talk about TV shows, movies, books, and boys. She went off to check things out, and usually came back and said Brenna was right. They watched TV and movies together, read the same books at the same time, sat on the wall outside school and watched boys together—when boys weren't coming over to hit on Nadia. This led to many discussions, but very few arguments.

Actually, the trusting-Brenna's-judgment thing might have been how *Nadia* caught *Brenna*. Having Nadia listen and agree with her was better than food. At home, everything Big Sister Amy said was gold, and everything Brenna said was ignored. Nadia let Brenna be a shadow when Brenna wanted, but let her step into the light, too.

"Try bending," said Nadia. "I want to make sure you can move."

Brenna bent and touched her toes. "It's fine."

Still, she felt strange, as though she were losing herself under the bandages. She felt more naked than she had

expected, even though every inch of her but hands and head was covered. The tight layers of gauze showed her real shape. She couldn't disguise the little bulge of her stomach, or hide her breasts the way she'd been doing since they appeared suddenly last summer. What would Jason think now that he could see what she really looked like?

She'd be in costume. Maybe he wouldn't recognize her. Maybe that was best: she'd just be the mummy and forget she was Brenna. But Jason had told her he'd meet her tonight, that she was supposed to save him a dance. He'd never said anything remotely like that before: she'd always thought he was another guy who just talked to her because she was with Nadia.

Well, wait and see what he thought of the costume, and if he seemed to like it, *then* let him know she was the one inside.

"Ta-da," said Nadia as she pinned the last end of gauze. "You have gloves and a mask, right? You can put them on before we leave. Just let me pin your hair." Nadia led Brenna to the vanity and seated her. Brenna stared at her white-gauze self as Nadia brushed her hair into a ponytail and bobby-pinned it to the top of her head. Nadia could do that and the pins would stay. When Brenna tried it, the pins always slipped out.

"Wow. Thanks, Nadia. I never could have done it so neat. So come on and tell me. What's your costume?"

Nadia smiled. "Close your eyes, Bren."

Brenna closed her eyes. She wanted to peek, but she wouldn't. Her ears sharpened: she listened to rustling, the

slide of fabric on fabric, and then other sounds, fainter and harder to identify: ripping? A little slurpy noise? A sizzle, a hiss.

"You can look now," Nadia said.

Brenna opened her eyes.

Nadia's body glowed with ripples of red and orange. Her face looked like shaped glass with flame inside it. Her hair was a fiery halo, and her hands dripped flame that spiraled upward into smoke and vanished.

"Nadia," Brenna whispered.

"Yes? What do you think?"

"Nadia."

"I had this dream about Halloween. I was thinking I could finally be myself."

"Nadia."

"Bren, you're repeating yourself."

"But, Nadia—"

The flaming face leaned near to stare into Brenna's eyes. Or maybe not; since the firething's eyes were plain yellow-white, Brenna couldn't really tell where it was looking. Brenna blinked. Heat poured off the face. Was this really her best friend?

"Nadia?"

"Brenna?"

"Are you really there?"

"More than I've ever been. Too much?" Nadia paced, leaving black footprints on the red carpet. The smell of burning rose on the air. She glanced at the trail she had left. "Oh. I guess so."

Nadia strode to the bed and picked up some flat pink things. She sat on the bed and slid them onto her feet. Afterward, she had normal feet again, narrow and long-toed, the same feet Brenna had seen when they walked barefoot on the beach or dressed for gym together. Brenna held her nose against the scent of singeing silk. Nadia got up and looked at the smoking quilt. "There are some things about this dimension I really hate." She pulled more flattened pink things up over her legs to her belly. The bottom half of her looked normal again. She pulled on pink gloves. "Everything burns so easily."

This dimension, Brenna thought. *Everything burns.* She gulped a large, smoke-tinted breath and held it for a long moment.

Nadia had chosen Brenna for a friend, whatever she was. Something that could burn with a touch.

Something that watched movies with Brenna, let Brenna help her with her homework, watched boys, laughed at Brenna's jokes, grabbed her hand and dragged her along to places Brenna would never have gone by herself, made her talk to people she was afraid would ignore her. How many times had Brenna slept over in Nadia's big puffy bed? How many times had they talked long after they turned out the light? Too many to count. Nadia knew most of Brenna's secret fears and longings. Brenna knew what Nadia had said about her own desires.

Had Nadia ever told her the truth?

Nadia looked eerie, naked from the waist down, her normal-looking hands floating at the ends of flaming red arms, upper torso and her features aglow with fire, her eyes too

bright to look into. Brenna crossed her wickerwork white arms over her chest and hugged her mummified self. A touch from Nadia could set her on fire.

"What are you?" Brenna whispered.

"A visitor. A student."

"The Woods—"

"My host family. They're lovely to me. I was lucky to find them."

"Do they know what you are?"

"They know I'm from somewhere else," Nadia said. "They don't know what I really look like, but now you do."

"What you really look like," Brenna whispered.

Nadia's normal-looking hand scratched her fiery nose, came away unburned. Nadia sighed, an exhalation of flame. "It isn't going to work, Bren," she said at last. "I can't be myself here." Tiny flames leaked from the inner corners of her eyes.

"Oh, Nadia. I'm sorry," Brenna said.

Nadia picked up the rest of the flat pink things on the bed. She pulled them on until she had covered herself. The last thing she pulled on was the head, with hair attached. The hair looked dull and brown until she tugged the head down to connect with her neck. Then the hair took on a red glow. She opened her eyes. Amber again, with only a hint of flame behind. She sat slumped on the bed, head hanging.

"Oh, Nadia." Brenna hugged her.

Nadia rubbed her eyes. "Well, I was stupid," she said. "I should have known that wouldn't work. What am I going to wear now?"

She stood, flung open the closet door. "Help me, Bren. I can't decide."

Is this what we do next, now that she's told me she's a creature from another dimension? Pick a costume? *Don't I scream and run away now, or something?* Brenna wondered.

Questions could wait.

Feeling strange and ghostly in her white wrappings, Brenna went into the closet and slid clothes hangers sideways. She loved Nadia's clothes. Sometimes Nadia let Brenna borrow something, but Brenna was too shy to wear the really wild outfits. Brenna pulled out a midnight-blue floor-length evening dress in shiny satin, sprinkled with rhinestones like tiny stars. "What about this one?" She handed it to Nadia and shifted clothes until she found something else she remembered: a fringed silvery shawl, crocheted spiderwebs. "And this. And—could you, uh, just take off your head? Maybe with that part showing, you won't burn anything, and everybody will think it's some kind of costume."

Nadia smiled.

Nina Kiriki Hoffman is the author of a number of acclaimed novels, including *A Stir of Bones* (a *Locus* Recommended Reading Selection, a Bram Stoker Award Finalist, and an Endeavour Award Finalist) and its two sequels: A *Red Heart of Memories* (a World Fantasy Award Finalist) and *Past the Size of Dreaming*. Her first book, *The Thread That Binds the Bones*, won the Bram Stoker Award for First Novel. She has also written and sold over two hundred short stories, which have appeared in both anthologies and magazines.

Nina Kiriki Hoffman lives in Eugene, Oregon, with cats, friends, and many creepy toys.

Author's Note

"Unwrapping" started out as a Halloween story for my Tuesday-night writers' workshop, the Eugene Wordos. We have a practice of writing theme stories for Halloween and Christmas/winter holidays, and then getting together to read them aloud and share holiday treats. I wrote "Unwrapping"on the theme of costumes.

I have a wall of masks in my office where I write, and when I'm stalled, I look at those strangers' faces. I love thinking about the masks we wear, both around holidays and in everyday life. I wonder who's hiding behind your mask. Sometimes I wonder about my own.

Alison Goodman

The Real Thing

The mind experiment had seemed like a good idea an hour ago. Now I wasn't so sure; Mavkel and I barely had the basics of telepathy covered, let alone this kind of thing.

"Are you prepared, Joss-partner?" Mav sang, the tips of his double-jointed ears quivering with excitement. He was Chorian, a mainly telepathic race, but when he did speak he used his two mouths to harmonise the words.

He flicked back his second eyelids. I stared into the dark, pupilless eyes of my time-jumping partner and nodded. Maybe this time the mind connection wouldn't hurt so much.

"Then execute the experiment," he sang.

A fiery spike stabbed through my temple. I grabbed the edge of the table and held my breath, exhaling as the pain eased into the soft warm weight of Mav in my mind. Concentrating on the fragile connection, I slowly lifted the real-bacon sandwich and took a bite.

"Well?" I said through the mouthful.

THE REAL THING

Salt? Lipids? Smoke? the pale green of his mind-voice said. *Chew more.*

I chewed. His primary mouth grimaced.

"You enjoy this food?" he sang out loud.

I winced as our connection broke and his pale green presence vanished from my mind. It had only been a few months since Mav and I first joined during a *Rastun,* a Chorian mind-weapon, and we weren't too slick in the connecting and disconnecting department. I still couldn't initiate proper contact with him—Mav had to set up the link—but considering everyone kept telling us that humans and Chorians aren't meant to join minds, we were doing okay. It was getting a bit easier each time we tried. According to Mav, my mind-voice was developing into a nice shade of orange, which apparently is about the level of a Chorian toddler.

"A girl needs a bit of real-meat now and again," I said, taking another bite and rolling the rich bacon and mayo juices around my mouth. "So, you could really taste it?"

"Not for long, but taste some, yes," he sang, holding up his two-thumbed hand. I slapped it in victory, my palm stinging as it met his squat, immoveable strength.

"Wait till you try a curry," I said.

"If this can be done with food, then it can be done with other things," he sang excitedly. "I am interested in experiencing your sex."

I stared at him, the sandwich halfway to my mouth. "*What*?"

"Your reproductive act. It involves much sensory input, yes?"

"No way, Mav," I said, shaking my head. "Forget it. It's not going to happen." I dropped the sandwich onto my plate. "You Chorians may like an audience, but I don't. And anyway, a human needs a partner and I don't have one."

I couldn't help sneaking a look at Kyle Sandrall. He'd just bought a couple of coffee cans at one of the machines and was heading towards the large table of cadets at the far end of the busy mess hall. It was the unwritten code of the University of Australia Centre for Neo-Historical Studies that the back table in the mess was reserved for the comp-kids, the genetically engineered students. A few weeks ago, Kyle had asked me to join them, but I'd said no. Not because I didn't want to, but because I knew I wasn't a real comp-kid. My mother had only used one gene donor with minimal engineering. She didn't want to risk too many donors or gene manips in case I developed CGD—Cascading Gene Defect Syndrome, a nasty collapse of pleiotropic genes. So, I wasn't a comp-kid, but I wasn't a real-kid either. And a few months ago I'd discovered I also had a bit of Chorian DNA in my mix, too. I didn't feel like trying to explain all that to Kyle, the poster boy for tailor-made kids. He'd probably only asked me to sit with him because he thought I was a real comp.

I watched him slide the coffees onto the table and sit down, hooking his long legs under the stool. He passed a can to the girl beside him, a blonde with her hair twisted into a flawless pleat and her chest in the tightest red halter top this side of an X-vid. Tarrah something-or-other; she was in sixth year with Kyle. I touched my own dark scraggly ponytail. It

needed a cut again. And I could probably do with a few new tops, something a bit more feminine than my usual black T-shirts. I brushed sandwich crumbs off my chest, chancing another look at Kyle.

He was looking at me.

He smiled.

He nodded.

I smiled back . . . then realised my hand was still resting on my boob.

"What is wrong, Joss-partner?" Mav sang. "Why do you redden? Are you ill?"

I snatched my hand away. Terrific. Kyle probably thought I was so hot for him I couldn't control myself in public. Out of the corner of my eye, I saw him stand up.

"I'm okay," I said to Mav. "Want to get out of here?"

"No." Mav flattened the tops of his ears and leaned across the table. "Something is wrong. What is wrong?"

"Nothing," I said, waving him back to his seat.

Kyle was definitely heading towards us. I wiped the corners of my mouth with the back of my hand and pushed my hair out of my eyes.

"Have I got mayo on my face?" I whispered.

"No," Mav whispered back. "Should you?"

Then Kyle was standing beside the table.

"Hey, Joss," he said. "Hey, Mavkel."

Mav bowed, his ears lifting. "Kyle Sandrell, this pair greets you most cordially."

Kyle grinned. "Good to see you, too, Mavkel." He turned to me. "How are you, Joss?"

"Terrific," I said. "Fantastic. Brilliant. You know, really good."

I smiled widely, trying to cover my sudden morph from eighteen-year-old college student into babbling idiot.

"Are you two taking Chenowyth's time dynamics class this semester?" Kyle asked.

I nodded, puzzled. All first years had to take Professor Chenowyth's class—Kyle would know that. He licked his lips. They were great lips, kind of full, but not pouty. I dragged my eyes off them.

"Yeah, it's a tough class," Kyle said. "If you and Mavkel ever need any help, just let me know."

"Thanks," I said.

Mav beamed a double-barrelled smile. "You are very kind, Kyle Sandrell."

There was an awkward silence. Mav looked from me to Kyle, his ears hovering uncertainly.

"Why do you stare at one another?" he sang. "Is this a game?" He started jumping up and down in his chair, attracting stares from nearby tables. "This is a courting ritual, is it not?"

I glared at him. His ears collapsed like windless flags.

"I'm sprung," Kyle said, laughing. He rubbed the back of his head, scruffing up his dark hair. "I really came over to see if you'd like to go out Friday night."

"Friday night?" I echoed. Kyle Sandrell—sixth-year demigod and all-round nice guy—was asking me out on a date? I suddenly had an image of kissing him, and ducked my head.

"I thought we could grab something to eat," he said. "And

a friend of mine is throwing a party. We could drop in on that, too."

"Sure," I said, trying to sound casual. "Sounds good." Underneath the table, I dug my fingernails into my palms.

"Great." He grinned again. "Can you infra me your screen code?" He held out his wrist, a sleek armscreen wrapped around it.

"Sorry, I don't wear a screen," I said. "My stand against constant surveillance."

He laughed. "Not a prob. You're quartered in P3, aren't you? How about I come round sevenish?"

"Seven's good. You'll have to wait in the security office, though. Just get them to comm me."

Instead of the usual student housing, Mav and I had a suite in P3, the state-of-the-art security building. Mav was the first Chorian to study on Earth and he was getting the red-carpet treatment. As his time-travel study partner, I got to go along for the first-class ride.

"See you then." Kyle gave me one last lingering smile. I watched him walk back to the comp-kid table; his rear view was as fine as his front view. When he sat down next to Tarrah, I saw her say something, an impeccable eyebrow lifted. Was she asking about me? I grinned to myself. Who cared about Tarrah tight-top? Kyle Sandrell had asked me out!

"I have read about this," Mav sang. "This is a date, is it not? A first date. I read that it is very important that you do not 'put out' yet."

"'Put out'? Where did you get that from?"

"It is from a late 1900s text. A magazine for young females.

It says you must wait until you know it is 'the real thing.'"

"Wasn't that an old advertisement for some kind of drink?" I said.

I was sure I'd heard our professor mention it in our Beginnings of Pop Culture class. I was taking it because I wanted to specialise in music history, mainly twentieth-century blues and jazz. I couldn't wait to time-jump back to the mid-1900s and see some of the big gigs of the golden age.

Mav's ears flicked. "No, that is not correct. *Sparkle* says that 'the real thing' is a pairing that is fated."

"*Sparkle?*" I rolled my eyes. "You can't take something called *Sparkle* as an authority on human relationships."

"It is on the recommended reading list," Mav sang, crossing his arms.

I looked over at Kyle. He was stretching, the movement hitching his T-shirt up over a flat stomach and cut abs. I didn't know much about fate, but I wouldn't mind testing out the idea that Kyle was the real thing.

"Still sticking to your own kind, Aaronson?" a slimy voice asked behind me. "Comp freaks?"

I turned around. Chaney Horain-Donleavy was sitting at the table behind me with his usual posse of losers. He jerked his head toward Kyle. "I heard they made that model sterile."

His gang sniggered.

I knew that some of the girls in our course thought Chaney was good-looking. He had a whole Renaissance-archangel thing going on: dark red curly hair, high cheekbones, golden tan. But I knew that inside, he was a total snake. He'd made it clear that if you weren't from one of the big-money hyphen

families, you might as well not exist. Unless he felt like tormenting you.

"Don't you ever get tired of being a snorkwit?" I said.

His pale blue eyes were unblinking. "Someone's got to make sure you freaks don't get too up yourselves."

"Up yourselves?" Mav sang uncertainly. "What does this mean?"

"It means, flap-head, that comps are trying to stop us from getting into the time-jumping course," Chaney said. He turned to his friends. "They reckon they're better than us, so they should be the first and only choice."

There was a murmur of disgust.

"What a load of screte," I said. "The Centre has strict comp *and* noncomp quotas. It's law."

"Well, you should know," Chaney said slyly. "Aren't you and your mother major shareholders in the Centre?"

I stared at him. How did he know I'd inherited a controlling interest in the Centre? My donor father had left it to me, and I'd had to choose between sitting on the board and studying. It was a no-brainer; who wanted to worry about budgets when they could travel through time? But I thought the whole situation had been kept hush-hush by the Centre bigwigs.

Chaney glanced back at his friends. "That would explain why she got a place. There's no other reason why she's here."

They all laughed.

"I didn't get in because of that," I said.

"No, of course not," he said mockingly. "Come on, Aaronson. Quit zooming. You may be a comp, but you've been kicked out of nearly every school you've ever been in."

He shook his head. "No, you're here because you've got a rich, famous shareholder mother who donated a little admin building. Just like I'm here because my family name is on the library." So he didn't know the whole story. He picked up a veggie fry from his plate and jabbed it into a puddle of tomato sauce. "In the end, it's always who you know and how much you've got that's more important in this world."

"Only in your twisted mind, Chaney," I said.

He pointed his fry at the comp table. "Their parents scrimped and saved and risked CGD to make their kids prettier and smarter than Joe Average. And what for? Just to give them a shot at getting where we already are—at the top. Our families have done it all without any enhancements. Now, you tell me who's better?" He stuffed the fry in his mouth.

Jorel, Chaney's right-hand lout and jump-partner, leaned forward. "My dad says the comp lobby group is getting really strong. He reckons before you know it, the comps will be trying to take over."

Jorel's dad was in government; obviously not a liberal.

"I've heard there's an extremist comp group on campus," Pino said. As usual, he was trying to outdo Jorel. He nodded towards the comps. "Probably them."

Chaney's gang all turned to look at the table at the far end of the hall.

"You should be more careful," I said. "Someone will have you up on a civ charge."

Chaney snorted. "Not if it's true."

"Yeah, not if it's true," Pino echoed. "What about the graffiti painted on the Time Admin building wall: NOT COMP, NOT

GOOD ENOUGH. Bet that was done by comp extremists."

"Haven't seen it," I said, shrugging, but a little coil of unease tightened in my gut.

"Graffiti?" Mav sang. "Is this an artwork?"

"It's like a protest painted on a wall," I said.

"Maybe we should paint one ourselves," Chaney said. "DELETE THE COMP SCRETE."

His gang laughed, loudly repeating the slogan to one another.

Chaney leaned over to me. "I know you're not a real comp, Joss," he said under the cover of their noise. "One donor, enhancements kept to a minimum. You're almost pure. Why do you want go out with someone like Kyle Sandrell?"

I stiffened. Where was he getting all this info about me?

A sudden sharp pain in my head made me wince, but it was gone in a nanosecond. Mav's mind presence washed over me like warm water.

I am here. His mind voice was dark green, strident.

I shot a greasy look at him. I'd told him over and over again he couldn't just barge into my head whenever he felt like it. Especially since I couldn't barge into his head.

But you are alarmed, his mind presence said. *Of course I am here. Contact seemed easier this time, yes?*

It had been easier, but I was too annoyed to agree.

I turned back to Chaney. "I am comp," I said, keeping my voice low. "I may not have ten donors, but I'm still comp."

Why does Chaney alarm you? Mav rocked up in his chair towards the oblivious Chaney, his ears angled back aggressively.

No! No alarm!

Mav stopped and looked at me, then nodded reluctantly. I felt his mind warmth slip away.

"Are you sure the comps will think you're one of them?" Chaney asked. "For a bunch of freaks, they're getting real picky about who makes the grade." He raised his pale red eyebrows. "You should think carefully about who you want to be associated with, Aaronson."

I gritted my teeth, wanting to slap the smug smile off his real-kid-old-money face. He thought he had it all pinned.

"You're absolutely right," I said, standing up. "Come on, Mav, I don't want to associate with these scretes any more. Let's get out of here."

Mav stood up, his ears straight and tense.

"We do not leave you with any cordiality," he said to Chaney.

I couldn't have said it better myself.

"You've got to stop gate-crashing my head like that," I said, waving my security wristband across the lighted door panel. It flashed to green and the door to our quarters slid open.

Beside me, Mav hummed disconsolately with his ears at half-mast, but I wasn't going to fall for his "poor little alien" act.

"It's kind of like walking in on me when I'm getting dressed, except a lot worse."

"But you were alarmed, Joss-partner. I wished to be of assistance."

"I wasn't alarmed," I said brusquely, stepping into our lounge room. "Chaney doesn't alarm me."

55

The Real Thing

"Chorian pairs are always mind-joined," Mav sang plaintively. "We should always be joined, not this sometimes joined. It is a not a real pairing."

I knew why Mav wanted us to be joined all the time—all Chorians had a constant telepathic link to their birth pair as well as to the rest of their race, and Mav's birth pair, Kelmav, had died in an accident. But something in me balked at trying to maintain a constant link. The last thing I wanted was Mav in my head full-time. I didn't want anyone eavesdropping on that constant murmuring stream of reality, fantasy, dream and emotion that flowed through my head. It was my own private narration of my life. And I had a feeling it was an important part of being human.

I headed for my bedroom, Mav trailing behind me. I had dragged him back to P3 as soon as we'd left the mess hall. He had wanted to stop and look at the graffiti, but I was a woman on a mission: to seek out and discover if I had anything to wear on a date with Kyle Sandrall. Poor Mav didn't have a chance—I practically put him in a headlock and marched him past the Time Admin building.

I threw my bag on the bed and slapped my hand against the v-robe sensor. The two virtual wardrobe doors disappeared with a soft pop. I stared at my sad collection of clothes. Apart from the regulation T-shirts and dress uniform, I had three black T-shirts, two red T-shirts, another pair of black jeans and a black jacket. Great for fast packing, not so great for a first date. I picked up an old black cashmere jumper lying on the wardrobe floor and shook the dust out of it.

"What do you think?" I asked.

Mav took the jumper between his two thumbs and held it up. "It will keep you warm and covered."

"Great. Just what I want on a hot date."

"Then that is settled," Mav sang happily. "I would like to see the graffiti now."

I snatched back the jumper. "No, it's not settled. I can't wear that on Friday. I need something . . . sexy."

Mav's ears flattened at the top. "Sexy? The 2-D images in *Sparkle* indicate that human sexy is achieved with much skin and little cloth."

"That's not really me." I couldn't see myself in one of Tarrah's little red halter tops, or a skintight cling dress. "I need something that is . . . well, at least not totally sexless."

"Lisa," Mav said.

"What?"

"Lisa will help you. I heard Jorel tell Pino that Lisa was sexy."

I frowned, conjuring up a mental picture of our friend Lisa. Long brown hair, savvy grey eyes, nice teeth. Was she sexy? I had never really thought about it. When someone gets shot on your behalf, you never really think of anything but their courage and spirit. A few months ago, she'd helped Mav and me jump back in time to save Mav's life and had got a laser through her shoulder for her trouble. I suppose she always wore makeup, but not much, and her hair was always shiny. Her clothes weren't anything special, although they did kind of skim her body. In all the right places. Damn, Mav was right; Lisa was sexy. And classy.

"Good idea," I told him. "Maybe she'll be able to lend me something."

His ears lifted. "We will visit the graffiti now. If we leave now, we will have six minutes to view it and two minutes to travel to our next class."

Sure enough, by the time we were standing in front of the graffiti on the south wall of the Time Admin building, the clock tower showed we had exactly eight minutes before the start of class. Who needed an armscreen with Mav around?

I stared up at the large slogan. Someone had gone to a lot of trouble; the outline of each letter was sprayed in red and filled in with yellow. The colours of the Genetic Enhancement Lobby Group. The big, beautifully drawn letters boldly declared war: NOT COMP, NOT GOOD ENOUGH. My gut tightened again.

Mav rocked back on his hind claws. "It is very neat," he sang. "And the lettering is aesthetically pleasing. Is this not art?"

"No, it's trouble."

"Why?"

"There's a lot of comps who are wondering why they should apologise for being better."

Mav looked back at the wall. "Comps consider themselves superior to nonenhanced humans?"

"I suppose some do," I said reluctantly.

"Is this not the aim of their genesis. To create superiority?"

"Superior attributes, but not superiority."

"Ah"—Mav nodded—"a semantics problem."

"Sometimes," I said drily, thinking of all the times I had been called a freak or unnatural. "It's just that a lot of humans like to think we're all equal, or that we at least start off equal. Some people think comps have an unfair advantage. Like it's cheating."

"Cheating?" Mav wrinkled his noses. "But if an attribute is created by the fortuitous combination of two unknowns, then it is considered not cheating?"

"Then it's good luck."

Mav's ears flattened. "Luck is acceptable, but design is not?"

"Luck is better because it doesn't need tons of money. Anyone can have luck," I said. "Not everyone can afford to take the chance out of luck."

"I do not understand," Mav sang dolefully.

I turned away from the wall. I wasn't sure I understood either. I just knew that sometimes I felt guilty for being alive.

"Come on," I said, wanting to get away from the graffiti. "We've only got one and half minutes to get to class."

Mav took the bait. "Incorrect, Joss-partner," he shrilled behind me. "We have two minutes, six seconds and four one-hundredths."

"I brought a whole load of stuff," Lisa said, dumping a pile of clothes and shoes on my bed. "Didn't know where you and Kyle were going, so I figured I'd cover all possibilities." She absently adjusted her tank strap over her bandaged shoulder. "You should have commed me sooner. We could have gone shopping."

It was D-Day—Date Day—and Lisa had jumped at the chance to make me over.

I poked at the clothes. "It's not a big deal," I said. Maybe if I said it enough times I'd believe it. "It's only going to be some dinner somewhere and then maybe a party." I pulled a

bright blue slip of silky material out of the stack. "What's this? A scarf?"

Lisa snatched it out of my hand. "Very funny. It's a top. Looks great with blue jeans."

"I can still wear jeans?" I'd been imagining microshorts and cling tops.

"Of course. I don't think you should make any drastic changes. Just move away from wearing so much black and smarten things up a bit."

She pulled back her fall of brown hair and deftly twisted it into a loose bun, tying it into itself. Amazing. All I could ever do with mine was whack a band around it and hope it held, or stuff it under a beret.

I pushed the clothes aside and sat on the edge of the bed. "So, you've been studying here for five years. What's the Kyle story."

Lisa got down to business. "For the last year or so he's been a bit of a serial dater," she said. "But before that, he and Tarrah were a couple right through to fourth year." She made a wry face. "The golden comp couple. They were probably whipped up in the same laboratory." She realised what she'd said. "Screte. I'm sorry, Joss, I didn't mean anything by that." She touched my arm in apology. "I think I was channelling my stepfather."

"Not a comp fan, huh?" I said tightly.

"You could say that. Both Mum and Leo are old-line religious. You know, 'Love thy neighbour as long as thy neighbour isn't a comp.' They're always saying that the scientists are playing God and that we shouldn't be messing with the

Lord's creations." She met my eyes. "Look, I'm a big girl now. I don't buy into their beliefs. I say live and let live. Okay?"

I nodded. "Okay." I stood up, wanting to physically shake off the sudden awkwardness between us. "So what went wrong between Kyle and Tarrah."

"Not sure," Lisa said, obviously relieved to be talking about something else. "One rumour was that he found her in a clinch with another guy. Another one said Tarrah started getting a bit too intense about the Comp Lobby and Kyle wasn't so into it."

"They're still friends, though, aren't they? I saw them in the mess together."

"Absolutely. Kyle's a nice guy, he likes to be friends with everybody," Lisa said. She pulled out a top in a soft pink knit. "Try this on. We're about the same size, so it should fit you." She picked up a pair of jeans. "And these, too."

I took the clothes just as Mav loped through the doorway.

"Lisa," he sang. "This pair greets you with great pleasure." He gripped Lisa's hand and bowed, entwining her thumb in the complicated Chorian friendship grip.

Lisa bowed back. "Hi, Mav. You're looking good."

"Yes, I feel much equilibrium. Does your injury heal?" Mav asked, his hand hovering over her shoulder. He began to hum softly.

Before he became a time-jumping student on Earth, Mav had been studying to be a Chanter, the Chorian version of a doctor. He'd once tried to explain to me how he'd been learning to sense injuries and emotional states through sound vibrations, but I'd got lost about five minutes into it.

"It's a lot better," Lisa said. "The doctors say I'll be a hundred per cent in a month or so."

Mav nodded. "They are correct." He dropped his hand and looked at the clothes on the bed. "You bring much cloth for Joss." His ears flattened. "She says I cannot accompany her on her first date to observe human sexual courting behaviour."

"Not on the first date or any date," I said firmly, ignoring Lisa's snort of laughter.

"She feels much apprehension about this first date with Kyle Sandrell," Mav sang. "It is good that you are assisting her to be at least not totally sexless."

I covered my face with my hands. "Think I'll go and drown myself in the bather now."

"While you're in there, try those on," Lisa said, still laughing. She pushed me towards my ensuite. "And don't forget the shoes." She handed me some sandals.

I stepped into the bathroom. "For the record, I am not nervous about this date," I said loftily. I hit the sensor pad, closing the door. My reflection stared at me from the far mirror. "Not one bit," I told it. It nodded.

Eight clothes changes later, we had a winner. I stepped out of the bathroom in a crisp fitted white shirt with thin stripes of blue and silver, a pair of mem-jeans that were already settling themselves around my shape, and silver sandals.

Lisa nodded. "Oh yeah, that's it." She stood up. "Just one thing." She reached over and undid my top two shirt buttons, creating a deep V.

Mav walked around me, considering. "It is pleasing," he

finally announced. “However, it needs a decorative metallic neckpiece.”

Lisa and I stared at him.

“You know, he’s right,” Lisa said. “Have you got a silver necklace?”

I found a twisted silver chain and clasped it around my neck.

“So?” I asked. I changed the v-robe doors into mirror mode and looked at myself.

Lisa and Mav nodded. I smiled at them in the reflection of the mirror.

“You’re gorgeous,” Lisa said. “I’ve seen your mother reading the news tons of times, but I’ve never really noticed how much you look like her. Except she’s blonde and you’re dark, of course.”

“That’s what she ordered,” I said. “The Eurasian version of herself—wouldn’t want another blonde bombshell in the family, would we? And just enough multi-ethnicity to boost her audience numbers.”

Even I heard the bitter edge in my voice.

“I’m sure your mother didn’t want you just for that,” Lisa said softly.

I turned to look at her. “My mother chose to manipulate the genes that create symmetrical facial structure, athletic body type and good teeth. Looks, looks and looks. I think that says it all.”

Lisa and Mav looked at me solemnly.

“So all those brains you’ve got are natural?” Lisa finally said, smiling.

I reluctantly grinned back. “Must be.”

Lisa stood up. "Well, it doesn't matter what way you got that face and body. I say, if you've got it, flaunt it." She zeroed in on me. "Come on, we've got to do something with your hair and makeup."

I turned to face the mirror as she smoothed back my fringe. Lisa was wrong. How you got it was important, and my gut told me that flaunting it might soon be very dangerous.

A few minutes before seven, the CommNet jingle sounded from the computer on the bedside table. Lisa was holding a pair of silver hoops against my ears and we both jumped as the screen moved smoothly around to face us.

"Joss, you've got a comm message from Sergeant Vaughn at the P3 Security Office," the computer said.

I met Lisa's eyes. This was it. She snatched away the earrings and stepped back, nodding encouragingly.

I took a deep breath. "Okay, connect."

Vaughn's fashionably altered face appeared on the screen. "Well now, don't we look purty." He leered. "Your little boyfriend is waiting for you."

I gave him a cool death glare, but my heart was already picking up pace.

"Thank you. Tell him I'll be out in five. Disconnect." The screen flicked back to the CommNet logo.

"Okay, he's here," I said, standing up. "Looks like I'm going now." I felt strangely reluctant to leave.

"Are you sure I cannot accompany you?" Mav asked, his ears hiking up hopefully.

"She's sure," Lisa said. She handed me a ridiculously small silver evening bag. "Good luck. And have a great time."

That was the plan.

Kyle tapped his spoon against the toffee crust of the crème brûlée that sat between us on the table. "Want to help me break it?" he asked.

I nodded and picked up my spoon.

He sat up straight, holding his hand over his heart. "I dedicate this crème brûlée to all those who believed in it and held the dream in their hearts of a better, happier dessert."

Laughing, we broke through the thin layer, exposing the smooth pale custard underneath.

"I think we've struck gold," he said softly, and I had a feeling he didn't just mean the dessert. "You go first."

I dug out a spoonful of toffee and custard and tasted it.

"Ohmigod," I breathed, letting the honey vanilla melt on my tongue. "That is fantastic."

"Told you," Kyle said, helping himself.

I looked around the crowded café. It had been quiet when we arrived and the headwaiter had seated us in the open double windows that looked out into Mall 11, the boutique area of the Melbourne central mall network. Now the restaurant was buzzing, and the energy in the place was pumping through me.

Kyle and I had talked nonstop about the Centre, discussing our majors (history of architecture for him, music for me), the tough fitness program, the best and worst teachers, and the first terrifying ten seconds of a time-jump. We'd even discussed Mav and the mind link, although I had moved the conversation on fairly quickly—it felt too much like talking behind Mav's back. The arrival of dessert had created a natu-

ral break in conversation, but I sensed that we were about to shift into more personal territory. And for once, I didn't mind. I spooned out some more of the crème brûlée, concentrating on scooping up as much toffee as possible.

"That Horain-Donleavy kid from your class cornered me yesterday," Kyle said.

That made me look up—Chaney had never been high on my list of romantic dinner topics.

Kyle shook his head. "One of these days someone's going to buck the civ laws and lay into that kid. And with that mouth on him, he'll deserve it. He wanted to have a 'little chat' about you."

I hurriedly swallowed my mouthful of dessert. "What did he say?"

Kyle shrugged. "That you weren't really comp."

The lingering sweetness in my mouth turned sour. The next time I saw Chaney, he'd better start running.

"I am comp," I said. "I may only have one donor, but I'm enhanced. I'm still comp." It came out more vehemently than I expected.

Kyle held up his hands. "Hey, I'm with you—if someone's enhanced, then they can call themselves comp. I know some comps wouldn't agree with that, but they're a bit hard-line." He picked up his glass and drained it. "You know Tarrah, don't you?"

"I've seen her around, but we haven't met," I said, trying not to sound too happy about it.

"She's well in with the Comp Lobby, and she told me they're trying to get some kind of criteria set for comp status.

A certain number of donors and things like that."

I looked at Kyle's beautiful face, a horrible thought hitting me like a hammer between the eyes. "Would it matter to you if I wasn't a comp?"

It was like everything in the café ground to a halt while I waited for his answer. Was this gorgeous, funny guy the flip side of Chaney? I had very specific ideas about where this evening was heading, and they would all disappear in a flick of a clean sheet if he said yes.

He shook his head. "Of course not."

The magic words. My evening was still intact.

"But I've kind of stopped dating noncomps now," he continued. "Not that there's anything wrong with them—it's just that they don't really understand what it's like. You know what I mean."

"Sure, but . . ." I had been about to say that anyone with an ounce of empathy would be able to work it out, and that went both ways. But earlier, Lisa had delicately suggested I tone down my attitude, especially on the first date. *Leave it to the second date*, she'd said. So, I swallowed the comment, although it kind of stuck in my throat.

Kyle looked at me expectantly. "But what?"

"But do you want coffee?" I said lamely.

"How about we skip coffee and head to the party?" Kyle said. "I promised we'd drop in, but we don't have to stay long."

I caught the lilt in his voice. My thoughts exactly.

We took the Venturi Loop back to campus. I've never been keen on the underground trans system—being sucked

through a tube in a metal capsule without windows always creeps me out—but it seemed like a good idea to get to the party as quickly as possible. The sooner we got there, the sooner we could leave.

It was being held in Trinity College, the sixth-year-student quarters. Kyle and I took the most direct route through campus, along the wide tree-lined central boulevard. The huge oaks had formed a canopy over the walkway and the University had installed old-fashioned streetlamps that created pools of buttery light and soft shadows. Although it was officially autumn, the night air was still warm, courtesy of the ever-expanding ozone hole, and a number of other couples were strolling hand in hand. It seemed like a good idea. I glanced across at Kyle. He met my eyes and smiled, both of us moving at the same time. I yelped as my finger mashed against his palm. We jumped apart then started laughing.

"I think we got our timing wrong," he said. "Let's try that again."

Our hands slid together. Something inside me lurched as I felt his long fingers curl around mine.

We walked up the steps to the arched entrance of Trinity College.

"What do you say we only stay for half an hour," I said, tightening my grip.

The door to the party dorm was opened by a sixth-year girl with short black hair intricately twisted back into beaded sections. She kissed Kyle on the cheek then pointed in the direction of the eating area.

"Drinks down there," she yelled over the pounding music.

I followed Kyle through a crowded living room and into the eating area. James, a cheerful fifth-year I'd met through Lisa, was manning the food dispenser.

"Hey Joss, how are you doing? I didn't know you belonged."

Belonged? To what? I opened my mouth to ask, but James had turned to Kyle.

"So what do you want to drink?" he asked.

"Beer?" Kyle said, turning to me for confirmation.

"Sure."

I took the cold glass and studied the group of people. Something was bugging me, but I couldn't work out what.

"Kyle!" a girl's voice yelled. We both turned around. Tarrah was heading towards us in a pale green cling dress, her blonde hair falling in VR star waves. She kissed Kyle on both cheeks, her bright hazel eyes on me.

"So glad you decided to come. And you, too, Joss," she said, smiling widely. "It's always good to have a new member."

Member? And then it clicked. Everyone in the room was a comp. I shot a look at Kyle.

"Member of what?" I asked.

"The Comp Lobby," Tarrah said. "Didn't Kyle tell you this is a meeting?"

"Me and Joss are just here for the beer," Kyle said.

"Come on, Ky, you're going to have to get off your fence one day." Tarrah turned around to face the crowd. "Hey, turn the music off," she called. "It's time to start."

There was immediate silence. I scanned the room; everyone had turned expectantly towards Tarrah.

"I'm not going to rave on for very long," she said. "This is just a prelim to see who is interested in the march on the Director's offices next week."

Four heavyset guys with rugby player necks raised their beers and cheered.

"Let's storm the place," one of them yelled. A few girls near them giggled.

"Thanks for your enthusiasm, Liam," Tarrah said. "But for the moment we're just marching. And that reminds me, although we all appreciate the sentiments of the graffiti on the admin building, it would be better if the artists played it cool for a while. Until the march is over."

"What are you marching against?" I asked.

Tarrah looked back at me and smiled. "Everyone, say hello to Joss. She's in first year, so all you old hands can give her some pointers about surviving the course," she said.

A friendly buzz of *hellos* rippled around the room. I caught a thumbs-up from the black-haired bead girl and a wink from James. I smiled, the warmth of the crowd surprising me.

Tarrah brushed back her hair. "We're marching against the quotas," she said, a strident note entering her voice. "It's just institutionalised prejudice against us. We're supposed to be living in a meritocracy, but potential comp students are being turned away, even though they're outstripping the noncomps in all areas."

"Don't the quotas work both ways?" I asked, curious.

Tarrah nodded. "It used to work both ways. But we're not just oddities any more. At the moment, five per cent of births are comps and that's rising. More and more comps are com-

ing through the school system. Why should they give way to the mediocre?" She turned back to the room of people and raised her voice into a rallying cry. "I say that if you're better, then you should get into the course. And I've seen the statistics—comps are better! Let's face it, that's why our parents took the chance."

The room erupted into a frenzy of whoops and cheers and clapping. Liam and his mates started chanting "Not comp, not good enough!"

"If you want to march, go see Birri over there," Tarrah yelled, pointing to a tall black woman at the back of the room. "Put your name down. Let's show them we mean business."

People started to move towards the sign-up. Beside me, Kyle drained his glass and put it on a nearby table.

"Want to get going?" he asked.

I nodded. "You don't seem very impressed with all this," I said, taking a last swig of beer.

"Are *you* impressed?"

I looked around the room. "I don't know. I suppose I'm impressed by the solidarity."

Kyle raised his eyebrows. "Yeah, Tarrah's good at that."

"Did I hear my name?" Tarrah said, moving away from the four rugby players.

"We're taking off now," Kyle said smoothly.

"Already?" Tarrah looked put out. "I hope you'll come again, Joss," she said. "We comps have to stick together, right?"

"Sure," I said.

She gave me an appraising look. "Think about it, Joss. I know you've had your fair share of screte from noncomps. Do

something about it." She quickly kissed Kyle on the cheek. "Don't be like Ky, here. He doesn't like to get involved. Do you, darling?"

"Only with the right person," he said lightly. And although he didn't look at me, I felt a rush of heat through my body.

Tarrah's laugh was brittle. "Always sidestepping the issue. See you tomorrow." Then she was gone, surrounded by her disciples, her voice urging and caressing towards the sign-up table.

Kyle took my hand and we made our way towards the door. I looked back at the milling group waiting to sign their names; arms draped over friends' shoulders, bursts of laughter, loud teasing, and underneath it all a real sense of camaraderie. Of belonging. James was standing at the back of the room and caught my eye. He motioned towards the sign-up table, his eyebrows raised. I shrugged. He nodded and smiled, mouthing "Next time." Perhaps I would, next time. I waved as Kyle gently tugged at my other hand.

Outside, in the warm night air, we paused at the top of the steps.

"Sorry about that," Kyle said. "I didn't know she was going to turn it into a rally."

"It's okay. I can sort of see where she's coming from. And I really liked the vibe."

"Yeah, it's nice to relax with your own kind," he said as we walked side by side down the steps. I felt a fleeting twitch of unease at his phrasing. "That's why I go," he continued. "To hang with other comps. I'm not so keen when Tarrah starts politicising."

"I wouldn't mind hanging with them again," I said.

As if we could read each other's mind, we both turned towards one of the smaller paths that branched off from the main boulevard. A more secluded path. The lamps were farther apart, creating soft-edged spotlights in the darkness. Kyle caught up my hand again and we walked in silence, the energy between us building. Every centimetre of my skin was aware of the warmth of his body, the flat smooth planes of his muscles, the soft curve of his lips. As we moved into the glow of one of the lights, I glanced up at him and saw him staring at me. The flare of his dark pupils pulled me towards him. I stopped and draped my arms over his shoulders. He leaned into me, his body firm against mine. As I rose to meet him, our bodies pressed closer together and I thought I could feel his heartbeat, as quick as mine. The kiss was gentle, a soft taste of each other, but I wanted more. I opened my mouth, feeling him move with me, all my focus on the shivering sensation running though my body.

I feel your desire, Joss-partner! It is beautiful!

I jerked back, the intrusion like the slash of a cold knife.

"What's wrong?" Kyle asked anxiously, his arms still around me.

My mind flamed into burnt orange fury.

No! Get out!

The link snapped, a whisper of lime green remorse colouring my consciousness.

I slammed my wristband across the security panel of our front door. Barely waiting for it to slide open, I stalked into

the hexagonal living room. Behind me, Kyle paused in the doorway.

"Mav, get out here," I yelled.

There was no answer. His bedroom door was closed, the lock panel glowing red. I slapped it anyway.

"Mav, don't you try and hide."

"I will come when you no longer shout," he sang.

I glared at the door. That was going to be a long time coming.

"Maybe I should go," Kyle said.

I turned back to him.

"Screte! I'm sorry, Kyle." I ran my hand through my hair, messing up Lisa's careful styling.

"Look, don't worry. You've got stuff to work out here. How about we catch up tomorrow night?" He hesitated. "That is, if you'd like to."

"I'd love to," I said. I walked over to him. "Thanks. And I'm sorry."

We kissed, brief but full of promise. I watched the door close behind him.

Damn it. I marched across to Mav's door again.

"You wrecked my date. You can at least come out and face me," I said, trying to modulate my voice.

The door slid open. Mav stood in front of me, his ears flat against his head.

"This is the correct time to say sorry, yes?" he sang meekly.

"'Sorry' doesn't cut it," I snapped. "I was having a fantastic time until you barged in!"

"I know," Mav sang.

"Do you know how creepy that is?" I said tightly. "To have someone in your mind when you're . . . " I stopped, not really wanting to describe what Kyle and I were doing.

Mav's ears raised placatingly. "On Choria, it is always an honour to be joined at such times."

"I don't give a damn if it's an honour on Choria," I yelled. "I don't want to share my love life with you. Do you understand?"

"Yes," Mav sang contritely. His ears flattened again. "But tell me why you still want Kyle when you do not trust him? I do not understand."

"What?" I stared at him, crossing my arms.

"You do not trust Kyle. I felt it through your desire."

"I don't know what you're talking about. You're just trying to change the subject."

"No, Joss-partner. Deep in you there is not-trust. Why do you fail to acknowledge this instinct?"

"Deep in me is pissed off. With you." I stamped across to my bedroom. "Don't even think about coming near me for a few days. I don't want to see you."

I didn't look back as my bedroom door slid shut. I slapped the lock panel then dived, full-length, onto my bed. I trusted Kyle, just fine. And anyway, what did Mav know about trust? I'd trusted him to stay out of my head for one night, and he couldn't even do that. Maybe this partnership wasn't going to work, after all.

The next day was Saturday, rest day, and Mav took me at my word; whenever I came out of my bedroom, he ducked back

into his room. I heard him leave the suite about midday.

As soon as I heard the front door slide shut, I commed Kyle and organised to meet him at the University basketball game at eight. Then I hotfooted it over to Lisa's quarters to borrow more clothes. She lent me a soft, sexy red jumper and red heels, then made me promise I'd go clothes shopping with her later in the week. I didn't mention my fight with Mav—he was wrong, but Lisa had a bad habit of looking at both sides of a situation.

At about a quarter to eight, I left our quarters. Mav was still out. We usually spent Saturday nights together at the Buzz Bar, catching up with our friend Lenny Porchino, the bar owner. Was that where Mav was now? In Lenny's private booth, listening to the house blues band? Sometimes I'd jam with the band on my blues harp and Mav would harmonise my line with intricate humming. We always got encores. It felt strange not being there with him.

I hurried over to the huge, central gym. The basketball game was between the University team and their old adversaries from Monash Uni. It was already crowded when I made it into the stadium. I scanned the seats for Kyle, but couldn't see him. This was one of the times when not wearing an armscreen backfired. Maybe I'd have to get one, now that I *wanted* someone to contact me. I saw Chaney and Jorel in the top row, throwing chips down at four big guys crammed together in the small seats: Liam and his friends from Tarrah's party. They already looked wasted. And now they also looked pissed off—Chaney liked to live dangerously.

I still couldn't see Kyle. Had he decided not to come? I

pushed down a hollow feeling and studied the rows, one by one. Finally I saw him guarding a spare seat in the far corner. A few girls were looking back at him, trying to catch his eye, but he was obviously on the lookout for me—bad luck, girls. I couldn't help grinning as I made my way across the bleachers.

"Hey, just in time," he called when he saw me climbing over legs and bags. He stood up to let me pass. As I brushed past him, I smelled hot man and citrusy cologne. It made me want to drag him out of the stadium.

I'm sure I cheered our team in the right spots and yelled at the refs' decisions, but I can't really remember. All I noticed was the energy between me and Kyle. He held my hand the whole time, softly stroking my palm, sometimes my arm. I pressed my thigh against his, and then my hip, until the whole of our sides were touching, the heat from our bodies only partly due to the crowd around us. By the end of the game, I felt like my whole body was vibrating against his and I knew, from the dark intent of his eyes, that we weren't going to be hanging around for the victory party.

By the time we made it out of the stadium, most of the crowd had cleared.

"It's still early," Kyle said. "Did you want to get a drink or something?"

I stared him in the eyes and shook my head slowly.

"No," I said, and smiled.

He grinned back. "My roomie has gone to stay with a mate," he said. "Want to come back to my place?"

"Why, thank you, Mr Sandrell. Don't mind if I do."

He laughed and squeezed my hand. "Let's cut through the science buildings. It's faster."

We started running, hand in hand, across the stadium quadrangle, leaving behind the last stragglers of the basketball crowd. Kyle led me in between the tall, dark science buildings, through a deserted arched walkway, and down a steep set of steps.

"Wait," I panted, laughing. "I can't run in these silly shoes."

I dragged on his hand. He stopped and we stood for a moment in a dark alleyway. I pulled him closer, angling my face to kiss.

The small space suddenly echoed with a sharp cry and the scraping sound of struggle.

I pulled back. "What's that?"

"Dunno, but it's from over there," Kyle said, turning towards the far end of the alley.

We started towards it, the sounds of heavy breathing and pain-filled gasps more insistent. I rounded the corner into a shadowy courtyard. For a second all I saw was a dark mass on the far edge. Then it became four heavy guys kicking two hunched forms on the concrete. Liam and his mates belting the screte out of two kids. Even before I saw the night-bleached flash of red curly hair, I knew it was Chaney. And Jorel.

Chaney covered his head with his arms as Liam savagely kicked him.

"Don't ever call me a freak again, you little bastard," Liam said.

I started forward, but Kyle's hand dug painfully into my arm, pulling me back.

"Don't," he whispered.

"What do you mean? We've got to stop it!" I jerked my arm away.

"It's not our fight."

"What's that got to do with it?"

Kyle's face was set. "You know Chaney and his friend were asking for it."

I stared at him. "You can't just walk away from people getting hurt."

"It's the only thing those type understand," he said harshly, stepping into the shadows of the alley. "Leave it, Joss. Don't get involved." He went to grab my arm again, but I jumped back.

"No, we have to do something. They're getting creamed."

"Look, I'll call Security," he said.

"They'll be too late."

He took a step back, shaking his head. "I'll call Security."

"Don't knock yourself out," I said as he disappeared down the alley.

I turned towards the fight, suddenly feeling very alone. One of the rugby thugs was down, writhing on the ground. Nearby, Jorel was lying very still on the concrete. Chaney was curled into a ball with the other three thugs on top of him.

"Oi," I yelled, running towards them. "Get off him."

Liam looked up. "Get lost."

He turned back to Chaney. His mistake. I punched him in the side of the head. My mistake. I should have gone for his gools.

"Bloody hell," he roared. And swung. I jumped back. He only grazed my shoulder, but it felt like a sledgehammer.

"Didn't I see you last night?" he demanded.

All three of his mates turned their attention to me. Not so good. On the ground, Chaney groaned, one side of his head covered in blood.

"So?" I said, slipping off my shoes. I couldn't fight in them and they had handy heels. Two of the guys had got up and were circling around me.

"You're comp," Liam said.

"So what?"

"So, these guys are lousy bigots. We're just teaching them a little lesson."

"No, you're not. You're bashing the screte out of them. Leave them alone."

"You're going to stop us, are you?" the thug on my right asked. He swung another kick into Chaney.

"Too right," I said. At least my voice was steady.

I felt the warmth of a body behind me just as Liam rushed me. I should have kept an eye on Left Thug. I zeroed in on Liam's crotch and kicked. Liam buckled as pain burst through my toes. Then I felt Left Thug's arms tighten around my chest.

"Silly bitch," Right Thug yelled.

The rush of adrenaline masked the pain of his first punch to my stomach, but it didn't soften the ground or the kick into my side. I heard Liam moaning near me, and saw Chaney try to get up and pull one of the thugs off me. Mav! I needed Mav! I strained every fibre of my being towards his mind, screaming as the burning pain in my body matched the orange

fire in my head. *Hear me! Mav, hear me!* The edges of my sight faded into grey haze as I gasped for breath. Something heavy on my chest. Can't breathe. *Mav!* I pushed against the human weight. Pushed against the confines of my mind. Screaming inside. Outside. Until there was no more breath.

Joss? His mind voice was startled, jubilant, darkening into anxiety. *I come.*

And then I knew why Mav wanted to be joined all the time. Waves of Mav, of everything that was Mav, broke over me, filling me with the certainty that I was not alone, would never be alone. A swirling, dizzying closeness, understanding, acceptance. Joss melding into Mav into Joss, a merging of minds and spirits. A joining of stories, thoughts, emotions, dreams. We flowed together; pasts, presents, futures fused into a rolling, endless stream. We were Pair.

We will be there soon. We will stop the pain. We will be together. We are Pair.

No!

Deep down, part of me struggled for separateness. A bolt hole of isolation. Nothing but the bare essence of Joss. Alone. Human. *One*.

I don't know if it was that, or the punch in the face that suddenly blacked out the world.

I heard humming. Insistent, annoying humming. I licked my lips. Dry. I tried opening my eyes. Bright, painful light. Antiseptic. White walls.

Hospital.

I focused on a hand hovering over my face. Two thumbs.

"Mav?"

The humming stopped.

"Joss-partner. I am here."

Mav's double-barrelled smile appeared in front of me.

"We've got to stop meeting like this," I croaked.

"You are bruised on your face and body and have one rib broken," Mav sang. "All will be well."

"Can't feel anything," I said. Must have been full of Alpheine. "How are Chaney and Jorel?"

"They both live," Mav sang somberly. "Jorel is still unconscious. He is injured inside and is now in the place of special care. Chaney is cut and swollen on his face and also has ribs that are broken. He is much grateful to you."

"What about Liam and his friends?"

"Those who attacked you? They are with your law enforcers. There is loud shouting and anger about comps and noncomps."

I tried to nod, but the effort was too great. The comp trouble had finally come.

"Kyle Sandrall wishes to see you," Mav sang. "He waits outside, asking about your health."

I closed my eyes. How did I feel about that? An image of Kyle disappearing down the alleyway flashed through my mind.

"All right, let him in."

Mav touched the wall panel and the door slid open. He motioned Kyle inside.

"Hi, Joss," Kyle said hesitantly.

He was holding a posy of flowers.

"Hey," I said, trying to summon up a smile. I shifted in the bed as my body remembered his arm across my shoulder, the warmth of his lips against mine.

Kyle looked across at Mav then back at me. "Could we have a moment alone?"

Mav's opaque eyelids flicked shut, shielding his eyes.

"I'd like Mav to stay," I said.

Kyle's face tightened. "Okay." He looked down at the flowers. "I just wanted to say I'm sorry."

"Why'd you take off like that? You left me there."

"I know. I'm sorry. I did call Security, though."

What had Tarrah said about him? Always sidestepping the issue?

Mav crossed his arms. "It was not proper courting behaviour," he sang stiffly.

Kyle nodded. "Joss has got a lot of guts," he said.

"It is not only guts," Mav sang, his ears high. "Joss has much generosity."

Kyle frowned. He didn't understand. He probably never would.

"Well, thanks for coming by," I said, suddenly feeling very tired.

He held out the posy. "Still friends?"

I took the flowers and laid them on the bed beside me. "Sure, Kyle. Maybe I'll see you round."

He smiled—he was still gorgeous, but something was missing. Honour, perhaps, or maybe empathy. Mav had been right about my instincts, after all. Not that I'd ever tell him that—I'd never hear the end of it.

Kyle walked out, the door sliding shut behind him.

Mav flicked back his second eyelids. "There is still much to like in Kyle Sandrell," he sang gently.

I blinked, trying to clear my eyes.

Mav peered at me. "You are weary. Shall I go?"

"No, stay." I swallowed against a dry ache. "Got any water there?"

Mav picked up a glass and held it to my lips. I took a small sip, the coolness slipping down my scratchy throat.

"Thanks."

He put the glass down.

I squinted with effort, trying to focus my mind. *And thanks for help.*

You called me. I came. His mind voice was bright green, pulsating with joy. *You called me!*

"I know. It was amazing," I said, picking up his hand and closing it around my fist. The closest I could come to the Chorian friendship clasp right now. "I feel honoured to know you in that way."

"It is my honour."

"But, Mav, I can't have you in my mind all the time," I said slowly. "I'm sorry, I just can't. Humans are separate. I have to think my own thoughts, narrate my own life."

Mav sighed. "I know, Joss-partner." He sat forward, his thumbs tightening around my hand. "But now you call me. We will make our own joining. And sometimes we will make a paired story. Is this good?"

Yes, it is good.

Alison Goodman is the author of *Singing the Dogstar Blues*, a science-fiction comedy thriller, which won the 1998 Aurealis Award for Best Young Adult Novel and was listed as a 1999 C.B.C. Notable Book. It was published in the United States in hardback by Viking and in paperback by Firebird, and was named an ALA Best Book for Young Adults.

Alison lives in Melbourne, Australia, with her husband, Ron, and their two exuberant Parson Russell terriers, Xander and Spike. She holds a master of arts and teaches creative writing at undergraduate and postgraduate level.

Alison is currently working on *Eon/Eona*, a fantasy duology based upon Chinese astrology; the first volume will be published by Viking in 2007.

Visit her Web site at **www.bssound.com.au/goodman**.

Author's Note

When Sharyn invited me to write a short story for *Firebirds Rising*, I jumped at the chance to continue the Joss and Mav story that I started in my novel *Singing the Dogstar Blues*. In the process of writing a novel, there are always interesting tangents that an author can't follow due to the necessities of plot streamlining or character development. One of the tangents I had to leave in *Singing the Dogstar Blues* was a short scene where Joss first meets Kyle Sandrall and decides not to accept his invitation to a "comp kid" party. "The Real Thing"

grabs that small interplay between Joss and Kyle and runs with it, taking Joss into a minefield of love, lust and prejudice. I was also keen to write about Mav's interest in human courting rituals—I loved writing his puzzled study of the strange processes that we humans go through when we fancy each other. Sometimes they puzzle me too! "The Real Thing" also expands on some of the questions raised in *Singing the Dogstar Blues*, such as what might happen to a society where some members have been engineered to be "better"? Would engineered people feel entitled? Would nonengineered people feel threatened? Science fiction specialises in asking "what if?" which is why I enjoy writing it. I believe that when we start thinking about the future, we are on our way toward understanding our present.

Charles de Lint

Little (Grrl) Lost

Scritch, scritch, scritch.

There it was again.

T.J. had first realised that something was living in the walls when she'd see the cat staring at the baseboards in her bedroom. It was as though Oscar could see right through the wood, and the plaster behind it.

Back when she still thought it was mice, she kept him out of her bedroom and didn't tell anybody. She liked the idea of mice sharing this new house in a new subdivision with her family. If she mentioned it, the traps would come out, just as they had in the old farmhouse where she'd grown up, and her brother, Derek, would be waving little dead mice under her nose again. Ugh. They were so cute with those big eyes of theirs. But they were also dead and gross.

So, no. Telling anyone that the new house had mice was right out.

Instead, she listened to the *scritch*ing at night, while lying in her bed. She'd flick on her bedside light, but of course

the sound immediately stopped when she did that. It started up again shortly after the light was turned off, but it was impossible to see anything in her shadowy room—even with the curtains open and light coming in her window from the streetlight outside.

So tonight, after Mom and Dad had come in to say their good nights, she pulled her sleeping bag from under her bed and rolled it out beside the part of the wall where she heard the sound most often. Grabbing her pillow, she'd snuggled into the sleeping bag and waited, almost falling asleep before the now-familiar sound brought her wide awake again.

Scritch, scritch.

Except it wasn't really like the sound of mouse claws running around inside the walls. This close . . . she leaned her ear right up against the baseboard . . . it sounded an awful lot like voices. Which was stupid. But then she remembered a story her uncle had told her once about how sometimes, when you heard crows in the forest, they could almost sound like human voices. Like real voices, but distant enough that you just couldn't quite make out what they were saying.

That's what the *scritch*ing sounded like.

Oh, right. Like there were crows living inside the walls.

There were a lot of things she didn't like about this new house in the suburbs, but she didn't think she could logically add wall-dwelling crows to the list.

Distracted, she rolled onto her back and stared at the ceiling. She could obsess for hours on the unfairness of having had to move from their farmhouse outside of Tyson to this stupid subdivision, where everything looked pretty much the

same from one street to the next. From one *house* to the next. The first time she'd gone out riding her bike, she'd actually found herself pedalling up the wrong driveway when she was coming back home. Could you feel more stupid?

So that was a big reason to hate being here.

Nobody was very friendly either. All the kids pretty much ignored her—when they weren't making fun of her accent. But she could live with that. The friends part wasn't totally bad. Sure, she'd had to leave hers behind, but she and Julie could instant-message and e-mail all day long, and Tyson was close enough that they could theoretically take the bus to stay with each other on the weekend, though they hadn't yet.

She didn't need a new best friend because she already had one, thank you very much.

But that wasn't totally good either, because talking by phone and computer couldn't begin to be the same. Not when they used to be able to simply cut across the cornfield and just *be* at each other's house.

She missed that. She missed the farm. But most of all, she missed Red. Her handsome, sweet-tempered, mischievous Red. He—okay, technically, it—had been the perfect horse, but she'd had to give him up.

That was what was so *totally* unfair.

So, maybe it wasn't her parents' fault. She didn't understand much about the stock market, except that if you had your money in the wrong kind of investment, you could end up losing it all if the market crashed. Which was what had happened to them.

But shouldn't you be able to see that coming?

Apparently not.

Apparently, you could lose all your savings, and your family home, and have to start over fresh again, where you were supposed to put on a good face, your best foot forward, soldier on. Even when it meant you'd lost the most important thing in your life.

When you hadn't lost so much, dealing with it wasn't so hard. Mom was happy with her new job at the hospital. Dad didn't seem to mind going to an office every day instead of working out of the spare room the way he'd done pretty much forever. Even stupid Derek was happy, because now he was in a place where he could start up a real band and there were clubs where he could play. He already had a new bunch of friends, though obviously no loyalty to old ones the way she did.

Red mattered to her. Julie mattered to her.

Did anyone ever consider *her* feelings? Of course not. She was only fourteen. No one cared about what *she* thought.

It was all, "You'll make new friends."

Like her old ones weren't important.

Or, "We can't afford to board Red, T.J. Maybe in a couple of years we can get you a new horse."

But a new horse wouldn't be Red.

It was all Dad's fault for losing their money.

And Mom's for taking this stupid job—which had brought them to the city in the first place—and then acting like the change would be good for the whole family.

And Derek's for being so happy to live here.

She could feel the tears welling up behind her eyes like

they always did when she thought of her beautiful Red. Like they did when she was "just feeling sorry for herself instead of embracing life's challenges," as Mom would say. Well, she had every reason to feel sorry for herself.

Scritch, scritch.

The sound brought her back. She wiped her sleeve against her eyes, and turned to stare at the wall. She wished she had Oscar's apparent X-ray vision, because it really did sound like voices. But now, instead of being curious, she was kind of bored and irritated. She raised her fist to bang on the wall, then froze.

Because the impossible happened.

A small section of the baseboard opened as though it was a tiny door, spilling out a square of light. A girl appeared in the doorway, looking back inside. She held a duffel bag in one hand and was wearing a jean jacket over a T-shirt, a short red-and-black plaid skirt, and black clunky shoes. Her hair was a neon blue. She looked to be about sixteen or seventeen.

And stood about six inches high.

"I'm not that person," she called back to someone inside, her voice hard and angry. "I don't want to be that person. I'm *never* going to be that person and you can't stop me!"

"Tetty Wood. You come back inside this instant!" a voice called from within.

"And my name's not Tetty!" the miniature girl shouted back.

She stepped outside and slammed the baseboard door shut.

The sudden loss of light made T.J. blink in the darkness.

I've fallen asleep, she thought. Fallen asleep and started to

dream that action figures can come to life. Because that was what the girl appeared to be. The size of one of Derek's old action figures, complete with duffel-bag accessory.

But her eyes had now adjusted to the low light and there the miniature girl was. She stared back at T.J., her eyes apparently adjusting at the same time, and suddenly realising that she wasn't alone.

"Oh, crap," she said. "Don't swat me."

T.J. realized that she still had her fist in the air from when she was going to bang it against the wall.

"I thought you were mice," she said, lowering her hand.

"Do I look like a mouse?"

"No, but when I could only hear you . . . "

T.J.'s voice trailed off. She felt stupid, like she did too much of the time since they'd left the farm. And why should she? People supposedly got that way when they were nervous or scared—according to her father—but she was a hundred times bigger than this uninvited guest glaring up at her. What did she have to be scared about?

And it was *her* bedroom.

"So what *is* your name?" she asked.

It seemed the most polite question. Better than what *are* you and why are you living inside my bedroom walls?

"Elizabeth."

"But whoever was inside—"

"My uptight parents."

"—called you Tetty."

"It's a stupid nickname. *Their* stupid nickname. My name's Elizabeth."

"I'm Tara Jane, but most people call me T.J." She waited a moment, then added, "I like having a nickname."

"Whatever works for you," Elizabeth said.

She'd dropped her duffel bag to the floor and stood looking up at T.J. with her hands on her hips, a challenge in her eyes.

"So what's your damage?" she asked.

"I'm sorry?"

"For what?"

"I meant, what do you mean?" T.J. said.

Elizabeth gave a wave of her tiny hand. "Why are you sleeping on the floor when you've got a perfectly good bed?"

"I was curious about the noises I was hearing . . . "

Elizabeth laughed. "See, they've got this huge worry thing going on. 'Don't be seen.' 'Always stay hidden.' But it turns out that all their yelling was just *attracting* attention."

"You mean your parents?"

"Oh yeah. There's, like, a hundred rules and regs, and they've been drilling them into us since the day we were born."

T.J. nodded. She knew all about parents. Like the kind who just gave away your horse and moved you to some ugly subdivision, and then expected you to be happy about it.

She peered more closely at Elizabeth.

"So do you have wings?" she asked.

"Do you see wings?"

"No. I just thought they might be folded up under your jacket."

"Why would I have wings?"

"Well, aren't you a fairy?"

"Oh, please. I'm a Little."

"I can see that."

"No, it's like you saying you're a human being. A Little's what I am."

"I don't think I'd ever say that. Who goes around saying they're a human being, except maybe the Elephant Man?"

"Whatever." Elizabeth cocked her head, reminding T.J. of a bird. "So you're okay with a little person just showing up in your bedroom like this?"

"I suppose I shouldn't be—I mean, it's totally unreal, isn't it?—but I don't feel surprised at all and I don't know why."

Elizabeth nodded. "And the 'rents get all in a twist about anyone even guessing that we exist. I knew it would be no big deal."

"Well, it *could* be a big deal," T.J. said.

"How do you figure?"

"Think about it. If the world found out someone like you is real, it'd be all over the news."

"Cool. I'm so ready for my fifteen minutes of fame. Look out, world, 'cause here I come."

"I don't think it would be like that. I think it'd be more like they'd put you in a terrarium in a laboratory to study you. And everybody'd be tearing up their baseboards looking for more of you." She paused for a moment, before adding, "Do you have, like, a house back there?"

"Oh, sure. It's just all small and secret, you know, and it stretches out through the walls. But we've got all the amenities. We only moved here a few years ago, when they first built these houses, but it's totally comfortable now. My brothers

and I even dragged in an old miniature TV that we found in the garage and hooked it up to the cable. It's like big screen for us."

"So why do you want to leave?" T.J. asked. "I mean, that's what you're doing right? Running away?"

"I'm not running. I'm old enough to make my own decisions about my life."

"You don't look much older than me."

"I'm sixteen."

"That's not old enough to live on your own."

"My mother was already married and had her first kid when she was my age."

"Gross."

Elizabeth shrugged. "It's no biggie." She looked around the room. "So do you mind if I crash here with you tonight? I'd kind of like to avoid going outside until it starts to get light."

She might be two years older than me, T.J. thought, but at least I'm not afraid of the dark.

"I like it outside at night," she said. "Sometimes I sneak out and just sit and look at the sky for a while, but it's not the same here as it was back home. The sky's way duller."

"That's because of the light pollution from the city. And I'm not scared of the dark."

"Then why won't you go out at night?"

"I didn't say I couldn't. It's just not safe with cats and owls and foxes and all."

"Oh, right."

"So are you staying here on the floor? Because I want to

bed down somewhere that you won't roll over on me in the middle of the night."

"No, of course not."

T.J. threw her pillow onto the bed and got up, being careful not to drop the flap of her sleeping bag on the Little or step in her direction.

"I'm going to put on the light for a minute," she said. "Is that okay?"

"It's your room. Knock yourself out."

The bright glare blinded both of them. Blinking, T.J. went over to her dresser and took her old teddy bear out of the little stuffed chair it was sitting in. She put the chair on her night table then turned to Elizabeth.

"You can use this," she said. "I guess it's big enough to be a couch for you."

"Thanks."

"Do you want a hand up?"

Elizabeth gave her withering look. "Do I look like a cripple?"

"No, it's just . . . "

T.J.'s voice trailed off as Elizabeth opened her duffel bag and took out a length of rope with a hook on the end. The hook folded out into three prongs so that it looked like an anchor. After a couple of swings over her head, up it went, catching in the cloth of the comforter at the top of the bed. She gave the rope an experimental tug. When she was satisfied it would hold her weight, she slung her duffel onto her back, using its handles as straps, and shimmied up the rope.

"Wow," T.J. said. "You're strong. I am so useless trying to do ropes in gym."

Elizabeth grinned, pleased. "We learn how to get around at an early age."

She worked the hook out of the comforter and coiled the rope, then walked across the top of the bed and jumped over to the night table. It was only a few inches, but when T.J. worked out the proportions, she realised it would be like her jumping over a gap as wide as her own height.

Elizabeth acted like it was no big deal. Dumping her duffel and the rope on the top of the night table, she stretched out on the chair. It wasn't quite a couch for her, but easily big enough that she could lounge comfortably in it.

T.J. got into bed and lay down with her head facing her guest.

"I still can't believe you're real," she said.

"Get used to it. The world's a big and strange place, my dad says, and just because you haven't seen a thing doesn't mean it doesn't exist."

"Obviously."

It was funny. Elizabeth said she hated her parents, but when she'd mentioned her dad just now, she seemed kind of proud of him.

"Will they come looking for you?" she asked. "Your parents?"

"I doubt it. They'll be totally freaking right now that you've seen me. They're probably packing up and moving the whole family out as we speak."

"They don't have to do that. I won't tell anyone."

"That doesn't mean anything to them. You could promise on

whatever you care for the most and they figure you'll tell anyway. 'Don't trust a Big.' That's, like, one of the major rules."

T.J. was insulted.

"Hey, don't look so bummed. It's not personal. That's just what they believe. And it's worse 'cause you're a kid, and in the world of my parents, kids only do what they're supposed to when you keep them under your thumb. God forbid you should have a thought of your own."

"Yeah, I know that feeling."

"So that's your horse?" Elizabeth asked, hooking a thumb in the direction of the picture of Red, which shared the night table with her chair and a small lamp.

"*Was* my horse."

"Yeah, I've heard you arguing with your parents about it. That sucks." She shook her head. "You know, it's funny, you thinking we were mice, because I had a pet mouse once. His name was Reggie."

A sweet-sad look came into her eyes and T.J. realized that this was the first time Elizabeth's features had softened. Up until that moment, she'd worn a look of steady confrontation, as though everything in the world was her enemy and she had to stand up against all of it.

"What happened to him?" she asked.

"Same as what happened to you. My parents made me get rid of him."

"But why?"

"Well, you know mice. They just poop and pee whenever they have to, no matter where they are. You can't train them. I'd take him out with me when we were foraging—for his exer-

cise and the company. The 'rents said that his pellets would make the Bigs think their house was infested with mice and they'd call in an exterminator or something, and then where would we be?"

"I like mice," T.J. said, feeling a little guilty for all the ones that had been trapped and killed back on the farm.

"What's not to like? Besides the pooping and peeing, I mean. I promised to clean up after him—like they cared or believed me. But I would have."

She sighed, then added, "I loved that old fellow. I really did. I think that's when I started to hate my parents."

"You don't really hate them."

"Don't I?" She had that hard look in her face again. "I'm surprised you don't hate yours—considering what they did."

T.J. thought about that. Her parents exasperated her, and she was still upset for what they'd done, but she didn't hate them. How could you hate your own parents?

"I just don't," she said.

"Whatever."

"So are you really going to go out into the world and let everyone know you exist?"

"No, I'm not crazy. I know it would be a horror show. When you're my size, being secret and sneaking around is about all you've got going for you. A Big could just smash me like a bug and there wouldn't be anything I could do about it."

"So what are you going to do?"

She shrugged. "I don't know. Get away from here and find someplace to live, I guess. Someplace snug, where I can have a mouse if I want one."

"You could stay here," T.J. said. "I don't know if having a mouse is the greatest idea, but I could get you a bunch of little furniture and sneak you food and stuff."

"Oh, so I could be your pet?"

"No, nothing like that. I just thought it would be fun and, you know, safe for you."

Elizabeth shook her head. "Not going to happen. Don't take this personally, but you're a little too Goody Two-shoes for my tastes and anyway, the whole purpose of going out on my own is to prove that I can do it."

T.J. would have felt insulted about being called Goody Two-shoes, except she knew she was. She did what she was told and tried to do well in school. She kept her blonde hair cut to her shoulders and she would never have worn a skirt as short as Elizabeth's.

"But who are you going to be proving it to if your family moves away?" she asked.

"That's a dumb question," Elizabeth told her.

But she had a funny look in her eyes as she said it—there for a moment, then quickly gone.

"You should turn out the light," she said. "I'd like to get some sleep before I take off in the morning."

"Okay."

T.J. reached for the light switch, then paused before turning the light off.

"I probably won't be awake when you go," she said. "I'm not much of a morning person. So, good luck, and you know, everything. I hope you find a way to be happy."

"Soon as I'm out of here, I'll be happy."

"And if you want to leave your family a note or something—to let them know that I really won't tell, I mean—you should, so that they won't move."

"Like they'd ever listen."

"Um, right. Well, good night."

"Sure. Can you get that light?"

T.J. flicked the switch and the room plunged into darkness.

Just before she fell asleep, she thought she heard Elizabeth say softly, "But just because you're a Goody Two-shoes doesn't mean I don't think you're okay."

But maybe that was only because it was something she wanted to hear.

T.J. awoke to find that Saturday had started much earlier without her; the sun was already well above the horizon. She looked at her night table. There was no Little sleeping in her teddy's stuffed armchair. There was no Little anywhere to be seen, nor any sign that there'd ever been one.

That's because you were dreaming, she told herself.

But it certainly felt as though it had been real.

She lay in bed for a while, remembering the punky six-inch-tall Elizabeth with her neon blue hair and enough attitude for a half-dozen full-size girls.

It would have been cool if she had been real.

After a while T.J. got up and turned on her computer. While she waited for it to boot up, she knelt on the floor where, in her dream, a door had opened in the baseboard. She couldn't see any sign of it now—except for maybe *there*. But that was probably only where one board had ended and another had been laid in.

When she returned to her computer, she went online and Googled the word "Little." Her screen cleared and then the first ten entries of two hundred and fifteen million appeared on her screen.

Well, that hadn't been a particularly good idea.

She tried refining the search by adding "people" and got links to toy lines, the Little People of America site, an archaeological news report on the finding of the remains of a miniature woman on an island in Indonesia—except since her head was the size of a grapefruit, she wasn't exactly tiny. T.J. scrolled through a few more pages, but nothing was useful, even if there were only some forty-seven million hits this time.

"Little magical people" got her thirty-seven hits that were closer to what she was looking for, but nothing that resembled Elizabeth.

What? she asked herself. You were expecting something from a dream to show up on the Net?

She tried "Littles" and that was no help either.

Finally, she tried "little people living behind the baseboards" and was surprised when something came up—a site called "Fairies, Ghosts and Monsters." It sounded pretty Game Boy-useless, but she clicked through anyway. It turned out to be run by a professor who used to teach at one of the local universities and contained an odd mix of stories and scholarly essays.

She found the Littles a few pages in, under "miniature secret people." The article cited literary references like *Gulliver's Travels* and *Mistress Masham's Repose*, the Borrowers of Mary Norton's books, the Brownies from a Sunday comic strip that was long gone, and the Smalls from a book written

by some old English guy named William Dunthorn.

There were two anecdotal entries, both about little people who lived behind the baseboards. One talked about "pennymen," who turned into pennies when people looked their way. And then there were the Littles. The way they were described seemed very close to what Elizabeth had told her. There was even a children's picture book about them: *The Travelling Littles*, written and illustrated by someone named Sheri Piper, who, like the professor whose Web site this was, also lived in town.

According to Piper's book, Littles had originally been birds who got too lazy to fly on after they'd found a particularly good feed. Eventually, they lost their wings and became these little people who had to live by their wits, taking up residence in people's houses, where they foraged for food and whatever else they needed.

She Googled the author, but the only links that came up were to eBay and used-book stores. Apparently, the book was long out of print, although she had written a number of others. None of those seemed to be about Littles. At least, she couldn't tell from the few links she clicked on to get more information.

She made a note of the author's name and the title of the one relevant book so that she could look them up at the library, then went to have a shower and some breakfast.

When she came into the kitchen her mother was just about to let Oscar out the back door.

"Don't let him out!" T.J. cried.

What if he came upon Elizabeth's scent and tracked her down to where she was hiding?

Her imaginary scent, the logical part of her corrected.

"Why ever not?" her mother asked.

"Because . . . I . . . I want to brush him first."

Her mother gave her a look that said, "When have you *ever* willingly brushed the cat?"

"Can you just leave him in?" T.J. asked. "Just until I've had breakfast and can brush him."

"Stop you from taking on a responsibility?" her mother said. "Not this mom."

"Ha ha."

But her mother left the cat inside. Oscar complained at the door, then shot T.J. a dirty look as though he was well aware of who was responsible for his lack of freedom before he stalked off down the hall.

T.J. poured herself some orange juice and took a box of cereal from the cupboard before joining her mother at the kitchen table.

"We're almost out of milk," her mother said. "Better use it before your dad gets up and takes it for his coffee."

"I will."

"So what has you up so early? Surely not just to brush the cat."

Saturday morning everyone in the house slept in except for T.J.'s mother. Back on the farm, T.J. had gotten up early, too, but she didn't have Red to look after anymore, and so had gotten into the habit of staying up late at night and sleeping in as long as possible.

T.J. shrugged. "Maybe I'm turning over a new leaf."

"Well, I'm happy for the company."

T.J. shook cereal into her bowl. She looked over at her mother as she reached for the milk.

"So, when you were a kid," she said, "did anyone ever take something away from you that you really, really cared about?"

Her mother sighed. "Please, T.J. I know you feel terrible about having to give up Red. Believe it or not, *I* feel terrible about it, too. But we have to move on."

"No, I didn't mean that. I was wondering about *you*. What did you do? How did you move on?"

Did you make up imaginary six-inch-high Littles to help you cope? she added to herself.

"Why are you asking me this?"

"I don't know. I . . . "

T.J. knew she couldn't talk about the Littles. For one thing, she'd promised not to. For another, her mom would think she was nuts. So she improvised.

"It's just there was this girl in the park yesterday," she said, "and we got to talking about . . . you know, stuff. And it turns out she was running away from home because she hates her parents, and the reason she hates them—or at least the main one, I guess—is that they made her get rid of her . . . um, pet dog that she'd had forever. So I was wondering—"

"What's her name?" her mother asked. "We need to tell her parents."

"*Mom*. We can't do that. It's not our business."

Her mother shook her head. "Sometimes we have to

involve ourselves in other people's lives, whether they want us to or not."

"Well, I don't know anything about her. I don't even know if she lives around here. I just met her in the park and she was already on her way."

"T.J., this is serious."

"I know. But it's something that's already done, and that wasn't the point of it anyway."

Her mother studied her for a moment.

"Do you hate us?" she asked.

T.J. shook her head. "I get mad whenever I think of how you made me lose Red, but . . . I don't know. It's not like it'd make me hate you."

"Thank God for that."

"Not like I hate living here."

"We've been through the why of it a hundred times."

"I know. I was just mentioning it, since you brought it up."

Her mother gave her a look.

"Okay," T.J. said. "So I did. But you still didn't answer my question."

"What exactly are you worried about?"

"That I'll end up hating you like this Elizabeth does her parents. So that's why I was wondering if something like this had ever happened to you."

"No," her mother said. "It never did. And don't think either your father or I are even remotely happy that things have turned out this way. We know how much you loved that horse."

"Red. His name's Red."

T.J. had to look down at her cereal and blink back the start of tears. Her mother's hand reached across the table and held hers.

"I know, sweetheart," she said. "I really am so sorry."

"I guess."

"And I don't think you'll start hating us—at least I hope to God you won't, because that would be just too much to bear. But if we can still have a talk like this, then I think we're okay."

Except they weren't, T.J. thought. At least she wasn't.

She didn't hate her parents. But that didn't help the big hole in her chest where Red used to be.

T.J. dutifully brushed Oscar after breakfast—a chore that neither of them appreciated very much—then reluctantly, she let him outside. Surely, Elizabeth would have taken cats into account and hidden herself away in some place where they wouldn't be able to find her. Assuming Elizabeth was even real.

And speaking of real . . . once she'd closed the door behind the cat, she went up to her room and knelt down by the wall where last night a little door had opened in the baseboard.

"I don't know if you're still in there," she said, "or if you can even trust me—but I just want you to know that no matter what happens, your secret's safe with me. I mean, it's not like someone hasn't already written a book about you, and you *can* be looked up on the Web. But I won't add my two cents—not even if someone asks me, point-blank. I already

lied to my mother about you, and I hated having to do that. I've never done it before. But that's how seriously I take keeping my word."

There was no reply.

Well, she hadn't exactly been expecting one. It was just something she felt she'd needed to say.

A week went by, and then another. T.J. didn't hear any more noises behind the baseboards. She didn't see any little people, or even signs of them. She did find *The Travelling Littles* at the library and read it. The book didn't tell her any more than she'd already known from Elizabeth and the Web site. It was kind of a little kids' story, but she liked the artwork. The Littles in the pictures were old-fashioned, but old-fashioned in an interesting way.

Goody Two-shoes, she remembered Elizabeth saying.

Maybe she should get a new haircut—something cooler.

She laughed at the thought. Right. Get a makeover because of a put-down by an imaginary, miniature girl.

But that was the odd thing about it. Although she was about ninety-five percent sure she'd just dreamed the whole business, the memory of it didn't go away the way dreams usually did. She kept finding herself worrying about Elizabeth, out there in the big world on her own. And what about her family? What had happened to them? Had they moved? They must have moved, because it was so quiet behind the walls now. Even Oscar had stopped staring at the baseboards.

But maybe they were just being really, *really* careful now.

They had some of Sheri Piper's other books in the library,

and she was surprised to find a second book about the Littles. It was called *Mr. Pennyinch's Wings* and was about how the Littles regained their ability to turn into birds. She wondered if Elizabeth and her family knew about it.

Of course, it was just a book. That didn't mean the story was real.

It didn't even mean Littles were real. Just that someone was writing about them.

She was true to her word and never said anything to anyone. The only time she felt guilty was when she was talking on the phone to Julie. They'd never had secrets before and now she had a Big One.

Maybe this was what happened when best friends were separated by a distance. You started keeping things to yourself, then you started calling each other less. And then finally, you stopped being best friends. She hoped that wasn't going to happen, but there'd already been a day last week when she hadn't phoned or messaged Julie.

The thought made her feel sad and sent her into a whole blue mood that started with Julie, and took her all the way back to the memory of the day they'd had to walk Red into the horse trailer and take him to his new home.

The closest she came to telling Julie was a week after she'd had her encounter with Elizabeth, when they were on the phone.

"Have you ever seen a fairy?" T.J. found herself asking.

"Oh, sure. Duncan's father is supposed to be one."

"Really?"

"That's what Melissa told me. But you shouldn't call them that. Just say they're gay."

"No, I meant a real fairy."

Julie started to laugh. "What, with little wings and everything? God, what's that city doing to you? I thought only country bumpkins like me were supposed to believe in things like that."

"I still feel like a bumpkin."

"So does that mean *you* believe in fairies?" Julie asked.

Elizabeth hadn't had wings, T.J. thought, so technically, she couldn't be considered a fairy and there was no need to lie.

"Of course I don't," she said.

"So are there *any* cute guys there or what?"

"There's lots of cute guys. They just never think *I'm* cute."

"The dummies."

"Totally."

T.J. had taken to brushing Oscar on a regular basis.

It had started out as a continuation of her cover-up that first morning when Elizabeth had run away, but now they'd both come to enjoy it. T.J. would sit with Oscar out on the back porch, where the view of the one maple and three spruce in the yard let her pretend she was still back on the farm. At least, it worked if she looked up into their branches, instead of across at the neighbour's backyard.

She'd hold the cat on her lap and brush him with long gentle strokes, carefully working out the mats. Oscar would soon start purring and T.J. would slip into the same sort of

contemplative mood that used to come over her when she was currying Red.

She was staring dreamily off into space one morning, hand on a sleeping Oscar, the brushing long finished, when her brother, Derek, interrupted her.

"Hey, doofus," he said. "Still playing with dolls?"

When she looked up, he tossed something at her. She caught it before she could see what it was, startling Oscar, who bolted across the lawn.

"You are such a moron," she started to tell him.

But then she looked at the small duffel bag she held in her hand and she could feel her face go pale. Luckily, Derek didn't appear to notice.

"Where did you get this?" she asked him, standing up.

"In the shed. Or should we start calling it the dolly house?"

"In the shed?"

"Yeah. I needed to replace the brake on my in-line skates and was looking for my spare. That thing fell off a shelf when I was moving some boxes around. What were *you* doing in there with your dollies?"

"Nothing."

He cocked his head, then asked, "So it's not yours?"

"Did you look inside it?"

"Sure. It's full of doll clothes."

Of course it would seem that way, T.J. thought. It belonged to Elizabeth. Who was real. How long had she been living in the shed? Was she even still there? Had Derek crushed her, moving around boxes?

Derek was still looking at her. To cover for Elizabeth, T.J. swallowed her pride.

"Of course it's mine. I was just . . . you know . . . "

Derek laughed. "Nope, I don't. And I don't want to either."

He grinned at her and walked off, shaking his head.

She waited until he'd gone around the side of the house and into the garage, then ran for the shed. It was hard to see in there, shadows deepening the farther she looked. It smelled icky, like machinery and the gas for the mower.

"Elizabeth?" she called softly. "Are you in here?"

There was no answer.

Oh God. She'd been eaten by a cat. Or a . . . a weasel or something.

"Elizabeth, please say something."

She looked everywhere, but there was nobody to be found. Especially not a six-inch Little with bright blue hair.

It was all T.J. could think about for the rest of the day.

She went back into the shed twice more with no better luck. That night, lying in bed, she couldn't stand it. She certainly couldn't sleep. So she got dressed, found a flashlight, and went back out to the shed once more, the little duffel bag stuck in the pocket of her jacket.

She'd never been afraid of the dark, but it was spookier than she liked at the back of the yard. The shed door made a loud creak when she opened it and she stood silent, holding her breath. But no lights came on in the house behind her. Allowing herself to breathe again, she flicked on the flashlight and stepped inside.

The first thing its beam found was a disheveled Elizabeth sitting on a spool of wire on the middle shelf. She blocked the light from her eyes with one hand and frowned.

T.J. aimed the light at the floor.

"Thank God you're okay," she said.

"Piss off."

"What?"

"I said, piss off. I don't need your stupid sympathy. I'm doing just fine, okay?"

"But why are you still here?"

"Maybe I like it here."

T.J. never liked to make trouble or impose where she obviously wasn't wanted. It was what was making it so hard for her to make new friends in the neighbourhood and at school. So her first inclination was to leave Elizabeth alone. But then she remembered what her mother had said.

Sometimes we have to involve ourselves in other people's lives, whether they want us to or not.

"I don't think you do," T.J. said. "God, what have you been living on out here?"

She didn't add that it was obvious Elizabeth could really use a bath and to wash her hair.

Elizabeth shrugged. "I found an old bag of birdseed and put out a container to catch rainwater."

"You have to come back to the house with me. I'll get you some real food."

"They're gone, aren't they?"

"You mean your family?"

"No, the zits on your butt. Of *course* I mean my family."

"I don't know," T.J. said. "Maybe they're just being really quiet."

"No, they're gone."

"I guess . . . "

"So what's the point of going back? It would have been horrible going back, having to admit they were right. I *can't* survive out here on my own. But now they're not even there."

"So what's the point of staying out here?" T.J. asked.

Elizabeth shrugged. "It's what I deserve for being such an idiot."

"Now you're just talking stupid."

Elizabeth looked up at her, eyes flashing.

"Remember what I said when you came in?" she asked. "Why don't you just do it? Piss off and leave me alone."

T.J. didn't move.

"Look," Elizabeth said. "You have no idea what it's like being me. Not having friends. Living somewhere you don't want, with people who don't understand you. Okay? So don't pretend *you* understand and can somehow make it better."

"You are so full of crap," T.J. said.

"What?"

"You act so brave, but here you still are, hiding out in my shed."

"You don't think I'd go if I could? But the night's full of owls and cats and the day's full of hawks and dogs and more cats. The few times I've tried to get away, I almost got eaten alive!"

"So what? You think you're the only person to feel scared or alone? Do you think I have all kinds of kids falling over me, wanting to be my friend? Do you think I don't miss the farm and Red?"

"At least you're a normal size."

"Oh yeah. That makes it really easy."

Elizabeth glared at her. "So what's your big point?"

"God, you are such a piece of work," T.J. snapped. "I should just wrap some tape around that big mouth of yours, stick you in a padded envelope and mail you somewhere."

Elizabeth's eyes widened a little. And then she actually smiled.

"Wow," she said.

"Wow what?'

"You do have some backbone."

T.J. wasn't sure if she should feel complimented or insulted. That old "Goody Two-shoes" comment still rankled.

"Sorry, I wasn't being snarky," Elizabeth added.

"Did I just hear you apologise?"

Elizabeth went on as though T.J. hadn't spoken. "It's just you go around and let everybody walk all over you."

"I don't. I just like to get along."

"Even if you don't get your way?"

T.J. sighed. "It's not like that. It's not all about getting your own way. Sometimes there's a bigger picture. Sure, I hate that we moved. And I really, really hated having to give up Red. But we're still a family and things had to change because . . . because they just did. It wasn't anybody's fault. It's just how it worked out."

"So you just go along with it?"

"Yes. No. I don't know. I'm trying to make the best of it, okay? Which is more than I can say for you. All you do is go around with a big chip on your shoulder. How does that make it better for you or anybody around you?"

"You're probably right."

T.J. blinked in surprise. "I am?"

Elizabeth shrugged. "Well, look where it's got me so far."

Neither of them said anything for a long moment.

"So do you want to come back to the house?" T.J. finally asked.

"I guess."

"We could try to find your family," T.J. went on. "Or some other Littles. I could carry you so that you don't have to worry about being attacked or anything."

"Like a pet."

T.J. rolled her eyes. "No, like a friend."

"I guess . . . "

"You know there's books about Littles."

Elizabeth nodded. "One, at least. None of us can figure out how she got the story so right."

"She's written a new one."

Elizabeth raised her eyebrows.

"It's about how the Littles have learned to turn back into birds. You know, like werewolves or something. They can just go back and forth and they don't even have to wait for a full moon."

"No way."

T.J. shrugged. "Well, it's just a book."

"Yeah, but her other one was dead-on."

"So maybe we could look her up. She lives here—or at least in the city."

Elizabeth got up and brushed the dust from her very short, very dirty skirt. It didn't do much good.

"I *am* kind of hungry," she said. "For real food, I mean."

"We've got plenty."

"And I'm dying to be clean again."

"We've got water, too."

Elizabeth nodded. "So . . . thanks, T.J. I guess I'll take you up on your hospitality."

"Do you . . . um, want to go under your own steam?"

"Instead of being carried like a pet?"

"It wouldn't be—"

Elizabeth smiled. "I know. I'm just pushing your buttons. Yeah, I'd appreciate the lift."

T.J. laid her hand palm-up on the shelf beside the Little. When Elizabeth climbed on, she carefully cupped her hand a little and stuck up a finger for Elizabeth to hang on to. Elizabeth didn't hesitate to use it.

"So where does this writer live again?" she asked as T.J. lifted her into the air.

"The librarian said somewhere downtown."

"I wonder how hard she'd be to find?"

"Shh," T.J. told her as she stepped out of the shed. "You're supposed to be a secret, remember?"

"Maybe you could mail me to her."

"Shh."

"But in a box. With padding and airholes . . . "

"Really, you need to shush."

"Can't you just imagine her face when she opens it and out I pop?"

"*Shh.*"

But they couldn't stop giggling softly as they made their way back into the house.

❧ ❧ ❧

Charles de Lint has been a seventeen-time finalist for the World Fantasy Award, winning in 2000 for the short story collection *Moonlight and Vines,* which is set in his popular fictional city of Newford. *Medicine Road, Quicksilver and Shadow,* and *The Blue Girl* are the most recent of his many novels, illustrated novellas, and story collections. He is also the author of *A Circle of Cats,* a children's picture book illustrated by Charles Vess.

De Lint is a respected critic in his field, and is currently the primary book reviewer for *The Magazine of Fantasy and Science Fiction.*

A professional musician for over twenty-five years, specializing in traditional and contemporary Celtic and American roots music, he frequently performs with his wife, MaryAnn Harris—fellow musician, artist, and kindred spirit. They live in Ottawa, Ontario, Canada.

Visit Charles de Lint's Web site at **www.charlesdelint.com** and MaryAnn Harris's at **www.reclectica.com**.

Author's Note

I've always had a fondness for little people living hidden on the periphery of our lives, from Gulliver's Lilliputians (both in Swift's book, and in T. H. White's *Mistress Masham's Repose*) to the Brownies from the old Sunday colour comics. I've explored the theme before in books such as *The Little Country*

(1991) and short stories like "The Pennymen" (which was reprinted in *Moonlight and Vines*, 1999) and "Big City Littles" (*Tapping the Dream Tree*, 2002), but this story is the first time I've done it with contemporary teenage characters, and I have to say, I had the best time visiting with them.

Diana Wynne Jones

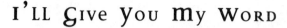

I'LL GIVE YOU MY WORD

People were always asking Jethro, "How do you *manage* with a brother like yours?"

Jethro mostly smiled and answered, "No problem. He makes me laugh."

This was not really a lie. Jethro used to laugh a lot in the days when he and Jeremy shared a bedroom and Jeremy used to kneel up in his bunk-bed every morning, rocking from side to side and singing—to a tune he had made up himself—"Computers, computers. Caramel custard computers." He sang until Dad banged on the wall and shouted that it was only *dawn,* for goodness' sake, and would Jeremy just *shut up!* At this Jeremy would turn his very knowing big blue eyes toward Jethro, a small smile would flit across his mouth, and he would sing in a whisper, "Collapsed cardinal caramel custard computers!" Jeremy had a way of making his face into a solemn egg-shape and staring crazily into the space between Jethro's head and the window while he uttered, "Sweet cervical béchamel with empirical gladiolus." This never failed

to send Jethro off into squeals of laughter. And their father banged on the walls again.

But Jethro's problem was that he was a worrier. In those days he worried that he would stop breathing in the night or that he would prick himself in his sleep and lose all the blood in his body, so that it was always a relief to be woken by Jeremy's singing. When eventually their father, Graeme, got so sick of the singing that he cleared out the box room at the end of the passage and their mother, Annabelle, made it into a bedroom for Jeremy, Jethro started to worry about Jeremy too. Jeremy took to wandering round the house then, saying things. "Ponderous plenipotential cardomum," he would say. "In sacks." And after a bit, "Sententious purple coriander."

"Does that come in sacks too?" Jethro asked him.

"No," Jeremy said. "In suitcases."

"What does *plenipotential* mean?" Jethro asked. "Or *sententious*?"

Jeremy just made his face egg-shaped and stared crazily over Jethro's head. At first Jethro thought that Jeremy was simply inventing these words, and he worried that his brother was mad. But then it occurred to Jethro to look them up in one of the many dictionaries in their house, and he found they were real. *Plenipotential* meant *possessing full power and authority* and *sententious* meant *tending to indulge in pompous moralizing*. And it was the same with all the other words Jeremy kept coming up with: they were always in one dictionary or another, although Jethro was fairly sure Jeremy had no idea what any of the words meant. He began worrying about how they got into Jeremy's head.

Their house was full of dictionaries. Graeme and Annabelle's main work was running an agency called Occult Security, which protected clients of all kinds from magical dangers, exorcised haunts and cleansed evil from houses; but this agency did not pay very well and there were long intervals between commissions. So when they were not getting rid of malign spirits or clearing out gremlins from factories, they both did other things. Annabelle wrote little books called Hall's Guides to Witchcraft and Graeme feverishly composed crossword puzzles for several newspapers. There were three computers in the house, one devoted to Occult Security, one on which Annabelle pattered away, frowning and murmuring, "Now is that strictly shamanism, or should it go under folk magic?" and a third full of hundreds of black and white square patterns and lists of words. Graeme was usually to be found in front of this one, irritably tapping a very sharp pencil and muttering, "I want something Q something something *K* here and I'm not sure there *is* a word." Then he would reach for one of the wall of dictionaries behind his desk.

Jethro began to suspect that these dictionaries—or maybe the computers or the crosswords—were leaking into his brother's brain.

Meanwhile Jeremy was marching round the house chanting, "Borborygmata, borborygmata!"

Jethro looked this one up too and found that it meant *rumblings of the stomach.* "Mum," he said. "Dad, I think this is serious."

Graeme shook his head and laughed. "You'd think he had a direct line to a dictionary somewhere."

"Yes," said Jethro, "but *how*?"

"You worry too much, my love," Annabelle said. "He probably only wants his lunch. I'd better stop this and find him some food."

"But it's not *natural*!" Jethro said. "And he doesn't know what any of his words *mean*. *Ask* him!"

Graeme bent down to Jeremy and said, "Jeremy, old son, have you any idea what *borborygmata* means?"

Jeremy went egg-shaped and angelical and answered, "Avocado pears."

"That's just your favourite food, old son," Graeme explained. "It means tummy rumblings."

"I know," Jeremy said, looking crazily over Graeme's right shoulder. "With pendulous polyps."

"You see!" said Jethro. "He can't go on like this! What happens when he starts school?"

"I think school will cure him," Annabelle said. "You have to remember we're a rather special household here. When Jeremy discovers that none of the other children talk like he does, he'll stop doing it—you'll see."

Jethro had nothing like Mum's faith in this. The week before Jeremy started school, Jethro took his brother outside and tried to explain to him that school was very different from home. "You have to speak normally there," he said, "or everyone will laugh at you."

Jeremy nodded placidly. "You laugh at me."

"No, *not* like I laugh at you," Jethro said. "I mean they'll *jeer*. Some of them may hit you for being peculiar."

"Cacophonous incredulity," Jeremy retorted. "Turnip

fondue." And then went back indoors. Jethro sighed.

He worried a lot about Jeremy when school actually started. Jeremy was put in Miss Heathersay's class. Miss Heathersay was known to be a really nice, understanding teacher. If anyone could deal with Jeremy, Jethro hoped it was Miss Heathersay. He watched anxiously that afternoon as Jeremy came out with the rest of the class, ready to go home. Jeremy sauntered out, serene and angelic, as if nothing at all had happened to disturb him, and smiled blindingly when he saw Jethro. Jethro noticed that a crowd of other little kids followed after Jeremy, looking awed and maybe even respectful.

"What happened?" Jethro asked. "Did you talk normally?"

"Replenishment," Jeremy replied. "Hirsute haplography."

Whatever that meant, it was all Jeremy would say. Jethro never did manage to find out how his brother got on in Miss Heathersay's class, except that it seemed perfectly peaceful there. No one complained. Nobody seemed inclined to bully Jeremy. All that happened was that more and more people came up to Jethro and asked, "How do you *manage* with a brother like that?" Jethro got very used to answering, "No problem. He makes me laugh." Which was only half a lie, because Jethro *did* laugh at Jeremy even while he worried about him more than ever.

All through the summer holidays that followed Jeremy's first school year, Jethro laughed and worried. Annabelle and Graeme were very busy sitting over the Occult computer, trying to solve the problem of a lady Town Councillor who kept hearing voices, and whether it was because that computer was leaking or for some other reason, Jeremy came up

with a new set of strange words every half hour or so.

"Impermanent epistemological urethra," he remarked to Jethro in exactly the same tone of voice ordinary people would say, "Nice day, isn't it?" At Jethro's worried stare, the knowing look came into Jeremy's round blue eyes and he added, "Febrile potlatch, don't you think?"

Jethro's worry turned to giggles as he looked these words up in several dictionaries. *Urethra* meant *the canal that in most mammals carries urine from the bladder out of the body*. He told Jeremy it did and Jeremy answered, "Obloquy," with a cheerful smile.

"Do go and laugh somewhere else, you two," Annabelle implored them. She and Graeme were leaning over a recording they had managed to make of the Town Councillor's voices. It was faint and far off and ghostly.

"These are real," Graeme said. "Mrs Callaghan is certainly not imagining them."

"And she's not going mad either," Annabelle agreed. "I'm so glad for her, Graeme."

"No, they're being broadcast to her somehow," said Graeme. "Someone's playing a very unkind psychic trick on the poor lady. Now, how do we make life bearable for her while we track down who's doing it?"

"Earplugs?" Jethro suggested, on his way to the dictionary to find out what *obloquy* meant.

"Now that's a very good idea," Graeme said. He pointed his beautifully sharpened pencil at Jethro in the way that meant "Congratulations!"—which was almost exactly the opposite of *obloquy,* Jethro discovered. "Occult earplugs," Graeme said.

"How do we go about making some, Annabelle?" He and Annabelle began tapping keys and bringing up diagrams.

"Scrutinizing congenial tinnitus," Jeremy remarked, coming in to look at the diagrams. "Pending conglomerate haruspication."

"Shut up, Jeremy! Go away!" both his parents commanded.

"Toads," Jeremy said disgustedly, "implicated in paradigms of exponential frogspawn."

He went away, and Jethro pulled down the dictionary again. But Jeremy kept coming back while his parents were doing delicate wiring on two deaf-aids and leaning between them to make remarks such as, "Subaverage nucleosis," or, "Tendentious bromoids."

At last Graeme said, "Jeremy, we are very busy with something very small and delicate that we have to get *right.* If you don't want your neck wrung, go *away*!"

"Halitosis," Jeremy said. "You never have time for *me.*"

"Play with him, Jethro," Annabelle said, "and I'll double your pocket money."

"But he's so boring," Jethro objected. "He only knows Snap."

"So teach him a new game," Graeme said "Just get out, the pair of you."

Jethro gloomily took Jeremy away and tried to teach him to keep goal in football. It was no good. Jeremy always dived the wrong way like a goalkeeper missing a penalty and the football kept going over into the road. But Jethro had to keep playing with Jeremy, all that summer, because Graeme and Annabelle soon grew busier yet. While they were still trying to trace the person who was broadcasting Mrs Callaghan's voices, trekking

out at night with earphones and backpacks of equipment, Mrs Callaghan was wearing the deaf-aids. These earplugs cut out the broadcast so effectively that Mrs Callaghan became convinced that Occult Security had already solved her problem. She recommended Graeme and Annabelle to everyone else on the Council. The consequence was that the Lord Mayor ordered psychic protection around the Council Building, several Councillors requested their homes made safe against occult invasion, and—while Annabelle began worrying that she was not going to meet her deadline with her latest Guide to Witchcraft—Jack Smith, the local Member of Parliament, came to visit them in person.

"Elephantiasis," Jeremy said. Jack Smith was indeed rather fat.

Jack Smith was convinced that he was being persecuted by a coven of witches. "It's hard to explain—it's so nebulous," he said, rubbing his fat hands nervously together. "Most nights I wake up with a jump, thinking I've been hearing horrible strident laughter, and then I can't get to sleep again. Or I become quite sure someone is walking softly about in the house, when I *know* I'm the only person there. And if I have an important speech, or an urgent journey to make, I'm sure to get ill in some way. It happens too often to be an accident. By now I feel quite awful, and I'm getting a name for being a shirker too. The Party Chairman has said hard words to me—and all the time I feel as if something malevolent is watching me and sniggering at my misfortunes."

"It sounds more like a curse," Annabelle said. "What makes you think it's witches?"

"Stridently nebulous," Jeremy explained to her. "Perforated herrings."

Jack Smith shot him an astonished look. Graeme sighed. "Jethro," he said, "take your brother away and teach him another game, or I won't answer for the consequences."

"I've taught him everything I can *think* of," Jethro said sulkily. "I've even invented—Oh, all *right*," he said hastily as his father started to get up. "But don't blame me if we break something."

So they played cricket and Jeremy somehow bowled a ball backwards and broke the kitchen window. Jethro protested that it was not *his* fault. "I was only acting under orders," he said.

"Follow your orders out in the park next time," Annabelle told him, "or I might be tempted to use an unkind spell on you. Look at this mess! My saucepans all full of glass!"

"With you two about, who needs witches?" Graeme grumbled, fetching the broom. "As if we haven't enough to do with Jack Smith's coven."

By the end of that summer, Graeme and Annabelle were still nowhere near discovering Jack Smith's witches. "They're coming in out of the astral plane, obviously," they kept telling each other anxiously. "We have to protect him *there,* as well as physically."

"I suspect they're the same lot as Mrs Callaghan's," the other would reply. "We have to locate that coven and close it down."

But the witches proved to be very well hidden indeed. Graeme filled and surrounded Jack Smith's house with every

detection device he could think of, with tracers on each device to lead him to the coven. And no tracers led anywhere. Not one sniff or sound of a witch could be detected. In the end, he simply enfolded Jack Smith himself with a hundred different protections and went on looking. Jack Smith arrived, rubbing his hands and smiling, saying he felt much better now. "My dear fellow," he said to Graeme, "the two of you are like hounds. Never let go of a scent, do you?"

"We don't like to leave a thing like this unsolved," Graeme said. "Neither of us do. But you don't need to go on paying us. It's something we both feel we have to do."

"My dear fellow," Jack Smith said. "My dear lady."

Things were at this stage when the boys started school again. Jethro was now in the top class, the last one before he moved up into the senior school. Every lesson seemed to start with, "You'll be in trouble in Seniors if you don't learn this *now*," or, "Everyone in Seniors has to know this before they begin." To a worrier like Jethro this was seriously alarming. He lay awake at night worrying about the way he was going to arrive to Seniors knowing nothing and be punished for it. And as if this was not enough, Jeremy was put in Miss Blythe's class.

Miss Blythe was notoriously strict. People made rude drawings of her in her tight purple sweater and big round glasses. She had a beaky nose and thin black hair that frizzed out around her angry owl-face. All the best drawings did her as an owl with thick legs and clumpy shoes and these often looked very like Miss Blythe indeed. In Miss Blythe's class no one was allowed to talk or fool about, and they had to form

up in lines before they did anything. Miss Blythe called the ones who never talked or played and who formed up in lines quickest her little flowers. The best ones were called her little daisies. You could always tell someone who had been in Miss Blythe's class by their subdued, frightened look and by the way they sat with their hands primly folded and their feet side by side. It was said they were trying to be daisies. Jethro could not imagine Jeremy being made into a daisy. He worried about that almost as much as he worried about Seniors.

For a fortnight nothing much seemed to happen. Then, one lunchtime, Jethro stood in the playground and watched Miss Blythe's class come outside, walking in a line as usual. As usual, Jeremy was about halfway along the line, looking more than usually egg-shaped and angelic. Jethro paused long enough to see that Jeremy was there and turned away to his friends, who were worrying about Seniors too.

The next moment, Jeremy came charging out of the line straight towards Jethro. He flung both arms round Jethro and butted his face into Jethro's chest.

"Hey!" Jethro said. "What's up with you?"

Jeremy said nothing. He just butted harder. People began gathering round to stare.

"Now, look—" Jethro was beginning, when Miss Blythe came shooting out of the school and advanced on Jethro and Jeremy with big strides.

"Jeremy Hall, "Miss Blythe said, "did I or did I not order you to stay behind and wash your mouth out with soap?"

Jeremy just clutched Jethro harder. Jethro realised he was supposed to protect Jeremy, although he was not sure how.

He looked up at Miss Blythe. She was even more like the rude drawings than he had known. She glared like an angry owl.

"Jeremy Hall," said Miss Blythe, "let go at once and look at me!"

Jethro, feeling distinctly brave, said, "What has my brother done wrong?"

"Disobeyed me," snapped Miss Blythe. "Went out with the others when I *told* him not to, and now he's behaving like a baby! After he said such things!"

Jeremy turned his head sideways. He said, "I only said words."

"Don't you contradict *me*!" Miss Blythe said. "Indoors at once! Now!"

"Shan't," said Jeremy, and he added, "Hendiadys."

Miss Blythe gasped. "*What* did you call me?"

Jeremy repeated it. "Hendiadys."

At this Miss Blythe made a noise somewhere between a growl and a scream and seized hold of Jeremy's arm. "For this," she said, "you are going to come with me to the Headmaster this instant, my boy. Come along." She pulled, irresistibly. Jeremy was forced to go where she pulled. But, since he refused to let go of Jethro, Jethro was forced to go too. Like this, watched by nearly the entire school, Jethro shuffled with Jeremy's head in his stomach, into the school, along a corridor and to the door of the Headmaster's study. MR GARDNER, said the notice on this door. HEADMASTER.

Miss Blythe gave the notice an angry bang, flung the door open and dragged both boys inside. Mr Gardner looked up with a jump from his egg sandwich. Jethro could see he did

not like being disturbed in the middle of his lunch. "What is this about?" he said.

"Mr Gardner," said Miss Blythe, "I demand that you expel this boy from the school at *once*!"

"Which one?" Mr Gardner asked. "There are two of them, Miss Blythe."

Miss Blythe looked down and was clearly surprised to find she had brought Jethro along as well. "The small one of course," she said. "Jeremy Hall. He does nothing but make trouble."

Mr Gardner looked at Jeremy. Jeremy turned his face out of Jethro's stomach to give Mr Gardner an abnormally egg-shaped and angelic look. Mr Gardner gave the look a strong scrutiny and did not, to Jethro's alarm, seem to be convinced by it. "He's not a troublemaker, sir," Jethro said. "Honestly. He's just strange."

Mr Gardner looked at Jethro then. "And why are *you* here?" he said.

Jethro began to feel rather like a lawyer called in when the police have just arrested a criminal. "He's my brother, sir," he said.

"Can't he speak for himself, then?" Mr Gardner asked.

"Speak? I should just think he can speak," Miss Blythe burst out. "Do you know what this child has just called me, Mr Gardner? Hendiadys, Mr. Gardner. He said it twice too! Hendiadys."

A strange look came over Mr Gardner's face. "And what, exactly, Miss Blythe," he asked, "do you take 'hendiadys' to mean?"

"Some sort of bird, I imagine," Miss Blythe said. "It was an obvious insult anyway."

Jethro, feeling more like a lawyer than ever, cut in hastily, "My cli—er—brother—er, Jeremy never knows what any of his words mean, sir."

"Really?" said Mr Gardner. "Well, Jeremy, what *does* 'hendiadys' mean?"

Jeremy's eyes went round and gazed over Mr Gardner's shoulder. He contrived to look sweetly baffled. "Mouse eggs?" he suggested.

"Jethro," said Mr. Gardner. "Your turn to guess now."

"I—er—think it could be a kind of crocodile," Jethro guessed. He tried to ignore the venomous glare he got from Miss Blythe.

"Do you indeed?" Mr Gardner turned and picked up the dictionary lying beside his lunch. "Let's see what the truth of the matter is," he said, turning pages with an expert whip-whip-whip. "Oh yes. Here we are. 'Hendiadys, *noun*, a rhetorical device by which two nouns joined by a conjunction, usually *and,* are used instead of a noun and a modifier, as in *to run with fear and haste* instead of *to run with fearful haste*.' Did you know that?" he asked Jeremy.

Jeremy looked stunned and shook his head.

"Neither did I," admitted Mr Gardner. "But it isn't a kind of crocodile, is it? Miss Blythe, I fail to see that a rhetorical device by which two nouns et cetera can possibly be any form of insult, quite honestly. I suspect we have a personality clash here. Jethro, take your brother home. You can have the afternoon off. Jeremy, you are suspended from school for half a day

while Miss Blythe and I talk this matter over. Off you go."

They went, thankfully scooting under Miss Blythe's purple arm. Before they reached the door, Miss Blythe was slapping her hand down on Mr Gardner's desk and saying, "I don't care what that word means, it was *intended* as an insult! That child is nothing but trouble. I ask them all to say what flower they're going to be, and what does he say?"

"I said I'd be *Rhus radicans*," Jeremy said when they were outside. "That's a flower. She made me stand out in front all morning. I don't like her."

"I don't blame you. She's a hag," said Jethro. "What do we tell Mum and Dad?"

As it happened, they did not have to tell their parents anything. They arrived home to a scene of excitement. A lady called Pippa from Annabelle's publisher was there with a briefcase stuffed with letters, contracts, forms and maps. It seemed that Hall's Guides to Witchcraft had become so popular that Pippa was arranging for Annabelle to go on a world tour to covens and magic circles as far away as Australia to promote the latest Guide. She was to go in three weeks' time, in order to be in New York for a Hallowe'en book-signing, and Pippa was to go with her. Such was the excitement that Jethro nearly forgot to look up *Rhus radicans*. When he did, he found it was poison ivy. Hm, he thought. Perhaps Jeremy *does* know what his words mean, after all. He thought it was lucky he had not discovered this before they were hauled in front of Mr Gardner.

Altogether he felt a fierce mixture of relief and worry: relief that neither of his parents had asked why he and Jeremy

were home so early, worry that Jeremy was in bad trouble; relief that something nice had happened for a change, worry because Mum had never been away so far or for so long before; relief that his father was taking the plan on the whole quite well—

"Of course I can manage," Graeme was saying, a touch irritably. "I've no wish to stand in your way, and Jethro is pretty sensible these days." This brought on Jethro's worry again as he realised he would have to look after Dad and Jeremy while Annabelle was away. "But," Graeme continued, "if we haven't located this coven before you leave, I can always go on looking by myself. You go and enjoy yourself. Don't mind me."

While Jethro was trying to decide whether this meant he could feel relieved, Annabelle said to him, "Don't look so worried, love. I'll be back by Christmas."

"Hirsute intropic ampoules," Jeremy said gloomily.

Did Jeremy know what this meant? Jethro wondered. Worry came out on top. And there was always Seniors to worry about as well.

They went back to school next day to discover that Jeremy had been transferred from Miss Blythe's to the parallel class taught by Mr Anderson. Mr. Anderson was young and jolly. When Jethro had been in Mr Anderson's class, he remembered, Mr Anderson's favourite saying had been "Let's have fun looking this up together, shall we?" He wondered if this would suit Jeremy. Or not.

Anyway, Jeremy did not complain. Nor, more importantly, did Mr Anderson. Life rolled on quite peacefully for three weeks, until Annabelle departed for the airport in a flurry of

schedules, maps and lecture notes. The house felt amazingly quiet and rather sombre almost at once. Jeremy went round saying "Calisthenic ketchup" in a small dire voice and sighing deeply. Both of them missed Annabelle badly.

Graeme tried to make it up to them. He put in a real effort for a while. He took them to the cinema and the zoo and he provided pizza and ice-cream for every meal until, after a week or so, even Jeremy began to get tired of pizza. "Dad," Jethro said, worrying about it, "this kind of diet is bad for you. We'll all be overweight."

"Yes, but you know I can't cook," Graeme said. "I'm much too busy with this witch hunt to spend time in the kitchen. Bear with me. It's only till Christmas."

"That's *two months,* Dad," Jethro said.

"Proverbial bouillabaisse," Jeremy said, and sighed deeply.

The next day they had a cook. She was a large quiet lady called Mrs Gladd who came silently in while the boys were having breakfast. Graeme seemed as surprised as they were to see her. "I don't do dishes," she said, putting on an overall covered with sunflowers. "Or," she added, tying the belt, "beds or cleaning. You might want to get someone else for that."

Mrs Gladd was still there when the two of them came home from school, cooking something at the stove which smelt almost heavenly. The kitchen table was spread with cakes, jam tarts and sticky buns.

"Herbacious anthracite," Jeremy said, sniffing deeply. "Hagiography," he added, nodding appreciatively at the table.

Mrs Gladd just shrugged. "Eat up," she said.

They did so. Everything was superb. It almost made up for

the fact that Mrs Gladd was living in and had to have Jethro's room, while Jethro moved in with Jeremy in the little room down the corridor. Graeme had to break off his witch hunt in order to heave beds about—Jethro spent several uncomfortable nights because his father had somehow twisted Jethro's duvet inside its cover. It was like sleeping under a knotted sheep. And Jethro didn't do beds any more than Mrs Gladd did. Even with Jeremy trying to help him he only succeeded in giving the duvet a second twist, so that he now seemed to be sleeping under a rather large python.

But this was straightened out by the end of that week when Rosie, Josephine and Kate arrived, Rosie to wash up the stacks of plates and pans in the kitchen, and Josephine and Kate to make beds and clean the house. Consequently, when Annabelle phoned from Los Angeles that Sunday, Jethro and Graeme were able to assure her that they were doing splendidly. Jeremy said, "Curdled phlogiston," which may or may not have meant the same thing.

On the Monday, however, Josephine and Kate said the work was too heavy for just the two of them and were joined by Gertie, Iris, Delphine, and Doreen. As Jethro and Jeremy left for school, all six ladies were hard at work mopping floors from steaming buckets. Graeme had turned all the computers off and was composing crosswords instead. Jethro spared a worry about how Graeme was going to tell which lady was which. Nearly all of them had blonde hairdos and smart jeans. Iris, Doreen, and Josephine wore pink sweaters and two of the others had glasses, but they were otherwise hard to tell apart. All were slim and very talkative. The house rang with happy

chatter, the clanking of buckets and the drone of vacuum cleaners.

Jethro could only spare a few seconds for Graeme's problems, however. This week there were going to be Tests on All Subjects, and if you had bad results, your life was going to be not worth living in Seniors. He was far too nervous to think much about anything else.

On Tuesday, three terrifying tests later, Jethro came home trying to forget the tests by wondering what cakes and fat buns Mrs Gladd had made today for tea. He found their car out on the drive in a puddle of water, surrounded by three ladies with cloths tied round their heads. Two had large sponges and the third had a hose. They were shrieking with laughter because one of them had just had her shoes hosed by mistake. Jethro thought at first this one was Rosie and that the others were probably Katie and Iris, but when he looked closely, he saw they were three quite new ladies.

"Perspicuous colonization," Jeremy remarked to him.

Jethro took him along to find Graeme. Graeme's study was knee-deep in sleeping bags. Graeme himself, already noticeably plumper from Mrs Gladd's cooking, was sitting at a new table in the corner of the kitchen. Crossword patterns and dictionaries were heaped on the table, but Graeme was busy eating a large sticky bun. Someone had provided him with new, wider jeans and a wide bland sweater. He hardly looked like Dad any more.

"Dad, who are the new ones washing the car?" Jethro asked.

Graeme smiled, again quite unlike himself. "Two Kylies

and a Tracy," he said. "They do the outside work, garden, wash the windows, all that. Aren't we lucky?"

"Troglodytic contralto," Jeremy said.

"Yes, but," Jethro said, eyeing the sheets of half-made crosswords, "can you get on with your witch hunt with all these people about?"

"Not at the moment," Graeme admitted. "But it's only temporary—only till Christmas—after all."

But *was* it only temporary? If Jethro had had any worry to spare from the tests, he thought he would have been quite worried about this. There were ten new chairs round the kitchen table—which seemed much bigger than it ought to be, somehow—and here Mrs Gladd served succulent meals for fourteen. Jethro ate with his head down, avoiding elbows, and his hearing filled with screams of laughter at jokes he didn't understand. All eleven ladies seemed to be living here now, not only Mrs Gladd. There were sleeping bags everywhere, in the airing cupboard, behind the sofa and bundled to the sides of the upstairs corridor. On Friday, when Jethro had done a test on everything possible from spelling to cookery, the ladies turned the living room and Graeme's study into hairdressing salons and did one another's hair. The booming of vacuum cleaners was replaced by the roaring of hair dryers. The house filled with strong perfumes.

Almost the only place that was empty of ladies was Annabelle's deserted study. Jethro took to sitting there beside Mum's blank turned-off computer, worrying about the results of the tests and wishing he knew the password to get into that computer. He thought he might feel better if he could read

some of the things Annabelle had been writing before she left. But when Annabelle rang that Sunday from Sydney in Australia, Jethro had not the heart to tell her about the tests or the ladies either. He was sure he had failed all the tests and there was nothing he could do about the ladies. Graeme, beaming all over his newly plump face, said they were getting along marvellously. Jeremy said, "Hypno-therapeutic distilled amnesia. In blue bottles." At which Mum laughed and said, "Oh *really*, Jeremy!"

Jethro came home from school the next day in a worse worry than ever. None of the results of the tests were ready. Every teacher he asked told him to be patient: it took time to mark them all, they said. He made for Annabelle's study, tripping over sleeping bags on the way, longing for some peace and quiet to worry in, only to find Jeremy in there. Jeremy was sitting at the computer, playing a computer game.

"How did you find the password?" Jethro demanded.

Jeremy turned to him, angelically egg-shaped. "Imperfect clandestine logistics," he said.

Jethro stumped away to consult a dictionary, which was not easy. Mrs Gladd pushed him aside when he tried to reach the one in the kitchen, and Delphine and Rosie said, "Not in here, please!" when he tried Dad's study. When he took down one of the dictionaries in the living room, Josephine moved the small table away in order to do her toenails on it and he was forced to spread the heavy book out on the floor. The sofa was filled with Tracy, one of the Kylies and Josephine, who were all laughing about something. Jethro had to push away a heap of sleeping bags to make room for the dictionary, from

which he discovered that *logistics* meant *the science of moving, supplying and maintaining of military forces in the field.* It had nothing to do with logging on, as Jethro had supposed. He went back to Annabelle's study. "I want to use the computer after you," he told Jeremy. "Or it's not fair."

"Fulminating lohan," Jeremy said.

Jethro tried to do without a dictionary, this time by going and asking Graeme when *lohan* meant. But Graeme simply crouched at his corner table and tapped with his pencil. "Don't bother me now," he said. "I have to find a proper clue for *stethoscope*."

Sighing, Jethro collected all the dictionaries the ladies would let him get near and took them up to the little room he was forced to share with Jeremy. It was really annoying, he thought, turning pages, the way he and Jeremy and Graeme were getting pushed away into the corners of their own house. The ladies seemed to feel it belonged to them now. A *lohan*, he discovered, was a rather good Buddhist—something he himself would never be, Jethro knew. He was too worried about those tests. He sat on his bed and worried.

It was an awful week. None of the tests got marked and Jethro began to fear that he was not going to be allowed to go to Seniors. When he got home, the house was always full of vacuum cleaners and shrieks of laughter, and however early he arrived, Jeremy had somehow managed to get to Mum's computer before Jethro did. He tried complaining to Graeme, but Graeme simply tapped his pencil on his teeth and said, "I can't find a decent clue for *stethoscope*." After five days of this, Jethro said to Jeremy, "Dad isn't listening to a word I say."

Jeremy astonished him by saying, "Yes, I know," before turning back to his game.

"No long words?" Jethro asked.

"Not yet," Jeremy said, and killed a swathe of aliens with one burst of gunfire.

"Supper! Hurry up!" Mrs Gladd called from the kitchen.

Jeremy left the computer running, and as they both went down to the kitchen, Jethro was determined to get back to that computer before Jeremy did or die in the attempt.

Supper seemed to be over very quickly. Graeme went straight to his corner then. Jethro and Jeremy edged through the bustle of clearing up, each with an eye on the other, each ready to make a dash for the computer as soon as the other did. They had only just reached the door when someone rang the doorbell at the front door. Josephine and one of the Kylies pushed them aside, right up against Graeme's table, rushing to answer it.

Jeremy looked at Jethro. "Penultimate epiphany," he said. They stayed to see who it was.

It was Miss Blythe. She came striding in, all owl face and purple bosom, and rapped on the kitchen table. "Everybody gather round," she said. As Mrs Gladd turned from the fridge and Kate from the sink and the nine other ladies came back into the kitchen, most of them carrying hair dryers, Jethro had one of those horrible moments when you realise you have been worrying about quite the wrong thing. He had spent all the last fortnight worrying about tests at school, when he should have been looking at what was going on in his own house. He stared at Miss Blythe, feeling empty.

"Now, my flowers," Miss Blythe said, when everyone was gathered by the table, "most of you have been here a full two weeks. I want full reports on progress made and objectives achieved. Mrs Gladd?"

"The way to a man's heart is through his stomach," Mrs Gladd said. "I've cooked up three spells daily and four at weekends. All three of them should be well under by now."

"So I see," Miss Blythe said. Her glasses flashed towards Graeme sitting chewing his pencil in his corner, and then travelled quickly, with evident dislike, across Jethro and Jeremy. "Well done," she said. "Kylie, Kylie and Tracy?"

One of the car-cleaners, the one who wore glasses, said, "We've made absolutely sure that none of their neighbours even see us, Miss Blythe, and we've stopped all communication from outside."

"So have we," said Rosie, stroking her blond hairdo. "Not a soul has been able to consult Occult Security since we came here. The only phone calls we allow in are from Mrs Hall."

"We're working on making everyone forget the Halls exist," Josephine added. She giggled. "Mr Hall's forgotten already."

They all looked over at Graeme, who frowned at his crossword and did not seem to notice.

"Good," said Miss Blythe. "Occult Security isn't going to bother us any more then—none of them are going to bother us much longer. We'll be able to sell this house soon. Have you worked out how much we'll get for it?"

"We priced it up," Kate said. "A quarter of a million seems about right."

A very satisfied expression came across Miss Blythe's face

at this. "Then we're in business," she said, "except for one little matter." Her satisfaction faded rather. "Have any of you worked out what we do about getting rid of *Mrs* Hall? Coven Head will be here any minute, and he'll want to know what we're doing about her."

Mrs Gladd said, "She's leaving Australia later today and flying to Rome."

"Lots of nice deep ocean on the way," said Doreen.

Iris added, "What say we simply bring the plane down while it's over the water?"

Miss Blythe nodded. "Yes, that should do it. It sounds like the neatest way. You can start setting that spell up as soon as Coven Head gets here."

The doorbell rang again.

"Here he is now," Miss Blythe said. "One of you let him in."

As Josephine scudded away to the front door, Jethro stood next to Jeremy thinking, What are we going to do? They're behaving as if we don't exist. *Do* we exist any more?

Just as if thinking that was a signal, Miss Blythe's big owl spectacles turned Jethro's way. She pursed her lips irritably as if he were something offensive like a very dirty sock someone had dropped on the floor. Then she turned with an effusive smile as Josephine ushered Jack Smith into the kitchen. "Oh, Coven Head," she said. "Good to *see* you!"

Jack Smith was fatter and more tightly packed into his expensive suit than ever. He beamed round at the ladies and nodded happily at Graeme in his corner. "Good, good, all going to plan, I see," he said. Looking very humorous, he reached into his waistcoat and then into his pockets and fetched out

hundreds of charms, protections and wires, which he threw into a heap on the table. "No need to carry these silly things about any more," he said, tossing a couple of batteries onto the heap. "I see the Hall family is pretty well obliterated."

"Not quite," Miss Blythe said, pointing at Jethro and Jeremy. "Those two don't seen to me to be quite under yet."

"Oh, we'll soon settle that." Jack Smith rubbed his hands together and came to stand over Jethro and Jeremy, smiling down at them, exuding such good cheer that he could have been Santa Claus in a dark suit. "Boys," he said, "this is very important. I need you both to give me your solemn word that you will never, ever say one thing about any of us here—about me, or Miss Blythe, or any of these charming ladies. You." He beamed at Jethro. "Give me your word. Now."

Jethro felt some sort of huge numbness spreading his brain out, squashing it flat, combing away all feelings until there was nearly nothing but a blank white space where all his thoughts usually were. Almost the only thing left was frantic worry. This is *awful*! he thought. If I give him my word I shall be like this for *ever*!

"*I'll* give you my word," Jeremy said from beside Jethro. He stared up towards Jack Smith, past Jack Smith and into empty space deep beyond Jack Smith, and his face was more egg-shaped and angelic than Jethro had ever seen it before. "I'll give you my word," Jeremy said, "and my word is FLOCCIPAUCINIHILIPILIFICATION!"

Jethro suddenly felt much better. Jack Smith said, *"What?"*

"Take no notice," said Miss Blythe. "He's a naughty little boy. He's always doing this."

"All right," Jack Smith agreed. "Forget the kids. Fill me in. What have we decided to do about dispensing with Annabelle Hall?"

"Bring down her plane between Australia and Italy," Miss Blythe told him. "Over the sea if we can. Does that seem good to you?"

Jack Smith said, "Perfect. Let's get on and set the spell then." He strode over to the table and sat himself in the chair next to the sink, rubbing his hands together gladly. Miss Blythe and the other ladies hurried to pull out chairs and sit round the table too. Amid the squawking of chair legs on floor, Jethro bent down to his brother and whispered, "What does floccipaucinihilipilification *mean?"*

Jeremy shrugged, egg-shaped and innocent. *"I* don't know."

Jethro snatched a look at everyone sitting at the table and staring respectfully at Jack Smith and whirled round to Graeme, smiling vaguely at his table just behind them. "Dad!" he said urgently. "Dad, what does floccipaucinihilipilification mean?"

"Eh?" Graeme said. "Floccipaucinihilipilification? Supposed to be the longest word in the language. It means—" Jethro held his breath and watched the smile drain from his father's face into the pinched, grumpy and attentive look he was much more used to. "It means, Jethro, *the act of regarding something as worthless,*" Graeme said. Now he looked almost his usual self. He seemed to have gone thinner, with lines where he had had smooth fat cheeks before. He stared silently at the twelve ladies seated at the table and at Jack Smith sitting by the sink, facing them. "My God!" he said. "A full coven! What are they doing?"

"Casting a spell to make Mum's plane crash," Jethro said.

"Right," said Graeme. None of the coven had even noticed him. He leapt up from his corner and went with long, noiseless steps, through the kitchen doorway and round into his study, where he kicked aside three sleeping bags and dived into the chair in front of his Occult Security computer. "Exorcism programme," he muttered as the machine hummed and flickered, "spell cancellation, expulsion of alien magics programmes, all of them I think, block and destroy magics . . . what else am I going to need?"

Jeremy's voice rose up from the kitchen. "Wanton aquamarine steroids. Epigrammatic yellow persiflage with semiotic substitution."

"Oh yes, personal protection for both you boys," Graeme said. "Go and get Jeremy *out* of there, Jethro!" The exorcism programme came up and he began stabbing at keys, furiously and at speed.

Hendiadys! Jethro thought. Instead of *with furious speed*. He sped back to the kitchen to find everyone sitting in a fixed, spell-making, concentrating silence, except for Jeremy. Jeremy was marching up and down beside the cooker, chanting. "Haloes and holograms, ubiquitous embargoes, zygotes and rhizomes in the diachronic ciabatta." Miss Blythe kept turning her spectacles towards him venomously, but she did not seem to be able to interrupt the spell-making in order to stop Jeremy.

Jethro seized his arm. "Come away. It's dangerous!"

"No, I've got to stay. *Gladiolus!*" Jeremy shrieked, bracing both feet. "Rosacea! Dahlias and debutante begonias.

Recycled stringent peonies. Pockmarked pineapples, tormented turnips, artichokes with acne. Let *go*, Jethro! Cuneiform cauliflowers. It's *working*!"

Right in front of Jethro, Mrs Gladd shrank to nothing in her chair. Where she had been sitting there was now a fat clod of earth with a small spiked shoot sticking out of it.

"See!" Jeremy shouted. Rosie winked out downwards as he yelled, into a smaller clod with two green leaves glimmering on top of it. "Monocotyledenous, dicotyledenous, myrtle and *twitch*!"

Almost at once—blink, blink, blink—Kate, Doreen, Josephine and both Kylies shrank likewise and became clumps of earth with tiny seedlings growing in them. Though Jethro had no doubt that Graeme's programmes were now running, he was also equally sure that Jeremy was somehow directing what these programmes did. Blink, blink, blink, all round the table. Gertie, Iris, Delphine and Tracy shrank into seedlings too, until only Jack Smith and Miss Blythe were left. Jack Smith was staring around in bewilderment, but Miss Blythe flopped forward with her face in her hands, looking tired and defeated.

"It's Miss Blythe's magic, see," Jeremy explained out of the corner of his mouth, and turned back to shriek at Jack Smith, *"Defenestration!"*

Jack Smith sailed up out of his chair and hurtled backwards towards the window.

"Oleaginous defenestration, I meant," Jeremy said quickly, just as Jack Smith's fat back met the glass.

Jethro watched, fascinated, as the glass went soft and

stretched like elastic to let Jack Smith shoot through into the flower bed outside. Then it snapped back into unbroken glass again. Through it, Jethro watched Jack Smith pick himself up and shamble off, looking puzzled, to the big car parked in their driveway.

"You appalling little boy!" Miss Blythe said faintly. "How did you know all my girls were flowers from my garden? And just look at what you've done to that poor dear man, Jack Smith! He was going to be Prime Minister with our coven for a Cabinet."

"Questionable offal," Jeremy retorted. "*You* were going to kill my mum."

"Well, we had to neutralise your parents," Miss Blythe said, in a tired, reasonable way, "or they would have spoilt all his plans, poor man. They are far too good at their job."

Jethro felt he had had enough of Miss Blythe. He went up to her and took hold of her by one purple arm. "The front door's this way," he said. "You'd better go now."

Graeme's programmes were obviously running sweetly by then. Miss Blythe stood up quite meekly and let Jethro lead her out of the kitchen and through the hall. "He was going to let me be his private secretary," she said sadly as they went.

Jethro felt the school could probably do without Miss Blythe too. "Why don't you give up teaching and be his secretary anyway?" he suggested, opening the front door and giving her a push.

"What a good idea!" Miss Blythe exclaimed. "I think I will." She turned round on the doorstep. "Jethro Hall, you're a very understanding boy."

Jethro shut the door on her, wondering if he really wanted to be called understanding by someone like Miss Blythe, and scooted to Graeme's study to check on his father.

Graeme, looking lean and irritable and entirely his usual self, was bending over the computer, where programme after programme was racing downwards on the screen. "I don't know which flight your mother's going to be on," he told Jethro. "I'm having to put protection round every plane that comes into Rome for the next twenty-four hours. Go and shut Jeremy up. He's distracting me."

In the kitchen, Jeremy was still chanting words, although they now seemed to have become a song of triumph. "Highly benevolent botulism," he howled as Jethro came in. "Crusading gumbo extirpated by chocolate pelmanism. Transcendent aureate thaumaturgy!" Jeremy's eyes blazed and his cheeks were flushed. He had worked himself into quite a state.

"Stop it!" Jethro told him. "It's over now."

"Creosote," Jeremy said, the way other people might use a swear word. "Ginseng. Garibaldi biscuits." His cheeks faded to a normal colour and he looked humorously up at Jethro. "I've never done real magic before," he said. "Has Dad made Mum's plane safe?"

"He's just fixing it now, " said Jethro. "What do we do with all these seedlings? Throw them away?"

"No, plant them of course," Jeremy said. "Tomorrow."

So, when Annabelle rang up from Rome the next day, after Graeme had said as usual that they were all fine, Jethro took the phone and told her that he and Jeremy had been

gardening. Then Jeremy snatched the phone to say, "And we got rid of those witches for you. They weren't attacking Jack Smith because they didn't exist really."

"Oh good!" Annabelle said. "And *I* want to tell you that Pippa and I have had enough. There was no one at all at the signing this morning. We're going to cancel the rest of the tour and fly home tomorrow." She stopped in a surprised way. "What's this, Jeremy? No more of your big words?"

"No," said Jeremy. "I've used them all up."

Jethro let his breath out in a long, gentle sigh. There was nothing to worry about any more. He was not even worried about the tests, he found. What was done was done.

Graeme wrestled the phone from Jeremy's fist. "Give me your flight number," he said. "I'll put protection round it, just in case."

"If you feel you need to," Annabelle said. "It might make Pippa feel better. She turns out to be terrified of flying."

Diana Wynne Jones was born in London, England. At the age of eight, she suddenly *knew* she was going to be a writer, although she was too dyslexic to start until she reached age twelve. There were very few children's books in the house, so Diana wrote stories for herself and her two younger sisters. She received her B.A. at St. Anne's College in Oxford before she began to write full-time.

Her many remarkable novels include the award-winning *Archer's Goon*, *Howl's Moving Castle* (recently made into a major animated feature by Hayao Miyazaki), *Fire and Hemlock*, the Dalemark Quartet, *Dark Lord of Derkholm, Year of the Griffin, The Merlin Conspiracy*, and the Chrestomanci books (*Charmed Life, Witch Week, The Lives of Christopher Chant, The Magicians of Caprona,* and her most recent novel, *Conrad's Fate)*.

Diana Wynne Jones lives with her husband, the medievalist J. A. Burrow, in Bristol, England, the setting of many of her books. They have three grown sons and five grandchildren.

Her Web site is **www.leemac.freeserve.co.uk**.

Author's Note

This story started with my love of dictionaries, not just for being full of words—and I love words—but because of the wildly different words that occur side by side in them. You find *shire horse* next to *shoestring* and *cutwater* beside *cynical*. My grandson Thomas loves words too, the more preposterous

the better. I was trying to teach him "borborygmata" when I got the idea. He was delighted with the word, particularly when he discovered it meant your tummy rumbling, but he couldn't say it. The nearest he got was "babagatama," which ought to be a word anyway. But the main character in the story is in fact another of my grandsons, Gabriel, who spends much of his time away in a distant part of his own head. Then he comes back and tells you something extraordinary. I suspect him of having uncanny powers. This worries his brother, who is Jethro in the story, and a worrier.

Ellen Klages

In the House of the Seven Librarians

Once upon a time, the Carnegie Library sat on a wooded bluff on the east side of town: red brick and fieldstone, with turrets and broad windows facing the trees. Inside, green glass-shaded lamps cast warm yellow light onto oak tables ringed with spindle-backed chairs.

Books filled the dark shelves that stretched high up toward the pressed-tin ceiling. The floors were wood, except in the foyer, where they were pale beige marble. The loudest sounds were the ticking of the clock and the quiet, rhythmic *thwack* of a rubber stamp on a pasteboard card.

It was a cozy, orderly place.

Through twelve presidents and two world wars, the elms and maples grew tall outside the deep bay windows. Children leaped from *Peter Pan* to *Oliver Twist* and off to college, replaced at Story Hour by their younger brothers, cousins, daughters.

Then the library board—men in suits, serious men, men of money—met and cast their votes for progress. A new

library, with fluorescent lights, much better for the children's eyes. Picture windows, automated systems, ergonomic plastic chairs. The town approved the levy, and the new library was built across town, convenient to the community center and the mall.

Some books were boxed and trundled down Broad Street, many others stamped DISCARD and left where they were, for a book sale in the fall. Interns from the university used the latest technology to transfer the cumbersome old card file and all the records onto floppy disks and microfiche. Progress, progress, progress.

The Ralph P. Mossberger Library (named after the local philanthropist and car dealer who had written the largest check) opened on a drizzly morning in late April. Everyone attended the ribbon-cutting ceremony and stayed for the speeches, because there would be cake after.

Everyone except the seven librarians from the Carnegie Library on the bluff across town.

Quietly, without a fuss (they were librarians, after all), while the town looked toward the future, they bought supplies: loose tea and English biscuits, packets of Bird's pudding and cans of beef barley soup. They rearranged some of the shelves, brought in a few comfortable armchairs, nice china and teapots, a couch, towels for the shower, and some small braided rugs.

Then they locked the door behind them.

Each morning they woke and went about their chores. They shelved and stamped and cataloged, and in the evenings, every night, they read by lamplight.

Perhaps, for a while, some citizens remembered the old library, with the warm nostalgia of a favorite childhood toy that had disappeared one summer, never seen again. Others assumed it had been torn down long ago.

And so a year went by, then two, or perhaps a great many more. Inside, time had ceased to matter. Grass and brambles grew thick and tall around the fieldstone steps, and trees arched overhead as the forest folded itself around them like a cloak.

Inside, the seven librarians lived, quiet and content.

Until the day they found the baby.

Librarians are guardians of books. They guide others along their paths, offering keys to help unlock the doors of knowledge. But these seven had become a closed circle, no one to guide, no new minds to open onto worlds of possibility. They kept themselves busy, tidying orderly shelves and mending barely frayed bindings with stiff netting and glue, and began to bicker.

Ruth and Edith had been up half the night, arguing about whether or not subway tokens (of which there were half a dozen in the Lost and Found box) could be used to cast the *I Ching*. And so Blythe was on the stepstool in the 299s, reshelving the volume of hexagrams, when she heard the knock.

Odd, she thought. It's been some time since we've had visitors.

She tugged futilely at her shapeless cardigan as she clambered off the stool and trotted to the front door, where she stopped abruptly, her hand to her mouth in surprise.

A wicker basket, its contents covered with a red-checked cloth, as if for a picnic, lay in the wooden box beneath the Book Return chute. A small, cream-colored envelope poked out from one side.

"How nice!" Blythe said aloud, clapping her hands. She thought of fried chicken and potato salad—of which she was awfully fond—a Mason jar of lemonade, perhaps even a cherry pie? She lifted the basket by its round-arched handle. Heavy, for a picnic. But then, there *were* seven of them. Although Olive just ate like a bird, these days.

She turned and set it on top of the Circulation Desk, pulling the envelope free.

"What's *that*?" Marian asked, her lips in their accustomed moue of displeasure, as if the basket were an agent of chaos, existing solely to disrupt the tidy array of rubber stamps and file boxes that were her domain.

"A present," said Blythe. "I think it might be lunch."

Marian frowned. "For you?"

"I don't know yet. There's a note . . ." Blythe held up the envelope and peered at it. "No," she said. "It's addressed to 'The Librarians. Overdue Books Department.' "

"Well, that would be me," Marian said curtly. She was the youngest, and wore trouser suits with silk T-shirts. She had once been blond. She reached across the counter, plucked the envelope from Blythe's plump fingers, and sliced it open it with a filigreed brass stiletto.

"Hmph," she said after she'd scanned the contents.

"It *is* lunch, isn't it?" asked Blythe.

"Hardly." Marian began to read aloud:

This is overdue. Quite a bit, I'm afraid. I apologize. We moved to Topeka when I was very small, and Mother accidentally packed it up with the linens. I have traveled a long way to return it, and I know the fine must be large, but I have no money. As it is a book of fairy tales, I thought payment of a first-born child would be acceptable. I always loved the library. I'm sure she'll be happy there.

Blythe lifted the edge of the cloth. "Oh, my stars!"

A baby girl with a shock of wire-stiff black hair stared up at her, green eyes wide and curious. She was contentedly chewing on the corner of a blue book, half as big as she was. *Fairy Tales of the Brothers Grimm.*

"The Rackham illustrations," Blythe said as she eased the book away from the baby. "That's a lovely edition."

"But when was it checked out?" Marian demanded.

Blythe opened the cover and pulled the ruled card from the inside pocket. "October 17th, 1938," she said, shaking her head. "Goodness, at two cents a day, that's . . ." She shook her head again. Blythe had never been good with figures.

They made a crib for her in the bottom drawer of a file cabinet, displacing acquisition orders, zoning permits, and the instructions for the mimeograph, which they rarely used.

Ruth consulted Dr. Spock. Edith read Piaget. The two of them peered from text to infant and back again for a good long while before deciding that she was probably about nine months old. They sighed. Too young to read.

So they fed her cream and let her gum on biscuits, and each of the seven cooed and clucked and tickled her pink toes when they thought the others weren't looking. Harriet had been the oldest of nine girls, and knew more about babies than she really cared to. She washed and changed the diapers that had been tucked into the basket, and read *Goodnight Moon* and *Pat the Bunny* to the little girl, whom she called Polly—short for Polyhymnia, the muse of oratory and sacred song.

Blythe called her Bitsy, and Li'l Precious.

Marian called her "the foundling," or "That Child You Took In," but did her share of cooing and clucking, just the same.

When the child began to walk, Dorothy blocked the staircase with stacks of Comptons, which she felt was an inferior encyclopedia, and let her pull herself up on the bottom drawers of the card catalog. Anyone looking up Zithers or Zippers (*see "Slide Fasteners"*) soon found many of the cards fused together with grape jam. When she began to talk, they made a little bed nook next to the fireplace in the Children's Room.

It was high time for Olive to begin the child's education.

Olive had been the children's librarian since before recorded time, or so it seemed. No one knew how old she was, but she vaguely remembered waving to President Coolidge. She still had all of her marbles, though every one of them was a bit odd and rolled asymmetrically.

She slept on a daybed behind a reference shelf that held *My First Encyclopedia* and *The Wonder Book of Trees,* among others. Across the room, the child's first "big-girl bed" was

yellow, with decals of a fairy and a horse on the headboard, and a rocket ship at the foot, because they weren't sure about her preferences.

At the beginning of her career, Olive had been an ordinary-sized librarian, but by the time she began the child's lessons, she was not much taller than her toddling charge. Not from osteoporosis or dowager's hump or other old-lady maladies, but because she had tired of stooping over tiny chairs and bending to knee-high shelves. She had been a grown-*up* for so long that when the library closed, she had decided it was time to grow *down* again, and was finding that much more comfortable.

She had a remarkably cozy lap for a woman her size.

The child quickly learned her alphabet, all the shapes and colors, the names of zoo animals, and fourteen different kinds of dinosaurs, all of whom were dead.

By the time she was four, or thereabouts, she could sound out the letters for simple words—*cup* and *lamp* and *stairs*. And that's how she came to name herself.

Olive had fallen asleep over *Make Way for Ducklings,* and all the other librarians were busy somewhere else. The child was bored. She tiptoed out of the Children's Room, hugging the shadows of the walls and shelves, crawling by the base of the Circulation Desk so that Marian wouldn't see her, and made her way to the alcove that held the Card Catalog. The heart of the library. Her favorite, most forbidden place to play.

Usually she crawled underneath and tucked herself into the corner formed of oak cabinet, marble floor, and plaster walls. It was a fine place to play Hide-and-Seek, even if it was

mostly just Hide. The corner was a cave, a bunk on a pirate ship, a cupboard in a magic wardrobe.

But that afternoon she looked at the white cards on the fronts of the drawers, and her eyes widened in recognition. Letters! In her very own alphabet. Did they spell words? Maybe the drawers were all *full* of words, a huge wooden box of words. The idea almost made her dizzy.

She walked to the other end of the cabinet and looked up, tilting her neck back until it crackled. Four drawers from top to bottom. Five drawers across. She sighed. She was only tall enough to reach the bottom row of drawers. She traced a gentle finger around the little brass frames, then very carefully pulled out the white cards inside and laid them on the floor in a neat row:

She squatted over them, her tongue sticking out of the corner of her mouth in concentration, and tried to read.

"Sound it out." She could almost hear Olive's voice, soft and patient. She took a deep breath.

"Duh-in-s—" and then she stopped, because the last card had too many letters, and she didn't know any words that had *X*s in them. Well, xylophone. But the *X* was in the front, and that wasn't the same. She tried anyway. "Duh-ins-zzzigh," and frowned.

She squatted lower, so low she could feel cold marble under her cotton pants, and put her hand on top of the last

card. One finger covered the *X* and her pinkie covered the *Z* (another letter that was useless for spelling ordinary things). That left *Y*. *Y* at the end was good: funnY, happY.

"Duh-ins-see," she said slowly. "Dinsy."

That felt very good to say, hard and soft sounds and hissing *S*s mixing in her mouth, so she said it again, louder, which made her laugh, so she said it again, very loud: "DINSY!"

There is nothing quite like a loud voice in a library to get a lot of attention very fast. Within a minute, all seven of the librarians stood in the doorway of the alcove.

"What on earth?" said Harriet.

"*Now* what have you . . . " said Marian.

"What have you spelled, dear?" asked Olive in her soft little voice.

"I made it myself," the girl replied.

"Just gibberish," murmured Edith, though not unkindly. "It doesn't mean a thing."

The child shook her head. "Does so. Olive," she said, pointing to Olive. "Do'thy, Edith, Harwiet, Bithe, Ruth." She paused and rolled her eyes. "Mawian," she added, a little less cheerfully. Then she pointed to herself. "And Dinsy."

"Oh, now, Polly," said Harriet.

"Dinsy," said Dinsy.

"Bitsy?" Blythe tried hopefully.

"*Din*sy," said Dinsy.

And that was that.

At three every afternoon, Dinsy and Olive made a two-person circle on the braided rug in front of the bay window, and had

Story Time. Sometimes Olive read aloud from *Beezus and Ramona* and *Half Magic*, and sometimes Dinsy read to Olive, *The King's Stilts*, and *In the Night Kitchen,* and *Winnie-the-Pooh*. Dinsy liked that one especially, and took it to bed with her so many times that Edith had to repair the binding. Twice.

That was when Dinsy first wished upon the Library.

A note about the Library:

Knowledge is not static; information must flow in order to live. Every so often one of the librarians would discover a new addition. *Harry Potter and the Sorcerer's Stone* appeared one rainy afternoon, Rowling shelved neatly between Rodgers and Saint-Exupéry, as if it had always been there. Blythe found a book of Thich Nhat Hanh's writings in the 294s one day while she was dusting, and Feynman's lectures on physics showed up on Dorothy's shelving cart after she'd gone to make a cup of tea.

It didn't happen often; the Library was selective about what it chose to add, rejecting flash-in-the-pan best-sellers, sifting for the long haul, looking for those voices that would stand the test of time next to Dickens and Tolkien, Woolf and Gould.

The librarians took care of the books, and the Library watched over them in return. It occasionally left treats: a bowl of ripe tangerines on the Formica counter of the Common Room; a gold foil box of chocolate creams; seven small, stemmed glasses of sherry on the table one teatime. Their biscuit tin remained full, the cream in the Wedgwood jug stayed fresh, and the ink pad didn't dry out. Even the little pencils stayed needle sharp, never whittling down to finger-cramping nubs.

Some days the Library even hid Dinsy, when she had made a mess and didn't want to be found, or when one of the librarians was

in a dark mood. It rearranged itself, just a bit, so that in her wanderings she would find a new alcove or cubbyhole, and once a secret passage that led to a previously unknown balcony overlooking the Reading Room. When she went back a week later, she found only blank wall.

And so it was, one night when she was sixish, that Dinsy first asked the Library for a boon. Lying in her tiny yellow bed, the fraying *Pooh* under her pillow, she wished for a bear to cuddle. Books were small comfort once the lights were out, and their hard, sharp corners made them awkward companions under the covers. She lay with one arm crooked around a soft, imaginary bear, and wished and wished until her eyelids fluttered into sleep.

The next morning, while they were all having tea and toast with jam, Blythe came into the Common Room with a quizzical look on her face and her hands behind her back.

"The strangest thing," she said. "On my way up here I glanced over at the Lost and Found. Couldn't tell you why. Nothing lost in ages. But this must have caught my eye."

She held out a small brown bear, one shoebutton eye missing, bits of fur gone from its belly, as if it had been loved almost to pieces.

"It seems to be yours," she said with a smile, turning up one padded foot, where DINSY was written in faded laundry-marker black.

Dinsy wrapped her whole self around the cotton-stuffed body and skipped for the rest of the morning. Later, after Olive gave her a snack—cocoa and a Lorna Doone—Dinsy cupped her hand and blew a kiss to the oak woodwork.

"Thank you," she whispered, and put half her cookie in a crack between two tiles on the Children's Room fireplace when Olive wasn't looking.

Dinsy and Olive had a lovely time. One week they were pirates, raiding the Common Room for booty (and raisins). The next they were princesses, trapped in the turret with *At the Back of the North Wind,* and the week after that they were knights in shining armor, rescuing damsels in distress, a game Dinsy especially savored because it annoyed Marian to be rescued.

But the year she turned seven-and-a-half, Dinsy stopped reading stories. Quite abruptly, on an afternoon that Olive said later had really *felt* like a Thursday.

"Stories are for babies," Dinsy said. "I want to read about *real* people." Olive smiled a sad smile and pointed toward the far wall, because Dinsy was not the first child to make that same pronouncement, and she had known this phase would come.

After that, Dinsy devoured biographies, starting with the orange ones, the Childhoods of Famous Americans: *Thomas Edison, Young Inventor.* She worked her way from Abigail Adams to John Peter Zenger, all along the west side of the Children's Room, until one day she went around the corner, where Science and History began.

She stood in the doorway, looking at the rows of grown-up books, when she felt Olive's hand on her shoulder.

"Do you think maybe it's time you moved across the hall?" Olive asked softly.

Dinsy bit her lip, then nodded. "I can come back to visit, can't I? When I want to read stories again?"

"For as long as you like, dear. Anytime at all."

So Dorothy came and gathered up the bear and the pillow and the yellow toothbrush. Dinsy kissed Olive on her papery cheek and, holding Blythe's hand, moved across the hall, to the room where all the books had numbers.

Blythe was plump and freckled and frizzled. She always looked a little flushed, as if she had just that moment dropped what she was doing to rush over and greet you. She wore rumpled tweed skirts and a shapeless cardigan whose original color was impossible to guess. She had bright, dark eyes like a spaniel's, which Dinsy thought was appropriate, because Blythe *lived* to fetch books. She wore a locket with a small rotogravure picture of Melvil Dewey and kept a variety of sweets—sour balls and mints and Necco wafers—in her desk drawer.

Dinsy had always liked her.

She was not as sure about Dorothy.

Over *her* desk, Dorothy had a small framed medal on a royal-blue ribbon, won for "Excellence in Classification Studies." She could operate the ancient black Remington typewriter with brisk efficiency, and even, on occasion, coax chalky gray prints out of the wheezing old copy machine.

She was a tall, rawboned woman with steely blue eyes, good posture, and even better penmanship. Dinsy was a little frightened of her, at first, because she seemed so stern, and because she looked like magazine pictures of the Wicked Witch of the West, or at least Margaret Hamilton.

But that didn't last long.

"You should be very careful not to slip on the floor in here,"

Dorothy said on their first morning. "Do you know why?"

Dinsy shook her head.

"Because now you're in the nonfriction room!" Dorothy's angular face cracked into a wide grin.

Dinsy groaned. "Okay," she said after a minute. "How do you file marshmallows?"

Dorothy cocked her head. "Shoot."

"By the *Gooey* Decimal System!"

Dinsy heard Blythe tsk-tsk, but Dorothy laughed out loud, and from then on they were fast friends.

The three of them used the large, sunny room as an arena for endless games of I Spy and Twenty Questions as Dinsy learned her way around the shelves. In the evenings, after supper, they played Authors and Scrabble, and (once) tried to keep a running rummy score in Base Eight.

Dinsy sat at the court of Napoleon, roamed the jungles near Timbuktu, and was a frequent guest at the Round Table. She knew all the kings of England and the difference between a pergola and a folly. She knew the names of 112 breeds of sheep, and loved to say "Barbados Blackbelly" over and over, although it was difficult to work into conversations. When she affectionately, if misguidedly, referred to Blythe as a "Persian Fat-Rumped," she was sent to bed without supper.

A note about time:

Time had become quite flexible inside the library. (This is true of most places with interesting books. Sit down to read for twenty minutes, and suddenly it's dark, with no clue as to where the hours have gone.)

As a consequence, no one was really sure about the day of the week, and there was frequent disagreement about the month and year. As the keeper of the date stamp at the front desk, Marian was the arbiter of such things. But she often had a cocktail after dinner, and many mornings she couldn't recall if she'd already turned the little wheel, or how often it had slipped her mind, so she frequently set it a day or two ahead—or back three—just to make up.

One afternoon, on a visit to Olive and the Children's Room, Dinsy looked up from *Little Town on the Prairie* and said, "When's my birthday?"

Olive thought for a moment. Because of the irregularities of time, holidays were celebrated a bit haphazardly. "I'm not sure, dear. Why do you ask?"

"Laura's going to a birthday party, in this book," she said, holding it up. "And it's fun. So I thought maybe I could have one."

"I think that would be lovely," Olive agreed. "We'll talk to the others at supper."

"Your birthday?" said Harriet as she set the table a few hours later. "Let me see." She began to count on her fingers. "You arrived in April, according to Marian's stamp, and you were about nine months old, so—" She pursed her lips as she ticked off the months. "You must have been born in July!"

"But when's my birth*day*?" Dinsy asked impatiently.

"Not sure," said Edith as she ladled out the soup.

"No way to tell," Olive agreed.

"How does July fifth sound?" offered Blythe, as if it were a point of order to be voted on. Blythe counted best by fives.

"Fourth," said Dorothy. "Independence Day. Easy to remember?"

Dinsy shrugged. "Okay." It hadn't seemed so complicated in the Little House book. "When is that? Is it soon?"

"Probably." Ruth nodded.

A few weeks later, the librarians threw her a birthday party.

Harriet baked a spice cake with pink frosting, and wrote DINSY on top in red licorice laces, dotting the *I* with a lemon drop (which was rather stale). The others gave her gifts that were thoughtful and mostly handmade:

A set of Dewey Decimal flash cards from Blythe.

A book of logic puzzles (stamped DISCARD more than a dozen times, so Dinsy could write in it) from Dorothy.

A lumpy orange-and-green cardigan Ruth knitted for her.

A snow globe from the 1939 World's Fair from Olive.

A flashlight from Edith, so that Dinsy could find her way around at night and not knock over the wastebasket again.

A set of paper finger puppets, made from blank card pockets, hand-painted by Marian. (They were literary figures, of course, all of them necessarily stout and squarish—Nero Wolfe and Friar Tuck, Santa Claus and Gertrude Stein.)

But her favorite gift was the second boon she'd wished upon the Library: a box of crayons. (She had grown very tired of drawing gray pictures with the little pencils.) It had produced Crayola crayons, in the familiar yellow-and-green box, labeled LIBRARY PACK. Inside were the colors of Dinsy's world: Reference Maroon, Brown Leather, Peplum Beige, Reader's Guide Green, World Book Red, Card Catalog Cream, Date Stamp Purple, and Palatino Black.

It was a very special birthday, that fourth of July. Although Dinsy wondered about Marian's calculations. As Harriet cut the first piece of cake that evening, she remarked that it was snowing rather heavily outside, which everyone agreed was lovely, but quite unusual for that time of year.

Dinsy soon learned all the planets, and many of their moons. (She referred to herself as Umbriel for an entire month.) She puffed up her cheeks and blew onto stacks of scrap paper. "Sirocco," she'd whisper. "Chinook. Mistral. Willy-Willy," and rated her attempts on the Beaufort scale. Dorothy put a halt to it after Hurricane Dinsy reshuffled a rather elaborate game of Patience.

She dipped into fractals here, double dactyls there. When she tired of a subject—or found it just didn't suit her—Blythe or Dorothy would smile and proffer the hat. It was a deep green felt that held slips of paper numbered 001 to 999. Dinsy'd scrunch her eyes closed, pick one, and, like a scavenger hunt, spend the morning (or the next three weeks) at the shelves indicated.

Pangolins lived at 599 (point 31), and Pancakes at 641. Pencils were at 674 but Pens were a shelf away at 681, and

Ink was across the aisle at 667. (Dinsy thought that was stupid, because you had to *use* them together.) Pluto the planet was at 523, but Pluto the Disney dog was at 791 (point 453), near Rock and Roll and Kazoos.

It was all very useful information. But in Dinsy's opinion, things could be a little *too* organized.

The first time she straightened up the Common Room without anyone asking, she was very pleased with herself. She had lined up everyone's teacup in a neat row on the shelf, with all the handles curving the same way, and arranged the spices in the little wooden rack: ANISE, BAY LEAVES, CHIVES, DILL WEED, PEPPERCORNS, SALT, SESAME SEEDS, SUGAR.

"Look," she said when Blythe came in to refresh her tea. "Order out of chaos." It was one of Blythe's favorite mottoes.

Blythe smiled and looked over at the spice rack. Then her smile faded and she shook her head.

"Is something wrong?" Dinsy asked. She had hoped for a compliment.

"Well, you used the alphabet," said Blythe, sighing. "I suppose it's not your fault. You were with Olive for a good many years. But you're a big girl now. You should learn the *proper* order." She picked up the salt container. "We'll start with Salt." She wrote the word on the little chalkboard hanging by the icebox, followed by the number 553.632. "Five-five-three-point-six-three-two. Because—?"

Dinsy thought for a moment. "Earth Sciences."

"Ex-actly." Blythe beamed. "Because salt is a mineral. But, now, chives. Chives are a garden crop, so they're . . ."

Dinsy bit her lip in concentration. "Six-thirty-something."

"Very good." Blythe smiled again and chalked CHIVES

635.26 on the board. "So you see, Chives should always be shelved *after* Salt, dear."

Blythe turned and began to rearrange the eight ceramic jars. Behind her back, Dinsy silently rolled her eyes.

Edith appeared in the doorway.

"Oh, not again," she said. "No wonder I can't find a thing in this kitchen. Blythe, I've *told* you. Bay Leaf comes first. QK-four-nine—" She had worked at the university when she was younger.

"Library of Congress, my fanny," said Blythe, not quite under her breath. "We're not *that* kind of library."

"It's no excuse for imprecision," Edith replied. They each grabbed a jar and stared at each other.

Dinsy tiptoed away and hid in the 814s, where she read "Jabberwocky" until the coast was clear.

But the kitchen remained a taxonomic battleground. At least once a week, Dinsy was amused by the indignant sputtering of someone who had just spooned dill weed, not sugar, into a cup of Earl Grey tea.

Once she knew her way around, Dinsy was free to roam the library as she chose.

"Anywhere?" she asked Blythe.

"Anywhere you like, my sweet. Except the Stacks. You're not quite old enough for the Stacks."

Dinsy frowned. "I am *so,*" she muttered. But the Stacks were locked, and there wasn't much she could do.

Some days she sat with Olive in the Children's Room, revisiting old friends, or explored the maze of the Main Room. Other days she spent in the Reference Room, where Ruth and Harriet

guarded the big important books that no one could ever, ever check out—not even when the library had been open.

Ruth and Harriet were like a set of salt-and-pepper shakers from two different yard sales. Harriet had faded orange hair and a sharp, kind face. Small and pinched and pointed, a decade or two away from wizened. She had violet eyes and a mischievous, conspiratorial smile and wore rimless octagonal glasses, like stop signs. Dinsy had never seen an actual stop sign, but she'd looked at pictures.

Ruth was Chinese. She wore wool jumpers in neon plaids and had cat's-eye glasses on a beaded chain around her neck. She never put them all the way on, just lifted them to her eyes and peered through them without opening the bows.

"Life is a treasure hunt," said Harriet.

"Knowledge is power," said Ruth. "Knowing where to look is half the battle."

"Half the fun," added Harriet. Ruth almost never got the last word.

They introduced Dinsy to dictionaries and almanacs, encyclopedias and compendiums. They had been native guides through the country of the Dry Tomes for many years, but they agreed that Dinsy delved unusually deep.

"Would you like to take a break, love?" Ruth asked one afternoon. "It's nearly time for tea."

"I *am* fatigued," Dinsy replied, looking up from *Roget.* "Fagged out, weary, a bit spent. Tea would be pleasant, agreeable—"

"I'll put the kettle on," sighed Ruth.

Dinsy read *Bartlett's* as if it were a catalog of conversations, spouting lines from Tennyson, Mark Twain, and Dale

Carnegie until even Harriet put her hands over her ears and began to hum "Stairway to Heaven."

One or two evenings a month, usually after Blythe had remarked "Well, she's a spirited girl," for the third time, they all took the night off, "for Library business." Olive or Dorothy would tuck Dinsy in early and read from one of her favorites while Ruth made her a bedtime treat—a cup of spiced tea that tasted a little like cherries and a little like varnish, and which Dinsy somehow never remembered finishing.

A list (written in diverse hands), tacked to the wall of the Common Room.

10 Things to Remember When You Live in a Library

1. We do not play shuffleboard on the Reading Room table.
2. Books should not have "dog's ears." Bookmarks make lovely presents.
3. Do not write in books. Even in pencil. Puzzle collections and connect-the-dots are books.
4. The shelving cart is not a scooter.
5. Library paste is not food.
   [Marginal note in a child's hand: True. It tastes like Cream of Wrong soup.]
6. Do not use the date stamp to mark your banana.
7. Shelves are not monkey bars.
8. Do not play 982-pickup with the P-Q drawer (or any other).

9. **The dumbwaiter is only for books. It is not a carnival ride.**
10. **Do not drop volumes of the Britannica off the stairs to hear the echo.**

They were an odd, but contented family. There were rules, to be sure, but Dinsy never lacked for attention. With seven mothers, there was always someone to talk with, a hankie for tears, a lap or a shoulder to share a story.

Most evenings, when Dorothy had made a fire in the Reading Room and the wooden shelves gleamed in the flickering light, they would all sit in companionable silence. Ruth knitted, Harriet muttered over an acrostic, Edith stirred the cocoa so it wouldn't get a skin. Dinsy sat on the rug, her back against the knees of whomever was her favorite that week, and felt safe and warm and loved. "God's in his heaven, all's right with the world," as Blythe would say.

But as she watched the moon peep in and out of the clouds through the leaded-glass panes of the tall windows, Dinsy often wondered what it would be like to see the whole sky, all around her.

First Olive and then Dorothy had been in charge of Dinsy's thick dark hair, trimming it with the mending shears every few weeks when it began to obscure her eyes. But a few years into her second decade at the library, Dinsy began cutting it herself, leaving it as wild and spiky as the brambles outside the front door.

That was not the only change.

"We haven't seen her at breakfast in weeks," Harriet said as she buttered a scone one morning.

"Months. And all she reads is Salinger. Or Sylvia Plath," complained Dorothy. "I wouldn't mind that so much, but she just leaves them on the table for *me* to reshelve."

"It's not as bad as what she did to Olive," Marian said. "*The Golden Compass* appeared last week, and she thought Dinsy would enjoy it. But not only did she turn up her nose, she had the gall to say to Olive, 'Leave me alone. I can find my own books.' Imagine. Poor Olive was beside herself."

"She used to be such a sweet child." Blythe sighed. "What are we going to do?"

"Now, now. She's just at that age," Edith said calmly. "She's not really a child anymore. She needs some privacy, and some responsibility. I have an idea."

And so it was that Dinsy got her own room—with a door that *shut*—in a corner of the second floor. It had been a tiny cubbyhole of an office, but it had a set of slender curved stairs, wrought iron worked with lilies and twigs, which led up to the turret between the red-tiled eaves.

The round tower was just wide enough for Dinsy's bed, with windows all around. There had once been a view of the town, but now trees and ivy allowed only jigsaw puzzle–shaped puddles of light to dapple the wooden floor. At night the puddles were luminous blue splotches of moonlight that hinted of magic beyond her reach.

On the desk in the room below, centered in a pool of yel-

low lamplight, Edith had left a note: "Come visit me. There's mending to be done," and a worn brass key on a wooden paddle, stenciled with the single word: STACKS.

The Stacks were in the basement, behind a locked gate at the foot of the metal spiral staircase that descended from the 600s. They had always reminded Dinsy of the steps down to the dungeon in *The King's Stilts*. Darkness below hinted at danger, but adventure. Terra Incognita.

Dinsy didn't use her key the first day, or the second. Mending? Boring. But the afternoon of the third day, she ventured down the spiral stairs. She had been as far as the gate before, many times, because it was forbidden, to peer through the metal mesh at the dimly lighted shelves and imagine what treasures might be hidden there.

She had thought that the Stacks would be damp and cold, strewn with odd bits of discarded library flotsam. Instead they were cool and dry, and smelled very different from upstairs. Dustier, with hints of mold and the tang of vintage leather, an undertone of vinegar stored in an old shoe.

Unlike the main floor, with its polished wood and airy high ceilings, the Stacks were a low, cramped warren of gunmetal gray shelves that ran floor to ceiling in narrow aisles. Seven levels twisted behind the west wall of the library like a secret labyrinth that stretched from below the ground to up under the eaves of the roof. The floor and steps were translucent glass brick, and the six-foot ceilings strung with pipes and ducts were lit by single caged bulbs, two to an aisle.

It was a windowless fortress of books. Upstairs the shelves were mosaics of all colors and sizes, but the Stacks were filled

with geometric monochrome blocks of subdued colors: eight dozen forest-green bound volumes of *Ladies' Home Journal* filled five rows of shelves, followed by an equally large block of identical dark red *LIFE*s.

Dinsy felt like she was in another world. She was not lost, but for one of the few times in her life, she was not easily found, and that suited her. She could sit, invisible, and listen to the sounds of library life going on around her. From Level Three she could hear Ruth humming in the Reference Room on the other side of the wall. Four feet away, and it felt like miles. She wandered and browsed for a month before she presented herself at Edith's office.

A frosted glass pane in the dark wood door said MENDING ROOM in chipping gold letters. The door was open a few inches, and Dinsy could see a long workbench strewn with sewn folios and bits of leather bindings, spools of thread and bottles of thick beige glue.

"I gather you're finding your way around," Edith said, without turning in her chair. "I haven't had to send out a search party."

"Pretty much," Dinsy replied. "I've been reading old magazines." She flopped into a chair to the left of the door.

"One of my favorite things," Edith agreed. "It's like time travel." Edith was a tall, solid woman with long graying hair that she wove into elaborate buns and twisted braids, secured with number-two pencils and a single tortoiseshell comb. She wore blue jeans and and vests in brightly muted colors—pale teal and lavender and dusky rose—with a strand of lapis lazuli beads cut in rough ovals.

Edith repaired damaged books, a job that was less demanding now that nothing left the building. But some of the bound volumes of journals and abstracts and magazines went back as far as 1870, and their leather bindings were crumbling into dust. The first year, Dinsy's job was to go through the aisles, level by level, and find the volumes that needed the most help. Edith gave her a clipboard and told her to check in now and then.

Dinsy learned how to take apart old books and put them back together again. Her first mending project was the tattered 1877 volume of *American Naturalist*, with its articles on "Educated Fleas" and "Barnacles" and "The Cricket as Thermometer." She sewed pages into signatures, trimmed leather, and marbleized paper. Edith let her make whatever she wanted out of the scraps, and that year Dinsy gave everyone miniature replicas of their favorite volumes for Christmas.

She liked the craft, liked doing something with her hands. It took patience and concentration, and that was oddly soothing. After supper, she and Edith often sat and talked for hours, late into the night, mugs of cocoa on their workbenches, the rest of the library dark and silent above them.

"What's it like outside?" Dinsy asked one night while she was waiting for some glue to dry.

Edith was silent for a long time, long enough that Dinsy wondered if she'd spoken too softly, and was about to repeat the question, when Edith replied.

"Chaos."

That was not anything Dinsy had expected. "What do you mean?"

"It's noisy. It's crowded. Everything's always changing, and not in any way you can predict."

"That sounds kind of exciting," Dinsy said.

"Hmm." Edith thought for a moment. "Yes, I suppose it could be."

Dinsy mulled that over and fiddled with a scrap of leather, twisting it in her fingers before she spoke again. "Do you ever miss it?"

Edith turned on her stool and looked at Dinsy. "Not often," she said slowly. "Not as often as I'd thought. But then I'm awfully fond of order. Fonder than most, I suppose. This is a better fit."

Dinsy nodded and took a sip of her cocoa.

A few months later, she asked the Library for a third and final boon.

The evening that everything changed, Dinsy sat in the armchair in her room, reading Trollope's *Can You Forgive Her?* (for the third time), imagining what it would be like to talk to Glencora, when a tentative knock sounded at the door.

"Dinsy? Dinsy?" said a tiny familiar voice. "It's Olive, dear."

Dinsy slid her READ! bookmark into chapter 14 and closed the book. "It's open," she called.

Olive padded in wearing a red flannel robe, her feet in worn carpet slippers. Dinsy expected her to proffer a book, but instead Olive said, "I'd like you to come with me, dear." Her blue eyes shone with excitement.

"What for?" They had all done a nice reading of *As You*

Like It a few days before, but Dinsy didn't remember any plans for that night. Maybe Olive just wanted company. Dinsy had been meaning to spend an evening in the Children's Room, but hadn't made it down there in months.

But Olive surprised her. "It's Library business," she said, waggling her finger, and smiling.

Now, that was intriguing. For years, whenever the Librarians wanted an evening to themselves, they'd disappear down into the Stacks after supper, and would never tell her why. "It's Library business," was all they ever said. When she was younger, Dinsy had tried to follow them, but it's hard to sneak in a quiet place. She was always caught and given that awful cherry tea. The next thing she knew it was morning.

"Library business?" Dinsy said slowly. "And I'm invited?"

"Yes, dear. You're practically all grown up now. It's high time you joined us."

"Great." Dinsy shrugged, as if it were no big deal, trying to hide her excitement. And maybe it wasn't a big deal. Maybe it was a meeting of the rules committee, or plans for moving the 340s to the other side of the window again. But what if it *was* something special . . . ? That was both exciting and a little scary.

She wiggled her feet into her own slippers and stood up. Olive barely came to her knees. Dinsy touched the old woman's white hair affectionately, remembering when she used to snuggle into that soft lap. Such a long time ago.

A library at night is a still but resonant place. The only lights were the sconces along the walls, and Dinsy could hear the faint echo of each footfall on the stairs down to the foyer.

They walked through the shadows of the shelves in the Main Room, back to the 600s, and down the metal stairs to the Stacks, footsteps ringing hollowly.

The lower level was dark except for a single caged bulb above the rows of *National Geographics*, their yellow bindings pale against the gloom. Olive turned to the left.

"Where are we going?" Dinsy asked. It was so odd to be down there with Olive.

"You'll see," Olive said. Dinsy could practically feel her smiling in the dark. "You'll see."

She led Dinsy down an aisle of boring municipal reports and stopped at the far end, in front of the door to the janitorial closet set into the stone wall. She pulled a long, old-fashioned brass key from the pocket of her robe and handed it to Dinsy.

"You open it, dear. The keyhole's a bit high for me."

Dinsy stared at the key, at the door, back at the key. She'd been fantasizing about "Library Business" since she was little, imagining all sorts of scenarios, none of them involving cleaning supplies. A monthly poker game. A secret tunnel into town, where they all went dancing, like the twelve princesses. Or a book group, reading forbidden texts. And now they were inviting her in? What a letdown if it was just maintenance.

She put the key in the lock. "Funny," she said as she turned it. "I've always wondered what went on when you—" Her voice caught in her throat. The door opened, not onto the closet of mops and pails and bottles of Pine-Sol she expected, but onto a small room paneled in wood the color of ancient honey. An Oriental rug in rich, deep reds lay on the parquet

floor, and the room shone with the light of dozens of candles. There were no shelves, no books, just a small fireplace at one end where a log crackled in the hearth.

"Surprise," said Olive softly. She gently tugged Dinsy inside.

All the others were waiting, dressed in flowing robes of different colors. Each of them stood in front of a Craftsman rocker, dark wood covered in soft brown leather.

Edith stepped forward and took Dinsy's hand. She gave it a gentle squeeze and said, under her breath, "Don't worry." Then she winked and led Dinsy to an empty rocker. "Stand here," she said, and returned to her own seat.

Stunned, Dinsy stood, her mouth open, her feelings a kaleidoscope.

"Welcome, dear one," said Dorothy. "We'd like you to join us." Her face was serious, but her eyes were bright, as if she was about to tell a really awful riddle and couldn't wait for the reaction.

Dinsy started. That was almost word for word what Olive had said, and it made her nervous. She wasn't sure what was coming, and was even less sure that she was ready.

"Introductions first." Dorothy closed her eyes and intoned, "I am Lexica. I serve the Library." She bowed her head once and sat down.

Dinsy stared, her eyes wide and her mind reeling as each of the librarians repeated what was obviously a familiar rite.

"I am Juvenilia," said Olive with a twinkle. "I serve the Library."

"Incunabula," said Edith.

"Sapientia," said Harriet.

"Ephemera," said Marian.

"Marginalia," said Ruth.

"Melvilia," said Blythe, smiling at Dinsy. "And I, too, serve the Library."

And then they were all seated, and all looking up at Dinsy.

"How old are you now, my sweet?" asked Harriet.

Dinsy frowned. It wasn't as easy a question as it sounded. "Seventeen," she said after a few seconds. "Or close enough."

"No longer a child." Harriet nodded. There was a touch of sadness in her voice. "That is why we are here tonight. To ask you to join us."

There was something so solemn in Harriet's voice that it made Dinsy's stomach knot up. "I don't understand," she said slowly. "What do you mean? I've been here my whole life. Practically."

Dorothy shook her head. "You have been *in* the Library, but not *of* the Library. Think of it as an apprenticeship. We have nothing more to teach you. So we're asking if you'll take a Library name and truly become one of us. There have always been seven to serve the Library."

Dinsy looked around the room. "Won't I be the eighth?" she asked. She was curious, but she was also stalling for time.

"No, dear," said Olive. "You'll be taking my place. I'm retiring. I can barely reach the second shelves these days, and soon I'll be no bigger than the dictionary. I'm going to put my feet up and sit by the fire and take it easy. I've earned it," she said with a decisive nod.

"Here, here," said Blythe. "And well done, too."

There was a murmur of assent around the room.

Dinsy took a deep breath, and then another. She looked around the room at the eager faces of the seven librarians, the only mothers she had ever known. She loved them all, and was about to disappoint them, because she had a secret of her own. She closed her eyes so she wouldn't see their faces, not at first.

"I can't take your place, Olive," she said quietly, and heard the tremor in her own voice as she fought back tears.

All around her the librarians clucked in surprise. Ruth recovered first. "Well, of course not. No one's asking you to *replace* Olive, we're merely —"

"I can't join you," Dinsy repeated. Her voice was just as quiet, but it was stronger. "Not now."

"But why *not,* sweetie?" That was Blythe, who sounded as if she were about to cry herself.

"Fireworks," said Dinsy after a moment. She opened her eyes. "Six-sixty-two-point-one." She smiled at Blythe. "I know everything about them. But I've never *seen* any." She looked from face to face again.

"I've never petted a dog or ridden a bicycle or watched the sun rise over the ocean," she said, her voice gaining courage. "I want to feel the wind and eat an ice-cream cone at a carnival. I want to smell jasmine on a spring night and hear an orchestra. I want—" She faltered, and then continued, "I want the chance to dance with a boy."

She turned to Dorothy. "You said you have nothing left to teach me. Maybe that's true. I've learned from each of you

that there's nothing in the world I can't discover and explore for myself in these books. Except the world," she added in a whisper. She felt her eyes fill with tears. "You chose the Library. I can't do that without knowing what else there might be."

"You're *leaving*?" Ruth asked in a choked voice.

Dinsy bit her lip and nodded. "I'm, well, I've—" She'd been practicing these words for days, but they were so much harder than she'd thought. She looked down at her hands.

And then Marian rescued her.

"Dinsy's going to college," she said. "Just like I did. And you, and you, and you." She pointed a finger at each of the women in the room. "We were girls before we were librarians, remember? It's her turn now."

"But how—?" asked Edith.

"Where did—?" stammered Harriet.

"I wished on the Library," said Dinsy. "And it left an application in the Unabridged. Marian helped me fill it out."

"I *am* in charge of circulation," said Marian. "What comes in, what goes out. We found her acceptance letter in the book return last week."

"But you had no transcripts," said Dorothy practically. "Where did you tell them you'd gone to school?"

Dinsy smiled. "That was Marian's idea. We told them I was home-schooled, raised by feral librarians."

And so it was that on a bright September morning, for the first time in ages, the heavy oak door of the Carnegie Library swung open. Everyone stood in the doorway, blinking in the sunlight.

"Promise you'll write," said Blythe, tucking a packet of sweets into the basket on Dinsy's arm.

The others nodded. "Yes, do."

"I'll try," she said. "But you never know how long *any*thing will take around here." She tried to make a joke of it, but she was holding back tears and her heart was hammering a mile a minute.

"You will come back, won't you? I can't put off my retirement forever." Olive was perched on top of the Circulation Desk.

"To visit, yes." Dinsy leaned over and kissed her cheek. "I promise. But to serve? I don't know. I have no idea what I'm going to find out there." She looked out into the forest that surrounded the library. "I don't even know if I'll be able to get back in, through all that."

"Take this. It will always get you in," said Marian. She handed Dinsy a small stiff pasteboard card with a metal plate in one corner, embossed with her name: DINSY CARNEGIE.

"What is it?" asked Dinsy.

"Your library card."

There were hugs all around, and tears and good-byes. But in the end, the seven librarians stood back and watched her go.

Dinsy stepped out into the world as she had come—with a wicker basket and a book of fairy tales, full of hopes and dreams.

ELLEN KLAGES lives in San Francisco. Her story "Basement Magic" won the Nebula Award for Best Novelette in 2005. Her short fiction has appeared in *The Magazine of Fantasy and Science Fiction* and *SCI FICTION*, and has been on the final ballot for the Hugo and Spectrum Awards. She was also a finalist for the John W. Campbell Award, and is a graduate of the Clarion South writing workshop.

In 2006, Viking will be publishing her first novel, *The Green Glass Sea*, about two eleven-year-old girls living in Los Alamos during World War II while their parents are building the Bomb.

Ellen also serves on the Motherboard of the James Tiptree, Jr. Award (www.tiptree.org), and is somewhat notorious as the auctioneer/entertainment for the Tiptree auctions. When she's not writing fiction, she sells old toys on eBay and collects lead civilians.

AUTHOR'S NOTE

This story came bubbling up in the Well of Ideas from a couple of different sources.

During a psychic reading about four years ago (a birthday gift from my sister), I was told that my spirit guides were seven librarians, who would help me find the answers to the questions in my life. I'm not sure I believed that, but I liked the idea, because the library was always my favorite refuge, and there have been many significant librarians in my life.

I have always lived with and around books. There was a battered, blue buckram-bound copy of *Heidi* on the bookshelf in the upstairs hall of the house I grew up in. Old book, with nice color plates, dating back to my mother's childhood.

When I was about eight I discovered that *Heidi* had a library-card pocket inside the cover. Overdue library books were a capital crime in my family, and this one had been checked out in 1933, when my mother would have been eight herself. I asked her about it, and to my surprise, she looked very embarrassed and said, in a determined but apologetic voice, "I *am* going to return it."

She'd checked it out of the Bristow, Oklahoma, library and her family had moved out of the state two weeks later. It had gotten packed by mistake. She'd been carting it around, from house to house, to college, into her marriage, feeling guilty about it for thirty years.

Sometime in the mid-1970s, she and a friend were planning a road trip, and Mom looked at the map and realized that if they made a 150-mile detour (each way), they could stop in Bristow. So that summer, my mother marched up the steps of the Bristow Public Library, plunked *Heidi* down on the circulation desk, and said, "This is overdue." An understatement. It was more than *forty years* overdue.

The librarian looked at the book, looked at my mother.

"I'll pay the fine, whatever it is." Mom pulled out her checkbook.

"That won't be necessary," the librarian said. Then she got her DISCARD stamp, whacked *Heidi,* and handed the book back.

It's sitting on my desk as I type this.

When I started thinking about a story for *Firebirds Rising,* my guiding librarians picked up *Heidi* and wandered into my brain again. They puttered around in there for months before the story began to gel. I wrote most of the first draft in a little cottage in the desert outside Tucson, with downloaded photos of old libraries on my laptop. When I got home, the manuscript and I visited a dozen old Carnegie libraries in northern Ohio, where I sat and wrote and looked at old wooden wainscoting and Craftsman-tiled fireplaces and pebbled-glass office doors. I spent a week sitting on the floor of the Stacks in a Case Western University library, making notes about the smells and the textures so that I could give them to Dinsy.

Sharon Shinn

Wintermoon Wish

All the way from Wodenderry to Merendon, I sat alone in the coach and scowled. I couldn't believe that no one, not even my cousin Renner, was willing to leave the royal city and miss the queen's ball.

But I had never spent a Wintermoon away from my grandparents' inn in Merendon, and I was not about to start now. Now that the whole world was bleak and my life nothing but a blighted promise.

My aunt tells me I am a fanciful girl with a flair for the dramatic. My mother says more plainly that I overreact to everything. In this instance, at any rate, I was sure I had a broken heart and nothing would mend it except a trip to Merendon, and even that didn't seem likely to do the trick. But who would want to stay in Wodenderry, when Trevor was in love with Corrinne and taking her to the Wintermoon ball?

The weather was bitterly cold and even my father's well-built carriage could not keep out the drafts. Our frequent stops for hot tea at little inns along the way were still not enough to warm me all the way through. By the time we

arrived in Merendon, just around sunset, my feet were icicles in their fashionable fur-lined boots and I couldn't feel my fingers in my gloves. We pulled up in front of the Leaf & Berry Inn and my heart sank: there were no welcome lights pouring from the front door or the upper-story windows. The inn looked as dark and cold as the interior of the coach.

But when the driver carried my luggage around back to the kitchen door, my spirits rose again. I could see my grandmother through the window, working at the stove, her white hair piled on top of her head, her hands busy, her face serene. I could smell the baking bread and roasting chicken. The very shape and scent of the scene before me matched the picture of *home* I always carried in my heart.

I was almost in tears as I burst through the door, and my grandmother dropped her spoon with a clatter. "Lirril! You startled me. Oh, look at you, you're half-frozen. Come sit by the stove. Bob! Build up a fire in the parlor! Lirril's here and she's a little ice-child."

I felt better than I had for days.

My grandfather bustled in, gathered me in a big hug, paid a handsome tip to the driver, and made sure the man had a place to spend the night. I sat at the kitchen table, sipping tea and inhaling the smells of the house. Dinner and wine and pie in here; wax and polish and soap drifting in from the other rooms. Overlaying it all, a sharper, sweeter odor, the very scent of Wintermoon.

"You've started the wreath already, haven't you?" I said, my voice just a touch accusatory. "You knew I was coming, and you couldn't wait until I got here?"

My grandmother looked amused. "We've gathered some

spruce and some rowan, and I've put some greens over the banister, but we haven't finished braiding the wreath," she said. "Don't worry, you'll have plenty to do."

"A mighty cold Wintermoon it's going to be," my grandfather observed, stepping out the door to fetch another pile of wood. "Glad you made it here before the snow. Supposed to start falling tomorrow afternoon."

In a few moments, the three of us were gathered cozily around the kitchen table, eating my grandmother's excellent meal and catching up on events. Well, mostly *I* told *them* everything that had been happening to me lately. Their lives tended not to hold much excitement or variation. *Oh, we had three guests come through last week, and a family of five stopped here the week before. Things were slow over the summer, but that gave us time to sew new curtains and finish the floors in the back bedroom on the second floor.* I had far more to relate.

I hadn't planned to bring up Trevor's name, but my grandmother had an uncannily good memory, which sometimes came in handy and sometimes did not. "What about that boy?" she asked as she served the pie. "The one you were so keen on this summer? Trevor? Was that his name?"

"Oh, I'm not interested in him anymore," I said, my voice quite airy. "He's—well, he's—anyway, Corrinne has been flirting with him most shamelessly. So of course he's practically infatuated with her. He even wrote her a poem a couple of weeks ago. A poem! Did you ever hear of such a silly thing?"

I had been shockingly jealous when Corrinne showed it to us—to me, and the other girls from my school who had formed a circle of friends. It wasn't a very good poem, it

didn't even rhyme, but you could tell by its extravagant praise how much Trevor adored her. I had been in love with Trevor all my life—or, at least, since he had danced with me two years ago when I was fourteen and allowed to go to my first Summermoon ball at the palace. But he had never so much as written my name on a calling card to be left at my parents' house.

My grandparents looked amused. "Never was much of one for poems myself," my grandfather said. "Still, that seems like a powerful sign of attraction. Man who'd write a poem for a girl would do anything for her, I suppose."

"I wonder if your father ever wrote a poem for your mother," my grandmother said to me.

"He would have if she'd asked him to," my grandfather spoke up. "That man would have done anything she wanted. He courted her for months. He's still courting her, all these years later."

Revolted, I put up my hands. "Please. Stop."

"I'm going to ask him about that poem," my grandfather said, teasing me.

My grandmother stood. "I'm going to clear the dishes. You two get started on the wreath."

The best part of Wintermoon: braiding the wreath. I happily settled on the floor beside my grandfather and helped him plait the long, whippy branches together, tying them at intervals with red and gold cords. My fingers were soon sticky with sap and I had sharp little needles all over my dress. My grandmother joined us about thirty minutes later, carrying a basket of odds and ends.

"Oh, here's a few pearls from that necklace that broke . . . let's tie those on. Those will be for—well, what do you think? A wedding? Yes, pearls for a wedding. And some of that blue silk from the back bedroom. How about serenity? Now don't forget the dried fruit—that's for prosperity, Lirril, never make a wreath without it."

My grandfather had his own contributions—dried cedar chips and a bird's wing and a scrap of fabric from a ship's ripped sail—though sometimes his connections between object and the magic they could confer seemed tenuous at best. I had only one extra bit to bind into the wreath, a long ribbon embroidered with alternating hearts and birds.

"That's for love," I said, knotting it around the woven branches.

"That's something everyone needs every year," my grandmother said.

When we were done, my grandfather hung the great wreath over the fireplace and it made a dense shape of promise over the mantel. Tomorrow night we would build a bonfire in the back, between the chatterleaf and kirrenberry trees that gave the inn its name, and we would throw the wreath into the blaze. All our hopes for the new year written in flame. Guaranteed to come true.

I slept deeply and well—for the first time in days—in the small bedroom on the third floor. It was the room that had belonged to my mother and her twin when they were growing up. Even once I woke, I didn't realize how far advanced the morning was, because so little light was coming in the double

windows. When I finally rose and dressed and peeked outside, I understood why: snow was falling so heavily that the sky was leaden and gray. The clouds were piled so deeply overhead that I couldn't imagine the sun would ever shine.

I skipped downstairs, calling, "Look at the snow! Look at it! There must be two feet on the ground already!" I didn't care much for snow on the crowded streets of Wodenderry, but here in Merendon, where I didn't need to leave the inn for a single necessity, snow was a delight.

"No one will be traveling far this day," my grandmother observed. "So anyone who has somewhere to get on Wintermoon had better be there by now."

I danced around the kitchen. "No one's here—we've got the inn all to ourselves," I exclaimed. "We can eat all the pie—and drink all the cider—and stay up as late as we want. No guests! No chores!"

My grandmother laughed. My grandfather said, "I'll just go chop some more wood."

Half an hour later, the stage from Oakton arrived.

It came feeling its way through the blizzard like a blind child down a tunnel and arrived at the front door like an omen of doom. My grandfather ran out to exchange a few words with the coachman. I watched as the door to the coach pushed open—a maneuver that took some effort against the wind—and a single figure stepped out, landing knee-deep in the drift of snow. He was tall and reedy, wearing an inadequate coat against the searing chill of the weather, and his head was uncovered. I could see his face, angular and thin, and his eyes, dark and devoid of hope. He couldn't have

been more than a year or two older than I was, but he looked weighed down by cares or disappointments. A more pitiful, dispirited, unwelcome visitor you could not imagine having arrive on your doorstep on Wintermoon.

"Oh no," I breathed as he fought his way up the walk toward the front door. "Oh *no*."

My grandmother had materialized beside me and was looking out the front door, serene as always. She said, "Looks like we've got company for Wintermoon."

His name was Jake. That was about all we learned about him during dinner that night, and I wasn't even interested in that much information. The four of us sat around the bigger table in the dining room and passed around food while we made labored conversation. His name was Jake, he was headed toward Thrush Hollow. He was sorry to be caught in the storm, yes, ma'am, so glad there was a place that could take him in, he was sorry if he was any trouble. He had the money to pay. He was polite and, once he'd warmed up a little, not unattractive in an intense and moping fashion. But who wanted strangers around on Wintermoon? Wintermoon was a time for family! For being with the people you loved most in the world! There was almost never anyone at the inn for Wintermoon. Why hadn't he started his journey a day or two earlier if he was so eager to join up with his parents or siblings or cousins or whomever he was off to visit? Why was he *here, now,* with *my* family, spoiling *my* Wintermoon? I could not have been unhappier if I had still been in Wodenderry.

Well, yes, I could have. But not much.

"So, Jake, would you like to help me build the bonfire?" my grandfather asked in his genial way as we finished the pie. I had to admit, even though we'd had to share it, there was plenty of pie for everyone. "It's dark enough now."

Jake came to his feet, looking uncertain. "You build a bonfire? Do you burn a wreath, too?"

"Well, goodness, doesn't everybody?" my grandmother exclaimed.

Jake gave her a crooked grin and looked, for the first time, boyish. "I haven't. Not for years."

"You don't have to help," my grandfather said.

"He wants to," my grandmother replied briskly. "Go on out there, you two. Lirril and I will clear the dishes. We'll come out when the fire's good and hot."

Jake put on his threadbare coat and followed my grandfather out the kitchen door to where most of the fire had already been laid. I watched from the window as they brushed away the accumulated snow and searched for dry kindling. Jake moved slowly, like a man at an unfamiliar task, but willingly, as if learning something he would like to know. Twice I saw him smile at something my grandfather said. He had only smiled once throughout the entire meal.

"He seems like a nice boy," my grandmother said, scrubbing at the dishes.

I sniffed. "How can you tell? He hardly said a word."

"Looks like he's had a hard life, though."

"He's so wretched he's pathetic."

My grandmother gave me one of her rare looks of disapproval. Her eyes were an odd blue, pale but pretty; my own

eyes were exactly the same color. "Better to be pathetic than to be cruel," she said.

My eyes widened. "I wasn't mean to him!"

"See that you aren't," she said.

I had just wiped down the table when Jake came back inside. "Bob says I should get the wreath down," he said in an apologetic voice, as if he thought it was something that would upset us. My grandmother just nodded, but I was instantly antagonized.

"It's not *time* to burn the wreath yet," I said. "We *never* burn it till midnight."

Jake nodded somberly. "No. That's what he said. He thought maybe I'd have something to bind to the branches."

I was frowning, but my grandmother was nodding. "That's a good idea. What would you like to add in?"

Jake looked despondent. "I don't know. Nothing I can think of."

"Nonsense. Everyone has a wish at Wintermoon," my grandmother said. "Come help me take it down, and Lirril and I will tell you all the wishes we've tied on to it so far. Then you can tell us what it's missing."

We put this plan into action, although—as I could have foretold—none of our blue silk and bird feathers and cedar chips inspired Jake to articulate his own desires. He did finger my embroidered ribbon and look wistful when my grandmother told him it represented love.

"Man-and-woman love or home-and-family love?" he asked.

"Either. Both," my grandmother said firmly.

"And these dried apricots—these mean a happy home?"

"A prosperous one," my grandmother corrected. "But, now, I like that. Let's find something to stand for a warm house, filled with joy. Jake, what did you bring that we can tie to the wreath?"

His expression was a little bitter. "Nothing you can use for that, I'm afraid."

"No, I'll pull a splinter from the front sign and tie that on with some ribbon. No place happier than the Leaf & Berry! Though that sign is a disgrace. More than twenty years old now, so weathered you almost can't read the lettering. There's paint in the barn, but Bob hasn't had a minute to sit down and put on a fresh coat." She paused, remembered why she had started her sentence, and continued. "But that's not what I meant. We need something of yours to wrap around the wreath. So you're part of the celebration. So your own wishes will catch on fire. Then, you know, they're more likely to come true."

Smiling a little, Jake investigated his pockets to reveal them almost empty. It didn't take much imagination to picture his single duffel bag to be the same. I couldn't imagine that he would have a thing worth contributing to our wreath, but I knew my grandmother well enough to know she would not be satisfied until we had *something* of Jake's to throw in the flames tonight.

"What about the top button on your shirt?" I asked. "It's about to fall off, anyway." My grandmother gave me a look that I couldn't interpret, so I added, "Or I could get a needle and thread and sew it back on for you."

Jake lifted a hand and yanked the button off with one quick pull. "No, I'll be happy to donate it to the wreath," he said. "It's metal, though—I don't know if it will burn."

"Then you can rescue it tomorrow morning and sew it on then," my grandmother said. "Something that survives the fire is always luck."

Soon enough we had attached our last contributions and leaned the wreath against the wall. My grandfather came stamping in, alternately rubbing his ears and blowing on his fingers. "*Mighty* cold out," he observed. "Believe I'll come in for a spell and warm up. Lirril, do you and Jake want to go out and watch the fire for a while?"

Jake looked surprised at the invitation, but I was already on my feet; I'd known it was coming. That was the tradition at the Leaf & Berry. My grandfather always started the fire, then he let someone else tend it till midnight, when the wreath was thrown on. Then he and my grandmother stayed up till dawn, watching the flames, shooing everyone else back inside so they could be alone before the dying fire. I had always wondered what made Wintermoon such a special holiday for the two of them. Neither my mother nor my aunt knew the answer.

"Go on. You two young ones keep the fire going," my grandmother said, waving us toward the door. "We'll come out later."

So I pulled on my gloves and my winter coat and my fur-lined boots and followed Jake out the kitchen door. The snow had stopped falling but lay thick on the ground like acres of profligate diamonds. The bonfire was a brilliant living jewel against the sere dark. The air was so cold that for a minute I

lost the ability to breathe. I ran through the snowdrifts and hovered as close to the fire as I could bear. Jake followed more slowly but came just as close. For a while we stood in silence, stretching our hands out to the flames, inhaling the scents of cedar and spruce and snow.

It occurred to me that Jake was not the most talkative of people, and that the night was going to be extremely dull and extremely long if we passed it in silence, and that if I wanted conversation, I was going to have to initiate it myself. I glared resentfully into the dark, and then sighed and glanced over at him.

"So, Jake," I said. "I take it your family lives in Thrush Hollow?"

He eyed me uncertainly. "Some of them. An uncle and some cousins."

"Do you always spend Wintermoon with them?"

"No."

I waited, but he had no more to add. "Where do you come from? Did you ride the stage all the way from Oakton?"

He nodded.

I found myself starting to wish I was keeping the Wintermoon vigil by myself. "What do you do there? I'm guessing you have a job?"

He nodded again. "Had one. Worked in a carpenter's shop. I did a lot of the staining and painting. I wasn't that good with the lathe and tools."

I could hardly miss his use of the past tense. "But you don't work there now?"

"Now I'm moving to Thrush Hollow."

"To be with your uncle?" That elicited another nod. "That'll be nice." He shrugged.

I let the silence run out for a good long while. Long enough for the flames to die down and for Jake to carefully pile on a few more logs. Long enough for him to glance at me, glance away, look back at the house, cut his eyes in my direction again. I was feeling anything but kindly, but I gave him a nod meant to be encouraging. *Go ahead. Your turn to ask questions.*

"Um," he said. "So they call you Lirril?" I nodded. He said, "I never came across that name before."

"It's a mirror name," I said. He looked blank. "It's the same forward and backward. My grandmother's and grandfather's names, too. Hannah and Bob. It's something our family does."

"And you live here with your grandparents?"

"No. I live in Wodenderry with my mother and father. But we always come to Merendon for Wintermoon and I didn't want to miss it this year just because—" I shut my mouth with a snap.

"Because?"

I shrugged. "Oh, there's a ball there, and everyone wanted to attend, but *I* didn't want to go, I wanted to be *here,* and so I came to the inn while they stayed behind. They'll be here tomorrow, though, with my aunt and my uncle and my cousin Renner." I shot a look up at the sky. "If it's stopped snowing. If the roads are clear."

"Why didn't you want to go to the ball?" he asked.

Why would he think to ask that? And his voice was so soft, so serious, as if he really cared to know the answer. I shrugged

again, not quite so pettishly. "Because my feelings were hurt. Because I was afraid it would make me sad. There's a man I know and he—" I hunched my shoulders. "And I'd rather be here. I love it here."

"I would, too," he agreed. "If I had a place like this to go to? I wouldn't wait till Wintermoon. I'd stay here all the time."

I was starting to think I could guess the answer for myself, and I didn't even want to *know* it, but I asked anyway. "So where are your parents?"

"Dead," he said flatly.

He added nothing to the single word. "I'm—that's—I'm sorry," I stammered. "When did—what happened?"

Now he was the one to give a shrug. "My mother died a long time ago. My father last year."

I could scarcely imagine such a thing. "What did you do without them?"

A ghost of a smile. "Worked. Found a place to stay. I did all right."

"But what about your family? Your aunts and uncles and grandparents? Why didn't you go to them?"

"I'm going now. To my uncle."

I had a sudden dreadful premonition. "Does he know you're coming?"

Jake almost laughed. "No."

"Will he be happy to see you?"

Jake looked lost for a moment, young. My age or even younger. "I don't know. He and my father hadn't spoken for years. He doesn't even know my father's dead. I just thought—it was worth a try. I don't have anywhere else to go."

"Why couldn't you stay in Oakton?"

"I could. I'll go back, I guess, if things don't work out in Thrush Hollow. But the carpenter I worked for sold his shop and the new owner had sons of his own to do the work and I—there wasn't a place for me there. I was always curious about my uncle. Seemed like as good a time as any to find out what he was like."

I felt so sorry for him that I almost despised him. Who could be so wretched and alone? Who could be so adrift in the world? I didn't want to wonder what his life might be like, so different from my own. I closed my heart and glanced away.

"I'm sure you'll like Thrush Hollow," I said, my voice indifferent. "Everyone says it's very pretty." He caught my tone, rebuffed as I meant him to be. He merely nodded and did not answer. He watched the fire a little longer, then added a few more logs. The old ones collapsed in a shower of sparks, which flung themselves into the snow and hissed out. Neither of us so much as winced away.

Now a determined silence held us both. My feet were numb inside my plush boots, and my cheeks ached with cold. Overhead, the sky was impossibly clear; the hard stars looked merciless. The full moon was so white and so brilliant it could have been sculpted from fresh snow. I wondered how much longer we had till midnight.

Jake added more fuel to the fire, then stood a moment with his back to the flames, as if to warm the other half of his body. I noted crossly that his coat was too thin. He must be even colder than I was.

"You should be wearing something heavier than that," I said.

He just looked at me for a moment. "This will do," he said.

I shrugged. Fine. If he didn't want to go in and put on a sweater, I didn't care.

We were quiet for another long stretch. The fire shifted again and the flames contracted, licking their small orange tongues around the charred embers of the bottom logs. Jake knelt to poke at the templed branches, teasing the fire back out. I accidentally glanced down at the bottoms of his feet.

"You have *holes* in your *shoes*!" I exclaimed. "What are you—you could get *frostbite* out here on a night like this!"

He gave me a dark look but didn't answer, merely continued prodding at the fire till the blaze caught again. He knelt there awhile longer to make sure the fire was really going, then he stood up. "I'm fine," he said. "I rarely feel the cold."

I stared at him. "*Everybody* feels the cold on a night like this! Why don't you—I'll watch the fire. You go put on another pair of shoes."

"This is the only pair I have," he said quietly.

I stared at him a moment, hating him more than I had ever hated anyone in my life. "Very well," I said, through gritted teeth. "You watch the fire." And I stomped back into the house, so angry that I almost slammed the door behind me, so furious that I was almost blinded by the emotion. Or blinded by something. I bumped into the kitchen door and stumbled a little as I turned into the hallway. I wasn't crying, though. No, I certainly wasn't. I brought a candle with me and set it on the hall table, then peered into the closet and began to root around.

Ten minutes later I was back outside, and I practically

flung a few items to the ground at Jake's feet. "Here. Put that on. It's my father's coat." No surprise that Jake didn't answer. I continued in a hard, fast voice. "He never wears it unless he's here and the weather's so cold he can't endure it. He says it's the most unfashionable cut imaginable and no man with any taste would ever wear it." I nudged the other pieces over with my toe. "Same thing about the boots. He won't put them on. He keeps trying to give them away, but no one will take them. They're ugly, but they're warm. I brought you some socks, too."

Jake didn't make a move. "I can't take those things."

"Well, you can wear them for a night, can't you? No one else needs them this very minute. It's stupid not to put them on and then freeze to death because you were proud and stubborn."

His eyes dropped; he looked longingly at the warm wool coat. "I could pay you something," he said.

"No, you couldn't! You could just be reasonable and put this coat on. *And* these boots. Here. Give me your coat. Give it to me right now."

And I stepped up to him and started unbuttoning his own garment, tattered and miserable as it was. Two of the buttons came off in my hands; something else to tie to the wreath if we had a little time and some extra ribbon. He resisted a moment, his face creased with doubt, but I started yanking at the sleeves, and he gave in. A few moments later, wearing his new coat, he was sitting on his old one and tugging off his shoes and his thin socks.

"Socks first," I said, handing him a thick, scratchy roll.

He hesitated. His bare feet looked so white and so cold that my own toes curled in sympathy. "No man wants to lend his socks to someone else," he said. "He'd never want them back."

"Fine. Don't give them back. My father won't mind." My father wouldn't mind because he didn't even know he owned this particular pair. I'd bought them as a rather uninspired Wintermoon gift. "Jake. *Put them on.*"

Either my tone convinced him or he was too cold and tired to argue. He pulled on the socks, then laced up the boots, then rose to his feet. Unfashionable it may have been, and too big for him it definitely was, but the long dark coat gave Jake some needed weight and a certain air of grace. He looked taller, broader, older, and very, very serious.

"I wish you would let me pay you something," he said.

I stamped my foot, almost bruising it against the iron-hard earth. "It's just a stupid extra coat!" I exclaimed. "You don't owe me anything!"

"Still, I should—"

"Shovel the walk, then! Chop some firewood. My grandparents will be delighted."

"Yes, but you're the one who—"

I was so *furious.* He was so *stupid.* I gave him impossible tasks. "Make me a necklace of icicles."

"I meant something I could actually—"

"Find roses in the snow. Write me a poem." Why had I said that? I rushed on. "Bring a bluebird to breakfast."

He was silent, merely watching me with those earnest eyes. I couldn't tell if he thought I was cruel or ridiculous. "Or just say thank you," I said. "That's all that's required."

He made a stiff little motion that could have been a bow. "Thank you," he said. "Lirril. You are—thank you. This was truly kind."

Now I really did want to weep. "It wasn't kind. It was mean," I said in a muffled voice. "I just didn't want to have to feel sorry for you. So there."

Now he smiled a little. "A generous impulse born of an ungenerous thought," he said. "But I'm still warm."

"It's so unfair," I burst out.

"What is?"

"That I have—it shouldn't be that way! I have so many people who love me, and you don't have any."

"That's the way the world goes," he said.

I stared at him. If I cried, I thought my tears might freeze to my face. "But don't you want more than what you have?" I whispered.

"Of course I do," he replied. "I want a place where I fit in, people who love me, friends who come when I cry for help. I want to do work that matters, make a home that's full of happiness. I want to be the friend who goes to others when they call out. I want all those things. Who doesn't? Maybe I'll find them in Thrush Hollow. I haven't given up. I'm going to keep looking."

My mouth had formed a little O, and I stared at him by ragged firelight. Who would have expected such a passionate speech from him? He must have realized how much he aston-

ished me, for his face softened as he looked down at me.

"And what do you want, Lirril? What wishes did you tie to the Wintermoon wreath?"

Everything I had ever wanted in my life now seemed trivial and trite. Trevor to notice me. My friends to envy me. My parents to buy me explicit and expensive presents. "I wished—just—for little things," I stammered.

"That man," he said. "The one you didn't want to see at the ball. Did you wish for him to fall in love with you?"

Nothing so specific, though it had been Trevor's face I envisioned when I wrapped the ribbon around the wreath. "Even if I did, he never will," I said. "He's very fond of another girl."

"You don't need to worry," Jake said. "You probably have no idea how many others are just standing ready, waiting for you to notice them."

It was so untrue that I had to laugh. "When I'm back in Wodenderry, I'll look around," I said.

After that, strangely, it was easy to talk to Jake. He told me a little about his father, a somewhat feckless man who had painted lovely landscapes and sold them for pennies. I told him about my own father, filled with such laughter, and my mother, whose standards of honesty I had always found it hard to live up to. He liked music but did not know how to dance; I was an excellent dancer but could not play an instrument if it would save me from hanging. We had nothing in common and yet, somehow, much to discuss. I was a little shocked when my grandfather pushed through the kitchen door, the wreath in his hands. Midnight already? My grand-

mother was right behind him, carrying mugs of hot tea.

"Gracious, it's cold out here!" she exclaimed, as if we might not have noticed. "Here, I brought something to warm you both up."

We gratefully gulped the steaming liquid, and then Jake set down his cup so he could help my grandfather hoist the greenery onto the fire. The flames shot up, greedy for a taste of our heartfelt desires. I saw my embroidered ribbon turn to red fire, to black cinder, to gray smoke. My dreams of romance drifted through the star-scattered sky and crossed the face of the wide-eyed moon.

"That was a good wreath," my grandfather said approvingly. "There'll be a lot of wishes come true next year."

"You two go on into the house," my grandmother said. "We'll watch the fire till dawn."

"Are you sure?" Jake asked. "It's so cold. I could come back out in a few hours and spell you."

"They always stay out from midnight till morning," I said, stepping up to my grandfather and kissing his cheek. "May all your Wintermoon wishes come true," I murmured in his ear. He replied in kind.

Then I kissed my grandmother's soft skin, and we exchanged wishes as well. I was so cold and so tired that I wasn't absolutely certain I could cross the lawn and find my way back inside the inn. I yawned and my grandmother gave me a little push toward the door.

"Go in, now," she repeated. "You're about to fall asleep on your feet. Oh, and show Jake to his room! He's on the second floor, in the green room."

I nodded and hurried for the house, Jake behind me. Candles awaited us in the kitchen, and we carried them upstairs, their flames wavering against the hands that we had lifted to shield them. The green room was right off the stairwell, a big and cheerful chamber with the most comfortable mattress in the house. Still yawning, I pointed out the amenities.

"If you need anything else, the rest of us all sleep on the top floor. No one gets up much before noon, but you can help yourself to food in the kitchen tomorrow morning. If there's a commotion anytime, don't worry—it'll probably be my family arriving from Wodenderry. My father has a loud voice. That's how you'll know it's him."

Jake had set his candle down on the dresser across the room, and now he was watching me with those grave, intent eyes. "Thank you so much for everything you've done," he said.

I shook my head, too tired to argue. "I didn't do anything."

I turned for the door, but he surprised me by catching my arm and turning me back to face him. Bending slightly, he blew out my candle, so that we were standing in nearly total darkness. I looked up, surprised, and he took the opportunity to kiss me. His mouth was warm. His hands, raised to cup my cheeks, were cold. Fire and moonlight.

I pulled back, too amazed to say anything, either to scold or flirt. Even in the darkness, I could tell he was laughing silently. "Good night, Lirril," he said. "May all your Wintermoon wishes come true."

⊠ ⊠ ⊠

The noonday sun came through my bedroom window the next day with such force that it seemed to be muscling its way into the house. I lay drowsing in my bed a few moments, allowing myself to slowly remember the evening before. Wintermoon. My grandmother's richly satisfying meal. The glacial vigil at the bonfire. With Jake. Who had kissed me at the door just before I ran out of his room—

Well, that might make for an awkward moment or two at the dining room table. I felt a small smile play around my mouth. Jake would be more embarrassed than I. He would expect me to be angry or distant or cool. Instead, I would treat him exactly as I had at dinner the night before, as if he were a not very interesting stranger. He would not know what to think by the time he left on the stage for Thrush Hollow.

That made my smile disappear. I had forgotten. Jake would be moving on as soon as the roads were clear. He wouldn't be staying in Merendon long enough for me to tease him.

Well, who cared, anyway? Stupid old Jake. Sad, stupid, misfit Jake. It wouldn't bother me if I never saw him again.

Sounds and smells from downstairs convinced me that my grandmother was up and cooking. My room was cold, so I rose, washed, and dressed in the fastest possible time. As I skipped down the steps, I glanced at the door to Jake's room, visible from the stairwell. His door was closed, and I gave a little sniff. Still sleeping, like a man with no responsibilities or appointments. No ties, no one depending on him, not even his uncle eager to see him. No wonder he had no incentives to get out of bed.

My foot had just touched the floor at the bottom of the

steps when my grandfather called to me. "Lirril, come see this! I'm so tickled."

I followed the sound of his voice to the parlor, where the Wintermoon gifts were stacked before the fireplace. I had put my own out the night before, and, as was tradition, my grandparents had added theirs to the pile while the rest of the house lay sleeping. There were dozens of presents laid out before the fire, and there would be dozens more by the time my parents, my aunt, and my uncle made their own contributions.

My grandfather was holding up a wide, flat board, and it took me a moment to recognize it. "Look at this," he said, and turned it so I could see the other side. It was the Leaf & Berry sign, lovingly repainted, the red words laid in crisply against a stark white background, small curlicues decorating the four corners.

I came closer to admire it. "When did you have time to do that?" I asked. The oily, pleasant smell of fresh paint drifted to my nose.

"I didn't! I'm guessing it was that young man. He must have stayed up all night to do this."

I felt my face suddenly heat with an unidentifiable emotion. "Jake? Did this? Last night after we were all in bed?" I remembered that he told me he had done painting and staining for the carpenter in Oakton. But I hadn't expected this.

"Must have," my grandfather said, turning the sign this way and that as if to detect hidden subtleties. "Or even while Hannah and I were watching the fire. He cleared the walks, too, front and back."

I felt a shiver go down my back. Which of the other tasks

that I had suggested to him had he also decided to accomplish? "That's—well. What a nice thing for him to do," I said.

My grandfather nodded toward the pile of gifts. "He left you something, too. I didn't open it, of course."

My eyes were pulled irresistibly to the bounty laid out on the hearth. In all that welter, I instantly spotted it—a scroll bound with what looked like a shoelace. My name had been carefully lettered on a scrap of paper. What would I find inside?

"I've got to go thank him again," my grandfather said, carrying the sign toward the kitchen.

"I think he's still asleep."

"No, he's out back, chopping firewood for your grandmother. I must say, I do like that boy," my grandfather said, and disappeared through the swinging door.

There was no way I could keep myself from dropping to the floor and untying the makeshift ribbon. I unrolled the single sheet of paper. In handwriting that I instantly knew was Jake's, I found a poem. I read it as if I were gulping it down.

Longest night, and coldest, of the year.
Lights beat back the blackness of the sky:
Bonfire blazes, jubilantly garish;
Full moon rises, perfect as a pearl.
I do not know what fortune brought me here—
Good or ill—and yet I know that I
Will not forget, until the day I perish,
Wintermoon, and the kindness of a girl.

I could not breathe. My cheeks were so hot I thought they

might scald my fingers if I touched my own skin. I read the poem again.

I heard voices and I leaped to my feet, not sure where to lay the poem so no one could see it, not sure how to hold my hands or what expression to summon to my face. But the voices stayed outside as my grandfather and Jake came around to the front of the inn and began to discuss the best way to hang the fresh sign. A minute after they decided the old hooks would work just fine, my grandfather was hailed by a new voice.

"Hullo there, Bob! Warm Wintermoon to you and yours!" It was Adam Granger, who owned a tannery a few streets over. He was getting a little frail with age, and there was some talk he might be hiring a younger man to take over his business soon. "Your grandson in town yet?"

"No, the girls are coming in a few days. Maybe longer, if the roads aren't clear."

"That's too bad. I had some work I needed done over at the house and I was hoping to hire Renner for a few hours."

"Jake, here, he's good with his hands," my grandfather said. "What do you want done?"

"Oh, I need a couple windows reframed and there's a table that's missing a leg. Small things, but I recall that your grandson helped me out last summer, so—"

"I can do all that," Jake spoke up. His voice was quiet and confident. He didn't sound like a man who had stayed up all night, thinking up ways to show people his appreciation.

Adam sounded pleased. "Really? I got two, three more things like that you could do if you had the time."

"Stage to Thrush Hollow probably won't be through till tomorrow or the day after," my grandfather said. "Good chance for you to earn a little extra money."

"When could you come over?" Adam asked.

"Soon as the sign's hung," Jake replied. "Give me a minute."

I felt myself start to breathe again. Adam could come up with a million tasks for a strong young man. Jake might not be taking the first stage out of Merendon after all, even if it came tomorrow.

I heard some clattering above the front door as the sign was put in place, and then the fading sound of voices as Jake and Adam walked down the street. I crossed to the front window to watch them go, but all I could see was Jake's back, slim but somehow sturdier in my father's rejected coat.

My grandmother stepped into the parlor just as my grandfather came in through the front door, bringing icy air with him. "Well, I was about to ask where everyone's gone off to," my grandmother said. "I've got a meal almost ready. Where's Jake?"

"Headed out with Adam Granger to do a few chores. Seemed mighty happy at the idea of earning a few coins, too," my grandfather said.

My grandmother looked pleased. "Now, that's good for both of them," she said. "I do like that young man. Did you see all that wood he split and set up against the door? You're not going to have to lift an ax all winter."

My grandfather grinned. "Fine by me. I've got a few chores of my own I can set Jake to when he's done at Adam's."

I looked up at that, feeling even more hopeful. My hand was behind my back, holding the poem so no one could see

it, but I had a feeling that my grandfather knew what I was hiding, anyway. My grandmother almost certainly realized I was concealing something, and could guess that it was a token of someone's affection. She had probably even figured out whose. She was very good at sorting out secrets.

"Do you think Jake'll stay, then?" my grandmother asked. "Here in Merendon?"

My grandfather glanced at me and he almost laughed. "Oh, I think he might," he answered. "If we give him a little encouragement."

My grandmother nodded. "I'm going to set the table. Lirril, you can run out and check the ashes if you like. See if anything's survived the fire."

"Oh—yes—that is—I will," I said, and they both turned away to hide their smiles at my disjointed speech. I waited till they were out of the room, then carefully rolled up my poem and tied it with the shoelace. Grabbing my coat from the hall closet, I hurried through the kitchen and out into the cold air, which was not at all warmed by the cheerful sunshine. Shivering a little, I knelt beside the coals and began sorting through the remains of the bonfire.

I was really only looking for one thing, and I found it almost immediately—the small metal button from Jake's shirt. The heat of the fire had contorted it to a strange shape and darkened its shiny surface, but it was whole, recognizable, too stubborn to give way to neglect and misuse. I cleaned it in the snow and slipped it into my pocket. I would only give it back if Jake thought to ask for it, but I was sure he wouldn't.

The button had carried a wish that wasn't mine, but I could make it come true.

Sharon Shinn has won the William C. Crawford Award for Outstanding New Fantasy Writer, and was twice nominated for the John W. Campbell Award for Best New Writer. She is the author of *Archangel* and four other books in the Samaria world, which have all been *Locus* best-sellers. Her many other books include three set in the world of this story: *The Safe-Keeper's Secret* (an ALA Best Book for Young Adults), *The Truth-Teller's Tale*, and the forthcoming *The Dream-Maker's Magic*.

A graduate of Northwestern University, Sharon Shinn now works as a journalist for a trade magazine. She has lived in the Midwest most of her life.

Author's Note

I had been thinking for some time that I wanted to write a Christmas story—or at least the kind of Christmas story that would unfold in a fantasy setting. The world would be full of cold, snow, and darkness, but small, determined lights and acts of simple charity would provide moments of hope and luminous beauty.

I had already written three novels that featured the Wintermoon ceremony, my own amalgamation of solstice, the Yule log, and New Year's resolutions. So I decided to set my tale at Wintermoon, when a self-absorbed young woman comes to realize that a material gift given to a desperate stranger will be repaid a thousandfold.

Kelly Link

The Wizards of Perfil

The woman who sold leech-grass baskets and pickled beets in the Perfil market took pity on Onion's aunt. "On your own, my love?"

Onion's aunt nodded. She was still holding out the earrings she'd hoped someone would buy. There was a train leaving in the morning for Qual, but the tickets were dear. Her daughter Halsa, Onion's cousin, was sulking. She'd wanted the earrings for herself. The twins held hands and stared about the market.

Onion thought the beets were more beautiful than the earrings, which had belonged to his mother. The beets were rich and velvety and mysterious as pickled stars in shining jars. Onion had had nothing to eat all day. His stomach was empty, and his head was full of the thoughts of the people in the market: Halsa thinking of the earrings, the market woman's disinterested kindness, his aunt's dull worry. There was a man at another stall whose wife was sick. She was coughing up blood. A girl went by. She was thinking about a man who had

gone to the war. The man wouldn't come back. Onion went back to thinking about the beets.

"Just you to look after all these children," the market woman said. "These are bad times. Where's your lot from?"

"Come from Labbit, and Larch before that," Onion's aunt said. "We're trying to get to Qual. My husband had family there. I have these earrings and these candlesticks."

The woman shook her head. "No one will buy these," she said. "Not for any good price. The market is full of refugees selling off their bits and pieces."

Onion's aunt said, "Then what should I do?" She didn't seem to expect an answer, but the woman said, "There's a man who comes to the market today, who buys children for the wizards of Perfil. He pays good money and they say that the children are treated well."

All wizards are strange, but the wizards of Perfil are strangest of all. They build tall towers in the marshes of Perfil, and there they live like anchorites in lonely little rooms at the top of their towers. They rarely come down at all, and no one is sure what their magic is good for. There are balls of sickly green fire that dash around the marshes at night, hunting for who knows what, and sometimes a tower tumbles down and then the prickly reeds and marsh lilies that look like ghostly white hands grow up over the tumbled stones and the marsh mud sucks the rubble down.

Everyone knows that there are wizard bones under the marsh mud and that the fish and the birds that live in the marsh are strange creatures. They have got magic in them.

Children dare each other to go into the marsh and catch fish. Sometimes when a brave child catches a fish in the murky, muddy marsh pools, the fish will call the child by name and beg to be released. And if you don't let that fish go, it will tell you, gasping for air, when and how you will die. And if you cook the fish and eat it, you will dream wizard dreams. But if you let your fish go, it will tell you a secret.

This is what the people of Perfil say about the wizards of Perfil.

Everyone knows that the wizards of Perfil talk to demons and hate sunlight and have long twitching noses like rats. They never bathe.

Everyone knows that the wizards of Perfil are hundreds and hundreds of years old. They sit and dangle their fishing lines out of the windows of their towers and they use magic to bait their hooks. They eat their fish raw and they throw the fish bones out of the window the same way that they empty their chamber pots. The wizards of Perfil have filthy habits and no manners at all.

Everyone knows that the wizards of Perfil eat children when they grow tired of fish.

This is what Halsa told her brothers and Onion while Onion's aunt bargained in the Perfil markets with the wizard's secretary.

The wizard's secretary was a man named Tolcet and he wore a sword in his belt. He was a black man with white-pink spatters on his face and across the backs of his hands.

Onion had never seen a man who was two colors.

Tolcet gave Onion and his cousins pieces of candy. He said to Onion's aunt, "Can any of them sing?"

Onion's aunt indicated that the children should sing. The twins, Mik and Bonti, had strong, clear soprano voices, and when Halsa sang, everyone in the market fell silent and listened. Halsa's voice was like honey and sunlight and sweet water.

Onion loved to sing, but no one loved to hear it. When it was his turn and he opened his mouth to sing, he thought of his mother and tears came to his eyes. The song that came out of his mouth wasn't one he knew. It wasn't even in a proper language and Halsa crossed her eyes and stuck out her tongue. Onion went on singing.

"Enough," Tolcet said. He pointed at Onion. "You sing like a toad, boy. Do you know when to be quiet?"

"He's quiet," Onion's aunt said. "His parents are dead. He doesn't eat much, and he's strong enough. We walked here from Larch. And he's not afraid of witchy folk, begging your pardon. There were no wizards in Larch, but his mother could find things when you lost them. She could charm your cows so that they always came home."

"How old is he?" Tolcet said.

"Eleven," Onion's aunt said, and Tolcet grunted.

"Small for his age." Tolcet looked at Onion. He looked at Halsa, who crossed her arms and scowled hard. "Will you come with me, boy?"

Onion's aunt nudged him. He nodded.

"I'm sorry for it," his aunt said to Onion, "but it can't be

helped. I promised your mother I'd see you were taken care of. This is the best I can do."

Onion said nothing. He knew his aunt would have sold Halsa to the wizard's secretary and hoped it was a piece of luck for her daughter. But there was also a part of his aunt that was glad that Tolcet wanted Onion instead. Onion could see it in her mind.

Tolcet paid Onion's aunt twenty-four brass fish, which was slightly more than it had cost to bury Onion's parents, but slightly less than Onion's father had paid for their best milk cow, two years before. It was important to know how much things were worth. The cow was dead and so was Onion's father.

"Be *good,"* Onion's aunt said. "Here. Take this." She gave Onion one of the earrings that had belonged to his mother. It was shaped like a snake. Its writhing tail hooked into its narrow mouth, and Onion had always wondered if the snake was surprised about that, to end up with a mouthful of itself like that, for all eternity. Or maybe it was eternally furious, like Halsa.

Halsa's mouth was screwed up like a button. When she hugged Onion good-bye, she said, "Brat. Give it to me." Halsa had already taken the wooden horse that Onion's father had carved, and Onion's knife, the one with the bone handle.

Onion tried to pull away, but she held him tightly, as if she couldn't bear to let him go. "He wants to eat you," she said. "The wizard will put you in an oven and roast you like a suckling pig. So give me the earring. Suckling pigs don't need earrings."

Onion wriggled away. The wizard's secretary was watching,

and Onion wondered if he'd heard Halsa. Of course, anyone who wanted a child to eat would have taken Halsa, not Onion. Halsa was older and bigger and plumper. Then again, anyone who looked hard at Halsa would suspect she would taste sour and unpleasant. The only sweetness in Halsa was in her singing. Even Onion loved to listen to Halsa when she sang.

Mik and Bonti gave Onion shy little kisses on his cheek. He knew they wished the wizard's secretary had bought Halsa instead. Now that Onion was gone, it would be the twins that Halsa pinched and bullied and teased.

Tolcet swung a long leg over his horse. Then he leaned down. "Come on, boy," he said, and held his speckled hand out to Onion. Onion took it.

The horse was warm and its back was broad and high. There was no saddle and no reins, only a kind of woven harness with a basket on either flank, filled with goods from the market. Tolcet held the horse quiet with his knees, and Onion held on tight to Tolcet's belt.

"That song you sang," Tolcet said. "Where did you learn it?"

"I don't know," Onion said. It came to him that the song had been a song that Tolcet's mother had sung to her son, when Tolcet was a child. Onion wasn't sure what the words meant because Tolcet wasn't sure either. There was something about a lake and a boat, something about a girl who had eaten the moon.

The marketplace was full of people selling things. From his vantage point Onion felt like a prince: as if he could afford to buy anything he saw. He looked down at a stall selling apples and potatoes and hot leek pies. His mouth watered. Over

here was an incense seller's stall, and there was a woman telling fortunes. At the train station, people were lining up to buy tickets for Qual. In the morning a train would leave and Onion's aunt and Halsa and the twins would be on it. It was a dangerous passage. There were unfriendly armies between here and Qual. When Onion looked back at his aunt, he knew it would do no good, she would only think he was begging her not to leave him with the wizard's secretary, but he said it all the same: "Don't go to Qual."

But he knew even as he said it that she would go anyway. No one ever listened to Onion.

The horse tossed its head. The wizard's secretary made a *tch-tch* sound and then leaned back in the saddle. He seemed undecided about something. Onion looked back one more time at his aunt. He had never seen her smile once in the two years he'd lived with her, and she did not smile now, even though twenty-four brass fish was not a small sum of money and even though she'd kept her promise to Onion's mother. Onion's mother had smiled often, despite the fact that her teeth were not particularly good.

"He'll eat you," Halsa called to Onion. "Or he'll drown you in the marsh! He'll cut you up into little pieces and bait his fishing line with your fingers!" She stamped her foot.

"Halsa!" her mother said.

"On second thought," Tolcet said, "I'll take the girl. Will you sell her to me instead?"

"What?" Halsa said.

"What?" Onion's aunt said.

"No!" Onion said, but Tolcet drew out his purse again.

Halsa, it seemed, was worth more than a small boy with a bad voice. And Onion's aunt needed money badly. So Halsa got up on the horse behind Tolcet, and Onion watched as his bad-tempered cousin rode away with the wizard's servant.

There was a voice in Onion's head. It said, "Don't worry, boy. All will be well and all manner of things will be well." It sounded like Tolcet, a little amused, a little sad.

There is a story about the wizards of Perfil and how one fell in love with a church bell. First he tried to buy it with gold and then, when the church refused his money, he stole it by magic. As the wizard flew back across the marshes, carrying the bell in his arms, he flew too low and the devil reached up and grabbed his heel. The wizard dropped the church bell into the marshes and it sank and was lost forever. Its voice is clappered with mud and moss, and although the wizard never gave up searching for it and calling its name, the bell never answered and the wizard grew thin and died of grief. Fishermen say that the dead wizard still flies over the marsh, crying out for the lost bell.

Everyone knows that wizards are pigheaded and come to bad ends. No wizard has ever made himself useful by magic, or, if they've tried, they've only made matters worse. No wizard has ever stopped a war or mended a fence. It's better that they stay in their marshes, out of the way of worldly folk like farmers and soldiers and merchants and kings.

"Well," Onion's aunt said. She sagged. They could no longer see Tolcet or Halsa. "Come along, then."

They went back through the market and Onion's aunt bought cakes of sweetened rice for the three children. Onion ate his without knowing that he did so: since the wizard's servant had taken away Halsa instead, it felt as if there were two Onions, one Onion here in the market and one Onion riding along with Tolcet and Halsa. He stood and was carried along at the same time and it made him feel terribly dizzy. Market-Onion stumbled, his mouth full of rice, and his aunt caught him by the elbow.

"We don't eat children," Tolcet was saying. "There are plenty of fish and birds in the marshes."

"I know," Halsa said. She sounded sulky. "And the wizards live in houses with lots of stairs. Towers. Because they think they're so much better than anybody else. So above the rest of the world."

"And how do you know about the wizards of Perfil?" Tolcet said.

"The woman in the market," Halsa said. "And the other people in the market. Some are afraid of the wizards and some think that there are no wizards. That they're a story for children. That the marshes are full of runaway slaves and deserters. Nobody knows why wizards would come and build towers in the Perfil marsh, where the ground is like cheese and no one can find them. Why do the wizards live in the marshes?"

"Because the marsh is full of magic," Tolcet said.

"Then why do they build the towers so high?" Halsa said.

"Because wizards are curious," Tolcet said. "They like to be able to see things that are far off. They like to be as close

as possible to the stars. And they don't like to be bothered by people who ask lots of questions."

"Why do the wizards buy children?" Halsa said.

"To run up and down the stairs," Tolcet said, "to fetch them water for bathing and to carry messages and to bring them breakfasts and dinners and lunches and suppers. Wizards are always hungry."

"So am I," Halsa said.

"Here," Tolcet said. He gave Halsa an apple. "You see things that are in people's heads. You can see things that are going to happen."

"Yes," Halsa said. "Sometimes." The apple was wrinkled but sweet.

"Your cousin has a gift, too," Tolcet said.

"Onion?" Halsa said scornfully. Onion saw that it had never felt like a gift to Halsa. No wonder she'd hidden it.

"Can you see what is in my head right now?" Tolcet said.

Halsa looked and Onion looked, too. There was no curiosity or fear about in Tolcet's head. There was nothing. There was no Tolcet, no wizard's servant. Only brackish water and lonely white birds flying above it.

"It's beautiful," Onion said.

"What?" his aunt said in the market. "Onion? Sit down, child."

"Some people find it so," Tolcet said, answering Onion. Halsa said nothing, but she frowned.

Tolcet and Halsa rode through the town and out of the town gates onto the road that led back toward Labbit and east, where there were more refugees coming and going, day

and night. They were mostly women and children and they were afraid. There were rumors of armies behind them. There was a story that, in a fit of madness, the King had killed his youngest son. Onion saw a chess game, a thin-faced, anxious, yellow-haired boy Onion's age moving a black queen across the board, and then the chess pieces scattered across a stone floor. A woman was saying something. The boy bent down to pick up the scattered pieces. The king was laughing. He had a sword in his hand and he brought it down and then there was blood on it. Onion had never seen a king before, although he had seen men with swords. He had seen men with blood on their swords.

Tolcet and Halsa went away from the road, following a wide river, which was less a river than a series of wide, shallow pools. On the other side of the river, muddy paths disappeared into thick stands of rushes and bushes full of berries. There was a feeling of watchfulness, and the cunning, curious stillness of something alive, something half-asleep and half-waiting, a hidden, invisible humming, as if even the air were saturated with magic.

"Berries! Ripe and sweet!" a girl was singing out, over and over again in the market. Onion wished she would be quiet. His aunt bought bread and salt and hard cheese. She piled them into Onion's arms.

"It will be uncomfortable at first," Tolcet was saying. "The marshes of Perfil are so full of magic that they drink up all other kinds of magic. The only ones who work magic in the marshes of Perfil are the wizards of Perfil. And there are bugs."

"I don't want anything to do with magic," Halsa said primly.

Again Onion tried to look in Tolcet's mind, but again all he saw were the marshes. Fat-petaled, waxy, white flowers and crouching trees that dangled their long brown fingers as if fishing. Tolcet laughed. "I can feel you looking," he said. "Don't look too long or you'll fall in and drown."

"I'm not looking!" Halsa said. But she *was* looking. Onion could feel her looking, as if she were turning a key in a door.

The marshes smelled salty and rich, like a bowl of broth. Tolcet's horse ambled along, its hooves sinking into the path. Behind them, water welled up and filled the depressions. Fat jeweled flies clung, vibrating, to the rushes, and once, in a clear pool of water, Onion saw a snake curling like a green ribbon through water weeds soft as a cloud of hair.

"Wait here and watch Bonti and Mik for me," Onion's aunt said. "I'll go to the train station. Onion, are you all right?"

Onion nodded dreamily.

Tolcet and Halsa rode farther into the marsh, away from the road and the Perfil market and Onion. It was very different from the journey to Perfil, which had been hurried and dusty and dry and on foot. Whenever Onion or one of the twins stumbled or lagged behind, Halsa had rounded them up like a dog chasing sheep, pinching and slapping. It was hard to imagine cruel, greedy, unhappy Halsa being able to pick things out of other people's minds, although she had always seemed to know when Mik or Bonti had found something edible; where there might be a soft piece of ground to sleep; when they should duck off the road because soldiers were coming.

Halsa was thinking of her mother and her brothers. She was thinking about the look on her father's face when the soldiers had shot him behind the barn; the earrings shaped like snakes; how the train to Qual would be blown up by saboteurs. She was supposed to be on that train, she knew it. She was furious at Tolcet for taking her away; at Onion, because Tolcet had changed his mind about Onion.

Every now and then, while he waited in the market for his aunt to come back, Onion could see the pointy roofs of the wizards' towers leaning against the sky as if they were waiting for him, just beyond the Perfil market, and then the towers would recede, and he would go with them, and find himself again with Tolcet and Halsa. Their path ran up along a canal of tarry water, angled off into thickets of bushes bent down with bright yellow berries, and then returned. It cut across other paths, these narrower and crookeder, overgrown and secret looking. At last they rode through a stand of sweet-smelling trees and came out into a grassy meadow that seemed not much larger than the Perfil market. Up close, the towers were not particularly splendid. They were tumbledown and lichen-covered and looked as if they might collapse at any moment. They were so close together one might have strung a line for laundry from tower to tower, if wizards had been concerned with such things as laundry. Efforts had been made to buttress the towers; some had long, eccentrically curving fins of strategically piled rocks. There were twelve standing towers that looked as if they might be occupied. Others were half in ruins or were only piles of rocks that had already been scavenged for useful building materials.

Around the meadow were more paths: worn, dirt paths and canals that sank into branchy, briary tangles, some so low that a boat would never have passed without catching. Even a swimmer would have to duck her head. Children sat on the half-ruined walls of toppled towers and watched Tolcet and Halsa ride up. There was a fire with a thin man stirring something in a pot. Two women were winding up a ball of rough-looking twine. They were dressed like Tolcet. More wizards' servants, Halsa and Onion thought. Clearly wizards were very lazy.

"Down you go," Tolcet said, and Halsa gladly slid off the horse's back. Then Tolcet got down and lifted off the harness and the horse suddenly became a naked, brown girl of about fourteen years. She straightened her back and wiped her muddy hands on her legs. She didn't seem to care that she was naked. Halsa gaped at her.

The girl frowned. She said, "You be good, now, or they'll turn you into something even worse."

"Who?" Halsa said.

"The wizards of Perfil," the girl said, and laughed. It was a neighing, horsey laugh. All of the other children began to giggle.

"Oooh, Essa gave Tolcet a ride."

"Essa, did you bring me back a present?"

"Essa makes a prettier horse than she does a girl."

"Oh, shut up," Essa said. She picked up a rock and threw it. Halsa admired her economy of motion, and her accuracy.

"Oi!" her target said, putting her hand up to her ear. "That hurt, Essa."

"Thank you, Essa," Tolcet said. She made a remarkably graceful curtsy, considering that until a moment ago she had had four legs and no waist to speak of. There was a shirt and a pair of leggings folded and lying on a rock. Essa put them on. "This is Halsa," Tolcet said to the others. "I bought her in the market."

There was silence. Halsa's face was bright red. For once she was speechless. She looked at the ground and then up at the towers, and Onion looked, too, trying to catch a glimpse of a wizard. All the windows of the towers were empty, but he could feel the wizards of Perfil, feel the weight of their watching. The marshy ground under his feet was full of wizards' magic and the towers threw magic out like waves of heat from a stove. Magic clung even to the children and servants of the wizards of Perfil, as if they had been marinated in it.

"Come get something to eat," Tolcet said, and Halsa stumbled after him. There was a flat bread, and onions and fish. Halsa drank water that had the faint, slightly metallic taste of magic. Onion could taste it in his own mouth.

"Onion," someone said. "Bonti, Mik." Onion looked up. He was back in the market and his aunt stood there. "There's a church nearby where they'll let us sleep. The train leaves early tomorrow morning."

After she had eaten, Tolcet took Halsa into one of the towers, where there was a small cubby under the stairs. There was a pallet of reeds and a mothy wool blanket. The sun was still in the sky. Onion and his aunt and his cousins went to the church, where there was a yard where refugees might curl up and sleep a few hours. Halsa lay awake, thinking of the

wizard in the room above the stairs where she was sleeping. The tower was so full of wizards' magic that she could hardly breathe. She imagined a wizard of Perfil creeping, creeping down the stairs above her cubby, and although the pallet was soft, she pinched her arms to stay awake. But Onion fell asleep immediately, as if drugged. He dreamed of wizards flying above the marshes like white lonely birds.

In the morning, Tolcet came and shook Halsa awake. "Go and fetch water for the wizard," he said. He was holding an empty bucket.

Halsa would have liked to say *go and fetch it yourself,* but she was not a stupid girl. She was a slave now. Onion was in her head again, telling her to be careful. "Oh, go away," Halsa said. She realized she had said this aloud, and flinched. But Tolcet only laughed.

Halsa rubbed her eyes and took the bucket and followed him. Outside, the air was full of biting bugs too small to see. They seemed to like the taste of Halsa. That seemed funny to Onion, for no reason that she could understand.

The other children were standing around the fire pit and eating porridge. "Are you hungry?" Tolcet said. Halsa nodded. "Bring the water up and then get yourself something to eat. It's not a good idea to keep a wizard waiting."

He led her along a well-trodden path that quickly sloped down into a small pool and disappeared. "The water is sweet here," he said. "Fill your bucket and bring it up to the top of the wizard's tower. I have an errand to run. I'll return before nightfall. Don't be afraid, Halsa."

"I'm not afraid," Halsa said. She knelt down and filled the bucket. She was almost back to the tower before she realized that the bucket was half empty again. There was a split in the wooden bottom. The other children were watching her and she straightened her back. *So it's a test,* she said in her head, to Onion.

You could ask them for a bucket without a hole in it, he said.

I don't need anyone's help, Halsa said. She went back down the path and scooped up a handful of clayey mud where the path ran into the pool. She packed this into the bottom of the bucket and then pressed moss down on top of the mud. This time the bucket held water.

There were three windows lined with red tiles on Halsa's wizard's tower, and a nest that some bird had built on an outcropping of stone. The roof was round and red and shaped like a bishop's hat. The stairs inside were narrow. The steps had been worn down, smooth and slippery as wax. The higher she went, the heavier the pail of water became. Finally she set it down on a step and sat down beside it. *Four hundred and twenty-two steps,* Onion said. Halsa had counted five hundred and ninety-eight. There seemed to be many more steps on the inside than one would have thought, looking at the tower from outside. "Wizardly tricks," Halsa said in disgust, as if she'd expected nothing better. "You would think they'd make it fewer steps rather than more steps. What's the use of more steps?"

When she stood and picked up the bucket, the handle broke in her hand. The water spilled down the steps and Halsa threw the bucket after it as hard as she could. Then she

marched down the stairs and went to mend the bucket and fetch more water. It didn't do to keep wizards waiting.

At the top of the steps in the wizard's tower there was a door. Halsa set the bucket down and knocked. No one answered and so she knocked again. She tried the latch: the door was locked. Up here, the smell of magic was so thick that Halsa's eyes watered. She tried to look *through* the door. This is what she saw: a room, a window, a bed, a mirror, a table. The mirror was full of rushes and light and water. A bright-eyed fox was curled up on the bed, sleeping. A white bird flew through the unshuttered window, and then another and another. They circled around and around the room and then they began to mass on the table. One flung itself at the door where Halsa stood, peering in. She recoiled. The door vibrated with pecks and blows.

She turned and ran down the stairs, leaving the bucket, leaving Onion behind her. There were even more steps on the way down. And there was no porridge left in the pot beside the fire.

Someone tapped her on the shoulder and she jumped. "Here," Essa said, handing her a piece of bread.

"Thanks," Halsa said. The bread was stale and hard. It was the most delicious thing she'd ever eaten.

"So your mother sold you," Essa said.

Halsa swallowed hard. It was strange, not being able to see inside Essa's head, but it was also restful. As if Essa might be anyone at all. "I didn't care," she said. "Who sold you?"

"No one," Essa said. "I ran away from home. I didn't want to be a soldier's whore like my sisters."

"Are the wizards better than soldiers?" Halsa said.

Essa gave her a strange look. "What do you think? Did you meet your wizard?"

"He was old and ugly, of course," Halsa said. "I didn't like the way he looked at me."

Essa put her hand over her mouth as if she were trying not to laugh. "Oh dear," she said.

"What must I do?" Halsa said. "I've never been a wizard's servant before."

"Didn't your wizard tell you?" Essa said. "What did he tell you to do?"

Halsa blew out an irritated breath. "I asked what he needed, but he said nothing. I think he was hard of hearing."

Essa laughed long and hard, exactly like a horse, Halsa thought. There were three or four other children, now, watching them. They were all laughing at Halsa. "Admit it," Essa said. "You didn't talk to the wizard."

"So?" Halsa said. "I knocked, but no one answered. So obviously he's hard of hearing."

"Of course," a boy said.

"Or maybe the wizard is shy," said another boy. He had green eyes like Bonti and Mik. "Or asleep. Wizards like to take naps."

Everyone was laughing again.

"Stop making fun of me," Halsa said. She tried to look fierce and dangerous. Onion and her brothers would have quailed. "Tell me what my duties are. What does a wizard's servant do?"

Someone said, "You carry things up the stairs. Food. Firewood. Kaffa, when Tolcet brings it back from the market.

Wizards like unusual things. Old things. So you go out in the marsh and look for things."

"Things?" Halsa said.

"Glass bottles," Essa said. "Petrified imps. Strange things, things out of the ordinary. Or ordinary things like plants or stones or animals or anything that feels right. Do you know what I mean?"

"No," Halsa said, but she did know. Some things felt more magic-soaked than other things. Her father had found an arrowhead in his field. He'd put it aside to take to the schoolmaster, but that night while everyone was sleeping, Halsa had wrapped it in a rag and taken it back to the field and buried it. Bonti got the blame. Sometimes Halsa wondered if that was what had brought the soldiers to kill her father, the malicious, evil luck of that arrowhead. But you couldn't blame a whole war on one arrowhead.

"Here," a boy said. "Go and catch fish if you're too stupid to know magic when you see it. Have you ever caught fish?"

Halsa took the fishing pole. "Take that path," Essa said. "The muddiest one. And stay on it. There's a pier out that way where the fishing is good."

When Halsa looked back at the wizards' towers, she thought she saw Onion looking down at her, out of a high window. But that was ridiculous. It was only a bird.

The train was so crowded that some passengers gave up and went and sat on top of the cars. Vendors sold umbrellas to keep the sun off. Onion's aunt had found two seats, and she and Onion sat with one twin on each lap. Two rich women sat across

from them. You could tell they were rich because their shoes were green leather. They held filmy pink handkerchiefs like embroidered rose petals up to their rabbity noses. Bonti looked at them from under his eyelashes. Bonti was a terrible flirt.

Onion had never been on a train before. He could smell the furnace room of the train, rich with coal and magic. Passengers stumbled up and down the aisles, drinking and laughing as if they were at a festival. Men and women stood beside the train windows, sticking their heads in. They shouted messages. A woman leaning against the seats fell against Onion and Mik when someone shoved past her. "Pardon, sweet," she said, and smiled brilliantly. Her teeth were studded with gemstones. She was wearing at least four silk dresses, one on top of the other. A man across the aisle coughed wetly. There was a bandage wrapped around his throat, stained with red. Babies were crying.

"I hear they'll reach Perfil in three days or less," a man in the next row said.

"The King's men won't sack Perfil," said his companion. "They're coming to defend it."

"The King is mad," the man said. "God has told him all men are his enemies. He hasn't paid his army in two years. When they rebel, he just conscripts another army and sends them off to fight the first one. We're safer leaving."

"Oooh," a woman said, somewhere behind Onion. "At last we're off. Isn't this fun! What a pleasant outing!"

Onion tried to think of the marshes of Perfil, of the wizards. But Halsa was suddenly there on the train, instead. *You have to tell them,* she said.

Tell them what? Onion asked her, although he knew. When the train was in the mountains, there would be an explosion. There would be soldiers, riding down at the train. No one would reach Qual. *Nobody will believe me,* he said.

You should tell them anyway, Halsa said.

Onion's legs were falling asleep. He shifted Mik. *Why do you care?* he said. *You hate everyone.*

I don't! Halsa said. But she did. She hated her mother. Her mother had watched her husband die, and done nothing. Halsa had been screaming and her mother slapped her across the face. She hated the twins because they weren't like her, they didn't *see* things the way Halsa had to. Because they were little and they got tired and it had been so much work keeping them safe. Halsa had hated Onion, too, because he *was* like her. Because he'd been afraid of Halsa, and because the day he'd come to live with her family, she'd known that one day she would be like him, alone and without a family. Magic was bad luck, people like Onion and Halsa were bad luck. The only person who'd ever looked at Halsa and really seen her, really known her, had been Onion's mother. Onion's mother was kind and good and she'd known she was going to die. *Take care of my son,* she'd said to Halsa's mother and father, but she'd been looking at Halsa when she said it. But Onion would have to take care of himself. Halsa would make him.

Tell them, Halsa said. There was a fish jerking on her line. She ignored it. *Tell them, tell them, tell them*. She and Onion were in the marsh and on the train at the same time. Everything smelled like coal and salt and ferment. Onion ignored her the

way she was ignoring the fish. He sat and dangled his feet in the water, even though he wasn't really there.

Halsa caught five fish. She cleaned them and wrapped them in leaves and brought them back to the cooking fire. She also brought back the greeny-copper key that had caught on her fishing line. "I found this," she said to Tolcet.

"Ah," Tolcet said. "May I see it?" It looked even smaller and more ordinary in Tolcet's hand.

"Burd," Tolcet said. "Where is the box you found, the one we couldn't open?"

The boy with green eyes got up and disappeared into one of the towers. He came out after a few minutes and gave Tolcet a metal box no bigger than a pickle jar. The key fit. Tolcet unlocked it, although it seemed to Halsa that she ought to have been the one to unlock it, not Tolcet.

"A doll," Halsa said, disappointed. But it was a strange-looking doll. It was carved out of a greasy black wood, and when Tolcet turned it over, it had no back, only two fronts, so it was always looking backward and forward at the same time.

"What do you think, Burd?" Tolcet said.

Burd shrugged. "It's not mine."

"It's yours," Tolcet said to Halsa. "Take it up the stairs and give it to your wizard. And refill the bucket with fresh water and bring some dinner, too. Did you think to take up lunch?"

"No," Halsa said. She hadn't had any lunch herself. She cooked the fish along with some greens Tolcet gave her, and ate two. The other three fish and the rest of the greens she

carried up to the top of the stairs in the tower. She had to stop to rest twice, there were so many stairs this time. The door was still closed and the bucket on the top step was empty. She thought that maybe all the water had leaked away, slowly. But she left the fish and she went and drew more water and carried the bucket back up.

"I've brought you dinner," Halsa said, when she'd caught her breath. "And something else. Something I found in the marsh. Tolcet said I should give it to you."

Silence.

She felt silly, talking to the wizard's door. "It's a doll," she said. "Perhaps it's a magic doll."

Silence again. Not even Onion was there. She hadn't noticed when he went away. She thought of the train. "If I give you the doll," she said, "will you do something for me? You're a wizard, so you ought to be able to do anything, right? Will you help the people on the train? They're going to Qual. Something bad is going to happen if you won't stop it. You know about the soldiers? Can you stop them?"

Halsa waited for a long time, but the wizard behind the door never said anything. She put the doll down on the steps and then she picked it up again and put it in her pocket. She was furious. "I think you're a coward," she said. "That's why you hide up here, isn't it? I would have got on that train and I know what's going to happen. Onion got on that train. And you could stop it, but you won't. Well, if you won't stop it, then I won't give you the doll."

She spat in the bucket of water and then immediately wished she hadn't. "You keep the train safe," she said, "and I'll

give you the doll. I promise. I'll bring you other things, too. And I'm sorry I spit in your water. I'll go and get more."

She took the bucket and went back down the stairs. Her legs ached and there were welts where the little biting bugs had drawn blood.

"Mud," Essa said. She was standing in the meadow, smoking a pipe. "The flies are only bad in the morning and at twilight. If you put mud on your face and arms, they leave you alone."

"It smells," Halsa said.

"So do you," Essa said. She snapped her clay pipe in two, which seemed extravagant to Halsa, and wandered over to where some of the other children were playing a complicated-looking game of pickup sticks and dice. Under a night-flowering tree, Tolcet sat in a battered, oaken throne that looked as if it had been spat up by the marsh. He was smoking a pipe, too, with a clay stem even longer than Essa's had been. It was ridiculously long. "Did you give the poppet to the wizard?" he said.

"Oh yes," Halsa said.

"What did she say?"

"Well," Halsa said. "I'm not sure. She's young and quite lovely. But she had a horrible stutter. I could hardly understand her. I think she said something about the moon, how she wanted me to go cut her a slice of it. I'm to bake it into a pie."

"Wizards are very fond of pie," Tolcet said.

"Of course they are," Halsa said. "And I'm fond of my arse."

"Better watch your mouth," Burd, the boy with green eyes,

said. He was standing on his head, for no good reason that Halsa could see. His legs waved in the air languidly, semaphoring. "Or the wizards will make you sorry."

"I'm already sorry," Halsa said. But she didn't say anything else. She carried the bucket of water up to the closed door. Then she ran back down the stairs to the cubbyhole and this time she fell straight asleep. She dreamed a fox came and looked at her. It stuck its muzzle in her face. Then it trotted up the stairs and ate the three fish Halsa had left there. *You'll be sorry,* Halsa thought. *The wizards will turn you into a one-legged crow.* But then she was chasing the fox up the aisle of a train to Qual, where her mother and her brothers and Onion were sleeping uncomfortably in their seats, their legs tucked under them, their arms hanging down as if they were dead—the stink of coal and magic was even stronger than it had been in the morning. The train was laboring hard. It panted like a fox with a pack of dogs after it, dragging itself along. There was no way it would reach all the way to the top of the wizard of Perfil's stairs. And if it did, the wizard wouldn't be there, anyway, just the moon, rising up over the mountains, round and fat as a lardy bone.

The wizards of Perfil don't write poetry, as a general rule. As far as anyone knows, they don't marry, or plow fields, or have much use for polite speech. It is said that the wizards of Perfil appreciate a good joke, but telling a joke to a wizard is dangerous business. What if the wizard doesn't find the joke funny? Wizards are sly, greedy, absentminded, obsessed with stars and bugs, parsimonious, frivolous, invisible, tyrannous,

untrustworthy, secretive, inquisitive, meddlesome, long-lived, dangerous, useless, and have far too good an opinion of themselves. Kings go mad, the land is blighted, children starve or get sick or die spitted on the pointy end of a pike, and it's all beneath the notice of the wizards of Perfil. The wizards of Perfil don't fight wars.

It was like having a stone in his shoe. Halsa was always there, nagging. *Tell them, tell them. Tell them.* They had been on the train for a day and a night. Halsa was in the swamp, getting farther and farther away. Why wouldn't she leave him alone? Mik and Bonti had seduced the two rich women who sat across from them. There were no more frowns or handkerchiefs, only smiles and tidbits of food and love, love, love all around. On went the train through burned fields and towns that had been put to the sword by one army or another. The train and its passengers overtook people on foot, or fleeing in wagons piled high with goods: mattresses, wardrobes, a pianoforte once, stoves and skillets and butter churns and pigs and angry-looking geese. Sometimes the train stopped while men got out and examined the tracks and made repairs. They did not stop at any stations, although there were people waiting, sometimes, who yelled and ran after the train. No one got off. There were fewer people up in the mountains, when they got there. Instead there was snow. Once Onion saw a wolf.

"When we get to Qual," one of the rich women, the older one, said to Onion's aunt, "my sister and I will set up our establishment. We'll need someone to keep house for us. Are you thrifty?" She had Bonti on her lap. He was half-asleep.

"Yes, ma'am," Onion's aunt said.

"Well, we'll see," said the woman. She was half in love with Bonti. Onion had never had much opportunity to see what the rich thought about. He was a little disappointed to find out that it was much the same as other people. The only difference seemed to be that the rich woman, like the wizard's secretary, seemed to think that all of this would end up all right. Money, it seemed, was like luck, or magic. All manner of things would be well, except they wouldn't. If it weren't for the thing that was going to happen to the train, perhaps Onion's aunt could have sold more of her children.

Why won't you tell them? Halsa said. *Soon it will be too late.*

You tell them, Onion thought back at her. Having an invisible Halsa around, always telling him things that he already knew, was far worse than the real Halsa had been. The real Halsa was safe, asleep, on the pallet under the wizard's stairs. Onion should have been there instead. Onion bet the wizards of Perfil were sorry that Tolcet had ever bought a girl like Halsa.

Halsa shoved past Onion. She put her invisible hands on her mother's shoulders and looked into her face. Her mother didn't look up. *You have to get off the train,* Halsa said. She yelled. *GET OFF THE TRAIN!*

But it was like talking to the door at the top of the wizard's tower. There was something in Halsa's pocket, pressing into her stomach so hard it almost felt like a bruise. Halsa wasn't on the train, she was sleeping on something with a sharp little face.

"Oh, stop yelling. Go away. How am I supposed to stop a train?" Onion said.

"Onion?" his aunt said. Onion realized he'd said it aloud. Halsa looked smug.

"Something bad is going to happen," Onion said, capitulating. "We have to stop the train and get off." The two rich women stared at him as if he were a lunatic. Onion's aunt patted his shoulder. "Onion," she said. "You were asleep. You were having a bad dream."

"But—" Onion protested.

"Here," his aunt said, glancing at the two women. "Take Mik for a walk. Shake off your dream."

Onion gave up. The rich women were thinking that perhaps they would be better off looking for a housekeeper in Qual. Halsa was tapping her foot, standing in the aisle with her arms folded.

Come on, she said. *No point talking to* them. *They just think you're crazy. Come talk to the conductor instead.*

"Sorry," Onion said to his aunt. "I had a bad dream. I'll go for a walk." He took Mik's hand.

They went up the aisle, stepping over sleeping people and people stupid or quarrelsome with drink, people slapping down playing cards. Halsa always in front of them: *Hurry up, hurry, hurry. We're almost there. You've left it too late. That useless wizard, I should have known not to bother asking for help. I should have known not to expect you to take care of things. You're as useless as* they *are. Stupid good-for-nothing wizards of Perfil.*

Up ahead of the train, Onion could feel the gunpowder charges, little bundles wedged between the ties of the track. It was like there was a stone in his shoe. He wasn't afraid, he was merely irritated: at Halsa, at the people on the train who

didn't even know enough to be afraid, at the wizards and the rich women who thought that they could just buy children, just like that. He was angry, too. He was angry at his parents, for dying, for leaving him stuck here. He was angry at the King, who had gone mad; at the soldiers, who wouldn't stay home with their own families, who went around stabbing and shooting and blowing up other people's families.

They were at the front of the train. Halsa led Onion right into the cab, where two men were throwing enormous scoops of coal into a red-black, boiling furnace. They were filthy as devils. Their arms bulged with muscles and their eyes were red. One turned and saw Onion. "Oi!" he said. "What's he doing here? You, kid, what are you doing?"

"You have to stop the train," Onion said. "Something is going to happen. I saw soldiers. They're going to make the train blow up."

"Soldiers? Back there? How long ago?"

"They're up ahead of us," Onion said. "We have to stop now."

Mik was looking up at him.

"He saw soldiers?" the other man said.

"Naw," said the first man. Onion could see he didn't know whether to be angry or whether to laugh. "The fucking kid's making things up. Pretending he sees things. Hey, maybe he's a wizard of Perfil! Lucky us, we got a wizard on the train!"

"I'm not a wizard," Onion said. Halsa snorted in agreement. "But I know things. If you don't stop the train, everyone will die."

Both men stared at him. Then the first said angrily, "Get

out of here, you. And don't go talking to people like that or we'll throw you in the boiler."

"Okay," Onion said "Come on, Mik."

Wait, Halsa said. *What are you doing? You have to make them understand. Do you want to be dead? Do you think you can prove something to me by being dead?*

Onion put Mik on his shoulders. *I'm sorry,* he said to Halsa. *But it's no good. Maybe you should just go away. Wake up. Catch fish. Fetch water for the wizards of Perfil.*

The pain in Halsa's stomach was sharper, as if someone were stabbing her. When she put her hand down, she had hold of the wooden doll.

What's that? Onion said.

Nothing, Halsa said. *Something I found in the swamp. I said I would give it to the wizard, but I won't! Here, you take it!*

She thrust it at Onion. It went all the way through him. It was an uncomfortable feeling, even though it wasn't really there. *Halsa,* he said. He put Mik down.

Take it! she said. *Here! Take it now!*

The train was roaring. Onion knew where they were; he recognized the way the light looked. Someone was telling a joke in the front of the train, and in a minute a woman would laugh. It would be a lot brighter in a minute. He put his hand up to stop the thing that Halsa was stabbing him with and something smacked against his palm. His fingers brushed Halsa's fingers.

It was a wooden doll with a sharp little nose. There was a nose on the back of its head, too. *Oh, take it!* Halsa said. Something was pouring out of her, through the doll, into

Onion. Onion fell back against a woman holding a birdcage on her lap. "Get off!" the woman said. It *hurt*. The stuff pouring out of Halsa felt like *life*, as if the doll was pulling out her life like a skein of heavy, sodden, black wool. It hurt Onion, too. Black stuff poured and poured through the doll, into him, until there was no space for Onion, no space to breathe or think or see. The black stuff welled up in his throat, pressed behind his eyes. "Halsa," he said, "let go!"

The woman with the birdcage said, "What's wrong with him?"

Mik said, "What's wrong? What's wrong?"

The light changed. *Onion,* Halsa said, and let go of the doll. He staggered backward. The tracks beneath the train were singing *tarà-ta tara-ta ta-rata-ta.* Onion's nose was full of swamp water and coal and metal and magic. "No," Onion said. He threw the doll at the woman holding the birdcage and pushed Mik down on the floor. "No," Onion said again, louder. People were staring at him. The woman who'd been laughing at the joke had stopped laughing. Onion covered Mik with his body. The light grew brighter and blacker, all at once.

"Onion!" Halsa said. But she couldn't see him anymore. She was awake in the cubby beneath the stair. The doll was gone.

Halsa had seen men coming home from the war. Some of them had been blinded. Some had lost a hand or an arm. She'd seen one man wrapped in lengths of cloth and propped up in a dogcart that his young daughter pulled on a rope. He'd had no legs, no arms. When people looked at him, he cursed them. There was another man who ran a cockpit in

Larch. He came back from the war and paid a man to carve him a leg out of knotty pine. At first he was unsteady on the pine leg, trying to find his balance again. It had been funny to watch him chase after his cocks, like watching a windup toy. By the time the army came through Larch again, though, he could run as fast as anyone.

It felt as if half of her had died on the train in the mountains. Her ears rang. She couldn't find her balance. It was as if a part of her had been cut away, as if she were blind. The part of her that *knew* things, *saw* things, wasn't there anymore. She went about all day in a miserable deafening fog.

She brought water up the stairs and she put mud on her arms and legs. She caught fish, because Onion had said that she ought to catch fish. Late in the afternoon, she looked and saw Tolcet sitting beside her on the pier.

"You shouldn't have bought me," she said. "You should have bought Onion. He wanted to come with you. I'm bad-tempered and unkind and I have no good opinion of the wizards of Perfil."

"Of whom do you have a low opinion? Yourself or the wizards of Perfil?" Tolcet asked.

"How can you serve them?" Halsa said. "How can you serve men and women who hide in towers and do nothing to help people who need help? What good is magic if it doesn't serve anyone?"

"These are dangerous times," Tolcet said. "For wizards as well as for children."

"Dangerous times! Hard times! Bad times," Halsa said. "Things have been bad since the day I was born. Why do I see

things and know things, when there's nothing I can do to stop them? When will there be better times?"

"What do you see?" Tolcet said. He took Halsa's chin in his hand and tilted her head this way and that, as if her head were a glass ball that he could see inside. He put his hand on her head and smoothed her hair as if she were his own child. Halsa closed her eyes. Misery welled up inside her.

"I don't see anything," she said. "It feels like someone wrapped me in a wool blanket and beat me and left me in the dark. Is this what it feels like not to see anything? Did the wizards of Perfil do this to me?"

"Is it better or worse?" Tolcet said.

"Worse," Halsa said. "No. Better. I don't know. What am I to do? What am I to be?"

"You are a servant of the wizards of Perfil," Tolcet said. "Be patient. All things may yet be well."

Halsa said nothing. What was there to say?

She climbed up and down the stairs of the wizard's tower, carrying water, toasted bread and cheese, little things that she found in the swamp. The door at the top of the stairs was never open. She couldn't see through it. No one spoke to her, although she sat there sometimes, holding her breath so that the wizard would think she had gone away again. But the wizard wouldn't be fooled so easily. Tolcet went up the stairs, too, and perhaps the wizard admitted him. Halsa didn't know.

Essa and Burd and the other children were kind to her, as if they knew that she had been broken. She knew that she wouldn't have been kind to them if their situations had been

reversed. But perhaps they knew that, too. The two women and the skinny man kept their distance. She didn't even know their names. They disappeared on errands and came back again and disappeared into the towers.

Once, when she was coming back from the pier with a bucket of fish, there was a dragon on the path. It wasn't very big, only the size of a mastiff. But it gazed at her with wicked, jeweled eyes. She couldn't get past it. It would eat her, and that would be that. It was almost a relief. She put the bucket down and stood waiting to be eaten. But then Essa was there, holding a stick. She hit the dragon on its head, once, twice, and then gave it a kick for good measure. "Go on, you!" Essa said. The dragon went, giving Halsa one last reproachful look. Essa picked up the bucket of fish. "You have to be firm with them," she said. "Otherwise they get inside your head and make you feel as if you deserve to be eaten. They're too lazy to eat anything that puts up a fight."

Halsa shook off a last, wistful regret, almost sorry not to have been eaten. It was like waking up from a dream, something beautiful and noble and sad and utterly untrue. "Thank you," she said to Essa. Her knees were trembling.

"The bigger ones stay away from the meadow," Essa said. "It's the smaller ones who get curious about the wizards of Perfil. And by 'curious,' what I really mean is hungry. Dragons eat the things that they're curious about. Come on, let's go for a swim."

Sometimes Essa or one of the others would tell Halsa stories about the wizards of Perfil. Most of the stories were silly, or plainly untrue. The children sounded almost indulgent, as if they found their masters more amusing than frightful. There

were other stories, sad stories about long-ago wizards who had fought great battles or gone on long journeys. Wizards who had perished by treachery or been imprisoned by ones they'd thought friends.

Tolcet carved her a comb. She found frogs whose backs were marked with strange mathematical formulas, and put them in a bucket and took them to the top of the tower. She caught a mole with eyes like pinpricks and a nose like a fleshy pink hand. She found the hilt of a sword, a coin with a hole in it, the outgrown carapace of a dragon, small as a badger and almost weightless, but hard, too. When she cleaned off the mud that covered it, it shone dully, like a candlestick. She took all of these up the stairs. She couldn't tell whether the things she found had any meaning. But she took a small, private pleasure in finding them nevertheless.

The mole had come back down the stairs again, fast, wriggly, and furtive. The frogs were still in the bucket, making their gloomy pronouncements, when she had returned with the wizard's dinner. But other things disappeared behind the wizard of Perfil's door.

The thing that Tolcet had called Halsa's gift came back, a little at a time. Once again, she became aware of the wizards in their towers, and of how they watched her. There was something else, too. It sat beside her, sometimes, while she was fishing, or when she rowed out in the abandoned coracle Tolcet helped her to repair. She thought she knew who, or what, it was. It was the part of Onion that he'd learned to send out. It was what was left of him: shadowy, thin, and silent. It wouldn't talk to her. It only watched. At night, it

stood beside her pallet and watched her sleep. She was glad it was there. To be haunted was a kind of comfort.

She helped Tolcet repair a part of the wizard's tower where the stones were loose in their mortar. She learned how to make paper out of rushes and bark. Apparently wizards needed a great deal of paper. Tolcet began to teach her how to read.

One afternoon when she came back from fishing, all of the wizard's servants were standing in a circle. There was a leveret motionless as a stone in the middle of the circle. Onion's ghost crouched down with the other children. So Halsa stood and watched, too. Something was pouring back and forth between the leveret and the servants of the wizards of Perfil. It was the same as it had been for Halsa and Onion, when she'd given him the two-faced doll. The leveret's sides rose and fell. Its eyes were glassy and dark and knowing. Its fur bristled with magic.

"Who is it?" Halsa said to Burd. "Is it a wizard of Perfil?"

"Who?" Burd said. He didn't take his eyes off the leveret. "No, not a wizard. It's a hare. Just a hare. It came out of the marsh."

"But," Halsa said. "But I can feel it. I can almost hear what it's saying."

Burd looked at her. Essa looked, too. "Everything speaks," he said, speaking slowly, as if to a child. "Listen, Halsa."

There was something about the way Burd and Essa were looking at her, as if it were an invitation, as if they were asking her to look inside their heads, to see what they were thinking. The others were watching, too, watching Halsa now, instead

of the leveret. Halsa took a step back. "I can't," she said. "I can't hear anything."

She went to fetch water. When she came out of the tower, Burd and Essa and the other children weren't there. Leverets dashed between towers, leaping over one another, tussling in midair. Onion sat on Tolcet's throne, watching and laughing silently. She didn't think she'd seen Onion laugh since the death of his mother. It made her feel strange to know that a dead boy could be so joyful.

The next day Halsa found an injured fox kit in the briar. It snapped at her when she tried to free it and the briars tore her hand. There was a tear in its belly and she could see a shiny gray loop of intestine. She tore off a piece of her shirt and wrapped it around the fox kit. She put the kit in her pocket. She ran all the way back to the wizard's tower, all the way up the steps. She didn't count them. She didn't stop to rest. Onion followed her, quick as a shadow.

When she reached the door at the top of the stairs, she knocked hard. No one answered.

"Wizard!" she said.

No one answered.

"Please help me," she said. She lifted the fox kit out of her pocket and sat down on the steps with it swaddled in her lap. It didn't try to bite her. It needed all its energy for dying. Onion sat next to her. He stroked the kit's throat.

"Please," Halsa said again. "Please don't let it die. Please do something."

She could feel the wizard of Perfil, standing next to the door. The wizard put a hand out, as if—at last—the door

might open. She saw that the wizard loved foxes and all the wild marsh things. But the wizard said nothing. The wizard didn't love Halsa. The door didn't open.

"Help me," Halsa said one more time. She felt that dreadful black pull again, just as it had been on the train with Onion. It was as if the wizard were yanking at her shoulder, shaking her in a stony, black rage. How dare someone like Halsa ask a wizard for help. Onion was shaking her, too. Where Onion's hand gripped her, Halsa could feel stuff pouring through her and out of her. She could feel the kit, feel the place where its stomach had torn open. She could feel its heart pumping blood, its panic and fear and the life that was spilling out of it. Magic flowed up and down the stairs of the tower. The wizard of Perfil was winding it up like a skein of black, tarry wool, and then letting it go again. It poured through Halsa and Onion and the fox kit until Halsa thought she would die.

"Please," she said, and what she meant this time was *stop*. It would kill her. And then she was empty again. The magic had gone through her and there was nothing left of it or her. Her bones had been turned into jelly. The fox kit began to struggle, clawing at her. When she unwrapped it, it sank its teeth into her wrist and then ran down the stairs as if it had never been dying at all.

Halsa stood up. Onion was gone, but she could still feel the wizard standing there on the other side of the door. "Thank you," she said. She followed the fox kit down the stairs.

The next morning she woke and found Onion lying on the pallet beside her. He seemed nearer, somehow, this time.

As if he weren't entirely dead. Halsa felt that if she tried to speak to him, he would answer. But she was afraid of what he would say.

Essa saw Onion, too. "You have a shadow," she said.

"His name is Onion," Halsa said.

"Help me with this," Essa said. Someone had cut lengths of bamboo. Essa was fixing them in the ground, using a mixture of rocks and mud to keep them upright. Burd and some of the other children wove rushes through the bamboo, making walls, Halsa saw.

"What are we doing?" Halsa asked.

"There is an army coming." Burd said. "To burn down the town of Perfil. Tolcet went to warn them."

"What will happen?" Halsa said. "Will the wizards protect the town?"

Essa laid another bamboo pole across the tops of the two upright poles. She said, "They can come to the marshes, if they want to, and take refuge. The army won't come here. They're afraid of the wizards."

"Afraid of the wizards!" Halsa said. "Why? The wizards are cowards and fools. Why won't they save Perfil?"

"Go ask them yourself," Essa said. "If you're brave enough."

"Halsa?" Onion said. Halsa looked away from Essa's steady gaze. For a moment there were two Onions. One was the shadowy ghost from the train, close enough to touch. The second Onion stood beside the cooking fire. He was filthy, skinny, and real. Shadow-Onion guttered and then was gone.

"Onion?" Halsa said.

"I came out of the mountains," Onion said. "Five days ago, I think. I didn't know where I was going, except that I could see you. Here. I walked and walked and you were with me and I was with you."

"Where are Mik and Bonti?" Halsa said. "Where's Mother?"

"There were two women on the train with us. They were rich. They've promised to take care of Mik and Bonti. They will. I know they will. They were going to Qual. When you gave me the doll, Halsa, you saved the train. We could see the explosion, but we passed through it. The tracks were destroyed and there were clouds and clouds of black smoke and fire, but nothing touched the train. We saved everyone."

"Where's Mother?" Halsa said again. But she already knew. Onion was silent. The train stopped beside a narrow stream to take on water. There was an ambush. Soldiers. There was a bottle with water leaking out of it. Halsa's mother had dropped it. There was an arrow sticking out of her back.

Onion said, "I'm sorry, Halsa. Everyone was afraid of me, because of how the train had been saved. Because I knew that there was going to be an explosion. Because I didn't know about the ambush and people died. So I got off the train."

"Here," Burd said to Onion. He gave him a bowl of porridge. "No, eat it slowly. There's plenty more."

Onion said with his mouth full, "Where are the wizards of Perfil?"

Halsa began to laugh. She laughed until her sides ached and until Onion stared at her and until Essa came over and shook her. "We don't have time for this," Essa said. "Take that

boy and find him somewhere to lie down. He's exhausted."

"Come on," Halsa said to Onion. "You can sleep in my bed. Or if you'd rather, you can go knock on the door at the top of the tower and ask the wizard of Perfil if you can have his bed."

She showed Onion the cubby under the stairs and he lay down on it. "You're dirty," she said. "You'll get the sheets dirty."

"I'm sorry," Onion said.

"It's fine," Halsa said. "We can wash them later. There's plenty of water here. Are you still hungry? Do you need anything?"

"I brought something for you," Onion said. He held out his hand and there were the earrings that had belonged to his mother.

"No," Halsa said.

Halsa hated herself. She was scratching at her own arm, ferociously, not as if she had an insect bite, but as if she wanted to dig beneath the skin. Onion saw something that he hadn't known before, something astonishing and terrible, that Halsa was no kinder to herself than to anyone else. No wonder Halsa had wanted the earrings—just like the snakes, Halsa would gnaw on herself if there was nothing else to gnaw on. How Halsa wished that she'd been kind to her mother.

Onion said, "Take them. Your mother was kind to me, Halsa. So I want to give them to you. My mother would have wanted you to have them, too."

"All right," Halsa said. She wanted to weep, but she scratched and scratched instead. Her arm was white and red

from scratching. She took the earrings and put them in her pocket. "Go to sleep now."

"I came here because you were here," Onion said. "I wanted to tell you what had happened. What should I do now?"

"Sleep," Halsa said.

"Will you tell the wizards that I'm here? How we saved the train?" Onion said. He yawned so wide that Halsa thought his head would split in two. "Can I be a servant of the wizards of Perfil?"

"We'll see," Halsa said. "You go to sleep. I'll go climb the stairs and tell them that you've come."

"It's funny," Onion said. "I can feel them all around us. I'm glad you're here. I feel safe."

Halsa sat on the bed. She didn't know what to do. Onion was quiet for a while and then he said, "Halsa?"

"What?" Halsa said.

"I can't sleep," he said apologetically.

"Shhh," Halsa said. She stroked his filthy hair. She sang a song her father had liked to sing. She held Onion's hand until his breathing became slower and she was sure that he was sleeping. Then she went up the stairs to tell the wizard about Onion. "I don't understand you," she said to the door. "Why do you hide away from the world? Don't you get tired of hiding?"

The wizard didn't say anything.

"Onion is braver than you are," Halsa told the door. "Essa is braver. My mother was—"

She swallowed and said, "She was braver than you. Stop ignoring me. What good are you, up here? You won't talk to

me, and you won't help the town of Perfil, and Onion's going to be very disappointed when he realizes that all you do is skulk around in your room, waiting for someone to bring you breakfast. If you like waiting so much, then you can wait as long as you like. I'm not going to bring you any food or any water or anything that I find in the swamp. If you want anything, you can magic it. Or you can come get it yourself. Or you can turn me into a toad."

She waited to see if the wizard would turn her into a toad. "All right," she said at last. "Well, good-bye then." She went back down the stairs.

The wizards of Perfil are lazy and useless. They hate to climb stairs and they never listen when you talk. They don't answer questions because their ears are full of beetles and wax and their faces are wrinkled and hideous. Marsh fairies live deep in the wrinkles of the faces of the wizards of Perfil and the marsh fairies ride around in the bottomless canyons of the wrinkles on saddle-broken fleas who grow fat grazing on magical, wizardly blood. The wizards of Perfil spend all night scratching their fleabites and sleep all day. I'd rather be a scullery maid than a servant of the invisible, doddering, nearly-blind, flea-bitten, mildewy, clammy-fingered, conceited marsh-wizards of Perfil.

Halsa checked Onion, to make sure that he was still asleep. Then she went and found Essa. "Will you pierce my ears for me?" she said.

Essa shrugged. "It will hurt," she said.

"Good," said Halsa. So Essa boiled water and put her needle in it. Then she pierced Halsa's ears. It did hurt, and Halsa was glad. She put on Onion's mother's earrings, and then she helped Essa and the others dig latrines for the townspeople of Perfil.

Tolcet came back before sunset. There were half a dozen women and their children with him.

"Where are the others?" Essa said.

Tolcet said, "Some don't believe me. They don't trust wizardly folk. There are some that want to stay and defend the town. Others are striking out on foot for Qual, along the tracks."

"Where is the army now?" Burd said.

"Close," Halsa said. Tolcet nodded.

The women from the town had brought food and bedding. They seemed subdued and anxious and it was hard to tell whether it was the approaching army or the wizards of Perfil that scared them most. The women stared at the ground. They didn't look up at the towers. If they caught their children looking up, they scolded them in low voices.

"Don't be silly," Halsa said crossly to a woman whose child had been digging a hole near a tumbled tower. The woman shook him until he cried and cried and wouldn't stop. What was she thinking? That wizards liked to eat mucky children who dug holes? "The wizards are lazy and unsociable and harmless. They keep to themselves and don't bother anyone."

The woman only stared at Halsa, and Halsa realized that she was as afraid of Halsa as she was of the wizards of Perfil. Halsa was amazed. Was she that terrible? Mik and Bonti and

Onion had always been afraid of her, but they'd had good reason to be. And she'd changed. She was as mild and meek as butter now.

Tolcet, who was helping with dinner, snorted as if he'd caught her thought. The woman grabbed up her child and rushed away, as if Halsa might open her mouth again and eat them both.

"Halsa, look." It was Onion, awake and so filthy that you could smell him from two yards away. They would need to burn his clothes. Joy poured through Halsa, because Onion had come to find her and because he was here and because he was alive. He'd come out of Halsa's tower, where he'd gotten her cubby bed grimy and smelly, how wonderful to think of it, and he was pointing east, toward the town of Perfil. There was a red glow hanging over the marsh, as if the sun were rising instead of setting. Everyone was silent, looking east as if they might be able to see what was happening in Perfil. Presently the wind carried an ashy, desolate smoke over the marsh. "The war has come to Perfil," a woman said.

"Which army is it?" another woman said, as if the first woman might know.

"Does it matter?" said the first woman. "They're all the same. My eldest went off to join the King's army and my youngest joined General Balder's men. They've set fire to plenty of towns, and killed other mothers' sons and maybe one day they'll kill each other, and never think of me. What difference does it make to the town that's being attacked, to know what army is attacking them? Does it matter to a cow who kills her?"

"They'll follow us," someone else said in a resigned voice. "They'll find us here and they'll kill us all!"

"They won't," Tolcet said. He spoke loudly. His voice was calm and reassuring. "They won't follow you and they won't find you here. Be brave for your children. All will be well."

"Oh, please," Halsa said, under her breath. She stood and glared up at the towers of the wizards of Perfil, her hands on her hips. But as usual, the wizards of Perfil were up to nothing. They didn't strike her dead for glaring. They didn't stand at their windows to look out over the marshes to see the town of Perfil and how it was burning while they only stood and watched. Perhaps they were already asleep in their beds, dreaming about breakfast, lunch, and dinner. She went and helped Burd and Essa and the others make up beds for the refugees from Perfil. Onion cut up wild onions for the stew pot. He was going to have to have a bath soon, Halsa thought. Clearly he needed someone like Halsa to tell him what to do.

None of the servants of the wizards of Perfil slept. There was too much work to do. The latrines weren't finished. A child wandered off into the marshes and had to be found before it drowned or met a dragon. A little girl fell into the well and had to be hauled up.

Before the sun came up again, more refugees from the town of Perfil arrived. They came into the camp in groups of twos or threes, until there were almost a hundred townspeople in the wizards' meadow. Some of the newcomers were wounded or badly burned or deep in shock. Essa and Tolcet took charge. There were compresses to apply, clothes that had

already been cut up for bandages, hot drinks that smelled bitter and medicinal and not particularly magical. People went rushing around, trying to discover news of family members or friends who had stayed behind. Young children who had been asleep woke up and began to cry.

"They put the mayor and his wife to the sword," a man was saying.

"They'll march on the King's city next," an old woman said. "But our army will stop them."

"It *was* our army—I saw the butcher's boy and Philpot's middle son. They said that we'd been trading with the enemies of our country. The King sent them. It was to teach us a lesson. They burned down the market church and they hung the pastor from the bell tower."

There was a girl lying on the ground who looked Mik and Bonti's age. Her face was gray. Tolcet touched her stomach lightly and she emitted a thin, high scream, not a human noise at all, Onion thought. The marshes were so noisy with magic that he couldn't hear what she was thinking, and he was glad.

"What happened?" Tolcet said to the man who'd carried her into the camp.

"She fell," the man said. "She was trampled underfoot."

Onion watched the girl, breathing slowly and steadily, as if he could somehow breathe for her. Halsa watched Onion. Then: "That's enough," she said. "Come on, Onion."

She marched away from Tolcet and the girl, shoving through the refugees.

"Where are we going?" Onion said.

"To make the wizards come down," Halsa said. "I'm sick and tired of doing all their work for them. Their cooking and fetching. I'm going to knock down that stupid door. I'm going to drag them down their stupid stairs. I'm going to make them help that girl."

There were a lot of stairs this time. Of course the accursed wizards of Perfil would know what she was up to. This was their favorite kind of wizardly joke, making her climb and climb and climb. They'd wait until she and Onion got to the top and then they'd turn them into lizards. Well, maybe it wouldn't be so bad, being a small poisonous lizard. She could slip under the door and bite one of the damned wizards of Perfil. She went up and up and up, half running and half stumbling, until it seemed she and Onion must have climbed right up into the sky. When the stairs abruptly ended, she was still running. She crashed into the door so hard that she saw stars.

"Halsa?" Onion said. He bent over her. He looked so worried that she almost laughed.

"I'm fine," she said. "Just wizards playing tricks." She hammered on the door, then kicked it for good measure. "Open up!"

"What are you doing?" Onion said.

"It never does any good," Halsa said. "I should have brought an ax."

"Let me try," Onion said.

Halsa shrugged. Stupid boy, she thought, and Onion could hear her perfectly. "Go ahead," she said.

Onion put his hand on the door and pushed. It swung open. He looked up at Halsa and flinched. "Sorry," he said.

Halsa went in.

There was a desk in the room, and a single candle, which was burning. There was a bed, neatly made, and a mirror on the wall over the desk. There was no wizard of Perfil, not even hiding under the bed. Halsa checked, just in case.

She went to the empty window and looked out. There was the meadow and the makeshift camp, below them, and the marsh. The canals, shining like silver. There was the sun, coming up, the way it always did. It was strange to see all the windows of the other towers from up here, so far above, all empty. White birds were floating over the marsh. She wondered if they were wizards; she wished she had a bow and arrows.

"Where is the wizard?" Onion said. He poked the bed. Maybe the wizard had turned himself into a bed. Or the desk. Maybe the wizard was a desk.

"There are no wizards," Halsa said.

"But I can feel them!" Onion sniffed, then sniffed harder. He could practically smell the wizard, as if the wizard of Perfil had turned himself into a mist or a vapor that Onion was inhaling. He sneezed violently.

Someone was coming up the stairs. He and Halsa waited to see if it was a wizard of Perfil. But it was only Tolcet. He looked tired and cross, as if he'd had to climb many, many stairs.

"Where are the wizards of Perfil?" Halsa said.

Tolcet held up a finger. "A minute to catch my breath," he said.

Halsa stamped her foot. Onion sat down on the bed. He apologized to it silently, just in case it was the wizard. Or maybe the candle was the wizard. He wondered what hap-

pened if you tried to blow a wizard out. Halsa was so angry he thought she might explode.

Tolcet sat down on the bed beside Onion. "A long time ago," he said, "the father of the present King visited the wizards of Perfil. He'd had certain dreams about his son, who was only a baby. He was afraid of these dreams. The wizards told him that he was right to be afraid. His son would go mad. There would be war and famine and more war and his son would be to blame. The old King went into a rage. He sent his men to throw the wizards of Perfil down from their towers. They did."

"Wait," Onion said. "Wait. What happened to the wizards? Did they turn into white birds and fly away?"

"No," Tolcet said. "The King's men slit their throats and threw them out of the towers. I was away. When I came back, the towers had been ransacked. The wizards were dead."

"No!" Halsa said. "Why are you lying? I know the wizards are here. They're hiding somehow. They're cowards."

"I can feel them, too," Onion said.

"Come and see," Tolcet said. He went to the window. When they looked down, they saw Essa and the other servants of the wizards of Perfil moving among the refugees. The two old women who never spoke were sorting through bundles of clothes and blankets. The thin man was staking down someone's cow. Children were chasing chickens as Burd held open the gate of a makeshift pen. One of the younger girls, Perla, was singing a lullaby to some mother's baby. Her voice, rough and sweet at the same time, rose straight up to the window of the tower, where Halsa and Onion and Tolcet stood looking

down. It was a song they all knew. It was a song that said all would be well.

"Don't you understand?" Tolcet, the wizard of Perfil, said to Halsa and Onion. "There are the wizards of Perfil. They are young, most of them. They haven't come into their full powers yet. But all may yet be well."

"Essa is a wizard of Perfil?" Halsa said. Essa, a shovel in her hand, looked up at the tower, as if she'd heard Halsa. She smiled and shrugged, as if to say, *Perhaps I am, perhaps not, but isn't it a good joke? Didn't you ever wonder?*

Tolcet turned Halsa and Onion around so that they faced the mirror that hung on the wall. He rested his strong, speckled hands on their shoulders for a minute, as if to give them courage. Then he pointed to the mirror, to the reflected Halsa and Onion, who stood there staring back at themselves, astonished. Tolcet began to laugh. Despite everything, he laughed so hard that tears came from his eyes. He snorted. The wizard's room was full of magic, and so were the marshes and Tolcet and the mirror where the children and Tolcet stood reflected, and the children were full of magic, too.

Tolcet pointed again at the mirror, and his reflection pointed its finger straight back at Halsa and Onion. Tolcet said, "Here they are in front of you! Ha! Do you know them? Here are the wizards of Perfil!"

Kelly Link is the author of two story collections, *Stranger Things Happen* and *Magic for Beginners.* She and her partner, Gavin J. Grant, live in Northampton, Massachusetts, where they publish books as Small Beer Press, produce the zine *Lady Churchill's Rosebud Wristlet* (www.lcrw.net), and coedit (the fantasy half of) *The Year's Best Fantasy and Horror* with Ellen Datlow.

Kelly once won a free trip around the world by answering the question "Why do you want to go around the world?" with "Because you can't go through it."

Her Web site is **www.kellylink.net**.

Author's Note

For about five or six years, I've had this picture in my head of a city of wizards. They live at the very top of impossibly tall towers and employ children to run up and down the stairs, fetching water and food and books and letters. But it wasn't really a story. It was just a very strange picture.

The first time I wrote "The Wizards of Perfil," it was Onion's story. He went off with Tolcet, and then the story just sat there. This wasn't Onion's fault: he was so happy to be working for wizards that the story got kind of boring. And I was sorry that Halsa and her brothers and mother went off on the train to be killed. So I put "The Wizards of Perfil" aside and went and wrote another story, "The Constable of Abal," which takes place in the same world, I think, although

it's either somewhat earlier or later. It's a story about gods, ghosts, and a murder, and I was still so preoccupied with the problem of Onion that it was a breeze to write. And by the time I'd finished the new story, I'd figured out some things about "The Wizards of Perfil."

So I came back, looked at the beginning again, and realized that I liked Halsa as much as I liked Onion, partly because she wasn't a likable character at all. So I sent her off with Tolcet instead, put Onion on the train, and then I could write the story.

I should also say that I wrote this story while sitting in the Haymarket (a coffeehouse in Northampton) and drinking smoothies with the writer Holly Black. I don't think I could have finished it without her or the smoothies.

Patricia A. McKillip

Jack O'Lantern

Jenny Newland sat patiently under the tree in her costume, waiting for the painter to summon her. Not far from her, in the sunlight, one of the village girls sneezed lavishly and drew the back of her wrist under her nose. A boy poked her; she demanded aggrievedly, "Well, what do you want me to do? Wipe me nose on me costume?" Jenny shifted her eyes; her clasped fingers tightened; her spine straightened. They were all dressed alike, the half-dozen young people around the tree, in what looked like tablecloths the innocuous pastels of tea cakes.

"Togas?" her father had suggested dubiously at the sight. "And Grecian robes for the young ladies? Pink, though? And pistachio . . .?" His voice had trailed away; at home, he would have gone off to consult his library. Here, amid the pretty thickets and pastures outside the village of Farnham, he could only watch and wonder.

He had commissioned the renowned painter Joshua Ryme to do a commemorative painting for Sarah's wedding.

Naturally, she couldn't wear her bridal gown before the wedding; it was with the seamstress, having five hundred seed pearls attached to it by the frail, undernourished fingers of a dozen orphans who never saw the light of day. Such was the opinion of Sylvester Newland, who claimed the sibling territory midway between Sarah, seventeen, and Jenny, thirteen. It was a lot of leeway, those four years between child and adult, and he roamed obnoxiously in it, scattering his thoughts at will for no other reason than that he was allowed to have them.

"Men must make their way in the world," her mother had said gently when Jenny first complained about Sylvester's rackety ways. "Women must help and encourage them, and provide them with a peaceful haven from their daily struggle to make the world a better place."

Jenny, who had been struggling with a darning needle and wool and one of Sylvester's socks, stabbed herself and breathed incredulously, "For this I have left school?"

"Your governess will see that you receive the proper education to provide you with understanding and sympathy for your husband's work and conversation." Her mother's voice was still mild, but she spoke in that firm, sweet manner that would remain unshaken by all argument, like a great stone rising implacably out of buffeting waves, sea life clinging safely to every corner of it. "Besides, women are not strong, as you will find out soon enough. Their bodies are subject to the powerful forces of their natures." She hesitated; Jenny was silent, having heard rumors of the secret lives of women, and wondering if her mother would go into detail. She did, finally,

but in such a delicate fashion that Jenny was left totally bewildered. Women were oysters carrying the pearls of life; their husbands opened them and poured into them the water of life, after which the pearls . . . turned into babies?

Later, after one of the pearls of life had finally irritated her inner oyster enough to draw blood, and she found herself on a daybed hugging a hot water bag, she began to realize what her mother had meant about powerful forces of nature. Sarah, tactfully quiet and kind, put a cup of tea on the table beside her.

"Thank you," Jenny said mournfully. "I think the oysters are clamping themselves shut inside me."

Sarah's solemn expression quivered away; she sat on the daybed beside Jenny. "Oh, did you get the oyster speech, too?"

She had grown amazingly stately overnight, it seemed to Jenny, with her lovely gowns and her fair hair coiled and scalloped like cream on an éclair. Sarah's skin was perfect ivory; her own was blotched and dotted with strange eruptions. Her hair, straight as a horse's tail and so heavy it flopped out of all but the toothiest pins, was neither ruddy chestnut nor true black, but some unromantic shade in between.

Reading Jenny's mind, which she did often, Sarah patted her hands. "Don't fret. You'll grow into yourself. And you have a fine start: your pale gray eyes with that dark hair will become stunning soon enough."

"For what?" Jenny asked intensely, searching her sister's face. The sudden luminousness of her beauty must partially be explained by Mr. Everett Woolidge, who had already spo-

ken to Sarah's father, and was impatiently awaiting Sarah's eighteenth birthday. "Is love only about oysters and the water of life? What exactly was Mama trying to say?"

Sarah's smile had gone; she answered slowly, "I'm not sure yet, myself, though I'm very sure it has nothing to do with oysters."

"When you find out, will you tell me?"

"I promise. I'll take notes as it happens." Still a line tugged at her tranquil brows; she was not seeing Jenny, but the shadow of Mr. Woolidge, doing who knew what to her on her wedding bed. Then she added, reading Jenny's mind again, "There's nothing to fear, Mama says. You just lie still and think of the garden."

"The garden?"

"Something pleasant."

"That's all it took to make Sylvester? She must have been thinking about the plumbing, or boiled cabbage."

Sarah's smile flashed again; she ducked her head, looking guilty for a moment, as though she'd been caught giggling in the schoolroom. "Very likely." She pushed a strand of hair out of Jenny's face. "You should drink your tea; it'll soothe the pain."

Jenny stared up at her, fingers clenched, her whole body clenched, something tight and hot behind her eyes. "I'll miss you," she whispered. "Oh, I will miss you so. Sylvester just talks at me, and Mama—Mama cares only about him and Papa. You are the only one I can laugh with."

"I know." Sarah's voice, too, sounded husky, ragged. "Everett—he is kind and good, and of course ardent. But I've

known you all your life. I can say things to you that I could never say to Mama—or even to Everett—" She paused, that faraway look again in her eyes, as though she were trying to see her own future. "I hope he and I will learn to talk to one another . . . Mama would say it's childish of me to want what I think to be in any way important to him; that's something I must grow out of, when I'm married."

"Talk to me," Jenny begged her. "Anytime. About anything."

Sarah nodded, caressing Jenny's hair again. "I'll send for you."

"Why must he take you so far away? Why?"

"It's only a half day on the train. And very pretty, Farnham is. We'll have long rides together, you and I, and walks, and country fairs. You'll see."

And Jenny did: the village where Mr. Woolidge had inherited his country home was charming, full of centuries-old cottages with thick stone walls, and hairy thatched roofs, and tiny windows set, with no order whatsoever, all anyhow in the walls. The artist, Mr. Ryme, had a summer house there as well. Jenny could see it on a distant knoll from where she sat under the chestnut tree. It was of butter-yellow stone with white trim, and the windows were where you expected them to be. But still it looked old, with its dark, crumbling garden wall, and the ancient twisted apple trees inside, and the wooden gate, open for so long it had grown into the earth. The artist's daughter Alexa was under the tree as well, along with four comely village children and Jenny. The village children with their rough voices and unkempt hair would have horri-

fied Mama. Fortunately she had not come, due to undisclosed circumstances that Jenny suspected had to do with oysters and pearls. Sylvester was away at school; Mr. Ryme would add their faces to the painting later. The governess, Miss Lake, had accompanied Jenny, with some staunch idea of keeping up with her lessons. But in the mellow country air, she had relaxed and grown vague. She sat knitting under a willow, light and shadow dappling her thin, freckled face and angular body as the willow leaves swayed around her in the breeze.

The artist had positioned Jenny's father on one side of the little rocky brook winding through the grass. The wedding guests, mostly portrayed by villagers and friends of the painter, were arranged behind him. The wedding party itself would be painted advancing toward him on the other side of the water. A tiny bridge arching above some picturesque stones and green moss would signify the place where the lovers Cupid and Psyche would become man and wife. Papa wore a long tunic that covered all but one arm, over which a swag of purple was discreetly draped. He looked, with his long gold mustaches and full beard, more like a druid, Jenny thought, than a Grecian nobleman. He was smiling, enjoying himself, his eyes on Sarah as the artist fussed with the lilies in her hands. She wore an ivory robe; Mr. Woolidge, a very hairy Cupid, wore gold with a purple veil over his head. At the foot of the bridge, the artist's younger daughter, golden-haired and plump, just old enough to know how to stand still, carried a basket of violets, from which she would fling a handful of posies onto the bridge to ornament the couple's path.

Finally, the older children were summoned into position

behind the pair. Mr. Ryme, having placed them, stood gazing narrowly at them, one finger rasping over his whiskers. He moved his hand finally and spoke.

"A lantern. We must have a lantern."

"Exactly!" Papa exclaimed, enlightened.

"Why, Father?" the artist's daughter Alexa asked, daring to voice the question in Jenny's head. She thought Mr. Ryme would ignore his daughter, or rebuke her for breaking her pose. But he took the question seriously, gazing at all of the children behind the bridal pair.

"Because Cupid made Psyche promise not to look upon him, even after they married. He came to her only at night. Psyche's sisters told her that she must have married some dreadful monster instead of a man. Such things happened routinely, it seems, in antiquity."

"He's visible enough now," one of the village boys commented diffidently, but inarguably, of Mr. Woolidge.

"Yes, he is," Mr. Ryme answered briskly. "We can't very well leave the groom out of his own wedding portrait, can we? That's why he is wearing that veil. He'll hold it out between himself and his bride, and turn his head so that only those viewing the painting will see his face."

"Oh, brilliant," Papa was heard to murmur across the bridge.

"Thank you. But let me continue with the lantern. One night, Psyche lit a lantern to see exactly what she had taken into her marriage bed. She was overjoyed to find the beautiful face of the son of Venus. But—profoundly moved by his godhood, perhaps—she trembled and spilled a drop of hot

oil on him, waking him. In sorrow and anger with her for breaking her promise, he vanished out of her life. The lantern among the wedding party will remind the viewer of the rest of Psyche's story."

"What was the rest, Mr. Ryme?" a village girl demanded.

"She was forced to face her mother-in-law," Alexa answered instead, "who made Psyche complete various impossible tasks, including a trip to the Underworld, before the couple were united again. Isn't that right, Father?"

"Very good, Alexa," Mr. Ryme said, smiling at her. Jenny's eyes widened. She knew the tale as well as anyone, but if she had spoken, Papa would have scolded her for showing off her knowledge. And here was Alexa, with her curly red-gold hair and green eyes, not only lovely, but encouraged to reveal her education. Mr. Ryme held up his hand before anyone else could speak, his eyes, leaf green as his daughter's beneath his dark, shaggy brows, moving over them again.

"Who . . ." he murmured. "Ah. Of course, Jenny must hold it. Why you, Jenny?"

Behind him, Papa, prepared to answer, closed his mouth, composed his expression. Jenny gazed at Mr. Ryme, gathering courage, and answered finally, shyly, "Because I am the bride's sister. And I'm part of Psyche's story, as well, like the lantern."

"Good!" Mr. Ryme exclaimed. His daughter caught Jenny's eyes, smiled, and Jenny felt herself flush richly. The artist shifted her to the forefront of the scene and crooked her arm at her waist. "Pretend this is your lantern," he said, handing her a tin cup that smelled strongly of linseed oil from his paint box. "I'm sure there's something more appropriate in

my studio. For now, I just need to sketch you all in position." He gestured to the dozen or so villagers and friends behind Mr. Newland. "Poses, please, everyone. Try to keep still. This won't take as long as you might think. When I've gotten you all down where I want you, we'll have a rest and explore the contents of the picnic baskets Mr. Woolidge and Mr. Newland so thoughtfully provided. I'll work with small groups after we eat; the rest of you can relax unless I need you, but don't vanish. Remember that you are all invited to supper at my cottage at the end of the day."

Jenny spent her breaks under the willow tree, practicing historical dates and French irregular verbs with Miss Lake, who seemed to have been recalled to her duties by the references to the classics. At the end of the day, Jenny was more than ready for the slow walk through the meadows in the long, tranquil dusk to the artist's cottage. There, everyone changed into their proper clothes, and partook of the hot meat pastries, bread and cheese and cold beef, fresh milk, ale, and great fruit-and-cream tarts arrayed on the long tables set up in the artist's garden.

Jenny took a place at the table with Sarah and Mr. Woolidge. Across from them sat Papa and Mr. Ryme, working through laden plates and frothy cups of ale.

"An energetic business, painting," Papa commented approvingly. "I hadn't realized how much wildlife is involved."

"It's always more challenging, working out of doors, and with large groups. It went very well today, I thought."

Jenny looked at the artist, a question hovering inside her. At home, she was expected to eat her meals silently and grace-

fully, speaking only when asked, and then as simply as possible. But her question wasn't simple; she barely knew how to phrase it. And this was more like a picnic, informal and friendly, everyone talking at once, and half the gathering sitting on the grass.

"Mr. Ryme," she said impulsively, "I have a question."

Her father stared at her with surprise. "Jenny," he chided, "you interrupted Mr. Ryme."

She blushed, mortified. "I'm so sorry—"

"It must be important, then," Mr. Ryme said gently. "What is it?"

"Psyche's sisters—when they told her she must have wedded a monster . . ." Her voice trailed. Papa was blinking at her. Mr. Ryme only nodded encouragingly. "Wouldn't she have known if that were so? Even in the dark, if something less than human were in bed with her—couldn't she tell? Without a lantern?"

She heard Mr. Woolidge cough on his beer, felt Sarah's quick tremor of emotion.

"Jenny," Papa said decisively, "that is a subject more fit for the schoolroom than the dinner table, and hardly suitable even there. I'm surprised you should have such thoughts, let alone express them."

"It is an interesting question, though," Mr. Ryme said quite seriously. "Don't you think? It goes to the heart of the story, which is not about whether Psyche married a monster—and, I think, Jenny is correct in assuming that she would have soon realized it—but about a broken promise. A betrayal of love. Don't you think so, Mr. Newland?"

But his eyes remained on Jenny as he diverted the conversation away from her; they smiled faintly, kindly. Papa began a lengthy answer, citing sources. Jenny felt Sarah's fingers close on her hand.

"I was wondering that, myself," she breathed.

Mr. Woolidge overheard.

"What?" he queried softly. "If you will find a monster in your wedding bed?"

"No, of course not," Sarah said with another tremor—of laughter, or surprise, or fear, Jenny couldn't tell. "What Jenny asked. Why Psyche could not tell, even in the dark, if her husband was not human."

"I assure you, you will find me entirely human," Mr. Woolidge promised. "You will not have to guess."

"I'm sure I won't," Sarah answered faintly.

Mr. Woolidge took a great bite out of his meat pie, his eyes on Sarah as he chewed. Jenny, disregarded, rose and slipped away from her father's critical eyes. She glimpsed Miss Lake watching her from the next table, beginning to gesture, but Jenny pretended not to see. Wandering through the apple trees with a meat pie in her hand, free to explore her own thoughts, she came across the artist's daughter under a tree with one of the village boys.

Jenny stopped uncertainly. Mama would have considered the boy unsuitable company, even for an artist's daughter, and would have instructed Jenny to greet them kindly and politely as she moved away. But she didn't move, and Alexa waved to her.

"Come and sit with us. Will's been telling me country stories."

Jenny glanced around; Miss Lake was safely hidden behind the apple leaves. She edged under the tree and sat, looking curiously at Will. Something about him reminded her of a bird. He was very thin, with flighty golden hair and long, fine bones too near the surface of his skin. His eyes looked golden, like his hair. They seemed secretive, looking back at her, but not showing what they thought. He was perhaps her age, she guessed, though something subtle in his expression made him seem older.

He was chewing an apple from the tree; a napkin with crumbs of bread and cheese on it lay near him on the grass. Politely, he swallowed his bite and waited for Jenny to speak to him first. Jenny glanced questioningly at Alexa, whose own mouth was full.

She said finally, tentatively, "Country tales?"

"It was the lantern, miss." His voice was deep yet soft, with a faint country burr in it, like a bee buzzing in his throat, that was not unpleasant. "It reminded me of Jack."

"Jack?"

"O'Lantern. He carries a light across the marshes at night and teases you into following it, thinking it will lead you to fairyland, or treasure, or just safely across the ground. Then he puts the light out, and there you are, stranded in the dark in the middle of a marsh. Some call it elf fire, or fox fire."

"Or—?" Alexa prompted, with a sudden, teasing smile. The golden eyes slid to her, answering the smile.

"Will," he said. "Will o' the Wisp."

He bit into the apple again; Jenny sat motionless, listening to the crisp, solid crunch, almost tasting the sweet, cool juices.

But these apples were half-wild, her eye told her, misshapen and probably wormy; you shouldn't just pick them out of the long grass or off the branch and eat them . . .

"My father painted a picture of us following the marsh fire," Alexa said. "Will held a lantern in the dark; I was with him as his sister. My father called the painting *Jack O'Lantern*."

"What were you doing in the dark?" Jenny asked fuzzily, trying to untangle the real from the story.

"My father told us we were poor children, sent out to cut peat for a fire on a cruel winter's dusk. Dark came too fast; we got lost, and followed the Jack O'Lantern sprite, thinking it was someone who knew the path back."

"And what happened?"

Alexa shrugged slightly. "That's the thing about paintings. They only show you one moment of the tale; you have to guess at the rest of it. Do you want to see it? My father asked me to find a lantern for you in his studio; he won't mind if you come with me."

Jenny saw Miss Lake drifting about with a plate at the far end of the garden, glancing here and there, most likely for her charge. She stopped to speak to Sarah. Jenny swallowed the last of her meat pie.

"Yes," she said quickly. "I'd like that." It sounded wild and romantic, visiting an artist's studio, a place where paint turned into flame, and flame into the magic of fairyland. It was, her mother would have said, no place for a well-brought-up young girl, who might chance upon the disreputable, unsavory things that went on between artists and their models. Jenny couldn't imagine the distinguished Mr. Ryme doing unsavory things

in his studio. But perhaps she could catch a glimpse there of what nebulous goings-on her mother was talking about when she said the word.

"You come, too, Will," Alexa added to him. "You don't often get a chance to see it."

"Is there a back door?" Jenny asked, her eye on Miss Lake, and Alexa flung her a mischievous glance.

"There is, indeed. Come this way."

They went around the apple trees, away from the noisy tables, where lanterns and torches, lit against insects and the dark, illumined faces against the shadowy nightfall, making even the villagers look mysterious, unpredictable. Alexa, carrying a candle, led them up a back staircase in the house. Jenny kept slowing to examine paintings hung along the stairs. In the flickering light, they were too vague to be seen: faces that looked not quite human, risings of stone that might have been high craggy peaks, or the ruined towers of an ancient castle.

Will stopped beside one of the small, ambiguous landscapes. "That's Perdu Castle," he said. He sounded surprised. "On the other side of the marshes. There's stories about it, too: that it shifts around and you never find it if you're looking for it, only if you're not."

"Is that true?" Jenny demanded.

"True as elf fire," he answered gravely, looking at her out of his still eyes in a way that was neither familiar nor rude. As though, Jenny thought, he were simply interested in what she might be thinking. He was nicer than Sylvester, she realized suddenly, for all his dirty fingernails and patched trousers.

"When you saw it, were you looking for it?"

"Bit of both," he admitted. "I was pretending not to while I searched for it. But I was surprised when I found it. I wonder if Mr. Ryme knew it was there before he painted it."

"Of course he did," Alexa said with a laugh. "Great heaps of stone don't shift themselves around; it's people who get lost. My father paints romantic visions, but there's nothing romantic about carrying a paint box for miles, or having to swat flies all afternoon while you search. He'd want to know exactly where he was going."

She opened a door at the top of the stairs, lighting more candles and a couple of lamps as Jenny and Will entered. Paintings leaped into light everywhere in the room, sitting on easels, hanging in frames, leaning in unframed stacks against the walls. The studio took up the entire top floor of the house; windows overlooked meadow, marsh, the smudges of distant trees, the village disappearing into night. Richly colored carpets lay underfoot; odd costumes and wraps hung on hooks and coatracks. A peculiar collection of things littered shelves along the walls: seashells, hats, boxes, a scepter, crowns of tinsel and gold leaf, chunks of crystals, shoe buckles, necklaces, swords, pieces of armor, ribbons, a gilded bit and bridle. From among this jumble, Alexa produced a lamp and studied it doubtfully. One end was pointed, the other scrolled into a handle. Gleaming brass with colorful lozenges of enamel decorated the sides. It looked, Jenny thought, like the lamp Aladdin might have rubbed to summon the genie within. Alexa put it back, rummaged farther along the shelves.

Will caught Jenny's eye then, gazing silently at a painting propped against the wall. She joined him, and saw his face in

the painting, peering anxiously into a wild darkness dimly lit by the lantern in his hand. Alexa, a lock of red hair blowing out of the threadbare shawl over her head, stood very close to him, pointing toward the faint light across murky ground and windblown grasses. Her face, pinched and worried, seemed to belong more to a ghostly twin of the lovely, confident, easily smiling girl searching for a lamp behind them.

Something flashed above the painting. Jenny raised her eyes to the open window, saw the pale light in the dense twilight beyond the house and gardens. Someone out there, she thought curiously. The light went out, and her breath caught. She stepped around the painting, stuck her head out the window.

"Did you see that?"

"What?" Alexa asked absently.

"That light. Just like the one in the painting . . ."

She felt Will close beside her, staring out, heard his breath slowly loosed. Behind them, Alexa murmured, "Oh, here it is . . . A plain clay lantern Psyche might have used; no magic in this one. What are you looking at?"

"Jenny!"

She started, bumped her head on the window frame. Miss Lake stood below, staring up at them. Will drew back quickly; Jenny sighed.

"Yes, Miss Lake?"

"What are you doing up there?"

"I'm—"

"Come down, please; don't make me shout."

"Yes, Miss Lake. I'm helping Alexa. I'll come down in a moment."

"Surely you're not in Mr. Ryme's studio! And was that one of the village boys up there with you?"

Mr. Ryme appeared then, glanced up at Jenny, and said something apparently soothing to Miss Lake, who put a hand to her cheek and gave a faint laugh. Jenny wondered if he'd offered to paint her. They strolled away together. Jenny pushed back out the window, and there it was again, stronger this time in the swiftly gathering dark: a pulse of greeny-pale light that shimmered, wavered, almost went out, pulsed strong again.

"Oh . . ."

"What is it?" Alexa demanded beside her, then went silent; she didn't even breathe.

Behind them, Will said softly, briefly, "Jack O'Lantern."

"Oh," Jenny said again, sucking air into her lungs, along with twilight, and the scents of marsh and grass. She spun abruptly. "Let's follow it! I want to see it!"

"But, Jenny," Alexa protested, "it's not real. I mean it's real, but it's only—oh, how did my father put it? The spontaneous combustion of decayed vegetation."

"What?"

"Exploding grass."

Jenny stared at her. "That's the most ridiculous thing I've ever heard."

"It is, a bit, when you think about it," Alexa admitted.

"He obviously told you a tale to make you stay out of the marshes." Her eyes went to the window, where the frail elfin light danced in the night. "I have to go," she whispered. "This may be my only chance in life to see real magic before I must

become what Mama and Miss Lake and Papa think I should be . . ."

She started for the door, heard Will say quickly, "She can't go alone."

"Oh, all right," Alexa said. Her cool voice sounded tense, as though even she, her father's bright and rational daughter who could see beneath the paint, had gotten swept up in Jenny's excitement. "Will, take that lantern—"

Will put a candle in an old iron lantern; Jenny was out the door before he finished lighting it. "Hurry!" she pleaded, taking the stairs in an unladylike clatter.

"Wait for us!" Alexa cried. "Jenny! They'll see you!"

That stopped her at the bottom of the stairs. Alexa moved past her toward the apple trees; Will followed, trying to hide the light with his vest. As they snuck through the trees, away from the tables, Jenny heard somebody play a pipe, someone else begin a song. Then Alexa led them through a gap in the wall, over a crumbled litter of stones, and they were out in the warm, restless, redolent dark.

The light still beckoned across the night, now vague, hardly visible, now glowing steadily, marking one certain point in the shifting world. They ran, the lantern Will carried showing them tangled tussocks of grass on a flat ground that swept changelessly around them, except for a silvery murk now and then where water pooled. Jenny, her eyes on the pale fire, felt wind at her back, pushing, tumbling over her, racing ahead. Above them, cloud kept chasing the sliver of moon, could never quite catch it.

"Hurry—" Jenny panted. The light seemed closer now, bril-

liant, constantly reshaped by the wind. "I think we're almost there—"

"Oh, what is it?" Alexa cried. "What can it be? It can't be—Can it? Be real?"

"Real exploding grass, you mean?" Will wondered. The lantern handle creaked as it bounced in his hold. "Or real magic?"

"Real magic," Alexa gasped, and came down hard with one foot into a pool. Water exploded into a rain of light, streaking the air; she laughed. Jenny, turning, felt warm drops fall, bright as moon tears on her face.

She laughed, too, at the ephemeral magic that wasn't, or was it? Then something happened to the lantern; its light came from a crazy angle on a tussock. She felt her shoulders seized. Something warm came down over her mouth. Lips, she realized dimly, pulling at her mouth, drinking out of her. A taste like grass and apple. She pushed back at it, recognizing the apple, wanting a bigger bite. And in that moment, it was gone, leaving her wanting.

She heard a splash, a thump, a cry from Alexa. Then she saw the light burning in Will's hand, not the lantern, but a strange, silvery glow that his eyes mirrored just before he laughed and vanished.

Jenny stood blinking at Alexa, who was sitting open-mouthed in a pool of water. Her eyes sought Jenny's. Beyond that, neither moved; they could only stare at each other, stunned.

Alexa said finally, a trifle sourly, "Will."

Jenny moved to help her up. Alexa's face changed, then;

she laughed suddenly, breathlessly, and so did Jenny, feeling the silvery glow of magic in her heart, well worth the kiss snatched by the passing Will o' the Wisp.

They returned to find the villagers making their farewells to Mr. Ryme. Mr. Woolidge's carriage had drawn up to the gate, come to take Sarah and Jenny, Papa and Miss Lake to his house.

"There you are!" Sarah exclaimed when she saw Jenny. Alexa, staying in the shadows, edged around them quickly toward the house. "Where have you been?"

"Nowhere. Trying to catch a Will o' the Wisp."

Her father chuckled at her foolishness, said pedantically, "Nothing more, my dear, than the spontaneous combustion—"

"Of decayed grass. I know." She added to Mr. Ryme, "You'll have one less face to paint in the wedding party. Will won't be coming back."

"Why not?" he asked, surprised. His painter's eyes took in her expression, maybe the lantern glow in her eyes. He started to speak, stopped, said, "Will—" stopped again. He turned abruptly, calling, "Alexa?"

"She's in the house," Jenny told him. "She slipped in a pool."

"Oh, heavens, child," Miss Lake grumbled. "It's a wonder you didn't lose yourselves out there in the marsh."

"It is, indeed, a wonder," Jenny agreed.

She stepped into the carriage, sat close to Sarah, whose chilly fingers sought her hand and held it tightly, even as she turned toward the sound of Mr. Woolidge's voice raised in some solicitous question.

Patricia A. McKillip was born in Salem, Oregon, received an M.A. in English literature from San Jose State University in California, and has been a writer since then. She is primarily known for her fantasy, and has published novels both for adults and young adults. She is a two-time winner of the World Fantasy Award: for *The Forgotten Beasts of Eld* and *Ombria in Shadow* (which also won the Mythopoeic Award). Her many other novels include the Riddle-Master trilogy, *The Changeling Sea*, and the science fiction duo *Moon-Flash* and *The Moon and the Face* (reissued by Firebird as *Moon-Flash*). Her recent books include *Winter Rose, Od Magic*, and *Solstice Wood*. She and her husband, the poet David Lunde, live on the Oregon coast.

Author's Note

I've been doing research lately into the Pre-Raphaelite painters, who worked in mid-1800s England, and who dedicated themselves to reviving fantasy and wonder with their art. One of the paintings I learned about, by Arthur Hughes, is called *Jack O'Lantern*. This surprised me because I thought that was a particularly American term signifying fiery, grinning pumpkins on Halloween. So I did more research, and incorporated that painting into my version of the Pre-Raphaelite world, with its mystical, romantic, and otherwise unconventional views occasionally hampered by the stricter and stodgier beliefs of the Victorians.

Carol Emshwiller

Quill

Mother says, "Don't sing. Don't dance. Don't wear red." She says, "Simplify!" She says, "We don't eat bugs. We don't eat crawdads." Aren't they simple enough? She says, "We . . . our kind . . . doesn't do *that,* doesn't do *this.*" We heard it in the egg—so to speak. So to speak, that is.

We do eat eggs.

Sometimes when we're playing too vigorously, Mother says, "No high notes."

Mother says we're unique. We don't know whether to feel left out or included in with special people. We keep wondering, if we climbed high enough up or far enough down, we'd find another group like us just as special and if they'd be all right to make friends with. We plan to go find out but right now the littlest one of us would need help.

A stranger came out of the woods and stared at us. We were dressed right, yet he watched as if we were strange. We acted

normal. We played human-being games just to prove we were completely proper. I'm too old for this kind of play but the little ones like me to do it. I was the man this time, though I'm female. I stamped around and took big steps. But how many times have we seen a man?

But this stranger isn't the first, though he's come the closest to our houses. Not long ago we saw three men, climbing up along the stream. At first we didn't know what they were. We thought some sort of humped-back creatures. But then they took their packs off and we saw they were men. They didn't see us, though we followed them all the way up.

They had beards. We laughed but only afterwards so they wouldn't hear. Mother wondered what was so funny. We made up something else even sillier than beards.

Tom, though. He's getting hair on his upper lip. I saw him cutting it off with little scissors he stole from Mother's sewing kit. They don't work very well for that, so there's some of it still there. That's called a mustache.

This other man that stared . . . We saw him first from across the lake, the one we call Golden because of the golden eyes of the frogs. Mother doesn't like us to call it that. The idea of gold makes her gloomy. The river we call Silver, though that's where gold is. We found some but we knew better than to tell Mother. We hardly tell her anything in case what we do "just isn't done." Or maybe "just isn't talked about."

We have to be out here by ourselves so as not to be tempted by the way other people live. We might do what they do and "they're not our kind." But we couldn't be a different kind if we wanted to. We don't know how.

Mother says, "Every day is a lesson." We knew that a long time ago. Jumping rock to rock is a lesson, especially when we fall. Not testing stepping-stones before you step on them—that's a lesson. Watching lightning strike the tallest trees, though not always. Building a little hut of reeds. Making fires in the rain. You have to know how.

Mother doesn't know any of those lessons. I'll bet she couldn't even make a fire when it *wasn't* raining. I wonder if she even knows how to swim. I've never seen her near the lake except to gather rushes for mats or cattails for supper—those, our kind is allowed to eat. She hates to get her feet muddy.

We have secret places for dancing and singing. We stole a pan for a drum. We have scraping sticks. We clack stones. We only make our music beside the stream so as to hide the sound in case Mother should come out that far, though that's unlikely.

Morning is lessons. Numbers mostly. You can't fault numbers. Some of us are not good at them. If we complain, Mother says, "That's the way it is." Spelling . . . I'm not good at that. Geology I'm good at. It's all around us. I like to know how things got this way.

Mother wants us to know things such as honesty and generosity, but we had that all figured out on our own a long time ago. We know what's fair and what's not. We know you have to give to get. Sometimes we argue all afternoon about the rules of whatever we're playing and never get to play it, so we know we have to give up and give in.

Afternoons, when Mother takes a nap, we rush out before she can think of something else for us to do. We don't come

back till dusk and sometimes later. Now and then some of us spend all night in the woods. We've built ourselves little houses of reeds or twigs and branches. We know all the caves and cozy piles of rocks. She doesn't worry if a few of us are missing. We wonder, though, if she knows how many we are.

Every day, first thing, we're supposed to give thanks for what we have, but also that we have but little. Thanks for beans and corn and apples, and especially for living right here in a safe place. And thanks to Mother for the simple life. And thanks to Mother for Mother.

That stranger walked into our part of the forest, sat down, and stared. He has paper and pencil. He might be writing or drawing. We can't tell from here.

But we quacked when we should have cawed.

He knows there are no ducks around. We came out in plain view then. Across the lake from him. That's when we did what people do. Except instead of talking, we quacked.

It's not far across the lake at that point. He got a good view. He watched the whole time. He must like our looks. We liked his looks, too. We liked his big hat. His shirt is red. Except for our collections of feathers and flowers, we don't have any red.

Tom is the best at everything. Of course, since he's the oldest. He dances now. Just look at Tom's fast footwork and how he can leap. The man stares. He even looks at us through things Tom says are binoculars. And he has another thing. Tom says that's a camera and he's taking our picture. We've seen pictures in our books. He'll have us on paper to take home to his house.

Where the river comes down to the lake, you have to cross on the stepping-stones to get to our side. It looks as if that man is coming over. There's a couple of wobbly stones we set up on purpose. We didn't want Mother crossing without us knowing it.

Those flat stones look as if they're there to be stepped on, but they're really there to trip you up. So down he goes right in the middle of the stream, backpack and all. I'm not happy about him getting his paper wet. How much paper is there in the world? I'll ask Tom. Or maybe I'll ask this man.

We save our laughing for later. We only caw a little bit.

He sloshes out.

He knows that was on purpose—that those two middle rocks were set there so as to teeter.

He takes off his big black hat and empties out the water, puts it back on. Then he sits on the bank and examines his ankle.

We crowd around and look, too. His ankle is already starting to swell and turn black. Others of us skip back and forth across the stream. We don't avoid the center stones, we just go really fast over them.

He has tape just for this. He wraps up his ankle, twisting the tape here and there. He's better at it than Tom ever was with our sprained ankles. Here's another lesson for all of us.

What if we bring this man to our little homemade huts or our cave? We could hide him from Mother and have him to ourselves. Or what if we bring him home to Mother?

When he gets up, we get up, too. He limps. He follows our path from the stepping stones. If we don't watch out he'll be

right at Mother's in ten minutes. Well, at this rate, twenty.

Tom says, "Lean on me," but he won't. Tom says he's angry. Tom says, "If we had fathers, that's who he'd be limping off to see. He wants us punished."

We do wonder about fathers. Why don't we have them? Even Tom doesn't know, and Mother won't talk about it.

We can let him limp along the path to home, or sidetrack him to our cave. Tom says, "Let him go on home. We'll get to see what Mother does."

Pretty soon our regular houses come into view. They're good houses, not only thatched roofs, but thatched sides, too. Maybe we shouldn't call it thatch. It's made of tule rushes. Mother's house is made of stone and is much bigger. Tom says she made it by herself. He remembers thinking he was helping, though now he doesn't think he could have helped much. He was only three or four.

At our clearing, the man stops and looks.

Chickens in the yard have already cackled a warning that a stranger is coming—or a fox. We know Mother's hiding behind the door of her house looking out the little peephole. I'll bet she has the bar down.

The man keeps standing at the edge of our clearing, just looking.

Usually we hear the clanking of her loom, but lately she's been making moccasins. The simple life seems awfully complicated to Tom. The rest of us don't know any other way, though we try to guess. Tom says you don't even have to build a fire or light the lamps. He says clothes and shoes are just there, and he's told us all about electricity.

"Mother!" That's Tom. He goes to the door. "Don't worry. He's hurt."

"Tell him to go away."

"We want him."

"He's not the right sort."

"Come and see for yourself."

"I can tell from here."

"Please come. He can hardly walk. He has paper and pencil."

"We don't need it."

How can she say that? It's what I want the most.

"And he has a camera."

We hear the bar fall away and the door opens. Out she comes.

She's pretty much covered up, big baggy shirt. She's the only one we know with breasts, though I seem to be getting something like that now. I hide it from the others. I wish she'd give me a shirt like the one she's wearing. If I get any lumpier, I'll need that. It's a wonder I even know about them, but we do have books with pictures. Mother gave me a talk. It sounded silly. I don't know whether to believe her or not.

Usually Mother dresses so you can tell more about her body. Now she's different. And her hair is pulled back tight like it never is. She looks angry and worried. We just can't keep track of all the things we're not supposed to do. As we think up new things, new ones keep turning out to be bad. It even surprises us older ones. But now we do know. We never should have let the man come this far. Mother knows to blame Tom and me.

QUILL

⊠ ⊠ ⊠

Tom and I are getting sick of not knowing more things about more places. It's a good thing Tom once was someplace else or we wouldn't even know there was another place. He came up here with Mother before any of us were born. He says Mother was looking for the simple life. He says that's what we're doing now.

He remembers lots of things from before. He had a father who left and Mother went around punching things when she wasn't lying on the couch. Finally she came up here with Tom. She said she didn't like the world the way it is and she was going to live a different way. But Tom doesn't know where the rest of us come from. He doesn't remember me coming. Suddenly I was here.

The man must like Mother. He looks relieved. As if everything is all right now.

When Mother steps out, Wren, right away, grabs Mother's skirt and Loon hides behind her. Mother couldn't save us from anything. Only Tom could do that. You'd think they'd know by now.

Mother looks horrified. "You can't stay here. Tom, take the camera."

"I've sprained my ankle—maybe broken it," says the man. "I need to impose on you. I don't think I'll be able to climb down for a while."

"You can't stay!"

Tom says, "We'll keep him with us. You'll hardly know he's here."

"He can't stay. You know that as well as I do. Think, for heaven's sake!"

The rest of us say, "Why?" but Tom says, "All right, all right. We'll send him on his way."

We didn't know Tom would be so cruel, nor Mother either.

The man looks upset. He hands Tom the camera. He says, "It got wet."

Tom gives it to Mother. Mother opens it and pulls out the insides.

The man says, "I can't climb down now."

Mother says, "You have to."

"Can I at least stay the night?"

"That's impossible."

We all say (except Tom), "Why not?"

But right away the man turns and starts hobbling down the trail.

Tom goes to help him and this time the man lets him. Tom is exactly as tall as the man.

A little ways down we turn off the path. Tom tells the man, "Only a little farther now." Then, to the younger ones, "If anybody says anything to Mother, I'll take your gold."

I know what's happening. It's off to our cave, sitting around the campfire, and crawdads for supper. Maybe even frog's legs. Nothing better. Nothing more fun.

Our cave has thick beds of ferns. Much better than our beds at home. And we have really soft rabbitskin blankets we made ourselves. Tom and I sewed them up. We chipped out little

pockets in the walls so we could have feathers and flowers all over. But it's shallow. When it rains the rain blows all the way in, but when it's clear, if you lie with your head toward the entrance, you can see the stars as you go to sleep. Sometimes the moon's so bright it wakes you up when it pops up over the mountain. There's a sort of porch in front where we made a fireplace and put logs around it to sit on. That porch has a good view over the whole valley.

I say, "Isn't this nice?" The man is impressed.

We build a little fire and send everybody out to catch things or dig things up. They're so excited to be doing it for the man. On the way back they pick big stalks—taller than they are—of fireweed in bloom just for looks.

He can't stop saying, Thank you, and keeps asking what can he do for us. We say, Don't worry, we'll think of things. He asks our names. His is Hazlet, but people call him Haze. He asks our ages but we're not sure. Asks where our fathers are. We say we don't have any.

"One mother for all these little ones?"

We don't know. Sometimes little ones just appear—in the chicken coop. Mother takes them in.

We talk about paper. He'll set his out to dry tomorrow. We'll help. He's going to draw us all as presents to each of us. And he'll give us all the leftover paper when he leaves.

Tom and I stay out all night with the man but we make the little ones go home.

Haze asks a lot of questions. Some are the same ones we ask ourselves, like, "Where's our father? How long have we lived up here? Why are we here in the middle of nowhere?"

(We think it's as much a place as anyplace else.)

We tell him Mother doesn't want us to get to be like other people.

He thinks that can't be the only reason, though he sees her point. He says we're turning out a lot better than some.

We like him. We say, "Stay. We need another grown-up. The only one we know is Mother."

He says both I and Tom are not far off from being grown.

Of course he has to stay until his ankle gets better, but we want him after.

Next day first thing he spreads the paper out to dry with a rock on each one. We help. It hurts him to walk, so he mostly crawls. Then he picks good pieces of charcoal out of the fireplace. He'll show us how to use them for drawing.

The little ones come rushing down. Some wanted to come so badly they didn't even have their breakfast.

As soon as the paper dries, Haze draws. He draws me and Tom first, and then Henny and Drake. Then the little ones sitting in a row on the logs on the stone porch. Sometimes he draws with the charcoal he picked out of the fireplace. "They'll smear," he says. "Be careful."

We hang the drawings at the back of the cave, high so the little ones won't mess them up. Me he draws again in pencil and rolls it up and puts it in his pack.

We want to show them to Mother, we wonder if she's seen anything like it, but we don't dare. It might be one of those things we're not supposed to do. Besides, the man is supposed to be gone by now.

Haze shows us how to use the binoculars. We look around at everything. To the side we see those three men . . . or, rather, their little tents—up along the silver river. We're good at taking turns. When we're not looking, we draw. He gives us lessons. I'm good at it already. I thought I would be.

We have lots of days of drawing and looking while Haze gets better. He even shows us how to make paper out of weeds. Lumpy, but better than nothing.

Tom makes a good strong staff for Haze. Haze says that'll be good even when his ankle is better. The rest of the time we gather cattail roots and lily roots and Solomon's seal along with the frog's legs and crawdads.

Then one time when Haze is much better he says, "I always wanted to go up to your glacier. Have you ever gone that high?"

We haven't, but we've thought about it. "We see lights up there sometimes."

"Good, we'll go. You and Tom. The little ones can spend the day with your mother."

"They won't unless we threaten to take away their gold."

"Gold?"

But we're not thinking gold, we're thinking how we'll be getting out of here, farther than we ever have. We're so happy we put out our traps and catch rabbits. Mother doesn't need to know about it. We stretch the skin for ourselves and dry the meat for our trip.

Tom and I skip morning lessons all the time now and stay down with Haze. We're learning more from him in just a few

weeks than we ever did from Mother. He shows us all about maps on his maps. We pick out what looks like the best route up to the glacier. He shows us all about his compass. He thinks it odd that we never saw a flashlight till now. He's got two, one you fit on your head and another you hold.

We start out while it's still dark. Haze wears the flashlight on his head and goes first. He gives the other to me and I go last. Tom and I each carry a little rabbitskin blanket. Haze has a bag for sleeping. He has the cane Tom made him and his maps. His backpack is full. He even brought paper in case he wants to draw. He has this waterproof stuff that he wrapped his food in before. Now he wraps the paper in it. He feels about paper as we do. We'd rather have paper than gold. He says he would, too.

We top our pass and dip into the next valley at sunrise, or what would have been sunrise if it hadn't been for the mountain in the way. This mountain is much higher than the ones near us. That's why you can see the glacier from our house.

Tom and I had hoped to find people in this valley, but there's nobody. Still the path goes on. From here you get a really good view of the glacier. It's been melting away. Haze gives us a lesson on glaciers. There's a lot of debris at the sides. That's called lateral moraine, at the end it's called terminal. I already knew that, though I never saw it until now.

The glacier's a lot bigger than we thought. Back home we can only see the top. We had no idea it had all this junk around it and came down so far into this other valley.

We spend the night right where we are, partway down the

second pass, and by afternoon next day, we're at the glacier and its river trickling out.

This valley has a lot fewer trees in it and those are all stunted. Haze points out odd stuff. To us everything is odd. He says, "Look at the peculiar shapes of those rocks. They look like a whole row of skyscrapers."

They sure seem like they're scraping the sky, but we know the sky is way, way, way up, all the way to the stars.

We climb the sideways debris to get a good look around. Then Haze sees what he thinks might be the mouth of a cave.

He tells us to stay back, but we don't want to. "Why come all this way and not see everything?"

"All right, but stay behind me."

It's not a cave but a doorway of some sort into a big, long, long bluish white house, hugging up close to the glacier. Until you get close, it just looks like more glacier.

At the door, Haze doesn't even knock. He just opens it in a careful sneaky way.

Mother never likes that. She wants us to know how to be courteous. Tom and I look at each other. Haze doesn't know how to be polite.

Haze opens the door all the way and we go in. Tom and I don't want to be sneaky, but we don't know what else to do except go with him.

It's warm in there. We were getting cold. We had wrapped our rabbitskin blankets around us. Haze is wearing his jacket filled with little feathers. He showed us. "Down is the warmest there is," he said, "but you know that already." Only we

didn't. He wanted me to trade my rabbit skins with his jacket so I'd be warm as we crossed the high places but I said maybe later, and we should all have a turn with it.

Through that door, we aren't anywhere at all, but there's another door. We open that one and it's even warmer. It's large and dim. At first we don't know what the room is all about, then we see it's a whole room full of eggs. Really big ones. There must be ten or fifteen. They're nested in white stuff. Warm air blows over us and them. Tiny feathers are flying around. Not a lot, just here and there.

Haze keeps saying, "My God. My God."

We're not as surprised as he is—after all, we gather chicken's eggs every day, just not such big ones. And there's feathers in our henhouse, too, but these are all the ones Haze calls "down." They're like what's on my head, but mine are black. Tom told me that when I first came, mine started out yellow.

Then we're even more surprised. Haze takes off his jacket, grabs the closest egg, wraps it in the jacket, and we hurry out. It's so big it'll be a meal for more than just us three. But we have plenty of food with us. Besides, no pan to cook it in.

It's not like our usual eggs. It has a leathery shell.

Haze holds the egg close to his chest to keep it warm. We go back to the edge of the valley.

Tom says, "Are you going to hatch it?"

"Well, I'm not going to eat it. Did you think I would?"

We like Haze. We didn't think he would but we weren't sure.

It's getting dark. It's too late to start home now. We build a little fire and eat our dried rabbit. Haze keeps the egg in his

lap and takes out paper and sketches the big room full of eggs from memory. He also marks on the map where the cave is. Tom and I curl up by the fire. I fall asleep right away but then I hear Haze ask, "Does your mother know about all this?"

That's what I was wondering. I think she does. But I won't say. Tom says, "Maybe."

And I know . . . I *think* I know what's in this egg. My little brother or little sister, I suppose.

Haze says, "It's a smart way to get a lot of them . . . of you . . . in a hurry." Then: "Maybe only takes one mother for the lot."

Just when I'm falling back to sleep he says, "Not clones either. Easy to see that."

The egg hatches next day when we're on the way home. The cutest little thing I ever saw. All golden. It's cute even before it dries off. It's one of the scaly ones with a feathered cap like I have, though I don't have many scales. Just in a few spots. It's a little on the duck-like side. Much more than me. We don't know yet if it's a boy or girl. Mother can tell right away.

Since I'm a girl I think I ought to get to carry it, but Haze thinks it's safer if he does.

"What do they eat?" he asks.

"Just regular food. Like everybody else. We can give it some of our rabbit. Look, it has all its baby teeth."

Now Haze is saying, "My God, my God, my God," again, then, "I suppose they crashed."

He says Mother is right to keep us away from the rest of

the world. He says, again, he has to admit we're, all of us, very nice children.

He jumps from one idea to another. He says, except for Tom we're all half-breeds. He says, "It's a good way to endure here. He says, "Maybe they think we won't kill any creatures that are half our own." Then he says, "When has that ever stopped us? Killing our own is what we do best."

Haze says I was hatched up there. He says he can't imagine what kind of creature my father is.

I get to feed the baby. (Those sharp little teeth are better at chewing rabbit than mine.) I get to have his first smile. And I get to sleep with him. Haze wraps us both in his down jacket. He keeps the fire going all night. I don't think he sleeps much. I don't sleep well either, but that's because the baby is wiggly. It doesn't seem to know it's night. Or maybe it's been sleeping so much in the egg so that now it wants to do things.

One of those funny things Mother told me turns out to be true. There's blood. So not only do I have to figure out how to keep the messes of the baby from getting all over, but I have to figure out what to do about my mess. I take pieces from our rabbit skins. I pretend it's all for the baby, but some is for me. I wonder if those breast things are any bigger than they were. I hope not. But I guess Mother is right about that, too. They will get bigger. This baby, though, is one of the ones that doesn't need them.

I lag behind though Haze carries the baby and we've already eaten most of our food so nobody has much to carry.

I'm cold even in Haze's jacket. My stomach feels funny. I sit down on a rock to rest and think.

But somebody is coming from behind. A tall creature with long thin legs that bend the way fox legs do. At first I think it's wearing a beautiful feathered hat, red and gold, but as it gets closer I see it's a topknot and that what I think is a black and red suit is feathers all over. When it sees me, the topknot lifts higher, widens. It's iridescent. There's blue and green in it, too. The creature spreads its arms. There's a row of red along its sides. I never saw anything so beautiful.

Someone has been in the nest. Our soft warmth has been intruded upon. Entered by they of those that can't smell. They think we won't know. As if we don't smell everything that happens.

Worst of all, my own little loved one, on the edge of hatching, stolen. A precious being in the making.

Strange and stranger land of much pain and so little softness in it. So few spots in which to hesitate and love.

I go to speak of my love for my own kind and even for their kind if need be speaking of it. Say it with nodding of head sky to ground, sky to ground, as if their yes and not sideways, east and west.

I lean forward so as to speed. Also lean so as to catch the scent. I smell not only my little one but also my biggest one, and she's ready to lay. Our first layer among the half-ones. A precious dear. I can't wait to speak of the future of us all. So much depends on her willingness, though why not? Offspring this way is so much easier than the way of mammals.

My tender feelings come with the good smell of myself on her. I breathe of myself all along the trail. Strange and dangerous as this

place is, I'm happy. Strange as even my own is, I'm happy.

But what of these harsh creatures? Even without moving from our wreckage, we've seen what they do—seen from their own technology. We know who they are. We've heard both war and music. Dance. At least they dance.

Now a whole new way to egg which only our knowledge makes possible. Not as pleasurable but necessary. But here's my daughter, though she, my dear one, is more of them than of me.

Our kind is not unknown here, though they never had a chance to develop. Had they come to full flower, we'd have landed among friends instead of among these odd intelligent mammals. It's too bad we didn't come earlier to help those like us achieve their full potential. We could have egged with them and raised them to our level.

Strange that this world took such a different turn. Hardly logical that eggless ratlike things would grow so large. Though even our own mammals get into everything, and some are smart enough to have made themselves into the little companions of our kitchens and the darlings of the nurseries.

I have wished my first daughter could be beautiful—more like me. Still I love her. I can be in love by smell alone. So much love I found it hard to bring her down to her mother. And when she smiled, like ours always do—the first conciliation, the first appeasement—I found myself in every way, her doting father.

It was Quat called us. The intruding mammals didn't see him in the dim nesting light. One of them was half us—Quat could smell that—and two were of their kind. One a full grown male not known to us. Quat said that male knows too much. Everything is vulnerable.

I've watched the offspring dance. Life will be hard for them, but at least they have the joy of dance. Now, to my own young one, I'll display. I'll strut. Though with these creatures it seems it's more the female's role to lure with colors and tall shoes. Still, I will *display.*

It calls, "Quill, Quill." It sounds like quacks but I'm used to that from some of the little ones—I can tell it's my name. It has a loud echoing voice. I don't know how far Tom and Haze have gotten, but for sure they'll hear. For sure they'll come, though I wonder if I want them to.

At first it doesn't come close. It stands, silent, below me on the trail so as to let me get used to it. I look. That's what it wants me to do. Its scales only show at its neck and clawed hands and feet. It turns sideways and shows off its topknot, up and out and then down, then up and out again. None of the little ones have anything at all like that topknot, though I realize now that some have the beginnings of one.

It comes closer. It makes more quacking sounds. Again, not too different from the way lots of the little ones talk. It says, "I'm your father."

I shout, *"Yes!"* He's so beautiful I can't help it. I've been wondering and wondering all this time. I can't conceive of a better father than this one.

"May I sit beside you for talking?"

I move to make room. He sits on my rock and we both look back toward the glacier.

He touches my hand with his and it feels terrible. His claws prick and his skin is scaly. That's all right, except when he turns it the wrong way it scratches. Some of the little

ones are like this, too. I hide that I don't like it like I do with them.

He says he loves me. I can see that in the way he looks at me. He calls me consort, but I don't know what that means. He says I'm old enough now. I don't know what that means either. But maybe I do. It's about the crazy things Mother told me. Which are coming true.

Then he asks about the baby. "He hatched. Did he? I saw where it happened. Or was that a . . . killing?"

"No, we wouldn't. I wouldn't let them. He hatched. He's fine."

I hope so. I think Haze will keep him safe. But Haze seemed pretty worried. He never stopped saying *My God,* and he couldn't sleep. Maybe I should have made him let me carry the baby.

"Did the baby smile at you first?"

"I guess so."

"Are you caught in his smile?"

"Yes, but I liked him even before he smiled."

"Excellent!"

Then he grabs my wrist, hard. It hurts.

"Come. You'll like it. Keep warm in the nursery. My friends will make you happy."

I try to twist away, but he's too strong, and twisting makes his hand scratch all the more. I think how glad I am that I hardly have any scales at all except a little on my back and the backs of my hands.

"I saw how you were. You like little ones. Come and make more."

"No!"

"We're from a far place. We crashed. We thought the glacier, so white and blue, was a dump of discarded nursery feathers. We slammed and slid and died. We can't go home. We made our conveyance into a nest. Had we even one female of our own kind, it would have changed everything. But here was your mother. Willing. Like you are."

But I'm yelling, "No. No!" and I'm yelling for Haze.

"You've no place on this world but with us. They'll never accept you. They hate the different. They never heard of one like you."

"Is that true?"

"The whole world is them."

"It's not. It can't be. How can that be?"

"My dear, dear one, it *is*! You're the first of your kind. Your mother has kept you hidden from the world so as to save you for us and save you for yourself."

He's loosened his grip and I manage to twist away and start running—up the trail toward Tom and Haze, but he catches me with no trouble. His legs are so long.

But Tom and Haze have turned back. They see me struggling. I yell for them to help.

Haze has something he never showed us. I've heard of that, it's like Mother's rifle but smaller. *Pop, pop,* and my father falls. Just like that. Into a fancy bundle of shiny black and red and iridescent. His hand still grips me. Haze has to pry open his fingers.

Tom sits me down and gives me a drink from the canteen. Haze is looking over my father's body. Examining everything,

the clawed hands and feet, the topknot. I see him looking at the sex, which is mostly covered with down. Then Haze actually sits down and starts to draw him. I'm not sure how I feel about this. It's true, he's beautiful, but Haze isn't drawing a portrait like he did of us. It's more diagrams, my father's different parts all laid out, a hand, then a foot, the topknot, the beak.

But I want to get away from here. I want to get home tonight. I need to talk to Mother—mostly about myself. I didn't listen when she talked about blood. It sounded too ridiculous. And how come my father knew that right away? Or maybe it was these lumps on my chest that made him say I'm ready for egging.

But I'm shaky and I do need to rest. I don't say, "Let's go." Not even to Tom.

We're so late we have to camp again. And practically right away, as soon as we leave my father's body. Haze says we should camp off the trail and hide. We find a place in among rocks.

I'm still all trembly. I just found a father and lost him right away. Some of the little ones squeak when they're sad and don't have tears, ever, but I'm one of the ones that cries. I cry, but I don't think the others know. I sleep with the baby. I need to. I need something warm and cuddly to hug.

The baby isn't as wiggly as he was when he was so happy to be out of the egg. I guess he stayed awake all day, looking around at everything, and now he's tired. Haze props himself against a rock and puts the gun in his belt, ready to shoot

somebody. He looks as if he's going to stay awake to guard us, but he starts to snore right away.

I cry for a while. The baby clings to me as though he wants to comfort me. After I stop I look up at the starry sky. It's so beautiful it makes me cry all over again. No matter what it looks like from down here, it's full of faraway suns, some even bigger than our own. We know all that because Mother taught us. "Who knows," Mother said, "what other kinds of life swirl around those suns?" She said, "Who knows, there might be a world where the dinosaurs didn't die out." I think now she was preparing us for strangers like my father. I wish I'd listened instead of looking out the window and wanting to be off in the woods.

Just when I finally start to fall asleep, Tom wakes me. He says Haze will tell about what we found. That's why he made the drawings. Tom says at first nobody will believe him . . . that there could exist creatures like us, so Haze will take us down to the real people. We'll get examined by policemen. Tom doesn't want that to happen. He likes us and he's always taken care of us—more than Mother has. He says he's not sure if Mother isn't crazy. Now that *we're* here, he knows why she has to live out here, but in the beginning she was angry at everybody and everything.

He talks as if my father was right. We won't be let anywhere near our nice home. There'll be nothing but buildings, and we'll never be able to come back. We might even be put in a zoo. The best thing to do is to get rid of Haze and then our life will stay the same.

"But how?"

"Easy. We'll just use that gun he has."

"I don't want to. I like him."

"Liking has nothing to do with it. It's your whole future. Mother's future, too."

"Let's wait and see what happens when we get back. We can always do it later if we have to."

"It might be too late then."

"I don't see why. Mother doesn't want him around either. She'll be on your side. She'll get out her hunting rifle and kill him herself."

So Tom says, "All right. We won't do it yet."

Next morning we come down, all of us together, straight to Mother's. Even Haze walks right in with us.

Mother comes out from her stone house looking shocked. I start crying right away. I never used to cry much, but now I seem to cry at everything. I don't even know why. I wonder if that's because I'm a grown-up now. I hope that's not the reason.

I run to Mother and hug her tight. We're breast against breast. I say, "I have to talk," and she says, "I should think so! What are you thinking? Can't you see? Couldn't you tell?"

She pulls away and slaps me. So hard she almost knocks me over. She's never done that before. I've never seen her so angry. I'm afraid to ask her anything, but there's nobody else to ask the kind of things I need to know. I don't think she'll ever want to talk to me—especially not about what I want to talk about. I wonder if it's in our anatomy book and I didn't notice it before because I didn't want to.

She snatches the baby from Haze—so hard the baby starts to squeak and won't stop. Talk about high notes! That's the first he's squeaked in all the time he's been with us. I snatch him right back and he stops squeaking right away, which is a relief to all of us. I stop crying, too. That's the end of me crying. I won't do it anymore, especially not in front of Mother.

Mother tries to snatch him back but I won't let her. She says, "You have no idea. None of you do. Look what you've done! All our lives I've worried this would happen—someone like this man would come. It's over and done for. Do you think we can live the way we do after this? It's *over*!"

I don't know who we ought to get rid of, Mother or Haze or maybe both.

Haze says, "It doesn't have to be over. It can be just begun. I can take Quill and the baby down and bring them right back."

Mother says she doesn't want us made into a sideshow. She says they'll wipe out the whole enterprise. She says what she's always said before, that she knows how the world is, which is why she's living up here. "My innocent Quill," she says. (She never has called me hers before. I don't know what to think, and just after she slapped me.) "My little Quill, corrupted."

Little! Can't she see anything? Not even my breasts?

Tom says, "It doesn't have to be over. It can be like it always is. Wait! Mother! Everything will be like you want it to be. I can fix it." He gives Mother a look. Says, *"Wait!"* again.

I go stand in front of Haze just in case it happens right now. But I don't want Haze to get suspicious. I don't *think* I want Haze suspicious. I'm not sure of anything anymore.

I'm not even sure if I might not want to go down and see the zoo.

Haze says, "You'll be found out sometime no matter what I do. Strange that you've lasted all this time as it is."

I don't see why Tom gets to be the only one who knows about down there. I might go with Haze, like he said, just me and the baby. Down to Haze's home forest. Who would have to know about us? Maybe it would be like our cave. Nobody but us would ever go there.

I should tell Haze to go home to his home right away, and he should keep watch over his little gun.

But I don't have a chance to tell him anything. He knows. We . . . Tom and I and Haze and the baby . . . We say we're going down to spend the night in the cave and that we'll eat supper there, but Haze goes right on past, without a word, not even to me. We're all worn out, but he just goes, even without supper, and he's going fast. Tom follows without a single word to me, and I follow Tom. I keep well back because of the baby, though the baby doesn't sound any different from the birds. The birds are settling down for the night so there's lots of chirping. The baby's settling down, too, with little night songs.

Haze has his lights, both of them, and Tom and I don't have anything, so we're a lot slower.

Pretty soon I decide I just have to rest. I think Haze will have to rest, too. I hope he finds a place where Tom can't get at him.

The baby and I move off the trail and cuddle up.

⊠ ⊠ ⊠

When I wake and look out, I'm way up on the side of a mountain and I can look down on a whole other valley with a big town there. I'm so happy. I start chirping to myself along with the baby. I'm getting somewhere really interesting. I'm going to know things Tom knows.

The baby and I pick elderberries and mountain currants for breakfast. I'm not in a hurry anymore. There's the town and I have plenty of time to get there. I don't care if I ever catch up to Haze or Tom.

But Tom waits beside the trail and jumps out at me. And right away tells me I have to go home. "You mustn't let people see you and especially not let anybody see the baby. He'll scare them to death."

"How can a baby scare anybody?"

"He, and even you, but he especially . . . you don't belong on this world."

How can he say such a thing? "Of course I do."

"You don't understand anything."

"I wasn't going to show myself right away. I thought to take a look around and maybe go to the zoo and see the animals. And then come home."

"People will see you for sure."

"What's so bad if they do see us?"

"Quill!"

"We're just other human beings."

"Well, that's the problem."

"Aren't we?"

"You've been protected from the real people."

"I'm real."

"Look at yourself. You're them. You may be a *being* but you're not a *human* being."

"I am so."

"You belong in the zoo."

"I wouldn't mind."

"There's no zoo in that little town anyway. They're only in big towns."

"That doesn't look little to me."

"Believe me, it is."

I suppose he's right. He usually is.

"Well, I won't go home. Not when I'm so close to seeing new things."

"You won't get far with that baby on your back."

"Lots of people must have babies down there."

"Not one like that."

"I'm not going to argue, I'm just not going to go home until I see this town."

"Go ahead, then, but it's the end of all of us. Though . . . I'm tired of it, too. Let's end it. Or I'll tell you what, go on down. Wear my hat pulled low and see if you can get away with it. And they might have a little zoo with maybe four or five animals in some park or other, but don't go into town till it's dark. I'll keep the baby. You'll never get away with it with him."

"All right, if the baby doesn't mind."

I do want to see that town. I start right away. It'll be getting dark by the time I get there.

Pretty soon the trees get fewer and there's fields of stuff growing. I begin to see cows and horses. I've only seen those in

books. I stop at the edge of one of the fields and two horses come over to me as if to say hello. At first I think they might bite, but there's the fence between us and you can tell they're friendly right away. They lean to be touched and I touch them.

Right after, there begins to be houses. All nicer even than Mother's. Some with one floor on top of another. I know all about that. I've seen pictures. There's some with different colors and bobbles hanging all over them. I never knew a house could be so pretty. I'm already glad I came.

When I get to the edge of town it's pretty dark. I pull my hat down even lower and walk on. The people are all Tom's kind of people just like he said. Nobody is as beautiful as my father. There aren't any feathers at all.

I come to a little park with swings and slides. I've seen pictures of those. There's nobody there. I guess it's too late for young ones to be out. I try all the things. I can't believe I'm learning so much in such a hurry. These last few days it's been one new thing after another.

There's streetlights. You don't need those lights Haze has. I come to a big street with stores all along it. Most of them closed. Some have prices in the windows. Money! I hadn't thought of that.

I walk all the way down the main street. It must be a mile long. Shops all along the way. I don't care what Tom says, it's a big town to me. I look in the store windows. The clothes look different from the ones Mother makes. And shoes . . . so fancy and slick, some with funny little heels. There's a store full of beautiful shiny pots and pans never used, cups and plates neither tin nor wood nor clay.

There's a bigger park at the other end of town. It even has a swimming pool. All blue and smells funny. I'm thirsty but I don't drink there. There's a river running through the park and that's where I drink. There's no zoo that I can find. I was so hoping there'd be one. I want to see monkeys and tigers and elephants. I wonder how far a bigger town is. If I knew which direction to go in, I might head for that town.

I see people on the porch of an eating place eating with forks. I see two women clacking along in high-heeled sandals. I see cars and trucks. All this even though you'd think people would be in bed. I get honked at. I jump away and quack back.

Then Haze is here. He must have been following me all this time. Even though my hat is pulled down low, he knows it's me.

I say, "Don't tell," and he says he won't. I don't know if I should believe him or not, but it looks as if he won't tell *right now,* anyway.

"You look exhausted. Are you hungry? Come home with me."

Haze's house is like I've never seen before. There's rugs and a couch. There's even a little room that's just for me, but I don't want it. I've never slept by myself before and I'm scared to. Haze makes me up a mattress on the floor next to him. The food is odd, too. I don't know what it is but I eat it anyway. Except for bugs, Haze ate what we ate. That was like Mother, too. She hated for us to eat bugs. There's also a little room for an outhouse that's not even *out*. I learn to flush. I learn to turn on the water, cold *and* hot.

⁂

But next morning breakfast is just like at home, oatmeal. I ask Haze, "What are you going to do about us? You killed my father. You might do anything."

"You were yelling, Help. Your father was trying to take you back. I thought I was helping. I didn't know it was your father. But I don't know. What *should* I do?"

"I don't know either."

"You're going to be discovered no matter what I do. Might as well be now as later. Might as well be me as somebody out to make a buck."

"How come we've not been discovered all this time?"

"Your mother picked a good hiding place."

"Tom said it was the end of all of us. Tom said our lives depend on you."

"I won't let anybody hurt you."

"You have drawings of everything."

"You're scientifically important. You're *all* important. They'll need to study you."

You wouldn't think so many things could happen so fast. It all comes about in a couple of days. Even the destruction of the fathers, which they did to themselves. I'm glad the regular human beings didn't do it. I don't know what I would have thought if they had.

The fathers knew what would happen. They know about human beings. When Haze and the others . . . the scientists and the army and police get out to the ship, it's destroyed. The nest and eggs and all the creatures with it. There's nothing left of them but us.

Mother must have known. Even if we didn't hear the blast

down in town, she's so much closer she must have heard and known. They found her body washed down our Silver river. She had made us all moccasins and lined them up along the table, all exactly the right size. She loved us but she needed for things to stay the same.

Now she'll never find out how we got taken into this school. A farm kind of school off in the middle of nowhere, with all kinds of animals. But also a scientific school with lots of geology and biology, so someday I can be a scientist in a zoo. I'll probably have to be *in* the zoo myself. I know that. Even now people keep coming to take blood and study us. I don't mind. I'm studying myself myself and them, too.

Haze took all our gold, but he's using it for us. He's paying for the school.

He says, "The fathers were scared of us." When he says "us," he means the human beings. He says, "And rightly so. They thought we wouldn't accept them and we wouldn't. They knew their nests and eggs were easy to destroy. But having living dinosaurs . . . Feathered . . . Think of the experiments . . . And studying . . . them and their ship . . ."

And he keeps saying, "Just think . . . think, there's been contact with aliens all these years and nobody knew it."

I don't feel like an alien. I think I belong here just as much as anybody.

Carol Emshwiller is the author of many acclaimed novels and story collections, including *Carmen Dog*, *The Start of the End of It All* (winner of the World Fantasy Award), *I Live with You*, *The Mount* (winner of the Philip K. Dick Award and a Nebula Award Finalist), and *Mister Boots*. She divides her time between homes in New York City and California.

Her Web site is **www.sfwa.org/members/emshwiller**.

Author's Note

Quill's strong voice made the tone—the *surface* of the story—interesting to me, so it was fun writing it. It was because of her voice that I went on with the story.

I usually don't write such a science fiction-y story, but the idea of beautiful, feathered dinosaurs pleased me. That is, after I got to them. I didn't know there were going to be dinosaurs in the story until I got to their cache of eggs. Then I had to go back and make the earlier parts match.

I always write that way: give myself hints of a mystery and then have to solve it after I've set it up. That means there's almost always an OH MY GOD NOW WHAT'LL I DO place in every story. I find my plots come out better when I don't know where I'm going.

Francesca Lia Block

Blood Roses

Every day, Lucy and Rosie searched for the blood roses in their canyon. They found eucalyptus and poison oak, evening primrose and oleander, but never the glow-in-the-dark red, smoke-scented flowers with sharp thorns that traced poetry onto your flesh.

"You only see them if you die," Lucy said, but Rosie just smiled so that the small row of pearls in her mouth showed.

Still, the hairs stood up on both their arms that evening as they sat watching the sunset from their secret grotto in the heart of the canyon. The air smelled of exhaust fumes and decaying leaves. The sky was streaked with smog and you could hear the sound of cars and one siren, but that world felt very far away.

Here, the girls turned dollsize, wove nests out of twigs to sleep in the eucalyptus branches, collected morning dew in leaves and dined on dark purple berries that stained their mouths and hands.

"We'd better get home," Lucy said, brushing the dirt off her jeans.

They would have stayed here all night in spite of the dangers—snakes, coyote, rapists, goblins. It was better than the apartment made of tears where their mother had taken them when she left their father.

Their mother said their father was an alcoholic and a sex addict, but all Lucy remembered was the sandpaper roughness of his chin, like the father in her baby book *Pat the Bunny,* when he hugged her and Rosie in his arms at the same time. He had hair of black feathers and his eyes were green semiprecious stones.

Lucy and Rosie loved Emerson Solo because like their father he was beautiful, dangerous and unattainable. Especially now. Emerson Solo, twenty-seven, had stabbed himself to death in the heart last month.

You really have to want to die to be successful at that, their mother said before she confiscated all their Solo albums and posters. Lucy understood why she'd done it. But still she wanted to look at his face and hear his voice again. For some reason he comforted her, even now. Was it because he had escaped?

Lucy and Rosie were in the record store looking through the Emerson Solo discs. There was the one with the black bird on the cover called *For Sorrow* and the one called *The White Room*. There was a rumor that the white room was supposed to be death. The store was all out of *Collected* with the photo

of Emerson Solo holding a bouquet of wildflowers with their dirty roots dragging down out of his hands.

A man was standing across the aisle from them, and when Lucy looked up he smiled. He was young and handsome with fair hair, a strong chin.

"You like him?" he asked.

Rosie said, "Oh, yes! Our mom threw out all his CDs. We just come and look at him."

The man smiled. The light was hitting his thick glasses in such a way that Lucy couldn't see his eyes. Dust motes sizzled in a beam of sunlight from the window. Some music was playing, loud and anxious-sounding. Lucy didn't recognize it.

"My uncle's a photographer. He has some photos he took of him a week before he killed himself."

Lucy felt her sinuses prickling with tears the way they did when she told Rosie scary stories. Her mouth felt dry.

"You can come see if you want," he said. He handed Lucy a card.

She put it in her pocket and crumpled it up there, so he couldn't see.

One of Emerson Solo's CDs was called *Imago*. The title song was about a phantom limb.

She wondered if when you died it was like that. If you still believed your body was there and you couldn't quite accept that it was gone. Or if someone you loved died, someone who you were really close to, would they be like a phantom limb, still attached to you? Sometimes Rosie was like another of Lucy's limbs.

Rosie was the one who went—not Lucy. Lucy was aware enough of her own desire to escape, to let herself succumb to it. But Rosie still believed she was just looking for ways to be happier.

When Lucy got home from school and saw her sister's note, she started to run. She ran out the door of thick, gray glass, down the cul-de-sac, across the big, busy street, against the light, dodging cars. She ran into the canyon. There was the place where she and Rosie had seen a rattlesnake blocking their path, the turn in the road where they had seen the baby coyote, the grotto by the creek where the old tire swing used to be, where the high-school kids went to smoke pot and drink beer. There was the rock garden that had been made by aliens from outer space and the big tree where Lucy had seen two of them entwined in the branches early one Sunday morning. Lucy skidded down a slope causing an avalanche of pebbles. She took the fire road back down to the steep, quiet street. She got to the house just as Rosie knocked on the tall, narrow door.

Rosie was wearing a pink knit cap, a white frilly party dress that was too small, too-short jeans, ruby slippers, mismatched ankle socks—one purple, one green, and a blue rhinestone pin in the shape of a large butterfly. No wonder people teased her at school, Lucy thought. She wanted to put her arms around Rosie, grab her hand, and run, but it was too late to leave because the man opened the door right away as if he had been waiting for them all that time.

He didn't ask them in but stood staring at them and twisting his mouth like he wanted to say something. But then another man was standing at the top of the steep staircase. The girls couldn't see his face. He was whited out with light.

Lucy knew two things. She knew that she and Rosie were going to go inside the house. She knew, too (when she saw it in a small alcove as she walked up the stairs) that she would take the screwdriver and put it in the pocket of her gray sweatshirt.

The walls were covered with plastic. So was all the furniture. Plastic was stretched taut across the floor. The walls were high, blond wood. There were skylights between the ceiling beams. Fuzzy afternoon sun shone down onto the plastic skins.

There was a long table. The older man stood at one end, watching. It was still hard to see what he looked like. The young man offered the girls pomegranate juice in small opalescent glasses. Lucy put her hand on Rosie's arm, but her sister drank hers anyway. Then Rosie walked out of the room.

"Rosie," Lucy whispered.

The young man said, "Do you know there's this dream that Jeffrey Dahmer had? He dreamed he was in this big, fancy hotel lobby with all these beautiful people wearing evening dresses and tuxedos. They were all pounding on the marble floor and screaming. But he was just standing there, not moving, not saying anything. He had on a leather jacket. It was like his skin."

Lucy felt for the screwdriver in her pocket. "I'm going to get my sister," she said.

But Rosie was back now. Her eyes looked brighter. She sat on a stool next to Lucy. She kept wetting her lip with her tongue.

The older man left the room.

"He's going to check on his photos," the younger man said. "You didn't take anything, did you?"

Rosie shook her head no.

"I have another story. It's about Richard Ramirez. When he went to this one lady's house, she kept him there like half an hour talking. Then he left. He didn't touch her. Do you know what she said to him? She said, 'My God, what happened to you?' And she listened. That was the main thing, she listened."

"What happened to you?" Lucy whispered.

The light in the room changed. It turned harsh. Emerson Solo was reclining on a chair. His skin was broken out, his hair was greasy, hanging in his eyes, and he had a bottle in one hand. His long legs were stretched out in front of him. A blue butterfly was inside the bottle.

"Get the fuck out of here," the younger man said, very softly. He was not looking at Lucy. The light was in his glasses. He was being swallowed up by the strange light.

Lucy felt the spell crack apart like an eggshell. She grabbed Rosie's hand. She pulled Rosie up from the stool. Rosie felt heavier, slower. Lucy dragged her sister out of the room. There was another staircase leading down to a back door.

Lucy flung herself down the staircase, pulling Rosie behind her.

"Lucy!" Rosie said.

A photograph had fallen out of Rosie's pocket. It was of Emerson Solo sitting on a chair with his legs stretched out in front of him.

Rosie tried to grab the photo but Lucy kept dragging her down the stairs. Their footsteps pounded, echoing through the house. Lucy fell against the door with her shoulder and jiggled the lock. The door opened.

They were in a strange, overgrown garden. They tore through brambles. Lucy saw a crumbling stone staircase. She pulled Rosie down it, deeper into the bottom of the garden. A palm tree was wearing a dress of ivy. There was a broken swing moving back and forth. A white wrought-iron bench looked as if it had been thrown against a barbed wire fence. The bougainvillea had grown over it, holding it suspended.

The barbed wire was very intricate, silvery. It was like metal thorns or jewelry. There was one small opening in the bottom. Lucy crawled through. Rosie followed her. But then she stopped: her ankle was wreathed in a circlet of spikes. Lucy dropped to the ground and carefully slipped the anklet off her sister, not cutting her, not even catching her mismatched socks.

She pulled Rosie to her feet. They were standing on the road, across from the wilds of the canyon. There were no cars. Not even the sound of cars. The sky was blue and cloudless. Lucy felt a buzzing sensation in her head like bees or neon.

She dragged Rosie across the road into the trees. The light kept buzzing around them.

Lucy reached into the pocket of her gray sweatshirt. It was empty. She reached into the other pocket and felt around. Nothing. The screwdriver was gone.

Gone, Lucy thought.

Rosie dropped to her knees on the soil.

"Lucy, look."

"What?" Lucy said. Her mouth felt numb, it was hard to talk.

"Blood roses."

"They don't grow here."

"I know that. "

The two sisters looked at each other, waiting for the shivers to graze their arms, making the hairs stand up, but instead they felt only a strange, unnatural warmth as if spring had seeped into them and would stay there forever.

FRANCESCA LIA BLOCK is the acclaimed, best-selling author of over fifteen works of fiction and nonfiction, including the beloved Weetzie Bat books, and has received the Margaret A. Edwards Award for the body of her work. Her latest novel is *Necklace of Kisses*. She lives in Los Angeles.

Visit her Web site at **www.francescaliablock.com**.

AUTHOR'S NOTE

"Blood Roses" came to me in a dream, even down to the details, like the screwdriver and the chain link fence. I rarely dream so vividly, and certainly never with this much plot. I had been experiencing a lot of conflicts in my life. I am sure this stress added to the dark tone of "Blood Roses." My response to Elliott Smith's death was another factor in the dream and the story. By writing this piece I believe my brain was trying to create some grace, order, and beauty out of sorrow. That is the power of art, and of dreaming.

I am grateful to Sharyn November for asking me to write something; the dream came right after this request. I believe that a wonderful editor is a huge part of the alchemy of creativity. Sometimes just a word can spark something that might never have come into existence.

Kara Dalkey

Hives

The girl curled up on the battered couch wanted to die. I understood. I'd been there myself.

"Get me her rig, doc," I said.

The thirtysomething juvie psychologist standing beside me turned and scowled. "That'd be giving a junkie a fix, wouldn't it, Mitch?"

I couldn't blame her 'tude. Dr. Sophie McGlynn had seen bad stuff in her work. Me, I was Michelle Rodriguez, a seventeen-year-old smart-ass who just happened to be the niece of the head detective in the Chelliwah Police Department. Uncle Ted had asked me to come down to the station, thinking I could help the girl on the couch. He liked Dr. Sophie, though, so I'd promised him I wouldn't act up . . . much.

"Works if you want the junkie's attention," I said. "Look, I can reach her, doc. But I need her rig."

Doc Sophie sighed and rubbed her face. "Can't you just talk like a normal person?"

My turn to sigh. "Once you've been a hive-girl, Doc, out-

side talk doesn't seem as real. She could tune me out like I was no more than a fly buzzing. An ESP call, though, she can't ignore."

Something I said must have connected. Doc Sophie drew her lips tight with a quick nod. "Guess we have to try." She walked out, shoulders slumped. Couch girl must have been a hard case.

I walked across a floor of peeling paint, a floor that had felt the feet of too many sad people on their last legs. The girl on the couch didn't deserve to be here. Her only crime had been wanting to belong.

I crouched down beside her. Her name was Angela and she was fourteen. She had honey-brown hair and a face that was an ordinary sort of pretty. Probably she only saw the ordinary part when she looked in the mirror. Angela had tried to make herself into an all-meat patty by jumping off the 605 overpass. But a cop watching for speeders had seen her straddle the railing and got to her in time. She was lucky, though I bet she didn't think so.

I gently stroked her hair and said, "Hi, Angela." She curled up tighter, pretending she didn't hear me.

Doc Sophie walked back through the door and handed me Angela's headset, still looking dubious. "This better be legit or your uncle Ted will hear about it. Don't think I don't know *your* history, girl."

"Thanks for the vote of confidence," I said, reaching up to take the coppery pink headset. I was proud that my hand only shook a little and that I stared for only a few moments, caught up in the junkie's fascination with her drug.

A wonder of technology is the ESP, the Ebisu SonoPhone. It looks like an old-style set of music headphones, but instead of earpieces, it has a pair of pads that press against the skull behind the ears. The ESP conducts sound waves through the bone, so that the voice or voices calling you sound like they're in your head. Clear and close as your own thoughts. The added features include the throat pad that allows you to subvocalize. With practice, you can talk with no one "outside" hearing you. To dial, you can use a wafer-thin tongue pad that sits on the inside of your lower jaw or up on your palate. My generation is as quick with our tongues as our parents were with their thumbs. And, yeah, I've heard the nasty jokes so stuff 'em.

Girls love phones. Girls love friends. Girls love being tight with the coolest clique. Put it all together with an ESP private network and you've got yourself a hive. All friends, all the time, right there with you, no matter where you are. Some hive-girls even sleep with their rigs on. I had, for a while. The ESP has really caught on—everyone from gangbangers to cops to biz-geeks to chatline callers love the ESP. Its popularity is even moving down the age ladder. There's a company that sells a clip-on accessory that looks like a princess's tiara. Oh yeah, they know their market. Bastards.

Being in a hive is the sweetest thing in the world to a lonely girl. If you don't like yourself or your life, you don't have to think about it. Your friends are always there to fill your thoughts, to make you feel like you belong. Until something happens. Maybe you say the wrong thing, or your Queen Bee suddenly decides you're not cool enough. You get Cut. Your

conference code no longer works. And then you go crazy. Because the voices in your head *stop*. You're left with that horrible silence, those lame, desperate thoughts. Nothing but you, despicable you. And you just want to die.

I put the speakers on Angela's scalp, behind her ears. She stirred a little. Using my thumbs (okay, so sometimes I'm old-fashioned), I called up a readout on her mouth pad and got her rig's number. I slung my backpack off my back, unzipped it, and pulled out my old silver-and-powder-blue rig. It looked clunky compared to Angela's newer model.

My heart began to pound. I'd begged Uncle Ted to let me keep the ESP rig, even after my own crash and burn. "For emergencies," I'd said. I swore I'd never do a hive again, and I meant it. And I'd been good, really good—hadn't used it since. I'd kept it mostly as a reminder . . . of just how horrible some people can be. And Uncle Ted had trusted me. But he probably had checked the rig now and then to keep me honest.

I slipped the rig on quick, turning to face the wall so that Doc Sophie wouldn't see how hard I was controlling my breathing. *I can do this,* I thought. *It's just one girl. Not a hive thing. I'm maybe saving her life. It'll be okay.*

I popped in the tongue pad (I wear mine left-lower). I tasted the sharp tang of the embedded disinfectant—the most delicious taste in the world to a hive-girl. I dialed Angela's number and heard a riff from Frivolous Genocide's latest track. *The tone quality has gotten better,* I thought, though that one was probably an illegal download. A click of connection. "Angela," I said.

Her whole body jerked. She blinked and sat up, eyes wide,

suddenly very alive. Now somebody was home. "Who are you?" she asked. It was strange hearing her voice in front of me and inside my skull at the same time. Like her voice totally surrounded and soaked through me. Sweet/scary memories of hive life flooded back. I didn't know whether to scream or cry.

I closed my eyes, clenched my palms, and tried to ignore the rush of adrenaline. "My name's Michelle Rodriguez," I said. "Most people call me Mitch. I wanted to talk to you."

"Me? Why?" She didn't say it, but I could hear the "I'm nobody" loud and clear.

"Because you're going through something awful. And I've been through the same thing."

"What, being rescued when you didn't wanna be?"

I shook my head and grasped Angela's shoulder gently. "You got cut out of a hive, didn't you?"

She stared at me as though I'd accused her of eating baby seals for lunch. Then she looked down and gave a slight nod.

"It's okay, Angela. That happened to me, too, about three years ago. I know how it feels. It was the worst thing that ever happened to me, worse even than losing my parents. I know what it's like, Angela—that awful silence in your head."

Angela looked away, her face screwed up like she was going to cry. What she finally blurted out, though, surprised me. "It's all my own fault!" The wail echoed through my head, bringing back even more memories. Helplessness. Rejection.

"It is *not* your fault, Angela!"

"Yes, it is! There was this boy I liked, and this girl that Sarah liked was all flirty with him. So I . . . I called her a slut!"

"Well, calling other girls sluts isn't a good thing, but it doesn't get you the death penalty, last I heard. So. You think you made your queen bee mad, huh?"

Angela shrugged. "I guess. I guess I wasn't good enough for them. I should have known."

"Bullshit."

"No, really, I should have *known*!" She pounded her fist against the old couch, and I had to turn down the volume on my headset.

"Stop blaming yourself."

"That's not it." She looked down again. "I should have known because . . . I wasn't the first."

"The first what?"

Her fingers tore at the already shredded upholstery. "Wasn't the first girl Sarah cut from the hive."

"You mean, just suddenly, no warning, like you were?"

Angela nodded. "Two other girls, one of them about three months ago, the other just last month. But I thought I'd be different."

Yeah, don't we all? I thought in sympathy. "Sounds like your queen bee is a flaky bitch. Well, you can find new friends. Join a school club or something."

"Hah. Not at Condoleezza Rice."

"Oh. Shit." A public school. A holding pen for kids not rich enough to go to a Corp or Church school. Poor Angela. Maybe her folks weren't rich enough for Microsoft Academy, but they could have at least tried for Wal-Mart High. Hell, even some Jimmy Bob Jones Praise Jesus school would've been better.

In public school, you were lucky if there were only fifty students per class. Lucky if you could hear the teacher talking through the bulletproof glass. Lucky if the teacher got to teach at all and not just be floor warden until the bell rang and the doors unlocked. No arts, no sports, no frills. No wonder she'd been desperate to join a hive.

"Mom doesn't have much money," Angela said, shrugging. "Dad left when I was ten. It was so cool when Sarah and the others . . . they seemed to really like me. And they watched my back. Made sure I didn't get beat up." Tears started to roll down her cheeks.

I put my arms around Angela and let her head fall onto my shoulder. "It wasn't your fault and you're not alone, Angela. Getting cut from a hive is like heartbreak. Lots of girls go through it. Just like I did." Not all people get addicted to ESP networks, just like not every beer drinker becomes an alkie. And not every heartbroken lover becomes a police statistic. Just the lonely ones, the shy ones, the geeky ones, the ones who think they deserved the rejection. The ones who had never felt such intense closeness—and figure they never will again.

My memory tossed up a vision of my former queen bee, Patty Nguyen's cute, freckled sneer as she told me I wasn't getting the new conf code. Her laughter had been like knives in my chest. All I did was cry as she and Cynthia and DaShauna and the others walked away, tossing their heads and laughing.

"Ow?"

I pulled back, realizing that I'd been gripping Angela's shoulders way too hard. "Sorry."

"Yeah. Must have been easy for you. You didn't kill yourself."

"I tried. I woke up that night in a hospital with my stomach being pumped."

Angela raised her head from my shoulder and looked me in the eye. I didn't really like the props I saw her giving me. "No shit?"

"No shit. No fun either. I learned my lesson."

Angela sat back, disappointed. "So you didn't try again."

"Still here, aren't I? No, I got too pissed off at what my hive did to me. What they nearly made me do. Anger kept me alive, Angela. Get mad at this Sarah person, that's what you have to do. What your hive did wasn't right. They promised to look after you and they didn't."

Angela sighed and rested her head back on my shoulder. "No. It's someone else's turn now."

"Hey, survival is the best revenge. Get a zPod, fill your head with your favorite music—"

"It's not the same."

"Well, then, find those other girls that your queen bee cut, be friends with them. Make a new hive."

"I can't. They're dead."

A prickle danced down my spine and my stomach went cold. "Whoa, whoa, whoa, *what*?"

"They succeeded," Angela went on with a grim smile of respect. "One hung herself. The other slit her wrists in a bathtub. They weren't stupid like me."

"Stop this!" My grasp on her wrist grew tighter and I shook her a little. "My God, didn't anyone at your school notice this was happening?"

"'Leezza Rice, remember?"

I sighed. "Shit. They probably get three dead kids a week from one thing and another. And kids run away all the time. Nobody'd fuss about two or three more, would they?"

Angela shrugged. "They'd be happy for the space."

My thoughts started clicking together like a Tau-Ka-Chi puzzle. After moving in with Uncle Ted the Detective, I read a lot of his books that weren't exactly kid-appropriate. Psychological profiles, rambling prison confessions, tabloid tales of murder. "Angela, before you joined this hive, when the other girls who were cut . . . died, how did this Sarah and the other girls react when they found out? Were they sad at all?"

"Ha. Sad?" Angela snorted. "No. Maybe the others, but not Sarah. She was kinda . . . smug. Like she knew a cool secret. I think she liked it."

"Uh-huh." This queen bee was a killer bee. Angela was right. If this Sarah had gotten a taste for taking lives, it was going to be some other poor girl's turn soon.

Doc Sophie walked in once more and her face brightened with surprise. She gave me a nod of respect before saying, "Hello, Angela. I'm Dr. McGlynn. Your mom is here. She'll be taking you over to Seacrest Hospital in just a little bit. Mitch, let me talk to Angela privately for a few minutes?"

"Sure. You stay strong, Angela, okay?" I gave her arm one last squeeze and stood up to walk out.

"Oh, and Mitch," Doc Sophie added, "take off the rig."

"But I . . ."

"Detective Rodriguez will have my hide, and yours, if he sees you wearing it."

I sighed loudly, wanting to say something really nasty back.

She was sweet on Uncle Ted, I knew it, and I could—but then realized it was my phone jones reacting. "Yeah. Sure. Okay." I reached up for my headset.

"Don't leave me!" Angela cried out, her voice so full of pain, it was like a physical punch to my chest. I felt hot tears start to well up in my own eyes.

"It'll be okay, Angela," I said softly. "Hold on. Just hold on. Remember, get angry. Survive. It'll be worth it." It was hard, but I did it. I took off the rig.

Doc Sophie reached for Angela's headset. "No!" Angela wailed. She fell over sideways on the couch and curled up again. I stuffed my rig in my backpack and left to the sound of Doc Sophie's gently cajoling voice, which now seemed weirdly flat and phony after the resonance of Angela in my head.

I almost slammed the holding room door behind me as I walked out into the busier station area. I leaned back against the cold painted-plaster wall beside the door and closed my eyes a moment. I breathed deeply, trying to ignore the echoing silence in my skull. It was all I could do not to jam the rig back on and call somebody, anybody—a phone psychic, a porn line, some stupid corporate voice-mail system. Anything.

I opened my eyes and saw a sad-faced woman wearing a faded coat sitting in one of the station's cheap plastic chairs. She was staring, absorbed, into her Styrofoam coffee cup, completely ignoring the raving Oxy-head going by on the arm of a cop. I went and sat in the chair next to her. "You must be Angela's mom, right?"

She looked up with the same "lights on" expression Angela had when I called her rig. "Oh! Yes . . . how is she?"

"She'll be okay," I said, totally lying. "She just needs, you know, some time."

"Of course, of course," murmured the woman.

What were you thinking? I wanted to scream at her, *Sending your precious girl to 'Leezza Rice?* But, as Detective Uncle Ted always says, "Don't get mad, get information." So instead, I asked her, "Was Angela happy at school?"

She did the one-shoulder shrug thing. Like daughter, like mom. "No more than other kids. Until recently, like a month ago? She'd found some new friends. Suddenly she was happier than I'd seen her, well, since she was just a little girl. She got that new phone in a school raffle drawing—"

Probably stolen by her hive sisters, I thought sourly.

"—and her grades went up and she couldn't wait to get to school. I always knew she was a real smart kid and I was so pleased to see her finally applying herself. That's what I don't understand about all this. She was so happy."

"Uh-huh." It was odd that Angela's grades had gotten better; usually hive-girls become total slackers. They're having too much fun in their heads. Unless Angela wasn't just studying for one. "Do you happen to remember a name or have a phone number of her new friends because, you know, I'd like to contact them. Maybe they could cheer her up or at least explain why she suddenly changed. It could really help."

"No . . . she hadn't brought her new friends home yet. I remember one of them was named Sarah. Angela seemed in awe of her. What we used to call a girl-crush, I guess. Do you go to Condoleezza Rice, too?"

"Uh, no. Homeschooled. Passed my GED last year." There

had been just enough money left from my parents' life insurance that Uncle Ted could hire tutors after my one-night stand with Mr. Death. I was hoping to get into Skagawit Community College next year. They have a great preforensics program.

"Well, good for you, I guess," Angela's mom rambled on. "I think it's such a shame that so much of the country has given up on public education."

Reality check, lady. It's your daughter's life you're playing politics with here. But I didn't say that aloud. My folks taught me some manners.

The holding room door opened again and Doc Sophie peered out. "Mrs. Smith? Would you like to speak to Angela now?"

"Oh! Oh yes! Thank you!" She stood suddenly, and the Styro cup fell to the floor, spilling the few remaining drops of her coffee. She remembered her own manners at the last minute, turning to say, "Nice to meet you, um . . ." and then hurrying off for some long overdue bonding with her daughter. Doc Sophie gave me a tired smile before going in after the mom.

I looked down and saw a colorful backpack leaning against the wall. It had a 3-D photo of the latest pop-hottie, Aramus James, printed on it. Hmmmmm. I doubted it was the mom's. As my uncle Ted once told me, I'm a good girl with bad girl instincts. I wondered how long the mom would be in the holding room. Well, couldn't let some Oxy-head walk off with Angela's backpack, could we?

I picked it up, set it on my lap, unzipped it, looked around. Nobody was watching me. I hang out in the station all the

time, I'm like furniture there. I pulled a battered old e-pad out of the backpack. Mrs. Smith must have bought it used—stores don't even sell 'em anymore.

I pressed the "on" button and selected *Search: Sarah*. The screen shimmered and scrawled writing flowed to the surface. Right there I found what I wanted. Girls get name fetishes. Angela had written over and over, "Sarah Potosi is cool!" and "Sarah Potosi Rules!" and "Callie Harris + Angela Smith = friends forever!"

I checked the memory use. Sheesh, hardly forty gig. I don't have the freshest wrist pad, myself, but it's got fifty times the space of an old e-pad. Fortunately Angela's was just new enough to have wireless tech. I was able to beam the entire contents into my wrist pad in less than five minutes. Then, being the good girl, I slipped the e-pad back into the backpack and walked up to the front desk.

Betsy Huang was just coming on duty. She's no nonsense. I like her. I handed her the backpack, saying, "The lady visiting her daughter in the holding room left this out here. Could you keep it up here for her?"

Betsy nodded once and that was that.

I went across the street and waited in Harriet Mizuki's diner for Uncle Ted to get off work, as I often did when I came down to the station. I sipped at a lemon mushroom tea and did a few searches on my download of Angela's e-pad. I checked her calendar. Pretty blank, except for a few notes here and there, like "4:30 see Mr. Wasserman about test. 8:00 ask Mrs. Cambert about homework. Zeek—4:00 Comp Lab 201!" whatever that meant.

Angela had a "Poetry" file full of haikus of confusion and self-hate. I felt a pang at the all-too-familiar words that mostly added up to a big *why me?* Why were you born with a "kick me" sign on your back, kid? Don't know, but it happens to more of us than you'd think.

The poems turned suddenly hopeful, warm odes to togetherness and friendship and I looked at their entry date. Jeez, she'd only been in her hive six weeks.

There was a photo file, though it was awkward to look through it on my wrist pad's tiny pop-up screen. Pre-hive, Angela's pictures were of houses, parks, cats, anything but people, except for a few of her mom. Then there were several pics of a group of girls in a tight hug grinning at the camera. A couple of them had fashionable gold tooth rings and circular cheek scars. Yeah, this was the hive. I was betting the tall girl with long black hair in the middle was Sarah. Maybe it was just what Angela had said, or my imagination, but their smiles reminded me of a pack of wolves staring at a trapped rabbit.

"Hey, Mitch!" Uncle Ted slapped his hand down on my shoulder and I jumped.

"Hey, hi! God, you startled me!" I switched off my wrist pad and let the screen sink back into the unit.

"Ready to go home?" He must have had a court day because he was wearing a suit. Uncle Ted's fortyish face was more rumpled than his jacket and that's saying a lot. But it's the handsomest face I know, anyway.

"Longtime ready." I followed him out to his battered old Toyota Prius. I made myself comfortable in the passenger seat as he worked on coaxing the car to life.

"Sophie says you got somewhere with the girl from the freeway," Uncle Ted said as he pulled into traffic.

"Yeah, some." I still felt a strange lump of guilt in my stomach at having disconnected from Angela. From being disconnected at all. I sensed Uncle Ted's X-ray gaze on me. "What?"

"You don't look too happy. Was it a mistake, honey? Hit too close to home?"

I shrugged, "Nah, it was all right. Just . . . really sad, you know? I felt sorry for her."

"Uh-huh. Sophie said you didn't want to take your rig off."

Anger flashed through me. "Hey, I just forgot it was on, okay? I'm cool. No problem."

After a pause, Uncle Ted said, "You're a tough girl, Mitch, and I trust you. And you know you can trust me. You can tell me anything, whatever. You know I'll listen."

"'Course, Uncle Ted." I get a lump in my throat when he talks like that. Best uncle a girl could ever have. I cleared my throat and changed the subject. "So, you ask Sophie out yet? She's dying to date you, you know that."

He gave me a mind-your-own-business glare that could make a perp cry. Then he just growled "Awww," and flapped his long-fingered hand as he looked away. He still wasn't over Aunt Dolores. Cousin Rosa says he still calls Dolores once in a while, hoping she'll come back.

"So what's for dinner?" I asked.

"Macaroni and cheese," he announced, as if it were a special on the board at Delamino's.

"Cool." It's always either mac and cheese, tuna casserole, or chicken fingers. Uncle Ted squeezed every dime he could to send Cousin Rosa to St. Margarite's boarding school, even though it was way down in Tacoma, so we didn't get to see her much. God bless Uncle Ted.

"Sure there isn't something on your mind?" he said.

God damn Uncle Ted—it's like he's psychic sometimes. So I opened up. "Okay, so it's like . . . this queen bee of Angela's—that's her name, the girl who tried to jump off the overpass—anyway she, that is Sarah, the queen bee, like, cut two girls before Angela, just weeks before, and the girls *killed* themselves just like Angela was going to, and she's going to do it again, and—"

"Whoa, whoa, slow down, kid! That sentence is like a Christmas tree, you got so many clauses hanging on it. Start over. What's this about Angela?"

"The girl off the overpass."

"Right, the one you were talking to."

"Told me about Sarah, the queen bee of her hive."

"That's the girl who's kinda leader of the pack, right?"

"Right. Her name's Sarah Potosi. Anyway, Angela thinks Sarah deliberately cut two other girls out of the hive just because Sarah liked the power of making them go nuts."

"Well, that sounds pretty rude."

"*Rude?* Uncle Ted, those other girls killed themselves just like Angela tried to. This Sarah is a killer queen, Uncle Ted!"

"Whoa, don't be throwing words like *killer* around me."

"But it's true! Angela says Sarah's gonna do it again. We've got to stop her!"

At a red light, Uncle Ted turned and squinted at me. "Let me get this straight. Two other girls from the same hive have committed suicide?"

"Yeah."

"And Angela was going to be the third."

"Yeah. And there's probably gonna be more."

He sighed and stared out the windshield. "Shit."

"Isn't there some way you can charge this Sarah with murder? Or manslaughter at least?"

Uncle Ted sighed and shook his head. "No way you could prove it."

"Aw, come on! You mean she can get away with it? Think about it, Uncle Ted!"

"You think I didn't think about it after I picked you up from the hospital three years ago?"

I paused. "You did?"

"'Course I did. Nobody treats my favorite niece like that." He made a disgusted face and looked away from me as he drove. "But incitement to suicide as murder? Impossible to prove. Especially when the victim's a teen. Too many other factors the defense can bring up. You'd need a confession from the perp to even get it before a judge."

"Well, how about possession of stolen ESPs at least, or illegally setting up a cell network?"

He sighed heavily again. "Yeah, well. Let me talk to the guys. They'll work it, honey, but it'll take some time. Just don't expect much, okay?"

"Yeah. I understand." Like our cops don't have enough to do, what with mall bombings and ricin in the mail. Lonely

girls offing themselves weren't going to get much priority. I sighed, and stared out my window, watching the decaying suburb roll by. "What's it take to get people to pay attention? Does another girl have to die?"

"You don't know that's gonna happen."

"My gut tells me it's true, and you always said I should trust my gut."

"Yeah, well, guts aren't always right. And as *Papá* used to say, they often lead to something messy."

"I'm right, Uncle Ted. I know it."

He stopped the car in the middle of the street and turned to me, angry. "Look, what are you saying we should do? I asked you to be a friend to that girl, not be her avenging angel. You didn't promise anything to that Angela, did you?"

"I didn't promise nothing!"

"All right, then. Forget about it. Sometimes you gotta let other people take care of their own problems, okay?"

I let a long, silent moment pass before saying, "So there's no justice, huh?"

"Leave perfect justice to the next world, *chica*. We just do what little we can in this one."

"After all you've been through, you still believe?"

"If I didn't, I'd go crazy."

"Lotta that going around," I said softly. I remembered the sight of Angela falling back on the couch. I felt awful. "Every school has suicide awareness alerts. You can at least do that, can't you?"

"Yeah." He sighed heavily again. "Yeah, I guess I can put one of the boys on that. What school does she go to again?"

"Condoleezza Rice."

"Shit. It'll have to go through the mayor's office. But, yeah, I can do that. First thing tomorrow, okay?"

"Okay. You're the best, Uncle Ted."

"Yeah, right."

That night, we were pretty quiet over our mac and cheese. Uncle Ted left shortly after because he was meeting his cousin, former colonel "Skip" Alvarez, for a beer. Cousin Skippy was one of those guys every cop knows--someone who says he's former Special Forces, SEAL, CIA spook, what-have-you. Half the stories they tell you're sure aren't true, and the other half you're scared sick just might be. Cousin Skippy was the Black Ops sheep of the family, and I wished I could go along, but Uncle Ted said, "You don't have the clearance rating for his secrets, and you aren't old enough to drink. Don't wait up for me."

We live in a highly secure condo, so I feel safe when he has to leave me alone. I'd told Uncle Ted I was going to spend the evening studying the want ads online. See, I have a hard time keeping summer jobs. The last one Uncle Ted got me, data entry at the district attorney's office, well, I lost that one when I got caught paying too much attention to the data. Turns out the attorneys don't like their admins playing girl detective. Who knew?

But instead of the want ads, I spent the evening studying my download of Angela's e-pad. I was hoping she'd entered the name of the spyder that had set up the network for Sarah's hive. Techie kids made a lot of side money and loads of new friends by becoming spyders- setting up the illegal webs,

the free hive conference connections. The really clever ones pirated satellite relays, sometimes hosting it all themselves over their family TV dish and computer, some piggybacking on their neighborhood cell tower. I'd heard rumors of one girl at 'Soft Academy who'd been caught with a transmitter in her backpack. The network provider corporations are rabid over this, but even their hired PIs learn that spyders are tough to find.

I Googled under *spider, spyder, spidey,* anything, but all I found were gushing love notes about the hottie new actor in *Spider-Man* X. I flung myself down on my bed in frustration.

What I hadn't told Angela was that, though I'd gotten over getting cut, I hadn't let the anger go. Last I'd heard about Patty Nguyen, she'd moved down to L.A. and was dating movie stars.

I threw a pillow against the wall, but it didn't help. Another girl was going to die. Like I almost did. Like Angela almost did. Like two girls already had. And what was I going to do about it?

I went to my desktop. Yeah, still got one of those. I'm so prehistoric. It's got a nice old plasma monitor that still works well, though. I went online and looked at the Ebisu Web site. Not sure why. Maybe hoping to see a confession of guilt, some hint that they knew what their little toy was doing. A pretty Asian anime lady popped up wearing a rig, purring, "With an Ebisu headset and wireless network, now you can get closer than ever before!" Yeah, helping to crush the egos of girls worldwide.

The home page had a cute little story about Ebisu's latest

promotional contest, for the farthest separated conf group. The runner-up team had a person on each continent. But the winners were a group of Chinese scientists with a man at each pole and one taikonaut on the moon. Kinda seemed like cheating, to me.

There was much burbling about how Ebisu's stock was taking off and would be "a wise choice for savvy investors." Farther down the page was a nice picture of the Ebisu North American CEO shaking hands with the director of Homeland Security. "Ebisu is helping to make the world safer!" the caption said. Right. How effective would it be for an interrogator or torturer to be speaking in your head? Bet Cousin Skippy would have some ideas about that. But I didn't want to save the world, just the life of one girl.

I Googled the blogosphere for a spyder at 'Leezza Rice. No self-respecting net-weaver would out himself in public, but geek boys feud like pit bulls. From the slime they sling at one another you can sometimes tell who's up to what if you read between the lines. Sure enough, there was some jerk handled Snotwire ragging on a guy named Zeek who'd been getting all high and mighty. Zeek . . . where had I seen that before?

I went back to Angela's data on my wrist pad. It was that entry in her calendar . . . it was right about the date she would have gotten in the hive. "Zeek—4:00. Comp Lab 201." With a bright red exclamation point beside it. Well, well. Wonder if Zeek made a habit of hanging at the computer lab at Angela's school?

I made my decision. I was going in.

The next morning Uncle Ted woke me just before he left for work. He still smelled of cigarette smoke and beer. I got up and dressed for invisibility in gray sweats, black T-shirt, and a gray hoodie. I threw random books in my old backpack, wolfed down a couple of toaster tarts, and hopped the city bus to 'Leezza Rice.

The old brick school was surrounded by a high chain-link fence topped by razor wire. There were only two gates that I could see; each had a grimy white electronic sensor arch. Half the time, the sensors in the arches didn't work and the schools were too underfunded to fix them, so their deterrent factor was kinda lost. Besides, they mostly scanned for guns and sniffed for drugs or bombs and I was carrying none of that.

Supposedly students had to wave their IDs as they went in, but I arrived at crunch time just before the first period, when everybody crammed through the gates to get in before lockdown. I let myself be caught up in the crushing flow of bodies, getting the breath squeezed almost out of me as we stampeded through the gate. I waved my learner's permit card as if it was an ID, but nobody cared. I was in.

And I was reminded why I was so glad I left school. The halls were narrow, crammed with lockers and kids and reeking of wet clothing and sweaty bodies and girls overdoused with pheromone perfume. The girls shrieked their greetings and threats, the guys glowered and shoved one another—you almost couldn't tell a friendly hit from an angry one. Lots of them wore hive rigs, some with eye-screen attachments for TV or vid. One hulking gangbanger glared at me through a GPS display over his right eye. I felt my stomach tighten, even

though this was not my crowd, no longer my world. I hunched my shoulders and pulled the hood down on my head, slogging along like a slacker too lowered with seds or too short on sleep to be worth the bother.

I'd sussed out Angela's class schedule from the info I'd downloaded, so I followed that. First hour was Spanish. I'd have aced this if I cared. The class was huge . . . a hundred kids at least in a big stadium seating room. The party-hearties sat way up in the back, the kids who wanted to learn anything sat way down front. I sat upper middle with the sleepers and stoners who gave me a companionable nod as I joined them. "You a narc?" one of them slurred at me.

"No. New transfer."

"Oh. S'cool."

There was a ruckus down front and I saw a posse of girls swagger in, just as the hour chimed. Well, well. I recognized the tall girl with long black hair and circular cheek scars. Angela's notes hadn't mentioned she shared classes with Sarah. The killer queen bee was holding hands with a small Asian girl who was staring up at Sarah with near adoration. The rest of the hive—a redhead, a blonde, and two black girls standing behind the Asian girl—could barely hide their cruel amusement. *So she's the next one*, I thought, my skin going cold.

The teacher, a haggard, thin woman with short gray hair, stepped into the safety booth at the front of the room and called for order. Hardly anyone listened. Somebody dropped a book, and the woman flinched. "Ha!" cackled the boy beside me. "Gun-shy."

The teacher called out *"Buenos días,"* in a shrill voice. Only half the class responded. She asked everyone to put their thumb on the chair pad for roll call. I noticed the glowing blue circle on the chair arm. I noticed a lot of other chairs had blue circles that weren't glowing. I noticed a lot of students weren't bothering to log in, so I didn't feel so bad about not doing it either.

Sarah and her posse sat down front with their new pet, brazenly ignoring the teacher. I wondered what the hell I was going to do, how was I going to warn the new girl? If I could just get her name, I might be able to get her e-mail address. I could write: "Hi, you don't know me but you are in grave danger." Yeah, like she'd believe that. These were the happiest moments of her short, miserable life. But she wasn't wearing a rig yet, so there still might be time.

I nudged the slumped-over guy next to me. "Who's that girl down there with Sarah Potosi?"

"I dunno," the guy slurred at me with a rude glare.

'Course not. Who knew anybody in this hell pit?

I suffered through the Spanish class as the poor teacher tried to get some *palabras* through to a class that didn't care. I hunched down in the too-small seat and watched Sarah and her hive fuss and coo over the new girl like she was the latest Supersinger. Oh yeah, Sarah had It, the coolness that attracts no matter what they're like on the inside. I stuffed my fists in my pockets and ground my teeth. Jealous, me? Nah, just a little pissed off. Sarah turned her heavily made-up face my way, her eyes squinting. Uncle Ted had told me that people have this animal sense—they know when they're being stared

at. One predator knows another. I looked away, hoping she hadn't seen me.

When the chime ended the class, I was suddenly sorry I'd chosen to sit in the back. The aisles were jammed with kids fleeing for the door and a few moments of freedom. I'd hoped to follow the hive, maybe pull the Asian girl into a doorway when no one was watching and give her the whole story. She could believe me or not, but at least I'd have tried. I squeezed through the crowd, getting called bitch and worse, but by the time I got to the front of the classroom, Sarah, the hive, and their new prey were gone.

I followed the rest of Angela's schedule for the day, but didn't see any of the hive again. Not even in the lunch room or lavatories. I didn't feel like asking around after Sarah. Word might get back to her, along with a description of me. As Uncle Ted says, sometimes it pays to be paranoid.

Besides, I had a date with a datageek. Around 2:00, as most of the school was emptying out, I went down to the computer lab and hung out near Room 201. One of the scrawny guys passing by said, "Can I help you with something?" in that combination of arrogance and abject terror that geeks display around girls.

"Lookin' for Zeek," I mumbled.

His expression lost every shred of hope. "Yeah. 'Course you are. They're always looking for Zeek. Down there." He made a weird, exaggerated nod down the hall. "In the radio lab."

"This school has a radio station?"

"Not so's you'd notice." The kid wandered off and I walked down the hall. There was an open door to a ratty-looking

studio with an old-style soundboard and chewed-up foam padding on the walls. No one in it. The next door down was slightly open and I peered in.

It was no bigger than a closet, maybe five by five, walls floor to ceiling lined with electronic sound and computing equipment from I'd swear the last hundred years. Wouldn't have been surprised to see an old CD player or even an eight-track. The rest of the space inside the room was filled by a tall, skinny kid with brown skin and shoulder-length brown hair that couldn't decide whether to dread or 'fro, sitting on a rickety wheeled office chair. His big brown eyes gazed at me with wary intelligence and his smile wasn't exactly welcoming.

"'S up?" he asked.

"Zeek?"

"Maybe."

"Hear you know something about hive-nets."

"Maybe."

"Well, do you or don't you?"

"Who says I do?"

I paused. What the hell. "A friend of Sarah's."

"Sarah P.?"

"Yep."

"Well, this friend of Sarah P. better watch her mouth. Come in and close the door."

I squeezed in, feeling pretty uncomfortable in the tight space. "You like it in here?"

"More cozy than home. Now what you want?"

"I wanna start my own hive."

"Heh." He chuckled. "Hope you got the leafy, girl. You don't exactly look dressed for success."

"My 'rents are Frugies." They hadn't been Frugalists, actually, one of the most hated movements in America, but I figured it might get me some sympathy.

"Dude, that's ugly."

"Tell me."

"How many?"

"In my family?"

"In your *hive,* emptywig."

"Oh. Maybe four."

"Probably cost you four Ronnies, then. Not including the rigs."

"Four hundred dollars! I could get a legit net for that!"

"On setup, maybe, but then you'd keep paying every month. Not to mention DHS, NSA, PTA, and God knows who all able to listen in and track. Spyder nets you pay only once and there's no Big Brother hanging on. Got it?"

"Yeah. But I don't got that kind of leafy right now."

"Then why are we still talking?"

I was staring at all the equipment. What a perfect place to hide a phone net transmitter. Who would know, or even care? "Did Sarah pay that much?" I asked, stalling.

Zeek chuckled again and his eyes became sly and knowing. "Sarah takes some of it out in trade, know what I'm sayin'?"

I didn't want to know what Sarah traded. "Yeah, right. Probably all HUAC anyway."

"Hey, you doubt me, ask around at the Crazy C. See what it gets you."

Probably beaten the crap out of, was my guess. The Crazy C was a downtown hangout not known for checking ID too closely, or noticing what the patrons might be doing. It seemed to be protected by all sorts of strange zoning codes. Lots of towns have such a place, Uncle Ted says, and how long they last depends on how long they keep the money flowing to local politicos. Anyone asking too much about spyders or Sarah at the Crazy C was not going to be mistaken for a friendly. "Never mind. I gotta think about this."

"Get out, then, bitch, and don't come back until you're richer. Better yet, don't come back." This was said without anger, by a king secure in his kingdom, even if it's a five-by-five closet paneled with silicon and steel and smelling of ozone and sweaty socks.

I slipped out the door and slung the backpack over my shoulder. Leaving the school was easy, so long as it was after class hours. They only try to keep you in while they're being paid to. I trudged across the asphalt yard, feeling only semi-successful. I'd found the spyder, but so what? I'd seen the new victim-to-be, but so what? I hadn't solved anything yet.

Out of the corner of my eye, I saw a familiar car rolling up to the curb as I went out the security archway. A *real* familiar car. My stomach sank and I sighed as I got into the Prius. "Hey, nice of you to come pick me up, Uncle Ted."

As he glared at me, I could almost see the anger radiating off him like the squiggly heat lines in cartoons. He jerked the wheel hard and the car lurched back into the street. "What. The hell. Do you think. You are doing?"

"Well, I told you I was job-hunting. I thought maybe they might need a new lunch lady or something . . . "

"Michelle!" he roared. Uncle Ted never calls me Michelle. And he never roars. His fingers were white on the steering wheel.

I slumped down in the seat. "I was investigating Angela's hive."

"God damn it!" He struck the steering wheel so hard I could swear I heard it crack. A horn blared behind us. Uncle Ted leaned out his window and yelled stuff in Spanish and English that could cause a plaster Maria to burst into flame. The car behind sped around us with a squealing of tires. And then he turned back to me. "People. Get hurt. Doing this sort of thing. People. Get killed. Doing this sort of thing. I should know. I got scars. Most of my friends got scars. Some of them got headstones. You hearing me?"

"I hear you."

"So what the friggin' hell were you doing?"

I took a few deep breaths and said, "I know who Sarah's next victim is."

"No, you don't know!"

"Yes, I do! I saw her. I saw Sarah the killer queen fuss over her. I've been there. I know what's going on, Uncle Ted!"

"Did this Sarah see you?"

"I don't think so."

"Damn it, Mitch. Is that all?"

I paused a little longer. "I know who the spyder is."

"Did you talk to him?"

"Yeah."

"Shit."

"It's cool. He just thought I was an unhappy potential customer."

Uncle Ted shook his head. "You have no idea what you're doing. I should never have let you talk to that Angela."

"Uncle—"

"You are so grounded. Two weeks!"

"What? Uncle Ted, I'm not a child!"

"Then stop acting like one!"

"I am not! That's unfair!"

"I am one seriously pissed off grown-up! That entitles me to be unfair!"

I crossed my arms on my chest and let my jacket hood slip down over my eyes. "How did you know I was at the school?"

"I got a buddy who's a narc there."

"You're shittin' me."

"Watch your mouth. You would not make your mother proud saying such words."

Yeah, like he should talk. The powers that be could spare money to track down every ounce of weed but couldn't spare the time to save the life of one girl. I stared out the window, feeling a good sulk coming on. Then I noticed something. "Hey, this isn't the way home."

"I gotta stop by the office. Doc Sophie wanted to tell me something."

"She couldn't use the phone?"

"She wanted to talk in person."

On a better day, I would have teased him about Sophie wanting face time, but this was not that day.

We pulled up into the parking lot of the station. Doc Sophie was standing on the sidewalk and came over to the car,

her arms wrapped tightly around her chest. When she saw me her eyes widened. Uncle Ted got out even before the engine shuddered to a halt, asking, "Sophie, what's wrong?"

Still staring at me, Doc Sophie said, "You're even more psychic than usual, Theodore. Still, I guess it's just as well you brought her."

That extra sense must run in the family. I jumped out of the car, asking, "It's about Angela, isn't it?"

Sophie nodded and looked down at the ground. "She got up to the top floor of the hospital. No one knows how. She—"

"Is she okay?"

Sophie shook her head. "She's dead."

"No!"

Uncle Ted grabbed me and held me while I pounded his chest with my fists. "No, damn it, no!" I yelled, still hearing Angela in my head, saying, "Don't leave me!"

"I'm sorry," Sophie whispered. "You tried, Mitch. I know you did. Sometimes, when a person is just determined—"

"There was nothin' you could do, honey," Uncle Ted said.

"There was plenty I could have done! I should have stayed connected to her longer, I should have—"

"Could you have replaced her hive?" asked Sophie.

I stopped, remembering the emptiness. No one voice from the outside could have filled it. "No," I admitted. Then I turned to Uncle Ted. "So. Looks like Sarah bagged herself another victim, doesn't it?" I snarled at him.

"What?" asked Sophie.

"Mitch is just upset. Never mind. Thanks, Sophie. We'll talk later, okay?"

Sophie nodded and Uncle Ted practically forced me back into the car. I felt my old buddy Anger come roaring back, filling every bone and muscle.

"God, I'm sorry, Mitch. God, I'm sorry," Uncle Ted said as we drove on to the apartment. I wiped a few tears, but I didn't say anything. I was scared of what might jump out of my mouth.

Uncle Ted took a call on his cell—a job had come up. When he dropped me off at home, he turned and looked at me, worry all over his face. "I gotta go to work. You gonna be okay, honey?"

"Sure, fine," I growled. "Am I still grounded?"

"'Fraid so, honey, more than ever. You've got every right to be upset, but I don't want you doing anything stupid."

"I won't." I got out and slammed the car door.

He got out partway and shouted, "Mitch, I love you. I just . . . don't want you getting hurt."

That made me pause. Uncle Ted never says "I love you." I turned and looked back at his sad, weathered face. "Too late for that," I said. Then I added, softer, "Thanks," feeling the tears flow again. "Love you, too."

"I'll see you later, honey."

"Yeah."

He slipped back into the Prius and roared off. I dragged myself up into the apartment, wishing I had a boatload of tissues to wipe my face. Uncle Ted sure knew how to take the air out of a case of righteous rage. But it was still there, simmering below the surface. One way or another I was going to get Sarah and her hive. Just a matter of when and how.

I sat on my bed and tried to calm my thinking, trying to channel the anger into something useful, like a plan. The phone rang, jangling me out of my fine meditation of hate. I could have just let the machine get it, but I was hoping it was one of those phone evangelists now oh-so-protected by free speech amendments, 'cause I was spoiling for a fight.

"Hey," I snapped at the receiver as I picked it up.

"Sugar pie, is that you?" It was Skippy Alvarez. He'd spent too much time in a platoon of Southerners, and therefore called women by the most syrupy crap. "Is Teo there?"

"Naw, Unk is at work, you might try his cell."

"Don't wanna bother him. Just thought we might get together one more time before I left town. Tell him I called, will ya?"

"Wait! Cousin Skip, can I ask you something?"

"Sure, sweetie, ask anything."

"Skip . . . what do you know about cell phones?"

An hour later, Skippy was sitting in front of me in the living room. He was short and broad and looked like he could pick up a tank if he had to. His salt-and-pepper hair was cropped in a short flattop, and his eyes were flinty black, but held a glint of worldly amusement. He pushed a white cardboard box, about the size of a small brick, across the coffee table at me. "Just so you know, it's a felony to have one of these."

I didn't pick the box up right away. "A felony to carry a jammer?"

Skip nodded. "FCC takes its rights seriously. Doesn't keep them from coming in, though. This one's Italian make.

They use them in churches over there and in Mexico."

I gently opened the box, like it was a bomb or something.

"Mind you, that one's been a little . . . modified."

I jerked my hands away. "Modified how?"

Skip shrugged. "It's also a booster. Helps when the signal is weak in some areas."

"Spook modified?"

He winked at me. "It's got its tweaks. Mind you, I don't know all the mechanics of the ESP, so I can't guarantee how it will interact. This stuff you've been telling me about the girls dying . . ."

"Killing themselves, Skip. It's ugly."

He bit his lower lip and shook his head. "I always wondered when something like this would happen."

"What do you mean?"

He folded his thick fingers in his lap and leaned toward me. "Back in the 1960s, there was this guy, Dr. Allen Frey, who was involved in some studies called Project Pandora for the Department of Defense. He discovered a thing they called 'microwave hearing.' Seems you can beam radio frequencies at a person, do it just right it sounds like words inside their head. Artificial telepathy."

I sat back. "You don't even need a phone?"

"Not for limited purposes, no. They found there were all kinds of . . . effects you could get by using the right frequencies. It was a real active area of study for a while among the non-lethal weapons people. Almost mind control, you could say."

I sucked my breath in. "Holy shit."

"Pretty unholy, if you ask me. Anyway, Project Pandora is long gone and many of the scientists moved on to the corporate world. I guess it was only a matter of time until some of their findings found . . . commercial applications."

My thoughts spun like tires on ice. "The addictiveness of the ESP . . . do they know . . . did they plan . . . ?"

He shrugged again. "Who can say?"

"Do they *want* to kill girls?"

Cousin Skip shook his head. "It's not profitable to kill off your customers, sugar pie. No, I figure that's a side effect the developers hadn't counted on. There's a saying from back in your grandfather's time: 'The street finds its own uses for technology.' This hive queen of yours is just taking advantage of a hidden . . . feature."

"Shit," was all I could say.

He pushed the box closer to me. "Use it, but use it wisely and in good health. Maybe you can bring a little more attention to this whole mess." He took out the slim, black bar about the size of my grandfather's cell phone, and showed me the controls. "This switch is the jammer. The range is set at about a twenty-foot radius. You don't want larger than that, or you might call attention to yourself. That's the booster dial. Keep it low, if you need it . . . set too high, something might break. Got it?"

"Yeah."

He paused and looked at me. I had the feeling he was sizing up my courage. "Take care of yourself, Mitch. It's a more dangerous world than you know."

"So I'm learning."

“Good. I gotta scoot.” He stood and swiftly but quietly headed toward the door. “Oh, and remember . . .”

“You never gave me this and you were never here.”

“That’s my girl.” He kissed my forehead and slipped out the door. I watched from the living room window as he walked down the sidewalk, casually looking around, checking to see if he was observed. He’d probably parked a block or two away. Once a spook, always a spook.

I hid the jammer in a sock in my dresser drawer for the night. I had a weapon. I figured, if nothing else, maybe I could give Angela’s old hive-girls a taste of their own medicine. Maybe, if I timed it right, I could ruin their plans to cut the next girl. Now I just had to wait for those two things Uncle Ted relies on—luck and inspiration.

When Uncle Ted came home, late, I told him that Skip had called, but just left a message.

Uncle Ted nodded, distracted. “You okay?”

I shrugged. “As okay as anyone who couldn’t stop a murder.”

Uncle Ted sighed and rubbed his stubbly chin. “I had some boys check out that computer lab at ’Leezza Rice.”

My heart rose. “Yeah?”

He sighed more heavily. “They found nothing. No transmitter. Guess your guts aren’t always right, honey. Well, I gotta sleep. You too. Get to bed.”

“Oh. Yeah. Sure, Uncle Ted.” I went to bed but didn’t sleep for a long time. I was too busy hitting my pillow with my fist.

I slept in and vegged the next day, Saturday. Late afternoon, Uncle Ted called—he still had to work, said they’d found a big

meth lab, dealers shot, and he had to tie it all to terrorism to get enough funding from Homeland Security to tide the department over for the year. I commiserated, told him politics sucked while inwardly I crowed for joy. Grounding or no, I was going out tonight.

I dressed for blending in—jeans, camo T-shirt, and a scarred-up leather jacket. At about nine, I slipped out the back door of the apartment complex. Yeah, there were cameras and Uncle Ted could've requested the tape, but if things got that far he'd already know. I caught a bus two blocks away and took it downtown.

The Crazy C was in a low brick building, wedged between a shabby used bookstore and an even shabbier teriyaki place. I was early, for the crowd, so I had no problem slipping up to the bar and ordering a beer. Hey, I was already violating curfew, what was another broken rule? Besides, the bartender didn't even ask for my fake ID. I felt slightly insulted. I settled onto a stool in the corner and pretended I was a chameleon.

There was a small stage against the back wall and a group of gangly, scruffy guys were setting up band equipment. When they set up the stands with the funny-shaped knobs on top, I muttered, "Who uses mikes on stands anymore?"

"Didja bring your rig?" asked the barrie.

I jumped, spilling some beer. His question was a little too pertinent. "Uh, yeah. Matter of fact I did. Why?"

"Well, put it on, *chica*. Those are BrainBombs they're setting up. Make the music sound inside your head. Really cool. Band starts in about forty-five. Stick around."

"Yeah, think I will, thanks." I took another swig of beer to

hide my surprise. *The street finds uses for technology.* No wonder Zeek and the hive-girls liked this place.

A few minutes later, one of those same hive-girls strode in, but it wasn't Sarah. It was one of her underlings, whom I'd only seen in a couple of Angela's photos—a blonde with shoulder-length, curled hair, wearing a bangly crop top and jeans. Not the brightest of the bunch, according to Angela's notes. The blonde was also wearing her rig, and I could see her throat bobbing a bit. She was sub-voking, probably to the rest of the hive. I tried to practice some of Uncle Ted's technique of watching without seeming to. I fetched my old rig out of my backpack, now feeling self-conscious about how out-of-date the phone was. I slipped the headset on and flipped my hair over the pads.

The place was starting to fill up, but I still didn't see Sarah. Hive-girl was starting to look a little anxious, too. I wondered what was up. I saw her head to the bathroom, and on a whim, I followed her.

She stood by the sink, fussing with a make-up bag while I went into a stall. I heard her whisper audibly, "Are you there? Sarah? Renee?" Hmmm . . . reception problems. That gave me an idea. I took the jammer out of my backpack and clipped it on to my belt at the small of my back, beneath my leather jacket. Then I turned the jammer switch on.

"Hello? Hello, Sarah?" Hive-girl's voice became panicked and louder. "Sarah, don't *do* this! Shitshitshitshitshit!"

I gotta admit, for several seconds I drank in the delightful draft of vengeance. Poor miss co-conspirator now thinks she might be victim number four. Awwwww. I let her panic rise

a few seconds more, then my delicious joy made me bolder. Why stop at that?

I flushed and stepped out of the stall. Hive-girl was stabbing at her rig with the business end of a pair of tweezers. "Having problems?"

"Shut up."

I ignored her rudeness. "Oh, hey, you got one of those Cayce 1500s."

"I said shut *up*! Go away."

"I know how to fix those. These new rigs are touchy, they need a lot of tweaking. But I know a few tricks."

She finally looked up and noticed me, blue eyes slightly red around the rims. She looked so young—what, fourteen, maybe fifteen, tops? "You can fix it?"

"Maybe." I almost felt sorry for her…and then imagined Angela taking a nosedive off the hospital roof.

"But you're wearing an old rig."

"Yeah, well, I find the old ones are more stable. These new ones are hot, but they need a little extra loving care. Want me to have a look at it?"

She stared at me with fear, distrust, hope, and desperation warring in her eyes. "Yeah, okay, but do it fast." She yanked the rig off her head, pulling out a few golden hairs with it, and handed the rig to me.

"Sure. And ice out. It should just take a sec." I took her silvery-opalescent rig in one hand and slipped my other hand behind my back, to pull a toothpick out of my back jeans pocket. I slid open the panel where the headset widens to get at the command pad. Just like cell phones have always

had, there's a place you can look up the last number dialed. And thanks to hive-girl's desperation, I was pretty sure the six-digit number repeating over and over on the screen was the conf code. I quickly memorized it and the phone number, pretended to tweak some more, then slid the toothpick back in my back pocket, turning off the jammer as I did so. "There ya go. Should be workin' now."

Hive-girl swiftly slipped the rig back on, redialed with her tongue. "Hey? Hey?" I swear tears slid down her cheeks and a smile ten miles wide crossed her face. She jumped up and down and flashed me a high sign before dashing out the bathroom door giddy with joy.

I wasn't sure whether to laugh or puke. Sad thing was, I was jealous.

The room was packed when I came out, and a too-angular-to-be-cute young man was standing at the BrainBomb. "Are you ready to get Beamed?" he teased the crowd.

"Yeah!" they all cheered back as one.

"Headsets on, space cadets. Here comes the noise." He jammed his fist down across his guitar strings. The jangling chord resounded in my brain, filling every neuron. He played a long, trilling riff and I felt his fingers playing the nerves up my spinal column. I blinked in astonishment. The drummer began a rhythm on his bass drum pad that replaced my heartbeat in the center of my chest.

I didn't want to be distracted like this, not when there was information to get and deeds to be done. But the music might make good cover. Before my personality was completely wiped by waves of sound, I tongued in the phone

number of the hive, then, at the prompt, the conf code.

Just in time as another power chord washed through me.

"We're here," I heard Sarah's husky voice rasp amid the music. In my head, as if she spoke from the center of my cerebellum.

—"by the door," said another hive-girl.

—"was waiting so long. What *took* you?"

—"we had take care of—oh!"

Another chord crashed like an ocean wave in a storm. Thoughts flew from my brain and all that was left was the sound. The drums started their pulsing beat again and my body moved, no longer entirely under my control. I swayed and shook, my hair standing on end, my skin tingling. The hive-girls began chanting in my brain, "Yeah . . . yeah . . . yeah," over and over, an affirmation of the high of sound, the high of togetherness, "yeah . . . yeah . . . yeah," they sighed in ecstasy, and it was so good, this oneness filling the void in me, that I began to whisper with them, "yeah . . . yeah . . . yeah," my breath their breath, my words their words.

"Who's there?" Sarah snapped sharply, cutting across the music.

—"Who?"

—"What?"

—"Someone's cutting in . . . I don't know that voice."

—"That girl from the bathroom—"

Oh my God. It took all my will to force my waving arms up to my head to yank off my headset. I began to shake uncontrollably in panic. *How could I be so stupid? How could I?*

The music still reverberated inside me but no longer con-

trolled my limbs. I was able to slip, hunched over, through the writhing, oblivious bodies to the bar. I didn't see any of the hive-girls, so I hoped they couldn't see me. I drank down the last gulps of my beer, trying to calm my nerves. I must have looked like a spastic wreck, but the bartender was so caught up in the music, he didn't care. Desperate to get my brain cells back, after a couple of minutes, as the song the band played was ending, I put my rig in my backpack and slipped out the back door.

A chill northwestern drizzle was falling. I leaned back against the brick wall and let the drops flow down on my face and neck. It felt good, and I could finally think again. Okay, I'd been stupid, but they didn't know who I was. I hadn't learned anything useful about soon-to-be-victim girl. And Sarah was probably going to change the conf code right away. Oh, well, live to fight another day and think of something else. I sighed and stepped away, turned right into the small passageway beside the building.

They were waiting for me. By the few beams of light that escaped the painted windows of the Crazy C, I counted five of them, Blondie on my far right, Sarah in the middle. The others, two black girls and a redhead I recognized from Angela's Spanish class.

"That's her," said Blondie. "The one who fixed my phone."

"Stole our number, you mean," growled the redhead.

"Well, aren't you the clever bitch," said Sarah, striding languidly toward me.

"Let's rip her!" said one of the black girls.

Sarah stopped and held up her right hand.

"She don't do that to you," the black girl protested. "Nobody does that to you. Not and live to tell about it."

I thought hard about running, but I could hear the other black girl circling quietly behind me. I wouldn't get far.

There was a silent pause, which I figured was filled with them sub-voking at one another. Then Sarah tilted her head at me. "Before you receive your just punishment, bitch, I just want to know why. Are you such a loser that you have to hijack other people's hives?"

"I'm here for Angela," I snarled back.

"Angela?" Sarah acted as though she didn't recognize the name.

"You know who she is. You cut her, didn't you? Angela threw herself off a building and now she's *dead,* thanks to you."

"Oh. Angela. She's dead? Oh, I'm *so* sorry." Sarah didn't even try to hide her laughter. She was really enjoying the news.

Blondie chimed in, "Well, Angela was such a waste of skin."

"Pathetic. Better off dead, really," said the redhead.

"Shut up!" I yelled.

"Oh, was Angela a . . . *friend* of yours?" cooed Sarah, as if Angela couldn't possibly have had worthwhile friends.

That's when I reached back behind my jacket with my right hand. Time to give them a taste of their own medicine. And maybe distract them just long enough to have a chance to run away.

"Watch it, she's packing!" said the black girl now in front of me.

"It's not a gun." I sneered at her. My fingers touched the jammer switch.

"Better show us what it is, then, bitch." She grabbed my arm and yanked on it. My fingers scraped across the box, dragging against the booster switch and the volume wheel. I heard the band strike another chord inside the bar. A loud hum erupted in my head that I'm sure didn't come from the band's equipment.

For a moment, Sarah and the hive-girls stood absolutely still. Then their hands flew to their heads, but they didn't take off their rigs. Their knees buckled, and one by one, each girl sank to the ground. Blondie began to twitch as if in the throes of an epileptic fit. Sarah began mewling like a lost, confused kitten, her eyes wide. The other girls were shaking and flailing, too.

I fumbled for precious seconds with the jammer, my hands shaking horribly. Finally I toggled the booster switch and the volume wheel. The hum in my head went away. It was off.

But the girls on the ground didn't get up. Two of them stopped moving altogether. Sarah continued her strange, sick cries. I swallowed hard, and like a gutless coward, I ran. At a gas station I called 911, then I grabbed a bus for home.

Thank God Uncle Ted wasn't in when I got there. I dashed for the bathroom and puked my guts out. I threw the jammer back in the dresser, as if it were hot to the touch. Then I paced and paced the apartment, hugging myself to control my shaking. Then I crawled into bed. When the adrenaline was finally spent, I fell into sleep as fast as falling off a building.

When I woke up, it was already bright morning. I heard a

rustling sound and glanced up. Uncle Ted was standing in the bedroom doorway, staring down at me. I wondered how long he had been there. "Morning," I mumbled.

"I got news," he said, walking farther into my room. He turned his back to me and ran his gaze lightly over the poster-covered walls, the bookshelves. His fingers idly played with a few papers on my desk. As if he were seeing the place for the first time. As if examining a perp's lair.

"What . . ." My voice rasped and I had to clear my throat. "What sort of news?" I sat up, drawing my knees up to my chin beneath the covers.

"You know that Sarah Potosi, the one you thought was a killer hive queen?"

"Yeah?"

"Seems she and four of her hive mates were found in the alley beside the Crazy C last night."

"Is she . . . are they okay?" I really did want to know. And much to my own disgust, I also wanted to know . . . *did they talk?*

"No," Uncle Ted said, leaning heavily on my desk with both hands. He still didn't look at me. "They're not okay. Best as anyone can figure, something went wack with their ESPs. Girls got a huge jolt of RFs right to the brain." He waggled his hands over his ears. "Fried the synapses in their amygdalawhatsis. They got serious memory loss. Some loss of limb control. Worst of all, they got hit in the parts of the brain that deal with sound. They'll be totally deaf the rest of their lives. Not even able to hear their own thoughts, the docs say. Already the parents are screaming lawsuit and lawyers are

circling the hospital like buzzards. It's a crappy thing, but thanks to this there's a chance this whole hive addiction business will be blown into the open."

"Wow." I didn't know what else to say.

His gaze fell on my rig headset hanging out of my backpack on the floor. He snatched up the rig and began to methodically snap the plastic headgear in many places. "You. Will. Not. Ever. Wear. One of these. Again. Understood?"

"Y-yeah, Uncle Ted. Sure. I understand."

Uncle Ted flung the rig in the wastebasket, turned, and walked back to the door, still not meeting my eyes. Pausing in the doorway, he said softly, "You wanted justice, sweetheart. You got it." Then he left, closing the door behind him.

I should have felt righteous joy. I should have pumped my fist in the air, saying "Yes!" Instead, I felt sick to my stomach again, and I curled back up under the covers, hiding my face from the light of day.

A week and a half later, on a miserable May afternoon, I took the ferry from Seattle to Bainbridge. Halfway across, I dropped the jammer into Puget Sound. It didn't make a noise over the hiss of the wake and the rumble of the ferry's engine. I watched the churning water behind the boat as the ferry plowed into the fog ahead. Maybe I wasn't cut out for this girl-detective stuff. Maybe it was time to get some new goals.

I'd tried to tell Uncle Ted what happened, but he made it clear he did not want to hear it. Did he know? Did he not know and not want to know? It made my brain hurt. I wondered if I'd been set up by Cousin Skip. Had he used me to expose Ebisu? Seemed like a long shot to just give me the

jammer and hope for the best. Unless there was something to all this mind control shit . . .

I shook my head as if I could get the memories out of my mind. But they wouldn't leave, playing on endless loop. I could hear Angela saying "Don't leave me!", hear the power chords from the BrainBombs, replay the hive-girls chanting their glorious "yeah . . . ," replay Sarah's mewling as her brain melted down. Replay the stricken tone of Uncle Ted's voice as he told me the news about the hive, and the fact they couldn't hear their own thoughts anymore.

And I've decided that, those girls now living in utter silence? I envy them.

❖❖❖

Kara Dalkey is the author of fifteen novels and a dozen short stories, all fantasy, historical fantasy, or science fiction. Her most recent publications have been *Water,* a trilogy of young adult novels she describes as "the Atlantis and Arthurian myths in a blender." Her short story "The Lady of the Ice Garden," which appeared in *Firebirds,* was selected for the James Tiptree, Jr., Award shortlist. Kara lives in the Pacific Northwest, land of overly caffeinated creative people. On the side, she plays electric bass in an oldies rock band and spends too much time playing computer games.

Author's Note

"Hives" came about as the result of several ideas colliding. The little SF I write tends to be stories about ordinary folk, and how technology may enhance or, more likely, complicate everyday life. "The street finds uses for technology," as the saying goes, but those uses are not always benign.

There's been a lot of attention in the media in recent years on young girls in groups, and how the competition for status in the schoolyard pecking order can damage a girl's psyche. This theme is addressed in such books as *Odd Girl Out* by Rachel Simmons and *Fast Girls* by Emily White, as well as the movie *Mean Girls*.

Cell phones are a technological marvel whose unexpected consequences are showing up all over, from buses becoming rolling phone booths for commuters to the "flash crowds" that a certain candidate made use of in the last presidential pri-

maries. And, of course, cell phone use is growing fast among teenagers, whose need to connect to friends was already well established with old-style landline phones.

Curiously, one study I read about noted that most cell phone calls are not for emergencies, but instead for the most ordinary of communications—just keeping in touch. Like the *baaas* within a herd of sheep, indicating "I'm here. We're all here. It's okay. All's well." Constant reassurance for social creatures is key.

And young girls are intensely social. So for teen girls, especially the shy and awkward, wouldn't it be wonderful, even addictive, to be in constant, voice-in-head-close contact with their friends, their clique, their in-group? It would be like heaven . . . until it stops. And then it's hell.

The additional note of "telepathic sound" was something I came across on the Internet. Given the wide-open range of stuff you find on the Web, all must be taken with a grain of salt until corroborated, but there were enough other references that it carried the whiff of truth, and added a healthy dose of paranoia to the plot.

So all these factors came together in the writing of "Hives." Curiously, not long after I'd finished the first draft of the story, I saw a commercial on TV for A Major Phone Carrier. This ad described a woman setting up a prototype cell network on her home computer. Her teenage daughter notices and asks how it works. Then promptly borrows it to get her friends together for an afternoon outing. Gave me chills. Looks like phone "hives" could be just a few years away. I just hope the dark side of the story doesn't happen, too.

Alan Dean Foster

Perception

Stefan didn't want the assignment to Irelis. He didn't want to work at the Outpost. He'd seen pictures of Irelis, and the Outpost, and the Allawout natives, and found all of them unpleasant in equal measure. But advancing up the company ladder meant climbing the rungs in order. Skipping one now and then, if you were fortunate. For a young apprentice such as himself, Irelis was a rung that couldn't be skipped.

So it was that he found himself installed for a year at the Outpost, a self-contained subdivision of the larger Irelis station set in the middle of a swamp. It could as easily have been anywhere on Irelis except at the poles. Swamp or savanna, take your choice: they were what covered nearly all of Irelis except for the murky, algae-coated oceans. Of the two, the savannas offered the more pleasant prospect, with drier, cooler weather. Unfortunately, humans weren't the only ones who preferred the plains to the swamps. So did the several dozen species of ferocious biting arthropods that

drained body fluids without discriminating between planets of origin.

The Allawout got around the swamps on primitive flat rafts fashioned from fiberthrush and covango saplings fastened together with strong, red looporio vine. Ages ago, some Allawout Einstein had figured out that if you built the rafts with points at both ends, not only would they go faster through the tepid, turgid water, but you wouldn't have to turn them around to reverse direction. That discovery represented the height of Allawout nautical technology. The idea of a sail was beyond them. Ignoring directives that forbade supplying indigenous aliens with advanced knowledge, visiting humans who observed the locals struggling with poles and paddles had taken pity on them and introduced the concept of the rudder, an innovation that the natives readily adopted and for which they were inordinately grateful.

To the Outpost the Allawout brought the pleasures and treasures of the Irelis hinterlands: unique organic gem material; seeds from which exotic spices were extracted; sustainable animal products; barks and resins and flowers from which were derived uniquely unsynthesizable pharmaceuticals; and their own fashionable primitive handicrafts. Widely scattered and hard to find, located in disagreeable, dangerous country, these diverse products of Irelis found their way into the insatiable current of interstellar trade through the good offices of the dirt (literally) poor natives. Everyone benefited, and the Commonwealth government was happy.

Stefan was not happy. He did not quite hate Irelis, but he disliked the place intensely. The swamp, for one. There was

nothing in the way of entertainment. Worst of all was having to work with the locals. None of the Allawout stood taller than a meter in height—if you could call it standing. In the absence of anything resembling legs or feet, it was hard to tell. They slimed their way along, their listless pace in perfect harmony with their sluggish metabolisms. A quartet of narrow but strong tentacles protruded from their cephalopodian upper bodies. These were covered in a fine, hairless, slick skin not unlike that of a frog or salamander. From the center of the upper bulge that was not quite a proper head, two large round eyes marked by crescent-shaped pupils took in the swamp that was their world. They had no external ears, no fur or horns, and wore no clothing. Not that there was much to cover.

When they burbled at one another in their rudimentary, vowel-rich language, bubbles frothed at the corners of their lipless mouths. They had no proper teeth and subsisted on a wide variety of soft plant life, supplementing this with the occasional freshwater mollusk that did not require overmuch chewing. Soon after arriving, Stefan had had the opportunity to see them eat. It was not a pretty sight.

It did not take him long to learn from his three coworkers that the Allawout were as oblivious to human sarcasm as they were to much of the world around them. Making fun of the slow-moving, slow-thinking natives was one of the few spontaneous entertainments available to the Outpost's inhabitants. Except when a supervisor came visiting, it was a sport they indulged in shamelessly, taking care to do so only out of range of the station's largely humorless scientific complement. By the time Stefan's tour of duty was half over, his own personal

file of Allawout jokes had grown as fat as one of the natives.

Not that they were inherently unlikable, he mused as he lazed his way through his daily turn at the trading counter. On his right was a projector that could—magically as far as the Allawout were concerned—generate a three-dimensional, rotatable image of anything in the Outpost's warehouse. Visiting natives who made endless demands of the device simply for its entertainment value soon found themselves cut out of the trade loop. Once word spread among the local clans, this abuse stopped. The Outpost, they learned, was a place in which to conduct serious trade.

The tripartite clan that was now leaving carried between them several parcels sealed in the ubiquitous, biodegradable plastic wrap that was used to package all trade goods. As he watched them depart, Stefan directed the room's air purifier to grade up a notch. Allawout body odor was no more pleasing than their appearance. In a few minutes the atmospheric scrubber would have removed the last lingering traces of the clan's visit.

Pervasatha waited for the cheerful, noisily bubbling family to exit before coming in. Despite his special cooling gear, he was sweating profusely. A number of visiting supervisors and scientists felt that would have been a better name for the planet: Sweating Profusely. It was certainly more descriptive than Irelis IV.

"Got something for you, Stef." Perv, as his friends and coworkers called him, leaned on the counter. The corners of his mouth twitched. He seemed to be striving hard to repress a grin.

"Not another carved Ohrus tooth." Stefan eyed the other young man warily. "They're pretty, but we've already got a boxful."

"Nope. Better than that." The grin escaped its bounds. Perv gestured toward the door. "Enter! Come inside."

A native slid slowly inward on the familiar, disgusting trail of lubricating gunk. Behind it, the floor did its best to clean up after the visitor. Unfeeling mechanical though it was, Stefan still felt sorry for the autocleaner. Unlike the rest of them, it could never look forward to a day off. Not on Irelis.

Perv's grin was wider than ever. "You remember that directive? Not last week's—the one before. Page twelve. 'All company Outposts must strive where possible to encourage local life-forms to participate in the ongoing activities of a given station, with regard to maintaining and enhancing benign relations between the human and native populations.'"

"Yeah," Stefan replied guardedly. "I remember it. So what?" He slapped at his forehead, smashing something small, irritating, and resistant to the cocktail of insecticides that he had liberally applied earlier.

Perv gestured grandly at the newcomer, who was gazing around at the interior of the station with eyes that were even wider than normal. "Meet your new native assistant!"

Stefan blanched, recovered when he thought it was a joke, eyed his friend in disbelief when it began to sink it that it was not. "Don't try to be funny, Perv. It's too hot today."

"And it'll be too hot tomorrow, and the day after that, and the one after that also. But this is still your new assistant. Morey says so."

"Screw Morey!" As if the native were not present, Stefan gestured in its direction. "We don't have indigenous assistants. No local works inside the Outpost."

"We do now," Perv shot back. "They do now."

The other man's eyes narrowed. "Then where's *your* assistant?"

"Regulations say that, at this point in the Outpost's development, we only need one. She's it. She's yours." His smile flattened. "Lack of seniority says so."

"'She'?" A dubious Stefan studied the lumpish native, who continued to ignore the two young humans as she gawked at the interior of the trading room. "I thought the biologists hadn't figured out how to sex them yet."

Perv stood away from the counter. "Far as I know, they haven't. But that's the classification I've been given." He winked and turned to go. "I'll leave you two alone now."

The other man gestured wildly. "Hey, wait a minute! What am I supposed to do with this—with 'her'?"

Perv kept walking. "Not my concern. Morey says she's your new assistant. Get her to assist. Me, I've got work to do on the bromide concentrator or the delay'll go down on my record." He exited at a brisk clip, not looking back.

Stefan was once again alone in the room. Well, not quite.

Maybe if he ignored the native, it would go away. Sitting back down, he muttered the "unpause" command and resumed watching the game he had been engrossed in prior to the trading clan's arrival. Images danced in the air half a meter in front of his eyes. After a while, he became aware that he was not alone. As was often the case, it was the smell that tipped him off.

Advancing silently on its sheet of motive slime, the Allawout had sidled up as close behind him as it dared, and was dutifully gazing up at images whose origin, meaning, and purpose must be as alien to it as tooth gel.

Nostrils flaring in revulsion, he looked over his shoulder and down at the creature. Morey had declared it was his new assistant. Until he could make the notoriously gruff Outpost administrator see reason, Stefan realized with a sinking feeling that he was probably stuck with the creature. (But fortunately, he told himself, not *to* it.) If he abused it physically, there could be trouble. Members of the station's scientific contingent, who infrequently mixed with the much-younger and less experienced team of trader apprentices, would report him. His advancement up the company ladder would be questioned, and he might even be dropped down a rating or two. That could not be allowed to happen. Not after the horrid half year he had already been forced to put in on Irelis.

Swallowing his distaste, he asked in Terranglo, "Do you have a name?"

The dumpy alien quivered as if trying to slough off its skin. Flesh-protecting mucus oozed from pores and slid down its sides. "I am chosen Uluk."

At least it could talk a little, Stefan thought. Come to think of it, the staff would not have selected one to work inside the station, with humans, unless it had acquired at least some facility with the visitors' language. Then something happened that completely broke his train of thought.

Raising a tentacle, the Allawout pointed at the hovering wordplay image and said, "Pretty—what means it?"

It was the first time in nearly six months that Stefan had heard a local ask a question not directly related to trading. Minimal fluency he had expected; intellectual curiosity, if such it could be called, was something new. Without pausing to wonder why he was bothering to reply, he struggled to explain something of the subtle nature of a wordplay.

She did not understand. That was not surprising. Had she comprehended even his childishly simple explanation, he would immediately have passed her along to the scientific staff as an exemplar of Allawout acumen. On the indigenous scale of intelligence, she doubtless qualified as quite bright. About at the level of a human eight-year-old, only without any book learning to draw upon. It was unlikely she would grow any smarter.

But as the months progressed, she did. Or at least, her vocabulary increased. Struggling with the most fundamental concepts, she did everything he asked of her, from laboriously dragging trade goods into the back chamber to be sorted, cataloged, prepriced, and packaged for shipment off-world to making suggestions to visiting locals about what goods the strange dry-skin folk preferred and would pay well for.

It was funny to see how the other natives deferred to her. Even mature males, thick of tentacle and sharp of eye, seemed to shrink slightly in her presence. For a wild moment he thought she might be some kind of local equivalent of royalty, much as the notion of an Allawout princess seemed a contradiction in terms. Belleau Lormantz, one of the xenologists, assured him that could not be the case.

"In the nearly twenty years there has been a human

presence on Irelis, no evidence has surfaced of any level of government above that of the extended family or clan. They haven't even achieved the tribal level yet. They're just starting to emerge from the hunter-gatherer stage." Belleau had a nice voice, Stefan mused. About the nicest voice on Irelis. And unlike most of the scientists, she was nearly the same age as he was.

They were sitting together on one of the elevated walkways built atop balumina pilings that had been driven down through water and muck into the reluctant bedrock far below. Irelis's sun, redder than that of his homeworld, was setting behind red and yellow fiberthrush, the light peeking through the fronds to illuminate the station's sealed-together, prefabricated modules. Belleau was almost as reflective as the metal walls, he decided.

A voice sounded behind them, plaintive yet insistent. "Stef-han, what should I do with kaja bowls just buying today?"

He looked around irritably. "They go in the back, on the bottom shelves on the right-hand side. You know that, Uluk!"

Her tone did not change, and she had no expression to alter. "Yes, Stef-han. I will make it so." It took her several minutes to slip-slide back inside.

He returned to contemplating the sunset, the violet underside of the evening cumulus filling his head with thoughts that did not belong in as unpleasant a place as the Outpost.

"I hear that you're leaving the station."

She nodded. "Sabbatical. On Rhenoull V. To consolidate my reports, put some into book form, give lectures—that sort of thing. I think I'll be back, to start in on my advanced work.

There's a lot about these creatures we still don't know."

"Is there that much more to learn?" When she did not comment, he added, "How do I know you're coming back, Belle?"

"Because I say so. Because my work is here."

He peered deep into her eyes. Perspiration glistened on her forehead and cheeks. She was wet, tired, unkempt, and beautiful. "Is that the only reason?"

She turned away from him, to the sunset. "I'm not sure—yet," she replied candidly. "I like you, Stefan. I like you a lot. But I'm so deep into my work that much of the time I feel like I'm drowning."

"Drown in me," he told her with more intensity than he intended.

Her hand slipped sideways to cover his. "Maybe when I come back," she told him frankly. "When I have more confidence in my own future. Then, maybe—we'll see. You're a little young for me, Stefan."

"I'm not that young." When he reached for her, she leaned away, laughing affectionately.

"No, not now. As sweaty as we are, if we hold each other too tightly, we're liable to slip right past each other and into the water."

He laughed, too, and settled for squeezing her hand, and waiting for the alien sun to finish its day's work.

He sweated out another six months, her absence made all the more frustrating by his having to deal with Uluk. Just when it seemed she was acquiring some real skill, she would do something supremely stupid. He was forced to reprimand

her, sigh in exasperation, and explain the procedure all over again. She would listen patiently, indicate understanding, go along fine for a while, and eventually repeat the same mistake. Something about the Allawout seemed to render them incapable of retaining any pattern of information for more than a few weeks at a time. It was as if the entire species was afflicted with Attention Span Deficit Disorder.

To make matters worse, he had to endure the endless jokes and gags the rest of the staff enjoyed at his expense. His only compensation was the occasional reluctant, approving grunt from Administrator Morey, who recognized the strain his most junior employee was operating under, plus praise from the scientific staff. The behaviorists in particular would seek him out to query him endlessly about his conversations with the Allawout.

"Look," he would object in exasperation, "we don't have 'conversations.' I give the thing orders, and she carries them out. Except when she forgets what to do, which is all the time, and I have to explain them all over again. Slowly and repeatedly, in the simplest terms possible."

"But within those constraints," a much older xenologist had pressed him, "the native in question *is* capable of performing the complex tasks she is assigned by you."

"Sure," he said, "if you can call stacking carvings and sorting voull horns 'complex.' Anything that involves actually thinking I have to guide and help her with. Initiative doesn't exist among the Allawout. Except when it involves food and shelter, I personally don't think they have any understanding of the concept."

"Yet the other locals obviously respect her deeply," the persistent scientist had insisted.

"Sure!" Stefan agreed. "She's big stuff because she has a job in the House-of-Wonders-That-Stands-in-Water, and speaks freely to the visitors from the cloud rafts. I suppose," he conceded, "that gives her some kind of rank, or status, that raises her up a notch or two above her fellow weed munchers." A few such carefully chosen comments were usually sufficient to send the behaviorists on their contemplative way, muttering to themselves.

One nice thing about Stefan's assistant, as far as Morey was concerned, was that the native never questioned her status. She accepted payment in trade goods, never asked for a change in the amount or kind of remuneration, worked silently and steadily, and was a real help in communicating the wants of the human traders to the natives. She slept in an old concentrate barrel Perv had welded to one of the balumina stilts, just above the waterline. Each morning she would ooze out of the plastic cylinder, drop into the water to clean herself, and then squirm up the ramp that had been erected to provide her kind with easy access to the station. With their strong tentacles the Allawout could easily climb a ladder, but that would not allow them to bring goods into or take them out of the Outpost.

Stefan had despaired of ever seeing Belleau again. Then one day, slightly less than a month before his tour was up and he was due to be promoted off-world, suddenly she was there, having arrived without notice on the monthly shuttle. They did not exactly fall into each other's arms—not with Customs officials and everyone else watching. But their eyes met, spoke,

and smiled. Certain decisions were reached without the use of words.

"I told you I'd come back," she whispered to him later that morning.

"To resume your work?" He left the question hanging, too fearful to add the other question he was burning to ask.

"To do that, yes—and perhaps," she added mischievously, "to attend to other matters."

"I'm finished here in a few weeks." They were standing in the Outpost, its familiar hothouse surroundings for once the equal and not the excess of what he was feeling inside. "The Company has offered me promotion from apprentice and my choice of positions. On civilized worlds, at a proper salary. I have a lot of flexibility."

"Hmm. That does open certain possibilities, doesn't it? For example, I've taken a lectureship on Mathewson III."

His expression did not change. "There are two Company operations on Mathewson. Big ones."

She nodded thoughtfully. Then she leaned forward, kissed him once, adequately, and almost ran from the room. He remained behind, dazed and relieved and overflowing with satisfaction.

Behind him, a familiar odor preceded a question. "Stef-han is happy?"

His expression fell. The wondrous contentment rushed away like water out of the bottom of a broken jar.

"Yes, Uluk. Stefan happy. Stefan go away soon."

"Go away?" Crescent pupils swam within disk-like eyes. "Why Stef-han go away?"

"It's time to go," he muttered irritably. "All sky folk eventually go from Irelis. Go back to home." At her uncomprehending silence he added, "Back to own home-raft."

She considered this. "Outpost not Stef-han's raft?"

"No, dammit. Don't you have something to do?"

"Yes. I forget."

Lifting his eyes heavenward, he moved to check the duty scan for the day. But nothing, not even Allawout dullness, could entirely diminish the joy of Belle's return.

The next several weeks passed in a haze that was more a consequence of his reestablishing his relationship with Belleau than of the heavy atmosphere. They spoke of her science and his business, and how the two might complement each other on a world like Mathewson III. When it was clear that the positives outweighed the negatives, their delight was mutual. Though young, they were both very practical people.

When it was time to go, to finally leave behind Irelis and its miasmatic swamps, bug-ridden savannas, melancholy atmosphere, and multifarious stinks and smells, it was almost an anticlimax. Complaining a little less than usual, Administrator Morey was there to see them both off and to wish them well. The grumpy old Company man was unable to look his former apprentice in the face for fear of giving way to an actual smile. Pervasatha was long gone, having been promoted ahead of Stefan, but several others among the scientific and commercial community who had established friendships with the personable young trader on his way up turned out to see the two of them off.

They were waiting for the skimmer that would ferry them

out to the distant shuttle site, an artificial island built out in the middle of a spacious lake, when it occurred to Stefan that something was missing. A certain—stench.

"Funny," he mused aloud, "I thought she'd come to say good-bye."

"'She?'" Belleau's tentative tone mimicked one he himself had used some time ago.

"My native assistant. An Allawout named Uluk. You met her. Or at least, you encountered her."

"Oh yes, of course. I only saw her a couple of times. She was usually working in the rear storeroom whenever I came into the Outpost."

He found himself searching the station's walkways, then the grubby muck below. "I thought she'd be here." He shrugged. "Oh well. No matter. She probably forgot." Turning back to Belleau, he smiled affectionately. "After a year here I don't know how I'll cope with a normal, Earth-type climate."

"I give you about two days to become fully acclimated," she replied softly.

Henderson came huffing and puffing down the walkway. Reaching out, the panting behaviorist caught his breath as he shook first the apprentice's hand, then Belleau's. "Wanted to wish luck to you both. I'm sure you won't need it."

Stefan nodded his thanks, looked past the scientist. "Say, you haven't by any chance seen Uluk around today?" He hesitated slightly. "I sort of . . . wanted to say good-bye."

"Your native assistant?" Henderson's expression fell. "Oh. I thought you knew. They found her yesterday, about half a kilo-

meter from the station. On Islet Twelve. Dead. Self-inflicted killing wound, the biologists tell me. Sorry."

A very strange feeling tightened in the younger man's gut. The longer he thought about it, the worse it got. "That's—too bad. I wonder what happened."

Henderson cast a quick glance in Belleau's direction before replying. Though much younger, she was a fellow scientist, after all, and the incident was an interesting comment on indigenous behavioral patterns.

"You really didn't know, did you? No, you wouldn't, always paying attention to commerce, and trade balances, and the like. An Allawout's individual focus is on its extended clan. Alpha males and females, Beta juniors, and so on. Didn't you ever notice that Uluk was never seen interacting with a family grouping?"

Stefan looked blank. "You're right, I didn't. But I never thought about it. She lived at the station. That was her choice. Mr. Morey, myself, everyone else—we all thought that was her choice."

"Oh, it was, it was," Henderson hastened to assure him. "I spoke to her several times, you know. As part of my work," he added almost apologetically. "You didn't realize that instead of one of her own kind, she had chosen to focus on *you*?"

The apprentice eyed the behaviorist uncertainly. "On me? Why would I notice something like that?"

Belleau's response was more understanding. "Are you saying that this Uluk individual chose to imprint herself on Stefan in lieu of a normal Allawout extended family grouping?"

"They worked together. Almost every day." Henderson looked apologetic as he regarded the younger man. "I thought surely you would have perceived something, or I would have mentioned it to you. It makes for a very interesting case history."

Stefan swallowed hard. "You're not saying that in some crazy kind of way she got, uh, attached to me, or anything weird like that?" In his mind he conjured up an image of the misshapen, slimy alien. But for some reason, it did not repulse him quite as much as it once had.

He found himself scanning the vegetation of the distant, fetid swampland. He remembered how Uluk had hovered about him, lingering in his vicinity even when her work was done; watching him operate the projector and the viewers; asking questions to which he was sure she already knew the answers. How she was always there waiting for him in the mornings, and leaving reluctantly when it was time for her to retire to her barrel under the Outpost.

He thought about how he had treated it—her—with casual indifference, even contempt. Memories of the time he had spent in her company came flooding back to him. They did not make him feel better. Surely he wasn't—responsible. He forced himself to ask as much.

Henderson considered. "Your announcement that you were leaving, permanently, no doubt came as a shock. In the absence of any other extended family connection, it's not uncommon for an Allawout to opt for self-termination instead of attempting to impose himself on another family or clan."

"You're saying," Belleau ventured, "that what happened was something like a dog pining away for its master?"

"Well, hardly." Henderson drew himself up slightly. "The Allawout may be a little slow on the uptake, but they're far from unaware." He turned back to the suddenly silent, staring apprentice. "It's not your fault, you know. Happens all the time with these clans. Self-termination is a well-documented means of controlling the population and maintaining the available food supply."

"Oh, I know." Stefan pushed away the sad thoughts. "It's too bad. She was nice enough—except for the smell. I can't help it if she was somehow attracted to one of the 'sky people.' To me." The oddest sensation was spreading through him. It made him angry, but try as he might, he found he could not suppress it.

"'Attracted'?" Henderson stared at him. "You really *didn't* perceive much, did you? Uluk wasn't 'attracted' to you. We spoke about many such things, and I remember quite clearly that she told me once she thought you were the ugliest living thing she had ever set eyes upon. Even uglier than any of the other humans she had met. *That's* why she stayed at the Outpost so long, and close to you. She felt it was something she needed to do. And then when you ignored her, and what she was doing for you, I guess she felt that all her efforts on your behalf were being rejected."

"Rejected?" Stefan frowned. "'Doing for *me*'? I was tolerating *her.* What did she think she was 'doing' for me?"

Wiping his eyes, the behaviorist blinked back the unforgiving rays of the setting violet sun. "She didn't stay close to you because she was attached to you, Stefan. She stayed because she felt sorry for you."

Alan Dean Foster has recently published his one hundredth book. His wide-ranging writing career includes excursions into hard science fiction, fantasy, horror, detective, western, historical, and contemporary fiction. His short fiction has appeared in all of the major science fiction magazines as well as in original anthologies and several "Best of the Year" compendiums. Six collections of his short-form work have been published.

Foster's love of the far away and exotic has led him to travel extensively. He has camped out in the "Green Hell" region of the southeastern Peruvian jungle, photographing army ants and pan-frying piranha (lots of small bones; tastes a lot like trout); has ridden forty-foot whale sharks in the remote waters off western Australia; and was one of three people on the first commercial air flight into northern Australia's Bungle Bungle National Park. He has rappelled into New Mexico's fabled Lechugilla Cave, white-water-rafted the length of the Zambezi's Batoka Gorge, driven solo the length and breadth of Namibia, crossed the Andes by car, sifted the sands of unexplored archaeological sites in Peru, gone swimming with giant otters in Brazil, and surveyed remote Papua New Guinea and West Papua both above and below the water. His filmed footage of great white sharks feeding off South Australia has appeared on both American television and the BBC.

Alan Dean Foster and his wife live in Prescott, Arizona.

Visit his Web site at **www.alandeanfoster.com**.

AUTHOR'S NOTE

It's bad enough growing up without being one of the "in" kids. Not popular, not with it, not invited to parties, etc. What's even worse is being treated as though you don't exist. Having the boy or girl you worship from afar totally ignore you in the halls, in class, or out on the street. Sometimes all you want from someone is an acknowledgment that you're alive. A polite word or two would be fine . . . just a smile and a "hello" or "how you doin' today?"

But what happens when that special someone does acknowledge you . . . only not with a smile or a greeting, but with contempt. As if the world would be a better place if you didn't exist, because that person thinks you're too dumb, too ugly, or simply too not in the know to be worthy of anything less than a casual insult.

Life can be heartless.

Something to keep in mind when we start exploring the universe, lest we find another species out there that looks at us the way the captain of the football team or the head cheerleader looks at you.

Tanith Lee

THE HOUSE ON THE PLANET

PLANET DATE: YEAR 3

Part One—Pioneers: Zelda

The journey, even with FLJ,* took over three months. But the ship was okay. Lots of places to roam around, a huge game room with everything from flyball to Computace, a movie theater, and a solar garden that, if you didn't think too much about it, did just about resemble someone's really wonderful backyard.

Then they landed.

Zelda looked at the spaceport—bleak and windswept, with cold-eyed buildings.

The sky was green.

Oh, God.

"Tell me again why you wanted to come?"

"Oh, Zelda." Moth and Dad, exasperated.

The transport raced over rolling hills too fast to see a thing.

"When'll we *get* there?" sang Joe.

* Fast Light Jump

"Soon, honey."

"No, but *when*?"

Joe grinned secretly at Zelda. He was eight now. He only acted up to be annoying.

"One hour exactly. In fact"—Dad checked the speed monitor—"fifty-seven minutes."

Joe went back to his laptop game.

Zelda, who was fourteen, repeated her own unanswered question: "Why are we here?"

"It's an opportunity, the chance of a lifetime, Zel," said Dad. "We explained, didn't we? A whole new world to open up. Aren't you the least bit excited?"

"*I'm* excited!" sang Joe noisily.

Zelda thought of home, the whitewashed house on Anchor Street, of the sunny town, of saying good-bye to her friends at school, who had looked at her with a mixture of awe, jealousy, and sorrow. Zelda—off to another planet. Amazing Zelda, lucky Zelda, Zelda-who-was-doomed. Zelda thought of a *blue* sky.

"It'll be great," said Moth.

"Try to enjoy yourself," said Dad.

"Are we there yet?" added Joe.

They lived, ate and slept in the transport while the machines built the house. (The transport, unlike the ship, was cramped.)

Their robot, Plod, oversaw the building, now and then coming to Dad with a query—where the yard trees should go, how many windows in the kitchen, and so on.

Joe *liked* Plod. He tagged along with the seven-foot, gray, two-headed, four-handed metal man, asking endless ques-

tions. Plod never grew tired of Joe. Well. Plod was a robot.

Zelda, when not engaged in chores, sat on the stoop of the transport, looking narrowly at the view.

"Isn't it *beautiful,* Zelda?"

"Yes, Moth. I suppose." Was it? Or ugly?

"Oh, *Zelda.*"

The hills were behind the house. Machines were already out front, marking out the plan of fields and orchards, fencing in the herd animals that had arrived one day by helejet. The animals were *planet* animals. Dad thought they were terrific, Moth thought they were very big, Joe thought they were fascinating. Zelda stood at the neat white fence and stared.

"What *are* they? Are they supposed to be *cows*?"

"Tappuls. A type of bovine animal, yes."

The tappuls, one hundred in number, were each about the size of a small adult Earth elephant. They were brown, with large brown eyes, and long yellow horns. They could be machine-milked, and the milk was both calcium-rich and thick with benign amino acids. The tappuls had a heavy smell, not nasty but—weird.

"They're very docile, Zelda."

I'm docile, Zelda thought morosely. *I'm* spineless. *I let you bring me here against my will.*

There were other planet animals. The newly planted fields were soon full of plays, which looked like rabbits with one single upright ear. Unlike rabbits, they did little damage to the crops. In fact, their droppings gave useful natural fertilizer. Joe liked the plays. He kept trying to catch one as a pet.

"Suppose it bites you?" Zelda snapped at him.

"Wouldn't matter. They're not poisonous."

"How do you know? Everything here could be. Even the air could be full of some poison the machines just don't recognize. We may all get sick, or evaporate, or turn into mush."

Having said that, watching his bright face crunch up, she felt sorry in case she'd really scared him.

But then he poked out his tongue at her. "Balls," said Joe, as he was *never* allowed to.

Day followed day, and night followed night. Same old thing.

They moved into the new house with its wide, airy rooms and brilliant self-cleaning, shockproof glass windows. Moth and Dad hung up the new white drapes.

"Doesn't it look fine?"

Chilly evenings, they lit the self-renewing pine logs on the big stone hearth.

"It's really getting to be homey now."

Outside in the darkness, strange things whiffled and chattered, just as they did by day. But here, the birds sang all night.

There were no dangerous animals in the region. Even if there had been, the fences and the house area walls had infallible devices for keeping any bad problems out.

In every window, the rolling blue hills, the rolling blue plain dotted with fields of white or red alien grain, with trees that would make pink and orange fruits and were already covered with pink and staring purple blossom. Machines roved, walking the land. Above, the green sky, lit by a sun that was not the sun of Earth. And at night, a green-black sky, lit by two tiny moons. Even the stars were wrong.

One night, Zelda dreamed she flew out over the hills. In the dream she didn't mind them so much. When she woke, the dream disgusted her.

"You'll be at school soon," said Dad, riding in on the cultivator machine, so cheerful Zelda wanted to hit him.

"That'll be *so* nice."

"Now, why be sarcastic? Lots of new friends to make."

"I liked my old friends."

Dad frowned and swung off the machine. He came over and stroked her hair. "It takes a while for the Ipsi-mail* to come through. You'll have some letters soon."

"It's been over a month, Dad."

"Well . . . I guess maybe . . . "

"They don't know what to say to me. I don't either, Dad."

He sat beside her on the porch. She could smell the three Earth trees that had been planted in the yard, especially the pine—if she shut her eyes she could pretend. But what was the use? If she opened them, the truly blue hills reached to the truly green sky. The sun was sinking in the front, over the fields, turning the hills to a mauve as raucous as a loud noise.

"Honey, look. You know how tight money was. We tried to tell you. We couldn't have kept going—we'd have had to move—take some tiny apartment in the city—my firm folded, I'd lost my job, Zelda, remember? And then this opportunity—government sponsored—perfect . . ."

"Yeah, Dad. It's okay."

"I know it isn't, honey. Not for you. Not yet."

* Interplanetary Satellite Intercommunication

"I'll get used to it," said Zelda grimly.

Dad sighed, and went into the house, and again, seeing his bowed head, she was sorry. Till she heard him laughing with Moth at the stove.

In two years I'll be sixteen. I'll take some kind of job—who needs college? I'll save. I'll catch the first ship out I can. I'll go home.

If only the night birds would shut up. They sat on the trees along the wall, even came in and sat on the Earth trees in the yard below Zelda's window. *Twindle-twindle tweety trrr*, they went. "Our own nightingales," Moth had said, pleased. But their song was thin, like wires in Zelda's ears.

She put in her music plugs not to hear the birds.

Tomorrow the house transport would run her to the school in the nearby town. It was, by Earth measurement, miles and miles away, but the transport would get her there in twenty minutes. She dreaded it

The planet had no human life other than the human life that, for the past three years, had come here from Earth. Moth and Dad were two of the last batch of "settlers" who had taken up the government's offer to help develop the land. Everyone else at school would have been here a *long* time.

Aliens. Like everything else.

I'd run away, but where'd I go? There's only here now.

In sleep, one of the music plugs was dislodged. In sleep, she began to hear the *twindle-twindle* birds. In sleep, she threw stones at them, which, awake, she never would have done. In sleep, anyhow, she missed.

⊠ ⊠ ⊠

Joe dissolved in tears when Zelda started to leave for school. Astonished, they all stood gawping at him.

"What's wrong, baby?" cried Moth, trying to resist gathering him into her arms.

"Zelda!" wailed Joe. "Don't wan' Zelda go!"

"But, honey—she has to—"

"She don' wanna!" yodeled Joe, absurd, funny, heartbreaking. "Don' make 'er—"

Zelda stepped forward. She just knew how ashamed he would be of this in ten minutes' time. She grabbed him by the shoulders.

"I *do* want to, you pest. Do you think I want to hang around here all day with *you*? And where's that stupid play rabbit thing you promised to catch for us? When I get back tonight you'd better have caught one—or two, that'd be better. Get two, Joey. If you think you *can*."

Joe stared at her. The tears dried on his face in the heat of his fury. "What ya bet, huh?"

"Ten Earth bucks."

"Zelda!" shrieked Moth. Dad restrained her, grinning.

"You are *on,*" snarled Joe.

Zelda swept into the house transport and was whisked away.

She thought of Dad, his face so pale when he'd first told them he'd lost his job. She thought of Moth, being so determined to make the best of it. And Joey, always ready for something new. And herself, Zelda, sticking tight, refusing to move an inch.

She had never felt so alone. She couldn't even talk about her feelings now, in case she upset Joe. She just hated it when

he cried. She would have to pretend from now on everything was fine, just fine.

Zelda pretended.

She pretended she hadn't dreaded the school, had been looking forward to it. She marched in, looking coolly pleased. When spoken to, she was friendly. She absorbed all the new instructions, the new schedule, gazed at the subjects of the classes, pinned on her grade badge, did what everyone else did. At lunchtime she went into the school yard, which was absolutely an alien garden. On the soft blue grass court, she played flyball with a girl called Patty. They were both pretty good.

"What color would you say this grass is?" Patty asked as they ate their food under a tree like a giant zucchini.

"Blue?"

"What shade of blue?"

"Well—kind of dark blue—"

"*I'd* say," said Patty, "it's the shade of Todd Ariano's eyes."

"Who?"

"Look. Over there."

Zelda looked. Just then Todd Ariano looked back at them and smiled.

Patty was totally right.

The planet grass was Todd-Ariano's-eyes blue.

Zelda kept on pretending. She pretended very hard. She pretended to Dad and Moth and Joe. At school and at home. Indoors and out. Even to Plod, she pretended. "Listen, Plod! Those birds are really singing today!"

It grew easier. Like something she'd wear on her wrist, at first too tight, loosening up over time.

She joined the chess club and the drama club at school and the flyball team. Patty did, too. So, for that matter, did Todd Ariano. Why not? It was okay.

She thought about home—that was, the house on Anchor Street, which they would have had to leave anyhow. And about the town and the big city they'd have to have moved to, crowded, often dangerous, alarms going off and sirens every place, and police cordons. She thought of the blue sky of Earth that could also turn gray or yellow with heat and pollution. She thought of Dad, tired and sullen, Moth looking angry or sad. Joey had always been the happiest there, maybe—but Joey hadn't made any fuss at all. He'd just said, "When are we going?" and gone to pack his games and toys.

Zelda had started to notice some things, almost as if she hadn't seen them before.

How not only was the grass the color of Todd Ariano's eyes but the purple blossom was like raspberry Jell-O, or sometimes violets.

The new town was clean and painted in different colors, too, hot colors and refrigerated colors.

Here and there Earth plants, which had been put in a year or so ago, were beginning to grow to great height, glossy-leaved, liking the soil, and the sun that was always warm, never too hot.

"This place is like heaven, my mother says," admitted Todd as a group of them walked to the transport bay.

"Heaven?"

"Yeah, I know. Mom uses words like that. But I like it here."

"Me, too," said Zelda, pretending, since now she must never say, except to her own heart, that she *didn't* like the planet.

"Wait till you see the wild roses in the spring," said Todd, truly surprising her. "But, you know, there's something even better."

"What?"

"The new ice-cream place on the corner of Foundation."

Zelda sat and thought in the window of her room, too.

She wondered why there was no humanlike life, no so-called Higher Intelligent life here.

This, so far, had been common to all the planets discovered, which was why, apparently, it was all right to colonize them. Earth had gotten so small, so crammed with people. There had to be somewhere else to go.

Earth.

The sunset touched the hills. Mauve.

Zelda glared at the color. Outside, the *twindle-twindle* birds twittered and trilled.

A couple of plays were actually *playing* in the backyard, closely watched by Joe. He crept toward them. Zelda could see from the angle of the two single upright ears that they knew exactly what he was doing, but they let him get way close before they darted off under the gap in the fence Joe had made to lure them in. There they went, along the outer wall and through the gate—Zelda laughed. She guessed her ten bucks were still safe.

A few months more, she'd be fifteen.

I can wait. Fifteen, sixteen—then she could start to get ready to go—home.

The rains came, and high winds, and Zelda stayed at the house, doing schoolwork through the compulink.

In the evenings she saw how the twindle birds sat out, soaking and beak-dripping, in the cover of the stout planet trees by the wall. They still bravely sang, through wind and rain, *twindle-twindle tweety trrr.*

"Moth—do you think we should put out some food for them? They look so—*wet.*"

They put out food for the twindle birds. (Their real name was auxicaps—"twindle" was much better.) The birds fed, and fluttered around the yard. They never left droppings. Apparently they only ever had to—er—*drop* stuff about once every five or six days, so you were unlucky if it fell on you or the lawn.

It was that day when Zelda stopped hearing them. Worried, she glanced out the window. Then she could see—and hear—they still sang. She had simply stopped hearing it, unless she listened.

An Ipsi-mail torrent of letters to Zelda fell into the home computer as the torrents of rain drummed down. She answered them slowly, carefully. Everyone wanted to know everything—the way the planet was, the animals, the people. Zelda sat for hours, telling them, telling them all about it. Describing the colors, the moons, the sky.

Outside in the sheets of rain, the huge forms of the tap-

puls grazed and slowly moved, unconcerned, calm. Several had new calves.

Joe, unable to hunt plays in the weather, sat drawing up battle plans of capture. He and Plod—or, rather, Plod with Joe jumping around him—had already constructed a large, luxurious enclosure for the one-eared rabbits.

Seeing Joe hunched over his plans, just after she and Todd had read through their parts for the drama club on the voice-view link, Zelda said, "Joey—thanks."

"What? Thanks 'cause I didn't catch a play yet and cost ya ten bucks? Just wait."

"No. Thanks for caring about me."

"You?" he asked with utter scorn.

The wind and rain faded back up into the sky. The world was glassy and clear, smelling of salad and flowers.

Zelda walked between the fields, the wet, Todd's-eyes-blue grass tinkling with a few last cascades, the grain heavy in the head, tall now as any corn in the fields of Earth.

That night, her ears unstoppered by the music plugs, sleeping, Zelda heard the twindle birds singing again. She was glad they sang. Why shouldn't they?

She thought, in her sleep, *See, there* is *a poison in the air. It makes you* like *this place even when you hate it.*

In the dream, she flew up above the plain once more, gazing at the house below, lit not by moonlight but by the sunset. How—*beautiful* it was after all, the light of the sun on the faces of the house and the hills, not lurid, but a color like lavender.

Zelda flew over the dream hills. She watched the dream moons rise, one, two. She looked at the clever pattern of the stars.

Next week I'll be fifteen.

Only one more year then before she could begin to think about leaving the planet. She could get through it. Just a year.

Down in the dream she swooped, to peer into the house. She saw Moth and Dad and Joe sitting watching an old classic movie, *Pirates of the Caribbean*. Joe nearly *had* caught a play today. Better save her money.

She thought, *I'm dreaming this. It's so real. It's like—home.*

Something in the air, she thought.

In her sleep, she smiled, and turned over.

Outside the twindle birds sang solemnly on through the night.

PLANET DATE: YEAR 31
Part Two—Present Tense: Harrington

In the end the farmers on the plains made their money and moved away. Some went back to Earth, but most went to the great cities that now stood proudly up on the planet. Meanwhile, the little towns swelled. New streets bloomed and ran like vines. Stretching out over the plains and hills, they closed around the solitary houses of the first pioneers, turned their farmlands to parks and neat backyards, enclosed everything in neighborhoods.

The house stood on Pine Street now. On either side were other houses, and across the street Pioneer Park, with a fine view of the overhead train.

A nice area. Good to bring up kids.

Their mother had thought that, Harrington guessed, when she and Pop bought the house eight years ago. Mom usually went by "Annie," now that Harrington had turned fifteen. Pop, though, had ceased to have a name or to be Pop. He'd left them one month after they'd moved in.

Then eventually there had been Annie's other guy.

Harrington—thirteen back then—hadn't liked the Guy much. But he was soon gone, though he'd left behind a souvenir.

Harrington looked at it now, this keepsake of Annie's sudden short love affair.

It was crawling along the rug, looking adorable. Harrington wanted to throw up.

Its real name was Jasselly. It couldn't speak even, not

properly, not yet. A girl who was almost two, Annie's second daughter, Harrington's sister.

"Oh, Harry—couldn't you have kept an eye on her?"

"I have to practice piano, don't I?"

"Yes—but—oh—come here, baby baa-baa," cooed Annie, scooping the crawling atrocity off the floor.

Annie didn't—*couldn't*—see, apparently, that Harrington did not care about It, that frankly, if It had crawled right out the front door and away down the block, Harrington would not have been exactly *upset*. She knew she *should* be. But why tell yourself lies?

It was a pain.

"When I think," said Annie, rocking the object, "buying this house—do you remember?"

"Not much. I was seven."

"And their daughter was married—I remember the live-view showing it—what was her name? She's a writer—Zelda, that's it. Zelda Ariano—she married the male flyball champion . . . And the son, what was he doing? A naturalist with Government Survey. No wonder they all moved away to someplace more fancy. But it was so lucky for us. The house going so cheap and all—"

"Yeah, we were really lucky. We moved in, Pop moved out, you got together with that Guy and we ended up with *It*—" All this was under Harrington's breath as she began to let loose rills of Chopin from the piano.

Annie put It back in the enclosure.

Really, the enclosure was like the ones the plays had, Harrington thought.

They had two plays, mostly to amuse It, though Harrington

was quite fond of them, too. They were very affectionate and intelligent for one-eared rabbits, and you could let them roam free outside when they wanted, like cats. Unlike cats, they did no damage, though the people next door always seemed to think they would.

Not *It*, though. *It* must not roam free. *It* had to be protected.

Which was why the Hedge was coming today.

"It's so clever," said Annie. She didn't mean the baby, but the Hedge, or what the Hedge could do.

"Sure, Annie."

"What are you playing so loud?" cried Annie as Jasselly started to wail.

"Chopin, Mom. 'The Funeral March.'"

"You'd never know it wasn't real, would you, Mrs. Riveras?"

Mrs. Riveras stared through the eyehole in the Hedge.

"No, Annie. It sure blocks out the sun like it's real. I'd a thought you had enough big things growing in there already with that pine tree."

"Well, the Hedge is only for one hour in the morning and one in the late afternoon."

"I guess that'll have to be okay, then."

"What we agreed, Mrs. Riveras."

Mrs. Riveras frowned. She was a thin old woman with a bitter face. She didn't think much of Annie, and she lived right next door. On the other side were Mr. and Mrs. Oplough. When Annie had explained to them about getting the Hedge, they had both peered at her as if she were crazy.

"It ain't allowed," said Mr. Oplough. "No way on Earth."

He had cackled at his joke. He had been an engineer ten years back; now he was retired and he knew his rights.

"Twelve meters high, you say?" quavered Mrs. Oplough. "Virgil, that's thirty-nine feet, isn't it?"

"Yes," said Virgil Oplough, scowling.

"Just from nine till ten in the morning," pleaded Annie. "Then just four till five. It's to keep the baby safe."

"Babies!" snorted Virgil. "Some folks don't know when to call it a day with babies."

But it was nearly impossible to insult Annie when she was trying to be sweet.

Harrington had watched from the back door. She'd wanted to shout at Mr. Oplough. Yes, even though all this fuss was for *It*.

Now the Hedge had been put in. That had taken all morning, with the soft but intrusive buzz of subsaws and whine of electrasonics. The neighbors hadn't liked that, and the Oploughs had come out to squawk *How long would this racket go on?*

When the Hedge was installed, Annie hit the button to bring it alive.

The Hedge stayed invisible, and in fact actually not *there*, when it was switched off. Switched *on*, it leaped instantly into being. Thirty-nine feet of darkest green-blue foliage, so dense there were the preordered peepholes to see through. Among the mat wove the *appearance* of wild planet roses the color of strawberries, and Earth-type ivy. Then Mrs. Riveras's face had appeared, unroselike, in the little hole nearest the house. (At the same moment Harrington heard, on the Oplough

side, a door open, a gasp gasped, and a door slammed.)

"Only two hours a day," sweet-talked Annie. "Mrs. Riveras—there'll even be days it won't be on at all."

"I'm timing you, Annie," said Mrs. Riveras, worryingly. "I'll keep track of your hours. If you go over time—"

"I won't. I promise."

Harrington wanted to throw something at Mrs. Riveras, too. Yes, even though, again, it was all for *It*.

The Hedge was a molecule construct, one of the latest things, and had cost two thousand IPU dollars,* which they couldn't afford. But what the heck.

Harrington had to admit she was quite impressed.

There was *really* nothing there but airwaves, and the original low fence, just reinforced slightly to stop the plays straying into the neighbors' yards, and the plays preferred to go to the park anyhow. Yet when that button was pressed, the Hedge towered, casting a rich green shadow, cool and safe, for the baby to crawl out of the direct sunlight, and with no apparent way for her to get out. Or anything else to get in. The Hedge *felt* of hedge, too. If you touched it, it felt real—leaves, roses. They even had a scent. The Hedge felt as if you couldn't push through it—it resisted, held you back. It seemed to do that with the sun, too—though in fact there was only a shadow because of something to do with the activated molecules "bending light."

Annie was as strict as Mrs. Riveras. On a corner of the home computer she faithfully marked off the two hours, nine till ten, sixteen (four) till seventeen (five) in the afternoon—

* Interplanetary Union

except every tenth day when she left the Hedge completely switched off, and Jasselly had to stay inside.

The plays didn't bother with the Hedge at all. Ignored it.

But Harrington noticed that birds had started to fly over.

A lot of the birds and animals had been driven out of the area as the town grew. There wasn't enough space for them and human disturbance wasn't what they liked. People didn't seem to care. They had their pets. Sometimes in the parks you spotted wild plays or foxiles, a lizard or two.

Birds, though . . . there weren't many birds at all.

Harrington, gazing up at the birds dark on the pale green young summer sky, realized abruptly that she had only ever really seen birds in books or on a screen.

"Mom?"

Annie looked around. Being called "Mom" by Harrington usually meant something was going on—good or bad.

"What, Harry?"

"Come see."

Annie, despite her major faults of (1) losing Pop, (2) liking the Guy, and (3) producing It, still had some plus points. If you said something like "Come see" in the right kind of "come see" voice, she went with you to look.

They stood in the yard.

The Hedge was on, and Jasselly was lying asleep on a big cushion. Harrington, sitting outside to draw, had been "keeping an eye" on her. Sort of. *Touching, really, how Annie trusts me . . .*

"Up there."

They both gazed upward.

On top of the Hedge a large bird had perched, balancing on the joined-up molecules that felt like solid twigs and leaves, fanning its feathers in blissful ignorance.

"Wow," said Annie.

"It's been there fifteen minutes. Why 'wow'?"

"Well, when did we last see a bird that close?"

"It's forty feet up!"

"Yes."

"You're not scared it'll pounce and peck Jass's eyes out?"

"Oh no, honey," said Annie. "I recall these birds from years back when your pop—when I lived more outside the town. They're called—what are they called?"

The bird pecked at the Hedge, and though nothing came off it into the bird's beak, it seemed convinced and pecked a bit more. Another bird just like it flew down and settled by the first bird. They began to make a noise. *What* a noise.

"Like rusty nails on a glass," exclaimed Harrington.

"No, it's more like—like tuning a guitar—"

Twindle-twindle, went the birds, *tweety trrr.*

"Auxicaps!" cried Annie.

"Gesundheit!" Harrington laughed.

Annie laughed, too. They stood laughing, looking up at the birds singing their twindle song on the Hedge above the sleeping baby.

Mr. Oplough stood the other side of the right-hand bound-

ary, looming over the low fence. Demonstrating without meaning to how excellent it was when the Hedge was there and they didn't have to see him.

"I'd like a word with you, Annie."

"Yes, Mr. Oplough."

"I have a vegetable patch just along here."

"Yes, Mr. Oplough? That's great."

"No, it ain't. Your damned Hedge is cutting off my sun."

"Only for two hours a—"

"And my planet tomatoes are going blue."

"But—they *do*, don't they, Mr. Oplough?"

"Nah. I bred it outta the darn things, till you started with that Hedge." Mr. Oplough glowered. "And besides, it ain't hardly two hours now, is it?"

Annie all innocence, Harrington all astonished.

"No, I been countin' them hours, Annie. *Three* hours yesterday. And *two* this morning."

"It's because of the birds, Mr. Oplough," said Annie, beaming at him.

"What birds? What're you talking about? And who wants birds anyhow, dropping their dirt all over my yard—"

"Oh, they hardly ever do, Mr. Oplough—only every six days. No need for you to get all tense."

Annie pointed.

Twelve meters up, two birds flew over and over where the Hedge had been, circling like moving paintings of birds on a green plate of sky.

"You're nuts!" declared Mr. Oplough. "You're a darn nuisance. Why don't you get back to Earth where you belong,

causin' all this trouble for proper folks, litterin' this clean new world with fatherless kids—"

Speechless, they watched him tramp away, and the door slammed loud as thunder.

"I guess the gloves are off," said Annie thoughtfully. "Mrs. Riveras told me yesterday—after we had the Hedge on too long—she's going to L-mail* the Town Authority. She says she plans for us to be thrown out of the house. It seems we've ruined the neighborhood."

"She can't!"

"Maybe she can."

They too went back—into what was still their house.

Annie set the stove to fix tea and the Ice-it to ice it.

They sat on the living room floor while Jasselly played quietly with her fur bear. Annie and Harrington drank their tea and watched the birds circle over the lawn, through the wide window.

Annie put down her glass.

"Yes?"

"Yes," said Harrington.

Jasselly looked up at the excited voices of these people she had come to live among. She smiled. "Yeff," agreed Jasselly, nodding both her head and the toy bear's.

Annie rose in her graceful way. She had been a dancer in live theater before Pop and Harrington. She strode to the button panel on the wall and pressed the brand-new button.

Outside, the two walls of Hedge sprang gloriously sunward, and after about five minutes more, the auxicaps floated down.

"I've always liked my tomatoes blue," said Harrington.

* Local Mail

"Boo," said Jass with approval. "Thom-*aif*-oos."

Three persons united against the world.

They were building a nest. They thought the Hedge was completely there, but maybe not quite, because they brought in the nesting material from elsewhere—twigs and leaves from the park, hair from Mr. Brand's dog four doors down. The nest was a huge unwieldy thing, big enough for a legendary roc's egg, Annie remarked. The birds sat on the nest in turns by day. In the evening they groomed each other with their beaks and snuggled up. They sang all night—if singing was what you could call it.

"It says in this book that they nest for ten to fourteen days, and then the eggs will be laid."

"Is that quick?"

"I don't really know, Harry. I don't know anything about birds, just that I like them."

"How many eggs?"

"Between two and six."

"Hey!"

By night, as the birds sang, the stars and moons shone down, and the Hedge gleamed as if moon-polished and star-gemmed, unseen (they had closed the eyeholes), they heard Mrs. Riveras's silent purse-mouthed rage and Mr. Oplough's trumpetings of fury. The birds sang louder and louder.

"You know, it's not so bad, the way they sing."

"Like badly tuned nightingales."

"What's a nightingale, Mom?"

"A bird that sings."

"Come on!"

"I said. I don't know a thing about birds."

"Look," said Harrington, "she's asleep with the rabbits."

"Yes. Real rabbits—I don't know that I'd risk a baby around them. But plays are fine. Gentle. *Careful.*"

"Was I *ever* that small?" asked Harrington, staring at Jasselly in her molecule-guarded sleep.

"Was *I*?" said Annie. Harrington stared at her mother. Once Annie had been a kid, too. As if she read thoughts, Annie added, "Hated my younger sister and all. I used to plan to kill her. Never did. Decided she was okay in the end. She's on Earth—I'd love to see her again . . . Maybe one day."

The tall man walked into the house and looked about him. His name was Dennis Rooney. He was very good-looking, but he came from Town Authority. Mrs. Riveras and Mr. Oplough had summoned him.

"Is that the Hedge? Yes, it's high. You can get slightly shorter models, though not by much. The shortest is, I understand, eight meters. And the cost's the same. It would cause the same problem, too. Block out neighbors' view and sunlight. Not everyone wants to know everybody else's business, of course, or get fried."

"I didn't mean to upset them," Annie said. "But those are living things up there. They've produced *seven* eggs—that's unusual."

"How'd you know there are seven?" He smiled at Annie.

"I hired a tiny elevcam and sent it up. They didn't notice—I mean the birds."

"Seven," Dennis repeated. "That *is* impressive."

Harrington broke in. "You sound like you don't think we did anything wrong."

"Harry, sshh. Wait."

"No, it's okay, Annie—may I call you Annie?"

"Yes, Dennis," said Annie, and blushed.

"You see, I'm less interested in the neighbors' gripes than in someone who's gotten these birds to breed again. They seemed to be dying out. As for Oplough and Riveras, they've already told me they want to move. They don't like children or animals so close. We can always pay them compensation and buy them out—then we can locate people who'll be happy to live in the two houses with a big Hedge on one side and some rare birds."

"What about," said Annie, "the other neighbors—Mr. Brand and the rest of them?"

"Oh, they're fine. Mr. Brand actually asked me to ask you if he could drop by sometime, take a closer look at the auxies. Won't bring the dog, he swore to me. *Or* his robot."

"The dog is welcome," said Annie. "And Mr. Brand, too."

"So there's just this form on the carry-com to sign, if that's okay? Read it all first."

Annie began to read. She looked up, very pale where she had been pink. "You're *paying* us to look after the birds?"

"Sure thing. Government grant concession Number X112, Rare and Endangered Indigenes, subclause 6."

Harrington saw her mother was gazing at Dennis from Town Authority spouting jargon and numbers as if he were reading her an ancient love lyric from Lord Byron. Ever the

soul of tact she knew herself to be, Harrington led Jasselly into the Hedge-safe yard, where they sat in the cool and watched the birds nesting and twindling high above.

"How many do you think will hatch, Jass?"

"Eighfs," announced Jass.

"Don't be crazy—eight? There are only seven eggs."

"Eighfs," insisted Jass, who, having found speech, wasn't going to have it challenged.

In any case, she was right. When the eggs did hatch, out tottered eight balls of fluff with beaks, who solidified enough inside a few hours to fly down with their parents to the lawn, for the bird food TA had supplied. One egg had been a double. It made the planetwide NewsNet.

Planet Date: Year 103
Part Three—Thinking Future: Lute

Riding there in her single-person hoverjet, Lute heard the melody and words of old songs running through her brain.

The jet didn't go so fast she couldn't take in the rolling prairie, dotted with ripening fruit trees and untended stands of grain, the wild herds of tappuls grazing, and whitehawks idling over the sky.

It had been government policy since the fiftieth year on-planet to let certain areas go back to the wild, let the land renew itself and give the local animal life a chance to regain habitat.

The town of Pioneer Pines was the first of these projects. And by now, according to the information site, most of the town was gone, smothered in mutating trees and rioting vines, with creatures lairing in the remains of the houses. There were even some dangerous critters now, the site overview had told her—felinxes, for example, the nearest thing to bobcats the planet had. Lute had brought a Planet League Approved stunner along with her bag, her rob, and her guitar.

"Why in hell do you want to go there?"

That had been the question one or two had asked her, in the city.

Because, she thought, *it's about as far away as I can get from* here.

She was seventeen, adult status. Nobody could stop her.

To be polite, she said some of the truth: "It's where Harrington Rooney lived, before she moved south."

Harrington Rooney was the movie actress who had been the star of so many of the early planet-made movies. Lute had always admired her.

"Wasn't her sister a mathematician, Lute?" inquired one of the "bright" girls.

Lute didn't answer, but someone else did. "Jasselly? She still is."

"She must be old . . . They both must be—"

"Kicking eighty or ninety, I guess," said the someone else. "But Zelda Ariano lived in that house, too, didn't she—different time, same place, right, Lute?"

Once more Lute said nothing.

Inside she said this: *I just want to get away so bad.*

To get away—

But you couldn't. Not really. For wherever Lute went, the memory went with her. The memory of Cholan.

The rob was the first out of the jet. It trundled lightly down Main Street, navigating between arching tree roots, clumps of huge flowers, and heaps of metallic rubble. The houses and stores had been designed to break down over a period of years if unmaintained. But enough of them were still standing to get in the rob's way.

The town looked weird. Hollow, yet choked with growing stuff.

Having parked the jet, Lute toted her bag and the guitar, the stunner slung over her other shoulder.

The morning was peaceful. Nothing moved.

Then—

Out of the tunnel of trees shot the rob, its metal box shape whirring with dials and lights. It raced toward her in robotic panic. Lute dropped her bag and pulled the stunner around.

"What is it?"

A scarlet light lit: *unfriendly life form*—that's what the light meant.

The rob was flinging itself for shelter against her ankles.

Lute braced herself for the biggest felinx on-world to burst from the trees.

Next moment the unfriendly life did erupt out of there.

"Oh, rob. That's only—it's only *plays*, that's all."

The three one-eared rabbits dashed up, turned a couple of somersaults over one another, and darted away again into the undergrowth.

The rob made ticking complaining noises. Embarrassed?

Lute raised her eyebrow. "It looked like they were teasing you, pal!"

Guided by the old street plan, Lute found the Ariano-Rooney house just after noon. Like everything else, it was tented in by vines. One wall had crumbled down, and most of the strong, unbreakable window glass had given way, as it always did without mechanical care.

In what had once been a pretty backyard, now part of the neighborhood jungle, a single tall Earth pine, slightly tinged with blue, lifted its dark pagoda to the sun.

Lute made her camp in the house. She was not without company. Pale-furred rodents lived in various holes, and a

foxile kept a single-fox apartment on the top floor—she soon grew used to its slim orange shape padding to and fro. She would try not to disturb them all, but they might not mind her too much. It had been noted that the planetary animals had a great tolerance for small groups of people, only shying away from the vast sprawls of populated towns and cities. Even there, though, you sometimes found them, and they seemed prepared to adopt Earth humans. So many of them had become companionable pets, rivaling the cats, monkeys, mice, and dogs the settlers had first introduced.

This house had even been the site of a breeding pair of auxicaps, who had built their nest in a molecular Hedge for six years running, producing a whole flock of new birds that bred in turn.

The auxicaps had been thought to be an endangered species. They were the most selective, and would never go just anyplace. They avoided most fully built-up areas. But they had always seemed to like Pioneer Pines. It was now quite a center for them—another reason why people had been encouraged to move away. So far Lute, always a city girl, had never seen an auxicap, except in a book or on a screen.

In the fading light, Lute sat by her little portofire, cooking her hamburger in a responsible way, the prewashed salad in its bowl, the glass of sparkling Plancola to hand.

Now and then she touched the guitar. She didn't play it.

Not yet. One day. When I can.

She had been promising that for months.

The rob scuttled around. It had taken a dislike to the harmless white rats now. Whenever one appeared, the rob would

launch itself off its resting pad and trundle toward the rat over the roots and broken floor. She would have to reprogram it in the morning. A city machine. It had clearly gotten hysterical out here.

Machines did have personalities, robs definitely, especially if they were with you a long time. She had argued about that such a lot with—

Such a lot with—

With Cholan.

Lute thought about Cholan. Let herself do it. The memories poured in like a sea gushing from a giant faucet, drowning her. Before Cholan, despite her many friends—none of whom had been close—she had been alone. Her parents had left her college *in loco parentis* and had "gone home" to Earth.

Then, a year ago . . .

He'd come to see her at the stadium, one more fan of double-line soccer, with a program for her to sign. She was the Green Tigers' main striker, and she'd spun three balls in the net. She always tried to be decent to any fan. Happy with her score, she was laughing and joking with all of them. Then Cholan was in front of her. Lute had fallen silent.

He held out the program in his long, dark-fingered hand. She signed, and glanced up into his face, and he smiled. Lute smiled back. At first she wasn't sure she'd be able to. It was as if she recognized him—*knew* him. But they'd never met before. Their fingers brushed as he took the program back from her, and they both started. "Electric," he said. Lute nodded. That was it.

Few things had been so simple. So good.

That year. That perfect almost-year. With Cholan.

She saw him nearly every day, and in the evenings they went dancing at the rinks, or drank sodas, or sat listening to music in the clubs. Cholan taught her how to really play a guitar. He would move her hands, and where he placed them on the instrument, she could suddenly make music—music that *shone.* He, too, could play guitar, and asera, drums, sax, and seventeenth-century mandolin. They sang together. His voice—velvet, dark as coffee.

The ones who knew about them figured that, once Cholan and she were seventeen—their birthdays were only five days apart, hers first—they'd marry.

Simple.

They even talked about it sometimes, but it didn't seem to matter. Being *together* mattered. But the strange thing was, Lute felt she was with him even when they were apart. Somehow.

They seldom argued, except about things like robots, or soccer tactics.

Once he said to her, standing in daylight under the city clock, "You're like a part of me, Lute." And she replied, "Me, too."

She'd left him only two hours before. She was sitting up in her bed, reading a novel that never after would she remember, when something happened inside her head.

It scared her stupid. It was like a light going out. A kind of blindness.

She jumped out of bed, ran halfway across the floor, wishing that her parents had not left her on-planet without them,

wishing that someone in the sorority house was someone she could really confide in. She thought of her friends. They all seemed like cardboard cutouts. All but Cholan. But where she looked for *him* in her mind, she couldn't see him anymore. He had vanished.

That was when she knew he was dead.

An automated door on the city's overhead train had given way. Such an accident had never happened before, was thought impossible. Two or three people had been slightly hurt. Cholan was killed.

It was that *simple.*

Lute wrapped herself in steel. She was cool and hard and distant. No one could get in. She didn't *want* them in.

She wanted Cholan, and he was gone. Forever.

Her friends, teachers, teammates, all the people she knew, they were concerned about her, tried to help, grew tired with trying and with her new steel surface. They gave up.

On her own, Lute seldom cried, and then only quietly, not wanting to be heard.

She began to hate the city. The city had killed him. She would leave, go somewhere she could cry really loud if she wanted, somewhere she could scream, and no one would hear.

Odd, though, now she was here in Pioneer Pines, she couldn't cry at all. She had held it back so long, the pain, too, had changed to steel.

For several days Lute camped in the house on Pine Street that had had such famous people grow up in it.

She explored the town, striding up into the hills, which were going back to grass now, blue as Todd Ariano's famous eyes.

She was okay if she kept busy.

At night, worn out from her long treks, she let the rob run her a bath in the portable unfolding tub, cooked supper, ate it. Reprogrammed, the rob was now sulky. It knew it had been stopped from doing what it wanted, which was to have hysterics every time a rat walked past or the foxile trotted up the stairs.

Once Lute saw two felinxes down among the crumbled stores on Main Street. They paid her no attention.

It wasn't till twelve days had gone by that Lute saw her first auxi.

The bird flew in out of the green sky and landed in the pine tree. But the needles weren't to its liking, obviously. After a moment it sailed down to the back porch.

Strange birds, the auxies. Weird.

And then the song began.

Twindle-twindle tweety trrr.

Lute stared at the auxi. Her eyes bulged. She stood up, her mug falling to the floor, spilling the hot tea.

Twindle-twindle—

"No," said Lute. "I'm not going out of my mind. No. I'm just—imagining—"

"You're not," said the auxicap, poised in the open doorway. "You can hear me perfectly plainly. I said, 'Hi, there.'"

Lute shook her head. She turned in horror to stumble away.

That was when she felt the edge of the auxicap's wing brush, gentle and smooth, over the surface of her brain. Immediately Lute grew calm. Her eyes cleared.

She gazed back at the bird.

Twindle, it said.

No. It said, "That's more comfortable, I hope."

"I don't—"

"Most humans we talk to don't hear the words. They just pick up the ideas. But we can help them to feel a little better, if they're receptive. You, though, Lute, are *very* receptive. You have the musician's ear. Maybe that's why."

Lute sat down.

The bird hopped slowly through the room. Meeting the rob—which had frozen to the spot just as Lute had—the auxi tapped it with its beak. The rob let out a little twitter, went to its resting pad, and sat still.

"Machines sometimes respond, too," said the auxi.

"Uh—good . . ."

The auxi perched beside her. It began to tell her of many things about the past of the planet. And of its own kind. Higher Intelligent life existed here. It was the animals who were intelligent, all of them to varying degrees. But the strongest minds existed among the auxicaps. "That isn't our name, of course. Would you care to know the real name of my kind?"

"Y-es—"

"Naturally it's in a different language from those of your own planet, but I think you *do* hear me in your own language? Good, then. The real name for the auxicaps, what we call ourselves, is the Human Race. Shall I tell you," it added, gentle

and somehow smiling there in her ears and her mind, "what we call this planet?"

"What?" whispered Lute.

"Earth," said the human auxicap. "It's what most species call their own home place, you know."

When the bird went away, flying off into the sky, Lute still felt calm. But she told herself she'd been dreaming.

That night she did dream. She dreamed she and Cholan were flying together on broad wings over the sky. When she woke, she cried for hours. It was like rain after a dry season.

She saw the auxi—the *human*—only once more. It perched neatly on the top of the unprotesting rob, and told her that, along with the ability to help, its kind—the *human* kind of *this* planet—could often bring out the talents of the other humans, the colonists who had settled here. It told Lute she already had a major talent for music.

"I can't play anymore," said Lute.

She thought, *Here I sit, confiding in a bird.*

It's all right.

The human auxi said, "Is that since Cholan died?"

"Yes. I should forget—I should get over it—but I can't—how can I?"

"You will never forget Cholan, or loving him," said the auxi softly. "So your job now is to make all the world know and love and remember him, with you. Even all those he never met."

"How?" she asked.

"Through your talent. How else? Through songs you'll write and sing. Through the music of your guitar. Your love can't die, even though Cholan died. Let it live, then. Tell it

to the world. That's your future—think! Even your name is a musical instrument of your Earth—isn't it? A lute. Play it, then. Play all your music for *him*."

As she rode back toward the city, new shiny songs ran through Lute's mind.

She saw the rolling hills and plains, the prairies starred with fire-colored flowers under the wide green sky.

Pioneer Pines was full of humans again—*auxi* humans.

Who would ever believe it? No one. Don't try to tell.

The rob stirred in the back of the hoverjet.

Twindle, said the rob. *Twindle tweety trrr.*

Are we there yet? the rob had asked her, like a child. And she had understood.

"Soon, rob. Only a few hours. Go to sleep now."

See, Cholan, see, they're kind of alive, too. And maybe you're alive? Someplace else?

He was with her again. She could feel he was, there in her brain that the auxicap had brushed with its wing and opened up like a planet to new songs and new dreams. Cholan was with her. She wasn't alone.

Tanith Lee was born in 1947 in London, England. She was unable to read until almost the age of eight and began writing at the age of nine. After she left school, she worked as a library assistant, shop assistant, a filing clerk, and a waitress. She spent one year at art college.

To date she has published almost eighty novels, thirteen short-story collections, and well over 250 short stories. Four of her radio plays were broadcast by the BBC and she wrote two episodes of the BBC TV cult SF series *Blake's Seven*. She has twice won the World Fantasy Award for short fiction, and was awarded the August Derleth Award in 1980 for her novel *Death's Master.*

Tanith Lee lives with her husband, the writer and artist John Kaiine, on the southeast coast of England.

Her Web site is **www.tanithlee.com**.

Author's Note

The idea for this story came, like about half of what I write, out of "nowhere." First I got the image of the place—green sky, small township growing and then going back to the wild. *Then* the three heroines arrived, complete with their names and characters. Zelda is named for the wife of F. Scott Fitzgerald, Lute for her music . . . Harrington, I'm not sure. I think I just liked the sound of a girl with a guy's name! I wrote the story in a few days. But I really want to go back to that planet. So sometime it will feature in a longer work.

Pamela Dean

Cousins

Kisandrion's mother was fond of saying that water always rolled downhill. When Dri was smaller, this fondness had led to a number of juvenile attempts to cause water to do something else. Only twice had the water done anything else.

On the first of these occasions, Dri's older brother chose a sandy hill, and the water at once sank into the sand without a trace. After the argument about whether sinking down into the sand was the same thing as rolling downhill, and the conclusion that sinking was not rolling and that straight down for—here came a subsidiary argument about how far water would sink into sand—that straight down was not the same as downhill, the four of them, Dri and her older brother and younger brother and sister all took the broiling paved road to the top of Mystery Hill. There they conducted an argument about whether it might not be better just to drink the water, which was sensibly resolved by drinking most of it but leaving a spoonful for the experiment.

Dri was nine years old at the time, and believed firmly that any place called Mystery Hill must surely cause everything to behave differently from usual. The water, however, ran down into a crack in the pavement, and its faint trail had dried entirely by the time the other three were done rehashing the argument about how much more water they should have saved.

Later that day, while their mother was putting smeary stuff on their sunburns, she remarked, "You do know that's a metaphor, don't you?"

"It's an analogy, surely?" said their father.

Then it was necessary to go get out their books to find out what an analogy was; and the next day to go call upon a friend who worked in the Levar's Library. When they finally had the matter sorted out to their own satisfaction, Dri's mother attempted to explain over their usual Sunday dinner of fish and sea grass that when she said "water rolls downhill," she meant, roughly, that many small things could invisibly join together to suddenly fall on one's head in a surprising fashion, and that one might be less surprised if one bore this in mind.

The eldest child, Kiffen, and the youngest child, Sinja, had agreed, but Dri and Melandin, the middle children, as well as their father, argued that while resentment or a failure to react promptly might well be mitigated by bearing such things in mind, the initial moment of sheer surprise could not be so easily affected. The experience of Kiffen, who was a newly trained member of the Scarlet Guard, was sifted in the course of this discussion, as well as that of a neighbor

who was a retired City Guard. The discussion alone proving unsatisfactory, Dri and Melandin spent a week leaping out at the other members of their family from dark corners and from under the stairs and, once or twice, from behind trees or walls far from home, and then pointing out triumphantly that their beleagured family members ought to have expected them to do so by now and yet were still surprised. No conclusions were reached, but a house rule had to be made about leaping out at people while they were carrying fragile or liquid loads, and another about following family members about the city to surprise them while defaulting on one's own academic or professional duties.

Nobody else's family argued so much as the Dorlianishes did. The upstairs neighbors, who took a dim view of all the discussion even though very little of it involved shouting, felt that the Hrothvekan origins of Dri's mother must explain the Dorlianish family's strange tendency to talk so much and so directedly. Dri had once tried to tell them that her aunts hardly talked at all, let alone directedly, but the upstairs neighbors were too pleased with their own reasoning to notice that they were being argued with.

It was her experience with arguments that got Dri a position in the Red Temple. After a year or so in the Scarlet Guard, Kiffen became an enthusiastic convert to the Faith of the Twin Forces. There was not much religion in Dri's family. A visiting nonarguing aunt had once opined that argument was their religion. As a small child, Dri had found priests of any temple rather unnerving. They all dressed alike and looked so full of concentration. Seeing them made her feel as

if a collection of painted soldiers had grown to life size and was looking for her.

Kiffen, however, came home from his training overflowing with enthusiasm. "They give you your very own spiritual adviser!" he informed his intrigued family over their usual Rainday meal of potboil. "And she has to listen to whatever you say about yourself! And she has to figure you out! And if you don't argue she tells you to do it!"

"How would you know what she does if you don't argue?" said Melandin.

"Jairy told me. Jairy makes a mussel look wide open."

"Why does Jairy talk to you, then?" inquired Sinja.

"Because I just keep saying things until he can't keep still anymore."

"Goodness, child, what do you say?" asked his mother.

"I say nice things about people he hates," said Kiffen, with a limpid look.

"How do you know he hates them, if the only way you can get him to talk is to—"

"I observe his expressions."

"When I hate people," remarked Dri, "I don't let them have any expressions of mine."

"Why, Dri," said her mother, "whom do you hate, and why?"

Dri was thinking of a certain fruit merchant who did not fall in with the usual City custom of letting children take the bruised fruit without paying. But Kiffen said, "She hates our aunt Mininu."

"I certainly do not!"

"You certainly do," said Kiffen. "Whenever she comes to visit, your face looks just like a statue."

"Kisandrion Dorlianish! You must not hate your aunt!" said her mother.

"Why not?" said Kisandrion, who did not actually hate her aunt but was deeply in awe of her, which was a very uncomfortable feeling; hatred would have felt cozier. "I don't have to live with her."

"You may one day."

"Why?"

"Should the pot of Liavekan politics ever boil over," said her mother, "I'll send you all to her by the fastest way."

"If the pot boils over," said Kiffen, while Dri stared horrified, "will the water run downhill?"

"Indeed it will," said their mother.

"What if potboil runs downhill?" cried Sinja.

"What if Dri came to work with me after school?" said Kiffen.

"I don't want to be a guard," said Dri.

"They want another clerk in the library. You could do that."

"Would I get to read the books?"

"They haven't books, really, they have archives."

"But would I get to read them?"

"I don't know, Dri. Come to work with me and find out."

So Dri, whose childhood ambition had been to own and pull a footcab, catching nefarious villains in the process, came to work for the Red Temple. She did not ask about reading the archives. Mundri, the chief librarian of this branch of the

Red Temple's documents, was almost as forbidding as Dri's not-hated, nonarguing aunt. Mundri did not brook much argument either. When Dri pointed out that one's spiritual advisers told one to argue, Mundri said dryly that Dri could argue with the priests all she liked, but she was not to argue in the library.

Dri liked her priest, a young placid woman called Atliae. Atliae argued with her, but Atliae also let her talk. At home, unless one happened to be bleeding heavily or running a fever, it was more or less impossible to speak more than a sentence without having it discussed in detail. Their mother had had to be very firm repeatedly before the bleeding and the fevers were let off the general requirement of discussion. Dri enjoyed home quite a lot, but talking about herself in paragraphs was enchanting, like eating as many cinnamon cakes as you wanted and neither being scolded nor ending up with a stomachache.

This happy state of affairs lasted for a month or two, and then the stomachache showed up. Atliae greeted Dri one Luckday morning by saying, "You have got on so well that we can go on to the second chapter of your training sooner than usual."

In the second chapter, Dri did not get to talk about herself in paragraphs; instead, she got to tell Atliae about five choices she had made in the preceding week, and Atliae would then tell her why the choices were not good ones. For every choice she had made, whether it was to lie to her mother about whom she fancied at work or school, to tell her sister the truth about who ate the last cinnamon cake, to buy her mother a

bottle of lavender water or to adopt a litter of kittens that were living under the house, to read a poem or write one, to write a letter to her country cousins or to throw a tantrum about the necessity of doing so, she had to contrive a deed that was that choice's opposite in magnitude and nature, and then do that.

They had a terrific shouting match about the kittens. Dri's first suggestion was that she put them and their mother back under the house, and she had to suffer a long and, for Atliae, impassioned lecture about how impossible it was to undo anything, ever, under any circumstances. Dri did not much heed this at the time because she wondered whether Atliae had somehow divined her intention of continuing to feed and brush the kittens even when they were back under the house.

Her second suggestion, that she give away the cat puppets that had taken a lot of her time and thought before she found the kittens, evoked a much calmer but equally long lecture about the inefficacy of symbolism and substitution in such a situation. Dri finally suggested that she give Sinja away instead. Atliae said briefly, "Sinja is not yours to give." Dri had no way of telling whether Atliae knew the suggestion was not serious or whether, much more intriguing, she would have entertained it if Sinja had been Dri's child instead of her sister.

"What do you suggest, then?" demanded Dri.

"You could find another litter of kittens and drown it," said Atliae.

Dri got up. "No," she said.

"Sit down, Dri; we haven't finished."

"I am not sitting down with a drowner of kittens."

"No, indeed now you are not, though certainly you have done so many times unknowing."

"Good people don't let their cats have dozens of kittens!"

Atliae looked dubious. Dri, her belief in Atliae's wisdom eroding rapidly, said in exasperation, "All you have to do is give them Worrynot."

"Some people's cats don't like the taste," said Atliae. Dri opened her mouth to provide a list of methods of giving medicine to cats whether the cats liked the taste or not, but Atliae went on, "In any case, a person can be too good."

"Well, I know that," said Dri, thinking of her eldest cousin on her father's side, who was a model of deportment, according to himself and also to Dri's parents. Then she thought through this initial thought, as Atliae had taught her to do. What was good about deportment, after all? You could bet that it didn't feed anybody—in fact, it slowed down how well you could feed yourself at the table—and it didn't save any kittens either. "Good at what?" she said cautiously.

Atliae grinned at her. She did not look like a person who would drown kittens. "That is a useful distinction," she said—this being perhaps the highest praise Atliae could bestow on a remark as opposed to a deed, "but it is sideways to our purposes. Hark now."

At this signal of a long speech, Dri sat down with her feet on the floor and put a cushion firmly behind her back. Atliae did not like it if you let your feet go to sleep and then tried to wake them up again while she was talking.

"Here is the fashion of the world," said Atliae. She was not a very dramatic speaker, but her voice took on a faint tinge of the storyteller's rhythm. "Two great forces there are, continually at war. We call the one Good, and the other Evil; and yet they remain upright only by virtue of the pressure that they exert, the one upon the other. Should either of them vanish or be vanquished, the other would collapse. Whether the other force would vanish also or merely assume a form so alien that the world would fail, we do not know, though many rolls of paper and gallons of ink have been expended in essays to prove the inevitability of one or the other event."

Dri was thrilled. She thought of the two forces as astrological drawings, their forms imposed on the wandering patterns of the stars, one gold and one red, arms upraised, eyes shut in concentration, each forcing the other upright so that the world of kittens and sand and spicy lentils and family and rain and railroads might continue.

"We are all part of this struggle," said Atliae. "In each of us it goes on in miniature."

Dri thought of herself as a dollhouse with the sky painted on the wall. She was somewhat less thrilled.

"And though few of us could bring down the world entire, we can all bring down the world that is our particular self."

I'd rather bring down the world entire, thought Dri. Atliae probably knew this, but Dri preferred not to say it just the same.

"The Twin Forces of good and evil must be balanced," said Atliae. "They must be truly twins. You must strive to keep them equal in yourself."

That said, Dri was still deeply preoccupied with the kittens. She knew without having to consider the matter that she was going to keep them and was not going to harm them. If behaving so brought down the equally braced forces of her particular self, perhaps it would be interesting to see what that was like. But her decision did not matter to whether the argument must go on. "If I found a sick cat," she said, "and took it to a healer and it had to be put down . . ."

"I'm afraid you are very literal," said Atliae, shaking her head.

Dri had heard this before from her parents and was not much impressed. In fact, as usual, a comment upon her literalness made her take it further. "Well, if you won't let me do anything opposite," she said, "what if I rather sneaked up on the middle again in little steps by doing smaller and smaller good things until I did a not-good, not-bad thing?"

Atliae actually clapped her hands and exclaimed, "Well done, well done!" This was when Dri realized that the Faith of the Twin Forces was made for her.

Matters proceeded in this pleasing fashion for most of a year. The kittens grew long-legged and were given to the baker on Dri's street, whose cat was getting too old to be interested in mousing; to the healer two streets over, who looked lonely to Dri; and, astonishingly, to Mundri, who, it developed, liked cats much better than she liked people. Dri was left with the ugliest kitten, not having troubled to mention his patient disposition. He even let them see whether water would roll downhill on his fluffy unevenly striped tail. It was lucky that nobody thought of seeing if potboil would boil downhill on

his tail, because he would probably have let them try that, too. He was much interested in all family activities, and was so often tripped over that they named him after Ghologhosh, the god of small curses.

Not long after the making of this momentous decision, suddenly it was the twelfth day of the month of Flowers, and Dri turned fourteen years old. She was not interested in her inborn luck; the danger and trouble of investing it into a usable object so that she could perform magic did not seem to her worth the rewards. She thought that she would prefer to rely on her wits. There had been, naturally, a great deal of argument about this decision all through her childhood, but after this birthday, nobody brought up the subject again.

She did not talk about it with Atliae, and perhaps oddly, Atliae did not ask her about it either. Dri puzzled herself over the matter for some little time. Surely it was a momentous decision, to abandon one's birthright and decline the acquisition of power. But like the decision to take care of the kittens, it seemed to be beyond argument, a thing she would simply do, like breathing. She did, once her birthday was a week or so past, ask Atliae whether a thing that seemed as natural as breathing might be viewed as a choice by the Twin Forces.

Atliae, after a much longer pause than usual, said that one should strive to make as few of one's actions in life like breathing, and as many like taking a life or having a child, as possible. Dri remarked that many people did both those things pretty much as if they were the same as breathing, and Atliae was rather short with her instead of arguing. Dri put this down to the late Spring heat, which Atliae didn't like, and

thought that she would wait to bring the matter up again until Fog or even Frost.

Once her birthday was weeks and weeks past, her family became so embroiled in enthralling discussions of what should happen at her coming-of-age party that neither water's running nor potboil's boiling was mentioned at all except in purely practical terms.

When the pot did boil over, it was not the entire pot of Liavekan politics, but a different pot. It was the Red Temple.

Dri's experience of the Red Temple was limited to her brother, Atliae, Mundri, and her fellow clerks, who acquired their positions and left them with irregular frequency, usually after either repeatedly professing boredom or having a huge battle with Mundri over some minor detail. People did come to use the library, but it was always Mundri who talked to them. Kiffen, however, saw and spoke to ten times as many inhabitants of their faith as Dri did, and he always kept her well informed of all the gossip. So she knew quite well that the head of the whole affair, His Scarlet Eminence, Regent of all Liavek until the Levar came of age, was named Resh, and was both soft-spoken and much feared. She did not specifically fear him herself, since he did not seem to be interested in her library, and since Mundri's behavior and remarks implied strongly that among Mundri's high and sacred duties was the doling out of a proper amount of fear in His Scarlet Eminence's direction. He seemed more an eccentricity of Mundri's than an active force.

On a dazzlingly hot day in the month of Fruit, Kiffen came breathlessly into the library. Even in the midst of crisis, he

upheld Mundri's rules. He came in at the beginning of the recess allowed Dri for her luncheon, and he said nothing to her until they were outside the library proper. Then he took her elbow and hustled her out into Gold Street. "We're going home," he said.

"I haven't time to—"

"We must go home."

Dri contemplated him. He looked as if his cat had died. She hoped hers was all right. If not, though, surely he would just say so. She fell into step with him. She did not stop arguing, but she did not stop walking either. They went home through the empty noontime streets, squinting at the dancing of dust motes in the dry bright air.

Their mother was preserving garlic, but did not scold them for interrupting. She put down her knife.

"Resh is dead," said Kiffen.

Their mother slid off her high wooden stool, picked up the jug of vinegar, put it down again. "Quick, Dri, bring me my pen and ink," she said.

Dri, going, heard Kiffen say in a voice that began low and firm and squeaked halfway through, "I can't leave the City."

Sinja had borrowed the ink again, and had also sequestered the paper under her bed. While discovering these facts, Dri thought that she could not leave the City either. Her work, her cat, her coming-of-age party; the necessity of preventing Melandin from disgracing them all or killing himself accidentally; the necessity of educating Sinja not to be like Melandin; fireworks in the Levar's Park and the long-legged white cadies wading in the Salt Marsh; the escaped white

geese and the wild white ducks on the Cat River; her friends in the next street, all condemned to years more of school to become apothecaries, who listened so breathlessly to her tales of the real outside world. No, she could not leave the City.

When she returned to the kitchen with the objects she had been sent to fetch, Kiffen was sitting at the table with a lowering expression and her mother had filled up two more jars of garlic. "I am writing to your aunts," said her mother. "Go and fill one pack for each of you. Dri, I will be good to your cat."

"Why can't I take Golly with me?" demanded Dri, and was immediately aware of having made a mistake.

"Don't fret, Dri, I'll look after him," said Kiffen.

Dri opened her mouth and then shut it again. She had always felt, even before first Kiffen and then she came of age, that their arguments had force, that they were attended to, if sometimes laughed at, that they helped to keep the house standing and people in a right relation to one another. But the way her mother was writing and not attending, as if she had suddenly gone deaf, made speaking seem useless. Kiffen's blithe tactic, of speaking as if what he wanted had already been accomplished, usually got him just what he wanted, to Dri's intense annoyance; but it was not working now. She thought there must be a thing to say that would restore rightness, but she did not know what it was.

Sinja arrived at that moment with a tremendous noise of slapping sandals, ready for her lunch. She looked around and did not ask why it was not ready. She edged up under her mother's unoccupied elbow and announced, "I didn't do anything wrong."

"Sinja can help me look after your cat," said their mother, still writing.

"Why can't Dri—"

"Because she is going to the great plains on a visit."

"Why?"

"Because His Scarlet Eminence is dead."

"Dri! Did you kill him?"

Dri sat down and laughed. There was nothing else to do except pack. After half a moment's serious consideration, she packed her cat. If she carried the bag in her arms instead of pulling the drawstring tight and putting it over her shoulder, he would be able to breathe. She put only a shirt or two of her own in the bottom of the bag. She had the vague impression that farmers were very poor—a great many stories told in the marketplace began, *Once, my excellencies, there was a poor farmer who*—But if she must go about wearing a flour sack, it was all the same to her. Who would see her in the country, after all?

She got Sinja's attention while their mother was talking Kiffen out of taking his entire wardrobe, and showed her Golly curled in the pack, and told her to wait until after dinner and then tell her mother where the cat was. Sinja's ordinary response to being told anything at all was to balk, but she nodded solemnly, rubbed Golly's nose, and said, "After dinner and before sweets, or after sweets, too?"

"After sweets, too, unless she asks you," said Dri.

In other circumstances, the journey might have been exciting and full of interest. Dri did her best to be excited and

interested. Riding out of Liavek in a cart full of cloth and earthenware was nothing new. She had done it many times on her own, staying at the shore or in the marsh for the day and making her return trip in a cart full of cabbages or mint or fish. Kiffen had shown her how it was all done. He had shown her hawks, dragonflies, river rats, sea otters, blackbirds, bluebirds, redbirds, and mockingbirds. He had discoursed on the military difficulties of the desert and the tides in the Saltmarsh and the building of the railroad.

Now, however, as they rode in a small cart and then a large cart and then a very small cart, farther and farther into a huger and huger blue sky, while the accustomed shapes of the earth dwindled and flattened and the road narrowed to a point like an impossibly long waxed-paper cone of soup bought in some giants' version of the Levar's Park, Kiffen did not discourse. He sulked. Dri showed him a red hawk and a blue dragonfly and a running camel, possibly the one carrying a mailbag that included her mother's letter to the aunts, warning of her and Kiffen's coming. But he did not even look at her.

Her cat was not troubled by the first cart, from whose driver one could purchase tidbits of fried fish; nor by the larger cart, which was full of dried seaweed; but even though the smallest cart held jars of cream, oddly being driven away from the City rather than toward it, he protested about every bump and jostle, and did not purr at anything. By the time the driver put them down on a crossroads distinguished from all the others by a clump of three gnarled trees and a parcel of goats, they were a disheveled and grumpy bunch. Before they could also become lost, Mininu stood up from where she

had been talking to the goats and walked to meet them. In the City she had always looked to Dri like the goddess of night, so tall and so dark with flecks of white like stars in her crown of black hair. Under the empty sky of the country, in her brown tunic and leggings with a cap on her hair, she seemed smaller and more like a person.

They must both have looked quite fretful, because her first words were, "Never worry, I have your mother's letter." She added as she touched her forehead in greeting and then patted their shoulders, "She didn't say that you were bringing any more livestock."

"He's very clever," said Dri, "and I'll keep him out of trouble. He's very meek with other cats, they don't mind him."

"Oh, we have no cats. Your cousins will be happy to see him. I suppose he sleeps on your bed. You will want to talk to Numa about that." She relieved Kiffen of his huge pack, removed Dri's smaller one from her shoulder with her other hand, and walked off down the northern road, leaving them to follow. Golly bumped his head under Dri's chin, which was an improvement on his behavior of the previous day and night.

The walk took perhaps as long as it would to go from Dri's house to the far end of the Levar's Park, but it was otherwise unlike any walk she had ever taken. The road was made of gravel, like the gardens at the Tichenese Embassy, except that their gravel was black and red and green and pure white, and this was a dusty gray. The land looked as flat as a griddle, but from time to time one's legs would give notice that in fact the road was going up and then down and then up again, in a stealthy fashion.

Dri did not realize that they were near the house until they were almost upon it. It was screened from the north and east by a triple row of mixed cedar trees, which Dri recognized, and leafy ones shaped like an elongated drop of water, which she did not. The house was made of cedarwood and gray and white stone, with a roof of cedar. It had no upstairs, and was very well supplied with windows. When Kiffen remarked on this, Mininu said, "Yes, this country has never been fortified. We have been the cause of many wars, but they all took place on the seas."

Mininu, who came from Ombaya, was their thin aunt. Their other aunt, their round aunt, their mother's sister, was called Sinja, and Dri's sister had of course been named after her.

The elder Sinja came running out of the house, trailed by two people taller than she was and one much shorter. Mininu and Sinja were raising three children, two from Ombaya—the tall ones, a boy and a girl called Wari and Welo, respectively—and one from Liavek—the short one, a much younger girl who was called Numa.

Dri had expected a great many farmhands, and not only cats but dogs. There were none of these, and this seemed a small family to do the work of a farm. They were all usually busy doing something or the other, and whenever Kiffen and Dri, who stayed together like each other's shadow for the first few days, came across them, work was offered, but smilingly and offhandedly. Apples appeared in bins and goat's milk in churns, and sometimes even cheese upon the table, without Dri's being able to see that anybody had picked any apples or milked any goats.

Fields of tall grass were mown and the grass gathered in cunning hillocks that, Wari explained proudly, would shed even the heaviest rain. But Dri had seen none of the family in the hayfield. The goats moved here and there, but nobody seemed to be telling them what to do. Then again, they were goats. The chickens were another matter, though. She had been shown how to feed the chickens that first night, but two mornings later she forgot and rushed out in a panic, followed by a mewing cat also with a point to make about his own late breakfast, and the chickens were pecking at corn that she had not scattered. She knew where her cousins and aunts had been all morning. Perhaps they worked all night, sneaking out of the children's common sleeping room after their soft city cousins were asleep. Dri stayed awake as long as she could on the fourth night, but nobody left the room.

Dri settled down insofar as she knew how to pump water for a bath and where the woodpile was, but she felt, on the whole, unsettled. There seemed to be nothing in the house to read but schoolbooks. She missed the library and the orderly progression of her work there. She even missed Mundri. When she sat or worked with her thin cousins, she felt like one of many nails made without much thought by a skilled smith, or a paper lantern of the cheaper sort that nobody had bothered to paint a special flower or character on. It was Kiffen with his round face and heavy shoulders who looked special. She wondered if she should be eating twice as much as usual, but that had never made any difference before.

Besides, she hated the food. It was all animal stuff: chicken, eggs, chicken fat, egg fat for all she knew; milk and cheese

and milk fat; sometimes goat, and of course goat fat. And it had no flavor to speak of other than its own fat animal flavor. Once they had a dish of lentils and she pounced on it with glee, only to find it coated with chicken fat and bits of meat, and quite inedible.

Golly loved the food, and began to look rather round himself.

In addition to being thin while eating fat, her cousins did not talk. This was the way Dri put it to herself. They did talk, really. That first evening at dinner, they exclaimed over Golly and asked his history and his habits; they asked after young Sinja and Melandin and their parents; they asked about Kiffen's work and Dri's work and what the railroad was like. They seemed to want only description, though. Dri and Kiffen's energetic disagreement about the amount of money the Red Temple possesed elicited only a polite silence.

Ending this silence none too soon for Dri, Mininu said, "Your mother's letter was rather hurried. I see that the Red Temple is now without a leader."

"Well, of course Resh's deputy Pitullio would—" began Kiffen.

"I think it would be just as well," said Mininu, "if this news were kept within the family for the time being. It will arrive from the City by a myriad of means soon enough, but I would prefer that nobody speak of it to anyone until one of us has heard it as gossip first."

"But we may whisper it at bedtime," said Wari.

"I think not for the present," said Mininu.

"May I ask one thing?" said Numa, the youngest cousin.

Dri's only memory of her was of a two-year-old screeching because she was afraid of the black dragonflies in the Saltmarsh, but she seemed steadier now.

"If your question is kept nameless," said Sinja the aunt.

"Why did our cousins' parents send them out of the City?"

Dri was much interested, since she was the one whose life had been upended. She watched Sinja and Mininu exchange glances and then nods. How could they talk without talking?

"A great leader, good or ill," said Mininu after this silent communication was concluded, "is like the keystone of an arch. Remove her and stones will fall."

"Water always rolls downhill," said Numa.

"Very sensible, Numa," said Sinja.

"But how can you be prepared for that kind of surprise?" demanded Dri.

Her aunts and cousins looked at her as if she had spoken in Ombayan—except that they knew Ombayan. Tichenese, perhaps. Kiffen said thoughtfully, "Really, you know, how can it be a surprise if it always happens?"

"Well, silly," said Dri, exasperated, "if it happens whenever there is an occasion for it to happen but there is not often an occasion."

"It's better not to call names," said Sinja, very kindly.

Dri looked at Kiffen, who gave her a very slight shrug. Neither of them said anything else. There seemed a kind of resistance against speech in the room itself, so that to consider speaking was like pushing against a stuck door.

They had arrived on a Luckday, and after almost a week

of the relentless sameness of meals, Dri had begun to think that she would starve or survive on windfall apples and the occasional potato rescued from being boiled, mashed, and smothered in sour cream. Then Rainday came around. For breakfast, there was congee. Dri approached it warily, expecting a huge blob of butter or sour cream or chicken fat, but it was quite innocent of these embellishments. It was full of parsley, chives, and spinach rather than ginger, green onion, and seaweed, but she didn't care. She devoured three bowlfuls, and Mininu looked at her thoughtfully.

At lunch they had a stew of potatoes, green beans, carrots, and mushrooms, with garlic and brown sauce. Dri wondered if she could save the leftovers under her bed and eat them all week. Brown sauce was very preserving, her mother said. Unfortunately, Golly liked it. At dinner they had sour cabbage soup with wheat dumplings. Sour cream was offered, but it was not assumed to be everybody's favorite.

She was trying to concoct a way to ask about the abrupt change of menu, and whether it might last a long, long time, without sounding snooty, judgmental, whiny, or spoiled, when Wari, the eldest, heaved a gigantic sigh and proclaimed, "How I hate Raindays!"

Both aunts looked at him warningly; he pushed out his lower lip and, ostentatiously reaching for the bowl of sour cream, covered the surface of his soup with it. Welo rolled her eyes in a sisterly fashion.

That seemed to settle that. In a normal family, Dri would have asked what was so special about Rainday, but here that would probably be done in sign language of some sort. She

might raise her eyebrows, and perhaps one aunt or another would give her a little book for farm children, and the answer would be in the last chapter. This thought amused her so much that she laughed, and got two warning looks of her own.

"I love Rainday," she said calmly.

"There, Wari, you see," said Sinja.

Wari rolled his eyes again. Dri bit her tongue on the remark that he wouldn't see much for long if he kept doing that.

She tried to repeat this witticism to Kiffen later, but Kiffen was proving a frail reed. Not only did he love the fat animal food, he very shortly vanished into this new family culture as if he had been born to it. Dri wondered if he would even want to come home with her. She caught him in the apple orchard that Rainday evening and asked him outright.

"Do try not to be insane," he said, an old family remark that cheered Dri quite a lot. "Of course I wouldn't want to stay here always. It would be like one endless Festival Week—no proper work and rich food, day after day."

"And no proper talk," said Dri wistfully.

"Yes, truly, a fine meditative silence."

"There is nothing fine about it."

"Not being challenged to a duel every five seconds is fine."

"Do try not to be insane," said Dri, but her heart was not in it.

Kiffen said comfortingly, "I would like to be at my work this moment."

"Kiffen," said Dri, and had to pause and breathe as if she had been running. She wanted to ask a question, but it was

very hard. Finally she said, "I think that you know what happened to Resh, and I want you to tell me."

"I don't precisely know," said Kiffen. "I have an idea. One hears stories, you know, and perhaps I put them together in the wrong order. But Resh wanted the Red Temple to be first in Liavek. He wanted to drive the other temples out. When he was a little drunk, my captain said that Resh had given the orders that destroyed the Gold Temple. I think that perhaps he tried to drive out some faith or god that was stronger than he was."

"But, Kiffen! There is nothing one could do that would balance an act like that." Dri looked up at the sky; she felt that it ought to be falling.

"I don't believe that we really understand others' acts," said Kiffen. "We only understand how those acts would be if we had done them ourselves. So you or I, we couldn't balance a huge act like that. But we are not Resh."

"And Resh is dead," said Dri. She thought of a dollhouse, a tall and imposing and richly furnished dollhouse, its rooftree upheld by the striving figures. Resh had ordered the destruction of the Gold Temple; the red figure, then, might hook its heel behind the ankle of the gold one, and then the house would fall on them both. What need of a stronger god to seek revenge when one could bring down all by oneself? She shivered.

They were looking at each other, feeling at a loss, when they heard their names being called. Welo, who tended toward dreaminess, was trudging through the orchard, calling without bothering to look. Kiffen hailed her, and she looked

startled. “It’s Rainday,” she said. “Come back to the house for the Affirmation.”

She walked off again, and they followed after a moment. Dri said to her brother, “I wonder if the Twin Forces are here, too.”

“The Twin Forces are everywhere. They hold up the world. They are in all of us.”

“I wonder if they are in the Way of Herself.”

“Of course.”

“I think the Ombayans would say the Way of Herself was in the Twin Forces.”

“They can say what they like,” said Kiffen.

Dri glared at him. That was not a cooperative remark. It discouraged argument. He was ingesting more than the wrong food. The effort was great, but she said, as she would have said without a second thought at home, “I thought there were different gods in different places.”

“There are,” said Kiffen briefly, “but the Twin Forces are above gods.”

“There is no way to know that,” said Dri, who was not actually possessed of such firm opinions but could think of no better way to phrase her real question.

“It’s obvious,” said her brother loftily.

They had almost reached the house, and Wari was already holding the door open for them. This gesture looked polite but actually, Dri and Kiffen had privately agreed, indicated impatience. Dri said hurriedly, “We don’t know what they do on Rainday.”

“If they don’t tell us, it’s their fault,” muttered Kiffen.

This was not comforting. However, the Affirmation was

brief and wordless. Dri and Kiffen went to stand with the cousins in the big room with windows on three sides where the weaving and reading were done. Mininu and Sinja had taken a red cloth from a wooden chest and opened the lid to reveal a collection of candles and cups stored in a carved tray made of dozens of small sections. They bowed to the children and to one another, lit candles, poured water into various vessels and finally onto the floor, and then lifted a large wooden cup between them and drank from it one after the other. Sinja brought the goblet to Wari; he drank and passed it to Welo, who drank and passed it to Numa; and so it came finally to Kiffen, who sipped cautiously and gave Dri a reassuring wink along with the goblet.

Dri took a cautious sip of her own and almost gasped. The water was cold and had a complicated flowery flavor. The room was stuffy and warm, and she would have liked to gulp from the goblet, but nobody else had. So she refrained.

People separated to their various occupations without speaking, but Dri lingered in the big room while Sinja briskly packed everything into the trunk again. She had never participated in a religious ritual before and wanted to think about it. The Red Temple did have rituals involving the Twin Forces, but Atliae had told her that she was not ready for the large public ones, let alone anything smaller and more secret. This first experience had been so everyday and matter-of-fact, except for the shock of the water.

"I hope that you have something to do, Dri," said Sinja.

This meant, "Try not to be idle," but it was also an inquiry into her well-being.

"I was going to read some history while the light lasts," said Dri. Her cousins had settled on the idea that the library she worked in was for historians, and they seemed concerned that she would forget her knowledge if not gently nagged.

"Good, good. There are plenty of candles," said Sinja, and went out. She had not wiped up the spilled water.

Dri walked over to the place where Mininu and Sinja had been standing. The water had reached out a long finger toward the south, and another to the east. Dri was surprised. She took from her pocket a marble that she kept in case Golly should want more amusement than he could provide for himself. She bent and put the marble on the polished wide board next to the pool of water. It rolled north and fetched up under Sinja's loom. Having done this, Dri was not sure what she had discovered. After a moment she got the largest of the history books and studied the map in the middle of it. Ombaya was south of the plains the farm stood on, and Liavek was to the east. Dri retrieved Golly's marble and went to get herself a drink of ordinary water from the pump in the kitchen.

Then she went about the house, with the pewter cup of ordinary water in her hand. In all the rooms that she entered, the water from the pump that she poured out of the pewter cup spread slowly or ran eagerly in the same direction as the marble rolled. The floors of the house were like the land about it; they seemed flat but were really made of a great many small ups and downs. Golly appeared, stretching, about halfway through her activities, and aside from one moment when he rolled in the water and was affronted, he was useful in that he could always find the marble and bat it back to the center

of the room. His mishap also made her think of what would happen if anybody slipped on the water she had left, so she went about wiping up all the pools she had left behind. The pool of water from the Affirmation had somehow disappeared on its own.

She was obliged to omit the kitchen and the room where all the children slept from her roster, since that was where people were in the evenings. She dealt with the sleeping room the next morning by being late to breakfast, but she despaired of the kitchen's ever being empty. Someone was almost always cooking something or making bread or preserving fruit or using the large table for carving or writing.

Her natural impulse in such a puzzlement would have been to consult Kiffen, but she felt somewhat hurt over their conversation in the orchard. A little pondering, however, provided her with a very likely idea of what he would have suggested.

So that night she kept herself awake by reciting songs and poems to herself, and when her supply of these ran dry, by naming all the rivers and mountains in and around Liavek. Then she tried to list all the Levars of Liavek, and their Regents, where those had been necessary. Her knowledge was still too imperfect to let her make much of a list, so she considered instead her scheme to find out which way water ran in all the rooms of the house. She thought that perhaps she had been driven to action because it was so hard to simply ask questions in this house. But there was something homelike, too, in seeing what water would do, even if she had no family members to help her.

Her brother and cousins were asleep very soon, but she could hear Sinja and Mininu moving about the rest of the house, and then the murmur of their voices, and then silence. Some time passed. The air sliding through the open windows became cool, the leaves of the oak trees rustled, and finally, caught in their branches, she saw the tiny bright curve of light that was the waning moon. She got up carefully. Golly stood up from his position at her feet and settled onto her pillow while she was still looking for her slippers.

Even after such long staring into the dark, she could not see very much. It was fortunate that on account of the food's disagreeing with her in the first days of her visit, she had been told to change beds with Numa so that she might sleep nearer the door. She made her way very slowly, if not patiently, to the kitchen, mostly holding her breath. She had pumped a cup of water after dinner and left it behind a stack of bowls in a lower cupboard. She got it out with only a single ring of pewter against earthenware. It sounded like the largest gong owned by the Red Temple to her, but nobody seemed to stir after.

Dri tilted the cup, and stopped, wanting very much to laugh. She had forgotten that she would need light. What a pity I never invested my luck, she thought. Almost any street magician can make a little light. She put the cup down on the table and groped in the table's drawer for a candle. The fire in the stove never went out; Mininu had told her so, during that first day when it had been permitted for the cousins to ask about Liavek and for Dri and Kiffen to ask about the house. She opened the oven door. A red glow came out, but no heat. She hoped it would light her candle. It did, with a whoosh that

made her jump back, feeling glad that she had laid hold of a long, new candle rather than a stub.

Finally, finally, she was able to sit firmly on the worn stone floor with cup, candle, and marble, and make her investigation. The flickering thread of water moved, unsurprisingly, toward the hollow worn in front of the stove by several generations of cooks. The marble followed. Something white streaked through the candlelight, pounced on the marble, and knocked it with an enormous clang into the iron base of the oven. Dri muffled her squeak of surprise. I thought cats were stealthy, she thought at Golly. He was waiting for her to pick up the marble, and she did so, and put it in her pocket. Luckily for her, he was not a talkative cat and merely stared and followed her when she went to sit down at the table and get her breath back.

The big squares of the windows were pale. Dri looked up and out, over the flat land with no intervening towers or hills, and saw the crescent moon, now a thin curve of red, disappearing beyond the edge of the world. It would be dawn soon. Her startlement had thoroughly woken her up. She would go out with her cat and watch the sun rise.

There was a welcome chill in the air. All the grasses and little trees were drenched in dew. Golly came out of the grass after a single exploration, shaking his paws and ears, and thereafter stayed on the path with Dri.

In Liavek, if you wanted to watch the sun or moon rise or set, you went up a hill, or if you did not want to walk so far, you went up on the roof of any building you could get to, preferably one with a garden and seats. She was not sure what

to do here. The sky was so much larger that perhaps it hardly mattered. The apple orchard was on a south-facing slope of what passed for a hill. The eastern slope of that hill was a garden of onions, in raised beds. She could sit on the stone edge of a bed and have a good view.

When she had settled there, in the strange half-light, Dri felt exposed. It was as bad as the sea and somewhat worse than the desert. It was so very flat. Parts of Liavek were flat, but there were buildings and trees breaking up the sky, providing shade and concealment. She didn't know what she thought was going to catch her, but here, whatever it was, if it wanted to come out of the sky and pluck her up as a hawk does a mouse, where could she hide?

At least, she thought, sitting straight on the cold stone of the garden edge and glaring at the huge colorless bowl above her, she would hear the hawk coming. The silence was as enormous as the flatness. And yet her ears were so unattuned to it, perhaps she would not after all hear the hawk. Because she had always lived in the City, she knew how to listen for voices, footsteps, drunken brawls and drunken revelry; wheels, hooves, paws; windows opening, nails going into wood, water sloshing in buckets, students of music practicing the flute and professionals playing the drum; the clatter of dishes and tiles, the shriek of the train whistle and the singing rumble of the train. Here in the country, she knew that the wind was making a sound in the grass, but her ears dismissed it as a barrier to hearing the sounds that she wanted, which were not there.

But we are there, she did not hear but heard somehow, and then, not believably, *If we were there, she would hear us, so where*

are we? Or where is she? It was the kind of thing she thought all day long, taken out of her head and put into the rustle of the dry grasses in the ceaseless breeze. Was this how it was to be insane?

This thought upset her so much that she took a great breath and spoke to the grass and the apple trees and the empty air. If one were going to be mad, one might as well do the thing thoroughly. Mundri was always intent on doing anything thoroughly. "I want to know who you are," she said.

The wind stopped making the grasses hiss. Now it was truly silent, a silence that made Dri feel even more as if she might fall off the unsafe flat surface of the earth and into the great beckoning sky. Her cat had disappeared. She wanted to clear her throat, to shout, to scuff her boots in the dry grass. But something was waiting to speak; she felt it.

When it spoke it was much more like a voice, alive in the chilly moving air. "The stranger should rather say than ask."

Oh, thought Dri, is that why it is so hard to ask anything? They might have said something before. She said, "I am Kisandrion Dorlianish, and I come from the City of Luck."

"Ahhhhh," said the voice, said several voices, unless it was only the wind.

"You sound as if you know my city," she said.

"We are exiles therefrom."

"So am I," said Dri, and sighed.

"Why so?"

"My mother thought it wasn't safe for my brother and me to stay."

The wind began again, hiss, rustle, whisper, scratch. It

sounded like a gigantic grassy conference. Maybe it was. Dri did not know what lived out here that was not people or domestic animals and birds. In the mountains were the shy gray mountain folk; in the sea were Kil; in the desert were trolls. But here among the farms, all the stories were simple and prosaic. Magical beans, golden duck eggs, cows that gave an endless amount of cream, talking goats, silver apples, geese that riddled and pigs that sang. But wait, the wind voice was not a thing native here; it had said that it was an exile from the City. She frowned, thinking. The City was full of everything, of course, from far and near, and an exile might not mean a native creature, just an accustomed one. Still, what had the City itself that might speak with the voice of the grass, unseen? Chipmunks, she thought, and giggled.

The wind stopped at once; the grass was silent. The sun had come up; she had not noticed. Dri's impulse was to speak, to repeat her question, to explain why she was laughing. But people hereabouts did not seem to use speech as she and her family used it. She hugged herself in the chill and tried not to think of chipmunks. The oldest, most luck-soaked things in Liavek were all remnants of the older city on whose site Liavek was built; but older than that were the chipmunks. They had their own god, Rikiki, who was blue, and irresistibly funny as long as you stayed out of his way. Her imagination peopled the brown and green and golden landscape around her with blue chipmunks, and she giggled again.

"Is exile a matter for laughter?" said the voice.

"No," said Dri hastily.

"What is, then?"

"I was thinking of chipmunks," said Dri, feeling somewhat helpless. She was so tired of not being able to ask questions that it was a relief to answer anybody who did.

"Do you follow Rikiki?"

"No," said Dri. "But I like the chipmunks in the Levar's Park. Once one of them ran up my leg and stole a roasted potato from my hand."

She felt entirely foolish as soon as she had made this childish remark, but the voice said, "A wise denizen, indeed," and did not seem sarcastic.

Dri put her hand to her forehead in formal acknowledgment, and said, "I thank you."

There was a brief pause in which the sky seemed less full of threats.

"We had hoped for better news," said the dry voice suddenly; Dri jumped. "We had hoped to hear that the City was safer."

"Well, mothers have particular ideas, you know," said Dri. "The City seemed just the same to me. And if Resh was so dangerous, I would think the City was safer without him."

The drooping grasses around her stood up straight, like the hair on a cat's back when the cat is angry. "Do you tell us that Resh has left the City?"

"He's dead," said Dri.

The grass crackled. Dri was tolerably sure that it was not supposed to do that. She stood up.

"Rumor hath many tongues," said the voice.

"I know, but I work for the Red Temple and I was told this by my brother, who was in His Eminence's special guard."

The grass around her still crackled. She took a few steps, looking around her. She saw the small trees on the little hill shake, and then all the grass flatten as if a huge invisible beast were striding across the fields from west to east. All the grass within her view lay down. Dri sat down on the path herself, feeling it prudent, and just as she did so, a wall of air pushed her backward. She lay there for some time after it had passed, because it smelled of home. Not the dry grass, warm earth, leaf-mold smell of the plains, but wet stone, cold metal, hot oil and spices, roasted potatoes and roasted nuts, flowers grown out of season and put out in their pots on warm days, even a faint whiff of sewage unmodified by the application of luck—all flowed over her and lingered in the air when it was still again.

In time, the smell of home wore thin and vanished. Dri sat up, and stood up, and stood still. Everything was the same, and not the same. She turned slowly in a circle. The orchard, the onion garden, the small hill with oak trees and the mass of trees that marked the strange low farmhouse were all there. They looked the wrong color. She took a step or two, and a mouse ran across the packed dirt in front of her. Two more followed it, and another. Dri went on cautiously, wishing for her cat. She called him, but he did not appear.

Before she reached the house, she had seen several more dark-colored mouselike animals with short tails, several rabbits in several sizes, something that might have been a rat, and a smooth brown blunt-headed animal larger than a cat.

The house, like the landscape, looked as if some sparkle had gone from it, although it was basking in early sunshine.

Inside, it felt stuffy. Dri went into the kitchen. Everyone was there, sitting around the big table peeling apples. They looked as they often had before, and yet they did not. Dri slid into her assigned seat. Wari passed her a knife and bowl. They knew that she did not have the knack of peeling apples, but some feeling of invisible pressure in the air made her forbear to speak. This sensation of having inquiry stifled was much harder to bear after the free speaking in the orchard.

She made a slow careful start on the nearest apple, but had to stop. The atmosphere was so strong that she felt she must keep a close eye on everyone. Kiffen looked as she felt, alert and wary. Mininu and Sinja had serene faces, but they kept exchanging glances. Dri felt that in a more outward family, they would be talking at the tops of their voices and gesturing. All three of their children were watching them, and had a general air of injured virtue.

"Dri," said Sinja, in her usual gentle tones, "I have not seen Golly these two hours."

"He was in the onion beds just now."

Sinja smiled at her, and finished removing the peel from an apple in one long curling piece.

"I hope he hasn't done anything bad," said Dri.

"Not that I know of."

"I could go and fetch him."

"No, I think he will manage on his own."

"There was a very large wind just now," said Dri. When nobody made any reply, she pulled in the air for the enormous effort necessary and asked, "Did you feel it?"

"This is a very windy place," said Mininu.

If Sinja had said that, Dri might, she thought, have had the courage to describe the wind and how it was different from the ordinary wind of the plains; but Mininu was truly formidable, all without even raising her voice.

That was the most conversation they had all day. Dri had thought it a house devoid of conversation already, but that day even the nods and raised eyebrows and smiles and half sentences were absent. The faint pressure she had always felt, oppressing her desire to ask a thousand questions, to question every statement, and to dissect every definition, had grown heavier and firmer, and sat on her chest like an older brother in an evil mood.

When Dri went to take her bath, the tub was full of spiders and there was a mouse on the windowsill. She backed out slowly. Not much later she heard Numa cry from the big room, "Min, Min, there is a snake in my chair!" Mininu came striding past Dri and toward the big room, but no other words passed.

Dri sank down on her bed, checking it for previous occupants first, and marveled at a family that could be silent in the face of this invasion. After she had marveled, she felt grateful. Her conscience was not easy. Mininu had asked her not to tell anyone about Resh's death, and she had blurted it out the first chance she got. Whether a disembodied voice could be defined as "anyone" might be open to debate, if anybody ever would debate in this house, but she still was not easy. If the exiled Liavekan spirits had kept the spiders and other creatures away, and if they had gone back to the City on hearing that Resh was dead, the invasion of all the vermin was Dri's doing.

She wanted to lie down and take a nap, but somebody might think to ask her some pointed questions at any moment. Without thinking much about it, she climbed out of the window and went away toward the hill with the small oak trees atop it. There were piles of last year's leaves there, nicely dry by now. She could sleep and return to the house with more of her wits in working order.

It was a still day with no wind, but Dri kept hearing sounds anyway, rustlings and scrapings and slidings. She supposed the grass was full of spiders and mice and snakes now, just like the house. This made her think twice about curling up in a pile of leaves. When she got to the top of the hill she perched herself on a protruding boulder and tried to examine her intended bed from a safe distance. She was distracted from this pursuit by the sight of Sinja, Mininu, Kiffen, all the cousins, a flock of chickens, and some five or six goats, who were all gathered at the back of the house. Mininu was talking vigorously. Everyone looked very solemn, even the chickens. After Mininu had spoken, Sinja sang a song that sounded Ombayan, and then Mininu sang a song that Dri recognized. She could not make out the words, but the tune was that of "Potboil Blues," which Mininu had once irritably referred to as "that all-too-typically-Liavekan catch." Dri was afflicted with a desire to giggle.

A striped snake slid across the rock at her feet, which was not so funny. She watched the group near the house narrowly. If they went far enough off, perhaps she could sneak back in and sleep in her bed. A bed seemed unlikely to hold as many snakes as a pile of leaves, so she had better settle for that.

With luck, whatever they were doing would send the snakes and other creatures back to where they had been before, before, before Dri had told the exiled Liavekan voices the secret that Resh was dead. If others undid the results of one's choice, how did that affect the figures striving to keep one's self upright?

The party below was marching around the house rightward, scattering clouds of yellowish matter, except for the chickens and goats, who were eating it. Therefore, it must be grain. Numa had a shining object in her hand and might have been pouring water from it.

"Oh no," said Dri. Perhaps it was not her speaking to spirits, but her going about the house pouring water, that had let all the creatures arrive. Even ordinary Plains water. Perhaps it was both. She could not unpour water, she could not unspeak secrets. As Atliae had taught her, the only way was forward.

"I hope you are here," she said firmly. "Spirits of my city, I hope that you are." She was being as foolish as the people below, but at least nobody could see her.

"They are all gone into the world of stone," said a furrier, cracklier voice. Dri's breath unlocked. She could speak in her native language. I must be careful, she thought. She said, "Do you mean the City?"

"Verily."

"Oh, but the City isn't only stone. It's wood and tile and water and grass and trees and what it really is, is people."

"Do you taste and smell stone when it is by, does it dazzle your eyes and befuddle your mind?"

Dri, sorting swiftly through a number of remarks about jewels and avarice, finally answered, “Not entirely.”

“To us, the City is the world of stone.”

“I’m sitting on a stone.”

“You appear as a voice from a burning light.”

Dri got up and moved carefully to her left, since she thought that the voice might be more leftward than not.

“What am I now?” she asked.

“A voice in the quiet air.”

“Who are you? Can I see you?”

“We are before you in the air.”

“I guess I can’t,” said Dri, staring before her. She saw only the air, just as they did when they looked at her. She spared a glance for the group down at the house. They were now hidden by the windbreak, but she could hear them singing something.

“But who are you?” she repeated firmly.

“If you cannot see us, you will not hear our names.”

“What do you do?”

“What we are bid.”

“Really!” said Dri, entertained. “I know a great many parents who would trade their children for you.”

Several laughs overlapped in the empty air. The same voice said, “That is not bidding as we mean it.”

“Do you mean luck, magical bidding?”

“No, luck has no power over us.”

“Really!” said Dri. She felt warmed, released, returned to herself. All the questions she had suppressed since she arrived, in the shut-door pressure of that house below, seemed to make a pressure of their own in her heart, pushing these

new questions before them. "What about the Twin Forces?" she said. "Do they have power over you?"

"Power over us is held by water, word, and will."

Dri looked again at the house. The group of people and animals had come around to where they started, and Mininu was speaking again.

"Is that what they are doing down there? Getting power over you?"

The several laughs came again. Dri wondered how she knew it was laughter. It was more like, like, she was not sure what. But she felt laughter. The voice said, "They do not know us. They seek those who have fled."

"The city spirits?"

"Our cousins of the stone, indeed."

Dri swallowed hard. "Why did your cousins leave?"

"That which drove them out has in its turn been driven."

"Oh," said Dri.

To speak to the voices of the air had been an action like breathing, an unconsidered choice. But Atliae might say that it should have been considered more than it was. She was glad that Atliae was far away. She wished that she knew of a way to tell whether one of the striving figures in herself was about to hook the feet from under the other. What would it feel like? She felt more herself than she had since they left Liavek. Perhaps some previous choice had made her totter and now she had restored herself. Would Atliae know? Dri did not know what she thought.

"What did they do, your cousins," she asked, "when they were here?"

"All tasks of ours; to guide the grain, to guard the house from moth and mold and the garden from mouse and mold and moth, to guard all things and yet harm none."

"Is that really possible?"

"If we are well bid."

"But they didn't bid you, they bid your cousins from the City?"

"Their bidding is too—sly."

"Oh!" cried Dri, and clapped her hands. "It is, it is, it truly is! They say that they hope you have an occupation when they want you not to be lazy, they, they, oh, yes, *sly* is a grand word!"

"They have need of us now," said the voice, "but they know not how to make us love them."

Dri sobered at once. "Why don't they, do you suppose?"

"They do not know that they have the need; even knowing, their way is not our way."

"Is that the Ombayan way?"

"We have toiled and created for Ombayans who were not sly, but there are many Ombayan ways. What would you call a Liavekan way? Our cousins of the City were as sly as yours of the plains."

"Things are always more complicated than you believe they are," agreed Dri.

"Unless they are simpler."

"Do you think we never see things truly, then?"

"We do not know. When we say 'we,' we have not been accustomed to think of the creatures of the earth in that wind. And yet you speak as properly as could be wished."

"Not if you ask Mininu," said Dri.

"It is she who must ask us."

Dri sat down on a fallen branch, staring down at the antics of her family and the animals. She no longer wanted to laugh. Their way was not her way, but she could tell well enough from her week's stay that they were happy in it. It had fed and clothed them, and had put horrid goat cheese and disgusting chicken eggs in the market for people who liked them; it had tended apple trees and barley fields; it had put that now missing sparkle in the landscape. She had wrecked it. However her interior structure might feel, it was necessary to restore the wreckage. She wondered what Atliae would say, but, as with tending to the kittens, what Atliae would say did not matter. Dri rubbed her tired eyes and firmly addressed the air.

"Do you live here, on their—on this land that they live on?"

"We do, and have always."

"Do you like your tasks, when you are well bidden; do they please you and feed you, and make things beautiful?"

"They do, and have always."

"You can't have had a very happy time of it, can you, while your cousins were here," said Dri.

"We cannot."

"Tell me, then," said Dri, "who is it that may bid you well?"

Before she went down the hill and back to the house, she scuffed thoroughly through the brown tea-smelling oak leaves that she had thought to take a nap in. On the bare earth thus

revealed she saw a few affronted worms and some hastily retreating roundbugs, just as she might find in her father's garden at home. Those would be good for growing things, she supposed. There were no snakes or mice.

"Thank you," she said to the air, not for the first time, but she had no reply. Her companions were busy.

Dri started down the path with a sigh. If she were behaving in Mininu's way, she would need to say nothing of what had passed. But since she must behave in her own way to restore what she had damaged, she must tell Mininu everything. Now that order was restored, she could only feel chastened for a few moments before she wanted, once again, to laugh. Mininu would be able to do as she liked, as she always did, in her household, but to conciliate the resident spirits of the air, she would have to ask questions and make statements and even, from time to time, to argue. "I am in such a great leafpile of trouble," she said, having gotten used to talking to the air in the past few hours. "I wonder what they will do to me."

Perhaps they would send her home.

She smiled at the thought, and then stopped smiling. Perhaps they would call her back once every year, to speak as Mininu would not, and eat fat cheese except on Raindays.

Golly came trotting out of the tall grass with a mouse in his mouth.

"That will be the last of those you see hereabouts," Dri told him.

But perhaps they would send her home first.

Pamela Dean is the author of six fantasy novels and a handful of short stories; five of the stories are set in the same world as "Cousins."

Firebird has reissued her Secret Country Trilogy (*The Secret Country, The Hidden Land*, and *The Whim of the Dragon)* and *Tam Lin*; a reissue of *The Dubious Hills* is forthcoming. She is currently working on *Going North*, a sequel to both the Secret Country books and *The Dubious Hills*.

She lives in Minneapolis with some congenial people, a lot of cats, and an overgrown garden. You can find a few photographs, links to interviews with her, a bibliography, and the occasional announcement at **www.dd-b.net/pddb**.

Author's Note

Sharyn says I should tell you why I wrote this story. There isn't one reason, of course. I wrote it because she asked me to; and because I loved the first *Firebirds* anthology and wanted to be in such good company. But the reason that those other reasons could be gratified is that Kisandrion, my protagonist, had a story in her. She and her family come from a novel I'm writing. It's set in a shared world called Liavek, about which five volumes of stories were published in the 1980s. The other characters in that novel are people I've written about before, but she was new, and she had a lot of opinions. The novel is mostly about other people, so that her opinions about family

and food and how to conduct a conversation, about religion and how one chooses right actions, did not have very much room to grow. I wanted to give her a landscape to try her thoughts out on. I also wanted to write a story that did not have certain usual complications, so that other complications caused by Kisandrion's opinions could also have room. I wanted the story to have no romantic element and not much darkness in it. When I began to write, I thought that when Kisandrion got to the country she would learn to garden. I had no notion at all that she would talk to the air, or what would happen when she did.

Emma Bull

What Used to Be Good Still Is

Porphyry is a volcanic rock. Maybe that's why it happened. Maybe it was because the hill that became a pit was named Guadalupe, for the Virgin of Guadalupe, who appeared in a vision to a Mexican peasant a long time ago. Maybe it's because walls change whatever they enclose, and whatever they leave out.

And maybe it could have happened anywhere, anytime. But I don't believe that for a second.

I expect I wouldn't have taken too much notice of Sara Gutierrez if my pop hadn't. I was a senior at Hollier High School, varsity football first string, debating team, science club. Sara was the eighth-grade sister of Alfred Gutierrez, who I knew from football. But the Gutierrezes lived in South Hollier, down the slope from the Dimas shaft, on the other side of Guadalupe Hill, and we lived on Collar Hill above downtown with the lawyers and store owners and bankers. Alfred and I didn't see much of each other outside of football practice. The only time my father saw Alfred's father

was when Enrique Gutierrez had his annual physical at the company hospital, or if he got hurt on the job and Pop had to stitch him up.

But one night I was up studying and heard Pop in the kitchen say, "I don't know if that youngest Gutierrez girl is simple or plain brilliant."

Pop didn't talk about patients at home as a rule, so that was interesting enough to make me prick up my ears.

"Probably somewhere in between, like most," Mom said. Mom didn't impress easily.

"She came into the infirmary today with her chest sounding like a teakettle on the boil. If I can keep that child from dying of pneumonia or TB, I'll change my name to Albert Schweitzer." He paused, and I knew Mom was waiting for him to come back from wherever that thought had led him. She and I were used to Pop's parentheses. "Anyway, while I'm writing up her prescription, she says, 'Dr. Ryan, what makes a finch?'"

"I don't suppose you told her, 'God,'" Mom said with a sigh.

"I didn't know what to say. But when she saw I didn't get her drift, she asked why are house finches and those little African finches that Binnie Schwartz keeps in her parlor both finches? So I started to tell her about zoological taxonomy—"

"I just bet you did," Mom said. I could hear her smiling.

"Now, Jule—"

"Go on, go on. I won't get any peace till you do."

"Well, then she said, 'But the finches don't think so. We're human beings because we say we are. But the finches don't think they're all finches. Shouldn't that make a difference?'"

A pause, and the sound of dishes clattering in the wash water. "Sara Gutierrez spends too much time on her own," Mom said. "Invalids always think too much."

I don't remember what Pop replied to that. Probably he argued; Pop argued with any sentence that contained the word *always.*

By the time I came home for the summer after my first year of college, the matter was settled: Sara Gutierrez was bright. She'd missed nearly half her freshman year in high school what with being out sick, but was still top of her class. Pop bragged about her as if he'd made her himself.

She was thin and small and kind of yellowish, and you'd hardly notice if she was in the same room with you. The other girls in town got permanent waves to look like Bette Davis. Sara still looked like Louise Brooks, her hair short, no curl at all. But that summer I saw her at the ballpark during one of the baseball games. She looked straight at me in the stands. There was something in her eyes so big, so heavy, so hard to hang on to that it seemed like her body would break from trying to carry it.

Nobody ever suggested that Sara was bright at anything likely to be of use to her. A long while later I looked her up in the *Hollier Hoist*, the high school yearbook, to see what her classmates must have made of her. She'd been a library monitor. That was all. No drama society, no debating team, no booster club, no decorating committee for the homecoming dance.

I guess she saved her debating for me. And she danced, all right, but you won't find that in the yearbooks.

Hollier was a mining town—founded in the 1880s by miners and speculators. The whole point of life here was to dig copper out of the ground as cheap as possible, and hope that when you got it to the surface you could sell it for a price that made the work worthwhile. The town balanced on a knife edge, with the price of copper on one side, and the cost of mining it on the other.

And that didn't apply only to the miners and foremen and company management. If copper did poorly, so did the grocers, mechanics, lawyers, and schoolteachers. What came up out of those shafts fed and clothed us all. Pop was a company doctor. Without copper, there was no company, no one to doctor, no dinner on the table, no money for movies on Saturday, no college tuition. He used to say that Hollier was a lifeboat, with all of us rowing for a shore we couldn't see. The company was the captain, and we trusted that the captain had a working compass and knew how to read it.

Underground mining's expensive. The shafts went deeper and deeper under the mountains following the veins of high-grade ore, the pumps ran night and day to pump out the water that tried to fill those shafts, and the men who dug and drilled and blasted had to be paid. But near the surface, under what farmers call dirt and miners call "overburden," around where the rich veins used to run, there was plenty of low-grade ore. Though it didn't have as much copper in it, it could be scraped right off the surface. No tunnels, no pumps, and a hell of a lot fewer men to pay.

Guadalupe Hill was a fine cone-shaped repository of low-grade ore.

The summer after my sophomore year at college, I came home to find the steam shovels scooping the top off Guadalupe Hill. You could see the work from the parlor windows on Collar Hill, hear the roar and crash of it funneled up the canyon from the other side of downtown. Almost the first thing I heard when I got off the train at the depot was the warning siren for a blast, and the dynamite going off like a giant bass drum. From the platform I could see the dust go up in a thundercloud; then the machinery moved in like retrievers after a shot bird.

As Pop helped me stow my suitcase in the trunk of the Hudson, I said, "I'd sure like to watch that," and jerked my head at Guadalupe Hill.

"I'd take you over now, but your mother would fry me for supper."

"Oh, I didn't mean before I went home." I would have meant it, but I knew he'd be disappointed in me if I couldn't put Mom before mining.

Once I'd dropped my suitcase in my room and given Mom a kiss and let her say I looked too thin and didn't they feed me in that frat house dining room, Pop took me down to watch the dig.

It was the biggest work I'd ever seen human beings do. Oh, there'd been millions of dollars of copper ore taken out of the shafts in Hollier. Everyone in town knew there were a thousand miles of shafts, and could recite how many men the company employed; but you couldn't *see* it. Now here was Guadalupe Hill crawling with steam shovels and dump trucks, men shouting, steam screeching, whistles, bells. It went as

smooth and precise as a ballet troupe, even when it looked and sounded like the mouth of hell.

And the crazy ambition of the thing! Some set of madmen had wanted to turn what most folks would have called a mountain inside out, turn it into a hole as deep and as wide as the mountain was tall. And another set of madmen had said, "Sure, we can do that."

Later I wasn't surprised when people said, "Let's go to the moon," because I'd seen the digging of Guadalupe Pit. It was like watching the building of the Pyramids.

Pop stopped to talk to the shift boss. Next to that big man, brown with sun and streaked with dust, confident and booming and pointing with his square, hard hands, Pop looked small and white and helpless. He was a good doctor, maybe even a great one. His example had me pointed toward premed, and medical school at Harvard or Stanford if I could get in. But looking from him to the shift boss to the roaring steam shovels, I felt something in me slip. I wanted to do something big, something that people would see and marvel at. I wanted people to look on my work and see progress and prosperity and stand in awe of the power of Man.

Over dinner, I said, "It makes you feel as if you can do anything, watching that."

"You can, if you have enough dynamite and a steam shovel," Pop agreed as he reached for a pork chop.

"No, really! We're not just living on the planet like fleas on a dog anymore. We're changing it to suit us. Like sculptors. Like—"

"God?" Mom said, even though I'd stopped myself.

"Of course not, Mom." But I'd thought it, and she knew it. She also knew I was a college boy and consequently thought I was wiser than Solomon.

Conversation touched on the basketball team and the repainting of the Women's Club before I said carefully, "I've been wondering if I'm cut out for med school."

Guess I wasn't careful enough; Pop gave me a look over his plate that suggested he was onto me. "Not everyone is."

"I don't want to let you down."

"You know we'll be proud of you no matter what," Mom replied, sounding offended that she had to tell me such a thing.

"I'm thinking of transferring to the Colorado School of Mines."

"Might need some scholarship money—being out of state," said Pop. "But your grades are good. The company might help out, too." He passed me the mashed potatoes. "You don't have to be a doctor just because I am."

"Of course not." I needed to hear him say so, though.

We sat in the parlor after dinner. Pop got his pipe going before he said, "The Gutierrez family isn't doing so well. Tool nippers got laid off at the Dimas shaft, and Enrique with 'em. I think it hit Sara hard."

At first I thought he was talking about Mrs. Gutierrez; I don't know that I'd ever heard her first name. Then I remembered Sara.

"You might take the time for a chat if you see her." He took his pipe out of his mouth and peered at it as if it were a mystery. "She asks about you."

If there's a young fellow who can remain unmoved by the knowledge that a girl asks about him, I haven't met him.

Sara was working in the Hollier Library for the summer. I found an excuse to drop in first thing next day. I came up to the desk and called to the girl on the other side who was shelving reserved books, "Is Sara Gutierrez working today?"

Of course it was her. When I look back on it, it seems like the most natural thing in the world that the girl would straighten up and turn round, and there she'd be. Her hair still wasn't waved, and she wasn't pink and white like a girl in a soap ad. But she wasn't thin anymore, either. Her eyes were big and dark under straight black brows, and she looked at me as if she were taking me apart to see what I was made of. Then she said, without a hint of a smile, "She'd better be, or this whole place'll go to the dickens."

I'd planned to say hello, pass the time of day for a few minutes. But a little fizz went up my backbone, and I heard myself say, "Must be awful hard for her to get time off for lunch."

"She'd probably sneak out if someone made her a decent offer."

"Will the lunch counter at the drugstore do?"

Sara looked at me through her eyelashes. "Golly, Mr. Ryan, you sweet-talked me into it."

"I'll come by for you at the noon whistle."

She had grilled cheese and a chocolate phosphate. Funny the things you remember. And she said the damnedest things without once cracking a smile, until I told her about my fraternity initiation and made her laugh so hard she skidded off her stool. By the time I asked for the check, I'd gotten a good

notion of how to tell when she was joking. And I'd asked her to go to the movies the next night, and she'd said yes.

I picked her up for the movie outside the library, and when it was over, I proceeded to drive her home. But at the turn-off for the road to South Hollier, she said, "I can walk from here."

I turned onto the road. "Not in the dark. What if you tripped in a hole, or met up with a javelina—"

"I'd rather walk," she said, her voice tight and small.

I didn't think I'd said or done anything to make her mad. "Now, don't be silly." I remembered Pop saying that Sara seemed to take her father's layoff hard. Was that what this was about?

"Really—" she began.

In the headlights and the moonlight I could see two tall ridges of dirt and rock crossways to the road on either side, as if threatening to pinch it between them. Two corrugated iron culvert pipes, each as big around as a truck, loomed in the scrub at the roadside.

"Where'd that come from?"

She didn't answer. The Hudson passed between the ridges of dirt, and I could see the lights of the houses of South Hollier in front of me. I pulled over.

"Are they building something here?" I asked.

Sara sat in the passenger seat with her hands clenched in her lap and her face set, looking out the windshield. "It's Guadalupe Hill," she said at last.

"What?"

"They have to put it someplace. The tailings will make a

new line of hills around South Hollier on the east and south."

I tried to imagine it. North and west, the neighborhood ran right up to the mountain slopes. This would turn South Hollier into the bottom of a bowl with an old mountain range on two sides and a new one on the others.

"What about the road?"

"That's what the pipes are for."

"You mean you'll drive through the pipe, like a tunnel?"

"One for each direction," she answered.

"Well, I'll be darned." The more I thought about it, the cleverer it was. Wasn't it just like mining engineers to figure out a way to put a tailings dump where it had to go without interfering with the neighborhood traffic?

Sara shook her head and pleated her skirt between her fingers. I put the Hudson into gear and drove down the road into South Hollier.

At her door, I asked, "Can I see you again?"

She looked up into my face, with that taking-me-apart expression. At last she said, "'May I.' College man."

"May I?"

"Oh, all right." Her eyes narrowed when she was teasing. Before I knew what had happened, she was on the other side of her screen door. Based on her technique, I was not the first young man to bring her home. "Good night, Jimmy."

I drove back to Collar Hill with vague but pleasant plans for the summer.

She met me for lunch a couple times a week, and sometimes she'd let me go with her and carry her packages when she had errands to the Mercantile or the Fair Store. Once

she wanted sheet music from the Music Box, and she let me talk her into a piano arrangement of a boogie-woogie song I'd heard at a college party.

"Should I hide it from my mama?" she asked, with her eyes narrowed.

"I'll bet she snuck out to the ragtime dances."

"Oh, not a good Catholic girl like my mama."

"Mine's a good Catholic girl, too, and she did it."

Sara smiled, just the tiniest little smile, looking down at the music. For some reason, that smile made my face hot as a griddle.

Sara wouldn't go to a movie again, though, or the town chorus concert or the Knights of Columbus dance. I asked her to the Fourth of July fireworks, but she said she was going with her family.

"I'll look for you," I said, and she shrugged and hurried away.

The fireworks were set off at the far end of Panorama Park, down in the newer neighborhood of Wilson, where the company managers lived. Folks tended to spread their picnic blankets in the same spot every year. The park divided into nations, too, like much of Hollier. A lot of the Czech and Serbian families picnicked together, and the Italians, and the Cornishmen; the Mexicans set up down by the rose garden, at the edge of the sycamores. The Gutierrez family would be there.

I got to the park at twilight, and after saying hello to a few old friends from high school, and friends of Mom and Pop's, I pressed through the crowd and the smells from all those pic-

nic dinners. When I got to the rose garden it was almost dark, but I found Alfred Gutierrez without too much trouble.

"You looking for Sara?" he said, with a little grin.

"I told her I'd come round and say hi." I was above responding to that grin.

"She's around here someplace. *Hola, Mamá,*" he called over his shoulder, "where'd Sara go?"

Mrs. Gutierrez was putting the remains of their picnic away. She looked up and smiled when she saw me. "Hello, Jimmy. How's your mama and papa?"

"They're fine. I just wanted to say hello . . . "

Mrs. Gutierrez nodded over her picnic basket. "Sara said she had to talk to someone."

Was it me? Was she looking for me, out there in the night, while I looked for her? There was a bang—the first of the fireworks. "Will you tell her I was here?"

Alfred grinned again, and Mrs. Gutierrez looked patient in the blue light of the starburst.

I watched the fireworks, but I didn't get much out of them. Was Sara avoiding me? Why wouldn't she see me except when she was downtown; in the daytime, but never the evenings? Could it be she was ashamed of her family, so she wouldn't let me pick her up at home? The Gutierrez family wasn't rich, but neither were we. No, it had to be something about me.

It wasn't as if we were sweethearts; we were just friends. I'd go back to college in September, she'd stay here, and we'd probably forget all about each other. We were just having fun, passing the time. She was too young for me to be serious about, anyway. So why was she giving me the runaround?

By the time the finale erupted in fountains and pinwheels, I'd decided two could play that game. I'd find myself some other way to pass the time for the next couple months, and it wouldn't be hard to do either.

That was when I saw her, carried along with the slow movement of people out of the park, her white summer dress reflecting the moon and the streetlights. She was holding someone's little girl by the hand and trying to get her to walk, but the kid had reached that stage of tired in which nothing sounded good to her.

"Hi, Sara."

"Jimmy! I didn't see you there."

I wanted to say something sophisticated and bitter like, "I'm sure you didn't," but I remembered that I'd resolved to be cool and distant. That's when the little girl burst into noisy, angry tears.

"Margie, *Margarita,* I *can't* carry you. You're a big girl. Won't you please—"

I scooped the kid up so quickly that it shocked the tears out of her. "A big girl needs a bigger horse than Sara," I told her, and settled her on my shoulders, piggyback fashion.

We squeezed through the crowd without speaking until we got to Margie's family's pickup truck. The Gutierrez family was riding with them, and I had to see Alfred smirk at me again. Folks started to settle into the back of the truck on their picnic blankets. Something about Sara's straight back and closed-up face, and the fact that she was still not talking, made me say, "Looks kind of crowded. I've got my pop's car here . . ."

Mrs. Gutierrez looked distracted and waved her hands over picnic basket, blankets, sleeping kids, and folded-up adults. "Would you—? Sara, you go with Jimmy. I don't know how . . . " With that, she went back to, I think, trying to figure out how they'd all come in the truck in the first place.

Sara turned to me, her eyes big and sort of wounded. "If you don't mind," she mumbled.

We were in the front seat of the Hudson before I remembered my grievance. "Now look, Sara, you've been dodging me—"

She was startled. "Oh, no—"

"I just want to say you don't have to. We've had some fun, but if you think I'm going to go too far or make a pest of myself or hang on you like a stray dog—"

The force of her head shaking stopped me. "No, really, I don't."

"What's up with you, then? We're just friends, aren't we?"

Sara looked at her knees for a long time, and I wondered if I'd said something wrong. "That's so," she said finally. "We are."

She sounded as if she were deciding on something, planting her feet and refusing to be swayed. I'd only started on my list of grievances, but her tone made me lose my place in the list. "I guess I'll take you home, then."

We talked about fireworks as I drove: which we liked best, how we'd loved the lights and colors but hated the bang when we were kids, things we remembered from past July Fourths in the park. But as I turned down her road and headed toward South Hollier, Sara's voice trailed off. At the tailings ridge, I stopped the car.

"Darn it, Sara, why should I care where you live? Is that what this is about, why you go all stiff and funny?"

She stared at me, baffled-looking. "No. No, it's that . . . " She reached for the door handle. "Come with me, will you, Jimmy?"

In the glare of the headlights, she picked her way up to the foot of the tailings. I was ready to grab her elbow if she stepped wrong; the ground was covered with debris rolled down from the ridge top, rocks of all sizes that seemed to want to shift away under my feet or turn just enough to twist my ankle. But she went slow but steady over the mess as if she'd found a path to follow.

She stopped and tipped her head back. The stars showed over the black edge of the tailings, and I thought that was what she was looking at. "Can you tell?" she asked.

"Tell what?"

Sara looked down at her feet for the first time since she got out of the car, then at the ridge, and finally at me. "It doesn't want to be here."

"What doesn't?"

"The mountain. Look, it's lying all broken and upside down—overburden on the bottom instead of the top, then the stone that's never been in sunlight before. It's unhappy, and now it'll be a whole unhappy ring around South Hollier." She turned, and I saw two tears spill out of her eyes. "We've always been happy here before."

For an instant I thought she was crazy; I was a little afraid of her. Then I realized she was being poetic. Pop had said her dad's layoff had hit her hard. She was just using the tailings as a symbol for what had changed.

"You'll be happy again," I told her. "This won't last, you'll see."

She looked blank. Then she reached out toward the slope as if she wanted to pat it. "This will last. I want to fix it, and there's nothing . . ." She swallowed loudly and turned her face away.

I couldn't think of a way to fix things for her, and I didn't want to say anything about her crying. So I turned back to the tailings ridge, textured like some wild fabric in the headlights. "That gray rock is porphyry, did you know?"

"Of course I do." The ghost of her old pepper was in that. I suppose it was a silly question to ask a miner's daughter.

"Well, do you know it's the insides of a volcano?"

She looked over her shoulder and frowned.

"The insides of a want-to-be volcano, anyway," I went on. "The granite liquefies in the heat and pushes up, but it never makes it out the top. So nobody knows it's a volcano, because it never erupted."

Sara had stopped frowning as I spoke. Now she turned back to the tailings with an expression I couldn't figure out. "It wanted to be a volcano," she murmured.

I didn't know what else to say, and she didn't seem to need to say anything more. "I ought to get you home," I said finally. "Your mom will be wondering."

When we stopped in front of her house, Sara turned to me. "I only told you that, about the . . . about the mountain, because we're friends. You said so yourself. I wouldn't talk about it to just anybody."

"Guess I won't talk about it at all."

She smiled. "Thank you, Jimmy. For the ride, and everything." She slid out of the passenger side door and ran up to her porch. She ran like a little kid, as if she ran because she could and not because she had to. When she got to the porch she waved.

I waved back even though I knew she couldn't see me.

Mom asked me the next day if I'd drive her up to see her aunt in Tucson. We were halfway there before she said, "Are you still seeing Sara Gutierrez?"

I was about to tell her that I'd seen her the night before, when I realized that wasn't how she meant "seeing." "We're just friends, Mom. She's too young for me to think of that way."

"Does she think so, too?"

I thought about last night's conversation. "Sure, she does."

"I know you wouldn't lead her on on purpose, but it would be a terrible thing to do to her, to make her think you were serious when you aren't."

"Well, she doesn't think so." Mom was just being Mom; no reason to get angry. But I was.

"And it would break your father's heart if you got her in trouble."

"I'm not up to any hanky-panky with Sara Gutierrez, and I'm not going to be. Are you satisfied?"

"Watch your tone, young man. You may be grown up, but I'm still your mother."

I apologized, and did my best to be the perfect son for the rest of the trip. But the suggestion that anyone might think Sara and I would be doing things we'd be ashamed to let other

people know about—it hung around like a bad smell, and made me queasy whenever I remembered it.

Did people see me with Sara and think I was sneaking off with her to—My God, even the words, ones I'd used about friends and classmates and strangers, were revolting. Somewhere in Hollier, someone could be saying, "Jimmy Ryan with the youngest Gutierrez girl! Why, he probably dazzled her into letting him do whatever he wanted. And you know he won't think about her for five minutes after he goes back to college."

When Mom and I got back from Tucson, I rang up Sam Koslowsky, who I knew from high school, and proposed a little camping and fishing in the Chiricahuas. He had a week's vacation coming at the garage, so he liked the notion.

For a week, I didn't see Sara, or mention her name, or even think about her, particularly. I hoped she'd gotten used to not seeing me, so when I came back, she wouldn't mind that I stopped asking her out or meeting her for lunch.

It would have been a fine plan, if Mom hadn't wanted me to go down to the library and pick up the Edna Ferber novel she had on reserve. When I saw that the girl at the desk wasn't Sara, I let my breath out in a whoosh, I was so relieved. Maybe relief made me cocky. Whatever it was, I thought it was safe to go upstairs and find a book for myself.

Sara was sitting cross-legged on the floor in front of the geography section, her skirt pulled tight down over her knees to make a hammock for the big book in her lap. She looked up just as I spotted her. "Jimmy, come look at this."

It was as if she hadn't noticed I'd been gone—as if she

hadn't noticed I wasn't there five minutes earlier. She had a wired-up look to her, as if she had things on her mind that didn't leave room for much else, including me. Wasn't that what I'd wanted? Then why was I feeling peeved?

I looked over her shoulder at the book. At the top of the page was a smudgy photograph of Mount Fuji, in Japan. Sara jabbed at the paragraphs below the photo as if she wanted to poke them into some other shape. "Mount Fuji," I said, as if I saw it every day.

"But that's not just the name of the mountain. The mountain's a goddess, or *has* a goddess, I'm not sure which. And her name is Fuji. And look—" Sara flipped pages wildly until she got to one with a turned-down corner (I was shocked—a library assistant folding corners) and another photo. The mountain in this one was sending up blurry dark smoke. "Here, Itza—Itzaccihuatl in Mexico. Itza is sort of a goddess, too. Or anyway, she's a woman who killed herself when she heard her lover died in battle, and became a volcano. And there's a volcano goddess in Hawaii, Pele."

"Sure. All right," I said, since she seemed to want me to say something.

"And there's more than that. Volcanoes seem extra likely to have goddesses, all over the world."

I laughed. "I guess men all over the world have seen women blow their tops."

Instead of laughing, or pretending to be offended, she frowned and shook her head. "There's so much I need to know. Did you want to go to lunch? Because I'm awfully sorry, I just don't have time."

That reminded me that I was annoyed. "I just came to get a book. People do that in libraries." I pulled one down from the shelf above her head and walked off with it. The girl at the desk giggled when she checked it out, and it wasn't until I was outside that I found I was about to read *A Lady's Travels in Burma*. Between that and Mom's Edna Ferber, I figured I was punished enough for being short with Sara.

I waited a week before I stopped by the library again. Again she was too busy for lunch, but as I moved to turn from the desk, she said, "I really am sorry, Jimmy." She didn't look like a girl giving a fellow the brush-off. In fact, something about her eyebrows, the tightness of her lips, made her look a little desperate.

I could be busy, too, I decided, and with better reason. I wrote to the Colorado School of Mines to ask what a transfer required in the way of credits, courses, and tuition. I wrote to some of the company's managers, in town and at the central office, inquiring about scholarship programs for children of employees who wanted to study mining and engineering. I gathered letters of recommendation from teachers, professors, any Pillar of the Community who knew me. Pop helped, and bragged, and monitored my progress as if he'd never had visions of a son following him into medicine.

In mid-August, I got a letter from the School of Mines, conditionally accepting me for the engineering program. All I had to do was complete a couple of courses in the fall term, and I could transfer in January. I took it down to Pop's office as soon as it came, because he was almost as eager as I was.

He was with a patient. I sat in the waiting room for a

few minutes, but I felt silly; waiting rooms are for patients. I ducked into the little room that held Pop's desk and books and smelled like pipe tobacco. The transom over the door between it and the examining room was open, and the first words I heard were from Sara. I should have left, but I didn't think of it.

"See, Margarita? Just a sprain. But don't you go near the tailings again."

"*You* do," said a little voice with a hint of a whine.

"I'm grown up."

"When I'm grown up, can I?"

"Maybe," said Sara, something distant in her voice. "Maybe by then."

"Tailings dumps shift and settle for a while," Pop agreed on the other side of the door. "They're not safe at first for anybody. *Including* grown-ups."

"Have . . . have many people been hurt, in South Hollier?" Sara sounded as if she wanted Pop to think it was a casual question. But I knew her better.

"Some sprains and bruises. Probably some scrapes that I never see, but only minor things. Folks just can't seem to stay off a hill or a high building, whatever you tell 'em. Especially the little ones," Pop added in a new, dopey voice. Margie squealed, as if maybe Pop had tweaked her ear.

I was mostly packed and ready to head back to college when Lucas Petterboro, three years old, wandered away from his yard in South Hollier and out to the new tailings dump. From what could be told after the fact, it seemed he'd caused a little slide clambering up the slope, which had dislodged

a much larger rock, which had produced a still larger slide. Searchers found his shoe at the bottom of the raw place in the dump, which gave them an idea where to start digging.

Pop and Mom and I went to the funeral. Pop had delivered Luke. Everyone in South Hollier was there, and so were a lot of other people, mining families, since the Petterboros had been hard-rock miners down the Princess shaft for thirty years. Mom sat beside Mrs. Petterboro at the cemetery and held her hand; Pop talked to Joe Petterboro, and now and then touched him lightly on the shoulder. The pallbearers were South Hollier men: Mr. Dubnik, who'd won the hard-rock drilling contest three years running; Mr. Slater, who ran a little grocery out of the front of his house; Fred Koch, who'd been in my class and who was clerking in a lawyer's office downtown; and Luis Sandoval, the cage operator for the Dimas shaft. It was a small coffin; there was only room for the four of them. The children of South Hollier stood close to their parents, in their Sunday clothes, confused and frightened. Their mothers and fathers held their hands and wore the expression folks get when something that only happens to other people happens to one of their own.

And me? There wasn't a damned thing for me to do.

So when Sara came up to me, her eyes red in a white face, and slipped her hand into mine, I wanted to turn and bawl like a baby on her shoulder. If she'd spoken right away, I would have.

"So," I said at last, harsher than I'd meant to. "Guess that mountain's still unhappy, huh?"

She let go of my hand. "Yes. It is." She pulled her sweater

close around her, though the sun was warm. "It keeps me awake at night. The engineers say the ridge ought to be stable, but there was a slide last week that came within three feet of the Schuellers' back door."

"Too much rain this summer." That made her shrug, which made me look closer at her. "What do you mean, it keeps you awake? Worrying won't help."

Her eyes were big and haunted and shadowed underneath. "I can hear the mountain, Jimmy."

Her mom called Sara's name. Sara shot me a last frightened look and went to her.

I went back to college the day after the funeral. I sat on the train still seeing that look, still hearing Sara say, "I can hear the mountain." I told myself it was poetry again, and banished her voice. But it always came back.

I shut it out with work. By the time the term ended and I packed all my worldly goods on the train for home, I'd gotten top grades in my classes, a scholarship from the company, and an invitation to visit my fraternity's house on the School of Mines campus at my earliest convenience.

I walked in the back door of the house on Collar Hill and smelled pipe tobacco, ginger snaps, and baking potatoes. I saw the kitchen linoleum with the pattern wearing away in the trafficked spots, saw Mom's faded flowered apron and felt her kiss on my cheek. Suddenly I felt safe. That was the first I knew that I hadn't felt safe for a long time, and that the feeling building in me as the train approached Hollier wasn't anticipation, but dread.

"You'll have to go find us a Christmas tree," Mom said to

me over dinner. "Your father's been so busy lately that it's full dark before he gets home."

"And your mom won't let me buy a Christmas tree in the dark anymore," Pop added.

"Oh, the poor spavined thing you brought home that year! You remember, Jimmy?"

It was as if I'd been away for years. I shivered. "Why so busy, Pop?" If it was the tailings, if it was South Hollier . . .

"Mostly a bumper crop of babies—"

"Stephen!" Mom scolded.

"—along with winter colds and pneumonia and the usual accidents. Price of copper is up, the company's taken more men on for all the shifts, and that just naturally increases the number of damned fools who let ore cars run over their feet."

"Right before I left, the Petterboro baby—"

"Lord, yes. Nothing that bad since, thank God."

"Then the tailings are safe?"

Pop cocked his head and frowned. "Unless you run up to the top and jump off. It's true, though, that the South Hollier dump made more trouble in the beginning and less now than any others. I guess they know what they're doing, after all."

The tightness went out of my back. It was all right. Of course Sara hadn't meant it literally, what she'd suggested at the funeral. And now everything was fine.

When I saw Sara on Main Street the next afternoon, on her way to catch the trolley home, I knew that something wasn't fine at all. Her cheeks were hollow, her clothes hung loose on her, and the shadows around her eyes were darker than when I left.

"You've been sick again," I said, before I realized how rude it would sound.

"No. Ask your dad." She thumped her knuckles against her chest. "Lungs all clear."

"But—" I couldn't tell her she looked awful; what kind of thing was that to say? "Pop's car's down the block. Can I drive you someplace?"

"I'm just headed home."

"Why, I know right where that is!" I sounded too hearty, but she smiled.

"There's still room, with all that chemistry and geometry in there?"

"The brain swells as it fills up. My hat size gets bigger every year."

"Oh, so it's learning that does that."

When we got to the tailings, I saw that the culvert pipes were in place on the roadway, and the fill crested over them about six feet high. I steered the car into the right-hand pipe. I felt like a bug washed down a drain as the corrugated metal swallowed the car and the light. The engine noise rang back at us from the walls, higher and shrill. I wanted to crouch down, to put the Hudson in reverse, to floor it.

"Looks like they've moved a lot of stone since summer." I watched her out of the corner of my eye as I said it.

She nodded. It wasn't the old nervous silence she used to fall into near the tailings. She wasn't stiff or tense; but there was a settled quality to her silence, a firmness.

"Pop says the dump's quit shifting."

Sara looked at me as we came out of the pipe and into South

Hollier. "That's right." She made it sound like a question.

I didn't know what to answer, so instead I asked, "Is your dad back at work?"

"They brought him on as a mechanic at the pit. He likes it. And it means he'll get his full pension after all."

South Hollier was now enclosed in its bowl, a medieval walled town in the Arizona mountains. It looked constrained, like a fat woman in a girdle. But kids played in front yards, women took wash off their clotheslines, smoke rose from chimneys. Everything was all right.

Except it wasn't. Something was out of whack.

When I pulled up to Sara's front door, I said, "We're still friends?"

She thought about it. I realized I liked that better than if she'd been quick to answer. "We are."

"Then I'll say this, one friend to another. Something's eating you, and it's not good. Tell me. I'll help."

Sara smiled, a slow one that opened up like flower petals. We heard her screen door bang, and looked to see her mom on the front porch.

"Jimmy!" Mrs. Gutierrez called. "Jimmy Ryan, when did you get home? Come in for coffee!"

Sara gave a little laugh. "Don't argue with my mama."

I went in, and got coffee Mexican style, with a little cinnamon, and powdered-sugar-dusted cookies. Mrs. Gutierrez skimmed around her scoured red-and-yellow kitchen like a hummingbird. But here, too, something wasn't right.

Mrs. Gutierrez gave Sara a pile of magazines to take to a neighbor's house. When we heard the screen bang behind

her, Mrs. Gutierrez turned to me. "You see how she is?"

"Has she been sick?"

Mrs. Gutierrez twisted the dishrag between her hands, and I was reminded of Sara twisting at her skirt, the first night I'd driven her home. "When . . . At night, late, she goes to bed. She says she's going to bed. But I lie awake in the dark and hear her go out again. It's hours before she comes back."

I felt so light-headed I almost couldn't see. "Is it some boy?" I was scared at how angry I sounded. "Is she—" Everything else stuck in my throat. I had no business being angry. I was furious.

But Mrs. Gutierrez shook her head. "Do you think I would let that go on? Almost I wish it were. Then we'd have shame or a wedding, but not this—this fading away."

It was true. Sara was fading away.

"What can I do?"

"Find out what's happening. Make her stop."

So I began to meet her for lunch. She wasn't too busy anymore, but she was always tired. Still, she smiled at me, the kind of weary, gentle smile that women who work too hard wear, and let me take her to the drugstore lunch counter. I made her eat, which she didn't mind doing, but didn't seem to care much about either.

"Are you going to tell me what's wrong?" I asked every time. And every time, she'd say, "Nothing," and make a joke or turn the subject.

One day—I know the date exactly, December 12—I badgered her again.

"There's nothing wrong, Jimmy. Everything's fine now."

"That sounds like things used to be wrong. What's changed?"

Sara gave a little frustrated shrug that made her collarbone show through her blouse. "You remember I told you we used to be happy? Well, we're happy again. That's all."

"Your mom's not happy."

"Yes, she is—she's just looking for something to be unhappy about. Is that why you're always nagging me? Because she told you to?"

"Well, why shouldn't she? You're skin and bones, she says you don't sleep, you sneak out of the house—"

Sara's face stopped me. It was like stone, except for her eyes, which seemed to scorch my face as she looked at me. "You know what you are, Jimmy Ryan? You're a busybody old woman. Keep your nose out of my business from now on!"

She spun around on her counter stool and plunged out of the drugstore.

By the time I got out to the sidewalk, she was gone. She wasn't at the library, or the high school.

That night I picked at my dinner, until Mom said, "Jimmy, are you sick?"

"I had a big lunch, I guess. Pop, can I borrow the car tonight?"

"Sure. What you got planned?"

I felt terrible as I said, "Supposed to be a meteor shower tonight. I thought I'd drive out past Don Emilio and watch."

This time he didn't give me a look across the table. I almost wished he had.

I drove out the road toward South Hollier at about 9 P.M. I didn't know when the Gutierrez family went to bed, but I

didn't want to arrive much past that time, whatever it was. I parked the car off the road just before the culvert-pipe tunnels and walked the rest of the way.

The night was so clear that the starlight was enough to see by. I circled South Hollier, only waking up one dog in the process, until I found a perch where I could see the front and back doors of the Gutierrez house. That put me partway up the lower slopes of the tailings dump. I'd thought there was another house or two between theirs and the dump; had they been torn down to make room?

It got cold, and colder, as I waited. I wished I had a watch with a radium dial. Finally I saw movement; I had to blink and look away to make sure it wasn't just from staring for so long at one spot.

Sara was a pale smudge, standing in her backyard in a light-colored dress, her head tipped back to see the stars, or the ridgetop. She set out to climb the slope.

She wasn't looking for me, and I was wearing a dark wool coat. So I could follow her as she climbed, up and up until she reached the top of the ridge. I had the sense to stay down where I wouldn't show up against the sky.

Sara stood still for a moment, her head down. Then she lifted her face and her arms. She began a shuffling step, rhythmic, sure, as if the loose stones she danced over were a polished wood floor. About every five steps she gave a spring. Sometimes she'd turn in place, or sweep her arms over her head in a wide arc. I followed her as she moved along the ridge, until in one of her turns the starlight fell on her face. It was blank, entranced. Her eyes were open, but not seeing.

I couldn't stand it. "Sara!"

She came back to her own face; I don't know any other way to say it. She came back, stumbled, and stopped. I scrambled up the slope to her, and grabbed her shoulders as she swayed. They were thin as bird bones under my hands.

"Sara, what *is* this? What the hell are you doing out here?" My voice sounded hollow and thin, carried away by the air over the ridge.

"Jimmy? What are you doing here?"

I felt my face burn. The only true answer was "Spying." I felt guilty enough to be angry again. "Trying to find out what you wouldn't tell me. Friends don't lie to each other."

"I haven't . . . I haven't lied to you."

"You said everything was fine!"

She nodded slowly. "It is, now."

"You're sleepwalking on the tailings!"

Her face took on a new sharpness. "You think I'm sleepwalking?"

"What else?"

"Oh, God." She scrubbed at her face with both hands. "Don't you remember, when I told you about Fuji and the others?"

I let go of her shoulders. For the first time I felt, in my palms, the heat of her skin, that radiated through the material of her dress. "This isn't some bunk about the mountain?"

"I had to fix it. There wasn't anybody else who could."

"You're not fixing anything! This is just a pile of rocks that used to be a hill!"

"Jimmy. I *am* the mountain."

She stood so still before me, so straight and solid. And I was cold all the way through, watching the light of the stars waver through the halo of heat around her.

"Sara. Please, this is—Come down from here. Pop will help you—"

Her eyes narrowed, and her head cocked. "Can he dance?"

She was still there, still present in her crazy head. The rush of relief almost knocked me over. What would I have done if she'd been lost—if I'd lost her?

If I'd lost her. Before my eyes I saw two futures stretching out before me. One of them had Sara in it, every day, for every minute. The other . . . The other looked like bare, broken rock that nothing would grow on.

The shock pushed the words out of my mouth. "I love you, Sara."

She shook her head, wide-eyed. "Oh . . . "

"Marry me. I'm going to Colorado next month, you can go with me. You can finish school there—"

Sara was still shaking her head, and now her eyes were full of tears and reflected stars. She reached out a hand, stretching it out as if we were far, far apart. "Oh, Jimmy. I want—Oh, don't you see?"

"Don't you care for me, Sara?"

She gave a terrible wordless cry, as if she were being twisted in invisible hands. "I can't leave!"

"But for you and me—"

"There are more people than just us. They need me."

"Your folks? They've got your brothers. They don't need you the way I do."

"Jimmy, you're not listening. I *can't* leave. I'm the mountain."

Her face wasn't crazy. It was streaked with tears and a deep, adult sorrow, like the saints' statues in St. Patrick's Church. Sara reached out to me the way Mary's statue reached down from her niche over the altar, pity and yearning in the very fingerjoints. I saw the waving heat around her, and the stars in her eyes and her hair.

I stepped back a pace. I couldn't help it.

I saw her heart break. That's the only way I can describe what I watched in her face. But when it was done, what was left in her eyes and her mouth and the way she held her head was strong and certain and brave.

"Good-bye, Jimmy," she said. She turned, sure-footed, and ran like a deer along the tailings ridge into the night.

I think I shouted her name. I know that something set the dogs barking all over South Hollier, and eventually Enrique Gutierrez was shaking me by the shoulders.

When Sara hadn't come home by morning, we called the police. Mr. and Mrs. Gutierrez were afraid she'd broken her leg, or fallen and been knocked out. I couldn't talk about what I was afraid of, so I agreed with them, that that could have happened.

Every able-bodied person in South Hollier joined the search. Everyone thought it would be over in an hour or so. By afternoon the police had brought dogs in, and were looking for fresh slides. They didn't say they were looking for places where the rocks might have engulfed a body.

If she was out there, the dogs would have found her. Still, I had to go down to the station, because I was the last one to

see her, because the girl at the lunch counter had heard our fight. And God knows, I must have seemed a little crazy. I told them what I'd seen and what we'd said. I just didn't tell them what I thought had happened.

I didn't transfer to the Colorado School of Mines. Leveling mountains didn't appeal to me anymore. I went back to premed, and started on medical school at the University of Arizona. When Pearl Harbor was bombed, I enlisted, and went to the Pacific as a medic.

After the war, I finished medical school and hired on as a company doctor at the hospital in Hollier. Pop had passed, and Mom was glad to have me nearby. I couldn't live in the house on Collar Hill, though, that looked down the canyon to where Guadalupe Hill had been. I found a little house in South Hollier, small enough for a bachelor to handle.

The Gutierrez house was gone. As the dump grew, it needed a bigger base, and the company bought the house and knocked it down to make room for more rock. Mr. and Mrs. Gutierrez bought a place down at the south end of Wilson, and while they were alive, I used to visit and tell them how their old neighbors were getting on.

I'd lived in South Hollier for a couple of months before I climbed the slope of the tailings one December night and sat in the starlight. I sat for maybe an hour before I felt her beside me. I didn't turn to look.

"The mountain's happy now," I said. My voice cracked a little.

"I'm happy," she said. "Be happy for me, Jimmy."

"Who's going to be happy for me?"

"I'll do that. Maybe someday you will, too."

I shook my head, but it seemed silly to argue with her.

"What used to be good still is," she said. "Remember that." And after a minute, "I take care of everybody, but you most of all."

"I'll die after a while and save you the trouble."

"Not for a long time." There was motion at the corner of my eye, and I felt warm lips against my cheek. "I love you, Jimmy."

Then there was nothing beside me but a gust of cold wind.

I'd watched the mining of Guadalupe Hill, and thought men could do anything, be anything, conquer anything. I'd thought we'd cure cancer any day.

Now Guadalupe Pit is as deep as Guadalupe Hill once was high, and next to it there's a second pit that would hold three Guadalupes. Both pits are shut down, played out. There's no cure for cancer, the AIDS quilt is so big that there's no place large enough to roll the whole thing out at once, and diabetes has gone from a rarity to an epidemic.

But in South Hollier there's a ridge that could have been nothing more than a heap of barren, cast-off rock; and a cluster of buildings that could have slowly emptied and died inside their wall. Instead there's a mountain with a goddess, and a neighborhood that rests safe and happy, as if in her warm cupped hands.

—For Elise Matthesen, and the necklace of the same title

Emma Bull lives in Tucson, Arizona, in the twenty-first century, but is fond of road trips and time travel. She's the author of several fantasy novels, including *War for the Oaks, Finder, Bone Dance* (Finalist for the Hugo, Nebula, and World Fantasy Awards, and the second-place Philip K. Dick Award novel), and (with Steven Brust) *Freedom and Necessity*. With her husband, Will Shetterly, she edited the Liavek fantasy anthologies (see Pamela Dean's story "Cousins" for a window into Liavek). She's been in several bands, most recently the Flash Girls. Her cat, Toby, is teaching her to play tag. For more information, see **www.qwertyranch.com**.

Author's Note

If I were writing a term paper, I'd have to say, "Landscape and history are one of the author's most dependable sources of inspiration." For this story, one inspiration was Bisbee, Arizona, which seems to me to have more story ideas per capita than is reasonable. Bisbee's full of weird magic.

Inspiration was also provided by Elise Matthesen's named necklace, "What Used to Be Good Still Is." For glimpses of Elise's awesome jewelry, check out **www.lioness.net**.

acknowledgments

If a book can be compared to a theater production, a list of books like Firebird is basically a continuous repertory season. There are a lot of people behind the scenes who make it happen, and who are never thanked. Let me tell you who they are.

FIREBIRD

The editorial boards, both teen and other

Ginny Schneider was my 2005 summer intern and I wish she could've stayed

PUFFIN

(Note: Firebird is an imprint of Puffin)

Eileen Kreit: Vice President and Publisher

Gerard Mancini and Phil Airoldi: Associate Publisher and Utility Outfielder

Pat Shuldiner and Martin P. Karlow: Copy Editors

Deborah Kaplan, Linda McCarthy, Nick Vitiello, Kristina Duewell, Jeanine Henderson, Tony Sahara, Jay Cooper (in absentia), Sam Kim (who typeset this book and made all of the exhaustive changes), and Christian Fünfhausen: Art Directors and Designers

Lori Thorn: Creator of the Firebird logo, and designer of this book's cover

Amy White and Jason Primm: Production

Nally Preseault: Almost everything else

Viking

(Note: All of the other fantasy and sf books I edit are published by Viking first)

Regina Hayes: President and Publisher

Gerard Mancini and Laurie Perl: Managing Editorial

Denise Cronin, Nancy Brennan, Kelley McIntyre, Jim Hoover: Art Directors and Designers

Janet Pascal: Fellow Diana Wynne Jones fan and Executive Production Editor

Nico Medina: Copyediting

Penguin Group (USA) Inc.

Doug Whiteman: Head of the Children's Group

Mariann Donato: Director of Sales and Marketing

Jackie Engel, Jennifer O'Donohue, Nancy Feldman (in absentia), Mary Raymond, Annie Naughton, Robyn Fink, Allan Winebarger, Janet Krug: Sales

Our field and inside sales reps rock the house and should be worshipped (a special acknowledgment here to Dave Cudmore and Ron Smith)

Gina Maolucci (in absentia), Emily Romero, Gina Balsano, Katrina Weidknecht, Lucy Del Priore, Lauren Adler, Andrea Cruise, Jess Michaels, Ed Scully, Lara Phan, Kim Chocolaad, Courtney Wood: Marketing
George Schumacher and Camille DeLuca: Contracts
Susan Allison, Ginjer Buchanan, Anne Sowards: Ace Books
Betsy Wollheim, Sheila Gilbert, Debra Euler: DAW
Cindy Spiegel: Riverhead Books

OTHER NICE PEOPLE

Jude Feldman titled this book. She and Alan Beatts are the main people responsible for Borderlands Books in San Francisco (www.borderlands-books.com). Go there and buy things.

I remain amazed by the wholehearted support and friendship offered me by both fans and pros in the genre fiction field. Thanks to everyone who has e-mailed, come up to me at cons, and bought the books. And special thanks to Charles M. Brown and the staff at *Locus*, Ellen Datlow, John Douglas, Jo Fletcher and Simon Spanton, Diana Gill, Gavin Grant and Kelly Link, Anne Lesley Groell, Eileen Gunn, Greg Ketter and Lisa Freitag, Jaime Levine, Elise Matthesen, Shawna McCarthy, Farah Mendlesohn, Jim Minz, Patrick and Teresa Nielsen Hayden, Stella Paskins, Judith Ridge, Bill Schafer, Jonathan Strahan, Rodger Turner, Gordon Van Gelder, Jo and Sasha Walton, Jacob Weisman, and Terri Windling, among many others.

An honored thank you to the Minn-StF people for Minicon.

I want to again acknowledge all of the stellar authors in this book, and their agents.

Our cover artists are fantastic. Special thanks to Cliff Nielsen for another stunning piece of art for this book!

There are so many librarians, educators, and teachers who have gotten behind Firebird, and they all deserve applause.

And of course, I need to mention my father, Frederick November. Not only is he genetically responsible for my reading speed and somewhat bizarre sense of humor and dubious social skill, but he is one of the best people in the entire world. He even laughs at my jokes. Everyone should know someone like him; I get to be related to him!

About the Editor

Sharyn November was born in New York City, and has stayed close by ever since. She received a B.A. from Sarah Lawrence College, where she studied and wrote poetry; her work has appeared in *Poetry, The North American Review,* and *Shenandoah,* among other magazines, and she received a scholarship to Bread Loaf. She has been editing books for children and teenagers for over fifteen years, and is currently Senior Editor for Viking Children's Books and Puffin Books, as well as the Editorial Director of Firebird. Her writing about her work with teenage readers (both online and in person) has been published in *The Horn Book* and *Voice of Youth Advocates*, and she is currently working on an essay collection. She has been a board member of USBBY and ALAN, as well as being actively involved in ALA, NCTE, and SFWA. She was named a World Fantasy Award Finalist (Professional Category) in both 2004 and 2005—in 2004 specifically for Firebird, in 2005 for editing.

She has played in a variety of bands (songwriter, lead singer, rhythm guitar), and maintains an extensive personal Web site at **www.sharyn.org**. She drinks a lot of Diet Mountain Dew and likes to cause chaos in her wake.

The Firebird Web site is at **www.firebirdbooks.com**.